Voice & Vision

A CREATIVE APPROACH to Narrative Film and DV Production

MICK HURBIS-CHERRIER

Second Edition

AMSTERDAM • BOSTON • HEIDELBERG • LONDON
NEW YORK • OXFORD • PARIS • SAN DIEGO
SAN FRANCISCO • SINGAPORE • SYDNEY • TOKYO
Focal press is an imprint of Elsevier

ELSEVIER

Focal Press

Focal Press is an imprint of Elsevier
30 Corporate Drive, Suite 400, Burlington, MA 01803, USA
The Boulevard, Langford Lane, Kidlington, Oxford, OX5 1GB, UK

Notices
Knowledge and best practice in this field are constantly changing. As new research and experience
broaden our understanding, changes in research methods, professional practices, or medical
treatment may become necessary.

Practitioners and researchers must always rely on their own experience and knowledge in evaluating
and using any information, methods, compounds, or experiments described herein. In using such
information or methods they should be mindful of their own safety and the safety of others, including
parties for whom they have a professional responsibility.

To the fullest extent of the law, neither the Publisher nor the authors, contributors, or editors, assume
any liability for any injury and/or damage to persons or property as a matter of products liability,
negligence or otherwise, or from any use or operation of any methods, products, instructions, or
ideas contained in the material herein.

Library of Congress Cataloging-in-Publication Data
Application submitted

British Library Cataloguing-in-Publication Data
A catalogue record for this book is available from the British Library.

ISBN: 978-0-240-81158-1

For information on all Focal Press publications visit our website at
www.elsevierdirect.com

11   12   13   14   15   5   4   3   2   1

Printed in Canada

Working together to grow
libraries in developing countries

www.elsevier.com | www.bookaid.org | www.sabre.org

ELSEVIER   BOOK AID International   Sabre Foundation

This book is dedicated to Frank Beaver, Michelle Citron, and Dana Hodgdon—exceptional professors, mentors, and friends whose teachings have remained with me and whose voices echo throughout the pages of this book.

Contents

Companion Website Contents
www.voiceandvisionbook.com

When you see this hand pointer icon in the pages of this book, it indicates that material related to that section is available on-line at www.voiceandvisionbook.com

■ THE COMPANION WEBSITE TABS

All by chapters

This section contains *all* of the supplementary web materials in the book, listed by chapter and in the order they occur in each chapter. This includes:
- Short film examples.
- High resolution and color figures.
- Video figures.
- Interactive figures.
- Forms, logs and tables for preproduction, production and postproduction.

Short films

This section contains links to stream the example short films discussed in the book. The films are:
- *The Black Hole*. Directed by The Diamond Dogs Phil & Olly (3 min.).
- *Plastic Bag*. Directed by Ramin Bahrani (18 min.).
- *Waking Dreams*. Directed by John Daschbach (24 min.).
- *When I Was Young*. Directed by Huixia Lu (15 min.).
- *Vive le 14 Juillet*. Directed by Didier Rouget (4 min.).
- *Before the Making of Sleep Dealer*. Directed by Alex Rivera (12 min.).
- *Kiarra's Escape* (scene excerpt) (2 min.).

Forms, logs, tables

This section contains downloadable forms, logs and tables for preproduction, production and postproduction. These forms include:
- Storyboard forms.
- Location scouting report.
- Budget forms.
- Production call sheet.
- Script breakdown sheet.
- Camera and sound reports.
- Depth of field tables for the 16mm format.
- Film can labels for exposed film.
- Sound cue spotting sheet.

Web links

This section contains links to all of the film related websites listed in the web resources appendix and will be updated regularly to include additional web resources.

Raw footage downloads

This section includes download links for raw video footage to be used for editing exercises.

Misc. and new

This section includes miscellaneous materials from throughout the book and new material added to the website after publication. This includes:

- Sample paperwork for Chapter 5 film excerpt
- Sample location contract and talent release.
- The CSATF and Ontario production safety guideline publications.
- Screenplay formatting specifications.
- Video format tables.
- Instructions for calibrating monitors to color bars.
- Material deleted from the 1st edition of *Voice & Vision*.
- New materials added to the website after publication date.

Acknowledgments

A book of this scope and size could not have been accomplished without the kind help, contributions, and counsel of many reviewers, assistants, and colleagues—friends one and all. Warmest thanks to the team at Focal Press: Becky Golden-Harrell, Dawnmarie Simpson, and Robin Weston, and to the inimitable Elinor Actipis, whom I cannot possibly thank enough.

I was especially fortunate to have a lineup of excellent reviewers—Jacqueline B. Frost, Michael Kowalski, and Catherine Sellars—whose careful, thoughtful, and detailed comments quite simply made this book better.

I would like to thank my colleagues at Hunter College of the City University of New York for their support, advice, encouragement, and patience, especially President Jennifer Raab, Jay Roman, Joel Zuker, Andrew Lund, Ivone Margulies, Joe McElhaney, Shanti Thakur, Kelly Anderson, Michael Gitlin, Renato Tonelli, and Peter A. Jackson. And I thank my dear friend Michael Griffel for his wisdom, kindness, and guidance.

During the writing of this book I was especially touched by the way Hunter film students rallied to my aid. To all of those who gave so willingly of their energy, enthusiasm, and talent, I am grateful: Katherine Allen, Brian Ferrari, Randi Harris, Yae Mitomi, Alana Kakoyianis, Lucas Pruchnik, Mika Mori, Rosa Navarra, Brian Safuto, Zita Vasilisinova, Michael Gibbs, David Pavlosky, Matt Henderson, Jayan Cherian, Emogene Shadwick, and all those who let us onto their film sets to take photographs. But an extra special thank you is in order for the hard, dedicated, and superb work put in by Jessica Webb, Alessandra Kast, Josh Hill, Timothy Trotman, Claudia Didomenico, Gresham Gregory, and George Racz.

I'd also like to thank all the kind people who helped with the technical research and illustrations, including Pete Abel at Abel CineTech, Will Sweeney at Color Lab Film Corp., Jan Crittenden at Panasonic, Dave Waddell at Fujinon, Lisa Muldowney at Kodak, Charles Darby at DuArt Film & Video, Joe Hannigan at Weston Sound, Frieder Hochheim at Kino Flo, Inc., and John C. Clisham at Mole Richardson Co.

I would be remiss in not acknowledging some of the many other friends whose tangible and inspirational support is woven throughout the pages of this text, especially Abbas Kiarostami, Seifollah Samadian, Peter Scarlet, Raymond Cauchetier, Thelma Schoonmaker, Ellen Kuras, Freida Orange, Edin Velez, Dave Monahan, Pam Katz, Kim Doan, Paul Cronin, Timothy Corrigan, Catherine Riggs-Bergesen, Lynne Sachs, Laurent Tirard, and Wes Simpkins. Ken Dancyger deserves credit and special appreciation for prompting me to write a book in the first place and for remaining an encouraging and remarkably perspicacious mentor throughout the process.

Acknowledgments for the Second Edition

My first acknowledgement goes to the excellent team at Focal Press: Melissa Sandford, Anaïs Wheeler, Melinda Rankin and, of course, Elinor Actipis, whose support and friendship I value greatly.

I was again fortunate to have terrific reviewers for this second edition: Ece Karayalcin from Miami Dade College, Pablo Frasconi and Jed Dannenbaum of the USC School of Cinematic Arts, and Tomasz Malinowski of Edge Hill University (U.K). Thank you for sharing your time, expertise, and invaluable comments.

I am especially grateful to the filmmakers who generously provided their excellent films for the online resource of this book: John Daschbach, Huixia Lu, the Diamond Dogs Phil & Olly, Nicola Doring, Ramin Bahrani, Adam Speilberg, Didier Rouget, and Alex Rivera; and to Ricardo Miranda Zuñiga who created the interactive figures for the companion website.

Also, a warm thank you to all of the people who participated in the making of the online film and photo examples, especially Miles Adgate, Jordan Cooke, Nick Vega, Sharine Mohamed, Robert Youngren, Jessica Krueger, Victor Varela, Rick Varela, Tom Ashton, Matt Dickson, Matilde Dratwa, Layla Biltsted, Adam Kaplan, Nicole Pommerehncke, Ruomi Lee Hampel, Rommel Genciana, Maya Sheppard, Elvis Maynard, Melissa Hill, Matt Post, Nikki Hracs, Richard Unapanta, Tristan Allman, Eric Smith, Donna Chin, Brian Kolb and Alessandro Roveri.

I'd also like to acknowledge those friends who provided everything from photographs to inspiration: Mike Figgis, Shirin Neshat, Antoin Cox, Christine Vachon, Kim Fuller, Courtney Hunt, Don Harwood, Heather Rae, Cory McAbee, Becky Glupczynski, Rain Li, Walter Partos, Zachary Sluser, Michel Khleifi, Pierce Varous, Dag Bennstrom, Matt Anderson, Clarence Courtney, Claire Luke, Henny Garfunkel, and Aaron Pinto at LetusDirect.

And once again, I am profoundly grateful and indebted to Katherine Hurbis-Cherrier and my brother Gustavo Mercado, who were in the trenches with me each and every day of the writing and research. This book would not have been not possible without them.

Introduction

Where does one begin a journey into the world of filmmaking? Film is creative and it is technical. It's a form of personal expression and a universal language. It requires careful logistical planning and inspired spontaneity. It is the product of a single vision and collaborative energy. Film is also the quintessential hybrid art form, finding its expressive power though the unique amalgam of writing, performance, design, photography, music, and editing. And all of it matters. Every choice you make, from the largest creative decisions to the smallest practical solutions, has a profound impact on what appears on the screen and how it moves an audience emotionally.

The central principle behind Voice & Vision is the notion that all of the conceptual, technical, and logistical activity on a film project should serve the filmmaker's creative vision. Making a film begins with someone wanting to tell a story, wanting to bring an idea to the screen for the world to see. The next step then involves gathering together the people, equipment, and resources to produce the movie. However, it's quite common these days to hear people who don't want to bother themselves with the technical or conceptual fundamentals of filmmaking say that "it's not about tech, it's not about rules, it's all about the story." That's a little too facile. The fact is, it's not enough to just have a story, no matter how good it is; you have to be able to tell that story well. It's not simply "all about story," it's all about storytelling, and in this medium storytelling involves actors, a camera, lights, sound, and editing. To develop your ability to tell a story on film necessarily means understanding the basic visual vocabulary of cinema, the process of production, as well as the function and expressive potential of the tools; like a camera, a light meter, and editing software. In a recent filmmaker's master class the great director Abbas Kiarostami stressed the point that a mediocre idea brilliantly told is preferable to a brilliant idea poorly told. Film is a complex art form, and in order to make the right decisions and express oneself successfully you must be clear about what your ideas are and what you want to say, and you must gain control of the film language, tools, and production process in order to say just that. As James Broughton, one of cinema's great poets, once wrote:

> Every film is a voyage into the unknown. ... It is unwise to embark on the high seas without knowing a few of the laws of navigation. To have a shipwreck before you have cleared the port is both messy and embarrassing.

Voice & Vision elaborates on all of the essential information and skills necessary to ensure that the student filmmaker will acquire the technical, logistical, and conceptual authority needed to "speak in film" with cinematic eloquence and fluency. Think of the book like a map—it may not predict every wondrous sight or challenge you'll encounter on your voyage, but it'll get you sailing into open waters.

Obviously, it is not possible for one book on filmmaking to be a completely comprehensive resource on such a vast and evolving subject. In fact, all of the film books on the bookstore shelves put together don't even manage to say all there is to say—and thank goodness for that. Voice & Vision is written for the introductory and intermediate film student or independent filmmaker. This textbook aims to provide a solid foundation in narrative filmmaking, from idea to distribution. This includes essential and detailed technical information on film and digital production tools, a thorough overview of the filmmaking stages and process, and, of course, a discussion of the conceptual and aesthetic dimensions of telling a motion picture story.

■ FILM AS A COLLABORATIVE ART FORM

The act of making a film, on any scale, is an endeavor that requires enormous effort, concentration, and a broad range of knowledge. It also requires the execution of several tasks simultaneously. For this reason, narrative filmmaking is always a collaborative art form, requiring the collective energy and expertise of a team. A filmmaking team can be anywhere from two to two dozen (or more), but the basic dynamic is the same—a film becomes better when everyone on the team is allowed to make creative contributions and when everyone takes serious responsibility for their practical and technical duties. You will see these ideas of team creativity and responsibility emphasized throughout Voice & Vision. This book is also written with the understanding that not every film student will become, or even wants to become, a director. Knowing that students can follow so many creative and fulfilling paths in film (cinematography, sound design, editing, art direction, etc.), I have provided ample technical information, creative context, and discussions of aesthetics to thoroughly engage those many students who are enthusiastic about areas other than directing. Whether they are writing, directing, shooting, or editing, the ultimate goal of Voice & Vision is to guide each student of film to develop their own creative voice while acquiring the practical skills and confidence to use it.

■ FILMMAKING AND TECHNOLOGY IN THE 21st CENTURY

This book is being written in an era when film production is undergoing enormous transformation. Digital media are changing forever the technology and procedures for making movies at every stage of the process. When it comes to the question of film and digital video technology, Voice & Vision takes its cues from the professional industry and from students, who have both moved toward an understanding of the application and free integration of these technologies far more quickly than the academy. There is no battle between film and video. There are only movies to be made. The 21st-century filmmaker understands the inherent aesthetic characteristics and creative possibilities of originating on film and originating on digital video and will use whatever they have at their disposal to make great movies. This ambidexterity is demonstrated in the films of internationally renowned directors like Abbas Kiarostami, Lars von Trier, Rebecca Miller, Steven Soderbergh, Spike Lee, Michael Winterbottom, and many, many others. The modern cinematographer is conversant and expressive across the technologies. This can be seen in the work of trailblazers like Ellen Kuras, Robbie Müller, and Anthony Dod Mantle. The crafts of the editor, sound recordist, art director, and sound designer are not significantly altered if one is working on a film or DV project: just ask any working professional out there. It's all about storytelling! And you can tell stories either way. This book does not favor one technology over the other; instead, I try to provide an understanding not only of the different technologies, but of their inexorable convergence as well. One more note: I often use the word "film" as a synonym for movie or motion picture, which means, in my book, that it can originate on DV, be edited and projected digitally, and still be called a film, and the person who made it is a filmmaker.

■ TEACHING AND LEARNING FILMMAKING

Film writing and directing cannot be taught, only learned, and each man or woman has to learn it through his or her own system of self-education.

Alexander Mackendrick

The great film director Alexander Mackendrick (*The Ladykillers, Sweet Smell of Success*) raises a pertinent issue when he states in his book, *On Filmmaking,* that you cannot teach film, but you can learn it. The interesting twist, however, is that Mr. Mackendrick was also a legendary film teacher at the California Institute of the Arts for 25 years, so he must have believed that something about film could be taught, or at least conveyed, and that a teacher plays some role in learning about filmmaking. I believe that you can, in fact, teach a great deal about filmmaking. One can teach the essentials of technique, cinematic language, the technology, and the expressive capabilities of the instruments of the art form. One can teach an understanding of how the production process itself supports the creation of a movie. One can teach a student a method for recognizing and appreciating exceptional examples of filmmaking from the history of movies. All of this can bring the serious student right to the threshold. The rest of what is necessary, albeit the core of being an artist in any medium, must be learned through example and experience, and here a teacher, and a book, can serve as a guide. This core consists of imagination, visual intuition, initiative, an aesthetic sense, and personal style. These qualities can't be taught, but they can certainly be nurtured and developed.

So where do we go to learn those things that cannot be taught? The first thing an aspiring filmmaker must do is watch films, especially the films of the masters, old and new. Writers read great writers, painters look at paintings and, in fact, often copy the works of masters when developing their craft. It is imperative that young filmmakers look carefully at films for what they express and how the filmmaker actually achieves that particular mood or emotion, or that specific narrative point, or how they develop a theme, or move you to laugh, or cry, or vote, through images, actions, and sound. Movies themselves are our most useful textbooks. Think about it: not one cinematic storytelling technique in the history of film has become extinct. Every filmmaking technique that has been developed remains part of the lexicon of the art form and it's all there for you to learn from, rework, customize, and apply to your own story. Knowing this, I have included throughout the text numerous illustrations from movies (every one available on DVD). The "In Practice" feature provides brief analyses of scenes or techniques from films that illustrate how a specific technology, process, or technique is used to support a conceptual, narrative, or aesthetic impulse—in essence, the creative application of a principle or a technology. This encourages the student to look at films analytically and to use the wealth of material available for rent as a research tool. You will notice that I reference films from all eras and from all over the world as well as films shot on 35mm, 16mm, Super 16, HD, and standard DV. This book celebrates the vast diversity of voices, approaches, perspectives, and innovations in cinema throughout its history. A smart film student will understand that great movies and creative innovations are as likely to come from Taiwan, Denmark, Brazil, and Iran as Los Angeles. Film is truly a global art form, and every continent continues to make vital contributions.

The second way we can learn about filmmaking is to listen to the tales from the trenches of production. Everyone has on-set experience stories: challenges that they faced, puzzles that they solved, issues with which they struggled, ideas that they held on to and those that they had to let go, accounts of their crafty accomplishments, shrewd fixes, and innovative workarounds. It's important to listen to these stories. We learn from the experiences, ideas, ingenuity, solutions, knowledge, advice, strategies, difficulties, disappointments, and successes of other filmmakers, from students struggling with their very first film to seasoned pros struggling with their 30th movie–there are lessons in all of it. Pick up any trade magazine, like *American Cinematographer,* or go to a website like www.filmsound.org, or pick up a book like Laurent Tirard's *Moviemakers' Master Class* or Walter Murch's *In the Blink of an Eye,* and what you'll find are people with experience in cinematography, sound design, directing, editing, or any other creative aspect of filmmaking sharing what they've accomplished and what they've learned along the way. You can tuck all of these illuminating stories, all of this first-hand information, into your tool kit and bring it with you to your next project. Then, after you've spent even one day on a film set, you'll have your own stories to share. It's all about storytelling after all.

You will find real-world stories sprinkled throughout the book and also in the "In Practice" boxes, which often contain brief anecdotes detailing common and characteristic production challenges from professional film shoots as well as student productions. Many of these on-set stories come directly from the experiences of my students during my 13 years of teaching introductory and intermediate production courses. Some of them come from filmmakers ranging in experience from first-time feature film directors to legendary masters of cinema.

In the end, however, the best way to learn about filmmaking is simply to make films. Here is some advice from someone who's made a few himself:

The advice I would give today to anyone who wants to become a director is quite simple: make a film. In the sixties, it wasn't so easy because there wasn't even super 8. If you wanted to shoot anything, you had to rent a 16-millimeter camera, and often it would be silent. But today, nothing is as easy as buying or borrowing a small video camera. You have a picture, you have sound, and you can screen your film on any TV set. So when an aspiring director comes to me for advice, my answer is always the same: "Take a camera, shoot something, and show it to someone. Anyone."

Jean-Luc Godard (From *Moviemaker's Master Class*, by Laurent Tirard)

So there you have it. What are you waiting for? It's time to make movies!

(January 2007)

Introduction to the Second Edition

Early in the process of writing this second edition, I happened to run into a former student who was preparing to go into production on his first feature film. When he elaborated on the project, the very first thing he told me, quite excitedly, was that he was shooting on a RED ONE camera at 24p and 4K resolution and that the latest version of Final Cut Pro supported the REDCODE RAW codec without transcoding, and so on and so on. It took some time for the conversation to get around to the actual story and ideas in the film.

This is not an unusual conversation these days. I have seen countless students labor so mightily over the mysteries of production formats, transcoding, compression ratios, workflows, container formats, and codecs, that the creative dimension (the hard work of crafting a compelling story with convincing characters and expressive images) often takes a backseat. But they're not entirely to blame for this tendency. Since writing the first edition of *Voice & Vision*—not really that many years ago— the technology of filmmaking and film distribution has accelerated rapidly, oftentimes outpacing the end user's ability to fully absorb the new paradigms. American television broadcast standards are now completely digital and analog NTSC is a quaint antique. Standard definition video exists for no other reason than there is a lot of SD equipment out there that's still very usable, but HD has come down in price and saturated all market levels to the point where HD formats are now the new standard. Anything resembling tape stock, whether in sound recording or DV recording, is now considered archaic. Sound and picture production is file based and solid state with new recording media being introduced regularly. Elite film camera manufacturers like Aaton, Arriflex and Panavision have entered the digital cinema arena and introduced their own DV cameras. So many feature films are shot on HD or use digital intermediates or are finished as D-Cinema packages that these facts are hardly even mentioned anymore, and, of course, the 3D revival (for it is surely a revival and not a brand-new development) is predicted to change filmmaking as we know it. Additionally, the web, which has become an essential tool for promotion, fund raising, and distribution, requires yet another set of technical skills to successfully harness. And if the past five years has shown us anything, it's that we can expect the same rate of technological transformation in the *next* five years—perhaps even greater. So it's understandable why a young filmmaker would reel off the technical dimensions of his project before the story; getting a handle on all of it does constitute an accomplishment of sorts. But this is exactly why we must be extra vigilant not to let the tail wag the dog. Filmmakers must dig deep into the core of their creativity to find their true artistic voices, even while they are digging deep into product spec sheets, user forums, and software manuals. And this is very possible.

I believe that this avalanche of technology is actually having an impact in two ways. Some things are getting trickier, while other things are getting easier. Yes, the constant changes to workflows, shooting formats, frame rates, scanning options, sensor types, and codecs can be a veritable technological tar pit. At the same time, however, gorgeous, high-resolution images of broadcast or theatrical quality, which allow for precise creative control over lighting and exposures, are now within easy reach for even a novice with very little money. In the past, it was rare for a student to shoot a 35mm film, even a short one; now I have many advanced students shooting on the same D-Cinema rig used by commercial directors like Soderbergh or Fincher, and many more recent graduates are able to embark on feature films knowing that even midlevel camcorders (and DSLRs) and off-the-shelf editing software will yield professional results. Perhaps all this easy and relatively inexpensive access to very high production values, along with this state of constant technological flux, might just make the technology *less* precious and encourage filmmakers to place their best energies into what will truly distinguish them as visual storytellers—the script, the acting, the images and the ideas behind all of it.

So, yes, the technical information in this book *is* important—these are our tools, this is how we express ourselves in this technological medium after all—and it is my sincerest desire that this book give you the fundamental technical information you need to work successfully as a filmmaker. I hope that the technical discussion in these pages empowers you to make films, to make them look the way you want them to look, and to avoid costly technical detours and errors. But I also hope that this book inspires you artistically and encourages you to never lose sight of the fact that filmmaking is a creative endeavor. We tell stories to move people, to make them cry, laugh, shriek, sit on the edge of their seat, hold their lover a little harder, think about their actions, understand other people better, feel warmth, joy, fear or outrage. We do not tell stories to prove to the world that we know how to use a RED camera shooting 24p at 4K resolution.

The point is that it really doesn't matter what the equipment is. It really matters who the artist is, and what their attitude is.

Mike Figgis (from *Digital Filmmaking*, Faber and Faber, 2007)

PART I DEVELOPING YOUR FILM ON PAPER

From Idea to Cinematic Story

Our first job is to look,
Our second job is to think of a film that can be made.

Abbas Kiarostami (Marrakech, 2005)

There's no doubt about it. Filmmaking is exciting stuff. Working on a set, surrounded by the energy of a great production crew, collaborating with actors, setting up lights, lining up shots, calling out "Roll camera! Action!" Seeing a film project come to life can be an exhilarating experience. In fact, most aspiring filmmakers simply can't wait to get their hands on a camera and start shooting. Once they get an idea, they're ready to go! But wait. What are you shooting? What is your idea? Are your characters interesting? Does the idea have a shape? Just what do you want to say and how will you say it? What does all this activity on the screen add up to? What about the practical side of making this film? Are the subject and visual approach appropriate for your resources? Can you get it done?

Whether your project is a two-minute chase scene with no dialogue or a complex psychological drama, the first step in any narrative film production is coming up with an idea that is stimulating, engaging, and ripe with visual possibilities. The idea is the DNA of the entire filmmaking process—it informs every word written into the script, every shot you take, and every choice you make along the way. The better your basic idea is, the better your film will be. But an idea is only the first lightning bolt of inspiration. All ideas have to be developed—fashioned into stories that can be told through the medium of film. This means turning an idea into a story that can be captured and conveyed by that camera you're dying to get your hands on.

■ FINDING AN IDEA

At the beginning of any film, there is an idea. It may come at any time, from any source. It may come from watching people in the street or from thinking alone in your office. ... What you need is to find that original idea, that spark. And once you have that, it's like fishing: you use that idea as bait, and it attracts everything else. But as a director your main priority is to remain faithful to that original idea.

David Lynch (From *Moviemakers' Master Class*, by Laurent Tirard)

Where do we find ideas? Where does inspiration come from? As Lynch reminds us, ideas can come to us anywhere and at anytime: an act of kindness we witness on the street, an individual we watch on the bus, a piece of music that moves us, an experience a friend relates to us or a memory we can't let go. John Daschbach's *Waking Dreams* (one of the short films available for viewing on the *Voice & Vision* companion website) came from a particularly vivid dream, and Ramin Bahrani's 2007 feature film *Chop Shop* was inspired by an evocative location that struck him as a perfect setting for a dramatic story (see page 127). I once attended a reading by the fiction writer Raymond Carver, and someone in the audience asked him if he had any secrets to becoming a writer. He said simply, "You have to be a sponge, you have to constantly absorb the world you live in." If you keep your eyes and ears open, you will discover that material is all around you. Everyday life provides fertile ground for story ideas, visual ideas, and character ideas. Stay alert and connect to the world around you, then you'll be able to connect with your audience.

Figure 1-1 Director Abbas Kiarostami.

In an interview with Houshang Golmakani, the Iranian filmmaker Abbas Kiarostami (Figure 1-1), speaking about inspiration, shared the following thoughts:

Gabriel Garcia Márquez once said, "I don't choose a subject; it's the subject that chooses me." The same goes for me. The subject depends on whatever happens to be keeping me awake at night. ... I have dozens of stories stored away in my memory. There's a story happening in front of me every day, but I don't have the time to make a film out of it. In the course of time, certain stories start taking on importance; one of them will end up becoming the subject of a film.

Precisely what strikes us as a good idea, one that could develop into a great movie, is a highly individualistic thing. In fact, where you get your ideas, what strikes you as a good idea for a movie, is *the* thing that makes your films your films and not someone else's, which is why it is best that ideas come from your own observations and responses to the world around you. The only way that a movie will contain your individual voice is if your core idea comes from you, from your imagination, interests, and perspective. Only Martin Scorsese can make Scorsese films. You may love them, but to try and duplicate them, because they are successful or because you think Mafia violence is the *ne plus ultra* of drama, is to avoid the most important work a filmmaker can do, and that is to find out what your unique cinematic voice and contribution might be. Finding your own voice is not easy work, but it's essential, and that process begins with your very first film.

Here is an example from the screenwriter and director Peter Hedges, who is discussing where he got the idea for his 2003 feature film *Pieces of April:*

In the late 1980s ... I heard about a group of young people who were celebrating their first Thanksgiving in New York City. They went to cook the meal, but the oven didn't work, so they knocked on doors until they found someone with an oven they could use. I remember thinking that this could be a way to have all sorts of people cross paths who normally wouldn't.

(From *Pieces of April: The Shooting Script*, by Peter Hedges)

Hedges jotted the idea down, made a few notes, and then forgot about it. This idea is like many lightning bolts of inspiration—it's interesting and compelling, but not yet fully formed. Hedges would not find the story in the idea until ten years later.

■ FROM AN IDEA TO A STORY

One's initial idea—that first spark of inspiration—more often than not is vague. Sometimes it's no more than an observation or a feeling. In the case of Peter Hedges, the idea was a simple situation that was ripe for interesting interactions, but it wasn't a story yet. The most basic elements of film are images and sound, those things that we can capture with a camera and a microphone. Think about it: when you are in a theater watching a movie, everything you understand about a character, including the story, the mood, and the themes of the film, is delivered exclusively through sound and images. We cannot point our camera and microphone at ideas, desires, intentions, or feelings, but we can record characters who react, make decisions, and take action as they strive to achieve something, and through those actions we can understand who these characters are, how they are feeling, what they are after, and what it all means. This is the fundamental principle behind **dramatization,** transforming what is vague and internal into a series of viewable and audible actions and events (also see page 37).

■ THE VOICE & VISION ONLINE SHORT FILM EXAMPLES

The following section refers extensively to the five short films provided on the Voice & Vision companion website (**Figure 1-2**). These films illustrate many of the central storytelling considerations for fictional narrative films (especially in relation to the short form). Also, these five shorts were selected because they represent a broad range of characters, themes, and approaches to cinematic storytelling and technique. Go to www.voiceandvisionbook.com to screen these films.

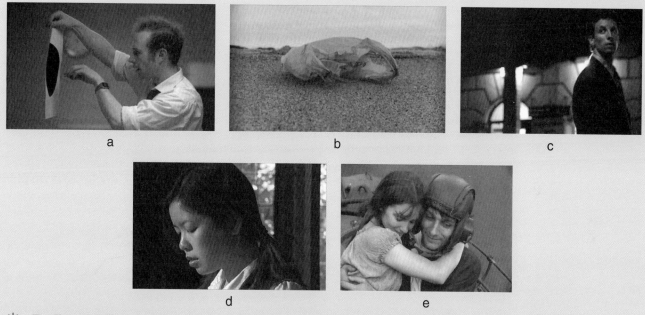

■ **Figure 1-2** The *Voice & Vision* online short film examples: (a) *The Black Hole* (Phil and Olly, 2009), (b) *Plastic Bag* (Ramin Bahrani, 2009), (c) *Waking Dreams* (John Daschbach, 2004), (d) *When I Was Young* (Huixia Lu, 2004), and (e) *Vive le 14 Juillet* (Didier Rouget, 2004).

■ FICTIONAL NARRATIVE BASICS I: ESSENTIAL STORY ELEMENTS

The next step in the process is to turn your initial inspiration into a dramatic story. In making this transition, it is important to understand the essential characteristics of a dramatic story. Most fictional narrative films have four basic and common elements:

1. A central character
2. A dramatic situation (the premise)
3. Actions and stakes
4. Resolution and what it all means

The Central Character

Drama is based on things that happen to characters, things characters do and ways characters change. Whatever the story is, it all starts with character. It doesn't matter if your film is about a single business executive (*Waking Dreams*), a recent Chinese immigrant (*When I Was Young*), a sweet, mild manner guy (*Vive le 14 Juillet*), a bored office clerk (*The Black Hole*), or even a plain brown plastic bag from the supermarket (*Plastic Bag*); the central character is usually the primary point of engagement for an audience—the element that encourages narrative involvement. If you really want your film to connect with an audience, you must create a central character who is compelling—a person people want to watch. One common way to do this is to create a central character a viewer can like or admire, someone who displays very human longings, needs, capabilities, vulnerabilities, and some noble qualities as well, like being fair, courageous, kind, or standing up for what is right; a figure with whom audiences can identify, empathize, or at least sympathize. This is called a **sympathetic character**. The main character in Ramin Bahrani's film *Chop Shop,* for example, is Alejandro, a 12-year-old boy, with no parents in sight, who is working hard to build an honest future for himself and his 16-year-old sister. He works adult manual labor jobs, he's resourceful beyond his years, he saves money, and he has noble, selfless goals. We easily like this smart, industrious, street-tough but open-hearted kid. We sympathize when he's not able to completely comprehend the nuances of the very adult situation he is in, and we feel for him when he stumbles. We want him to succeed, so we cheer him on (see page 127). And take a look at Bahrani's short film *Plastic Bag* and see how the first-person voice over imbues an inanimate object with painfully human traits, so much so that we feel immense sympathy for the desperate plight of a piece of trash, a brown plastic bag (read page 8).

However, *the* critical factor in building a main character is audience engagement, not necessarily likability. You can certainly engage an audience with a character who is unkind, unpleasant, mean, despicable, or even repulsive, if that character offers a glimpse at something fascinating, intriguing, and engaging (even if unsavory) to watch. This type of character is sometimes called an **antipathetic** character—but you can just call them unlikable—and boy, oh boy, can they be fun to watch. Mark Zuckerberg from Fincher's *The Social Network* is not likable in any traditional sense (**Figure 1-3**). In fact, he's kind of an immature, selfish, arrogant jerk with a superior attitude and a nasty ambition fueled by envy and spite. So why do we want to watch a story about this guy? Well, there is certainly something interesting about getting a behind-the-scenes glimpse at someone's speedy rise from an unpopular tech geek to CEO billionaire, especially if that achievement pushes the borders of ethics, scruples, and friendship. It's also fascinating to see a person with utterly no social skills become rich by creating a social network. Intellectually, Zuckerberg understands the zeroes and ones of a social network, but emotionally he cannot function in a social situation—a delicious central irony. But isn't there also something about this character that, despite his unsavory pettiness, we can understand on a human level? He's brilliant but he's awkward, terribly insecure and yearning to become someone people admire. He just doesn't know how to get there without being duplicitous and stomping on friends. We may

■ **Figure 1-3** Engaging central characters can be conceived as valiant and likable, like Ale (Alejandro Polanco) in Bahrani's *Chop Shop* (2007, *left*), or unsavory and vindictive like Mark Zuckerberg (Jesse Eisenberg) in Fincher's *The Social Network* (2010, *right*). It's also common to combine noble and ignoble qualities in a single character, as long as they remain compelling figures.

not go so far as to feel *sympathy* for America's youngest billionaire, but we can, on some level, connect to him and be engaged in his story. Also, keep in mind that these two character approaches, sympathetic and antipathetic, are only the extreme ends of a sliding scale. Many characters, like most human beings, are created somewhere between these two poles, with a few qualities we can admire and some qualities that are troubling.

You may have noticed in these examples that I mention both who the central character is and what happens to them. How an audience feels about a character is integrally linked to that character's dramatic situation and what that character *does*. This is, after all, the way we come to conclusions about anyone we meet in our lives. We know who people are by seeing what they do. So we cannot really talk about character without talking about what the character does.

The Dramatic Situation, Actions and Stakes

A dramatic narrative film involves a character in a situation, one that has a clear effect on them and provokes action. The character's response to that situation (what the character does) tells us who they are and moves the story forward. In the early stages of crafting a story, while we search for our character, we are also imagining the specific situation we can put that character in that gets them moving and reveals who they are. By moving I mean, reacting, making decisions, taking action. Without a situation that gets our central character moving, we don't have a movie. Also, you need to be clear about *what's at stake* for this particular character in this particular story. What does the character stand to lose, to win, to discover? How might the character change? These details form the **dramatic situation** or **premise**. The task of a film-maker in the early stages of conceptualization is to develop dramatic situations that can, in some way, change the character through a discovery, an accomplishment, an experience, an epiphany, an ordeal—whatever it is, the main character is not quite the same at the end of the film as they were at the beginning or the viewer's understanding of that character is not quite the same. What emerges from the chemical reaction between a particular character in a particular situation is a specific **central dramatic question**.

Resolution and What It All Means

In any film, all the narrative activity leads to a conclusion of some sort. This means that the dramatic situation you've established is resolved and the central dramatic question you've posed is answered, even if the viewer understands that life goes on for the character after the movie ends. This resolution can be positive or negative for your central character; you can have ironic endings, pyrrhic victories, unexpected outcomes, humorous twists, epiphanies, or any sort of conclusion that satisfies the questions you've raised. But resolutions must be carefully considered. Not only do they emerge from and answer back to the dramatic situation, but the way you resolve your movie is a significant part of what the ultimate meaning of your movie is. To find the most dramatically satisfying and thematically appropriate resolution, you need to ask yourself what the point of all this narrative activity (character/situation/action) was and what does it all add up to? This ultimate meaning can be as big as a universal theme or as small as a clever ironic point. Is your film an allegory with a broad moral lesson? Is it a mystery with a dramatic twist that will leave a viewer breathless? Is it a glimpse into a unique person's life that connects a viewer to a new perspective? Is it a comedy that will give viewers a great belly laugh? Knowing specifically, what the effect you want to have on an audience and what you want them to be left with will help you organize your material into a dramatically satisfying narrative shape and find the strongest conclusion to your story.

Now that I've laid out the essential elements for fictional narrative films, let's turn our attention to the short films from the companion website and see how these elements of cinematic storytelling play out. These movies were chosen specifically because they represent a variety of approaches, styles, and even running times, yet they all contain, in some form, the four basic narrative elements:

- In Phil and Olly's *The Black Hole* a bored, exhausted office clerk is wearily photocopying papers late into the night when he discovers a magic black hole that allows him to reach through solid bodies. This ability can clearly change his dreary life. Very quickly we understand the *central character*, the *dramatic situation,* and the *stakes*. The *central dramatic question*, what every viewer is wondering, is what's he going to do with this magical ability? Now he gets moving and his actions start small and get bigger (*narrative shape*): first he tests the hole with his hand, then he tries it on the vending machine and gets a free candy bar, then he uses it to get into the forbidden office, and finally he plunders the safe with it. Each step in this narrative activity reveals to us that the black hole stirs the avaricious impulses of this fallible but very human character. Each time he takes more, he wants more. I must admit, I wouldn't be satisfied with just a free candy bar (*identification*), would you? In the end he is defeated by his own desire to have it all (*resolution*). The major dramatic question is answered: he abuses the magical powers and dooms himself. So this film turns out to be a little morality tale. Like nearly every other allegorical story about a person given magical powers, the irony of the conclusion is that he is undone by the very magic that promised to make his life better.

- John Daschbach's short film *Waking Dreams* has a simple premise to express a complex idea. Office executive Mr. Saroyan (*central character*) is all set to go on a scuba diving vacation. But Becky, an eccentric office temp worker whom he doesn't know, tells him she had a dream in which he was in a yellow bathing suit scuba diving and was attacked by sharks. She's certain that this was a premonition and warns him that he's going to die if he goes in the water (*dramatic situation)*. The central dramatic question is, will he or won't he go in the water? In order for this premise to work, Daschbach must plant small seeds of possibility in her clairvoyant prediction (i.e., she could not have known he was going on a scuba diving vacation and she seems to predict an incoming call). He only needs a little bit of possibility precisely because the *stakes* here are so high, life and death, so there is no margin for error. In the end, the film's *resolution* answers the central question absolutely—yes he went scuba diving, and he didn't die. But *Waking Dreams* remains slyly open ended because it intentionally doesn't entirely answer another nagging question, was Becky's premonition accurate? Maybe yes, maybe no. He didn't wear a yellow bathing suit, so maybe she was correct, but he changed his fate? Or maybe the "premonition" was just the invention of a mentally unstable woman. Or maybe her next premonition, "don't take the subway," is a true portent. Without answering this question, our central character and the viewer are left with a larger, lingering existential question about fate, destiny and free will, which human beings will never adequately answer.

- The *central character* in *Plastic Bag* is, well, an ordinary plastic grocery bag, but Bahrani has given this particular bag human consciousness and character with which a viewer can empathize. The bag speaks and articulates its desires, fears, and hopes. The bag's *dramatic situation*, which unfolds quickly, is that it is at first put to constructive use by its "maker" and is truly happy. However, once his maker throws the bag away, it no longer has a purpose in life. This *situation* requires *action* because, like most humans, the bag wants its life to mean something. Obviously, the *central dramatic question* is, will it find a purpose for its existence? That larger goal is broken down into smaller, very specific goals (e.g., to find its maker, to find community in the vortex, etc.) and these *decisions* and *actions* make up its journey, its search for purpose. The journey is the narrative shape for the film; like most journeys, it is episodic in nature with each episode posing new conflicts and revelations. Along the way, the plastic bag encounters many complications: it gets caught in trees, the winds do not blow, it gets lost, it discovers that there are no people left on earth, not even its maker. Without people, how can it find a purpose? Also, it doesn't really understand the world it explores (*internal conflict*) and this causes confusion. The "humanity" of this plastic bag, however, also means that it is painfully cognizant of its terrible condition of loneliness, purpose-lessness, and immortality. In the end, after all its peregrinations, it does not find its purpose, and that's the tragedy and the thematic point of the film (*resolution*). A dis-carded plastic bag, with no purpose, is simply garbage, an unnatural thing floating around the natural world forever and ever. If only it could die. To find the ultimate point of this film we need to consider some of the ideas Bahrani has developed: a journey, looking for one's "maker," searching for meaning in life, immortality; these ideas tap into rich story traditions, and by doing so Bahrani has created an allegorical tale that follows one brown plastic bag but is not just about the plight of that one bag. Rather, it represents the trillions and trillions of plastic bags with no purpose that we've already created and thrown away. By the end of the film we come to feel that the consequence of discovering immortality in the form of plastic has precipitated the destruction of the human race. These are *huge* themes carried in a very small and poetic film.

■ Perhaps the subtlest film of the online examples is Huixia Lu's short *When I Was Young*. The *central character* of this film is Sue, a young Chinese immigrant in Philadelphia. Her task in the film is completely banal, to pick her husband up from work. There are no conflicts or obstacles to this task, so the real story isn't located here. Sue's *dramatic situation* arises when she hears her housemates, another married couple from China, arguing over the husband's inability to score TOEFL grades good enough to get into college. This moment, along with other triggers later on, cause her to remember an American boy she knew in China. The *dramatic tension* in this film centers on the disquiet and disappointment she experiences when she compares the optimism and excitement she felt about America when she was young (delicately represented by the figure of the American boy) and the way her actual life in America has turned out. The *central dramatic question* is under-stated, but it is there: How will this woman reconcile the dream with the reality? The shape of this film moves back and forth from her optimistic days in China to her dreary current life in America, but nothing in either location is overt or excep-tional. The ultimate idea and organizing principle for this film is that it is a small slice of life, an intimate portrait of a person who is disappointed with how things have turned out. The poignancy for this kind of film does not come from grand dramatic gestures; rather, the opportunity for an empathetic and human connec-tion comes from the accumulation of small, sharp, and truthful details—the close and accurate observation of someone who could be our next-door neighbor or any person walking down the street. By close observation I mean carefully chosen, small yet precise details that reveal much: sharing a cheap apartment with another couple in quarters so tight that she can hear their bickering, splitting the phone bill down to the penny, locking the car door, her husband's low-level prep job in a Chinese restaurant, the disrespectful way her husband is treated, the fact that he gives her all his earnings, the American flag hat he wears, and so on. The scenes in China are not explicit expressions of her immigrant dreams; rather they are poeti-cally associative of an emotional state of youthful hopefulness. During this clash of her current life and what she felt as a young woman in China, she decides to do something nice for herself and she buys a single rose (an *action* that is clearly and revealingly a financial splurge). That rose is hers and she makes this clear to the husband who just lost his job. But her next act brings this one small moment in her life to a *resolution* of sorts and satisfies the major dramatic question; she takes her husband's hand sympathetically in her own, meaning she doesn't reconcile her hopes with her reality but accepts the reality and carries on. True to the slice-of-life genre, Lu has just dipped in and out of a brief moment in a longer life of struggle: Sue's life will go on and on after the moment she takes her husband's hand. But the small moment Lu has chosen is so representative and revealing that it stands as a portrait of a woman (*the meaning*).

By now you should be able to see, given the interplay of the essential elements of dramatic narrative, how the engine of cinematic storytelling works: (1) a compelling character is placed in a situation that provokes a reaction or action, (2) what the character does (or doesn't do) reveals more about who that character is *and* (3) results in a new situation requiring new actions (etc.). With the right choices we get to have our cake and eat it too in that as the story moves forward we both reveal our character and develop complexity or intensity or nuance to the storyline.

Making Specific Choices

It is critical that the choices you make when creating a character and the dramatic premise are very specific. Vague situations or amorphous characters will not yield specific actions, a sharp narrative line, or a well-defined conclusion. A woman who is lonely and wants to escape loneliness may be the general subtext of your movie, but in terms of a storyline it is way too vague and open ended. Who is the woman, specifically? Is she a rich dowager in New York City? The wife of a mean farmer in a rural town? A young intellectual who is obsessed with, and lives within, her books? And what does it mean "to escape loneliness"? Specifically, what is her situation and what does she do? Leave her neglectful husband? Convince her gerontologist to start an intimate relationship? Join an exclusive singles club composed of much wealthier members? Convince an estranged son to move back home? Search for her lost dog? Although derived from the same general idea, each one of these specific choices will yield a significantly different story. So when moving from vague inspiration to an images-on-the-screen story, you need to define and develop those specific details that can generate the particular movie you wish to make (see the *Pieces of April* concept, discussed later).

■ FICTIONAL NARRATIVE BASICS II: CONFLICT-DRIVEN STORIES

One of the most common methods to get a character and a story moving is to create a situation of **direct conflict**. This is traditionally conceptualized as a story in which a character, who needs to accomplish something, encounters obstacles and must struggle to get what they need. The American playwright, screenwriter, and director David Mamet (Figure 1-4) wrote a description of this common story type in his book *On Directing Film:*

The story is the essential progression of incidents that occurs to our hero in pursuit of his one goal. ... It consists of the assiduous application of several basic questions: What does the hero want? What hinders him from getting it? What happens if he does not get it?

This sort of dramatic situation is referred to as a **conflict-driven story** because the story's forward momentum is generated by conflicts that keep your central character from achieving their identifiable goal (or want, or need, or task). This goal can be obvious (to get the job) or it can be subtle (to understand another person). It can be an extraordinary goal (to save the world) or an ordinary one (to get home). Goals can be professional tasks that must be accomplished (to solve the criminal case)

■ **Figure 1-4** American writer/director David Mamet works extensively in both film and theater.

or a personal need (to earn a mentor's respect). In feature films, where you have more time to develop characters, you can develop multiple layers to what a character wants or needs. For example, a main character's goal in the plot might be to get the big job, but his interior need is to win his father's love. In this sort of situation, the exterior goal is devised to reveal a deeply held interior longing.

Once you add some kind of **opposing force** (obstacles) to the progress of the central character, the dramatic question emerges: Will the central character achieve their goal? Will they complete their task? Conflicts that oppose our "hero's" progress can come from many places. An opposing force can be another character who stands in the way or is struggling for a contradictory goal. This sort of character is called an **antagonist**. External forces like weather, government bureaucracy, a traffic jam, an inhospitable landscape, or a physical injury can also be used as obstacles. And, of course, the opposing force can be even more subtle or complex than this. For example, you could create a situation where your central character is ambivalent or averse to a task they are obliged to accomplish (e.g., to prosecute a close friend who is corrupt). Thus, the conflict is built into the task itself. Or the obstacles can have an internal source, coming from the character; for example, a character might feel fear, insecurity, ambivalence, or lethargy in the face of the task at hand. However, when dealing with obstacles that come from within, a filmmaker needs to figure out ways to externalize the internal so that "feelings" are transformed into actions and decisions that we can put on film.

In David Mamet's quote he mentions an "essential progression of incidents." These are the events of the film. The moments, actions, reactions, and interactions, all of which make up the plot. The **plot** is the order of events in your film—the unfolding of the story in scenes and the order of those scenes. When a goal-oriented character encounters an obstacle, something that "hinders him from getting [his goal]," he is compelled to do something in order to find a way over, around, or through that obstacle to get what he wants. The exciting thing about conflict-driven drama is that deciding what characters do and how they do it reveals, in a dramatized way, who each character is. So I would add one more to Mamet's list of basic questions: *What is the hero willing and able to do to achieve their goal?* Now, if we pose a question like this, then it stands to reason that there are things a character is *not* willing or able to do. Keep in mind that what characters *don't* do, what they avoid and how they avoid it, can also be revealing of character. As the plot continues, the obstacles and actions usually increase in intensity because each action (or inaction) has *consequences*, and those consequences cause the tension to increase until the protagonist, in one last-ditch effort to get what they want, brings the film to a *resolution*. As I mentioned earlier, the resolution answers the central question: Did the hero get what they wanted after all? Did the hero accomplish what they needed to do? In a happy ending the goal is accomplished, and in a tragic ending the resolution is not what the hero had hoped.

Now, let's get back to *Pieces of April*. Hedges did not completely discover the full dimensions of the story until the late 1990s, when he was dealing with his own mother's cancer diagnosis. As he says in his book, "That's when I realized I had a story to tell." He also hung onto that initial spark—"this could be a way to have all sorts of people cross paths who normally wouldn't"—and it emerged as the central theme in the film. Hedges transformed his idea into a cinematic story by turning the "group of people" (too vague) looking for a working oven to cook their Thanksgiving turkey into the specific story of a girl named April, the black sheep of a family (*central character*) who decides to cook an all-out, traditional Thanksgiving dinner for her family in her New York City apartment (*plot goal*). Cooking is the way this iconoclastic character tries to reconcile with her mother, who is dying from cancer (*internal need and personal motivation*), but April's lovely gesture nearly fails because she has no cooking ability whatsoever (*obstacle*) and her oven doesn't work (*obstacle*). Her dysfunctional family, arriving from out of town, is fully anticipating a disaster (*pressure*). April elicits the aid of her neighbors (*actions*),

Figure 1-5 In Hedges' *Pieces of April* (2003), iconoclastic free spirit April (Katie Holmes) attempts to reconnect with her estranged family by preparing a Thanksgiving meal.

whom she doesn't know, to help her pull off the meal. In the end April completes the Thanksgiving dinner, forms a new family of friends, *and* manages to reconnect with her mom before her mom dies (*resolution*) (Figure 1-5).

A lot of Pieces of April *to me is about the family you're born into but also the family you find, and it was the family you find that really compelled me to write this particular story.*

(From an interview with Mark Pfeiffer, ***The Film Journal*, November 2003)**

Pieces of April shows that while the terms "hero," "goal," "conflict," and "action" sound hugely dramatic, they actually work for films of any size and any subject. You don't necessarily need to conceive of a film like *Raiders of the Lost Ark*, in which Indiana Jones (hero!) has to obtain the Arc of the Covenant (goal!!), and with the Nazi Army after it too (obstacle!!!). You can use these same dramatic principles on just about any scale project and with any degree of subtlety, such as a young woman who wants to connect with her mother by cooking a Thanksgiving turkey, or even a little boy who wants to get past a big dog to get home (see *Bread and Alley,* discussed later).

■ FICTIONAL NARRATIVE BASICS III: THERE ARE NO RULES

Conflict is immensely useful for a filmmaker because it provides narrative momentum and elicits revealing actions from characters. But does conflict always have to always be so overt? Is it always used as a direct obstacle, getting in the way of our character's goal? Not at all.

The goal and conflict approach is a mainstay for the feature length form because it must maintain dramatic tension and develop characters and storylines over an extended period of time. Naturally, the goal and conflict approach works perfectly well for short films as well, as we can see with *Plastic Bag* and *Waking Dreams* (and *Bread and Alley,* discussed later). But the brevity of short films makes it an extremely flexible story form, allowing a filmmaker to work with subtler forms of conflict, other sources of dramatic tension, and other approaches to a central dramatic question beyond "will the hero achieve a specific goal?"

Didier Rouget's film, *Vive le 14 Juillet* starts out with dramatic tension in the form of an unsupportable situation: a sweet, mild-mannered guy (*central character*) has a wayward girlfriend who is attracted to men in uniform. To make matters worse, he doesn't seem capable of doing anything about it (*situation*). What sends him into action is when he literally loses his girlfriend during the Bastille Day parade. In order to find her, he commandeers a tank, locates her with high-powered binoculars, and lifts her into his arms with the tank's canon barrel, all the while revealing the military mojo necessary to truly get his girlfriend back (*resolution*). There are, in fact, no real obstacles getting in the way of his dramatic goal; nonetheless, something significant is revealed in the end to his girlfriend and the viewer that was there all along—this sweet, mild-mannered guy can be a heroic man of action when he has to be. In *The Black Hole*, the dramatic situation does not include any direct conflict either; the clerk is mysteriously delivered a magic hole and nothing gets in the way of his using it. Nonetheless, dramatic tension exists because we wonder how he'll use the magic hole and how far he'll go with it. Before long (two minutes) the film delivers its ironic conclusion. Finally, *When I Was Young* does derive conflict from the friction between the optimism Sue felt in her past and the bleak reality of her current situation, but although this conflict provides a powerful undercurrent of tension to the story, it does not generate direct obstacles to the task she is undertaking in the plot, which is to pick up her husband.

When filmmakers eschew a conflict-driven plot, they must replace the goal-oriented dramatic question, "Will the protagonist get what they are after?" with something else equally compelling. Here are a few story types that can work without direct obstacles to protagonist goals:

- Mysterious or ambiguous activity that is explained in the end
- A discovery that changes the perceptions of a character or the viewer
- An experience or series of events that changes a character or reveals their true nature.
- A story that constitutes a puzzle to be solved
- Slice of life stories that are detailed, perceptive, and revealing portraits.
- An allegorical journey
- A setup/payoff plot structure (setup/ironic twist, setup/epiphany, setup/humorous punch line, setup/perception shift, etc.)

Here's another simple example. Maggie, a woman in her early fifties and her young daughter Maria (around 10) arrive at a cemetery and stroll to one of the graves. Along the way they talk casually about the girl's school, the cemetery, and a stray cat. When they get to the grave they set out a little picnic including sandwiches and grapes (Maria's favorite fruit). The feeling is that this is a regular, if infrequent, routine for them. The dramatic question is delicate (whose grave might they be visiting?) and there are clues in the dialogue that it could be the Maggie's father, whom she mentions in the past tense and whom the girl says she doesn't remember. There is absolutely no direct or overt conflict. In fact, nothing much out of the ordinary happens as they eat, chat about mom's hair, and play games, except for two small details: during their picnic Maggie drinks something from her thermos that appears to be more potent than orange juice and she uses the F-word in front of her little girl. This certainly doesn't constitute conflict, but it's a bit out of place. In any case, eventually, Maria needs to pee and goes behind a tree and here, additional subtle tension enters the situation, Maggie responds strangely during a guessing game Maria is playing, and when they play patty-cake, Maggie breaks down and cries. But her lovely little girl is there to comfort her and Maggie lays her head on her daughter's lap. Then camera briefly leaves them and scans the periphery of the cemetery before returning to the picnic site. But now Maggie is alone and folding her blanket getting ready to leave. When Maggie makes the small gesture of laying the grapes (Maria's favorite fruit) on the gravestone, we realize that this is Maria's grave and she had conjured the presence of her daughter for comfort (as it seems she does on each visit). This short film synopsis describes the *Maggie* episode from Rodrigo Garcia's film *Nine Lives* (2005), a feature-length movie comprising nine slice-of-life vignettes of nine different women. Each episode is a self-contained 10- to 12-minute short film that represents a particularly critical and revealing moment in each woman's life. Some of the segments involve traditional conflict driven storylines, while others, like the *Maggie* episode, do not (**Figure 1-6**).

The structure here is simple: setup/perception shift. The setup is filled with activity that seems completely commonplace but contains a few off-balance moments. Then in one stirring and surprising moment, the

■ **Figure 1-6** The *Maggie* episode from Garcia's *Nine Lives* (2005) contains very little in the way of direct obstacles, yet it delivers a devastating conclusion that inverts everything we thought we understood about the situation.

filmmaker unveils the total perception shift for the viewer: the grave is actually Maria's. What we assumed was real and true, wasn't. But the perception shift is narratively satisfying because as we reflect on the subtle clues embedded in the story we see that it makes perfect narrative and emotional sense.

This discussion of dramatic principles, of course, is only a basic guideline. As an emerging filmmaker, you should be testing these boundaries and possibilities yourself. Cinematic storytelling allows lots of flexibility and room for experimentation. The legendary filmmaker Jean-Luc Godard is commonly paraphrased as saying that films do indeed need a beginning, middle, and end, though not necessarily in that order. Just as the subject matter of drama is virtually unlimited, so, too, are the ways that we can approach these subjects in cinema. The way you tell stories on film can vary depending on what you want to say, how you want a viewer to feel along the way, and what is appropriate for the ultimate point of your movie. As one of my writing professors, the novelist Alan Cheuse, once said of writing in general, "There is only one absolute rule to telling stories—make it work." Nonetheless, an understanding of the basic principles and the conventions that inform most cinematic narratives is an essential starting point. Obviously, it is not even remotely possible to exhaust this subject in one short chapter, which is all a book like this can afford. There are countless books on the shelves exploring in great detail the form, structure, and elements of cinematic drama. I have included some of these books in the recommended readings and, of course, all the films cited throughout this book serve as excellent examples to study.

■ IDEAS WITHIN LIMITATIONS

The second sentence from the Kiarostami quote, which opens this chapter, "Our second job is to think of a film that can be made," refers to one of the most important skills a filmmaker can develop: identifying ideas that can both be great movies and be accomplished within the filmmaker's real-world limitations. No matter how good your idea, if it is beyond your resources and experience you will not have a movie to show in the end. Always keep in mind, from the very first stages, that there is a symbiotic relationship between ideas and resources. One must work, from the beginning, with *what one has* rather than what *one wishes one had.* Such resourcefulness will go a long way to ensuring that you will, in fact, make movies.

Every film project, from a student's first film exercise to huge-budget Hollywood productions, works within limitations. The smart filmmaker will take these limitations into consideration from the very conception of the idea and the earliest development of the screenplay. A filmmaker's job is always to make the best film possible within the realistic limitations of the particular circumstances. You may have a big-budget, epic film waiting to burst out, but if you are taking only your second film class, your film is due in three weeks, you're using sync sound for the very first time, and you lost one-third of your film funds fixing your car, it may not be the right moment to go for the Oscar. But every project, large or small, is an opportunity to show that you can master the craft of filmmaking, the art of cinematic storytelling, and your specific circumstances to deliver an effective film.

You do not need unlimited resources to be a successful filmmaker; you need to be smart about the resources you have. The following sections describe some real-world circumstances that a filmmaker should consider from a project's earliest conceptual stages.

Story Scale and Film Length

Running-time restrictions for a project can be imposed for a variety of reasons, from a professor setting a time limit, to standard television broadcast time limits, which demand accuracy to the fraction of a second. If an advertising agency hires you to make a 30-second commercial spot, you will not be allowed to hand in a 32-second spot, no matter how brilliant the extra 2 seconds are. If you've imagined a terrific idea for a feature film but only have the resources to make a 15-minute film, it's not a good idea to try to condense your long story into a short form. The story must fit the size and scope of your production.

Short films can be about almost anything, but they tell simple stories with a strict economy of means. They revolve around a single idea, quickly recognizable characters, and a sharp turning point to make one moment resonate. Short film concepts, of necessity, are narrowly circumscribed because they must be expressed in a matter of minutes. You do not have time to complexly develop or slowly transform a character, nor can you examine every angle of a situation or involve too many extra elements outside of the basic story engine. You don't have room for multiple story layers or for developing a historical context. What we look for in a short film is an idea that can be expressed with simple narrative elements and vivid imagery: characters and a situation that we can recognize quickly, a conflict that is streamlined, and actions that are revealing all on their own without explication. Short films can be just as profound as features, but they must be tight, simple, and efficient.

If you consider the short films I've gathered for the online examples, you'll see a wide variety of characters, themes, story types, visual styles, and running times; but they are all sharp, efficient, and clear in what they are trying to communicate. *Plastic Bag* is an allegorical journey with sweeping themes about mortality, existence, and pollution; in two and a half minutes, *The Black Hole* delivers a humorous story with a sharp ironic twist and a moral message; *When I Was Young* conveys a complex, detailed, intimate, and sympathetic understanding of a woman by representing only two very brief, and even mundane, moments in her life; and *Waking Dreams* explores a large existential theme in only a few quirky encounters between an unlikely duo. Not a single scene or detail or moment in any of these films is wasted or unnecessary and yet, as compact as they are, every one of them accurately reflects the unique artistic sensibility of the filmmaker.

Production Time

One of the most common mistakes young filmmakers make is underestimating how much time it takes to make a film and overestimating how much they can accomplish in a prescribed production period. Your production period can be defined by any number of factors: the limitations of a semester, the availability of an actor, changes in the weather, the availability of equipment or crew, delivery deadlines, and, of course, financial resources. Be realistic about the amount of time you have to complete a project and let this inform the idea you choose to develop and the scale of the story you write.

Financial Resources

Being realistic about your financial resources is a vital consideration because it determines many factors that figure into the film concept and, eventually, the screenplay, including the number of characters, the locations, and the props, as well as the time, crew, and equipment necessary to execute certain stories. But working with a limited budget should not stop you from making a great film.

It's obvious to anyone who goes to the movies that bigger budgets alone don't necessarily make better movies, so it also stands to reason that less money doesn't necessarily result in a film of inferior quality. Limited funds should never dampen your creativity; in fact, quite the opposite. The fewer financial resources you have, the more creative you have to be, and this often makes for ingenious filmmaking, which is why modest means have often led to enormous innovation. *La Jetée* (1962) by Chris Marker, *Two Men and a Wardrobe (Dwaj ludzie z szafa)* (1958) by Roman Polanski, and Maya Deren's *Meshes of the Afternoon* (1943) are all black-and-white shorts shot with tiny production crews, minimal financial

■ **Figure 1-7** Deren's *Meshes of the Afternoon* (1943, *left*) is a landmark American film shot on a minimal budget; it has no synchronized sound and is only 18 minutes long. Marker's *La Jetée* (1962, *center*), one of the great films of the French New Wave, tells its complex and compelling story in 28 minutes, almost exclusively through still images. Polanski won many international film awards with *Two Men and a Wardrobe* (1958, *right*) a short produced while he was a student at the Lodz film school. Despite nominal resources, all of these short films have an established place in the history of cinema because of their beauty and innovation.

resources, and no synchronized sound, yet they are considered classics of the short form for their incalculable contributions to the art of the cinema (Figure 1-7). The key with each of these films is that their basic idea was smart, sharp, and elegant and worked intelligently with minimal resources.

Equipment, Location, Props, and Other Resources

You may have a wonderful idea for a short film—say, about a timid oceanographer who wins the heart of his one true love by taking her on a deep sea dive and showing her the wonders of the ocean floor—but if that movie requires real underwater photography and you have no access to an ocean (because you live in South Dakota) nor the equipment you need to shoot underwater, then maybe it's not the best idea to go with, even if it is a winner. Also, keep in mind that there is a direct link between the number of locations and the amount of time and money you will spend. A short film idea conceived with two locations in mind is easier to accomplish than one that involves 12 locations.

Cast and Crew

Small crews can only do so much. There will be many times, especially on low-budget projects, when crew members need to double up on responsibilities, but you need to be aware, as you write your screenplay, that there is a law of diminishing returns when it comes to overextending your crew. Developing story ideas that require sync sound, moving cameras, careful lighting, crowd management, costumes, makeup, and so on will require crew to address each need. If you are expecting your cinematographer to take care of the camera and the logging and to set up all of the lighting alone and to do the special-effects makeup and arrange the furniture, don't be surprised if something goes wrong with the camera work.

Also, keep in mind that the number of characters you write into a film has a direct impact on the financial and logistical burden of the project. The more people you have in front of the camera, the more time and money you can generally expect to spend.

The enemy of art is the absence of limitations.

Orson Welles

Keep It Manageable

If you're just starting out in filmmaking, it's best to keep your projects manageable. A tight, effective, stylistically exciting five-minute film in which all of your story and technical elements work together to tell a convincing and involving little story is *always* preferable to a sloppy 30-minute film which loses its way because the filmmaker did not have command of all the cinematic details. Even worse is a film that cannot even be completed because its demands exceed the limits of the filmmaker's resources. Your first opportunity to establish the logistical, financial, and labor parameters of your production happens right in the beginning, as you develop your idea and begin scripting. It's wonderful and important to be optimistic about your projects, but you must also be realistic.

In general, novice filmmakers, still honing their craft, work on short films between 2 and 15 minutes in length. I do not use the word "novice" in any pejorative sense; every filmmaker is a novice in the beginning—even a celebrated master like Abbas Kiarostami. His first film was a 10-minute short called *Bread and Alley* (1970).[1] (**Figure 1-8**) The film is about a young boy, carrying a loaf of bread, on his way home from school (*goal*). To get home he must travel down a labyrinth of narrow and deserted alleyways. In one alley he is confronted by a big dog who chases him back and then lies down in the middle of the alley (*major obstacle/ conflict*). Frightened, the boy can't proceed home past the dog. He looks around and sees that there is no alternate route and that the alley is so narrow that he cannot sneak around the dog (*location as obstacle*). Other people travel past the dog without a problem, but he cannot (*inaction revealing his fear*). He's stuck and it's getting late. Just then an old man walks by and the boy decides to follow closely behind him to get past the dog (*action*). But just as they reach the dog, the old man turns down a side alley into his house, leaving the boy alone again and face to face with the dog (*conflict intensifies*). Knowing he must do something quickly, the boy breaks off a piece of bread and throws it to the dog (*action*). With the dog now distracted by eating the bread, the boy scampers past. Finished with the morsel of bread, the dog takes off after the frightened boy, who feeds the dog more bread as he heads toward home (*action*). Before long the dog's tail is wagging happily and the boy reaches his house, where the door is safely closed between him and the dog (*resolution*). The dog lies down in the alleyway until along comes another food carrying boy, the dog growls at him and the whole thing starts again… (*coda*).

Bread and Alley is a good example of a filmmaker following his own advice. The film involved only elements that were easy for Kiarostami to obtain, especially crucial because this was his first film. The movie is only 10 minutes long and it was shot in black and white, without sound, without lights, and, for Kiarostami, in an easily obtainable location. He shot the film in one day with only two crew members, one boy, and a couple of extras. Kiarostami needed some bread, some milk, and, the film's toughest requirement, a dog. But, of course, the most important thing he had from the outset was a simple yet elegant and touching story idea.

■ **Figure 1-8** *Bread and Alley* (1970), Abbas Kiarostami's first film as writer/director.

---

[1] Kiarostami's *Bread and Alley* is not on the *Voice & Vision* website, but it does show up on YouTube once in a while (no promises, though).

Robert Rodriguez' *El Mariachi* (1992), a feature film produced for $7,000, went on to win major awards and serious Hollywood studio contracts for its director. The first secret to Rodriguez' success is that he came up with an idea that he could make into a film using what he had at his disposal (**Figure 1-9**).

> *How do you make a cheap movie? Look around you, what do you have around you? … Your father owns a liquor store—make a movie about a liquor store. Do you have a dog? Make a movie about your dog. Your mom works in a nursing home, make a movie about a nursing home. When I did El Mariachi I had a turtle, I had a guitar case, I had a small town and I said I'll make a movie around that.*
>
> **Robert Rodriguez**
> **(From Robert Rodriguez'**
> ***10 Minute Film School)***

By doing the shooting, directing, and editing himself, he required only a small crew of five people; he used few artificial lights, did not shoot with synchronized sound, and used locations that were nearby and easily accessed. The small crew was so lean that Rodriguez could work fast—a method that he calls "frantic filmmaking." The second quality that made his film so successful is that he turned all of these "limitations" into an opportunity to create a flamboyant style that perfectly matched the story and mood of the film. Nowhere is this more apparent than in his energetic camera style, which swoops, pivots, glides, and shoots from a stunning variety of angles. Rodriguez had no lights, no sound (and therefore no sound crew), and a small camera.

Realizing that his camera was free of these shackles, he also freed it from the tripod, allowing it to move, handheld, anywhere and everywhere.

> *On Mariachi I had two lights, regular light bulbs; they were balanced for indoor film, so [they] look fine. In fact everyone said the lighting looked moody because there was very little light. Your mistakes, your shortcomings suddenly become artistic expression.*
>
> **Robert Rodriguez**
> **(From Robert Rodriguez'**
> ***10 Minute Film School)***

When Kelly Reichardt read the short story "Old Joy" by Jonathan Raymond, she knew right away that she not only *wanted* to adapt it into a film, she *could* actually make the film. The story, which is about two old friends who reunite for a weekend camping trip in the Oregon forests, attracted her on many levels. One was the idea of making a film that would involve bringing a very small cast and crew together for a condensed period of time in a very special, somewhat isolated, place—in this case, the old-growth forests of Oregon. The result was Reichardt's ultra-low-budget and intensely moving feature film *Old Joy* (2006) (**Figure 1-10**).

All of the requirements were within Reichardt's grasp: a small cast of two principal actors, a car, a dog, and the Pacific Northwest wilderness. She had one more crew person, six, than Rodriguez had, because she was shooting with sync sound and needed another person to record sound. She also brought to the project Peter Sillen, a cinematographer with extensive

■ **Figure 1-9** A turtle, a guitar case, and a town. Robert Rodriguez crafted the story of his successful *El Mariachi* (1992) around things he knew he had access to or could borrow.

experience on documentaries, so was expert at working with natural light and "working small." True to her original inspiration, Reichardt brought her small cast and crew to Oregon, where they lived together in friend's houses and in a church retreat in the Oregon forests. The film took a mere 10 days to shoot. Reichardt had only two lights, which she used in only two scenes. The rest of the time she shot in the magnificent old-growth forests of Oregon under cloudy skies. The location and the quality of natural light made her low-budget film look like a million bucks—nature itself (the birds, rivers, and foliage) became like another character in the film.

Working small also allowed the cast and crew to be especially agile and made it possible to work in the rugged terrain and around the sudden downpours, which were frequent in Oregon. However, the primary benefit to emerge from the limits of her working conditions involved the intimacy of the group. As Reichardt tells it, "Everyone schlepped equipment up and down the paths, even the actors. And when it rained, all of us would pile into the car and go over lines, do rehearsals, and discuss the film until it stopped." The intense and close working conditions created a strong collaborative energy between cast and crew, which encouraged everyone to contribute to the film. "We knew we were all in this together. We were in a special place having a great experience together. I knew something would come out of it." These sessions generated a deep understanding of the script and some powerful improvisational exchanges, which wound up in the film. So much of what goes on in *Old Joy* is only barely and delicately revealed, and Reichardt's close-knit, small-scale production approach created the perfect environment for nurturing this tone. "I think the intimate approach we took to making the film comes through in the film itself. The limitations all somehow work out for you in the end. Although I sometimes had my doubts, it did work out that way in the end" (**Figure 1-11**).

With both *El Mariachi* and *Old Joy*, the aesthetic and conceptual approach to the film necessarily responded to the real-world limitations of the production resources, yet each style is so perfectly integrated with the story being told that one doesn't feel pennies being pinched or corners being cut. The stories are right for the resources and the approaches are just right for the stories. We can't imagine these films told any other way.

■ **Figure 1-10** In *Old Joy* (2006), Reichardt maintained a minimal crew that was isolated in Oregon's Cascade Mountains for the duration of the shoot, creating an atmosphere that complemented the intimate tone of the story.

■ **Figure 1-11** Director Kelly Reichardt conferring with lead actor Daniel London. The bond developed by the close-knit crew and cast of *Old Joy* created an intimacy that was evident on screen.

The Screenplay

A **screenplay** is the literary expression of the story, characters, actions, locations, and tone of your film written in a specialized dramatic script format. Whether you write the script yourself or work with someone else's material, it's important to remember that the screenplay is not the final product. It is an intermediate step in the production of a film and serves many functions in all stages of the project's development. It is often said that the screenplay is the blueprint for the entire process of making a film, in the same way that an architect's rendering serves as the blueprint for the construction of a house. In many ways this is true; however, unlike an architectural blueprint, a screenplay should remain a rather more flexible document throughout the process. It's important to keep in mind that screenplays evolve. They should be revised and rewritten, at every stage of a film's progression, as new ideas or circumstances emerge.

■ STAGES OF SCRIPT DEVELOPMENT

There are a number of stages in the evolution of a screenplay, and each stage usually requires various drafts. Each stage has a specific purpose as you proceed, step by step, from a general outline of your story to a script that contains the full dimensions of your film, including locations, actions, dialogue, sounds, and movements. This process of working and reworking your film's story material, adding, cutting, or refining details along the way, is called **script development**.

Concept

The **concept** is a very brief outline of the basic elements involved in your story. It describes, in no more than a few sentences, the essential dramatic engine that will drive the movie: Who is your main character? What is the central dramatic question around which all the action revolves? And how does it end? A good concept outlines the general shape of the narrative material. These are the elements that translate an idea for a film into something that is in fact a dramatized, filmable story. The descriptions of the basic story elements for *Pieces of April* (page 11) and *Bread and Alley* (page 17) are good examples of concepts.

Here's an example from one of my students, George Racz, who was making his second film, his first with synchronized sound. George has a four-year-old niece and he was enchanted by her vivid imagination. He had the idea to somehow capture in a movie her belief in wondrous and magical things. His intention was to charm an audience by allowing us to see the world for a moment through the eyes of this innocent, imaginative girl and, as George told me, "Through Panna I want to invite the viewers to rediscover those small magical moments which they once believed in" (**Figure 2-1**). George's intentions were clear, but it was not yet clear how he would accomplish this on film. *What* would he point the camera at? *What* would the little girl do? *What* would the audience actually see on screen that would charm them or make them see the world as Panna sees it? In short, what's the story? George quickly turned his general idea into a specific film concept.

At a toy store, four-year-old Kate is enjoying all the toys when she sees a homeless woman digging through the trash outside the store. At that moment her parents lead her to a magic show in the store and she assists the magician with a trick. Kate believes she has learned how to perform real magic. Later she sees a panhandler on crutches unable to walk, and she decides to help the poor man with her new magical powers; and it works.

■ **Figure 2-1** Frame from *The Miracle* (2006), George Racz (writer/director).

Ideas in their raw form do not constitute a film story. Once you have an idea, you need to translate it into a film concept with basic, but specific, story elements (see page 5). This is the beginning of your script development process. Once your concept is working, then you are ready to write a treatment where you'll develop more specific details.

Treatment

The **treatment** is a prose description of the plot, written in present tense, as the film will unfold for the audience, scene by scene (Figure 2-2). A treatment is a story draft where the writer can hammer out the basic actions and plot structure of the story before going into the complexities of realizing fully developed scenes with dialogue, precise actions, and setting descriptions. The treatment is the equivalent of a painter's sketch that can be worked and reworked before committing to paint on canvas. It's much easier to cut, add, and rearrange scenes in this form than in a fully detailed screenplay. Generally, a treatment involves writing a few sentences for each major dramatic event, also called a narrative beat. A **narrative beat** is a dramatic event

■ **Figure 2-2**
A treatment is a simple but comprehensive prose description of a film's plot. George Racz' treatment for *The Miracle*.

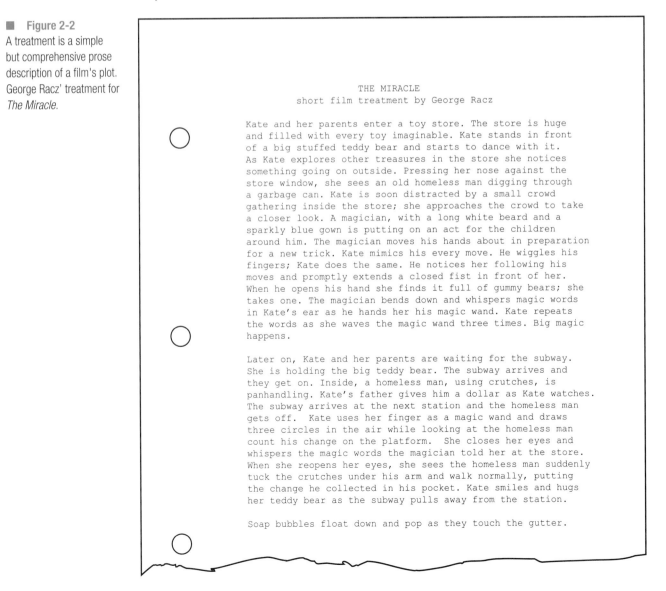

THE MIRACLE
short film treatment by George Racz

Kate and her parents enter a toy store. The store is huge and filled with every toy imaginable. Kate stands in front of a big stuffed teddy bear and starts to dance with it. As Kate explores other treasures in the store she notices something going on outside. Pressing her nose against the store window, she sees an old homeless man digging through a garbage can. Kate is soon distracted by a small crowd gathering inside the store; she approaches the crowd to take a closer look. A magician, with a long white beard and a sparkly blue gown is putting on an act for the children around him. The magician moves his hands about in preparation for a new trick. Kate mimics his every move. He wiggles his fingers; Kate does the same. He notices her following his moves and promptly extends a closed fist in front of her. When he opens his hand she finds it full of gummy bears; she takes one. The magician bends down and whispers magic words in Kate's ear as he hands her his magic wand. Kate repeats the words as she waves the magic wand three times. Big magic happens.

Later on, Kate and her parents are waiting for the subway. She is holding the big teddy bear. The subway arrives and they get on. Inside, a homeless man, using crutches, is panhandling. Kate's father gives him a dollar as Kate watches. The subway arrives at the next station and the homeless man gets off. Kate uses her finger as a magic wand and draws three circles in the air while looking at the homeless man count his change on the platform. She closes her eyes and whispers the magic words the magician told her at the store. When she reopens her eyes, she sees the homeless man suddenly tuck the crutches under his arm and walk normally, putting the change he collected in his pocket. Kate smiles and hugs her teddy bear as the subway pulls away from the station.

Soap bubbles float down and pop as they touch the gutter.

in which the action, decisions, or revelations of that moment move the plot forward either by intensifying it or by sending it in a new direction. In other words, a treatment sketches in the essential events. For a short film, a treatment might be one to three pages long. For very simple short films, you can simply write one sentence describing each narrative beat. This shorter version is called a **step outline** or a **beat sheet**.

Author's Draft

The **author's draft** is the first complete version of the narrative in proper screenplay format. The emphasis of the author's draft is on the story, the development of characters, and the conflict, actions, settings, and dialogue. The author's draft goes through a number of rewrites and revisions on its way to becoming a **final draft**, which is the last version of the author's draft before it is turned into a shooting script. The aim of an author's draft is to remain streamlined, flexible, and "readable." Therefore, technical information (such as detailed camera angles, performance cues, blocking, or detailed set description) is kept to an absolute minimum. It is important not to attempt to direct the entire film, shot for shot, in the author's draft. The detailed visualization and interpretation of the screenplay occurs during later preproduction and production stages. In this chapter we will look closely at some essential principles for script language and for formatting the author's draft.

Shooting Script

Once you have completed your rewrites and arrived at a final draft, you will be ready to take that script into production by transforming it into a shooting script. The **shooting script** is the version of the screenplay you take into production, meaning it is the script from which your creative team (cinematographer, production designer, etc.) will work and from which the film will be shot. A shooting script communicates, in specific terms, the director's visual approach to the film. All the scenes are numbered on a shooting script to facilitate breaking down the script and organizing the production of the film. This version also includes specific technical information about the visualization of the movie, like camera angles, shot sizes, and camera moves. Chapter 5 deals with the process of creating the shooting script.

■ FORMATTING THE AUTHOR'S DRAFT SCREENPLAY

The screenplay is a multipurpose document. It is both a literary manuscript, conveying the dramatic story for a reader, and a technical document that anticipates the logistics of the production process and allows everyone involved in your project to see what they need to do. The technical functions of a screenplay are realized in the format of the script, which is standardized to facilitate common film production processes. This is why a screenplay looks unlike any other literary manuscript.

Beyond the technical formatting of a script, the language of the author's draft screenplay, its style and detail, communicates the *spirit* of the visual approach, tone, rhythm, and point of view of the final film. Embedded in the author's draft are your first thoughts on visualizing the story for the screen without the use of camera cues and technical jargon. If written well, an author's draft script should help everyone involved in your project "see" what you are striving for, thematically and visually.

Elements of an Author's Draft Script

There are six formatting elements used in the screenplay form: title, scene headings, stage directions, dialogue, personal directions, and character cues. Let's look at *Kebacle* (2006), a simple screenwriting observation exercise written by my student Alana Kakoyiannis, and label each element. Alana was assigned to observe the people, activities, and interactions in the world around her for two weeks and then render one particularly interesting moment as a scene from a screenplay (**Figures 2-3** and **2-4**).

■ **Figure 2-3**
Screenplay formatting elements. *Kebacle* (2006); a typical moment on the streets of New York City, vividly written in screenplay form by Alana Kakoyiannis.

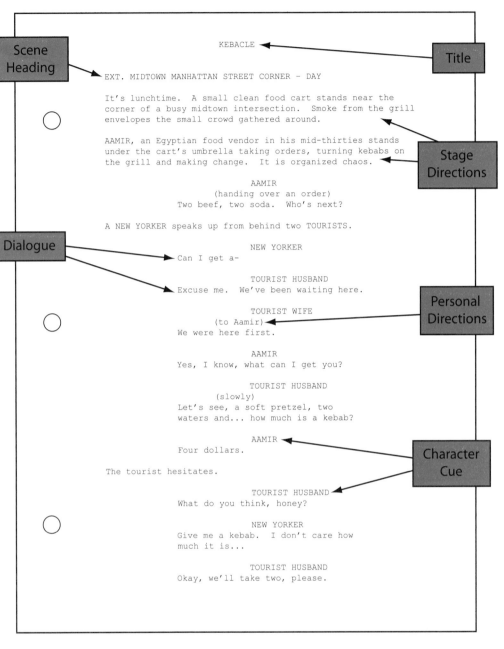

General Principles

A screenplay is written as the film would unfold to an audience. It is written in the present tense and must follow the progression of the film, moment by moment, scene by scene, as you wish it to appear before an audience. There is no literary commentary in a film script, and this necessitates two important practices:

1. The words on the page present each scene, action, image, character, and series of events to a reader as they would appear to the viewer of the film. Notice that Alana does not anticipate what is going to happen later by introducing Aamir saying:

Aamir is an unlicensed vendor who shouldn't be serving food to people on a public sidewalk.

We will get to that detail only when it is revealed to the audience. The screenplay builds its story one moment at a time in the same way the film will, and in the beginning all we see is a food vendor serving people.

2. *There should be nothing in the script that the film's audience will not see or hear.* In general, nothing goes on the page that cannot be realized on the screen in images and sounds. These are the fundamental tools of a filmmaker, and therefore they are the tools of the screenwriter as well. In prose fiction and poetry it is common for an author to explain to the reader what people are feeling, what personal history might be informing an action, what characters are secretly thinking, or even what subconsciously motivates them. In film we must dramatize these internal states. **To dramatize** is to externalize and reveal the internal, through actions, dialogue, and visual context. Notice that Alana does not describe what any character is feeling, their state of mind, or their intentions. She does not write, for example,

    The New Yorker is impatient and anxious to get back to work so he calls out his order out of turn.

If you are true to the moment and to the voices of the characters, the intentions behind each line should be apparent. We can already feel the impatience, verging on pushiness, in the words and actions of the New Yorker, so there is no need to announce them. It would, in fact, completely ruin the scene if Alana were to write something like

Aamir only pretends to close down by lowering his umbrella because he knows that as soon as the police van drives away, he can get back to business.

While these internal feelings and intentions may be part of what is going on in the scene, expressed this way, they are not cinematic. However, the filmable actions of Aamir folding his umbrella and watching the police drive away, then immediately reopening his umbrella to resume business without missing a beat, all vividly reveal what he was thinking and intending to do. Presented this way we also understand that this interaction is routine for him. It is far better to simply show it as it happens and let the audience discover his intentions for themselves—just as Alana did when she witnessed the scene.

Now let's look at each script element used in an author's draft individually.

Scene Headings (or Slug Lines)

The scene heading is our first introduction to each and every scene and establishes the fundamental time and location information in order to set the scene. What is a scene? **A scene** is a dramatic moment that has unity of both time and location. If you make a jump in time, say from day to night, you need to begin a new scene. Change location, and you must begin a new scene—even if that change is only from the living room to the kitchen of the same house. In addition, scene headings play a vital role in the disassembly and reorganization of the script in preparation for creating production shot lists and shooting schedules (see Chapter 5).

- *Interior or exterior setting:*
  EXT. Interior and exterior are always abbreviated and simply tell us if the scene takes place indoors or outdoors.
- *Location.* EXT. MIDTOWN MANHATTAN STREET CORNER–
  The next bit of information is a brief but specific name of the location. We do not describe the location in detail here, but we must be precise. For example, EXT. NEW YORK CITY is brief, but it lacks the specificity to establish the location accurately. Where in New York City does this take place? Brooklyn? Staten Island? Upper East Side? On the street? In a park? All of these are very different locations with very different associations. EXT. MIDTOWN MANHATTAN STREET CORNER gives the necessary information, as would EXT. TIMES SQUARE or EXT. CENTRAL PARK, for other scenes.
- *Time indication.* EXT. MIDTOWN MANHATTAN STREET CORNER—DAY
  The final bit of information is an indication of whether the scene takes place during daylight hours, nighttime, or in between. Do not get too specific by writing things like THREE AM or TEN-THIRTY PM. Only DAY, NIGHT, DAWN, or DUSK are generally used. If you need the audience to know the exact hour, then you must put it elsewhere, like an image (a clock) in stage directions or in dialogue.
- *Other time indicators.*
  CONTINUOUS, LATER, and SAME are additional time indicators that are commonly used. We use CONTINUOUS in cases when one scene follows the previous one (from one location to another) without any break in time whatsoever. LATER is used when we remain in the same location, but we leap forward a little bit in time (i.e., less than day to night), and SAME is used when two scenes are happening in different locations, but it must be understood that they are happening at precisely the same time:

INT. SCHOOL HALLWAY – DAY

Matt races down the empty hallway, past the sleeping hall monitor and turns into...

INT. CLASSROOM – CONTINUOUS

...a classroom full of students already working on their exams. Just as Matt takes his seat his teacher places a five-page exam on the desk in front of him.

Matt looks it over and swallows hard. He pulls out a pencil and gets to work.

INT. CLASSROOM – LATER

All the students are gone, except Matt who is still struggling with the exam. The only other person in the room is the teacher, who impatiently checks his watch.

EXT. SCHOOL PARKING LOT – SAME

Suzie sits in her idling car, with her friend Jill, watching as the last few students exit the school.

> SUZIE
> Where is he?

> JILL
> He's not coming. I told you Matt's no good.

> SUZIE
> Maybe you're right.

Suzie sighs, puts the car into gear and drives off.

Stage Directions

Stage directions are where most of your creative writing takes place. This is where you describe, always in present tense, the actions of the characters, the settings, the images, and all non-dialogue sounds. In short, this is where you write what we see and, other than dialogue, what we hear. We will discuss the role of style and the art of visual writing in more detail later, but as a general rule, you should not elaborate on actions, settings, and movements in extreme detail. Too much extraneous description will bog down your script. When you write a screenplay, words and space are at a premium, so include only the *essential details* to tell your story. Notice in the *Kebacle* example that Alana describes Aamir's pushcart simply as

> A small clean food cart.

Combined with Aamir's cooking actions, his professionalism, and the food details along the way, there's enough information for a reader (and a set designer and cinematographer) to conjure just the kind of pushcart this man would run and exactly how it would look down to the smallest detail. We don't need to know where the napkins are or which side the pretzels are displayed or list every item on the posted menu. Later, in the production process, these details and more will be decided, but in the script, they're not essential. The umbrella detail, however, is important to the story, but not, for example, its color.

In terms of essential actions, notice how the author doesn't trace every detail of every action. While we see Aamir give the tourists their order (to show that he doesn't stop working even as he's getting a ticket), we don't need to write out the entire transaction, including getting money and making change, for example. Also, the author says that he

> ...wraps up the New Yorker's order.

But we don't need to know if he uses foil or wax paper, nor do we need to describe him putting the kebab in a bag and then the soda, followed by two napkins and a straw. Sure, these details will need to be worked out on the set, but it's not essential to the script.

The *Kebacle* screenplay is exemplary because its language is lean and yet the scene is vivid. We'll look closely at how this is accomplished in the "Screenplay Language and Style" section.

Other Stage Direction Rules

There are certain instances when words and names need to be written in all capital letters in the stage directions. Again, this is part of the technical function of the screenplay:

1. *Character introductions.*

   The first time a character actually, physically appears in the film you must use all capital letters for their name in the stage directions. This allows a producer and casting agent to see at a glance how many characters there are in a given script, and it also allows actors to quickly find their first scene. Once you have introduced a character using all capitals, then you write the character's name normally for the rest of the screenplay. This rule apples to minor characters as well, but not to extras.

   In our Kebacle example, Aamir, the tourists, the New Yorker, and the officer are in all capital letters the first time they appear in the script, but they're never written in all caps again in the stage directions. The other customers are not capitalized because they are **extras**, which means that they are performers who do not have a dramatic role in the film; they simply populate the environment for atmosphere and authenticity.

2. *Sound cues.*

   Any time you have a sound that is not created by a character actually in the scene, like the SIREN BLIP in the example, it needs to be capitalized. This is a reminder that although the sound is not in the scene as you shoot, the performers will still have to account for it during shooting. If, for example, you are shooting a scene in which a character hears CHURCH BELLS in the distance, the bells will not likely be sounding during actual shooting, yet the characters still need to react as if they were. Also, this is an indication to the sound designer to find this sound effect for postproduction.

3. *Readable text.*

   Anything intended for the audience to read must be put in quotation marks. This reminds the director and cinematographer that they must compose the shot so that the audience is able to read the text of, say, a "Closed" sign on the door, a "Happy Birthday" banner, or a road sign that reads "WELCOME TO KANSAS" (**Figures 2-5** and **2-8**).

Character Cues

Character cues indicate which character speaks the lines of dialogue, which follow (i.e., AAMIR, OFFICER, TOURIST WIFE). These are simple, but there are a few rules to keep in mind:

1. *Keep the name consistent.*

   If my character's name is Aamir Hassan and I give him the character cue AAMIR, then it must remain AAMIR for the entire script. I can't change it to MR. HASSAN later on.

2. *Only one character per name.*

   If I have two characters, Aamir Hassan and Aamir Khan, then they both cannot have AAMIR as a character cue. You should refer to them by their last names.

3. *You may refer to characters by a role.*

   It is common to refer to minor characters by their role, such as OFFICER or TOURIST.

■ **Figure 2-5** Text that is meant to be read by the audience, as in this shot from Soderbergh's *Ocean's Eleven* (2001), should be put in quotation marks in a screenplay. (See Figure 2-8.)

4. *Additional information: Voice-over, off screen, and other delivery indicators.*
   The character cue line sometimes carries other information about the delivery of the dialogue. Occasionally you will have a character speaking off screen or in a voice-over, or the dialogue may come over radio. Kebacle has an example of this:

CUSTOMER (O.S.)
Shawarma here! No onions.

Off screen implies that the character is present in the time and place of the scene but is not visible from the camera's perspective (i.e., a voice from somewhere in the crowd or from behind a door). **Voice-over** implies that the person speaking is not speaking from that time or place, like a narrator commenting on the events of a scene from the perspective of memory (**Figure 2-6**).

Off screen and voice-over indications are always abbreviated—(O.S.) and (V.O.), respectively—and are located after the character cue. You can also indicate (TV) or (RADIO) if the dialogue is being broadcast.

INT. ANDREW'S BEDROOM – NIGHT

Andrew rushes into his bedroom, pulls his suitcase out from under the bed and starts stuffing it with clothes from his dresser. He hears a NOISE from the bathroom - he freezes.

ANDREW
Who's in there?

RUTH (O.S.)
It's just me Andy. I'll be right out.

Andrew goes to the window and cracks the blinds. He eyes a car passing slowly in front of his house.

ANDREW (V.O.)
After that phone call I started losing my mind. I was suspicious of everyone; even Ruth seemed to be spying on me.

Dialogue

Dialogue is what your characters say. Using proper margins and single spacing are pretty much the only formatting rules that apply here. However, dialogue is the other area where your creative writing and stylistic skills come into play. When you consider that dialogue is the "voice" of your character and that everything from the dialogue's content, tone, grammar, rhythm, and accent all serve to define the person speaking those lines and establish their credibility, then you begin to realize that determining "what your characters say" is not so simple. The main principle for stage directions—stick to the essentials—also applies to dialogue. One common mistake early screenwriters make is to overwrite dialogue. We will discuss working with dialogue in more detail later in the chapter.

Personal Directions

Personal directions are always very brief, placed in parentheses, and do not have any capital letters unless you use a proper noun. They refer only to the person speaking the lines within which they appear. Personal

■ **Figure 2-6** *The Thin Red Line* (1998). "Are you righteous? Kind? Does your confidence lie in this?" A Japanese soldier appears to communicate from beyond the grave through voice-over narration, a staple of Malick's films.

directions are one of the most misused elements in a screenplay. Novice writers tend to use personal directions to tell the actors how to perform their lines. This is a mistake in two respects. First, the line itself should evoke the emotional tone of the delivery (sorrowful, joyful, wistful, etc.) without you having to label it as such. If a line is not sarcastic, then labeling it with the personal direction (sarcastically) will not make it sarcastic. Also, generally speaking, actors will try to make the best emotional decisions for the lines and the scene. When you use an emotional cue like (sorrowfully), you are closing the door to an interpretation of the line that could, in fact, enrich the moment. The emotional approach should be evident in the situation and dialogue itself, and if there is room for interpretation, then this is worked out between the director and actors in rehearsal and should not be codified in the author's draft. So, when *do* we use personal directions?

1. *Important, but very small, actions that must happen on a precise line of dialogue.* For example, in *Kebacle:*

                    OFFICER
        C'mon now, pack it up. Show's over.
                    (hands Aamir the ticket)
        You know you're not supposed to be here.

    It's a nice touch that Alana placed this action right here. The officer's second line is slightly more personal than the others and indicates that they've been through this before. The fact that the ticket is exchanging hands at this moment makes the line seem even more person to person.

2. *Receiver of dialogue in group scenes.* Occasionally it may not be clear to whom your character is speaking, especially in group conversations, so instead of constantly embedding the name of the receiver of the dialogue in the lines, we can simply indicate it in personal directions. For example, in *Kebacle:*

A NEW YORKER speaks up from behind two TOURISTS.

                    NEW YORKER
        Can I get a-

                    TOURIST HUSBAND
        Excuse me, we've been waiting here.

                    TOURIST WIFE
                    (to Aamir)
        We were here first.

                    AAMIR
        Yes, I know, what can I get you?

                    TOURIST HUSBAND
                    (slowly)
        Let's see, a soft pretzel, two waters and... how
        much is a kebab?

                    AAMIR
        Four dollars.

The Tourist hesitates.

                    TOURIST HUSBAND
        What do you think, honey?

```
                    NEW YORKER
            Give me a kebab. I don't care how much it
            is...
```

One of the things that makes this moment so sharp is the way the Tourist Husband confronts the New Yorker while the wife appeals to Aamir. They attack on two fronts at once, a strategy that tells us that this is an important matter of principle to them and they *really* feel entitled to order first. If we had left out the personal direction (to Aamir) then the wife's dialogue would appear to be directed to the New Yorker and would have a different effect. Notice also how Alana understood that it was not necessary to write (impatiently) or (exasperated) when the New Yorker places his order. The emotional tone of the line is obvious in the words and context. (Slowly) is not so much an emotion as it is an indication of pace. Alana wants to really draw out this moment, knowing that it adds tension to the situation. Other nonemotional, personal directions you'll see are words like (whispers), (yells), and (stutters).

I have outlined only the basics of screenplay formatting in this chapter. It's definitely worth your time to locate one of the books I mention in the recommended readings section for more detail.

Margins, Fonts, and Spacing

Margins, fonts, and spacing are an important part of formatting because they ensure that each script page reflects 1 minute of screen time, more or less. A 15-page screenplay will yield a 15-minute film, approximately. There are several commercial software programs that automate this aspect of formatting (e.g., *Final Draft* and *Movie Magic Screenwriter*). You can also find free script formatting software online (e.g., *Celtx*). You could even set margins yourself manually on your computer or, if you like, a typewriter, but no matter how you do it, you must get the margins and spacing correct. (Go to www.voiceandvisionbook.com for formatting specs.)

■ SCREENPLAY LANGUAGE AND STYLE

Visual Writing, Character, and Action

"Show Me, Don't Tell Me"

In film, as in life, actions speak louder than words. Someone can announce, "I love you," and it sounds great, but can you trust it? "I really, really love you": pretty words but perhaps too easy to say. But if that person actually shows their love by leaving a great job, their beloved city, and all their friends to follow you to another state because they can't live without you, then you might think, "Gee, you did that for me? You must really love me."

When you write a script, try to do as much as possible with actions. Converting feelings, intentions, and character traits into actions and behavior is at the heart of screen drama and is essential to establishing an indelible understanding of character. In the *Kebacle* example, just the casual action of Aamir starting business up again after the police van drives away tells us a lot about his essential character: How afraid he is of the law, what he feels he needs to do to run his business, and what his work routine is.

Let's look at some principles for showing character through actions. The focus here will be on the craft of writing visually and on what is revealed through what we see and how it is presented. We will use a brief sequence from *Ocean's Eleven* (screenplay by Ted Griffin, 2001) (**Figures 2-7** and **2-8**).

■ **Figure 2-7** Excerpt
from *Ocean's Eleven.*
Granted courtesy
of Warner Brothers
Entertainment Inc.

31

```
49.  INT. CROWDED SUBWAY CAR (CHICAGO)

     Native Chicagoans demonstrate their indigenous sixth
     sense -- L-car balance -- as the TRAIN bends and SHAKES
     at a corner.

     One passenger in particular keeps his footing, a young
     man in a frayed jacket: LINUS. Two overgroomed
     STOCKBROKERS stand with their backs to the young man,
     yammering about high interest yields, and consequently
     they don't notice (and neither do we, not at first)
     that Linus is slowly picking one of their pockets.

     The thievery is glacier-paced: Linus, his face always
     forward and inscrutable, gingerly raises one tail of
     his target's Brooks Brothers jacket and then, with
     incomparable dexterity, unbuttons his wallet pocket
     with a flick of his thumb and forefinger.  From halfway
     down the train car, nothing appears amiss, and no
     passenger looks the wiser. Or so it seems...

     A copy of the Chicago Sun-Times, opened and upheld,
     lowers just enough to allow its reader a peek at Linus.
     It is Danny, smirk on his lips: he (and he alone) is
     aware of the ongoing heist.

     Back to Linus, his spoils (a Gucci wallet) now in
     sight, he waits for just the right moment, and
     then, when the train hits another curve...

     ... he stumbles forward, his left hand finding support
     on the Stockbroker's shoulder as his right relieves the
     man of his wallet.

                         LINUS
               Sorry 'bout that.

                         STOCKBROKER
               No problem, guy.

     The Stockbroker resumes his yacketing, oblivious, as
     Linus tucks his prize into his own jacket pocket, face
     betraying nothing.

     Only Danny appreciates the artistry performed here
     today. He folds the Sun-Times under his arm as...
```

■ *Write with precision.*
The first thing to remember is that when you are writing a screenplay, you are a writer. As a writer, your tools are words, so you need to be precise with your language and find the specific words that will convey not just the action, but also the tone or mood of the situation. The author of the *Ocean's Eleven* script does not say,

Linus lifts up the man's coat, opens his pocket, reaches in, and pulls out his wallet.

■ **Figure 2-8** Excerpt
from *Ocean's Eleven*
(cont'd). Granted courtesy
of Warner Brothers
Entertainment Inc.

```
                                                        32

   50. INT. UNION STATION / SUBWAY STATION - CONTINUED

        ... The SUBWAY SQUEALS to a stop. Linus jumps out,
        leaving his prey aboard, and a few moments later, Danny
        steps off, too.

   51. INT. UNION STATION - EVENING

        The hurly-burly of rush hour in Union Station.

        Commuters zig and zag, this way and that, all on
        furious schedules, and Linus slips blithely through
        them, in no hurry, a man who's pulled this job a
        thousand times before.

        He dodges and sidesteps crazed commuters, and except
        for a brief brush with one well-dressed man (the Sun-
        Times tucked under his arm), he escapes the station
        without incident.

   52. EXT. UNION STATION - EVENING

        Linus exits, casually reaching into his jacket to count
        his winnings. And his face falls.  All he finds where
        the stolen wallet once resided is a calling card. On
        one side, in engraved printing:

        "DANIEL OCEAN." On the flip side, in handwriting: "Nice
        pull. Murphy's Bar, Rush & Division."

   53. INT.  MURPHY'S BAR -
```

Yes, that's basically what happens, but put this way, the reader would imagine that Linus is a hapless clod who could not possibly get away with this. So instead he writes,

> Linus, his face always forward and inscrutable, gingerly raises one tail of his target's Brooks Brothers jacket and then, with incomparable dexterity, unbuttons his wallet pocket with a flick of his thumb and forefinger. [And he eventually] ... relieves the man of his wallet.

The author has written only the actions, but the precision of the passage allows us to really "see" the crime and it also shows us Linus's expert abilities at picking pockets, a skill he will need later on in the film.

Keep in mind that not all actions and details are equally important. In stage directions we stick with only the essentials. The amount of time and words you use to describe something determines its importance in the scene. Lavish special attention and language only on those moments that are really critical to the story line.

■ *Use images, not camera cues.*

In an author's draft, we avoid as much as possible the inclusion of camera cues—indications such as CLOSE-UP ... or ZOOM IN ON ... or CAMERA PANS TO REVEAL ..., etc. However, that doesn't mean you can't indicate a close-up or a wide shot if you really feel that it is necessary in the telling of the story. As a screenwriter you need to describe, in prose, an image or action that suggests to the reader or a director a close-up or a long shot or whatever else you intend. This is the essence of visual writing. In the *Ocean's Eleven* example, Ted Griffin writes:

(a) Linus, his face always forward and inscrutable, gingerly raises one tail of his target's Brooks Brothers jacket (b) and then, with incomparable dexterity, unbuttons his wallet pocket with a flick of his thumb and forefinger. (c) From halfway down the train car, nothing appears amiss, and no passenger looks the wiser.

This passage is written to invoke three different shot sizes. In order to show his inscrutable face and lifting up the coattail (a), we'd need something between a long shot (full body) and a medium long shot (from the knees up). Then, for us to really "see" the dexterity in something as small as the flick of a thumb (b), we would need an extreme close-up. Finally, to take in the image of other passengers and half the train (c), we'd need a long shot; we cannot visualize this image with the close-up. So the language shows us the shots in prose, rather than labeling them. Again, be careful not to overuse this technique. Invoke a precise image only when you really need it to tell the story.

- *Paragraphing stage directions and audience point of view.*
  We use paragraphing in stage directions for three reasons. The first is to distinguish different locations within a single location. Notice how each time the author shows Danny, who is standing at the other end of the train watching, there is a new paragraph. The paragraphing shifts the reader's point of view off Linus and onto Danny, who occupies a different end of the train car. The second reason we use paragraphing is to distinguish dramatic beats and shape the progression of the scene. Paragraphing helps the reader feel when one dramatic moment has ended and a new moment has begun. Yes, this episode on the train is one large dramatic unit; Danny watches Linus pick a businessman's pocket. But tension is created by breaking this task down into smaller dramatic beats and slightly rearranging the details to reveal the situation to the audience in a more suspenseful way.
- (Beat 1, paragraph 1) Average day on a Chicago subway. (Nothing is amiss.)
- (Beat 2, paragraph 2) Introduces Linus and the stockbrokers and Linus is picking this guy's pocket. (Uh, oh—a crime and now tension.)
- (Beat 3, paragraph 3) Shows us that Linus is skilled and cool. (Character development.)
- (Beat 4, paragraph 4) He's not alone; Danny is watching the whole thing and likes what he sees. (The plot thickens with this big shift in point of view; now Linus is not just picking a pocket, he's unknowingly being auditioned for a part in a bigger score.)
- (Beat 5, paragraphs 5 and 6 with dialogue and 7) Linus completes the lift and is even polite. (Mr. Smooth the whole way, a real pro.)
- (Beat 6, paragraph 8) Danny is very impressed (and so are we) (Figure 2-9).

The third reason to paragraph is to further highlight very important moments or details. *The dramatic question in this scene, for Danny, Linus, and the reader, is, will Linus successfully lift the wallet?* So *the* climactic moment and action is when he actually picks the pocket. For this reason, the screenwriter has set that moment off in its own paragraph.

■ **Figure 2-9** Linus (Matt Damon) and Danny (George Clooney) in the subway scene in Soderbergh's *Ocean's Eleven* (2001).

■ **Figure 2-10** In Demme's *The Silence of the Lambs* (1991), Dr. Lecter presents himself as a sophisticated gentleman when he greets Clarice. Later, we see Hannibal the Cannibal's true nature as he savagely murders his guards.

Character versus Voice

In the *Ocean's Eleven* example, the actions we see Linus perform tell us who he is. He's a thief, a skilled thief, who is using his abilities to pull off petty crimes. We believe it because we saw it. **Character** is defined through actions. **Voice**, on the other hand, is the way in which people present themselves to the world. This could be through their style of dress, the way they decorate their apartment, and, or course, the way they speak. Dialogue can be written in harmony with what we understand of that character through their actions, or it can provide another layer of complexity, or it can even be contradictory to what we see. With his "frayed jacket" and polite apology, Linus presents himself as an average, nice guy (which the brokers believe), but we know better because we've seen him in action.

Another good example is Hannibal Lecter (**Figure 2-10**) in *The Silence of the Lambs* (written by Ted Tally). Through his dialogue, Hannibal presents himself as an erudite, cultured, refined, courteous gentleman. At their first meeting he even tells Clarice Starling, "discourtesy is unspeakably ugly to me." This is no one we should fear, right? Until we see him literally rip the face off a police guard! Lecter is a great example of the tension you can create with the dissonance between character and voice. So if you are able to establish your character's essential nature through actions, then dialogue, your character's voice, can be used to add and refine other facets of their personality. Action = Character, Dialogue = Voice.

Working with Dialogue: Revealing Emotions, Not Announcing Them

Ideally, dialogue should *reveal* a character to us. It should illustrate what that person is thinking, feeling, and wanting instead of broadcasting these things directly. In this way, the *show me, don't tell me* principle also applies to dialogue. This scene from the Academy Award–winning screenplay for *Sideways* (2004), written by Alexander Payne and Jim Taylor, is a great example of dialogue that is, on the surface, about one topic, in this case wine, but in fact reveals an enormous amount about the internal yearnings and struggles of the lead character, Miles (**Figure 2-11**). Although Miles is clearly lonely, he is finding it impossible to get over his recent divorce and resume his life. In this scene, Miles, who is a wine aficionado, finds himself alone with Maya, an attractive acquaintance, while his buddy Jack is having casual sex in another room with a woman he only met that day. Miles and Maya are sitting on the front porch, drinking wine (**Figure 2-12**).

■ **Figure 2-11** Miles (Paul Giamatti) talks about pinot noir but reveals his soul. *Sideways* (2004).

```
                                                    38
                        MAYA
            Can I ask you a personal question?

                        MILES
                    (bracing himself)
            Sure.

                        MAYA
            Why are you so into Pinot?  It's
            like a thing with you.

    Miles laughs at first, then smiles wistfully at the
    question.

    He searches for the answer in his glass and begins
    slowly.

                        MILES
            I don't know.  It's a hard grape to
            grow.  As you know.  It's thin-
            skinned, temperamental, ripens
            early.  It's not a survivor like
            Cabernet that can grow anywhere
            and thrive even when neglected.
            Pinot needs constant care and
            attention and in fact can only
            grow in specific little tucked-
            away corners of the world.  And
            only the most patient and
            nurturing growers can do it
            really, can tap into Pinot's most
            fragile, delicate qualities.  Only
            when someone has taken the time to
            truly understand its potential can
            Pinot be coaxed into its fullest
            expression.  And when that happens,
            its flavors are the most haunting
            and brilliant and subtle and
            thrilling and ancient on the
            planet.

    Maya has found this answer revealing and moving.
```

Miles laughs at first because the "personal question" he braced himself for turns out to be *only* about wine, yet Maya finds his answer surprisingly revealing and so do we. Through Miles' passionate description about the pinot noir grape he unwittingly reveals his loneliness and that he, like the pinot grape, is difficult to nurture but ultimately well worth the time and care. So the question ends up being deeply personal after all and his subconscious revelation betrays his romantic interest in Maya. Also his answer poses questions of his own to Maya: are you patient and caring enough? Will you "take the time to truly understand [my] potential?"

The other interesting nuance in this monologue is the comparison of grape varietals, which serves as a comparison of Miles' personality with that of his friend Jack. His buddy in the other room, who easily picks up women to have sex, is clearly the cabernet grape, which can "grow anywhere and thrive," while he is more like the pinot, "thin-skinned, temperamental," and "needs constant care and attention."

Words and Grammar Define Voice
As with stage directions, your choice of language is crucial in dialogue. The words your characters use and the grammar they employ express their unique identity—both who they are and how they wish to be seen. Aamir's "my friend" and the officer's "C'mon now,

pack it up. Show's over" are precise and put flesh on the bones of their characters. Their lines also establish their credibility with the audience. We believe them as people.

Throughout *Sideways,* Miles is an exceptionally nervous and awkward character—especially around women. In the scene before our example, he stumbles over himself to describe the novel he is working on to Maya. However, in this scene, Miles is in his comfort zone. He is eloquent, even literary, when speaking of wine. This reveals to the audience that not only is he knowledgeable about wine but that, yes, hidden under all the anxiety, Miles also is a passionate, thoughtful, and interesting guy—but it's not easy for him at this moment in his life—he must be "coaxed into [his] fullest expression."

Dramatizing the Story

I am always reluctant to single out some particular feature of the work of a major filmmaker because it tends inevitably to simplify and reduce the work. But in this book of screenplays by Krzysztof Kieslowski and his co-author, Krzysztof Piesiewicz, it should not be out of place to observe that they have the very rare ability to dramatize their ideas rather than just talking about them. By making their points through the dramatic action of the story they gain the added power of allowing the audience to discover what's really going on rather than being told. They do this with such dazzling skill, you never see the ideas coming and don't realize until much later how profoundly they have reached your heart.

Stanley Kubrick (foreword to Kieslowski & Piesiewicz, *Decalogue: The Ten Commandments*, London: Faber & Faber, 1991)

In his response to the *Decalogue* screenplays written by the filmmaker Krzysztof Kieslowski and his screenwriting partner Krzysztof Piesiewicz, Stanley Kubrick succinctly sums up the primary dramatic task of the screenwriter. As I mentioned in Chapter 1, to dramatize is to tell a story about characters in conflict through action, dialogue, and visual detail and it applies to screenplays of any length or genre. Revealing a story through actions, being precise and true to your characters' voices, and using visual detail in meaningful ways are all part of what is necessary to dramatize a story. Audience involvement is diminished when characters discuss the conflict, their motivations, or thematic points in direct or expository ways. It's easy to undercut the believability of your story with characters who are too aware and verbally articulate of the dilemma they're in and their responses to that dilemma. Yes, of course, you can always get the basic point of an encounter across in a simple and utilitarian way like this:

```
INT. KITCHEN - NIGHT

A man and woman, both in their mid-fifties, sit in a dark kitchen drinking
whiskey.

                    WOMAN
         I'm so mad at you right now.

                    MAN
         Why?

                    WOMAN
         Because the baby's hungry, we're broke, and you lost
         one month's pay at a stupid card game, that's why.
         How could you do this to us again?

                    MAN
         I can win all my money back next week, and more.

                    WOMAN
         You have a gambling problem and I'm sick of dealing
         with it. I'm going to leave you - for good.
```

If characters announce their feelings and intentions, if they discuss the story they are in (rather than just being in it), then the audience has no reason to become emotionally involved in the unfolding tale. Believable and engaging characters inhabit, act, and react within the world of the film and the events that swirl around them. They "do things," and the viewer pieces together this display of human behavior to determine why they do what they do. This dynamic is critical to encouraging audience investment and involvement in our story. Many times a gesture or a look will expose, in much more eloquent and human ways, what someone is feeling than the verbal articulation of that feeling. Often what *is not said* speaks louder than an explanation ever could. Also, visual details like locations, clothes, and objects can reveal an enormous amount about the specific dramatic situation and context.

INT. KITCHEN - NIGHT

A man and woman, mid-fifties, sit in the shabby kitchen of an old single-wide trailer drinking whiskey as a baby whimpers from a crib in the corner. The man stares into his glass while the woman's gaze is fixed hard on his face.

                              MAN
              It's only one month's pay. I can win it back next
              week - and more. The odds will be better -

The woman knocks back her whiskey and throws the empty glass at him, narrowly missing his head. It shatters against the wall and the baby wails!

                              WOMAN
              You bastard!

She goes to the crib and comforts the screaming child as the man pours himself another shot.

INT. BEDROOM - DAY

The baby lies on the bed, sucking on an empty milk bottle. Next to him is an open suitcase packed with clothes. Crying to herself, the woman places one more item into the suitcase and closes it up. She looks at her little baby and wipes her eyes dry...

We know there is a baby, because we see the baby. We see a woman throw a glass at her husband and we can't help but feel that she is really mad. We know he has a gambling problem because his dialogue employs the logic of a habitual gambler. The woman packs her bags, and we realize that she's leaving him. She does not need to verbalize any of it, she simply feels it and acts on it and we get it.

in practice

Let's look at the principle of dramatization through actions and visual details in two of the short films I have provided as examples online: *The Black Hole*, by Phil and Olly, and *Waking Dreams*, by John Daschbach (see these films at www.voiceandvisionbook.com). *The Black Hole* is the most obvious example of a story revealed through action because it does not rely on dialogue at all to convey the step-by-step transition of its main character from bored office clerk to greedy thief. First, the drab office location, the way the character is dressed, and the act of photocopying late at night are all details that establish the character as a low-level office clerk within seconds. Then, this bored clerk simply responds to the cosmic delivery of a strange black hole and one action leads to the next. These actions are so revealing that we can easily imagine his thoughts at each critical dramatic beat: there is the "What is that?" moment when the black hole comes out of the photocopier and the "What the heck happened?"

moment when he drops the cup into the hole. Then he thinks, "Should I? Do I dare?" when he wonders if he should retrieve the cup, and, of course, the big "OMG, it's magic!" moment when he sticks his hand into the black hole for the first time. After he easily snags himself a candy bar, we clearly understand that greed is overtaking him. When he scans the office, we know exactly what he's thinking, "What else can I do with this? I want more!" He does not verbally express these feeling and no one is explaining this story to us, it is simply unfolding through actions that are revealing of character and intention, and therefore we are actively involved in putting the story together. We anticipate what he'll do based on what we'd probably do. So when he spies the locked door with the sign "Keep out" we can practically hear him say, "Oh, yeah, jackpot! Come to daddy!" We easily follow his trajectory, because his behavior (shown exclusively through actions) is painfully human: he discovers power, he tests power, he abuses power, and the ironic twist is that he is undone by his own power and greed (**Figure 2-13**).

In *Waking Dreams*, Mr. Saroyan never directly states the emotional turmoil he is in nor does he articulate the questions that hangs over his head: Do I or don't I believe this woman? Will I or won't I go in the ocean? Instead, we understand that this kooky proclamation of his impending death has rattled him because he can't simply dismiss it. We witness him call Becky back to his office several times, first to undercover a prank by a colleague, "who put you up to this?" (that would expose her premonition as a trick), then to imply that she's not in her right mind "How are you Becky?" (that would assure him that

she's just imagining things) and then to use reason "Premonitions are fate, right?" (as if logic is the antidote to ominous predictions). And then, in a very funny moment, he uses executive-speak to try and brush it aside with the standard bureaucrat's phrase, "Thank you for your input. I appreciate it, and I'll take it into consideration." These are not expository lines of dialogue; these verbal exchanges are active attempts to discredit Becky's premonition and each of these moments only further reveals to us that he is truly bothered by her predictions, so much so that he may indeed alter his vacation plans. The more he tries to deny it, the more we understand that he believes it. But why does he, on some level, believe her? And why do *we* too suspect she could be right? Here, small details plant the seeds for plausibility. Becky's slightly disheveled state (compared with his super controlled self-presentation), her idiosyncratic logic delivered with total assurance ("What people call fate is just time plus free will"), the small but essential moment when she looks at the telephone seconds before it starts ringing, the unexplained cigarette butt and shark's tooth in his mini Zen garden, and the fact that it is clearly established the he is a single man vacationing alone— all these details create an atmosphere in which a premonition of portentous events should be taken into consideration. Mr. Saroyan doesn't need to articulate his feeling of existential drifting—we see it in his response to this eccentric temp. So although *Waking Dreams* is a dialogue[driven film, the dialogue constitutes action and behavior rather than explanation. Again, the "show me don't tell me" principle does *not* mean "don't use dialogue"; it means reveal the story to me through behavior and not by explaining it to me.

■ **Figure 2-13** *The Black Hole (left)* and *Waking Dreams (right)* are two of the Voice & Vision short films examples that can be viewed at www.voiceandvisionbook.com.

■ REWORKING AND REWRITING

Whether a project is a three-minute chase scene with no dialogue or a complex, character-driven, emotional drama, narrative filmmakers are storytellers, and the unfolding of events that make up film stories are first hammered out and polished on the page. The first steps in narrative film production involve developing your ideas on paper in concept

in practice

Now that you've seen George's concept and treatment (pages 21 and 22), here is how his final script turned out. Keep in mind that this was a short film written and produced for an intermediate film production class. This was the first time George was working with color film and synchronized sound. In addition, he had a crew of four people and only one semester, 13 weeks, to go from a concept to a rough cut of the movie. So George kept it short and simple (**Figure 2-14**).

■ **Figure 2-14**
Screenplay for the short film *The Miracle* (2006), written by Georges Racz.

```
                              THE MIRACLE

             FADE IN:


             INT. TOY STORE - DAY

             KATE and her PARENTS enter the front door of a huge toy
             store, where every toy imaginable seems to exist.

             Kate wanders between the rows of shelves, touoching each
             toy.

             She stops in front of a big teddy bear and caresses its
             soft fur.  She dances with it, spinning in circles.

             She stops.  The bear slips from her grip as she walks over
             to one of the store's windows.

             EXT. STREET - DAY

             Kate's nose is pressed against the store's window.

             She watches as an OLD HOMELESS MAN digs through a grabage
             can.

             From behind Kate, two hands reach over.  One grabs one of
             Kate's hands while the other rubs her head lightly.

             Kate's parents lead her away from the window.

             INT. TOY STORE - DAY

             Kate notices a CROWD gathered in one of the corners of the
             store and approaches it to take a closer look.

             She squeezes her way between the crowd's legs and makes
             her way to the front.

             A MAGICIAN, wearing a long white beard and a sparkly blue
             gown is performing a magic trick.  He lifts up his hands
             in preparation for a new magic act.

             Kate lifts up her hands like the magician.  He sees this and
             approaches her.  He extends his hand in front of her and
             reveals that it is now full of gummy bears.  Kate takes one.

             As the crowd watches, the magician bows down and whispers in
             Kate's ear.
```

in practice

2

MAGICIAN
Siribi-siriba-pick-pack-puck!

Kate lifts her hand and moves the wand around.

KATE
Siribi-siriba-pick-pack-puck!

Suddenly. soap bubbles fill the air. Silence falls over
the crowd, then erupts into applause. Kate smiles.

EXT. SUBWAY STATION - DAY

Kate and her parents wait on the platform as a subway
train pulls up.

As they get on, a BEGGAR with crutches makes his way toward
them and holds his hand out for change. Kate's father
gives him a few singles.

Kate looks at the beggar as the subway pulls into a station
and he gets off.

Kate closes her eyes and using her finger as a wand draws
three circles in the air.

On the subway platform, the beggar counts the money he
collected.

KATE
Siribi-siriba-pick-pack-puck!

Kate opens her eyes and looks through the subway's window.

The subway slowly pulls away from the station.

The beggar puts his crutches under his arm and walks
unaided, the money clutched in his hand.

Kate smiles and embraces her bear.

EXT. CITY STREET - DAY

Soap bubbles touch the gutter as the train is heard passing
below.

FADE OUT

■ **Figure 2-14, cont'd**
Screenplay for the short
film *The Miracle* (2006),
written by Georges Racz.

and treatment forms and then writing a screenplay. Each of these steps constitutes a reworking of the story. When it comes to the script itself, an often-repeated axiom is that *writing is rewriting.* It's important to remember that a screenplay is not written in stone. It is not unusual for screenplays (shorts or features) to go through many rewrites. Students in my intermediate production class will typically pen five or six drafts of their 10-minute film before heading into production. Some of these rewrites are simply to improve the script, while others are in response to real-world exigencies (like losing an important location), which must be worked into the script in such a way that they *also* improve the script. Screenplays should remain flexible and can be rewritten at every stage in the production process— including the editing phase—to respond to new ideas, creative collaboration, production circumstances, practical concerns, and spontaneous inspiration. The better the script, the better your film will be. So it is essential not to shortchange these crucial creative steps out of impatience and eagerness to get on a set. It's better to postpone a shoot in order to give yourself the time to get your script in shape.

The Visual Language and Aesthetics of Cinema

Film is a medium. … A medium is based on an agreement, a contract that has developed over a long period during which the speaker and the listener, the picture maker and the viewer, performer and audience, have established a system of meanings: a vocabulary, syntax and grammar of the language being used. For this reason, language emerges slowly, and will continue to evolve for as long as audiences and authors develop new ways of expressing themselves.

Alexander Mackendrick (From *On Filmmaking*, 2004)

Filmmaking has its own grammar, just as literature does. Everybody knows what basic coverage should be and just because you have some idiosyncratic ideas that might work even though they're breaking rules, the fact remains that there are rules that are there and that work. … But of course, following the rules does not guarantee that the film will work. That would be too easy.

Ethan Coen (From *Moviemakers' Master Class*, by L. Tirard, 2002)

■ SHOTS, SEQUENCES, AND SCENES

Film scholars and practitioners alike have long referred to the cinema as a language, which means that it is a shared system of terms, symbols, and syntax used to communicate thoughts, feelings, and experiences. In written language we use letters, words, sentences, and paragraphs. In the visual language of cinema we have four basic elements: the **shot**, the **shot sequence**, the **scene**, and the **dramatic sequence**.

The **shot** is the smallest unit of the film language. A shot is a continuous run of images, unbroken by an edit. Technically speaking, a shot is the footage generated from the moment you turn on the camera to the moment you turn it off—also called a **camera take.** However, these shots are often divided into smaller pieces, which are used independently in the editing stage, and each one of these pieces is also called a shot. Shots can be as short as a few frames or as long as your imaging system will allow before you run out of film or tape or data storage space. The famous shower sequence in Hitchcock's *Psycho* (1960) lasts about half a minute, but contains more than 50 shots, while the film *Russian Ark* (2002), directed by Aleksandr Sokurov and shot on high-definition video, is a 96-minute feature film comprising only one continuous shot!

Crucial to understanding the potential impact of the shot is the concept of **mise-en-scène** (a term derived from a French theatrical phrase that means "put on stage"), which in film terms can be defined as everything visible in the frame of a shot: the subject, actions, objects, setting, lighting, and graphic qualities. The mise-en-scène of a shot contains information, a certain meaning, derived from a combination of what we see in the shot and how it is presented.

Take a look at the very first shot (after the credit sequence) from Darren Aronofsky's 2008 film *The Wrestler* (Figure 3-1). This shot, unbroken by any edits, introduces us to the main character, professional wrestler Randy "The Ram" Robinson, after a wrestling bout. The choices Aronofsky and cinematographer Maryse Alberti made for this critical shot are precise and convey specific information. The blackboard, toys, and children's drawings which dominate the mise-en-scène tell us that the location is an elementary school classroom, which means that his match was probably in a rented gym and he's forced to use the classroom

■ **Figure 3-1** The mise-en-scène of the opening image from Aronofsky's *The Wrestler* (2008) reveals much about the central character Randy "The Ram" (Mickey Rourke) in just a few seconds.

as a locker room. This is not the locker room of a big-time, national pay-per-view championship wrestling arena, so the narrative meaning of this location effectively places him on a very low tier local wrestling circuit, where matches take place in VFW halls, community centers, and school gyms. Randy's hunched posture and the accentuation of the slack aspects of his physique also tell us that this is not a wrestler in prime physical condition. The other aspect of the mise-en-scène that reveals his diminished stature as a wrestler is his position in the frame. Randy is far from the camera and appears very small. He does not command the frame any more than the toy dump truck does. To the right of the truck is another prominent feature of the mise-en-scène, a pair of little kid's stirrup tights. Costume is an important element in mise-en-scène, and Randy is wearing tights too, sequined tights. Sequined tights on big men makes sense in the ring, but in this setting, next to the kiddie's tights, they feel a little like child's play. Finally, the lighting of this scene does not reflect the show-time spectacle and theatrics of big-time wrestling; instead it is as bland and flat as one would expect in this environment, which only accentuates the banality of his dreary circumstances. Everything about the mise-en-scène of this one shot tells us, here is a small time wrestler, isolated and at rock bottom. The crucial concept behind mise-en-scène is that everything you put in a shot has the potential to add story information, so in a very real way you tell much of your story in the shot.

A **sequence** is an expressive unit made up of editing together multiple shots to define a unified action or event, or passage of time or place. Sequences can be designed to make multiple points. The *Psycho* shower sequence just mentioned not only shows us Marion's murder, but Hitchcock, a master of the macabre, also wants us to feel her terror and simultaneously wants to establish a new dramatic question: Who was that woman who killed Marion?

Each shot in a sequence builds on the others, so that by arranging shots in a particular order (or sequence), you can contextualize each individual image to create meaning that is greater than the sum of its parts. Film theorists refer to this concept as **montage** (from the French word "montage," which simply means editing). Broadly defined, montage is the film technique in which meaning is derived from the accumulation of information of the various shots in an edited sequence. (For a more on the term "montage," see page 468).

The term **juxtaposition** is often used when talking about sequences. This means placing two or more shots next to each other so that you highlight a link or contrast between the content in each shot. It's essential for a filmmaker to really understand and put to use the fact that a viewer does not simply interpret each image individually but almost

■ **Figure 3-2** In Malick's *The Thin Red Line* (1998), the long shot of a navy ship is followed by a shot of Private Witt (James Caviezel) in a dark location. Although there are no physical clues to indicate exactly where he is, we assume Private Witt is somewhere inside the ship, because of this juxtaposition.

instinctively creates additional connections between individual shots. If we first show a shot of the United Nations Building, followed by a shot of a group of people seated around a conference table, the audience automatically assumes that this is a conference being held inside the U.N. building. No one needs to announce it; it just becomes a presumed fact. This is a very simple example that, on the surface, seems completely common and obvious, and in fact it is, but on closer analysis you will come to understand the power in the mechanism and the broader creative implications between what's on screen and how an audience assumes connections and actively creates meaning (Figure 3-2).

Take a look at Figure 3-1 again. We've already analyzed the mise-en-scène information, but add to this the fact that this shot is juxtaposed with a previous shot (as the credits roll). The previous shot is a long, close-up pan over a collection of magazine and newspaper clippings revealing that Randy "The Ram" Robinson was a wrestling superstar in the 1980s; he fought in the biggest arenas, headlined star-studded events, was named "wrestler of the year," and had many fans. Then, when we cut to 20 years later and see that small, hunched, slack figure in the elementary school classroom, the juxtaposition of only two shots effectively traces 20 years of a man's wrestling career from the glory days to the skids. In two shots, without even seeing the man's face, we already know that this is a wrestler who had a glittering career but is now an old has-been.

The "meaning" derived by the juxtaposition of two shots need not only be logistical or expository, but the context created by putting one shot next to the other can also elicit an emotional understanding from the audience. The most famous examples of this phenomenon are the early film experiments of Lev Kuleshov, who in the early 1920s shot the expressionless face of actor Ivan Mozhukhin and juxtaposed the very same, emotionally neutral shot with various other images. When the face was juxtaposed with a bowl of soup, people saw the face as that of a hungry man; when the same shot was juxtaposed with a child's coffin, people read his expression as sorrowful. Each new juxtaposed image inflected Mr. Mozhukhin's neutral expression with a different emotion. It is important to always remember that images and editing are used in tandem to create meaning and communicate your story, in specific terms, to your audience (Figure 3-3).

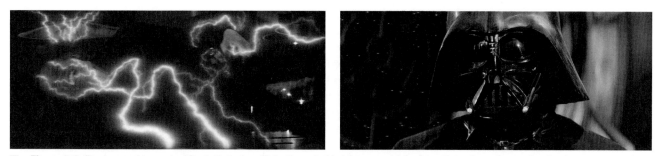

■ **Figure 3-3** The immovable mask of Darth Vader is sufficiently neutral to take on a variety of emotions, depending on the visual context created through juxtaposition. In this scene from Marquand's *Star Wars: Episode VI—Return of the Jedi* (1983), we detect feelings of sympathy, concern, and alarm on the ordinarily evil mask of Vader as he watches his son Luke Skywalker get electrocuted.

■ **Figure 3-4** The "Jack/Zak" scene from Jarmusch's *Down By Law* (1986) is 2 minutes and 45 seconds long and is accomplished in only one shot.

Because images and editing function in tandem, they must both be considered as we devise our visual strategy during **previsualization**. That's not to say that we try to precisely edit our film, shot for shot, before we go into production (although Alfred Hitchcock very nearly did just that on most of his films), but it does mean that we need to consider not only what we will shoot (mise-en-scène) but also how these shots might fit together (montage). This is what is referred to as **shooting for the edit**.

As stated in Chapter 1, **a scene** is a dramatic unit in which action ostensibly happens in continuous time and within a single location. A scene is usually composed of multiple shots, which guide the audience's attention, and there are principles of visual grammar that we employ in putting these shots together to make coherent sense of time, space, and actions (Chapter 4 explores these principles in detail). Depending on the style of the film, a scene, even those that include a variety of camera angles, can also be accomplished in a single shot (**Figure 3-4**). This approach has been used throughout the history of cinema, from Bresson to Hou Hsiao-Hsien, but is less commonly used.

A **dramatic sequence** is made up of a series of scenes that create a larger dramatic unit. The relationship between the scenes can vary, because of cause and effect (the result of one scene triggers the beginning of the next) or parallel action (in which the actions in two or more scenes, happening simultaneously, relate to each other), or the scenes can have other associative connections.

Just as in written language, where we put words together to create sentences, and sentences together to create paragraphs, in film we put shots together to create sequences and scenes, and scenes together to create the larger dramatic events of our story. Theoretically, one could certainly shoot any image at all and place it next to any other image, just as one could configure any string of letters to create sounds that resemble a word—for example, *fluugeproit*. This "word" *fluugeproit* doesn't directly communicate anything, and a sentence like "Bilious for at cake one" makes no sense at all either, even though the meaning of each individual word is perfectly understandable. Neither the "word" nor the "sentence" works within our language's shared system of practices.

Likewise in cinema, there are many commonly understood principles that we use for putting the visual pieces together to communicate coherently. This chapter and Chapter 4 explicate some of cinema's "shared systems of practices," including the most pervasive and fundamental visual system, known as *continuity style*. **Continuity style** shooting and editing provides tried and true principles for organizing our images to create a coherent sense of space, time, and movement in a way that is recognized and understood by nearly everyone. Keep in mind that, while continuity style is the fundamental cinematic language, there is always room for innovation and evolution. Only a few years ago "smartphone," "blog," "gastropub," and "carbon footprint" meant about as much as *fluugeproit,* but today you'll find them in the dictionary and most of us can actually understand a sentence like, "Today I was at my

Alfred Hitchcock is known as a master of montage for the way he was able to conjure complex mysteries through visual means—primarily the precise juxtaposition of simple shots that, with a few edits, accumulate complex meaning. In the second scene of Hitchcock's 1937 film *Young and Innocent*, we are presented with a series of shots that, on their own, don't mean so much, but together they mean murder and mystery! A perfect day, a beautiful beach, a lighthouse, and seagulls. These shots resemble kitsch postcards of a summer vacation spot. Wish we were here (shots 1 and 2)! Waves break along the shoreline and then an arm flops against the water. The shot tells us that there seems to be a swimmer in the ocean. The swimmer, it turns out, is an unconscious woman who is being tumbled by the waves (shots 3 and 4). Now the viewer starts to ask questions. The swimmer washes onto the shore. Her body is limp and clearly lifeless. Did she drown, or was she bitten by a shark? We can't know yet. But a question has been raised, "What happened to this poor woman?" Then, a belt washes up on the shore (shot 5)!

The shot of the belt all by itself simply means that a belt washes up on a beach—no big deal. Juxtaposed only with the first shot it could mean that the beach is more polluted than we thought, given the beauty of the "postcard" shot, but placed here, next to the shot of the woman's body, it seems to answer our question, "What happened to this poor woman?" The belt immediately and clearly becomes a murder weapon and Hitchcock suggests that the swimmer who washed up on the shore was murdered *with it!* In addition, that idyllic beach becomes an ironic image because, for all its natural beauty, the location has become a sinister crime scene. Suddenly, all those questions, essential to any good mystery movie, flood into the minds of the audience. Who is she? How did she wind up in the ocean? Why was she killed? Whodunit? All in just a few shots (**Figure 3-5**).

■ **Figure 3-5** In this sequence, from Hitchcock's *Young and Innocent*, each image efficiently adds vital visual information that guides the viewer to make specific and complex narrative assumptions.

favorite gastropub and used my smartphone to tweet about how staycations reduce your carbon footprint." Cinema, too, is a living language with an ever-expanding vocabulary and ever-evolving syntax—the fundamentals in this chapter are just the beginning of how we speak in film. Just as in writing, the cinematic language can be bland or expressive, prosaic or poetic, utilitarian or profound. The development of visual eloquence and your particular style begins with an understanding of the basic vocabulary and the creative possibilities of the film language. And the best place to begin is with the frame.

■ THE FRAME AND COMPOSITION

Cinema is a matter of what is in the frame and what is not.

Martin Scorsese

Dimensions of the Frame

Aesthetic considerations concerning the graphic and compositional aspects of your shots begin with the frame. **The frame** has two definitions. The *physical frame* is each, individual, still image captured on film or on video, which, when projected as a series, creates the illusion of motion (see Chapter 8). The *compositional frame* (Figure 3-6) is a two-dimensional space defined by its horizontal (**x-axis**) and vertical (**y-axis)** dimensions. Within this space we can perceive a third dimension, depth (**z-axis**); however, depth and distance are created through graphic illusion.

The frame is your canvas, the rectangular space in which you determine the parameters of the viewer's perspective. We refer to each of the four edges of the frame as **screen left, screen right, top,** and **bottom.** The frame essentially crops the real-world environment and determines what the audience sees (mise-en-scène) and doesn't see, referred to as **off screen.** Framing your shot, deciding what to show and what *not* to show, is a significant creative decision.

The relationship between the width and the height of the frame is called the **aspect ratio** and is derived by dividing the width of the frame by the height. There are several different aspect ratios used in film and video (Figure 3-7). The aspect ratio of a full frame of 35mm film, 16mm film, and broadcast standard video is 1.33:1. In film, this is called **Academy Aperture** (from the technical standards set by the Academy of Motion Picture Arts and Sciences). In video parlance, this ratio is expressed as 4 × 3. In any case, the horizontal (width) is one-third longer than the vertical (height).

Movies intended for theatrical release on film or HDTV broadcast are shot with a different aspect ratio, which elongates the horizontal dimension. The American theatrical release aspect ratio is 1.85:1, the European theatrical release aspect ratio is 1.66:1, and the HDTV broadcast aspect ratio is 16 × 9 (or 1.78:1). We will discuss film and video aspect ratios in more detail in Chapters 8 and 9.

Shot Composition and the Graphic Qualities of the Frame

Working within the parameters of a given aspect ratio, a filmmaker has a broad pallet of aesthetic choices when designing the composition of a shot. There are no absolute rules concerning visual style except that the choices you make should emerge from the dramatic needs of the script and should reflect your own creative ideas. Each compositional principle is expressed in precise terms, and it's important that you use the proper terminology when applying them to your script and communicating with your crew.

Closed and Open Frames

A **closed frame** means that all of the essential information in the shot is neatly contained within the parameters of the frame, and an **open frame** means that the composition leads the audience to be aware of the area beyond the edges of the visible shot (Figure 3-8). This is not necessarily an either/or choice. A shot can begin as a closed frame and then an unexpected intrusion from beyond the edge of the

■ **Figure 3-6** The compositional frame. Although we work with only two dimensions (the x- and y-axes), we can imply depth by emphasizing the z-axis. Still from Mercado's *Yield* (2006).

frame can suddenly disclose the larger off-screen environment. Also, sound or dialogue coming from off screen can serve to open a frame, because it asks the audience to imagine the space beyond the edges of what is visible.

Deep Frames and Flat Frames

We refer to a frame that accentuates the compositional element of depth (z-axis) as a **deep frame** and one that emphasizes the two-dimensionality of the image as a **flat frame.** The graphic factors that are used to create the illusion of depth are the same ones that are minimized to create a flat frame (Figure 3-9):

1. *Receding planes, overlapping objects, and diminishing perspective.*

    We can achieve a feeling of deep, receding space by creating a mise-en-scène in which there are objects placed along the z-axis that define foreground, midground, and background planes. By reducing the z-axis space to two or even a single plane, we flatten the perspective and the space appears shallow. Related to this is the idea of **object overlapping**, which is the understanding that objects nearer the foreground will partially cover or overlap objects farther in the background. Also, related to the notion of receding planes is **diminishing perspective**, which is the perceptual understanding that objects will appear to be smaller the farther they are from the viewer, and conversely, objects will appear larger the closer they are to the viewer. For example, a chicken walking across the foreground of a shot will appear larger than a locomotive far in the background. **Foreshortening** is the same compositional phenomenon but with respect to a single object in which one part of the object appears large because it is very close to the viewer, while another part of the same object appears small because it is farther away, creating a dynamic sense of depth within the frame.

2. *Horizontal and diagonal lines.*

    Shot head on, horizontal lines or objects in a horizontal arrangement will obviously look, well, horizontal. But shot from an angle, a horizontal line appears to recede into the distance on a diagonal. For example, if we shoot five people standing against a wall for a police lineup head on, the composition will appear flat; if we move the camera 45 degrees (or more) to the side, so that the lineup now recedes diagonally along the z-axis, then we've created depth in the frame (Figure 3-10). This is a simple yet powerful way to create a sense of deep space. Shooting horizontals head on minimizes the sense of depth.

16mm, 35mm full frame and SD video
1.33:1

Super 16,
European theatrical release
1.66:1

HD video
1.78:1

U.S. theatrical release
1.85:1

■ **Figure 3-7** Aspect ratios. The ratio of the width to the height of a frame depends both on the shooting and the exhibition formats of the film or digital video.

■ **Figure 3-8** A closed frame contains all essential information within the frame, as shown in Jarmusch's *Stranger Than Paradise* (1984) *(left)*. An open frame has a composition that necessarily implies the existence of space beyond what is contained within the shot, like the gunman's hand protruding into this frame from Melville's *Le Samouraï* (1967) *(right)*.

3. *Deep and shallow focus.*
   The depth of the focus range of a shot can add or eliminate attention to background and foreground information (**Figure 3-11**). When focus is deep we can see objects along the z-axis, from foreground to background, in crisp detail. Deep focus gives us an awareness of deep space because it is clearly visible. When focus is shallow, meaning that only a single vertical plane is sharply defined and objects in front of or behind that plane are blurry, our attention is limited to a narrow and flat area (see Chapter 10 for information on how to control "depth of field").

4. *Shadows.*
   Shadows add depth to just about any image because they accentuate the dimensionality of your subject and their environment (**Figure 3-12**). Eliminating shadows, therefore, conceals dimensionality and leads to a flatter image (see Chapter 13 for information about controlling light and shadows).

Although **3D filmmaking** utilizes exactly the same depth cue techniques as standard filmmaking (or 2D cinematography), the difference is that 3D technology replicates one additional element of our ability to visually perceive depth and dimension: stereopsis. **Stereopsis** is a visual perception phenomenon created by viewing objects with two eyes that physiologically are placed slightly apart—like human eyes. The distance between our two pupils is called the **interocular distance**, and the two lenses on a 3D video camera try to replicate this physical occurrence (see **Figure 9-40**). Hold your right finger, pointing at the ceiling, six inches in front of your nose. Look at your finger with the left eye only and you will see more of the creases on the underside of your finger. Now, use only the right eye and you will see more of the tops of your knuckles. Each eye has a different perspective because the angle from which we view an object is slightly offset between our two eyes. This horizontal discrepancy creates a strong dimension cue

■ **Figure 3-9** Accentuating depth by using receding planes (*left*, from Kalatozov's *The Cranes Are Flying*, 1957) or by the foreshortening of a subject (*middle*, from Malmros' *Slim Susie*, 2003) creates deep frames. Limited number of z-axis planes produces a flatter perspective, (*right*, from Godard's *Masculin/Féminin*, 1966).

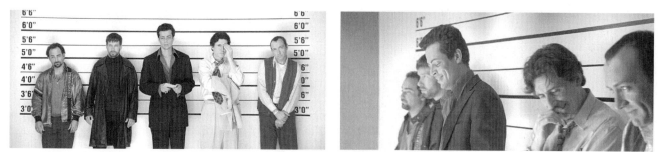

■ **Figure 3-10** Shooting horizontal lines head on creates flat compositions. Changing the shooting angle so that horizontal lines recede into the distance reinforces the depth of the frame, creating a sense of deep space (frames from Singer's *The Usual Suspects*, 1995).

■ **Figure 3-11** Manipulating depth of focus can direct the attention of the audience to selected areas of the composition. The deep focus in Zvyagintsev's *The Return* (2003) *(left)* lets the audience see the source of the subject's despair (his friends are leaving him behind), whereas the shallow focus used in Leigh's *Naked* (1993) *(right)* hints at the isolation that exists between the subject and society.

when our brains combine these two perspectives into one image incorporating both perspectives (creases and knuckles simultaneously). There are several different 3D technologies for filmmaking (anaglyph color filter glasses, polarization glasses, LCD shutter glasses, etc.), but they all involve some method of creating and then displaying two of the same image, a right eye signal and a left eye signal, slightly horizontally offset. During display, it is necessary to present each eye with one discrete signal isolated from the other (**Figure 3-13**). Despite the technology, however, the same compositional principles I've discussed apply if you wish to create deep frames in 3D.

Balanced and Unbalanced Frames

The principle of compositional balance begins with the understanding that objects in your frame carry a certain visual weight (**Figure 3-14**). Size, shape, brightness, and placement can all affect the relative weight of an object in the frame. How you distribute this visual weight within the frame, equally or unevenly, symmetrically or asymmetrically, gives your composition a sense of stability or instability. There is no value judgment attached to balanced and unbalanced frames; neither is "better" than the other. Like all of the other aesthetic principles in this section, the right choice is the one that is appropriate for the story you're telling and the mood you're creating.

■ **Figure 3-12** Lighting is critical to accentuating dimensionality in the frame. Eliminating shadows conceals texture, creating a flatter image *(top)*. Positioning lights to create deep shadows adds texture and depth to a subject *(bottom)*. Both frames from Coppola's *Tetro* (2009).

■ **Figure 3-13** Although Cameron's *Avatar* (2009) is a groundbreaking 3D film, it nonetheless uses all the same depth cues as regular cinema. Notice the receding and overlapping planes, the deep z-axis diagonal composition, and the use of shadows to create depth.

Rule of Thirds (Looking Room, Walking Room)

Cinematic composition, as with any other art form, has certain classic principles that have developed over time. Film, being a two-dimensional representational art form, developed after painting and photography, has been influenced by many of their ideas of classical form. One such idea is the **rule of thirds**, which is often used as a guide for framing human subjects and for composition in general.

First, we divide the frame into thirds with imaginary lines (sometimes referred to as "sweet spots") along the horizontal and vertical axes and then we place significant objects, focus points, and elements of interest along these lines. For the human form, for example, this would mean placing the eyes along the top third horizontal line. If your subject is looking or moving toward one side of the screen, then the vertical placement of the figure should be along the left or right vertical third line *opposite* the direction in which the subject is looking or moving (Figure 3-15).

This extra vertical space, to one side or the other, is called **looking room** (or **walking room** for a moving figure). This space provides a sense of balance because the direction of the gaze, or movement, itself carries a sort of compositional weight. This space also keeps the viewer from feeling like the subject is pushing, or about to go beyond, the edge of the frame. Of course, you may *want* to create that uneasy sense. For example, if you want to accentuate the urgency of a character running, you might want that person bumping up against the front edge of the frame, as if the camera itself can't keep up with them! But this is an expressive deviation (Figure 3-16), which is made possible by the common application of the rule of thirds. Again, the rule of thirds is just a guide, a convention, and not really a rule at all, and while it is often employed and can be a useful starting point, it is by no means a requirement for a well-composed shot.

Shot Size

Shot size refers to the size of your subject in the frame. The size of your subject is determined by two factors: (1) the proximity of subject to camera (the closer the subject is to the camera, the larger it will appear) and (2) the degree of lens magnification (the more your lens magnifies the subject, the larger the subject will appear). These two approaches are not the same and the differences in their visual perspectives are discussed in detail in

■ **Figure 3-14** The distribution of objects/subjects in the frame can create a sense of balance or imbalance, according to the needs of the narrative. In Greenaway's *A Zed and Two Noughts (left)*, the equal distribution of twins Oliver and Oswald (Eric and Brian Deacon) echoes the film's obsession with symmetry. In Antonioni's *L'Eclisse (right)*, the placement of the subjects at a corner of the frame hints at an uneasy relationship with their surroundings.

■ **Figure 3-15** Typical use of the rule of thirds. Note how the "sweet spots" created by the intersection of the lines located at the thirds of the image are used to position the subject, giving her proper headroom and viewing room. Still from Mercado's *Yield* (2006).

■ **Figure 3-16** Breaking the rule of thirds for dramatic impact. In this scene from Hooper's 2010 film *The King's Speech*, Prince Albert "Bertie" (Colin Firth) is boxed in by the bottom left edge of the frame and the corner of the sofa, reflecting his extreme discomfort at having to go to the office of a commoner to receive speech therapy. Notice how the elimination of looking room further accentuates his sense of unease.

Chapter 10. Dramatically speaking, one selects a shot size based of the narrative emphasis, visual information, and emotional impact needed from a particular shot at a particular moment in the story. As the following figures show, most films are made up of a wide variety of shot sizes.

The frame of reference for any discussion of shot size is traditionally the human form, but the following shot designations work for nonhuman subjects as well:

- An **extreme long shot** or **wide shot** (**ELS**) is a shot that shows a large view of the location, setting, or landscape (Figure 3-17). Even if there are people in the shot, the emphasis is on their surroundings or their relationship to their surroundings.
- A **long shot** (**LS**) is generally a shot that contains the whole human figure. It's a good choice when you need to show larger physical movements and activity (Figure 3-18).
- A **medium long shot** (**MLS**) frames your subject from approximately the knees up (Figure 3-19). This shot is sometimes called a "cowboy shot" because, as legend has it, of the need to always see a cowboy's gun belt in the western genre pictures. The French call this shot an "American shot" because of its frequent use in genre movies of the 1930s and 1940s.
- A **medium shot** (**MS**) frames your subject from approximately the waist up (Figure 3-20). This shot can show smaller physical actions and facial expressions, yet maintain some connection with the setting. However, location is clearly no longer the emphasis of the shot, as the viewer is now drawn closer to the subject.

■ **Figure 3-17** An extreme long shot (Scorsese's *Raging Bull*, 1980).

■ **Figure 3-18** The long shot (Scorsese's *Raging Bull*).

■ **Figure 3-19** The medium long shot (Scorsese's *Raging Bull*).

■ **Figure 3-20** The medium shot (Scorsese's *Raging Bull*).

- A **medium close-up** (**MCU**) is generally from the chest or shoulders up (**Figure 3-21**). The emphasis of this shot is now facial expression, but some connection to the broader physical "attitude" of the body is maintained.
- A **close-up** (**CU**) places the primary emphasis on the face or other part of the body (**Figure 3-22**). Small details in features, movements, and expressions are the subjects of this very intimate shot.
- An **extreme close-up** (**ECU**) is a stylistically potent shot that isolates a very small detail or feature of the subject (**Figure 3-23**).
- **Two shots, three shots,** and **group shots:** As these labels clearly state, the two shot includes two subjects, the three shot includes three subjects, and shots that include more than three people are referred to as group shots (**Figure 3-24**).

Shot Size and Character Identification

When framing a human subject, the shot size is especially important in establishing the level of intimacy and identification you wish the audience to have with that character. Obviously, an ELS and an LS cannot show a character's facial expressions with any detail and therefore these shots convey a feeling of distance and remoteness from the subject. With medium shots we are close enough to clearly see them, but we're still at an observation distance, which is why this frame is rather neutral in terms of creating an emotional connection with a character. When using an MCU and CU we enter the very intimate, personal space of a character allowing us see emotions and reactions through facial expressions. At this proximity, audience identification is quite strong. An ECU is so close that it can be either extremely intimate or, in its own way, mysterious and distancing—especially if the ECU obscures a character's eyes. It depends on the subject and composition of the shot. Understanding

■ **Figure 3-21** The medium close-up (Scorsese's *Raging Bull*).

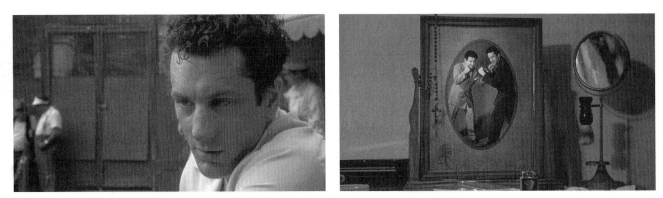

■ **Figure 3-22** The close-up (Scorsese's *Raging Bull*). Close-up of a person *(left)* and an object *(right)*.

■ **Figure 3-23** The extreme close-up (Scorsese's *Raging Bull*). ECU of an object *(left)* and a person *(right)*.

■ **Figure 3-24** Two shots, three shots, group shots. These shots are named according to the number of subjects included within the frame (Scorsese's *Raging Bull*).

this, a filmmaker is able to precisely modulate not only the focus of attention within the frame but also the degree of emotional involvement the audience has with any particular character at any given moment by carefully selecting shot sizes.

Camera Angles

The orientation of the camera to the subject, the horizontal and vertical angles you are shooting from, has a dramatic effect on your image no matter what size the subject is in the frame. Simply moving the horizontal or vertical position of the camera, relative to your subject, can be a powerfully expressive technique that establishes the viewer's relationship to your subject.

High and Low Angles

Let's look first at vertical angles (Figure 3-25). Again, using the human form for our reference, the **eye-level** shot is one in which the lens of the camera is positioned at eye level with your subjects, regardless if they are sitting, standing, or lying down. Raising the camera above eye level yields a **high-angle** shot and below eye level gives us a **low-angle** shot. An eye-level shot can encourage a connection with a subject, while extreme high or low angles tend to be more emotionally remote, but they can make for very dynamic frames.

■ **Figure 3-25** High-angle, eye-level, and low-angle shots. In an eye-level shot, the camera is positioned at the eye level of the subject *(middle)*, regardless if the subject is standing, sitting, or lying down. Positioning the camera above eye level produces a high-angle shot *(left)*, while putting the camera below eye level produces a low-angle shot *(right)*. Examples from Wenders's *Wings of Desire* (1987).

Figure 3-26 A character who looks straight into the camera appears to address the audience directly. Each time Amélie (Audrey Tautou) speaks to the camera, she is inviting the viewer into her thoughts and schemes as a secret accomplice to her acts of kindness. (from Jeunet's *Amélie*, 2001).

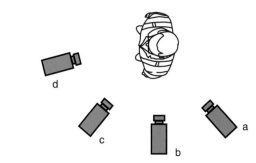

Figure 3-27 Front to back camera angle positions: (a) three-quarters back, (b) profile shot, (c) three-quarters lfrontal shot, and (d) frontal. Unless you want direct camera address, actors should look slightly off the side of the lens in a frontal shot. (For an interactive video example of these various camera angles, go to www.voiceandvisionbook.com.)

Front to Back Angles

The horizontal position of the camera can be anywhere from directly in front of your subjects to directly behind them. A shot in which the subject looks directly at the camera is called **direct address** (Figure 3-26). Even though music videos use direct address all the time, eye contact with the audience is rare and is especially powerful in narrative films because it shatters the fictive world by eliminating the separation between the watcher and the watched. Direct camera address is the cinematic version of the theatrical concept of breaking the fourth wall. Much more common are **frontal shots**, in which the camera looks directly at the face of your subject but the subject's sightline glances just off the edge of the frame. Moving the camera along a horizontal arc, we progressively move through **three-quarter frontal**, **profile shot**, **three-quarter back** (Figure 3-27), and finally to **shooting from behind** (see Figure 3-30). As we move the camera angle from frontal, to profile, to the back of the subject, we drastically change the relationship of the viewer with the subject. Looking directly at a subject's face (frontal and three-quarter frontal) is an intimate perspective and can elicit strong engagement; a profile shot is a somewhat neutral point of view, and hiding the face by shooting from behind can create a sense of distance, remoteness, or mystery. However, shooting from three-quarter back position can also encourage the audience to identify with a character by aligning their visual point of view with that of the subject.

One other camera angle that we can consider adjusting is the lateral positioning of the camera. Tilting the camera laterally so that the horizon of your composition is oblique is called a **canted angle** (or **Dutch angle**) (Figure 3-28). This sort of shot can create a feeling ranging from slight imbalance to extreme spatial disorientation, depending on the extremity of the lateral tilt of your camera. A canted shot can infuse tension, imbalance or disorientation into a scene.

Creating New Frames and Aspect Ratios

So far, we have been looking at working within the given aspect ratio of the film and video frame (1.33:1, 1.85:1, etc.), but you are not entirely restricted to these compositional dimensions. Many filmmakers find interesting ways to alter the aspect ratios of the area that frames their subjects. Because we cannot physically change the aspect ratio of the film or video frame, this technique involves using some element of the location or lighting to crop the existing frame to new proportions. This is called a **frame within a frame** (Figure 3-29).

Figure 3-28 In *The Crying Game* (1992), director Neil Jordan uses a canted angle when a desperate Jody (Forest Whitaker) shows Fergus (Stephen Rea) a picture of his "girlfriend" Dil. This imbalance adds to the sense of precarious tension as Jody struggles to survive.

■ **Figure 3-29** Frames within frames. The filmmaker is not restricted to the aspect ratio of the shooting format. Through careful use of composition or lighting, it is possible to alter the dimension of the frame to create a dramatically compelling way of presenting a subject. *Left* from Fassbinder's *Ali: Fear Eats the Soul* (1974); *Right* from Hausner's *Lourdes* (2009).

in practice

In their film *The Son* (2002), the Dardenne brothers tell the story of Olivier, a carpentry mentor at a rehabilitation center for juvenile delinquents. One day the boy who killed Olivier's son during a botched robbery is released from prison and winds up in his carpentry shop as one of his apprentices. On the boy's first day the camera follows Olivier, who is following the boy, as he tries to get a glimpse of the kid who killed his son years ago. For extended sequences the camera remains behind Olivier, shooting from a three-quarter back angle or completely from behind (**Figure 3-30**). This camera angle choice allows the audience to feel like they're peering over Olivier's shoulder, seeing the world from his perspective; however, this angle does not allow us to see how Olivier is reacting to seeing his son's killer. Through this camera angle, the Dardenne brothers and director of photography

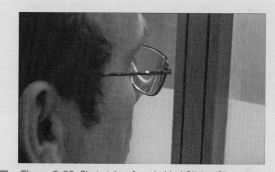

■ **Figure 3-30** Shots taken from behind Olivier (Olivier Gourmet) in the Dardenne brothers' *The Son* (2002) bring the audience into the point of view of the lead character but also serve to obscure his emotional response, because we can't make out his facial expressions.

Alain Marcoen build enormous tension and suspense by frustrating our need to see what emotions are playing across Olivier's face.

■ THE MOVING FRAME

A shot in which the framing remains steady on the subject without moving or shifting perspective is called a **static shot** (or **fixed frame**). We can certainly use two static shots edited next to each other to shift the viewer's perspective from, say, a man working at his desk, to the dark window behind him. But there are often important dramatic and stylistic reasons to shift the perspective of the frame and therefore the viewer's attention, horizontally, vertically, or even along the z-axis, during the course of a shot. This is called a **camera move**. Shifting the viewer's perspective, in one continuous motion—from the man at his desk, across the empty room, to the dark window behind him—might provide extra information or a visual connection, which could be vital to fully develop that particular dramatic moment. For example, by scanning the room between the man and the window, we can see that he is completely alone.

Camera Moves

There are two kinds of moves: stationary camera moves and dynamic camera moves.

Pivot Moves

Pivot camera moves (also **stationary camera moves**) involve pivoting the camera, horizontally or vertically, from a stationary spot while the camera is running. This can be done on a tripod or with a handheld camera as long as the location of the camera doesn't change, just its horizontal or vertical angle.

A **pan** scans space horizontally by pivoting the camera left or right (*pan left* and *pan right*). A **tilt** shifts the camera perspective vertically, with the lens facing up or facing down (*tilt up* and *tilt down*) (Figure 3-31). A pan or a tilt that moves from one subject to another is called **panning from/to** and **tilting from/to.** For example, you pan *from* the man at his desk, *to* the dark window across the room. A pan or a tilt that follows a subject as they move within the space is called a **pan with** or **tilt with** (this move is also called a **follow pan** or **follow tilt**). For example, the man at his desk thinks he hears a funny noise outside. We can pan *with* him as he walks from his desk to the window to look outside (Figure 3-32).

It is also possible to move in closer or farther away from a subject while your camera remains in a stationary spot. **Zooming in** or **zooming out** requires a variable focal length lens (see Chapter 10 for details). This lens is common on DV cameras but less common on film cameras. Just as with any other move, one can *zoom from/to* subjects or *zoom with* a moving subject.

Dynamic Moves

Dynamic camera moves involve a mobile camera, which means literally moving the entire camera in space, horizontally (left or right), closer or farther (forward or backward), or even vertically (up and down). These moves can be accomplished with special camera mounting equipment or with a handheld camera.

A **tracking shot** is a term used when you move the camera in order to *follow* or *track with* a subject (Figure 3-33). You can *track* left, right, forward, or backward to follow along with the movement of your subject. Gus Van Sant's film *Elephant* (2003) makes frequent use of long tracking shots, following characters as they walk through the hallways of their high school. Tracking shots can also be from/to shots. **Dolly shots** are generally moving shots in which the camera moves closer or farther away from the subject (Figure 3-34). To *dolly-in* or *dolly-out* means to move the camera closer to or farther away from, respectively. Dolly, however, is a slippery term because it also refers to the wheeled apparatus on which we mount the camera to move it. We can certainly move a camera closer or farther away from our subject without using a dolly, for example, with a handheld camera. So you'll also hear people say *push-in* or *pull-out* for this camera move, especially when an actual dolly isn't being used.

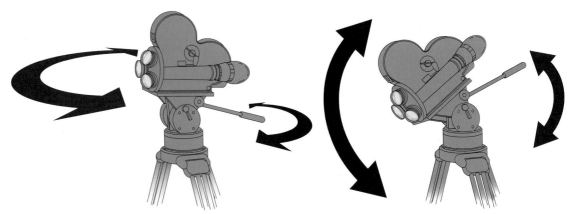

 ■ **Figure 3-31** Panning and tilting. In a pan, the camera scans space left or right on the tripod's axis. A tilt shifts the camera's perspective vertically on the tripod's axis.

■ **Figure 3-32** Pan with and pan to. In Cocteau's *Beauty and the Beast* (1946), the camera pans from right to left *with* Beauty (Josette Day) as she explores the Beast's castle. The camera keeps her centered in the frame as she moves from the door to the window *(top frames)*. In a later scene, the camera pans *from* Beauty *to* the Beast (Jean Marais) standing across the room. The camera move follows Beauty's look and reveals the Beast, which heightens the surprise and tension of their encounter.

Lifting the camera up and down is called **booming** (*boom up* or *boom down*). This can be done with a handheld camera or mechanically with a boom or jib arm (**Figure 3-35**). A **crane shot** is one in which the camera is raised very high in the air, certainly above a human subject's head. This usually requires a special, and expensive, piece of equipment called a crane. The specific equipment and techniques used for dynamic camera moves are discussed in more detail in Chapter 11.

All of these moves—pans, tilts, dolly, tracking, booming, and zooming—are often combined. For example, following the trajectory of a helium balloon just as a child lets go of it would require panning and tilting simultaneously—one might even want additionally to zoom in. Executing more than one move at a time is referred to as a **combination move** and is very common.

The Moving Frame and Perspective

Although the general directions of the frame shifts are similar (i.e., left to right or up and down), there is a big difference between stationary camera moves (pans and tilts) and dynamic camera moves (dolly, track, and boom). Think of the camera as essentially the seat from which an audience member views the world of your film. With pivoting camera moves this perspective point of reference remains fixed. Panning or tilting the camera is the equivalent of placing the

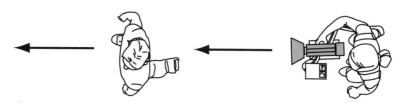

■ **Figure 3-33** Tracking is when the camera follows a subject as it moves. Tracking shots can be accomplished with dollies, wheelchairs, vehicles, handholding the camera, or, in the case of Van Sant's *Elephant* (2003), with the use of a Steadicam system.

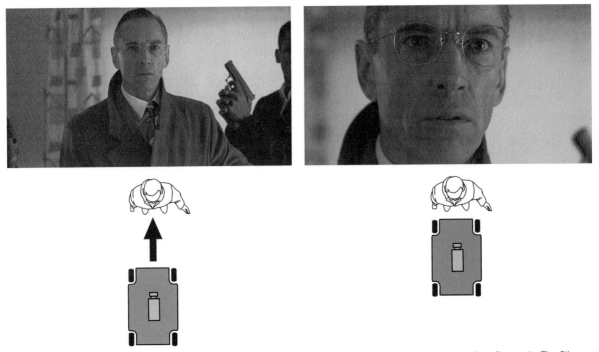

■ **Figure 3-34** In a dolly shot, the camera is moved away or closer to a stationary subject. In this example, from Demme's *The Silence of the Lambs* (1991), a dolly-in move was used to underline the dramatic moment in which Jack (Scott Glen) realizes they've just seized the wrong house and put Clarice (Jodie Foster) in grave danger.

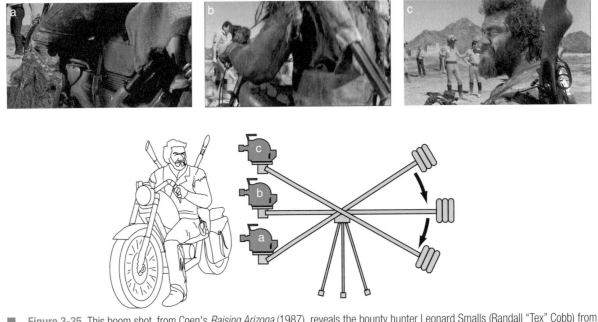

■ **Figure 3-35** This boom shot, from Coen's *Raising Arizona* (1987), reveals the bounty hunter Leonard Smalls (Randall "Tex" Cobb) from boots to beard. The camera move not only scans his arsenal of weaponry but also emphasizes his fearsomeness.

viewer in one spot and then having them turn their head left and right or up and down. Their viewer's seat becomes the pivot point as they scan the world horizontally or vertically. With a mobile camera, you are essentially moving the viewer's seat through the space of the fictive world of the film. This makes for an extremely dynamic feeling of traveling through space.

Here's an example of the difference. Let's say we are filming a runner, jogging down a street. First, let's shoot the run with a follow pan, placing the camera at the halfway mark along his path (**Figure 3-36**).

The beginning of the shot is quite frontal, looking into the runner's face. When he hits the midpoint mark, directly in front of the camera, he will be seen in profile and, continuing, when he reaches the end of his path, we will be looking at his back. It's the perspective of a stationary spectator—as if we were sitting on a bench watching him run past us.

Now, let's go back to the beginning of the runner's path and shoot his run with a tracking shot (Figure 3-37). We begin alongside the runner, in profile, and as he moves, our camera tracks along with him. As he reaches the midway point and then the end of the path, the runner remains in profile all the way because we have been following parallel to him. In this shot, the viewer, like the camera, is a runner too, a participant—moving through space just like the runner.

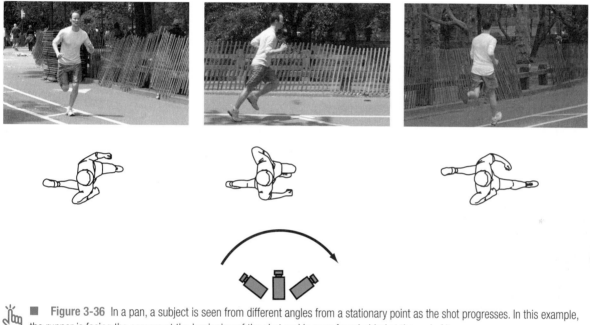

■ **Figure 3-36** In a pan, a subject is seen from different angles from a stationary point as the shot progresses. In this example, the runner is facing the camera at the beginning of the shot and is seen from behind at the end of it.

■ **Figure 3-37** Here the camera tracks with the runner, maintaining a consistent profile angle.

.in practice

For video examples of pivot and dynamic camera moves, go to www.voiceandvisionbook. com. Review pan and tilt (with and from/to) at interactive **Figure 3-27**; track, dolly and boom at interactive **Figures 3-33, 3-34,** and **3-35;** and a panning versus tracking comparison at interactive **Figures 3-36** and **3-37**.

Motivation and the Moving Camera

Camera moves can look very cool, and because they do, they are one of the most overused techniques in film. Your film, after all, should be about what happens to the characters and not about what's happening with the camera. So like all film techniques, you need a good reason to employ a moving camera. Camera moves should be **motivated** in two ways. First, conceptually speaking, a camera move must have a narrative function, meaning that it serves as an important storytelling technique. If it is included just because it looks snazzy, then it will be a distraction rather than and enhancement. Second, the moment the physical camera move actually begins needs to be motivated within the scene.

Narrative Motivation: Reveal, Conceal, or Dramatic Punctuation

A camera move, whether it's a pan, track, or zoom, is a promise—it promises the viewers that they are going to get a new piece of information, a new perspective or a new understanding by the end of the camera's little trip. Let's say we're shooting a wide shot of a mountain range and we pan right; the pan promises the viewer that we'll see something in addition to those mountains: maybe the pan reveals a forest fire raging on the south slopes or maybe a cowboy comes into view in the foreground, or perhaps the pan of the mountains goes on and on and on and the move reveals that our character is surrounded by mountains on all sides. But if you just pan from some mountains to a few more mountains and the move accomplishes nothing more than a static shot would, then the move breaks its promise of showing something else, and it is considered an unmotivated move. Although camera moves are often used to **reveal** new (and sometimes startling) information within a single shot, they can also be used to **conceal** actions and details for dramatic effect. What, how, and when you reveal or conceal details are very important factors to consider when you devise camera moves of any sort (see the "Reveal Conceal Camera Movement" box).

Short camera moves, like a short dolly-in to a character's face or a short arc around a character can be used to punctuate an important or highly emotional moment. These shots do not change the image composition very much; rather, they infuse a little jolt of energy at critical points in the narrative. Florian Henckel von Donnersmarck's 2009 film *The Lives of Others* revolves around East German Stasi (secret police) officer Captain Weisler (Ulrich Mühe) and his covert surveillance of a couple: the playwright Dreyman (Sebastian Koch) and his lover Christa-Maria (Martina Gedeck), an actress. Early in the film Captain Weisler starts to feel sympathetic toward the two "subversives" he's spying on and

■ **Figure 3-38** The short dolly push-in underscores a particularly dramatic and pivotal moment in a scene from von Donnersmarck's *The Lives of Others*.

■ REVEAL AND CONCEAL CAMERA MOVEMENT

The 2009 film *Creation*, directed by Jon Amiel and shot by Jess Hall, is about Charles Darwin as he struggles to complete his life's work on the origin of species. Although he believes absolutely in the scientific evidence of his theory of evolution, his inability to reconcile the death of his beloved daughter Annie with the brutal natural cycle of survival of the fittest, which he is espousing, has caused serious trauma to his health and his ability to complete the manuscript. The opening frame of this scene shows Darwin alone, procrastinating with research he doesn't really need to finish his book, but as the camera dolly-arcs around him (frame right), it reveals another figure in the room with him—the spirit of his deceased daughter. This small perspective shift effectively moves us right into Darwin's psyche. At first, Annie remains out of focus, but as Darwin shares deeply personal thoughts with her, she comes into sharper focus. Through this surprising dolly "reveal," Amiel manages to imbue a flesh-and-blood actor with the aura of an apparition who has just appeared, conjured by Darwin's troubled mind (**Figure 3-39**).

Camera moves that conceal space or action have been used since the very early days of cinema primarily to conceal a violent or sexual encounter that might run afoul of the censors. We've all seen it. A man and a woman enter a passionate embrace, kiss, and recline onto a bed as... the camera pans away to the window where a thunderstorm is raging. Quentin Tarantino and his director of photography Andrzej Sekula slyly wink at this tradition in *Reservoir Dogs* (1998). In this scene Mr. Blonde (Michael Madsen) has been dancing and taunting a captured cop with a straight edged razor. We know he'll use it, we just don't know when. The buildup to the horrific moment when Mr. Blonde moves in to slice off the officer's ear is nearly unbearable, but when the act finally happens, Tarantino dollies left, away from the action, to show a doorway with a sign along the top that reads, "watch your head." The conceal is humorously coy for a director who obviously has no qualms about showing graphic blood and brutality, and the sign above the door encourages us to chuckle at the little joke, but we also know that a man's ear is being sliced off. With this ironic, concealing camera move Tarantino reduces the gore but exaggerates the sadism of the moment (**Figure 3-40**).

■ **Figure 3-39** A subtle dolly-arc to the right in Amiel's *Creation* serves to reveal the presence of Darwin's (Paul Bettany) deceased daughter Annie (Martha West) in such a way that we understand her to be an apparition from his imagination.

■ **Figure 3-40** This dolly-left in Tarantino's *Reservoir Dogs* serves to conceal the physical torture in this scene, yet manages to emotionally amplify this horrifically violent moment.

actually comforts Christa-Maria at a local bar as if he were just a friendly stranger. However, later in the film Weisler is asked by his superior to interrogate her directly. Weisler knows that she will recognize him as the stranger who spoke kind words to her in her hour of despair and this recognition could put them both in grave danger. The scene is already suffused with tension, but the short dolly-in electrifies the exact moment he reveals himself to her in his official capacity as a Stasi officer (Figure 3-38). Notice also that as the camera pushes in, Weisler does not make eye contact with Christa-Maria until the very end of the movement, thus motivating the cut to her reaction.

Move Motivation

The moment the camera begins to move also needs motivation within a scene. A move that begins arbitrarily can feel artificial and make the camera apparatus itself very apparent to viewers, causing them to become aware of the filmmaker manipulating the world of the film. Camera moves can be motivated by the physical movements of a character or even simply by their gaze. In the example from Cocteau's *Beauty and the Beast* (Figure 3-32, *top*), which was photographed by the inimitable Henri Alekan, the pan-with is motivated by the movements of Beauty who crosses from the door to the window prompting the camera to follow her. Narratively speaking, the purpose of the pan is to reveal more detail of the Beast's castle, particularly Beauty's room at the castle. During the pan we see that this is a magical place, with mist and flora obscuring walls and ceiling this is neither inside nor outside, but more like a fantastical dream space. The pan-to example from the same figure (Figure 3-32, *bottom*) is from the scene where Beauty sees the Beast for the first time. The physical pan move is motivated by her seeing something off screen and the move follows her gaze to reveal the Beast. In cases like this we say that we "pan off her look." The purpose for a pan like this is to place the camera, and therefore the viewers, closer to the subject's point of view—we see what she sees because it is the force of her gaze that moves the camera.

◼ CONCLUSION

It is essential that anyone hoping to tell stories with moving images develop a deep working appreciation for the concepts of mise-en-scène and montage, because it is here where we truly connect with an audience on the level of story information, meaning, and emotion. In addition, being aware of the expressive power of camera angles and camera moves allows one to conceive of shots, sequences, and scenes that are narratively and emotionally eloquent. When it comes to the aesthetics of the frame—still or moving—we have only laid the groundwork in this chapter. There are many factors that contribute to the graphic qualities of your images—for example, choice of imaging format, lens selection, camera support, lighting design, exposure, frame rate, and the physical location to name a few. It's all integrated, and these aesthetic tools will be discussed throughout the chapters of this book.

Organizing Cinematic Time and Space

■ SINGLE-CAMERA PRODUCTION AND THE CONTINUITY SYSTEM

Whether you are shooting on film or digital video (DV), fictional narrative movies are generally shot using a single camera. This enables productions to be extremely mobile and to go to any location required by the script, as opposed to multicamera and control room productions like sit-coms and soap operas, which are produced in a studio. Single-camera shooting also allows the energy and expertise of the director and the entire creative team to be focused on each and every shot in the movie. Finally, shooting single-camera gives us maximum versatility in editing, because the film has been broken down into its smallest component parts—individual shots—whose intended sequence can be creatively rethought and rearranged throughout the postproduction process to improve the film.[1]

The scenes and shots of a narrative film are rarely shot in the order in which they appear in the script or in the final film. Because of the expense, time, and labor involved in film production, a script is divided and rearranged according to major locations, camera angles, and, finally, shots, and the actual shooting order is organized primarily for efficiency (see Chapter 5). This means that scenes, sequences, and even specific actions are often divided into different pieces and are shot at different times. **Continuity-style shooting and editing** is a system that assures us that individual shots, when cut together, will give us the illusion of smooth and continuous time, movement, and space, regardless of the order those shots were taken. The continuity system has been devised to present a scene without any confusion about the spatial and temporal relationships of people, objects, and actions. Also, the hallmark of continuity style is to render each edit, the link from one shot to another, as seamlessly as possible. Although the principles of the continuity system can, at first, seem a bit like a needlessly complex jigsaw puzzle, they are, in fact, quite simple and can be mastered with relatively little shooting and editing experience.

■ PRINCIPLES OF CONTINUITY STYLE

Any discussion about the continuity system necessarily concerns both shooting principles and editing principles; there is no way to separate the two; therefore, the requirements of the editing process must be acknowledged in the shooting process. In other words, a director needs to get more than just a collection of great-looking shots; directors need to get shots that will work together in the edit.

Let's start with two shots connected by one single edit. We want to cut shot A with shot B as seamlessly as possible. Invisible edits are the traditional goal of continuity style. Shot A is a long shot of two men at a chess table in the park starting a game of chess. Shot B is a medium close-up of the player with the white pieces making his first move and hitting the clock (**Figure 4-1**).

[1]There are some exceptions to this practice. Spike Lee's *Bamboozled,* for example, was shot with as many as 10 DV cameras simultaneously, but this is rare, even within the oeuvre of the director. Also, big action sequences that cannot be duplicated, like the spectacular train wreck in Andrew Davis' *The Fugitive,* are often shot with multiple cameras from different angles.

a   b

■ **Figure 4-1** A simple edit. Cutting from a long shot (a) to a medium close-up (b).

Because shooting a movie can take a long time, it's not uncommon that two shots like these might not be shot one right after the other. Perhaps after we shoot the long shot, we decide to break for lunch and shoot the close-up one hour later. Maybe during lunch our actor becomes ill and needs to go home. A week later he's better and we return to the park to get the close-up. To assure that these two shots cut together seamlessly, no matter when they were shot, our first consideration is that the shared visual and aural characteristics in each shot remain consistent.

Continuity of Mise-en-Scène
Costume, Props, Sets, and Lights
The clothes our character wears, the things he touches, and his surroundings need to remain the same from one shot to the next. For example, our actor is wearing a necklace in the long shot, but if he removes it during lunch, he might forget to put it back on when shooting commences. Cutting from a long shot with necklace to a MCU without a necklace will break continuity.

Consumable props and set pieces can also cause difficulty. Cigarettes that are short in one shot but longer in the next, or a glass of milk that is half empty in the master shot but is suddenly full again in the close-up, or a candle that is tall in the master but just a stub in the close-up—all of these discontinuities are common problems and avoiding them requires sharp eyes and lots of extra props on hand. In the case of our chess player, the clock needs to be watched carefully. If it starts out showing five minutes but in the one cut it's down to 1 minute, then the illusion of continuous time is broken in a very literal way. For exactly this reason, you must be careful of clocks that appear in the background of shots. You can easily find yourself cutting between 10 a.m. in long shots and 3 p.m. in close-ups.

The angle and quality of the light in shots A and B must also be consistent if you want to edit these shots together and create the illusion of continuous time. We might be able to shoot an hour later, especially if the chess table is in the shade of a tree, but we wouldn't want to shoot these two shots too far apart in the same day. If the sun is overhead in the master shot but it is setting in the close-up (creating long shadows), then continuity will be broken and the shots won't cut. The angle of the sun is not just a concern for exterior scenes. Let's say you shoot your first shot in an interior space with the sun streaming in through the windows, but when you finally get around to the close-up the sun has moved to the other side of the house or clouds have moved in. This is why it's common practice to block windows and then re-create the sunlight streaming in. If your "sun" is a 2,000-watt light on a stand, then that's a sun that'll never set. But even when using all artificial lights, you often tweak and rearrange a few lighting instruments between shots, so you need to remember to be consistent with lighting angles, exposures, and colors from shot to shot.

Not Looking

One of my students was shooting a film and took a break between a long shot and a close-up to solve an unrelated logistical matter. During the break, the actor decided to go over his lines and put his glasses on to read the script. When shooting recommenced, he got into position for his close-up and didn't even think about taking his glasses off. He had forgotten, and no one else noticed either, that he wasn't wearing his glasses in the long shot. So in editing, the student was unable to cut to the close-up without breaking continuity.

Not Thinking

Another story from a student shoot happened on an advanced thesis project. The art department team had done a beautiful job creating just the right look for a kitchen scene, including placing a lovely bowl of fruit on the dining table. During the crew's lunch beak, however, no one noticed that one of the production assistants, someone with very little filmmaking experience, decided to augment the meal provided by the producer with a few pieces of fruit from the set! Ultimately it wasn't a disaster—it was possible to cut around the missing bananas and grapes—but this does make a good case for using plastic food as set dressing and being careful whom you allow onto your set.

As much as we all try to maintain continuity as perfectly as possible, many films still have this sort of continuity error. In fact, there are dozens of "blooper" books dedicated to spotting, say, the stick that disappears and reappears in the reverse shots in *My Own Private Idaho* (Figure 4-2). But tiny continuity gaffes like this are often overlooked if your story is engaging, your performances are good, and the rest of your continuity technique is solid. The truth is, most people don't look for the little stuff if they're engaged in the drama of your film. However, glaring continuity errors can pull the audience completely out of the story. I remember the murmurs and chuckles in the theater during the opening chase scene in *New Jack City* (1991). The chase between Scotty and Pookie starts on a beautifully sunny day, not a cloud in the sky, but in one edit, as Pookie leaps over a fence, everyone on the street is suddenly holding umbrellas to shield themselves from the steady rain. No matter how exciting the chase is, it's hard to overlook a continuity error that big.

On a professional set, the **script supervisor** is responsible for keeping track of these continuity concerns, but small productions and student films rarely have a dedicated script supervisor, so it is important for everyone on the set (especially actors, the director, the cinematographer, and the art director) to be as vigilant and perceptive as possible to maintain the continuity of these mise-en-scène details. Digital still cameras are a great help for continuity of shot content. If you break before completing all of the shots in a continuity sequence, simply take a few pictures of the actors in costume, the props, and the sets to remind you what was in the scene and where it was. Shooting DV does allow you to back up and view the previous take—but a word of caution: I've seen many shots erased because the tape was not properly requeued.

■ **Figure 4-2** Continuity of mise-en-scène. In this shot/reverse-shot sequence from Van Sant's *My Own Private Idaho* (1991), the stick in Mike's (River Phoenix) hand *(left)* disappears when we cut to Scott (Keanu Reeves, *right*). Small continuity gaffes like this one are common, but audiences rarely notice them if they are fully engaged in the drama of the film.

Continuity of Sound

If you are shooting a film with sound, then the shared aural universe between shots A and B also must be consistent. This is especially difficult when it comes to ambient sound. **Ambient sounds** are the sounds that exist naturally in a given location. If you're at the beach, the ambient sound might include breaking waves, seagulls, and kids playing. However, the human perception of sound has developed such that we unconsciously ignore or "filter out" a lot of ambient sound and "focus" our ears on important sounds. This is a great ability for maintaining one's sanity, but it can be a disaster for the aural continuity of a film.

Let's say that all was quiet in the park when we took shot A and recorded our chess players' dialogue, but while we were setting up for shot B the grounds crew decided to trim the grass with a weed-wacker, or maybe a jet airplane is flying overhead at precisely the moment you shoot shot B. These are sounds that we can easily miss at the time, but they will break the illusion of continuous time when you cut the relative silence of one shot right next to the buzz of an off-screen weed-wacker in the next. For this reason, sound recordists are trained to hear absolutely everything in their environment, the same way a cinematographer observes everything in the frame. Many shots have been halted by a sound recordist who hears a plane flying overhead. There are ways to "fix" continuity sound problems, but fixes often involve time, money, and compromises. It's best to try to maintain the best possible sound match between the shots—so you should wait for the plane to pass before running the camera, or in the case of the weed wacker, maybe it would be a good time to break for lunch and shoot the medium close-up when the gardeners are done trimming. Issues concerning continuity and audio recording, editing, and mixing are discussed in detail in Chapters 17 and 23, respectively.

Continuity of Performance, Actions, and Placement

If we are to cut shot A seamlessly with shot B, then the *placement* and *physical actions* of our performer must be consistent. Our character moves the king's pawn with his left hand in the long shot, so he must move the same chess piece with the same hand in the medium close-up, if we are to successfully cut in that spot. This ensures that the visible actions in the two shots match. Also, our character is sitting upright with his right hand in his lap in the LS, so he cannot be leaning forward, resting his chin in his right hand in the medium close-up. Cutting these two shots together would make us feel like there was a chunk of film missing, the chunk in which the character leaned forward in his seat to prop his chin in his hand.

Performance pace is another factor to keep in mind for continuity. If our character in shot A is in a hurry—makes a quick move and hits the clock, BAM!—but is leisurely in the close-up, then it will seem strange that his pace has switched so abruptly, making the separateness of the shots very apparent. Also, the *emotional intensity* of a performance must be consistent from shot A to shot B. This can be very difficult to gauge, especially if a lot of time has elapsed between the various takes. Perhaps in shot A the actor is projecting a sense of chess mastery and confidence when he faces his opponent across the table. But during lunch he decides that his character at this point in the script should be fearful of his opponent and petrified to lose this game in public. Cutting directly from a man exuding confidence to a trembling, fearful wreck will break emotional continuity and confuse the audience. This sort of performance consistency issue is especially difficult when you are recording dialogue. The emotional range of the voice is very wide and it can be tricky to maintain consistency from shot to shot and day to day. Experienced film actors understand all of these issues and are trained to keep their performance consistent.

Spatial Continuity and the 180° Principle

Spatial continuity is a crucial tenet in the continuity system. For the viewer to understand the physical space of the scene and the relationships between characters and objects in that space, we need to maintain coherent and consistent spatial orientation. Spatial orientation begins with the **180° principle,** which, in basic terms, means that we must shoot all of the shots in a continuity sequence from only one side of the action. In other words, when we begin shooting an action from one side, we cannot place our camera on the other side of that action for subsequent shots, or else the orientation of our characters and their actions (in fact, the perspective of the viewer) will be reversed and the shots will not cut together seamlessly.

Let's say you're watching a chess game and the man playing with the white pieces is to your left. When he looks at his opponent, he faces left to right. The opponent playing the black pieces is to your right—he faces right to left. When white makes the first move it is from left to right, and black's first move is from right to left. This is your spatial orientation from your side of the table. However, for the onlooker who is watching the game from the other side of the table, across from you, everything is reversed. White is to the right, looking and moving from right to left. When we make a film, the camera is the spectator, and to shoot this scene we cannot take some shots from one side of the table and others from the opposite side because that would reverse both the direction of the moves and the direction the players' faces.

To understand and utilize the 180° principle, we draw an imaginary line along our action—called the **180° line** (also called the **axis of action**) (**Figure 4-3**). We draw this line following the directional bearing of our subject, which is the direction a character is looking, called their **sight line,** or the direction the character travels in the frame, called their **screen direction**. The 180° principle tells us that, to maintain consistent sight lines and screen direction, all shots used in a sequence must remain on one side of the line, giving us a 180° arc where we can place our camera. Crossing the 180° line with the camera reverses both looking and moving directions of our subject and breaks spatial continuity.

If we shoot our long shot from the near side of this line, then the viewer's perspective is defined by the man playing white facing screen right (shot A). To maintain this orientation, we must stay on the same side of the line for the medium close-up (shot B). If we place our camera anywhere on the far side of the line to take our close-up, the sight line of the character and the orientation of all actions will be reversed. This is called **jumping the line** (**Figure 4-4**).

Notice in shot C that our character now suddenly faces screen left and the chess move, which we anticipated going from left to right, is now going from right to left. This shot will not cut with the first shot without causing spatial confusion for the viewer. The viewer might think that the players, for some reason, suddenly changed places or the edit could be construed, perhaps, as moving us forward in time, hours later, after the two players have switched positions. In addition to the direction reversal of the action, the total shift in background and the position of the clock will also throw off the illusion of continuous motion.

Keep in mind that we could have equally chosen to shoot our long shot from the opposite side of the line, meaning that our character would be facing screen left, but then the close-up would also need to be shot from that side of the line of action. It doesn't matter which side you choose: what matters is that you are consistent with all of the shots that make up a continuity sequence.

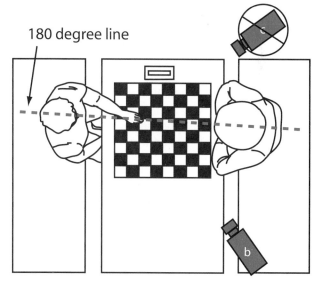

180 degree line

■ **Figure 4-3** Overhead of shots (a), (b), and (c). Character sightlines establish the 180° line of action and shot (a) establishes on which side of that line all shots must remain. Shot (c), crosses the line, effectively reversing all sight lines and movements and potentially causing spatial confusion (see Figure 4-4).

■ **Figure 4-4** The images taken from the overhead positions in Figure 4-3. Note that while shot (b) cuts seamlessly with shot (a), shot (c) will not cut smoothly with shot (a) because character positions, sight lines, and movements are abruptly reversed.

20mm/30° Rule

Now let's put a slightly finer point on invisible editing and continuity technique. When we cut from one shot of a subject to another shot *of the same subject,* we need to make sure that each shot is a distinct composition in terms of frame size and camera angle. If we try to cut together two shots of the same subject when the frames are very similar, then the viewer has the feeling that a single shot has simply lurched forward a little bit—like a battered, old newsreel with missing bits of footage. This is called a **jump cut,** and the awkwardness of the edit calls attention to itself (see "Cutting on Action" later). In some instances this may be a desirable aesthetic approach (see "Style Outside the Continuity System" later), but for the continuity system, it's to be avoided. The 20mm/30° rule ensures that each shot is a distinct composition. Basically, the rule tells us that in order to cut from shot A (the men sitting at the chess table) to shot B (white making his first move), we must change the size of shot B by at least 20mm and the camera angle by at least 30° from its position in shot A (Figure 4-5).

Although the 30° rule is easy to understand, the 20mm principle needs a little clarifying. The 20mm indicates a shift in the degree of magnification of the lens that alters the size of the subject in the frame, but since we can also change shot size by moving the camera, it's better to think about this part of the rule in broad terms. Essentially, the principle is to avoid making the sizes of each shot too similar. Notice how, going from shot A to B, I'm cutting together a long shot with a close-up, very different sizes. If I were to try and cut together, say, a medium long shot with a medium shot, we might get a jump cut (Figure 4-6, C).

Cutting on Action

Cutting on action is an effective technique for creating a smooth sense of continuous time and movement from one shot to the next. The **match action edit** means dividing a single movement between two shots in order to bridge the edit. In a match action edit, one part of a movement is in shot A and the continuation of that movement is in the adjoining shot B. Let's say our long shot includes the actions of the player with the white pieces walking into the frame, sitting down at the table, looking up and acknowledging his opponent with a nod, moving the first piece, and hitting the clock. When do we cut to the close-up? Technically there are four strong edit points where we can match the action from the wide shot to a tighter shot:

1. *Match action as he sits down.* Use an LS for the first half of his sitting action, then cut to the MCU for him landing in his seat.
2. *Match action as he looks up at his opponent.* Hold the LS until he tilts his head to make eye contact, then cut to a CU as he nods to his opponent. It could be a very small movement, but it's all we need for a smooth edit.
3. *Match action as he makes his first move.* Stay with the LS until he touches his first chess piece, then cut to a CU as he pushes it forward.
4. *Match action as he hits the clock.* Stay on the LS as he reaches for the clock, then cut to the MCU on the second half of that motion when he actually taps the button.

Action Overlapping

The ultimate decision for where to cut depends on the dramatic emphasis of the scene, meaning that we need to think about why we are drawing the audience closer to the character at this precise moment, but technically

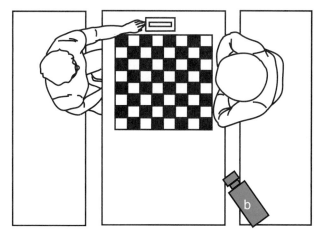

■ **Figure 4-5** The 20mm/30° rule. Two shots of obviously different sizes and angles such as shot (a) (LS profile) and shot (b) (CU three-quarters) cut together smoothly, but two shots that are nearly identical, such as shot (a) (LS profile) and shot (c) (LS shifted slightly to the right), will cause a jump cut.

■ **Figure 4-6** The images taken from the overhead positions in Figure 4-5. Shot (b) will cut seamlessly with shot (a), but shot (c) creates a jump cut.

speaking it should be obvious that in order to cut any of these actions we need to overlap or duplicate these action points when we shoot each shot. If we decide to cut to the CU of the clock when the man with the white pieces hits it (as in Figure 4-6, A and B), then we shoot that entire action in the long shot and duplicate the action again in the close-up. Doing this allows us to edit anywhere along that action. We can cut on white reaching for the clock, or when he hits the clock or when he pulls his hand back. Going into production, directors should have a sense for where they might want to cut, and shoot ample footage of shared actions so that, in the edit, there is a range of cutting possibilities.

In our chess player example, however, the possible edit points (1 through 4) are so close that I would probably choose to shoot the entire thing in the long shot (walking in, sitting, acknowledging, moving, tapping clock) and then repeat the actions, from sitting to clock, in the MCU. That would allow me even more flexibility in the editing room. Technically speaking, wherever we edit, we must be careful to make the cut such that the action is matched precisely. Be careful not to accidentally duplicate some part of the movement in both shots, creating double motion or eliminating a chunk of the motion, even just a few frames. Both cases will lead to an awkward edit that calls attention to itself.

in practice

A strong, tight cut on action creates such a smooth transition that it can effectively hide small continuity errors. In a scene from one of my own films (Figure 4-7), I shot an extensive MLS master shot of the architect and then later shot the CU of her hand reaching for the telephone. When I framed the CU, I didn't like the composition—there was just a bare white wall in the background and it seemed bland—so I repositioned the colorful pencil can on the drawing table to be behind the phone. Everyone on the set cried "Continuity! Continuity!" but I shot it anyway. I knew that by cutting on the strong action of her grabbing the phone and the relative brevity of the CU, no on would notice the pencil can jump from one side of the desk to the other. I've screened this film all over the country and dozens of times in class, and not one person has called me on this shot. That's how smooth and seamless cutting on action is.

Figure 4-7 A tight cut on action can cause viewers to overlook small continuity errors, like the moving pencil can in this edit from Hurbis-Cherrier's *Ode to Things* (1998).

Cutting on action can also smooth out transitions between shots in which the subject is entirely different. For example, what if your next shot (shot B) is not a match action edit, meaning that there are no shared actions between the two shots? What if we were to cut from the second shot (MCU shot B) to a woman at a park bench (MS) who has noticed that a game has begun? Cutting on an action—or perhaps more accurately, *cutting on movement*—in the first shot (i.e., moving the pawn) to the woman turning her head and noticing the game makes for a smoother edit than cutting together two perfectly static images.

■ SIX BASIC PRINCIPLES OF CONTINUITY

1. Continuity of mise-en-scène (shared shot content)
2. Continuity of sound
3. Continuity of performance
4. Continuity of spatial orientation (axis of action)
5. 20mm/30° rule
6. Cutting on action (match action edits)

■ SCENE STRATEGIES: PUTTING CONTINUITY TO USE

In this section we explore a range of scene and sequence constructions that work with the preceding continuity principles and that make up the fundamental visual approaches to dramatic visualization and scene structure. This is essential information for any filmmaker. One can certainly move beyond or add to these traditional methods, but these approaches are central to the expectations an audience brings to the experience of watching a film, and with these approaches one can find enormous communicative power. In fact, many great films have been made with not much more than the techniques I discuss for the remainder of the chapter.

Every concept in the following section involves the interrelationship between shooting technique (a production process) and editing technique (a postproduction process)—it is impossible to detach the two. In addition, these concepts inform both the creative approach and the production plan for your film, so they are vital preproduction concerns as well. Film is an interrelated art form; each stage of the process is intimately connected to the others.

Two-Person and Person/Object Interactions

One of the most fundamental relationships we construct within a scene is between two people, or between a person and an object, in the same space. We have, in fact, already done that with our two-shot sequence of the chess players. But let's make it a little more complicated than just one edit—let's look at a scene in which two people interact over the course of many cuts. The traditional and still most common way of approaching a two-person (or person and object) interaction is called **the master scene** or **shot/reverse shot technique**. **The master scene** consists of three basic shots that are later edited together—that is, the master shot and reverse shots of each person (or the person and the object). In addition, there is often a fourth type of shot in a master scene called a **cutaway**.

The Master Shot

The **master shot** clearly shows both subjects in the scene and defines the spatial relationship of the two to each other and the space around them, like the long shot (see Figure 4-1, A) of our chess players. For this reason, the size of a master shot is usually on the wide side. Often master shots are used to cover the entire scene from beginning to end and can be used as a safety shot, one that you can always stay on or cut back to if the other shots do not edit in smoothly. The side of the 180° line of action from which you choose to shoot the master shot determines on which side you must remain for your reverse shots.

Reverse Shots and Reaction Shots

Reverse shots (also called **singles**) are closer shots of the subjects in the scene, often a MCU or CU. Each time we move our camera to frame up a reverse shot, we observe the six basic principles of continuity so that the reverse shot will cut seamlessly into the master shot at dramatically motivated moments. Keep in mind that you have many possibilities concerning the size of your frame and the camera angle for the reverse shots, and these must be chosen carefully because they are central to the dramatic emphasis and style of your scene. You can shoot a reverse shot from anything between an extreme close-up to a medium shot and from a frontal shot to a three-quarter back angle. A reverse shot that is from an angle that includes a portion of the other person's shoulder or head is called an **over-the-shoulder shot** (OTS) or **dirty single** (Figure 4-8, B and C).

We can use the reverse of only one character in the scene or we can alternate between the reverse shots of both characters. Alternating between the two reverse shot angles is called **shot/reverse shot technique**. Reverse shots are not just about showing a person when they speak their dialogue; there are often times when we wish to see a character who is purely reacting to the moment. This type of reverse shot is called a **reaction shot** (Figure, 4-8 D).

As I mentioned before, reverse shots are edited into the master shot at dramatically motivated moments—for example, when you want to draw the audience into a closer identification with one character at a particularly pivotal moment. These pivotal moments depend on your script and how the director interprets the scene. It's also important to note that you can shoot more than one reverse shot of a single character, adjusting the framing and shot size in order to change the tone of the scene or the audience's engagement with that character as the scene evolves.

This example from Alexander Payne's *Sideways* (2004) demonstrates how this simple master shot, shot/reverse shot technique can be used to shape the dramatic impact of a scene (Figure 4-8). The scene involves the protagonist Miles, a wine aficionado still recovering from a two-year-old divorce, who finds himself alone with Maya, a woman he is attracted to but afraid to approach. The master shot that opens the scene is very wide and reveals that they are on a porch and quite alone. Even though the master shot is close to the 180° line, it is nonetheless clearly on one side and defines the space such that Miles is looking left-to-right and Maya is looking right-to-left (frame A). This is an intimate scene, so the director chose not to stay on the master shot for more than 10 seconds before bringing the audience into Miles and Maya's personal space by cutting to the reverse shots. The camera setups for all the reverse shots are also near the line of action, which means that they are frontal shots, an intimate perspective as the audience can look directly into a subject's eyes and see facial expressions clearly. The reverse shots begin as medium OTS shots (frames B and C) as Miles delivers his monologue, which ostensibly is about pinot noir but which actually reveals his soul (see page 36). Maya's response to him, however, ups the ante significantly as she subtly reveals, through her own monologue (about why she likes wine), that she is a perfect fit for Miles and is interested in him. Here, as the scene becomes increasingly personal and intense, Maya's reverse shots and Miles's reaction shots move closer with each edit until they are very tight close-ups (shots D through G). Although both characters are supposedly speaking about wine, the progressively tighter framing effectively ramps up the dramatic tension and reveals the emotions that are embedded in the subtext of the dialogue.

Eyeline Matching

An additional and important principle that applies to the camera placement for reverse shots is called the **eyeline match**. More exact than the general looking direction established by the 180° line (i.e., left to right or right to left), eyeline matching means being precise with camera placement and the focus of a character's gaze so that you accurately follow that person's sightlines from shot to shot, especially in an interaction. The sightlines established in the master shot are not only traced horizontally but they are also defined vertically, especially if there is a height discrepancy between the subjects (i.e., one looking down and the other looking up). Eyeline matching involves two critical details to keep in mind when setting up for reverse shots (two characters or a character and object). The first is simple and has to do with the eyes. If you intend for there to be eye contact, the looking direction of a subject in a reverse shot must be focused

■ **Figure 4-8** This scene from Payne's *Sideways* (2004) cuts from a master shot, to medium close-ups (OTS), to increasingly tighter shots as the conversation between Miles (Paul Giamatti) and Maya (Virginia Madsen) becomes more intimate.

Figure 4-9 Perfect eyeline matching in Jenkins' *The Savages*. Laura Linney (2007).

precisely where the audience understands the other person (or object) to be. For example, if we know from the master shot that character A is standing slightly to the right of character B who is sitting, then when we cut to character B's reverse shot (especially important if it's a CU single), they should be looking up and slightly to their right. If character B is looking straight ahead or if there is a horizontal stray to their visual focus, then it will not appear as if B is looking at A and the shot will feel very awkward. It is remarkable how just a little discrepancy can throw off the connection and prompt the audience to feel like the eye contact is askew. This discrepancy can occur especially when you shoot singles without the other actor sitting in (i.e., shooting reverse shots after one actor has gone home or at a later date). In these cases you should have a stand-in to give the on-camera subject the correct **focus point**. In this sequence from Tamara Jenkins' 2007 film *The Savages* (**Figure 4-9**), Wendy Savage (Laura Linney) is clearly less than involved in the "two-person interaction" she is having with a married man; instead her attention wanders and eventually her gaze fixes on something off-screen where she makes a more meaningful connection—with the man's dog, Molly. Notice how clear the eyeline match is. She looks at the dog and the dog looks back at her, though they are not in the same frame. It is very likely that both Wendy and her lover were not there for the dog's reverse shot, and that Molly was not off-screen for Wendy's reverse shot. It doesn't matter as long as their visual focus is precise enough to create the connection.

The second eyeline consideration has to do with the height of the camera. It's very common when shooting reverse shots to adjust the camera angle in order to approximate the vertical sight lines established in the master shot if there is a height differential between characters addressing each other, as in (**Figure 4-10**). This scene from Jason Reitman's *Up in the Air* (2009) shows a classic example of seamless master shot/reverse shot matching. Ryan (George Clooney) stands as he explains to the seated Natalie (Anna Kendrick) that the employee she has just fired will probably not commit suicide as she announced. The master shot clearly establishes their horizontal and vertical sightlines. Ryan's reverse shots are then shot from a slightly low angle (approximately as Natalie sees him) and Natalie's reverse shots are from a high angle (almost as Ryan would see her). Even when the camera pushes in closer (to clean singles), the angles remain consistent with their horizontal and vertical looking directions. You can see clearly in this example that reverse shots are not *directly* from the visual perspective of each character, but the sightlines of each character—where they are looking—is precise.

Cutaways

Finally, one additional shot commonly found in a simple two-person interaction scene is the **cutaway shot**. The cutaway is a shot of a detail within your scene other than the characters' faces. For example, in our scene of the chess players, one cutaway might be an extreme close-up of the clock counting down the seconds, and another could be a shot of a bystander watching their game. Generally, cutaways can have few continuity connections to the main action of your scene. The fewer details a cutaway shares with the other shots in the scene, the easier it is to cut it in. Cutaways are very useful in editing. They can be used for adding additional detail to the scene for patching together shots where continuity is problematic, as a way to hide postproduction alterations (like cutting out blocks of dialogue), or as a way to control the dramatic

■ **Figure 4-10** The eyeline matching in this exchange from Reitman's *Up in the Air* (2009) maintains both the horizontal and the vertical looking angles established in the master shot (a) in each respective medium close-up: (b) lower angle and (c) higher angle.

pace within a scene. **Figure 4-11** shows a sequence from the "emotional response" scene in Ridley Scott's *Blade Runner* (1982). Several times, this scene cuts to close-up details of the Voight-Kampff replicant detection device as an effective cutaway to add visual information, suture shots together seamlessly, add tension to the encounter, and regulate the pace of the scene.

Coverage

Practically speaking, typical master scene shooting technique involves shooting the entire scene in a master shot, then changing the placement of the camera to reshoot sections of the scene for all of the reverse shots of one character, and then changing again to shoot all of the reverse shots of the other character. It's very common to shoot the same moment in a scene from two or three different angles and shot sizes or even more. Shooting a scene from various angles is called **coverage**. The amount of coverage you can accomplish for any given scene is determined first by your visual conception of the scene and then, to a large degree, by your time and financial resources. Coverage from multiple angles takes time and continuity coordination, but being able to choose between several angles of the same moment also gives you great flexibility in shaping the dramatic arc and emphasis of the scene later in the editing. Shaping the master scene is a central skill in a filmmaker's dramatic vocabulary. The motivation for cutting back and forth between the reverse shots, for deciding where and when to utilize the master shot and

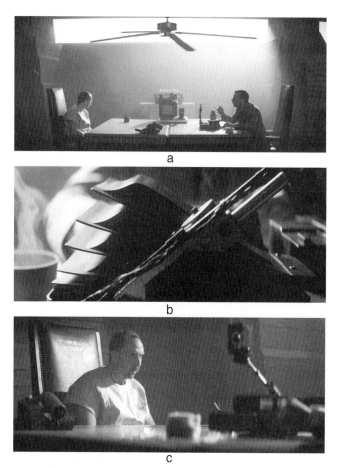

■ **Figure 4-11** The Voight-Kampff device (b) is used as a neutral cutaway in this scene from Scott's *Blade Runner* (1982).

■ **Figure 4-12** With no dramatic reason to cut to a closer angle, this scene from Payne's *Sideways* plays out in a single, unbroken long shot.

when to use a cutaway, is largely determined by the dramatic rhythms of action, dialogue, and emotions in the screenplay. These decisions are initially made in preproduction, but with standard continuity coverage, a modular, and highly flexible shooting system, these choices can change according to the dynamics of performance and discoveries made during rehearsals and shooting and they can change yet again during the editing process as you work with the reality of your actual footage. We will look at how to give dramatic shape to a master scene throughout this book, but especially in Chapters 5 and 21.

The story and directorial style of some films require extensive coverage, while others, like Jim Jarmusch's *Down by Law* (see Figure 3-4), don't use coverage at all, opting instead for one single long take to cover an entire scene. It is important to understand that not *every* scene requires the same amount of coverage; some scenes are shot from multiple camera angles, while others are presented from only one angle. For example, the pinot noir scene from *Sideways* (see Figure 4-8) involved numerous camera setups to cover, which requires extra time. In this case the time was clearly well spent, because this is one of the central moments in the film and each tightening of the reverse shots intensifies the moment. However, in an earlier scene, where Jack warns Miles not to "sabotage" him on their date with Maya and Stephanie, the exchange is presented only in a long, uncut master shot (Figure 4-12). Clearly the director felt that there was no dramatic reason to cut to a tighter shot for this relatively simple moment.

Coverage is often a matter of a director's style: their particular approach to a scene, to the film, and to filmmaking in general. So in the final analysis, there is no absolute right or wrong way to shoot a scene. As Ethan Coen states in his quote at the beginning of Chapter 3, "That would be too easy." Here are some directors discussing their approaches (all quotes from *Moviemakers' Masterclass*, by L. Tirard, 2002):

I don't do any coverage, and I try to shoot every scene in a single shot, or as close to that as I can. I don't cut as long as I don't have to, and I never shoot the same scene from a different angle …I never cover anything partly because I'm too lazy, and partly because I don't like the actors to do the same thing over and over.
Woody Allen

I tend to cover each scene a lot, mostly if they're dialogue scenes, because of matching problems. Sometimes I get a very straightforward scene,

where I know there is only one way to shoot it and I stick to that. But that's pretty rare.
Sydney Pollack

As a rule, I don't cover much. It depends on the scene, of course. Very often there is only one way to shoot it. But in some scenes, and especially if the scene is something of a transition, where the story can shift from one point of view to another, then I will do a lot of coverage because it is only in the editing that I will be able to know whether the story should follow this person or that person.
Wong Kar-Wai

When I shoot a scene I cover everything, from wide shots to close-ups, and then I choose in the editing, because that's the moment when I really know how I feel about a scene.
John Woo

Multiple Lines of Action

How do we organize space for a slightly more complex scene in which one of our characters moves around, disrupting the original line of action? What happens if a third person comes into the scene, causing our characters to shift their sight lines? The truth is, we are not once-and-for-all stuck with only one axis of action in every single scene. It's very common for there

■ **Figure 4-13** This scene from Baumbach's *The Squid and the Whale* (2005) illustrates a common shift in the line of action. Shots (a) and (b) maintain consistent sight lines: screen right for Joan (Laura Linney) and screen left for Walt (Jesse Eisenberg). However, when Walt passes in front of the camera (c) on his way down the steps, the sight lines are reversed and a new line of action is created (d).

to be shifts in the line of action, even several times, within a single scene. Each time there is a shift in sight lines within a scene, we simply need to be clear in showing how and when the axis shifted and then we redraw our line of action and shoot any reverse shots accordingly.

For example, you will often see a moving character cross the established line of action causing a complete shift in looking direction. In this case, it's important to show, in a single shot, the character move and cross the line while the other person follows them with their gaze. Very often this will involve the moving subject to pass in front of the camera. Once a character has crossed the axis and settled, a new axis of action is established from that point onward. Usually the movement that establishes the new line of action is shown in a master shot, although it is also possible for us to see a character cross in front of the camera in the reverse shot of the stationary character, where we can also see the sight lines shifting (Figure 4-13).

Another way we can change the line of action in a scene is to move the camera itself from one side of the action to the other, during a single, unbroken shot. For example, arcing the camera around and behind one of our chess players to shoot over the other shoulder as they contemplate a move would shift the line of action for subsequent reverse shots.

It's essential to understand that the line of action is not a fixed axis—rather, it shifts when characters and sightlines shift. Very active scenes, like a judo match or a swordfight in which characters circle each other, might involve reestablishing the line of action many times, as would a very active and mobile camera.

Creating Point of View

Establishing a character's **point of view** (POV) means representing the visual perspective of that character, what the character sees. By creating a point of view, the audience is not just looking *at* your character but *with* them. There are two ways to create shots that replicate a character's POV: using a **subjective camera** or constructing a **POV sequence**. Using a

■ **Figure 4-14** Large sections of Schnable's *The Diving Bell and the Butterfly* (cinematography by Janusz Kaminski, 2007) are presented through the subjective perspective of its main character, the stroke victim Jean-Do (Mathieu Amalric).

subjective camera implies that we are literally looking through the eyes of our character. To produce this effect, the camera is usually operated so that its motions are somewhat human (i.e., a handheld camera), and we do not see the character who is looking, just as we never really see our own faces. Because of the overt artificiality of the device, the subjective camera is not frequently used (**Figure 4-14**).

A much more common approach to creating POV involves a three-shot POV sequence, which, visually speaking, only approximates the true perspective of our character but which, in many ways, allows us even more intimate access to the character's perception. The three shots in the POV sequence are: the looking shot, the POV shot and the reaction shot. The **looking shot** shows your subject turning their gaze toward a person or object. At the precise moment their eyes rest on the target, we cut to the **POV shot,** which shows what they are looking at. The POV shot is taken from approximately the looker's perspective, including sightline matching, but it is not a true subjective shot. After the POV shot, we return to the character to see their response to what they've just seen (the **reaction shot). (Figure 4-15**). If this sequence is done correctly, the reaction of our character can be quite subtle because the POV shot puts us inside their perspective and the additional juxtaposition with the reaction shot creates all the necessary context.

POV sequences follow the same continuity principles as shot/reverse shots, with camera angle positions, to approximate the sight lines of the looker, being especially critical. Practically speaking, although the POV sequence includes three edited shots, we really

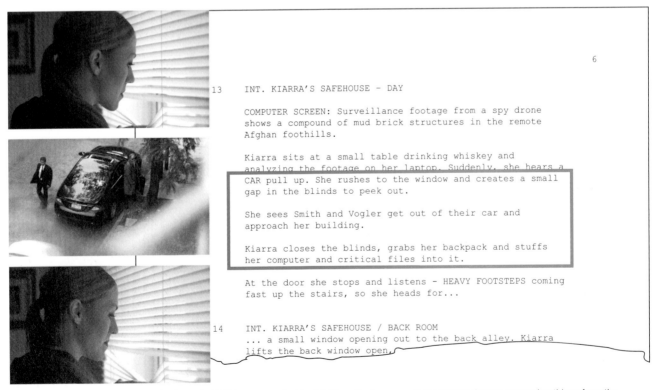

```
                                                                    6

13   INT. KIARRA'S SAFEHOUSE - DAY

     COMPUTER SCREEN: Surveillance footage from a spy drone
     shows a compound of mud brick structures in the remote
     Afghan foothills.

     Kiarra sits at a small table drinking whiskey and
     analyzing the footage on her laptop. Suddenly, she hears a
     CAR pull up. She rushes to the window and creates a small
     gap in the blinds to peek out.

     She sees Smith and Vogler get out of their car and
     approach her building.

     Kiarra closes the blinds, grabs her backpack and stuffs
     her computer and critical files into it.

     At the door she stops and listens - HEAVY FOOTSTEPS coming
     fast up the stairs, so she heads for...

14   INT. KIARRA'S SAFEHOUSE / BACK ROOM
     ... a small window opening out to the back alley. Kiarra
     lifts the back window open,
```

■ **Figure 4-15** By using the three-shot POV sequence (looking/POV/reaction), we create the illusion that we are seeing things from the perspective of a given character. In this example from *Kiarra's Escape,* the titular character observes her enemies, Smith and Vogler, approach her building. The script excerpt shows how POV sequences are written.

■ **Figure 4-16** A two-shot POV sequence from Jeunet's *Amélie* (shot by Bruno Delbonnel, 2001).

only shoot *two shots* during production. The looking shot and reaction shot are in fact just one take that we have divided by inserting the POV shot.

A very effective and common variation of the three-shot POV sequence is accomplished by shooting a subject from a three-quarters back view, essentially merging the looking and POV shots into one shot. This gives us the feeling that we are looking over a character's shoulder and seeing what they see. This shot is then juxtaposed with a reaction shot from a different angle (**Figure 4-16**).

Dramatically speaking, creating a specific point of view—that is to say, linking point of view to a specific character—is a strong device. It's powerful to have a character's look send the camera and the entire audience to see what they see! This is not an ability to be taken lightly. Establishing point of view signals to the audience who your main character is and from whose perspective the audience is supposed to experience the scene. It can also establish with whom an audience is supposed to identify. Giving the power of POV to one character or another can radically alter the meaning of a scene or even the entire film. Do not squander the intimate connection created through POV on just any character.

Group Interactions

There are many different approaches to shooting groups of people, and each approach is more or less complicated and time consuming. It's advisable for beginning filmmakers, with small crews, to approach these scenes as simply as possible. In general, it's simplest if you can divide your group into two smaller groups (i.e., single versus group, or half and half); then you can conceptualize the camera placement for the scene exactly like a two-person interaction. For example, take a scene involving a teacher interacting with a class of 20 students. If we conceptualize the teacher as character 1 and all the students as character 2, then we simply draw our axis of action and follow the basic rules of the continuity system. Even if we cut to different close-up reverse shots of various students, they will all follow the same sight line principles (**Figure 4-17**).

■ **Figure 4-17** Breaking up a group of people into two groups makes it easy to cover the dialogue of both, since each can be treated as simple shot/ reverse shot instances. In this example from Antonioni's *L'Awentura* (1960), the group was divided up as one versus the rest.

Moving a Person through Space
Movement and the 180° Line of Action

In the continuity system, the 180° line of action also applies to moving a character through space—that is, moving someone from one place to another in an edited sequence. The movement of a character (or a car, or animal, etc.) through the frame establishes their screen direction and the axis of action. For us to maintain a strict sense of continuity and progress toward a destination, we must maintain this screen direction from shot to shot by staying on the same side of the 180° line.

Let's create a simple, three-shot sequence. Jessica is sitting on a bench and decides to walk to a food cart, which is down the sidewalk, to get a soda (**Figure 4-18**). We decide that our three shots will be (A) getting up from the bench and heading toward the food cart, (B1) walking down the sidewalk, and (C) arriving at the food cart. When Jessica gets up in shot A and moves in one direction, say screen right, in order to get to the cart, the audience understands that the cart is off in that direction. When we cut to the shot of

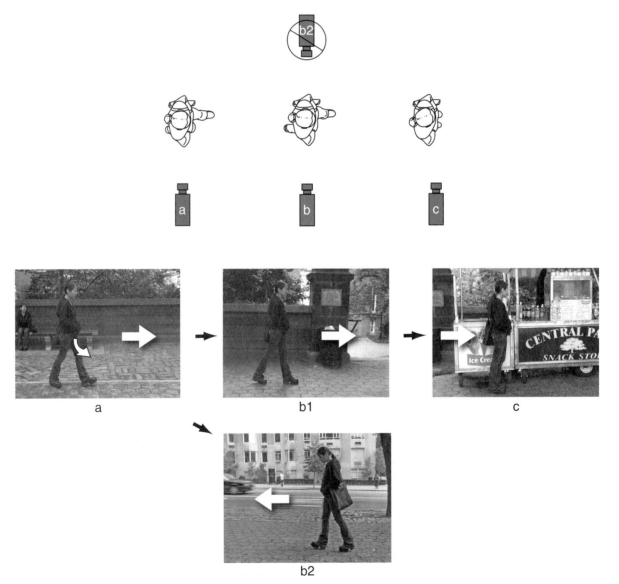

■ **Figure 4-18** The movement of a subject through the frame establishes their screen direction and the axis of action. Crossing the line of action (camera position b2) reverses the subject's movement through the frame creating the impression that the subject is suddenly moving away from the original destination.

her walking down the sidewalk, we must remain on the side of the action that will maintain her progress, toward screen right, and continue the same screen-right progression when she gets to the food cart. Notice that if we were to place the camera on the other side of the 180° line of action (B2) it would reverse Jessica's screen direction. This gives the viewer the feeling that she is returning to the bench or heading in the wrong direction rather than making her way to the cart.

Entering and Exiting the Frame

Allowing moving subjects to enter and exit the frame in each shot is especially useful when it comes time to edit a moving-through-space sequence. Cutting from the moment a subject exits the frame to the moment they enter the frame is a very smooth edit, although it is not necessarily the one you need make. By allowing a moving character to enter and exit the frame, you give the editor a range of possible places in which to cut into the action.

Movement and Elliptical Edits

Look at the three-shot sequence in Figure 4-18 and take out the middle shot. It still works. We can show this character going from bench to food cart in two shots, leaving and then arriving. In fact, we could show a person walking from New York City to Dallas, Texas, in the same two shots! However, we could show Jessica going from park bench to the cart in four shots or ten shots or even more! One important question for a director is, how much of a journey, from one place to another, do we want to show? The usual answer is, we show as much of the journey as is necessary to get our dramatic point across. If our character's progress to the food cart is not important, then two or three shots will do. If we need to show that Jessica is on a very rough street, then we might need many shots to show her walking past a snarling pit bull, two men fist fighting, and a police officer arresting a drug dealer, until she finally reaches the cart to buy a drink. In this case, the details of the journey and the additional shots have narrative importance.

For the most part, however, getting someone from one place to another usually means cutting out the nonessential time and terrain. If our point is simply that Jessica gets up to get a drink, then we need not belabor the journey and we can simply show two shots: Jessica getting up from the bench and Jessica arriving at the food cart. This sort of time compression is an extremely common cinematic technique. Removing extraneous time and territory in the edit is called **elliptical editing**. Some ellipses are designed to be extreme and obvious (e.g., the guy who walks from New York City to Dallas in two shots), but others, like Jessica walking to the vendor in two or three quick shots, are practically invisible. The remarkable thing about elliptical editing is that you can maintain the feel and seamlessness of strict continuity, even though you have lopped off a good portion of time (Figure 4-19). (For an example of the basic principles for moving a person through space, see the brief film excerpt from *Kiarra's Escape* at www.voiceandvisionbook.com.)

■ **Figure 4-19** In this elliptical edit from the Coen Brothers' *Raising Arizona* (1987), the bounty hunter Leonard Smalls (Randall "Tex" Cobb) is riding his motorcycle in the middle of a vast desert. When he crests a hill his motorcycle takes flight and in one edit lands in the middle of town. The edit maintains perfect spatial continuity while moving us far forward in time and location. The energy contained in this flamboyant edit also adds to the superhuman quality of this fierce character.

Changing Screen Direction

Maintaining only one screen direction over the course of a longer traveling sequence can get somewhat monotonous for a viewer. It's easily possible to change screen direction (i.e., the axis of action) and still maintain the feel of a character's progress toward the destination. Figure 4-20 shows three simple ways we can change screen direction for Jessica, who is walking across the park to her destination:

1. *Show the character change direction within a shot.* Given that our character leaves the first shot (A) moving screen right, we match screen direction and start the next shot with Jessica following a footpath screen right. But if that path curves around so that she ultimately crosses the front of the camera and exits screen left, she has now reestablished her screen direction (B1). Her journey from this point on can progress screen left (C).

2. *Use a neutral shot.* A neutral shot is a shot that has no specific horizontal screen direction, meaning the character is moving either directly toward or away from the viewer. We have not crossed the axis in this shot; rather we are shooting right on the 180° line (B2). Since there is no (left/right) screen direction in this shot to match, the following shot can be taken from either side of the axis of action, showing the character moving screen left or right, and it will cut in seamlessly.

b1

a

b2

c

b3

b4

■ **Figure 4-20** Three ways to reverse the screen direction of a subject while maintaining the feeling of forward progress. From shot a (moving screen right); changing direction within a shot (b1); cutting to a neutral shot (b2); or using another character's POV shot (b3 and b4) will allow us to continue the journey toward screen left (c).

3. *Use a POV shot.* Using a POV shot reestablishes the axis of action via a third character and can reverse your character's direction. For example, in shot A Jessica is crossing the field moving screen right. In the background is a mysterious man, sitting under a tree, watching her. We can redraw our line of action between Jessica and the man (B3). Now, if we cut to an over-the-shoulder POV shot (B4), Jessica's direction is reversed and her journey can proceed toward screen left (C).

There are, of course, other ways to strategize changing screen direction and to maintain coherent directional orientation. Although these things can be puzzling and even frustrating, at times it's often actually a fun conceptual challenge to devise elegant or even acrobatic approaches to keeping a character's journey as interesting as possible.

Moving People through Space: Following or Converging

Screen direction is a crucial concern when we create a sequence in which we move multiple people through space, principally in meeting (or converging) scenes and chase (or follow) scenes.

A **meeting scene** is one in which we intercut between two (or more) people (or other moving subjects) who are in different locations but appear to be moving toward each other. To create the impression that two people will meet, we must make sure that their screen direction is oppositional—meaning that one character is moving screen right and the other is moving screen left. Simply by presenting the movement of two people in oppositional (or converging) directions, you can create a very strong anticipation that these people will ultimately meet—long before they do or even if they never do! In shot A (Figure 4-21) we present a young man moving screen right, and we cut to a shot of a young woman (shot B) walking screen left, so the viewer will get the *sense* that these two might bump into each other at some point. With two shots, you have the audience imagining what might happen—in fact they are imagining the story. The more you intercut the characters' converging paths, the stronger this feeling becomes, and after a few cross-cuts the audience will *assume* that their meeting is inevitable.

The **chase** (or **follow**) **scene** involves cross-cutting the paths of two (or more) characters who are traveling in the same direction. Simply switch the direction of the young man in the preceding example, so that he is moving screen left, like the young woman, and it will now feel like she is following in his path (Figure 4-22).

■ **Figure 4-21** Meeting sequence. Maintaining a consistent and oppositional screen direction creates the expectation that two characters might eventually meet.

■ **Figure 4-22** To create a sense of one character following (or chasing) another, we shoot them moving in same screen direction. This can be emphasized further by shooting the characters against a shared landmark, in this case a flowerbed.

This feeling becomes even stronger if there are **shared landmarks** from shot to shot. For example, the young man passes by a bed of flowers and then we cut to a shot of the young woman, walking in the same direction, and she eventually passes the same flowerbed. Now it's clear she is following along the same path. If you add a POV shot from her perspective, in which she watches the young man and then moves in the same direction, you will have created a sense that she is *intentionally* following him. Further, if you give him a POV shot, looking over his shoulder at her, before he flees screen left, you will create a sense that he *knows* he's being followed and he's trying to elude his pursuer. Now we have a genuine chase scene—someone is fleeing from another person who is in pursuit. The screen direction of pursuer and pursued must be the same in order to preserve the feeling of a chase, while passing common landmarks offers clear points of reference for the proximity of the two. The expectation of a viewer concerning chase scenes is that they are very dynamic sequences. For this reason, chase scenes, especially long ones, often use many neutral shots (and other axis-switching techniques) so that they can change screen direction at any time. Controlling screen direction can allow us to alternate between a close chase (same direction and landmarks) to one in which the pursuer is losing the trail (screen directions become scrambled and landmarks are no longer shared).

Parallel Action Sequence

Parallel action is a narrative technique that involves intercutting between two or more separate areas of action (or scenes) in such a way that the viewer assumes the scenes are occurring simultaneously. Parallel action involves **cross-cutting,** which is an editorial term meaning to alternate between two or more scenes. Parallel action is a powerful technique because it invites the viewer to draw thematic connections or make other kinds of comparisons between the areas of action. Just as we discussed earlier with juxtaposing shots in a sequence (page 44), by juxtaposing the events of two or more scenes a film suggests more than the meaning of each scene individually, because the actions of one area inflect the actions of another area. In order to maximize the substantial potential of parallel action, it must be anticipated *before* shooting, and certainly long before editing, when and where the intercutting will occur. An effective parallel action sequence is devised in preproduction, followed through in the shooting stage, and constructed in editing.

A Classic Meeting Sequence

In the magnificent opening to Hitchcock's *Strangers on a Train* (1951), screen direction establishes the eventual meeting between Guy (Farley Granger) and Bruno (Robert Walker) by showing shots of their feet as the men make their way to a train (**Figure 4-23**). Guy consistently moves screen right while Bruno moves steadily screen left. In a display of typical Hitchcockian formalism, a shot of converging train tracks (frame E) foreshadows the course their lives are about to take.

A Classic Chase Sequence

The famous "man versus moped in the subway" (**Figure 4-24**) chase scene from Jean-Jacques Beineix's *Diva* (1981) uses many of the principles we've discussed, including:

A. Maintaining screen direction and shared landmarks between the shots of the chaser, a Parisian cop, and the chasee, Jules (note the poster on the subway wall).
B. A neutral shot, (B, left) to switch screen direction.
C. Changing screen direction within a single shot.
D. Toward the end of the chase the two characters are placed within the same frame to give us the sense that the cop is closing in on Jules and will catch him.

a b c

d e f

g h i

■ **Figure 4-23** A classic meeting sequence. Guy consistently moves toward screen right (frames a, c, f, and h) while Bruno moves toward screen left (frames b, d, and g).

■ **Figure 4-24** These frames represent only one small segment of the extensive "man versus moped" chase sequence from Beineix's *Diva* (1981).

The power of parallel action is not realized simply by intercutting areas of action willy-nilly, but by carefully selecting the specific moments, action, and objects, which are linked through the editing. This is what gives an audience the sense that these separate actions are happening simultaneously *and* that encourages intellectual or thematic comparisons as well. Here are five common ways to create provocative links in your parallel action sequences:

1. *Dramatic structure matches.* Intercutting on dramatic narrative beats, meaning that we alternate between the beginnings (intro), middles (development), and ends (result) of each area of action in the sequence. This provides a strong sense of simultaneous actions.

2. *Content and activity matches.* Cutting on similar activities or details that have different particulars encourages the audience to make direct comparisons between each scene.

3. *Matched action cuts.* We can make very strong associations, along with smooth editing transitions, between the different areas of action by using the matched action cutting technique. As discussed earlier, this would involve an edit that matches the gesture in one area of action to the same action, but performed by a different person, in another location. The second shot is the completion of a gesture from the first shot.

4. *Graphic matches.* We can create strong aesthetic associations from area to area through formal visual links, like matching color, shape, objects, frame compositions, camera or subject movement, and so on. Graphic matches also make for smooth editing.

5. *Sound bridges.* Finally, audio can create a bridge between various areas of action. The obvious example would be score music that continues under all of the intercut scenes, but shared sounds within each scene, or dialogue, can also be used as edit points and/or points of comparison and contrast.

Let's look at each juxtaposition technique one by one as they are used in two very different films: *Mama, There's a Man in Your Bed,* by Coline Serreau (1989), and *The Godfather,* by Francis Ford Coppola (1972).

The French film *Mama, There's a Man in Your Bed* opens with a parallel action sequence that cross-cuts between the morning routines of two Parisian families: the wealthy white family of executive Romuald Blindet and the struggling, African immigrant family of cleaning woman Juliette Bonaventure (Figure 4-25). By using both dramatic structure matches and content/activity matches to move back and forth between the same morning activities of each family (e.g., waking, cleaning, eating, leaving), Serreau is able to quickly and vividly reveal the stark contrast in economic status between these two families and instantly raises the issue as a central theme in the movie. In addition, by using parallel action, the filmmaker is able to anticipate the improbable but inevitable entanglement between these two families, who appear to have very little in common.

Dramatic Structure Matches
The narrative events of the sequence in Figure 4-25 are duplicated within each area of action, Romuald and Juliette's apartments. Each sequence begins with one of the mothers getting out of bed and waking up their children, who then get ready for the day in their respective bathrooms. Next, each of the women prepares breakfast. They then each see their families off to school, and work, and finally they both return to bed. Each of these specific narrative beats is deliberately and carefully paired. This approach not only maintains the sense of linear progression in each of the narrative lines, but it also strongly implies the simultaneity of actions. It feels like the activity of each household is happening on the very same morning and at the very same hour.

Content and Activity Matches
Because the morning rituals of each family are essentially the same, their juxtaposition encourages us to see the telling differences in their details. At Romuald's apartment, the mother must walk down long corridors to get to each of her children's separate rooms. In addition, each child has their own bathroom and brushes their teeth at their own private sink. This is juxtaposed with Juliette's apartment, where she enters her children's one single bedroom, just off her own, and simply claps her hands to wake up all six kids. Teeth brushing time at Juliette's apartment means five children crowded around one tiny sink to brush their teeth while the sixth is showering just behind them in the same bathroom. Simply witnessing the specific conditions of their respective morning routines back to back provides all of the evidence necessary to drive home the point that there is enormous economic disparity here. Add to this that Romuald and his children

■ **Figure 4-25** Efficiently illustrative and thematic juxtapositions through parallel action open Serreau's film *Mama, There's a Man in Your Bed* (1989).

step into a waiting limousine while Juliette's children wait for the bus. By the end of the sequence, when the two mothers return to bed, we understand that Romuald's wife does so because she can afford the luxury (she has a maid who cleans the kitchen), while Juliette does so out of necessity—she is a cleaning woman who works the grave-yard shift.

The justly celebrated "baptism sequence" from *The Godfather* is a masterpiece of paral-lel action technique (**Figure 4-26**). The overall idea behind the parallel action is the harsh juxtaposition of the brutality of cold-blooded murder with the indoctrination of an inno-cent new life into the spiritual tradition of the church. These are the worlds that the lead character, Michael Corleone, straddles. He is literally both the godfather to his sister's baby and the godfather of his "family business." The sequence follows more than six (!) lines of action and utilizes every one of the techniques mentioned, both to maintain a sense of coherence and simultaneity and to create a strongly ironic context that reveals the hypocrisy and true brutal identity of Michael Corleone. One can write an entire chapter

■ Figure 4-26 The famous baptism sequence from Coppola's *The Godfather* (1972) develops more than six lines of action simultaneously through exemplary parallel action technique.

on this scene alone, but here I'll just isolate the final three juxtaposition techniques mentioned on page 89.

Matched Action Cuts and Graphic Matches

Throughout the baptism sequence Coppola sutures together areas of action through matching gestures, shot sizes, movements, and camera moves. Some of these are perfect continuity matched actions, like the cut on two different hit men wiping their sweaty faces (B frames). One man starts the gesture in a medium close-up and the other completes the gesture in a long shot. This creates a seamless edit and provides a strong sense of the simultaneity of action. Other action juxtapositions have more thematic overtones to them, like the duplication of gestures and camera moves when the barber's hand brings shaving cream to the face of a mafia assassin (the face of evil), juxtaposed directly with the hand of the priest bringing the holy water to the face of the baby (the face of innocence) (A frames). These are not continuity matched action edits but are formal, graphic matches on camera and subject movement and shot size.

Sound Bridges

Perhaps the most overt thematic bridges in this parallel action sequence occur through Coppola's use of sound to connect the holy baptism to the unholy murders. Michael Corleone's rejection of Satan during the baptism is directly juxtaposed with the savage killings of all his enemies (C frames). Additionally, the somber ecclesiastical organ music from the church is heard throughout the entire sequence, adding an ironic context to the revelation that Michael's allegiance to a life of virtue is, in fact, a lie.

in practice

ONLINE FILMS AND THE BASIC TECHNIQUES OF FILMMAKING

In the preceding section I explored the basic techniques of continuity filmmaking. As I mentioned, many successful and wonderful films have been made with not much more than these simple techniques. In the companion website for this book, you will find five short films that provide a great opportunity to see and analyze many of these principles (go to www.voiceandvisionbook. com). *Waking Dreams* by John Daschbach develops the strange relationship between the executive Mr. Saroyan (Ben Shenkman) and Becky (Tina Holmes), a temp worker who may be able to predict the executive's death. Highly dialogue driven, this film revolves around five conversations Mr. Saroyan has with Becky and serves as a great example of shot/reverse shot technique. The two-person interactions in the office do not use any master shots per se, but the over-the-shoulder shots establish the physical proximity of the executive and the temp. Interestingly, Daschbach decided not to cut into the conversation that takes place in front of the elevator; rather he maintained the extreme awkwardness of this encounter by keeping it in an unbroken two shot. In their fourth office encounter you'll see a great example of shifting the 180° line when Becky crosses the line of action (passes in front of the camera) and changes their looking direction just before she delivers her significant line "There's no such thing as fate. What people call fate is just time plus free will." Also, the hospital encounter shows a classic example of cutting on action (sitting and standing) to move from the master shot into the reverse shots and back out to the master shot again. Finally, the rhythm of Daschbach's editing and how reaction shots are

used to invite the audience to imagine what a character must be thinking is especially important to observe in all these scenes (**Figure 4-27**, *left*).

Plastic Bag by Ramin Bahrani is the story of one bag's eternal journey across land and sea to find purpose and meaning in life. Visually, we follow a plastic bag as it travels across great distances. The screen direction and cutting (continuity and elliptical) is impeccable in this film. What's especially interesting is that for the most part the bag is not traveling to a specific destination (from point A to point B), but instead the journey is peripatetic; it floats this way and that, wanders here and there, and is often lost and blown about by the winds. To give us this feeling the screen direction is intentionally not consistent. The bag roams left to right in one shot and right to left in the next, and very often, Bahrani will use a succession of perfectly neutral moving shots. Given this, what becomes critical to the sense that this bag is, in fact, crossing great distances are the different landscapes from shot to shot and indications of the passage of time (night to day, summer to winter) (**Figure 4-27**, *right*).

In the short films online you'll also find many examples of the looking shot/POV/reaction shot sequence, but the sharpest and most revealing can be found in Phil and Olly's *The Black Hole* and Huixia Lu's *When I Was Young*. In the first film, after the office clerk (Napoleon Ryan) tests the special powers of his photocopied "black hole" by getting himself a candy bar, he scans the room for other uses. When he sees the locked door marked "Keep Out," his reaction shot tells us (without any need for dialogue) that greed is overtaking him and that he fully intends to get into that room. Lu's film, which is a subtle portrait of a Chinese immigrant's life in Philadelphia,

pivots on the moment the central character (Vicki Wang) enters a restaurant where her husband works as a prep cook. There is an intricately conceived sequence of shots between them through a tiny window in the kitchen door. This shared moment is a relay of looks, POVs, and reactions, which begins with him in the kitchen and ends with her in the restaurant. No words are spoken, but the sequence betrays their very different reactions to seeing one another (**Figure 4-28**).

■ **Figure 4-27** Daschbach's *Waking Dreams* (*left*, 2004) displays textbook shot/reverse shot technique and Bahrani's *Plastic Bag* (*right*, 2009) uses many techniques to move a plastic bag through space.

■ **Figure 4-28** Simple and intricate POV sequences can be seen in Phil and Olly's *The Black Hole* (*left*, 2008) and Lu's *When I Was Young* (*right*, 2004) respectively.

■ STYLE OUTSIDE THE CONTINUITY SYSTEM

At this point in the history of filmmaking, many films do not adhere strictly to the established principles of temporal and spatial continuity from beginning to end. It's common for a filmmaker to deviate from the conventions from time to time to make an especially strong narrative point or to elevate one dramatic moment, like a film's climax, over other moments. In these heightened dramatic scenes the conventional rules go out the window in order to jolt the audience visually to make a more direct and visceral emotional connection. For example, Martin Scorsese's fight sequences in *Raging Bull,* especially the "Sugar Ray Robinson: Round 13" sequence, are significant stylistic departures from the rest of the film (see page 451).

■ **Figure 4-29** Meirelles' *The Constant Gardener* (2005) freely mixes standard continuity technique with scenes shot in a loose, discontinuous, jump-cut style. The scene in which Justin (Ralph Fiennes) meets Tessa (Rachel Weisz) *(left)* maintains spatial and temporal continuity, whereas the scene in which the couple make love for the first time *(right)* eschews these conventions.

In the case of Fernando Meirelles's *The Constant Gardener* (2005), the moments that *do not* contain essential expository information are shot and edited with a very loose, disjunctive, and noncontinuity style, whereas the moments that include important verbal information (exposition) calm down considerably and adhere fairly closely to basic continuity principles (**Figure 4-29**).

It's important not to mistake fast editing or handheld camera work with jump cuts or disjunctive editing. As you have seen, the continuity system is founded on two central precepts. The first is the invisibility of the edit, which is accomplished by maintaining a coherent sense of space, motion, and movement through principles like the 180° line of action, the 20mm/30° rule, and cutting on action. The second is the expectation to eliminate extraneous time, action, and terrain through seamless elliptical edits. There are many techniques and aesthetic approaches to shooting and editing that challenge both of these assumptions. Two common approaches are the intentional use of jump cuts and the long take technique.

The use of **intentional jump cuts** directly challenges the precept of invisible edits by tossing out concerns like the 180° line of action, the 20mm/30° rule, and matching action edits. The legendary French film director Jean-Luc Godard has often been credited as the innovator of this technique, and his film *A Bout de Souffle* is generally regarded as the first film to make extensive and aesthetic use of the intentional jump cut. Today the intentional jump (**Figures 4-30** and **4-31**) is a fairly common formal technique in narrative films used freely by many filmmakers, including Wong Kar-Wai, Lars von Trier (in his DV movies), Danny Boyle, and Steven Soderbergh (especially in *The Limey*). The key to jump cuts is to utilize them as an *intentional technique,* a stylistic choice around which you plan and organize your shooting and which is fully integrated into the overall aesthetic approach of your project. There's a big difference between the intentional, aesthetic use of jump cuts and the accidental occurrence of jump cuts. One works and the other doesn't.

■ **Figure 4-30** Lars von Trier uses jump cuts as an aesthetic device throughout *Dancer in the Dark* (2000), adding a directness and immediacy to this DV film. The three frames shown here were taken from three consecutive shots.

Another technique that challenges the traditional continuity system is the **long take**. The long take technique eschews editing altogether and allows the actions and relationships of an entire scene to develop within a single shot, in real time. These shots are often five, eight, or even ten minutes long! Consider that the average shot length in a conventional motion picture runs around two to six seconds, and you'll have a sense of what a radical aesthetic departure the long take is. The irony is that the long take is actually the only technique that gives us true continuity of action, time, and space. Because one essentially never cuts into a master shot, there is no question about matching shot content or actions or spatial orientation. However, for that same reason we are not able to cut out extraneous actions, terrain, or time. This real-time unfolding of events gives the viewer a long time to ponder the image, and *this* is the power of the long take. Viewers are asked to look, think, and then consider again what it is they are seeing, as the film flows on in the real time of everyday life. They are also given the opportunity to choose for themselves what part of the scene to give their attention, rather than have the edit dictate what they should see and when. In the appropriate story, this immersion into a single perspective for a long unbroken period can communicate the feeling of truly being "in the moment" instead of witnessing an abbreviated construction of it, and this can be profound. A good example can be seen in the remarkable last scene from Tsai Ming-Liang's *Vive L'Amour* (1994) (**Figure 4-32**). One of the film's leads, May (Yang Kuei-Mei), first tries to contain her tears, then cries inconsolably. Afterward, she gathers herself and lights up a cigarette, but after a few moments she weeps once again. This unbroken shot lasts six minutes, and watching May's pain unfold in real time is utterly unforgettable. Many filmmakers make extensive use of this technique, including Tsai Ming-Liang, Jim Jarmusch, Cristi Puiu, Hirokazu Kore-edo (especially in *Mabaroshi*), and Gus Van Sant (especially in *Elephant*).

In the case of both the intentional jump cut and the long take, the filmmaker understands that the technique will call attention to the artifice of the filmmaking process. Making the process visible rather than invisible makes the audience aware that they are watching a movie, a fiction made by people and machines, and this can encourage active viewing, rather than passive reception. Both techniques, among many other alternative approaches to filmmaking, encourage a viewer not only to *feel* but also to *think*.

■ **Figure 4-31** In Wong Kar-Wai's film *Happy Together* (1997), the consistent use of jump cuts throughout the film conveys the feeling of disquiet, displacement, and a pervasive loneliness that denies our protagonist, Lai Yiu-Fai (Tony Leung Ka Fai), any emotional equilibrium.

■ **Figure 4-32** The long take from Tsai's *Vive L'Amour* (1994).

■ CHEATING ON FILM

Filmmaking is one arena where cheating is common and encouraged when necessary. What does it mean when we "cheat" a shot? It's important to realize that how a shot appears on the screen is more important than the true physical circumstances and layout of the real location. Understanding this concept is fundamental to shooting beyond the limitations of your situation and capitalizing on the small tricks filmmakers play all the time. There are many types of cheating, but the most common one involves moving people and objects around to accommodate a certain camera position. **Figure 4-33** shows a simple example of cheating from Reitman's *Up in the Air* (it also demonstrates perfect eyeline matching). As Ryan (George Clooney) packs to travel he comes across a cardboard cutout of his sister and her fiancé, which he is suppose to take with him to photograph at various locations. His reverse shot, which is shot from behind the cutout (like an OTS) reveals that he is not pleased with this thing that does not fit into his perfectly organized suitcase. But how is this angle possible given the fact that the cutout is laying on the pillows? Although no one would notice it in the theater, this shot was cheated. The bed was moved, the camera placed where the bed was, and the cutout held above the camera to position it in the foreground of the shot.

But cheating can be bigger than this. Take, for example, Didier Rouget's short film *Vive le 14 Juillet*, which is one of the short film examples on the *Voice & Vision* companion website. Didier's film is about a sweet, civilian guy who loses his girlfriend (a woman with an eye for men in uniform) during the Bastille Day military parade. In the film the guy joins a tank crew, cruises down the street in the turret gunner's position, and finds his girl.

When he finds her he stops the tank, lowers the tank's long barrel so that she can sit on it, and, as he raises the barrel, she slides into his arms. Without getting into the audacious and hilarious sexual references here, this sequence was not even remotely possible to accomplish with a real tank. He had neither that much access to a tank nor would it have worked anyway. It had to be cheated—a lot! The

■ **Figure 4-33** Simple "cheating" from Reitman's *Up in the Air* (2009).

reality was this: Didier's actor and camera operator were allowed to ride the real tank only twice—for a total of a few minutes. Once very briefly, during the parade rehearsal and another time as the tank was driven into position (**Figure 4-34**). Didier quickly got shots of the hero in the tank, the hero's POV of the tank commander, and down the barrel of the tank. The left frame is Didier's champion image, and he knew that he could work cheated shots around it. Understanding that the audience has *seen* the guy

■ **Figure 4-34** The real tank shot *(left)* and the "cheated" tank shot *(right)* from Rouget's short film *Vive le 14 Juillet* (1995).

in a tank, he can now create the *illusion* of the tank through careful cropping. So next to the few real shots he juxtaposed low-angle CU shots of the guy riding in a car with his head poking out of a sunroof, (right frame) which created the illusion that he is still in the tank. Later, the scene where the guy lowers the tank barrel to "pick up" his girlfriend was accomplished by using a painted carpet roll and a tee-ter-totter-like device (**Figure 4-35**). With careful cropping and matching of the angles from the real tank, he created a seamless illusion. It's remarkable to think that this film was shot in only six hours total.

■ **Figure 4-35** Cheating the tank barrel sequence in Rouget's *Vive le 14 Juillet* with a painted cardboard carpet roll.

From Screenplay to Visual Plan

Tell me and I will forget.
Show me and I will remember.
Involve me and I will understand.

Chinese Proverb

Once you're acquainted with the fundamental aesthetic and conceptual principles of the cinematic language, you're ready to transform a written screenplay into a story, told in images and sound playing out across a screen. This transformation is the heart and soul of filmmaking, and the visualization process is where directors do the lion's share of their creative work. However, this is also the beginning of the nitty-gritty logistical work necessary for you to have a successful production period, so a filmmaker needs to wear two hats at this stage: the creative, visual storyteller and the foreman of a production team who has a movie to construct.

Novice filmmakers tend to rush or overlook previsualization, but this is precisely the stage that, if done thoroughly and correctly, can ensure a successful production. When it is done right, a filmmaker goes onto the film set knowing what to shoot, what it should look like, and what everyone must do in order to achieve the unified vision of the film. Knowing your visual approach beforehand allows for two things. First, it makes the production process, the most expensive and stressful stage of making a film, much more efficient and calm. Second, because you are clear about what you are striving for aesthetically, you can more easily respond to the unexpected and improvise on the set. In other words, thorough preparation actually facilitates creative spontaneity during production.

[W]e basically make the movie before we even walk on the set. I mean she and I know so well what we want to accomplish and what we want to do that we know what the shots are. We know what we're going to do before we even get there. This kind of collaborative planning, instead of a one-sided approach, is what enables the flexibility on the set, the opportunity to make changes as the need arises. ... People who don't plan get themselves so worked up when they actually get to the location that they're so frantic to get something in the can that they're out of their minds.

Ellen Kuras (cinematographer) on preproduction with director Rebecca Miller (From *Taking the Digital Medium into Their Own Hands,* by Philippa Bourke)

There are three tools that we use to previsualize a film: the shooting script, overheads, and storyboards. We use these tools simultaneously to help us "see" our film and devise the visual and practical strategy that will make the script come alive and the film shoot progress smoothly.

■ THREE TOOLS FOR PREVISUALIZATION

The Shooting Script

The ultimate goal of the visualization process is the realization of a shooting script. The **shooting script** expresses the director's visual strategy for every scene in the film. It shows you what shots are used to cover a scene and how they connect together as an edited scene. Camera angles, shot sizes, and camera moves are marked right on the script itself. Not only does the shooting script clearly communicate the director's aesthetic approach, it also shows, at a glance, many practical and technical details, especially the coverage required for each scene. It's important to remember that the core creative team (cinematographer, art director, sound mixer, etc.) each get a copy of the shooting script on which they make their own notes. This is why you must be sure that all major revisions are completed. From the details in the shooting script, you will then devise the logistical strategy for your shoot—the organization of the order in which scenes will be shot. Considerable time, effort, collaboration, and creative attention are required at this stage, because the shooting script functions as both the creative and the technical blueprint for the entire shoot.

Creating the Marked/Shooting Script

1. The first step in creating a shooting script is to number each scene in the script sequentially by placing the scene number in the left margin next to each scene heading.
2. Next, indicate how every action and line of dialogue will be covered by **marking the script** (also called **lineup**), which means drawing a vertical line through the action and dialogue covered by a specific shot. The line represents the anticipated duration of the shot—where the camera starts rolling and stops (which is always longer than the anticipated edited shot). Each line is labeled with the type of shot desired (i.e., CU or MS PAN WITH or MLS, etc.). When you have finished marking a script, you should be able to see at a glance the anticipated coverage for each scene; you'll also easily see if you've inadvertently left any actions or dialogue uncovered by a shot. Keep in mind that some actions may be covered more than one time (drawn through with multiple vertical lines), allowing for options in the editing room. Also, keep in mind that actions on which you anticipate editing should be duplicated in each camera take to allow for a matched action edit (see **action overlapping** pages 71–72). The concept of starting a shot well before the anticipated edit point is known as **shooting with handles**.
3. Finally, give every shot a letter identifier. Shots are labeled with capital letters and in alphabetical order beginning with (A) in every scene. Each new scene begins with (A) again. For example, scene #1 will have shots 1A, 1B, 1C, etc., and scene #2 will have 2A, 2B, 2C, etc. One caveat is that we usually skip over the letters I and O because they can look like a one and a zero, especially written on a slate (e.g., is scene #5O scene five-O or scene fifty?). When you are done, every shot in every scene has a unique identification number and a basic shot description. This information will become very important when it comes time to organize your shot list and shooting schedule (see later, "Creating a Shot List").

The **marked shooting script** (Figure 5-1) for several sample scenes from the film *Kiarra's Escape* will serve to illustrate how we visualize and indicate some of the cinematic concepts discussed in previous chapters: especially 180° line of action, POV sequences, and moving characters through space. *Kiarra's Escape* is about Kiarra (Jessica Krueger), a skilled freelance undercover agent who discovers sensitive military surveillance footage she wasn't supposed to see. As a result, she is being hunted by the CIA and the corporation who hired her. Her principle nemesis is the capable, but sleazy, Vogler (Robert Youngren) who, along with his sidekick Smith (Rick Varela), is always just one step behind her.

In these six example scenes (scene #13 through #18), every action and line of dialogue has been marked through and is covered by at least one shot, and every shot is now identified with a scene number and letter. Notice also that for the POV sequence in scene #13 that shot 13C continues right through shot 13D, even though there will obviously be an edit from the looking shot to the POV shot. It doesn't make practical sense to separate the looking and reaction shots into two different shots when you can easily shoot the looking and reaction in one shot and then insert the POV shot later (see Figure 4-15). Also notice how scene #16 is covered first by a master shot (16A) and then again by the CU reverse shots of each character in the scene (16B an 16C); this is a typical coverage strategy for simple dialogue exchanges and gives you great flexibility in post to determine the pace of the exchange or cut around less than perfect acting. There is similarly duplicated

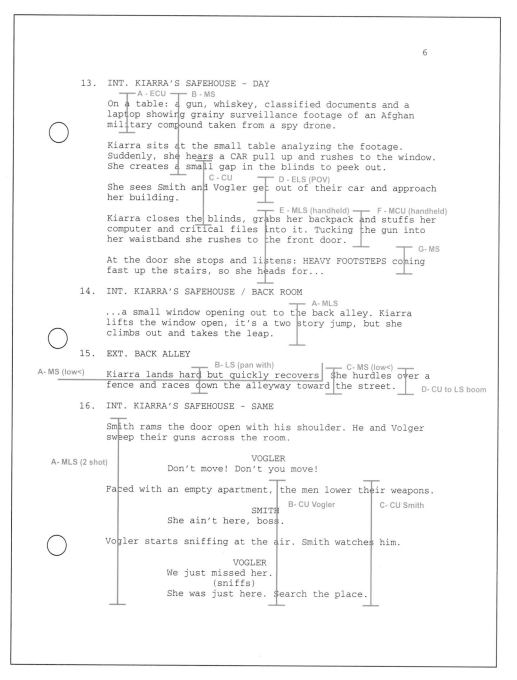

■ **Figure 5-1**
Marked shooting script. By drawing vertical lines across dialogue and action on a script to indicate shot coverage, the director can visualize how they will shoot the film. Scenes must be numbered and individual shots identified with letters.

■ **Figure 5-1, cont'd** Marked shooting script. By drawing vertical lines across dialogue and action on a script to indicate shot coverage, the director can visualize how they will shoot the film. Scenes must be numbered and individual shots identified with letters.

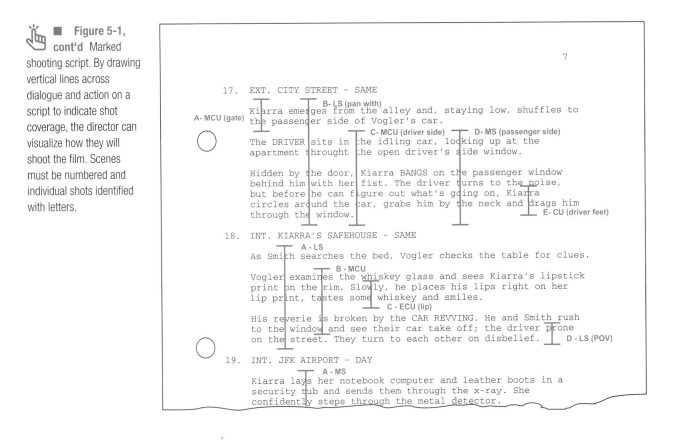

coverage for the action sequence in scene #17 when Kiarra sneaks up on the driver and drags him out of the car. Large chunks of this scene are covered by different angles so that the rhythm and energy of the attack can be precisely modulated through editing. Finally, look at scenes #14 and #15. Both are very short moments, but #14 is covered with one fairly neutral shot while #15 is covered by *five* very different and dynamic shots. This gives you a sense for which scene the director felt was more important or was doing more for developing the character, narrative, or tone (see these scenes from *Kiarra's Escape* at www.voiceandvisionbook.com).

For short films, the marked shooting script is certainly all you need to take your film into production. The marked script suffices as your shooting script. Feature films, however, often go through an additional process of rewriting the script to incorporate the shot information into the body of the screenplay itself (**Figure 5-2**). On short films, this is an unnecessary, non-creative step. It's best to simply work from your marked screenplay, as it also gives you a more immediate picture of scene coverage.

Overhead Diagrams

Overhead diagrams are essential previsualization tools worked out and used simultaneously with the development of the shooting script (**Figure 5-3**). **Overheads** are basically drawings of each scene from a bird's-eye perspective; they help the filmmaker figure out important details like the axis of action, camera placement, and character **blocking** (the movement of your characters in the space). Overheads are one of the most efficient methods for figuring out where the camera goes for each shot and for communicating the visual breakdown of a scene to your crew. You may

```
                                                                    6

   13      INT. KIARRA'S SAFEHOUSE - DAY

           CLOSE UP on a table: a gun, whiskey, documents and a laptop
           showing grainy surveillance footage of an Afghan military
           compound taken from a spy drone. Nails painted deep red, a
           hand takes the glass of whiskey and raises it.

           FOLLOW GLASS TO -

           CLOSE UP - Kiarra drains the whiskey and leans in for a good
           look at the footage. Suddenly, her attention shifts to the
           window, she hears a CAR pull up.

           TRACK WITH KIARRA as she rushes to the window and creates a
           small gap in the blinds to peek out.

           KIARRA'S POV: On the street, Smith and Vogler get out of their
           car and approach her building.

           WITH KIARRA as she closes the blinds, grabs her bag and packs
           her computer and critical files. Tucking the gun into her
           waistband she rushes to the front door.

           ANGLE ON DOOR: Kiarra pauses at the door, listens; HEAVY
           FOOTSTEPS coming fast up the stairs, so she heads for
```

■ **Figure 5-2** Shooting scripts for feature films often involve rewrites that incorporate shot angles. This is usually an unnecessary step for short films that can easily use a marked script as the shooting script.

sketch and throw away many preliminary overheads as you work and rework a scene during previsualization and rehearsals, but in the end you should always generate polished overheads of your final scene strategy to accompany the shooting script on the set of your film.

Each camera symbol represents a **camera setup**, which is the basic location and angle (e.g., angle on table) of the camera from which we shoot one or a number of similar shots from the shooting script. Camera setups communicate to the entire crew where equipment needs to be roughed in from shot to shot and which areas will be in the frame and therefore must be lit and prepped. Notice in Figure 5-3 *(left)* that four different shots are being taken from setup 3 (angle on the table: 13A, 13B, 13E, and 13F). By referencing those shots with the lined script, you'll see that the shots are of different sizes, but they all share the same basic angle and therefore the same lighting setup and mise-en-scène details. Camera setup 2, on the other hand, is used for only one shot, 13C. So in the end we are covering scene #13 *(left overhead)* with seven shots, but we have only four setups. One additional detail to note is that there are, in fact, *nine* shots on the overhead. This is because two shots from other scenes (16A and 18D) share these camera setups, so we'll also grab those shots while we're already lit and ready to go with those angles (see setup 1 and setup 4 in left overhead). Remember, a film shoot is usually organized for maximum efficiency. This idea of multiple shots taken from the same camera setup will be an important consideration in organizing your shoot (see later, "Creating a Shot List"). You'll also notice the indication of character movement in both overheads. This ensures that continuity of action is consistent and that, even though we're shooting out of sequence, it'll all cut together smoothly in the edit.

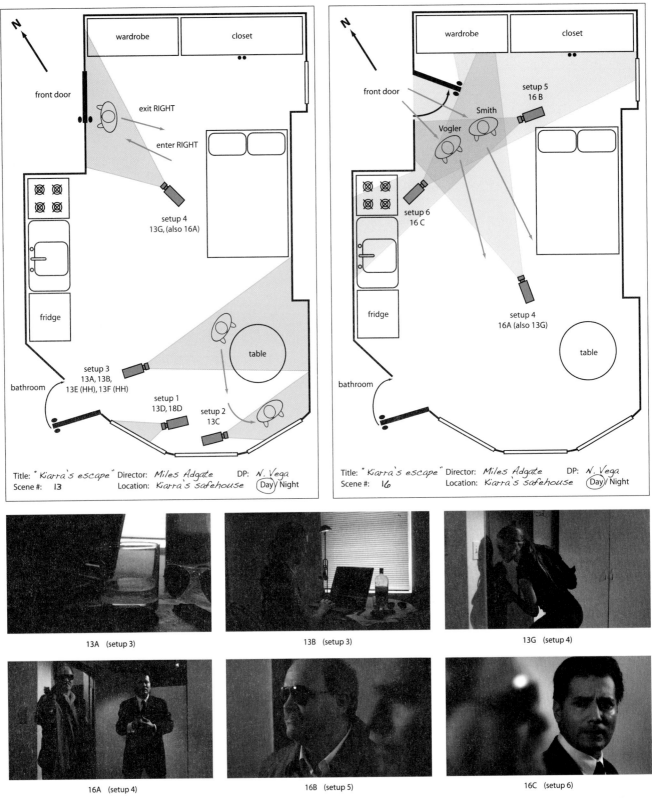

Title: "Kiarra's escape" Director: Miles Adgate DP: N. Vega
Scene #: 13 Location: Kiarra's safehouse Day / Night

Title: "Kiarra's escape" Director: Miles Adgate DP: N. Vega
Scene #: 16 Location: Kiarra's safehouse Day / Night

13A (setup 3) 13B (setup 3) 13G (setup 4)

16A (setup 4) 16B (setup 5) 16C (setup 6)

■ **Figure 5-3** Overhead diagrams are simple bird's-eye views of locations with camera positions and actor movement sketched in to allow everyone on the crew to know the basics of each setup.

For his film *The Miracle* (read the script in Chapter 2), George Racz managed to obtain permission to shoot in a famous toy store in New York City (scenes #1 and #2). But he was allowed only one hour (from 9 to 10 a.m) to get all of the shots he needed. To save time, George scouted the location 10 times before shooting day! He went alone and with his D.P. He imagined shots, actions, and character movements. He took copious notes and digital photos. He was aware of where all of the toys were and how many shoppers were usually there at that hour. Before production day arrived, he drew overheads of the toy store so that everyone on the set could see where the characters would be, how they would move in the space, and where the camera would be set up for every shot. George had eight setups (12 shots) to do in one hour, but he was so well prepared that he got what he needed on the first take, every shot (**Figure 5-4**).

One small note: Although scene #3 also takes place at the toy store, some of this scene was in fact shot in a studio, since the real location wasn't necessary and more time could be taken for lighting and shooting in a more controlled location.

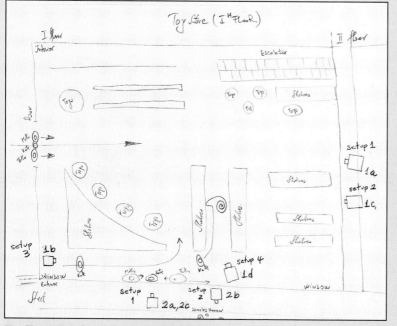

```
                    THE MIRACLE

        FADE IN:

    1-  INT. TOY STORE - DAY                 ⌐ a (LS)

        KATE and her PARENTS enter the front door of a huge toy
        store, where every toy imaginable seems to exist.

        Kate wanders between the rows of shelves, touoching each
        toy.                                 ⌐ b (LS)

        She stops in front of a big teddy bear and caresses its
        soft fur.  She dances with it, spinning in circles.
                                             ⌐ d (LS)
        She stops.  The bear slips from her grip as she walks over
        to one of the store's windows.       ⌐ c (ms)

    2-  EXT. STREET - DAY                  ⌐ a (ms)

        Kate's nose is pressed against the store's window.
                                           ⌐ b (LS)
        She watches as an OLD HOMELESS MAN digs through a grabage
        can.
                                         ⌐ c (cu)
        From behind Kate, two hands reach over.  One grabs one of
        Kate's hands while the other rubs her head lightly.

        Kate's parents lead her away from the window.
```

Figure 5-4 George Racz's thorough research, marked shooting script, and overheads for his short *The Miracle*, allowed him to be efficient and precise while shooting under extreme time pressure.

These examples should make it clear that in order to make accurate overheads, you need to have a good sense of the layout of your location, so it's important to do your location scouting ahead of time (see Chapter 6). Because overhead scene visualization involves character placement and movement, overheads often reflect work accomplished during rehearsals with the actors as you work out the blocking of the scene. Also, if it's available, this can be done in the actual location, but often blocking is done in a mockup location (see page 158). Finally, overheads can also incorporate rough lighting placement ideas for each scene and electrical distribution at each location as well (see figure 18-13). I think you can see how, once given an overhead with basic camera placement and character movement, the D.P. can start to sketch in a lighting scheme for each setup.

Storyboards

The third previsualization tool commonly used is storyboards. **Storyboards** are drawings of shots, arranged on paper in the order they appear in a sequence. Storyboards are always drawn in frames with the same aspect ratio as your camera frame. Written under each drawing is a description of the shot and the actions or lines of dialogue it covers. Usually, each frame of a storyboard represents one central moment within a single shot; however, long moving shots, which include different framings, might be represented by a number of frames. As the storyboards for *Kiarra's Escape* (scene #15) illustrate, the movement of characters within the shot is indicated with arrows inside the frame, and movement of the camera is indicated by arrows outside the frame (Figure 5-5).

Storyboards are the most direct way to see what your film will look like before you shoot it, but it is by no means necessary to storyboard an entire film. In the professional world, storyboard use is quite idiosyncratic. Some people base their storyboards on the shooting script; other people do just the opposite by previsualizing with storyboards first and then transcribing the results into the shooting script. Some people create storyboards with detailed and intricate renderings of costumes, sets, facial expressions, and lighting, to establish the style of the film, while others use bare bones sketches to do nothing more than figure out shot size, screen direction, and sequencing. Some people use storyboards for every scene, while others use them only for sequences that involve an intricate interplay of movement, action, and composition. It is true that once you get the hang of shot/reverse shot technique, you really don't need to storyboard these scenes; however, sequences that require tricky graphic or movement matches from shot to shot might require drawings. Several computer programs are available to help you create storyboards, including Frame Forge 3D or Storyboard Artist, but hand drawing is still by far the preferred method, especially with short films produced on tight schedules.

It's Only on Paper, Not Written in Stone

Once you have completed previsualization, resulting in a marked shooting script, overheads, and perhaps storyboards, then you have, in fact, already made your first, fairly complete, visualized version of your film—on paper. Now you are ready to go into production because you know exactly what shots are needed to tell the story of your film. For some directors the production process is mostly the realization of the creative decisions they've made in preproduction. For most filmmakers, however, the previsualization process is just the next step in the development of the film's visual strategy. It's not uncommon for a director to rethink choices made in preproduction based on the energy of production: being in the real location, looking through the camera, interacting with the actors, seeing the lighting, negotiating logistical problems, and seeing how the movie is actually coming together. It's common to hear a director on the set say things like, "Let's combine these three shots into one with a slow pan left and a tilt up" or "Lose the close-up and let's stay with the two shot; I prefer to keep the tension between the two of them in the same frame when he says that line" or "Look at those trees in the background! Instead of a medium close-up here, let's use a long shot to get them in the frame." This is the importance of having thorough and detailed previsualization. When you go onto a set knowing exactly what you need to realize your movie, you actually gain for yourself the freedom and confidence to respond to the moment and improvise with your camera from time to time.

■ **Figure 5-5** Storyboards for *Kiarra's Escape*. Storyboards are a useful tool for previsualizing the composition and editing of a film. They usually depict a central moment of a shot and include arrows to show actor movement or camera movement.

The award winning short film *The Black Hole* by Phil and Olly (a.k.a. The Diamond Dogs) is a little gem of a story. Told in less than three minutes, the narrative revolves around a bored office clerk who discovers the magical powers of a black hole bizarrely printed out by a photocopier. Since the film was so short and involved absolutely no dialogue, the directors decided to eschew the screenplay process altogether and work directly from detailed storyboards (**Figure 5-6**). Although the storyboard sketching itself is fairly simple, they have included every shot in the film, right down to the exact angle. They also include the basic actions contained in each frame

and even little exclamations like "?" "OMG!" and "Realizes what it can do" to provide the running internal thoughts of the main character (Napoleon Ryan). There is also a technical aspect to these boards, as you will see small notes to create the hole edge in postproduction for the inside-the-hole POV shot or how to shoot the green screen effect shots. What is especially remarkable about these storyboards is that, despite the simplicity off the renderings and the inclusion of technical information, the filmmakers managed to capture the style, tone, and spirit of the film (see *The Black Hole* film and storyboards at www.voiceandvisionbook.com).

■ **Figure 5-6** Phil and Olly's three-minute film *The Black Hole* (2008) was shot using storyboards in lieu of a screenplay (Storyboards courtesy of Phil and Olly and Nicola Doring.).

■ THE DIRECTOR AND PREVISUALIZING: A METHOD

Framing and editing determine the eye-path of the viewer. It might not be too much to say that what a film director really directs, is his audience's attention.

Alexander Mackendrick (From *On Filmmaking*)

Some people like to do it in the shower, some people like to do it lying in bed, others do it at their desks in the early hours of the morning when everyone else is asleep. Personally, I have always enjoyed doing it while jogging first thing in the morning: imagining how the film will unfold—shot for shot, moment by moment, and scene by scene. The ability to "see," in specific detail, how you want your film to play out in specific images and how sequences hold together to tell a story is a skill a director must practice and cultivate.

In general, when we first approach a script we begin from the broadest aesthetic concerns and work toward the details. We also want to find an approach that supports the ideas and intentions of the script, rather than imposing a style regardless of the script content. Your job in the previsualization process is to find a visual style that will add something to what is on the page, not simply illustrate it and certainly not clash with or undermine it.

The Big Picture

First, consider the overall tone, mood, and pace of the film and determine a general visual strategy. Does the narrative suggest an energetic style involving many quick shots cut together, or is a contemplative pace, with long takes playing out over time, more appropriate? Would a fluid, moving camera feel right, or are highly composed and graphically complex static shots more revealing? What is the overall point of view of the film, and how will the camera present this point of view? Will wide objective frames work better than tight, intimate angles, or vice versa? Remember, there is no universally "right" answer and no universally "better" approach. You need to find the style that works best with your specific story material and resources.

The Details

Next, working within your general aesthetic approach, look at each scene individually and determine how every scene and each moment in your film will be visualized, including shot compositions and sequence coverage. As you decide on shots, ask yourself three questions: What is this scene about/what really happens in this scene? Whose scene is this/from whose point of view should this scene be presented? And finally, are there any important moments, actions, or details that need to stand out above everything else? Answering these questions (and working with overheads and storyboard sketches) will help you to determine specifically what shots and sequences will best convey the content of the scene. Then you'll note them directly on the shooting script. For each shot, sequence, and scene, you are attempting to express a dramatic point through visual choices, so it's important to know what you want to express and then decide how you can best express it.

For example, take a look at the shooting script for the six-scene excerpt from *Kiarra's Escape* again (see **Figure 5-1**). You'll notice that there are two specific things that the visualization emphasizes over all the other action. The first is Vogler's general creepiness. His sniffing the air after he breaks into Kiarra's safehouse warrants a reaction shot of his partner Smith (a minor character) just to highlight Vogler's animal behavior; and, of course, the moment in which Vogler sees Kiarra's lip print on the glass and tastes it for himself is elevated as a character-defining action with three shots including an ECU of his mouth on her lip print. If the moment had remained in a wide shot, it may have seemed that Vogler just takes a swig of whiskey for himself, but after witnessing this act in close and closer detail, we know that this is not just an ordinary job for Vogler—he's getting some sort of intimate thrill from hunting Kiarra. The second character detail that is highlighted through previsualization is Kiarra's athletic physical abilities. The scene in which she jumps to escapes Vogler is defined by many dynamic shots, which help the viewer realize that she may be chased, but she will not be easy to catch.

Some moments are critical and need careful attention, special emphasis, or extra technique (Kiarra leaping from the window and escaping: five shots), while other moments get us from point A to point B and should be conceived with simplicity and efficiency (Kiarra getting to the window itself before she leaps: one shot). Where it gets *really* interesting is when a critical moment presents several valid coverage and emphasis options to consider. Here is a simple example: A young soldier is saying good-bye to his fiancée moments before he is to leave her to join his platoon on the front lines. Let's say we start with a MLS two-shot as he says goodbye and they kiss for the last time before he leaves. Then, at the moment he walks out the door, leaving his fiancée alone, we are faced with a choice: which shot is best for this highly emotional moment? Where do we put the camera? Should we cut to a close-up of her face to show her distress and sadness, or do you cut to a wide shot and show her as a small, lonely figure within the emptiness of her surroundings? The first option draws the audience into a close identification with the fiancée by bringing them into her intimate space, but the second option creates an equally valid and powerful understanding of her situation. Again, there is never one "correct" answer, but often there is a "best choice" for what you want to express and for the stylistic unity of your project. This is an example of an emotion that must be conveyed through an image, but you will face similar questions with other details, like visually presenting physical tasks in shots or sequences, or simply finding the right composition to match the scale and dynamism of an event or action. Thinking in visual terms like this allows the camera to become the storyteller—and that's what cinema is all about.

in practice

Figure 5-7 provides an example of a carefully visualized scene in which the camera is the primary storyteller. In the following interview of Alfred Hitchcock (A.H.) by François Truffaut (from Truffaut's book *Hitchcock*), Hitchcock discusses his carefully planned and considered shot strategy for a key scene in *Sabotage* (1936) and the role the camera plays in building the tension and revealing the inner thoughts and emotions of the characters. In the scene where Verloc is "accidentally" killed by his own wife, there isn't one aspect of any shot that is taken for granted. Notice, too, how Hitchcock anticipated editing the sequence as well as the audience's reactions to each shot.

A.H.: *We had a problem there. You see, to maintain the public's sympathy for Sylvia Sydney, [the actress playing Verloc's wife] her husband's death had to be accidental. And to bring this off, it was absolutely essential that the audience identify itself with Sylvia Sydney. Here we weren't trying to frighten anyone; we*

had to make the viewer feel like killing a man, and that's a good deal tougher.

This is the way I handled it. When Sylvia Sydney brings the vegetable platter to the table, the knife acts as a magnet; it's almost as if her hand, against her will, is compelled to grab it. The camera frames her hand, then her eyes, moving back and forth between the two until suddenly her look makes it clear that she's become aware of the potential meaning of that knife. At that moment, the camera moves [cuts] back to Verloc absently chewing his food as on any other day. Then we pan [cut] back to the hand and the knife.

The wrong way to go about this scene would have been to have the heroine convey her inner feelings to the audience by her facial expressions. I'm against that. In real life, people's faces don't reveal what they think or feel. As a film director I must try to convey this woman's frame of mind to the audience by purely cinematic means.

When the camera is on Verloc, it pans [cuts] to the knife and then back again to his face. And we realize that he, too, has seen the knife and has suddenly become aware of what it may mean to him. Now the suspense between the two protagonists has been established, and the knife lies there between them.

Thanks to the camera, the public is now living the scene, and if that camera should suddenly become distant and objective, the tension that's created would be destroyed. Verloc stands up and walks around the table, moving straight toward the camera, so that the spectator in the theater gets the feeling that he must recoil to make way for him. Instinctively, the viewer should be pushing back slightly in his seat to allow Verloc to pass by. Afterward, the camera glides back to Sylvia Sydney, and then

it focuses once more on the central object, that knife. And the scene culminates, as you know, with the killing.

F.T.: *The entire scene is utterly convincing! Someone else might have ruined the whole thing merely by changing angles when Verloc rises to his feet, and placing the camera at the back of the room for a full shot before going back to the close shot. The slightest mistake, like the sharp pulling back of the camera, would have dissipated all of that tension.*

A.H.: *That would ruin the whole scene. Our primary function is to create an emotion and our second job is to sustain that emotion.*

(From *Hitchcock*, by François Truffaut, Simon & Schuster, 1985.)

■ **Figure 5-7** The careful visual design of this scene from Hitchcock's *Sabotage* (1936) allows the audience to feel the fear that pushes Mrs. Verloc (Sylvia Sidney) to murder her own husband (Oskar Homolka).

One conventional way to visualize a scene is to start wide, with establishing shots (master shots), and then move in tighter (MCUs and CUs) when tension starts to mount. The tightest shots are reserved for the most climactic moments when seeing the emotional reaction of a character is vital. For example, in the scene from *Sideways* described in Chapter 4 (**Figure 4-8**) Alexander Payne starts with an LS (master shot) and moves in closer and closer as it becomes increasingly clear that Maya is interested in Miles. Toward the end of the scene, the tight close-up on Miles shows us that he is both very attracted and very nervous. The subsequent ECU of Maya laying her hand on his is the climactic moment in the scene and puts the question to Miles: "What are you going to do, Miles?" The next moment Miles balks and the shots become wider again. He blew it.

Even the Hitchcock sequence described in Chapter 3 (Figure 3-5) uses this pattern. We start with ELS establishing shots of the location, then an LS of the swimmer in the waves, and then an MLS of her washing ashore, and finally the sequence culminates in the close-up of the belt, which announces to us that there has been a murder.

This conventional pattern, however, is certainly not the only way you can visualize a scene. You could, for example, start with tight shots to create a sense of mystery about where we are or who is in the scene and then broaden out to fully contextualize the scene and answer the mystery. Scene #13 in *Kiarra's Escape*, for example, begins with an extreme close-up of the table. The shot is filled with a sense of espionage because it tells us in vivid detail: computers, surveillance, gun, whiskey; and it begs the question "Where are we?" The next shot reveals Kiarra and the question is answered, "This is Kiarra's domain." If we consider the hypothetical scene of the young soldier and his fiancée introduced earlier, we could start our scene of the young man leaving his fiancée with a close-up of the woman crying. The audience might wonder, why is she crying? What's going on? Then pulling out to a wide shot and seeing the young man next to her in a soldier's uniform might be all an audience needs to see in order to understand her tears. He's been inducted! The choice is yours.

Back to the Big Picture

Just as a painter will step back to see how the small details are working within the broader canvas, you, too, need to step back from time to time to look at the overall picture as you visualize each individual scene. The transitions from scene to scene are especially important to consider. Your scenes may be visualized beautifully, but scenes are not totally distinct dramatic units. You must look at the larger architecture of the film and determine how each scene will link with those on either side to create the overall shape and rhythm of the film.

For example, I had a student who made a simple chase film. A tourist in New York City thinks he is being chased by two young hoodlums but discovers in the end that they were only trying to *return* his wallet, which he had dropped. The chase takes us through several areas of Central Park and midtown Manhattan. This student carefully considered the larger shape of the film and decided that the pace of the film should speed up toward the end, in order for us to feel that the hoodlums were getting closer and closer. Each successive scene was constructed with increasingly quicker shots, more angles, and more dynamic frames than the previous one, to give us a sense of acceleration. The final sequence was done entirely with a handheld camera to reflect the main character's anxiety. This film was a success because the student did not think about each scene in isolation; rather he imagined the film, and composed it, almost as a single, unbroken piece of music.

■ PREVISUALIZATION AND COLLABORATION

In the professional world, a director is lucky to be able to make one film every two or three years, but it is not unusual for a cinematographer to shoot two or three films every year. It's important to understand that a director is not alone in the previsualization process and that a smart director will draw on the experience and expertise of his crew. The creation of a shooting script, overheads, and storyboards is often done in collaboration with the cinematographer. Cinematographers are trained to find visual solutions to narrative challenges, and this second set of eyes is invaluable. Cinematographers are also knowledgeable about practical techniques and technical capabilities (from film stocks to lenses), which the director might not know. Even on student shoots, where the director and cinematographer have equal experience, the pooling of knowledge and the additional perspective of the person who is responsible for lighting the scene, choosing the lenses, and using the camera can provide indispensable creative contributions (Figure 5-8).

The other important creative collaboration that informs previsualization is the one between the director and actors. During rehearsals, which often happen simultaneously with previsualization, the director and actors explore the emotional and psychological dimensions of the story, the characters, and specific scenes. This process often yields ideas for **blocking** (the movement of characters in the space) as well as an understanding for where critical moments in a scene are located. For action-oriented sequences, like most of *Kiarra's Escape,* it's fairly simple for actors to work within the visual design of the scene, but for longer, more emotionally involved scenes, it's not always easy for actors to perform at their best if their movements have been completely prescribed for them beforehand. If, for example, you were to block the intensely emotional scene I introduced on page 110 in which the young

■ Figure 5-8 George Racz, going over camera setups during a production meeting with his D.P., Tim, and his A.D., Kanako.

soldier gives his fiancée the news that his unit has been called to go to war and you tell the fiancée that she *must* cross over to the window and start to cry there because you've already planned for a nice close-up with great lighting at the window, you'll likely to get a mechanical performance. But if you rehearse the scene and watch carefully how the actors engage each other and discuss what feels best for the actor in terms of emotions and movement, then you'll start to get ideas for where to place the camera based on the strongest performances those actors can give you. You may discover through the actor's choices, for example, that it's best for the fiancée not to break down until after her soldier boy has left the room, where she then weeps all alone against the door he's just walked out of. One of the main functions of rehearsals is to help directors previsualize scenes by allowing performances to inform their visual design. (See Chapter 7 for more on rehearsals.)

During previsualization, it is also important to include someone from your team, like the producer, who is responsible for the practical and logistical aspects of your production. This person keeps an eye on the feasibility of the director's creative aspirations and helps the director stay within the practical parameters of the project, like how many shooting days there are, how big the crew is, what equipment is available, and so on. To imagine dolly shots in every scene when you have a budget to rent a dolly for only one day is counterproductive. To cover a scene with 25 shots when you have only two hours at the location is futile. It's very common for inexperienced directors to get overly optimistic during previsualization and forget to check their exuberant and expansive creative vision against the realities of production resources. Once, as a student, I was the cinematographer on a project with a four-person crew. The director had many great ideas and some that were not so great. One idea was to send me up on the roof of a six-story building to get a handheld, subjective camera shot for a nightmare sequence. In one swift movement I was supposed to transport the camera from behind a chimney, along the roof tiles, and hold it, suspended over the edge of the roof. "It'll be a great shot!" the director insisted. But the producer intervened, "Nope, can't be done." "Why?" the director asked. The producer replied calmly, "One, we don't have access to the roof and I doubt that the university will give it to us. Two, it's dangerous; Mick could fall and die! And three, if the professor sees on screen that we were dangling the school's camera over the edge of a roof, we'll all lose our equipment privileges for the year." The director said, "Oh, yeah. You're right," and he came up with a different shot. I think it was the idea of losing equipment privileges that ultimately convinced him.

In the professional world there is no shortage of people who perform the role of "reality checker." The production manager, assistant director, and associate producer all function as overseers of the practical, financial, and logistical feasibility and progress of the film. On small crews this could be the producer or associate producer's role. On very small shoots (with a crew of three or four), a director might ask everyone during previsualization to help keep an eye out for the impractical and unachievable and to devise alternative solutions that are equally strong and creative, but more practical. Additionally, everyone along the line should be considering the safety of the ideas proposed during the previsualization process. Red flags should go up if anything seems to remotely endanger the health and safety of the cast or crew, or the safety of the equipment (see Chapter 18 for more about project safety).

■ THE SHOT LIST: FROM VISUAL PLAN TO PRODUCTION PLAN

Once you have completed your previsualization (marked/shooting script, overheads, and storyboards), you should have a clear and specific idea of every shot you need to bring the script to the screen. Now you need to take the next step and transform your creative visual approach into a practical production plan. As we mentioned earlier, the scenes and shots in a film are rarely shot in the order in which they appear in the script or on the screen. Instead, actual shooting is organized to maximize efficiency of time and resources, which usually means shooting out of sequence. So how do we know what to shoot first? What setup follows after that? How do we organize the order of our shooting to be most efficient? The answer to these questions lies in understanding how to create a tight shot list. A **shot list** is a list of all of the shots that make up the film *in the order in which they will be shot*. A shot list contains exactly the same shots as in your marked scripted, but they have been rearranged according to the practical and logistical considerations of the production process. With a good shot list the entire crew knows, at a glance, what shot they need to set up for at any time.

Creating a Shot List

The shot list is usually created by the director and the production manager (or associate producer). The shot list is the first step in the larger task of scheduling the production, and the principal factor in organizing the shot list is efficiency. The considerations determining the organization of our shots, in more or less descending order of importance, are (1) major location (and time of day), (2) camera setup angle, (3) shot size, (4) on-set logistics, and (5) pickups. Additionally, there may be some (6) exceptional considerations that determine when certain shots must be scheduled.

For the following discussion, refer to the *Kiarra's Escape* marked shooting script (see Figure 5-1), overheads (see Figure 5-3), and shot list (Figure 5-9). These three preproduction documents work in concert with one another.

1. *Location and time of day.*
   The first and broadest organizing principle for ordering shots concerns location and time of day. In general, we organize our shooting schedule so that we shoot all scenes occurring in the same location together, regardless of where they appear in the script. For example, if we have a script with four scenes in a restaurant kitchen (one in the beginning, two in the middle of the film, and one at the end), we will, nonetheless, group all of these scenes together and shoot them back to back. This way, we minimize the number of times we need to travel to a location and set up lights, camera, sound, etc. Imagine the waste of time if we were to shoot the first kitchen scene, then strike the set to go shoot the next scene somewhere else, and then return to the kitchen location another day and set up all over again.

   Figure 5-9 shows the shot lists for two shooting days for *Kiarra's Escape*. Scenes #13, #16, and #18 all take place in KIARRA'S SAFEHOUSE around the same time of day, so these scenes were shot on the same shooting day, back to back, and then that particular location was no longer needed (see Figure 5-9, Shot List 7/20/10). Although Scene #14, KIARRA'S SAFEHOUSE/BACK ROOM is in the same apartment according to the script, in reality, the location chosen for the safehouse was a

SHOT LIST (7/11/10)

TITLE: Kiarra's Escape	**Dir.** Miles Adgate	**Scenes:** #14, #15, #17	**Shoot Date:** 7/11

SCENE: #17 EXT. CITY STREET – DAY
SET-UP 1: Angle on front gate to street
        1) 17A: MCU K. enters checks if coast is clear, exits left.

SCENE: #15 EXT. BACK ALLEY – DAY
SET-UP 1: Angle on window (low angle)
        1) 15A: MS K. opens blind, window and leaps out.
SET-UP 2: Angle on Kiarra
        2) 15B: / PAN WITH K. lands, recovers runs and leaps over fence.
SET-UP 3: Extreme Low angle from ramp
        3) 15C: MS X-TREME LOW ANGLE K. leaps over fence (and over camera)
SET-UP 4: Angle down alley
        4) 15D: CU – LS/BOOM UP K. lands in front of camera. BOOM as she sprints away.

SCENE: #14 INT. KIARRA'S SAFEHOUSE / BACK ROOM – DAY
SET-UP 1: Angle on window
        1) 14A: MLS K. enters left, open blind, window and leaps out.

SHOT LIST (7/20/10)

TITLE: Kiarra's Escape	**Dir.** Miles Adgate	**Scenes:** #13, #16, #17, #18	**Shoot Date:** 7/20

SCENE: #17 EXT. CITY STREET – DAY
SET-UP 1: ANGLE ON CAR - DRIVER'S SIDE
        1) 17B: LS/PAN WITH Kiarra. Start up street, pan with and follow action to end.
        2) 17C: MCU on Driver casual. K.'s hand hits window, roll down window. To end.
SET-UP 2: ANGLE ON CAR – PASSENGER'S SIDE
        3) 17D: MS on Driver casual, hand hits, window down, K. enters screen left, attacks!
        4) 17E: CU on Driver's Feet (hand held) Feet struggle as he is dragged out window.

SCENES: #13, #16 and #18 INT. KIARRA'S SAFEHOUSE – DAY
SET-UP 1: POV ANGLE ON STREET
        1) 13D: POV from west window.
        Start with blinds shut, cracked open, then snapped shut. (Kiarra's hand)
        2) 18D: POV from west window.
        Start with blinds shut, cracked open, then snapped shut. (Vogler's hand /stand in)
        *** *Car & Driver are done and can go home* ***
SET-UP 2: ANGLE ON WINDOW (EAST)
        3) 13-C: CU Kiarra enters left. Opens blinds, looks, reaction, close blinds. Exit left.
SET-UP 3: ANGLE ON TABLE
        4) 13A: ECU table top. K's hand lifts glass out of frame (top)
        5) 13B: MS K. looking at footage, noise, reaction. K. exit frame right.
        6) 13E: MLS *(hand held)* K. enters right. Packs up. Follow to door. Exit right.
        7) 13F: MCU *(hand held)* K. enters right. Packs up. Exit left.
SET-UP 4: ANGLE ON DOOR
        8) 13G: MS K. enters right w/backpack. Listens. Registers noise. Bolts right.

        ****Kiarra is done for day and can go home****

        9) 16A: MLS 2 SHOT MASTER Smith & Vogler. Break in. V. exit left. S exit right.
SET-UP 5: 10) 16B: ANGLE ON VOGLER: CU reverse shot
SET-UP 6: 11) 16C: ANGLE ON SMITH: CU reverse shot

CONTINUED:

■ **Figure 5-9** Shot list for two production days on *Kiarra's Escape*. A shot list is a list of all of the shots for each scene in the order in which they will be shot.

studio apartment with no additional room. Scene #14, in fact, was shot a week earlier and miles away in a different apartment where there was also the BACK ALLEY location (scene #15) and the front gate for the first shot in the scene #17. So all of these shots were placed on their own shooting day (see **Figure 5-9**, Shot List 7/11/10).

For scenes that use natural light, day or night becomes a significant organizing detail. These sample scenes all take place during the day, but for the rest of the film one would cluster all EXT. BACK ALLEY - DAY scenes together and then shoot all EXT. BACK ALLEY - NIGHT scenes at another time, regardless of where they occur in the script.

You'll also notice in **Figure 5-9** that each shooting day begins with the exterior locations and then the production moves indoors. If it's possible, we try to shoot exterior scenes first, taking advantage of fair weather when we can, but have an interior set ready to go as a backup should the weather turn inclement. An interior scene that can be used in case your exterior shoot is cancelled because of bad weather is called a **cover-set**. By scheduling exteriors first, we have our interiors as backups and we waste less time. But if we shoot all of our interiors first, then when bad weather strikes all we can do is postpone.

2. *Camera setup angle.*

As we mentioned earlier, a camera setup is the placement of the camera for each principal camera angle from which we can shoot one or multiple shots. Once a camera placement and angle is determined, a great deal of production time is spent dressing the set, lighting that area, and wiring it for sound. For this reason, we cluster all shots with the same general setup together on the shot list (the same way we did on the overheads; see Figure 5-3). This way we move the camera, position the lights and microphones, and all the rest of it, fewer times. Scene #13 has four shots taken from the camera angle on the table: shot 13A, 13B, 13E, and 13F. Even though there are shots (13C and 13D) between these shots, we will take the four shots in setup 3 back to back so that we set up the camera, lights, sound, etc. for the angle on the table only once. The same is true for the two shots from exactly the same POV angle out of the window even though they are from completely different scenes (setup 1: 13D and 18D) The two shots (13G and 16A) in setup 4 will also be taken back to back because they share the same angle on the door. (see Figure 5-9, Shot List 7/20/10).

3. *Shot size.*

Generally speaking, we further organize our shooting to go from wide shots to close-ups. For example, we would shoot a wide master shot, before we shoot the close-up reverse shots or cutaways in a two-person interaction. You can see this with scene #16 (see Figure 5-9, Shot List 7/20/10). The master shot 16A is first to be shot, followed by the reverse shots 16B and 16C. We do this for several reasons. First, the master scene generally covers more of the script and shows more of the space, so it therefore requires more attention to set details, lighting, and so on. If we run out of time and have to abandon a shot, it's usually easier to reshoot a close-up later or even do without it. Most close-ups also require fewer cast on camera, so fewer people need to be call back to reshoot. And it's also much easier to begin with the broadest lighting setup and slightly adjust lights as you move in closer than it would be to light a close-up and then have to relight the entire scene for a wide shot.

4. *On-set logistics.*

On-set logistics is where common sense comes into play. It is important to avoid keeping your cast waiting for hours needlessly until you get around to their shots. For example, if we have a scene in which a teacher is lecturing to a class of 25 students and we plan to cut back and forth between the teacher at the chalkboard and the class taking notes, we would shoot all shots that involve the class first (i.e., master shot of class with teacher and the reverse shots of the class). Then we can let the class go home—preferably before lunchtime to save on our food budget!—and shoot the reverse shots of the teacher without the 25 people hanging around on the set.

In the *Kiarra's Escape* example, we don't need to have Smith and Vogler on set while we shoot Kiarra's shots for scene #13. However, the camera setup that they all share is setup 4 (angle on door). This setup includes Kiarra's last shot of the day (13G) and she can go home, and then, using the exact same camera setup, we can shoot 16A, Smith and Vogler's first shot off the day. This is why that particular setup is placed where it is in the shot list.

5. *Pickup shots.*

Pickup shots are quick shots that are often not part of the original script previsualization but that are taken after (and sometimes during) production to fill in gaps, to make editing smoother, or to add something that, in retrospect, can improve the scene. Pickups are not to be confused with **reshoots**, which means reshooting significant shots or scenes for one reason or other. Pickups are usually taken with a skeleton crew and often don't require actors; pickups include shots of landscapes, location-establishing shots, and shots of objects and cutaways. There is no need to have a sound recordist on the set while you shoot cutaways that require no synchronized sound and no need to keep actors waiting while you shoot an ECU of some still-life detail. Often these shots are done after everyone goes home or on another day.

Kiarra's Escape has a good example of a pickup shot that you will not find in the lined script, overheads, or shot list, but you will see it in the film online. That's because the shot was an impromptu idea on the part of the director at the time of shooting. During the final takes of shot 13G (scene #13, setup 4, in **Figure 5-9**), Smith and Vogler were already in costume and makeup ready to go for the next shot in that camera setup (16A). According to the shooting script, shot 13A shows Kiarra at the front door as she hears "heavy footsteps coming fast up the stairs." She then dashes off to the back-room. But the director had a little extra time and thought, why not shoot a quick pickup shot of Smith and Vogler, guns drawn, stalking up the stairs? If he didn't like the shot, he could always just use the audio portion for the off-screen "heavy footsteps" sound effect. For slating and logging, when you add impromptu pickup shots to a scene they are marked "PU" for pickup. So the shot of the thugs coming up the stairs was slated as #13 PUa. If the crew happened to shoot another unscheduled pickup shot, then that would be logged and slated #13 PUb, and so on.

6. *Exceptional considerations.*

Every now and then (or a little more often than that) you'll have no choice but to organize your schedule around exceptional considerations. Actors' schedules, location restrictions, prop and equipment availability, location sound issues, weather conditions, and other factors can force you to stray from your ideally efficient shot list schedule. In these cases, you just roll with it and do what you need to do—but keep the rest of your scheduling as efficient as possible. While shooting the film *Chop Shop*, director Ramin Bahrani's location was an actual, working auto repair shop, so he had to be sensitive to the needs of the shop owner to run his business (see the box on page 127). He ended up shooting many interior scenes at night after the shop had closed and shooting day scenes around normal business activity, which could change unexpectedly from day-to-day. He was also always ready with contingency scenes at other locations.

In the case of *Kiarra's Escape*, the exceptional consideration was the car. The film needed an appropriate car for the "spy hunters" Smith and Vogler. Luckily, one of the crew knew a guy who worked at an auto dealership and was willing to provide the movie a floor-model, black Mercedes sedan for free. The catch was that he had to get the car back to work before noon. Shooting day 7/20/10 reflects this special case and all shots involving the Mercedes were taken first, from the scene #17 attack on the driver to the POV shots of the car (13D and 18D).

One other special circumstance to consider, and this one supersedes all others, is the directorial and performance approach. There are times when a director needs to preserve the momentum of the cast's creative and interpretive energy by shooting a scene more or less in order. It may be inefficient, but if you get better performances from sequential shooting, then it is worth the trade-off. This is especially a factor when dealing with nonactors or actors not familiar with single-camera-style shooting.

in practice

Scheduling around Extenuating Circumstances

A friend and colleague of mine, Andrew Lund, shot his short film *Finders Keepers* (2006) on the beaches of North Carolina. In the movie there are several scenes that take place under a long pier. Weather during the month of the shooting was wildly variable, so for continuity's sake all of the pier scenes had to be shot on the same day. Additionally, Andrew had to carefully consult the online tide charts and weather reports to determine the exact minutes when he could get the framing he wanted, which included a shot from the ocean to the beach, with the water's edge in the foreground. As they say, "time and tide wait for no man," and you can see in **Figure 5-10** that the margin of error was very narrow between getting the shot he wanted and having the shoot washed out.

Scheduling for Special Performance Considerations

Most of Andrew's earlier short film, *Snapshot* (2005), takes place in a much more controlled filming situation—two guys in one room. The drama unfolds around the kidnapping of a celebrated photographer by one of his subjects who is disgruntled about how he is portrayed in a widely reproduced photograph. Although it was not the most efficient use of time, Andrew chose to shoot the scenes in chronological order because he anticipated the real exhaustion of the actor, Henry Darrow, who portrays the photographer and who remains tied to a chair. The fact that his actor would truly be getting more and more fatigued (and anxious) as shooting progressed, Andrew felt, would add something to the scene. The extra shooting time to accommodate this performance strategy paid off. By the time they shot the ending, the lead actor was worn out and at the end of his rope, and the climactic scene contains a truly visceral sense of the frantic anxiety that only a man who has actually spent hours and hours bound to a chair can have.

■ **Figure 5-10** Sometimes it is necessary to accommodate the shooting schedule around location considerations, such as the depth of the tides in Lund's *Finders Keepers* (2006, *left*), or around the consistency of a performance, such as the one achieved by Henry Darrow *(right)* in Lund's *Snapshot* (2005).

■ DAY-TO-DAY PRODUCTION SCHEDULING

As you can see, creating a shot list already anticipates the day-to-day film production scheduling because it divides the script into the smaller production units of location, time of day, setup angle, and shot and then organizes them into an efficient order. The next step is to schedule your production by dividing up the shot list tasks into specific production days and to generate call sheets. **Call sheets** (Figure 5-11) are simply forms for each shooting day that they detail: what portion of the script is being shot on a specific day, who needs to be on the set, when each person needs to be there, and how to get to the set. Arrival times include setup times for the crew and makeup and rehearsal times for the cast.

On very simple shoots involving a crew of three and a cast of two, the "call sheet" might simply be an email to everyone involved. But on more elaborate shoots, it's good to hand the schedule out in hard copy form (and maybe follow up with emails). These days, filmmakers often create facebook pages for each project to keep cast and crew informed of the shooting and rehearsal schedules by posting call sheets online and to discuss other production details. It's the duty of the production manager (and assistant director [A.D.]) to create the call sheets, to see that everyone gets them, and to make sure that the production stays on schedule.

The length of time for a shooting day, of course, varies. You should never schedule a shooting day longer than 10 hours. On rare occasion you might need to schedule a 12-hour day. In these cases, do not schedule long days back to back. It's imperative that you allow time for your crew to rest. You must have a *minimum* of 10 hours of **turnaround time** between the

PRODUCTION CALL SHEET

Title: *KIARRA'S ESCAPE*		**Shooting Date:** 7/20	
Producer: Madgate Productions		**PM:** Sharine M.	
Director: Miles Adgate		**AD:** Michelle H.	

SET	SCENES	PAGES	LOCATION
EXT. CITY STREET	#17	pg. 6	867 Riverside Dr.,
INT. KIARRA'S SAFEHOUSE	#13, #16, #18	pp. 6, 7	Apt 3-G. NYC

CAST CALL TIMES

CAST MEMBER	ROLE	MAKEUP	SET CALL
Jessica Krueger	Kiarra	8:30 am	9:30 am
Victor Varela	Driver	8:30 am	9:30 am
Robert Youngren	Vogler	10:30 am	11:00 am
Rick Varela	Smith	10:30 am	11:00 am

EXTRAS & STAND INS	MISC. INSTRUCTIONS
N/A	Victor is also bringing car @ 8am

CREW CALL TIMES

CREW TITLE	NAME (S)	SET CALL
Director	Miles A.	7:30 am
P.M.	Sharine M.	7:30 am
A.D.	Michelle H.	7:30 am
Art Dept.	Gus M., Jenni P., Michael C.	7:30 am
Makeup & Wardr.	Michael C.	7:30 am
D.P.	Nick V.	8:00 am
A.C.	Richie U.	8:00 am
Elec. & Grips	Nico P., Jenni P.	8:00 am
Sound Dept.	Tristan A. (sound mixer), Eric S. (boom op.)	8:00 am
Other: P.A.	Donna C.	7:30 am

NOTES & DIRECTONS:
Location is between 158th & 159th streets. (take the 1 or 9 train) Very important: the building is not facing the water (west), it is facing east, on the other side of the complex.

Victor is bringing car @ 8am, must be done by 1 pm.

Fire, Police, Ambulance emergency: 911
NEAREST HOSPITAL:
Columbia Presbyterian 608 W 165th street New York, NY 10032-7901 (212) 781-8640

▪ Figure 5-11
Call sheet for *Kiarra's Escape*. Call sheets are printed for each shooting day and tell cast and crew when they are expected to arrive on set.

end of one call and the beginning of the next, but 12 hours is standard (12 hours is also the minimum for minors on the set). Don't expect your crew to pull all-nighters—they'll make sloppy mistakes and these mistakes can potentially put people at risk.

Deciding how much (or how many script pages) you can do on a particular day depends on many factors: the amount of coverage, the style of shooting (e.g., moving cameras take longer to set up than do stationary cameras), the shooting environment (e.g., controlled interior set versus uncontrolled exterior location), the size of the cast and crew, and the shooting style of the director. The more films you make, the more you will come to understand your own particular production pace and the better you will be able to predict how much you can get done in any given day. One general rule, however, is that it takes some time for a film crew to find its groove and work at maximum efficiency. For this reason, the first day is usually scheduled very lightly. It's a great morale booster for a film production to accomplish everything on the first day's schedule. Conversely, if you try to pack in too much on the first day and you do not succeed, your crew will feel like they're already falling behind on day 1, which can be a drag. But a light, accomplishable first day allows everyone to get to know each other, hit their stride, and fly for the rest of the project.

When you're creating call sheets, it's easy to write down that you'll do 30 setups in a day, but in reality that might be impossible to accomplish. So be realistic. It's counterproductive to be overly optimistic about how much can be accomplished in a day. If your film clearly requires six days to shoot, then budget for six days. Don't try and cram a six-day production period into four days.

Blank storyboard forms and production call sheets can be downloaded from the *Voice & Vision* companion website at www.voiceandvisionbook.com. In addition, you will find all of the production paperwork for *Kiarra's Escape* available to download as well as the video of the excerpted scenes used in this chapter.

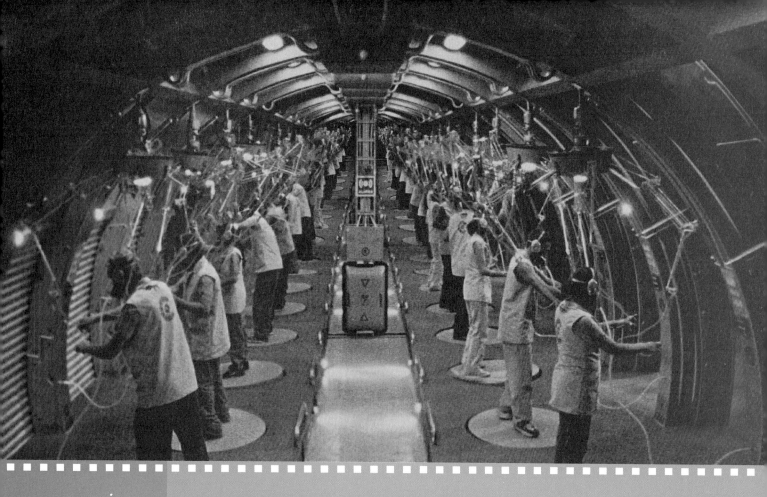

PART II PREPARING FOR PRODUCTION

Preparing for Production

■ LINE PRODUCING AND THE CREATIVE PROCESS

Making a narrative film, on any scale or in any format, is a multipronged effort. There is, of course, the creative dimension, which involves writing the script, visualizing the shots, working with actors, etc., and then there is the practical dimension of film production, which involves the organization of time and personnel; coordinating the locations, props, and costumes; dealing with film labs and other vendors; and working with budgets. We call these practical considerations the **line producing** or **production management** aspects of a film, and we cannot make a movie without them. However, it is essential to remember that these practical tasks are not divorced from the creative element of making movies. Selecting your crew, casting your actors, finding locations, selecting props, scheduling shooting time, and working within a budget are all tasks that will have an impact on what a filmmaker can achieve creatively and what the audience will see on the screen.

How much is enough? For narrative films, our shooting days are the most precious hours of the entire project. A great deal of coordination must happen in order to get everything we need—actors, crew, equipment, and props—on location, on time, and ready to go. It can be disastrous if something basic is forgotten or overlooked. Any film professor can list numerous film shoots that had to be scrapped because someone forgot to charge the camera battery, or no one secured the location, or no one thought to bring the film stock. Countless are the stories of actors getting hopelessly lost because no one gave them directions to the set, or of production being stalled because no one checked to see if there was enough electricity for the lights, or if there were enough crew members on the set to attend to all the technical duties required, and on and on. This is production management, and on every film set, someone must see to these details or you will have no movie.

However, while many film projects fall apart because not enough attention or care was devoted to production management, the converse can also become a problem. Many films wind up feeling lifeless or mechanical because of an overemphasis on line production, to the exclusion of creative inspiration and exploration. It's not unusual for a producer and director to get so wrapped up in logistics, paperwork, and technical factors that important creative steps like visualization, rewriting, and working with the actors get only cursory attention. One must not let the practical side of filmmaking overwhelm the creative side.

Line producing run amok can also result in a film being "overproduced," which means that the line-producing elements and production technology take precedence over the creative aspects of the film—like a good story, or vivid performances, or truly expressive camera-work. In some ways, it's easier to create a technically slick surface than it is to create a film with some depth, poignancy, and originality. In the absence of good ideas and creativity, money, big crews, and technological bells and whistles will not make a good film.

The creative side of filmmaking and the practical side of filmmaking remain in close dialogue for the duration of every film project, big or small. Balanced and proper attention as well as a healthy collaboration between the producer and director assure a successful process and satisfying project. Every film shoot, from the smallest to the largest, involves unforeseen challenges, extenuating circumstances, and unanticipated difficulties. To deal with these adequately, you must make sure that all of those production elements that you can control, plan, and prepare for are taken care of. The bottom line is that line producing is an essential part of filmmaking and it supports the creative efforts of the entire cast and crew.

Production Design

Production design is all too often overlooked on low-budget and student films. Many filmmakers just starting out recognize the importance of scriptwriting, directing actors, cinematography, and editing as essential creative elements, but they often reduce the process of production design (and sound, but we'll get to that later) to a purely utilitarian function. The **production design** of a film (also called **art direction**) determines the look of the environment in which your scenes take place (including locations, colors, textures, and space), the choice and design of the specific objects that are used in the scene, and indeed the presentation of characters through costume and makeup. All of these details have a profound impact on the tone, the characterizations, and the meaning of your movie. I'm constantly amazed at students who take great pains choosing just the right film stock, filters, and lighting scheme to achieve a specific look but end up shooting in utterly bland locations, with no thought to the color of the walls, the arrangement of objects in the space, or the background beyond the performers. Recently a student of mine screened a film in which he got great performances in a scene involving two people playing a tense game of cards, but just behind the head of one of the characters was a huge, ugly air conditioner that dominated the shot. I asked the student why he had that thing so prominently in the frame, distracting us from the subtle eye contact during the card game. He answered, "Wow, I didn't even notice that." He hadn't noticed it because he shot in his own apartment where he has become used to everything. All he needed to think about was a little art direction and simply moved the card table a few feet to one side. Remember, from the discussion on mise-en-scène in Chapter 3, the audience responds to everything that is in your frame—yes, obviously the audience sees the performances and camera angles, but they also see the background, the clothes people are wearing, the color of the walls, the kind of lighter a person uses to light a cigarette, and the air conditioner just behind the head of your lead character. Every detail the audience sees is part of the filmic world you are creating and therefore part of your expressive palette. You need to think carefully about what you want that location or costume to "say" and how we can use art direction to "say" just that (**Figure 6-1**).

Let's take a scene shot in a dorm room as an example and let's say you have easy access to a real one. A "real" or unprepped location may look fine to the human eye, but on camera it might not read the way you intend. A dorm room can look exactly like a prison cell if the walls are bare cinder block and the room contains nothing more than a bed, a desk, and a garbage can. *You* may know it's a dorm room, but on film it's not so clear. Beyond this, not all dorm rooms are alike. What sort of dorm room does the script require? What sort of student inhabits this dorm room? How would this student set up the room? Are they neat or a slob? What happens in this dorm room, and how is the audience supposed to respond to it? It is the job of the **production designer** (also called the **art director**) to make sure that every location, in this case a dorm room, has the appropriate look for the film (see page 148). Just as the cinematographer is responsible for the visual

■ **Figure 6-1** One glance at the stickers on the door of this neighbor in Hedges's *Pieces of April* (2003) tells us everything about her convictions, an example of an economical and effective art direction choice.

interpretation of the script in terms of lighting and camera work, the production designer is responsible for the interpretation of the script in terms of locations, set dressing, costumes, props, and makeup. Production designers don't simply hang a few posters on the wall and throw some dirty laundry on the floor; rather, it is their job to read the script, consult with the director, do some research, and imagine what this particular character would have in this specific dorm room—what objects, posters, details, and colors would support the character and the dramatic needs of the script.

Let's say our script is about Elise, a classical piano student at an elite music conservatory. The second scene shows Elise walking into her dorm room after expertly ripping through a Chopin polonaise for her professor. If we were to create a dorm room for her in which there is nothing but a grand piano, piles of sheet music, and a futon wedged under the piano as a bed, we would give the audience one impression of her. If we create a room covered floor to ceiling with rock posters, tie-dyed fabrics, beer bottles, candles, half-smoked cigarettes, and dirty laundry, we give the audience another impression entirely.

We should also consider what Elise is wearing—her wardrobe, how she presents herself to the world. Is she in ripped jeans and a leather jacket? Or does she wear modest wool skirts with a coordinated sweater set? How's her hair? Does she keep it in a neat ponytail, is it shaved close to her scalp, does she have a dyed streak that changes color every other scene? And what about props, like her book bag? Is it a canvas backpack, customized with patches, key chains, and a big "Save the Planet!" sticker? Or maybe Elise carries her sheet music in an expensive designer alligator skin case? What if that designer case were then plastered with a huge "Outkast" bumper sticker? And that's just the second scene! Making material decisions so that your character and the story come alive through your characters' surroundings (**location** and **set dressing**), the way they present themselves to the world (**wardrobe, hair & make-up**), and the things they use (**props**) is what production design is all about.

Locations and Set Dressing

On low-budget and student films, one always tries to find locations that are as close to the needs of the script as possible, but almost always a "real" location needs some degree of tweaking and fixing up so that it looks just right on screen. This is called **set dressing**. Set dressing includes things like rearranging, adding, or removing decorations, objects or furniture; painting or hanging things on walls; installing a specific window dressing, etc. Sets are dressed before the camera crew arrives to set up the lights. Always take photographs of a location before you dress it so that you know exactly how to return it to its original state when the shoot's over.

Never assume that you can use the things that are in your "perfect" location; you must always ask if you may use them. This was a huge lesson I learned as a film student. My classmate's aunt had a remarkable home packed with 19th-century furniture, antiques, etchings, lace curtains, and healthy plants. It felt like stepping into the 19th-century home of English gentry. I loved this location so I devised a short film exercise that was to be a period piece and I asked my friend's aunt if I could shoot in one room of her house for a day. She agreed and I was all set—or so I thought. When I got there on the day of the shoot, with cast, crew, equipment and wardrobe, I discovered that she had packed away all her precious antiques, lace, art, and plants to protect them from the upset of a film shoot. All that was left were four bare walls and some large pieces of wood furniture.

The flip side to this lesson is to not simply use any old place and then try to make it conform to your needs. Always try to get as close as possible to what you need for a scene so that you don't have to fight the location. I once had a student who wrote a scene in which a couple goes out to a "romantic dinner in a fancy restaurant," but he couldn't convince any "fancy restaurants" in town to let him shoot in their establishment. At that point he should have rewritten the scene for a location that he could actually get—a "romantic picnic in the park," for example, would have worked. Instead the director decided to dress his dorm room to make it look like a fancy restaurant. Let's just say it really didn't work.

Figure 6-2 shows two locations from Florian Henckel von Donnersmarck's *The Lives of Others* (2009). The production design team for *The Lives of Others* included Silke Buhr, production design; Christiane Rothe, art director; and Frank Noack, set decorator. Like all art department teams, they had to consider the tone, mood, and style of the film; the specifics of the historical era and location in which the story takes place; and the particularities of each character. This film takes place during the late 1980s in the former East Germany and revolves around two men who are strong believers in the socialist system. Georg Dreyman is a popular state-sponsored playwright and Captain Weisler is an agent of the East German secret police (Stasi). The film consistently contrasts these men—their fundamental characters—in many ways, and one vivid example is through their living environments. The left frame shows Weisler's apartment, located in a vast, multi-story apartment complex. It has the typical cold, industrial square lines of modern socialist architecture, which gives the impression of living in a sterile box or the factory housing of ideological conformity. Other than a few utilitarian pieces of furniture and two small posters from a communist military parade, there is nothing in this apartment: no art, no music, no books, no plants, no knick-knacks, no souvenirs, no clutter. His environment is obsessively orderly and barren, utterly devoid of warmth, personality, and passion. One feels that there is nothing else in Weisler's life but the work he does interrogating and spying on subversives. The right frame in **Figure 6-2** shows Dreyman's apartment, located in an older building with decorative moulding, wood floors, and wood trim. The furniture is warm and well used and even includes a piano. The walls are covered with posters, paintings, and photos, and everywhere there are books, personal trinkets, plants, and photos of loved ones. This is the abode of an artist and intellectual, someone who wants to surround himself with art and ideas—perhaps even subversive ones. Each of these environments efficiently and indelibly defines the character who lives there, and each provides tangible and visual evidence for contrasting these two central figures.

Sometimes a location in your script may be so specialized that you may not be able to find what you need, so you need to construct it (more or less). Building a set, whether on a sound stage or at an empty location, requires set design. **Set design** means the art director draws sketches for what they plan to build, and once approved by the director, they build that set. If it's an elaborate set, then they might create three-dimensional models to scale and hire a set construction crew of carpenters and painters. This process can be simple and cheap or elaborate and expensive (see **Figure 6-4**). For a short introductory film, one of my students needed a jail cell and managed to gain access to the decrepit basement of the student's apartment building. This gave the student great prison-like walls and a tiny window. The student brought in an old toilet and a cot and set it up in one corner then constructed a set of bars out of wood and painted it to look like iron. It was simple, inexpensive, yet totally convincing.

■ **Figure 6-2** Set dressing as the expression of character in Von Donnersmarck's *The Lives of Others* (2006). The austerity of Stasi Officer Weisler's apartment illustrates many of his personal characteristics *(left),* while the intellectual clutter of playwright Dreyman's apartment reflects the nature of its inhabitant *(right).*

Finding Locations

Ramin Bahrani's *Chop Shop* (2007) is a case where the director didn't find a location to work for an existing script; instead the location found him and the story emerged from there. Bahrani discovered the forgotten corner of New York City called Willets Point when he accompanied his friend and cinematographer, Michael Simmonds, to have his car repaired. Willets Point Queens comprises 20 blocks of scrap yards, cut-rate auto repair shops, and dirt roads adjacent to the Mets Shea stadium. Bahrani knew instantly that this was a great location for a movie, but he needed a story. Rather than write any old story to paste onto the location, Bahrani returned to Willets Point regularly for over a year and a half to explore the neighborhood, take photographs, and do research. He wanted to know in depth what went on there, who the people living there were, and what the rhythm of life was. He wanted the location to suggest a story to him so that the environment would be more than just a backdrop. He wanted Willets Point to be a character (**Figure 6-3**, *left*).

The story started to come together as he watched young kids working for the chop shops in this very tough neighborhood, while across the street, at Shea stadium, a huge billboard proclaimed, "Make Dreams Happen." The juxtaposition got him wondering, "What kind of dreams can happen in this location? What kind of dreams could these kids have?" As Bahrani and co-writer Bahareh Azimi incorporated more and more story details and characters gleaned from the location, the story—about a 10-year-old boy who works the chop shops and who has a dream to buy a food truck to provide a stable income for him and his sister—started to take shape.

But in order to portray Willet's Point on film with authenticity and to create the same powerful impression the area had on Bahrani himself, he would need the cooperation and trust of the people who worked there and owned the shops. This could have been a daunting obstacle, but he lucked out when Rob Sowulski, a longtime repair shop owner, one day walked up to this strange guy who had been hanging around for a year taking notes and asked him directly, "Whatchadoin'?" When Bahrani told him he wanted to make a movie about Willets Point, Sowulski pointed to his own shop in the middle of the busiest street and said, "You're gonna shoot your movie right there."

Sowulski's shop was not only an ideal central location for the film, allowing Bahrani to shoot in the real environment with minimal set dressing, but Rob's prominent stature among the auto shop owners opened many other doors for the project. Bahrani refers to Sowulski as "the angel and hero of the movie," because not only did he deliver the principal location and play one of the prominent roles in the film but he trained the lead actor (Alejandro Polanco) to work in the business, including sanding, priming, and painting cars. During the three-month rehearsal and shooting period, Alejandro virtually worked for Sowulski, who paid him for his labor, and often Bahrani would just roll camera and document the real action of the moment (**Figure 6-3**, *right*).

Building Locations

While most low-budget, independent filmmakers stick with locations that are easily available and close to complete in their detail, director Alex Rivera set himself a challenge for his first feature film, *Sleep Dealer* (2008). He wanted to make a science fiction

■ **Figure 6-3** Willets Point Queens is more than a central location in Bahrani's *Chop Shop* (2007); it becomes like another character in the film *(left)*. A working auto body shop provided a perfect location that needed little alteration and also gave Bahrani opportunities to shoot real, unscripted actions, like Ale (Alejandro Polanco) truly sanding a client's car *(right)*.

film that takes place on the Mexican-American border in the near future, but he had a very low budget. Rivera imagined a highly militarized future where the border is closed tight and Mexican workers travel to huge cyber-labor factories in Tijuana where their manual labor is exploited through a computer network transmitting their physical movements to robots in the United States—cheap labor and no immigration problem.

Rivera was able to find many of his locations in Mexico and create the futuristic context through set dressing, but clearly some locations had to be built as sets, particularly the futuristic cyber-labor factory. Rivera credits production designer Miguel Ángel Álvarez for working with his rough

doodles and designing sets that were absolutely convincing of a high-tech future yet relatively inexpensive to construct. **Figure 6-4** shows the progression from set design sketch *(a)*, to scale model *(b)*, to finished set *(c)*. The way the final location appears in the movie is a combination of the ingenious construction of a small space with digital manipulation to make it appear larger. The story of Rivera's low-budget preproduction and art direction process is remarkable, and he has graciously provided us with a highly informative behind-the-scenes documentary of his creative steps called *Before the Making of Sleep Dealer*. In this documentary he reveals, in detail, the evolution of his story ideas, costumes, locations, and sets. The documentary can be screened online at www.voiceandvisionbook.com.

■ **Figure 6-4** Rivera's cyber-labor factory set in *Sleep Dealer* (2007). The set design process proceeded from a sketch (a) to a small-scale model (b) and finally to the completed set (c).

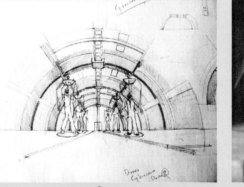

a

b

c

Location Scouting

A great deal of production design is done during preproduction so that everything is available, secured, and in place when the camera starts to roll. One of the first steps is finding your locations. Whether you're making a two-minute exercise or a feature film, you should never arrive at a location on a shooting day without first scouting and surveying that location ahead of time, or you will inevitably get some nasty surprises. Deciding where you want to shoot requires **location scouting**. This means visiting several location possibilities for each setting, to find the one that will work for your film. Here is a simple series of concerns, and questions you should ask as you scout each location to determine if it's right:

- *The look.* The most important aspect of selecting a location is what it looks like—the physical space, architecture, backgrounds, light, colors, etc.—and what that look can contribute aesthetically and thematically to the film. Is the location appropriate for the action of the script? Does the location add to the overall emotional tone of the script and scene? Is this place aesthetically what you are after? If the answer to any of these questions is "NO," then don't waste time; move on and scout another location. If the answers to all of these questions are "YES," then continue on to....

- *The access.* A location that looks perfect doesn't help you if you don't have access to it; this is the next step in determining if a location will work for you. Can you get access to that location? Can you get access to that location on the days and for the hours you need it? If there is rental money involved, can you afford it? If there are strings attached, do you really want to get involved in that way (e.g., you want to use your grandma's house, but she'll ask you to mow her lawn for one solid year in return)? If the answer to any of these questions is "NO," then don't waste time; move on and scout another location. If the answers to all of these questions are "YES," then continue on to...

- *The logistics.* Another factor in determining if a location is workable for you has to do with its functionality as a film set. Is the location safe for people and equipment? Is there adequate natural light, or if you need to use artificial light, is there enough power and access to electricity? Is there enough space to contain your crew, equipment, and cast? Is it possible for everyone to get to the location? Are there bathrooms accessible? If the answer to any of these questions is "NO," then don't waste time; move on and scout a different location. If the answers to all of these questions are "YES," then you might have found your location, if you don't later find an even better one.

- *The sound.* If your film involves synchronized sound recording, then you'll need to scout for the sound environment as well. Close your eyes and listen to the sounds that exist naturally in the environment (**ambient sound**). Do you hear noisy air-conditioning motors, a barking dog next door, or kids on a nearby playground? Is there a highway nearby that creates a constant drone of traffic, or is the location under the flight path of an airport? Is the location quiet enough for you to record sound, or is the ambient noise at least appropriate for the scenes you're shooting? How controllable is the sound environment? How are the acoustics of the location? Does the space have a lot of echo? (More on ambient sound and acoustics in Chapter 15.) If your film involves a lot of sync sound recording, like dialogue, and the sound environment is not conducive to location recording, then you should consider finding another location.

- *Securing the location.* Securing a location means making sure that you don't lose it between scouting and shooting and that you're not kicked out once you do start shooting. Public spaces often require a **location permit** for you to shoot. Every city has different requirements for obtaining a location permit, so it's best if you go to the City Hall or, if it's a larger city, the film and television office to find out the specific rules. Most places make it fairly simple for students to obtain shooting permits. In some cities there are fees involved; in other cities (like New York) it's free, but you must have production insurance and fill out the appropriate paperwork. I once scouted locations for a film in New Jersey and discovered that each township had completely different regulations for location permits. One township required only that you notify the chief of police, whereas the neighboring township required proof of a $2 million liability insurance policy and $250,000 in an escrow account. It was clear that the latter township was discouraging film productions within its borders. To find out more about shooting permits in your area, simply call the local City Hall.

■ **Figure 6-5** Permit hell. Even Al Pacino's celebrity was no match for the NYPD officers asking to see a shooting permit, which he did not have. This real-life event was cleverly integrated into Pacino's innovative narrative/documentary hybrid film *Looking for Richard* (1996).

Do you really need a permit to shoot on the street? Think of a permit as a kind of production insurance. No one can stop your shoot or chase you off your location if you have one. In New York, especially in recent years, at least two-thirds of my students' projects are scrutinized by the police. Without a permit, they are usually shut down, and this can be disastrous for a project timetable that allows for only three shooting days (**Figure 6-5**).

Shooting on private property often requires that you obtain either formal permission or a location contract. At the college where I teach, for instance, my students must obtain permission from the Office of Buildings & Grounds before they can shoot on campus. For locations like friend's houses, grocery stores, or local restaurants, it's necessary to have someone who is truly authorized to do so sign a location contract. (See the sample location contract at www.voiceandvisionbook.com.) Basically, the location contract protects both parties involved. The filmmaker is protected because the shoot is approved and secure and the owner of the property is protected because the contract releases owners from any liability should someone get hurt during the shoot. The contract also usually states that the filmmaker is responsible for any damage to the property.

Whether you are shooting in a public or private space, you must securely establish, well in advance, the availability and reliability of all locations. It's a serious setback for a film when cast, crew, and equipment show up at a location only to be kicked out.

The Location Technical Survey

Once you have secured your location, you may need to revisit the location to do a thorough survey. A **location technical survey** means closely scrutinizing the location for its technical and aesthetic capabilities. For minor locations the scouting and survey can be done in one visit, but major locations, especially those that require extensive visual planning and lighting, need another visit dedicated to the survey. The director, D.P., and production designer often go on location surveys together. If your scene involves critical sound recording in the field, then your sound recordist will want to check the location for sound. Also, if your scene involves available light, it is important to visit the location at the same time of day that you anticipate shooting.

During the survey, try to imagine what shots will work in the space. Think in terms of angles you would like to shoot from, and the size of your shots. Figure out roughly how much of the space will be visible. Is there movement in the shot? From where to where? What will be in the background? How many shots will you need in this location? Takes notes as visual ideas and impressions occur to you. Digital photos are extremely helpful for recalling location details or ideas for shot angles as you later visualize your screenplay or do rough blocking during rehearsals somewhere else.

After you have determined some rough ideas about where and how you'll shoot, the location starts to look more and more like a film set. A **film set** is a location that is being used, customized, and controlled to serve the needs of a film shoot. To establish the set, you need to consider the following aesthetic and practical elements:

- *Light.* How much of the room will you need to light? Will you be mixing light sources? Research the distribution of the electricity in the location and make sure you know how much power is available.
- *Art direction.* What does the setting look like in its unaltered state? What are the colors of the walls? What is on the walls? What are the furnishings? What is in the background of all of your imagined shots? And then, what art direction will you need? What will you need to add, remove, or change to make the space look the way you need it to look? Make sure you'll be allowed to do this. Of course, for low-budget films shooting on a tight schedule, so it's best to find locations that need as little art direction as possible.
- *Sound.* If you are shooting sync sound at the location, then you'll need to pause a moment, be quiet, and take note of the natural sounds of the location. Are there any sound issues that might pose problems on the shoot? For example, is there a construction site across the street or a German shepherd next door that barks his head off? Get a sense for the aural ambience and acoustic qualities of the location. Is the space acoustically "live" or "dead"? (See Chapter 15.)
- *Other concerns.* Make sure that there are bathrooms available and inquire about getting food to the location. Are there food stores nearby? Take the time to note the nearest hospital in case of emergency. Check to see that there is a safe and secure place to hold equipment during the shoot, called a staging area (see page 364). Also, make sure you know the "house rules," meaning the limits of manipulating the space. Are you allowed to move furniture around? Is there a carpet that you must cover? Are you allowed to paint a wall?

You will always run into surprises on the set, but the location survey should be thorough enough that those surprises are relatively minor. A location scouting form and a detailed location scouting "how-to" are available for downloading at the *Voice & Vision* companion website.

Wardrobe and Props

Wardrobe (**costumes**) and **props** are powerful and efficient elements in defining our character. Props are different from set dress in that props are those things that characters actually handle in a scene. A production designer (with the **costume designer** and **prop master** on larger films) will review every scene with the director to determine how wardrobe and objects can contribute to our understanding of each character.

Earlier we saw how von Donnersmarck used location and set dressing to define aspects of his two principal characters in his film *The Lives of Others* (see **Figure 6-2**). Now let's look a how he and the other members of the art department—costume designer Gabriele Binder and propmaster Olaf Kronenthal—used costumes and props to further build character. Captain Weisler, the State Security Stasi officer (**Figure 6-6**, *left*), is consistently dressed in shades of gray: light gray shirt, gray suits, and a gray jacket. He is almost never without a tie (gray, of course), and the few times we see him without his tie, he keeps the

■ **Figure 6-6** Wardrobe as the expression of character in Von Donnersmarck's *The Lives of Others* (2006). Stasi Officer Weisler *(left)* and playwright Dreyman *(right)*.

collar of his shirt buttoned, even when he is having sex with a prostitute! His style of dress is just as colorless as his apartment décor; however, it is also just as compulsively tidy and sharp. His shirts are always perfectly pressed, reflecting his military discipline. The playwright Dreyman, on the other hand, wears warm, brown corduroy jackets and loose white shirts (**Figure 6-6**, *right*). When he's at home writing, Dreyman goes without the jacket and his shirt is slightly wrinkled with collar and cuffs unbuttoned. Dreyman's collar is almost always open and he practically never wears a tie. In fact, one scene makes the point very clearly that he doesn't even know how to tie one. It's a socialist ideological thing with him; middle-class fetters is what he calls ties.

Costumes are so important to the expression of character that no filmmaker can leave the selection to chance. Young filmmakers will often typecast a friend in a role, thinking that he looks perfect for the part, and then assume that he'll arrive on the set dressed as he always is, say in jeans and a baggy sports jersey. But as the day of the shoot approaches, this friend becomes self-conscious about being in front of the camera and arrives dressed the way he wants to be seen instead, in a suit and tie, destroying the conception the director had in mind.

Student and independent films often plunder the wardrobes of their actors for suitable clothes. Why not? The clothes fit and the actor is comfortable in them. But you cannot assume that your actors will wear the right thing when the shooting day arrives. If you're using the actors' real clothes, you should go to their homes before the shoot, carefully look over their wardrobes with them, and once you find what you need for the film, mark those items "COSTUME." Either give the actors instructions to come to the set wearing those clothes or take the clothes away and hold them for the shoot.

Be careful of clothes that have logos on them. It's easy for us to overlook words and graphics on shirts, hats, or jackets, but they read very strongly in film. If there are words on your costumes, make sure they're appropriate for the character and the scene. I once had a student whose film included a dramatic scene in which a couple on the verge of breaking up was having an intense argument. It was difficult for the audience to feel the tension of the scene because the actress was wearing a T-shirt that read "C is for Crunk!" Instead of listening to the argument, I myself was trying to figure out what the heck a crunk is. When I asked the student why he chose that particularly distracting shirt, he replied, "That's all the actress brought with her." That was the very first film this student ever made and the very last time he'll overlook wardrobe considerations.

If you don't find the clothes you're looking for to really bring this character to life, then you'll need to get measurements and either buy, borrow, rent, or make the costume items you need. However, beware of slick costume tricks. I had a friend who needed a wedding dress for a scene. She bought an exquisite wedding dress on her credit card with the clever idea that she'd use it in the film then return it within two weeks and get her money back—a great idea until the actress spilled Kool-Aid on the dress during a break in shooting. I think my friend is still paying off that credit card debt.

When it comes to props, it is well worth a little extra time to find just the right object that will reflect something about the character using it, or about the time period, or that will carry any other inflection you'd like in your film. But you also must make sure that your props are on the set when you need them. This is the sort of detail that can get lost in all of the activity of putting a film together. Someone needs to be assigned the specific responsibility of getting particular props to the set on the days the props need to be there. I recently asked a student why, in his film, he chose to have a burglar tie up the owner of the house with one of the thick orange extension cords from the school's lighting kit. "He was supposed to tie him up with duct tape" came the explanation, "but no one brought any." He glared at the project's production manager, who defended himself by saying, "No one *told* me to bring duct tape!" If your film is about two guys who mix up their identical briefcases, then you need to find identical briefcases and make sure they're on the set when you need them. If your film involves a guitar-playing Don Juan, then you need to get a guitar (with strings) and make sure Romeo knows how to fake it enough that you can dub in romantic guitar playing later. And remember, props are not only crucial to the action, they can express character.

Getting back to our Stasi officer from *The Lives of Others,* we see a fantastic use of props for character definition (Figure 6-7). When Captain Weisler returns home to cook himself dinner, the choice of meal and preparation is not arbitrary. We see him in his austere kitchen where strangely there are no

■ **Figure 6-7** Props as the expression of character in Von Donnersmarck's *The Lives of Others* (2006). Captain Weisler in his kitchen making dinner—tomato sauce from a tube on gray noodles.

pots, pans, cooking utensils, spices, or anything that even looks like food. He just boils up some pale noodles, squeezes a red substance from a tube onto the noodles (presumably something tomato-ish), and that's dinner. Consistent with his environment and costumes, his eating habits are utilitarian, which is to say efficient and neat but devoid of flavor, pleasure, or sensuality. It's the perfect choice for Weisler who would only require basic fuel for the body. Consider now the total portrait created by the location and set dressing (his sterile apartment), the wardrobe (gray shirt, jacket, and tie), and props (the meal he makes). Through these details we understand that this man is barely flesh and blood; he functions as a piece of the bureaucratic state-run socialist machinery. Great! Now this character is perfectly set up for how the narrative will transform him and make him human.

The Script Breakdown Sheet

The **script breakdown sheet** (Figure 6-8) is the form used in film production to keep track of all the mise-en-scène details that are necessary for every scene, including set dressing, hand props, costumes, makeup, and atmosphere (rain, fog, smoke, etc.). Every scene gets its own breakdown sheet so that everyone can see, at a glance, what details are necessary for every scene and so that the responsibility for acquiring it all can be assigned in an organized way.

The script breakdown sheet is usually generated by the Assistant Director (or Production Manager), but since most of these details fall under the purview of the art department, the production designer will usually carefully double-check the list, adding specific details that are part of the designer's interpretation of the scene. For example, an A.D. might not know specifically what posters will hang on the walls of a character's dorm room or what kind of book bag the character will carry if it's not specifically mentioned in the script.

■ BUDGETING YOUR FILM

In many ways, the budget is, as they say, where the rubber meets the road. In a broad sense, **the budget** of a film is basically how much money (and other resources) one has available to make a movie. In a more specific sense, **budgeting** a movie means deciding what specific expenses you will incur and how your available funds will be distributed across the various needs of the project.

There are generally two ways of approaching your budget. One approach is to figure out how much money you have (or can reliably get) and devise the best film you can make with that amount. The other way to go about it is to write the script you want to produce, break it down, and find out how much it will cost to make that film. Then you go out and raise the necessary funds. The latter approach is common practice in the professional industry but can be risky for a student filmmaker who needs to produce a movie in a few weeks for a grade. There are, of course, many strategies between these poles; for example, you can shoot your film with all of the resources you have, getting it "in the can," and then raise

■ **Figure 6-8** A script breakdown sheet.

Scene #: **17**		Date: 8/18/2006
Script Page: 1	**BREAKDOWN SHEET**	Sheet: 1
Page Count: 1 7/8 pgs.	BECOMING	Int/Ext. EXT
		Day/Night: NIGHT

Scene Description: Anna and Sebastian get into car
Setting: DESERTED STREET
Location: FLUSHING PARK PROMENADE
Sequence: _____ Script Day: _____

Cast Members	**Set Dressing**	**Costumes**
1. ANNA	STREET SIGN "ONE WAY"	BLACK SKIRT (ANNA)
11. MAN	WET DOWN STREET AND PARKED CARS	FADED BLACK SHIRT (MAN)
6. OLD MAN		DIRTY SUIT (OLD MAN)
3. SEBASTIAN		VEST AND SUSPENDERS (SEB)
	Special Effects	**Vehicles**
	LITTLE SMOKE	PROP CAR (MIDSIZE)
	OCCASIONAL BREEZE	ROWS OF CARS
Props	LIGHT RAIN	
CRUMPLED PAPER BAG		
CLIPBOARD		
SMALL PIECE OF PAPER		
PEN		
Makeup	**Greenery**	**Special Equipment**
GLAMOUR MAKE UP		HOSE FOR RAIN
DROPLETS OF BLOOD		LADDER
		HOSE AND SPRINKLER
Mechanical FX	**Extras**	**Stunts**
	YOUNG MAN	

Page 1

This report was created with Gorilla™

money later for postproduction expenses. In any case, it is essential, before you begin production on your movie to know just how much it will cost you. Serious sticker shock awaits anyone who makes films on a spend-as-you-go basis. A detailed budget includes a price line for every item or service that costs money, and it will let you know how much your film will cost and where the money will go. It is not a good idea to be blindly optimistic about budgets and about how far a buck will stretch; it's always best to be bluntly realistic. As I mentioned in Chapter 1, resources and ideas are inextricably linked, so working up a budget often becomes an occasion for rewriting the script.

In student and independent productions. many items ordinarily costing money are generally free or can be borrowed. When budgeting a film you must consider *all* of your resources, not just the available cash. For example, in school your production crew, being students themselves, work for free, and the school generally provides basic equipment. A college often provides facilities like editing rooms and rooms for auditions and rehearsals and screenings. Introductory and interme-diate students also rarely pay actors or have a need for legal work requiring lawyers. But no school covers every expense of a simple film, so working up a bud-get is still essential (**Figure 6-9**). In the real world, when you're trying to raise money for a movie, every produc-tion company, grant-awarding agency, or investor will invariably ask to see not only the screenplay but also the budget for your movie, so it's a good idea to know what's involved and what it means to translate ideas into financial needs.

The major factors that go into working up an accurate budget are:

- Length of the film and shooting ratio (film stock and processing)
- Number of shooting days
- Workflow (acquisition and distribution formats and process)
- Equipment (rental and purchase)
- Materials and Supplies
- Facilities
- Personnel (cast and crew)
- Location Expenses (rental fees, food, insurance, transportation, etc.)

■ **Figure 6-9** The preparation of a realistic budget must include all projected expenses. These students are using a camera and a tripod provided by their school, but the mini-jib necessary for a dramatic shot had to be rented at a cost of $65 per day.

Obviously not every budget looks the same because not every film project has the same requirements. **Figure 6-10** is an example of a budget for a typical short, introductory student movie shot on film.

Film Length and Shooting Ratio

The **shooting ratio** of a film is the amount of footage we shoot compared to the final running time of the movie. If we shoot a total of 20 minutes of film for a 5-minute movie, then we have a 4:1 shooting ratio. How does this happen? Let's say we have a scene in which our actor, sitting at a bar, finishes his beer, puts his coat on, and leaves. In the first take the actor chokes on the beer: "Cut!" In the second take he drinks the beer but then leaves without putting the coat on: "Cut!" In the third take the performance is fine, but the camera operator fails to pan with him as he leaves: "Cut!" The fourth take goes just as planned—beer, coat, pan; perfect: "Keeper!" One good take out of four. We have our shot and we've accumulated a shooting ratio of around 4:1 without much effort at all. Also, the amount of coverage you choose to do on a scene—for example, shooting from multiple angles to give yourself editing options—also increases the shooting ratio. Finally, the more technically complicated your film is (field sound recording, dynamic camera moves, multiple actors, multiple angles, etc.), the more things can go wrong during each take and the higher your shooting ratio is likely to be.

Estimating the shooting ratio is important in budgeting because it helps us calculate how much raw film or tape stock we need to purchase and how many feet of film stock will be processed by the lab and transferred to DV. Keep in mind that many lab services are billed by the foot. This is why movies shot on video enjoy larger shooting ratios; there is no labo-ratory charging them by the foot for processing and transfer.

Shooting Days

The number of shooting days you need for your project is important to calculate in order to arrive at accurate budget figures for things that are paid on a per-day basis, includ-ing meals, transportation, equipment rentals, location rentals, and personnel who charge by the day. Again, it's best not to be overly optimistic about these figures. If your film will clearly take five days to shoot, then budget for five days. It would be pennywise and pound foolish to try and cram a five-day shoot into three days. Also, keep in mind that you must

■ **Figure 6-10**
A sample budget for a
five-minute project shot
on film.

SHORT FILM BUDGET

Title: *Random Predestiny*

Director: Jessica W.   D.P.: Timothy T.   Production Mgr.: Fannie M.

Length: 5 min	Shooting Ratio: 3:1	Shooting Days: 2

1) PRE - PRODUCTION BREAKDOWN:

Item / Service / Personnel	Unit price / rate	Cost:
Transportation (gasoline)	Allow	$ 25.00
Photocopying	5 copies of 5pp script @ $0.10/sheet	$ 2.50
Miscellaneous	2 @ $6/hr parking	$ 12.00
1) PRE - PRODUCTION SUB-TOTAL		$39.50

2) PRODUCTION BREAKDOWN:

Item / Service / Personnel	Unit price / rate	Cost:
SUPPLIES:		
Film Stock 1	6 100' rolls 7213 @ $30 ea. (w/student discount)	$180.00
Gels & Diffusion	6 sheet @ $9.00 ea.	$ 54.00
Misc. Production Supplies	*e.g.* 2' gaffer tape @ $20.00/roll	$ 38.00
	1' camera tape @ $12.00/roll	
	C-47's @ $1.00/dozen	
	Sharpies @ $5.00/pack	
EQUIPMENT RENTAL:		
Wide ange lens (8 mm)	1 @ $50.00/day	$ 50.00
Polarizing filter (4 x 4)	1 @ $10.00/day	$ 10.00
ART DEPARTMENT:		
Set dressing	1 lace curtain @ $10.00	$ 20.00
	1 "AutoBabes" wall calendar @ $10.00	
Props	1 "Rubix Cube" @ $12.00	$ 12.00
Wardrobe	1 Fez @ $10.00	$ 10.00
LOCATION EXPENSES:		
Transportation/Fuel	4 subway Metrocards @ $10.00/ea.	$ 40.00
Meals	8 lunches @ $10.00/each	$ 80.00
2) PRODUCTION SUB-TOTAL		$494.00

3) POST – PRODUCTION BREAKDOWN:

Item / Service / Personnel	Unit price / rate	Cost:
LAB WORK		
Film Processing	600' @ $0.19/ft (incl. leader, prep & clean)	$114.00
DV dailies	600' One-lite telecine @ $0.19/ft	$114.00
Syncing Dailies		N/A
DV tape stock	2 HDCAM @ $25.00 ea.	$ 50.00
FireWire Drive	(Provided)	N/A
DVD stock for copies	1 @ 30.00/ 25 pack	$ 30.00
3) POST – PRODUCTION SUB-TOTAL		$308.00
TOTAL		$841.50
Contingency allowance 10%		$ 84.00
GRAND TOTAL:		**$925.50**

allow time for your crew to rest. This is a safety issue and a morale issue. You must have at least 10 hours between the end of one call and the beginning of the next. Don't expect your crew to pull all-nighters—they'll make sloppy mistakes and, again, these mistakes can potentially be a safety risk.

Workflow and Budgeting

The choices you make concerning your acquisition format (film or digital video) and distribution format (film print, HD video, DVD, or Internet) have a significant impact on the budget for your project. Although it is a mistake to believe that shooting on digital video is, across the board, cheaper than shooting on film (the 2006 Michael Mann film *Miami Vice* was shot on high-definition video at a budget estimated around 150 million bucks!), it is possible to produce effective movies on digital video, with effects, dissolves, and complex sound tracks, for very little money; however, making your movie on film (especially finishing on film) is almost always a costly endeavor because of the unavoidable involvement of a film lab for intermediate prints, transfers, effects, optical track masters, and so on. Let's look at just the basic costs of shooting film and shooting standard definition (SD) digital video to the point of having footage ready to edit. A one-hour professional quality MiniDV tape runs around $8 (on the high side). When we are done shooting we are ready to download the footage directly into a nonlinear editing system and edit. Shooting one hour of film footage includes processing and transferring to a DV tape by a film lab before we can capture our footage. The total cost for one hour of edit-ready film footage comes in around $1,135 per hour of footage. It's harder to make comparative calculations for file-based (tapeless) HD media, but it's true that it can be somewhat expensive to start out (as I write this book, a 32-GB Panasonic P2 card, for example, costs around $580 and the Sony 32-GB SxS card comes in at $800), but these cards are reusable project after project after project, so it's a one-time expense for multiple films. So you can be sure that shooting HD video is significantly less expensive minute for minute than shooting film. Similar calculations are also made for the second half of the workflow equation. Do you plan to finish your movie on video or to make a film print? These different processes carry vastly different costs and are covered in detail in Chapter 19.

in practice

The formula for calculating shooting ratios for 16mm film is (L × R)36 = TF.

"L" is the anticipated final length of your film, "R" is your ratio, 36 is the number of feet of film per minute of screen time at regular sync speed, and "TF" is total footage. So an eight-minute film, shot on a ratio of 5:1 is calculated like this: (8 × 5)36 = 1,404 feet. We must buy 1,404 feet of film to make our movie.

The cost of one 400-foot roll of Kodak Vision2 16mm color negative film (around 11 minutes of footage) is approximately $105 after the 20% student discount.[1]

Because we must buy four of these rolls, adding up to 1,600 feet of film (our necessary footage with a little cushion), the cost of our raw film stock will be $420. Then, we need to calculate the cost of processing this film and having the negative transferred to DV tape by a film lab. Both services are charged by the foot, around 21¢ per foot (1,600 feet × 0.21), totaling roughly $295. So the cost of film, processing, and transferring for an eight-minute film shot on a 5:1 ratio will be around $715. There it is; no surprises later.

[1]If you are a student, always ask for the student discount on anything you buy or rent for the film. You may be surprised at how many places will give you 10% to 20% off the list price.

Equipment, Facilities, Materials and Supplies

Cameras, lenses, lights, digital editing stations, audition rooms, and screening facilities all require rental fees, but, happily, schools usually provide students with the basic equipment and facilities necessary to make their films. However, there will be times when something you need for your film can't be accomplished or obtained through the school. Maybe you're shooting a scene through the windshield of a moving car and you need a hood mount for the camera or maybe you're shooting an exterior night scene and require a portable generator to power a few lights. These are not items that schools usually provide, and so they must be rented. If you need a specialty item, then you must find an equipment rental house near to you and check its online catalog for rental prices when you draw up your budget (**Figure 6-11**).

The cost of digital editing software, like Final Cut Pro or Avid DV Express, has come down so drastically in recent years (especially with the educational discounts) that many students, frustrated by the limited access at their school's communal editing facilities, simply put editing software in the budget of their first film, and then they have it for

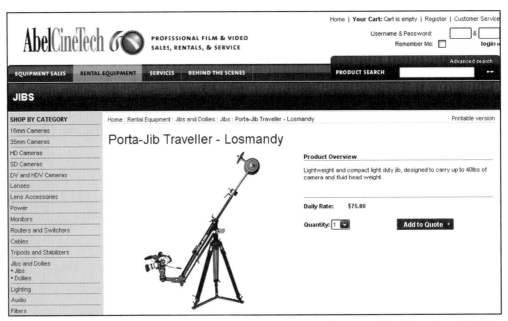

■ **Figure 6-11** Most equipment rental houses, like AbelCineTech, have their entire rental catalog online, making the preparation of a budget an easy task.

every subsequent project. They find the convenience of editing in their room worth the added expense.

Materials and Supplies are those expendable items that everyone needs on the set. Some are big ticket items, like set construction materials while others are relatively inexpensive items, like gaffer's tape, extra batteries, diffusion paper, color gels, sharpie markers, and so on. Take note: these small items can really add up, so make sure you anticipate them in your budget.

Personnel (Cast and Crew)

On a professional film, the fees for cast and crew are significant. Some people on the team are paid a flat rate for the project if they've negotiated their fee in this way, but usually most production personnel are paid a day rate. On small-budget films, any of the principal production team members (e.g., director of photography, art director, sound recordist) can make anywhere between $75 and $1,200 per day. Student productions on the introductory and intermediate level, however, usually use fellow students on the production team, which works out well for both the student filmmaker's pocketbook and the teammates' film experience and education.

Location Expenses

Location expenses are all the costs associated with being on location. This includes: rental and insurance fees to secure your location; truck rental, transportation and parking to get people and equipment to-and-from the set; and craft services (food and drinks) during the hours of shooting. It also includes the costs associated with returning a location back to its original condition after shooting (cleaning and repair). Location expenses can constitute a major percentage of a budget.

Hidden Costs

Finally, it's important that you think very hard to anticipate any exceptional or unusual expense that might crop up. It's obvious that you have to budget for film stock and processing, but what about transportation costs for crewmembers who live in different areas, or the cost of cleaning up the house you used as a location, or the dry-cleaning bill for the costumes you borrowed but must return cleaned and pressed? What about the special dietary needs of an actor who cannot function on the normal crew meal you're providing? How about the "one-time setup fee" the lab charges you on certain services, or the late fee you had to pay because you returned the equipment late, or the $70 replacement cost for the 2,000-watt bulb that blew during your shoot? What if you're shooting a simple exercise and budget for only 200 feet of film but discover later that the lab has a "minimum service fee" (as many do) that is nearly double what you anticipated? There are a thousand places where hidden costs can sneak up on you. Most unexpected costs occur because the filmmaker hasn't done thorough research, especially in the area of lab services, but a lot of budget overruns simply come from not accounting for the little stuff, which can really add up. However, you can never quite predict everything, and it's for this reason that many people figure in a 10% contingency allowance as a line item in the budget. This ensures that there is money on hand to cover unforeseen expenses.

Professional film production budgets are incredibly long and elaborate documents generated by professional accountants. For the purposes of small, low-budget films we can do with a lot fewer details. The short film budget sheets available on the *Voice & Vision* companion website should suffice for most small film projects. Keep in mind that you do not need to use every line item on the budget for every film and that you can add line items as you need them. **Figure 6-12** is another sample budget a low-budget short film shot on HD video.

in practice

■ PREPRODUCTION PAPERWORK

The key to a creatively successful shoot is organization and planning. Every film production, regardless of the size or budget, encounters extenuating circumstances, unforeseen challenges, and at least one brush with Murphy's law. Being organized and prepared will ensure that you can meet these challenges without the whole project going under. Here are the preproduction forms we've discussed; these will help you get organized in preproduction and stay organized throughout the production process:

- Marked shooting script (page 100)
- Overhead diagrams (page 102)
- Storyboards (page 106)
- Shot list (page 114)
- Scene breakdowns (page 133)
- Call sheets (page 118)
- Budget (page 133)
- Contact sheet (page 162)

Blank storyboard forms, call sheets, breakdown sheets, and short film budgets can be downloaded from the *Voice & Vision* companion website at www.voiceandvisionbook.com.

■ **Figure 6-12** A sample budget for a 12-minute project shot on HD video.

SAMPLE BUDGET FOR TWELVE MINUTE HD STUDENT FILM

Length: 12 min	Shooting Format: HD / P2	Shooting Days: 6

PRE - PRODUCTION BREAKDOWN:

Item / Service / Personnel	Unit price / rate	Cost:
Transportation (scouting)	3 days car rental @ $80 / day	$240
Photocopying	6 copies of 12pp script @ $0.10 / sheet	$8
Audition facility / equip.	*Provided through college*	0
Hospitality	(e.g. food, drinks, etc.) Allow	$75
Research	12 oz. fake blood @ $14 / bottle	$14
Miscellaneous	4 / 60 min. miniDV@$2.99 ea. (to record audition)	$12
PRE - PRODUCTION TOTAL		$349

PRODUCTION BREAKDOWN:

Item / Service / Personnel	Unit price / rate	Cost:
SUPPLIES:		
Video record media	32 GB E-series P2 card	$580
	500 GB portable hard drive for footage download	$175
Audio record media	16 GB Compact Flash card	$50
Batteries	1 @ $15 / 24 pack (AA)	$25
Gels & Diffusion	10 @ $6 / sheet	$60
Misc. Production Supplies	(e.g. gaffer tape, replacement bulbs, C47's) Allow	$75
EQUIPMENT RENTAL:	*Major equipment supplied by college*	
Camera Support (dolly)	1 @ $40 / day	$40
Misc. Camera Dept.	Polarizing filter & diffusion filter kit	$40
Microphones	2 mic. wireless lav. Syst. pack. @ $200/week	$200
Lighting rental	2 mini-flo kits @ $50 / day (3 days)	$150
Misc. Lighting & Grip	(e.g. genny, ladder, dimmer, etc.) Allow	$75
ART DEPARTMENT:		
Set dressing	Misc. furniture rental, curtains, wall dress. Allow	$200
Props	Prop gun rental, 1 day @ $50	$50
Wardrobe	Tuxedo rental, 2 @ $75 day	$150
Miscellaneous	(e.g. make-up, dry cleaning, tailoring, etc.) Allow	$75
LOCATION EXPENSES:		
Location Rental	6 @ $50 / day	$300
Van Rental	7 days @ 379.99/wk	$380
Transportation/fuel	Subway cards, gas, taxi fares. Allow	$75
Meals	6 @ $55 / day	$330
Miscellaneous	(e.g. trash bags, cleaning supplies, etc.) Allow	$25
PRODUCTION TOTAL		$3055

POST - PRODUCTION BREAKDOWN:

Item / Service / Personnel	Unit price / rate	Cost:
FILM EDIT SUPPLIES & FACILITY:	*Editing facilities supplied by college*	
Media Drive	1 500 GB Firewire 800 @ $150	$150
Misc. edit supplies	(e.g. firewire cable, DVDs, etc.) Allow	$25
SOUND POST & MIX:		
Sound Mix Suite	4 hours @ $85 / hour (student rate with mixer)	$340
Recording Studio Rental	1 day @ $150 / day (piano included)	$150
Musicians	Pianist $100 / flat rate	$100
FINISHING & RELEASE		
Digital Mastering	2 hours @ $90.00 / hour	$180
DVD copies	25 @ $2.25/each	$45
Packaging	25 cases & inserts @ $1.20 / dup	$30
POST - PRODUCTION TOTAL		$1020

TOTAL (Pre, Pro, & Post)		$4424
Contingency allowance 10 %		$440
GRAND TOTAL		**$4864**

The Cast and Crew

I think the secret to directing is collaborating and I had truly an extraordinary group of collaborators in my crew.
Kathryn Bigelow (From acceptance speech, 2010 Academy Award for Directing)

Filmmaking is a communal activity in the sense that an artist has to go out and interact with a lot of other people and inspire and energise them. Unless you have the ability to convey your internal vision to enough people in a way that enthuses them and makes them want to help you translate that vision back as cinema vision, you won't make the jump.
Mike Figgis (From *Digital Filmmaking*, Faber & Faber, 2007)

■ THE PRODUCTION CREW

Narrative filmmaking on any scale is a collaborative art form requiring the effort and creative expertise of a team of people. The filmmaking team is the crew and the cast, and choosing the right group of people to pull off the movie you are envisioning is a task of paramount importance. When you build your production crew, it is essential to remember that the size of the crew must fit the scale of the project; the size of your team must be adequate to pull off the film but not so large that it becomes cumbersome. Short narrative films are typically produced with as few as three and as many as fifteen people. The more technical production tasks your project requires, the more people you need. Take the time to build a crew that you can trust and with whom you can collaborate, because your production crew is your creative team. Even in a case where you are assigned a crew in a class, you should take whatever steps are necessary to foster cooperation and a collaborative spirit.

Production Departments

Whether you're shooting on film or video, making a five-minute short or a feature film, or working with a big budget or miniscule resources—the core production tasks for all narrative motion pictures are essentially the same. All film crews are divided up into departments. A **production department** can involve one person or many people who are responsible for a circumscribed set of tasks. In the professional world, where production crews can be very large, these tasks have become narrowly defined and department teams are therefore staffed with many specialists. For example, on a big-budget feature film, it's very common for there to be six or more people responsible for the cinematography and functioning of the camera alone (i.e., D.P., camera operator, 1st A.C., 2nd A.C., loader, Steadicam operator, video assist tech, camera P.A.—and then there is the second unit camera crew!). But if we consider the duties of the production departments *broadly*, it will give us a good idea for the fundamental tasks on any narrative film of any scope and with any size crew:

- Someone must be responsible for budgeting, scheduling, and the logistical coordination of the project (personnel, locations, production resources). This is the **producing team**.
- Someone must be the definitive creative decision maker of the movie, the person who makes sure that everyone's efforts are working toward a common and expressive end. This is the **director**.
- Someone needs to be in charge of lighting and capturing the image on film or video. This is the **camera department**.

- Someone needs to attend to the look of the physical space (locations and sets) for the movie and acquire the costumes and objects used by the actors in the film. This is the **art department**.
- Someone must be in charge of recording sound on location, if it's necessary. This is the **sound department**.
- Someone must appear on camera to perform the dramatic roles in the movie. This is **the talent**.

There is, of course, much more detail involved in the tasks of each department, but considering it in this general way can help you distribute the duties among smaller production teams on low-budget films, where people often need to perform multiple roles.

The Principal Production Crew: Creative Core

The **principal production team** includes those crewmembers with substantial responsibility and often direct creative input. These people are the heads of the various departments, and in the professional world these key positions are supported by technical teams with highly specific jobs. However, on short films, where budgets, technical demands, and production crews are much smaller, these people often work alone. For our purpose we'll look at the role of each position as it pertains to short projects on the introductory and intermediate levels.

The Producing Team

It's not easy to create a precise list of duties for a producer, because this role can be very different from film to film. The best definition I've seen comes from Christine Vachon's book, *A Killer Life*, which details her experiences as an independent film producer: "Producers are the ones who get movies made, from the concept to the contracts to bankrolling the folks at the craft services table" (see the In Practice box that follows). **The producer** oversees the logistics of the film from preproduction to distribution, including funding, personnel, scheduling, equipment, locations, and other production resources. The producing team makes sure that the project is accomplished on time and on budget. The producer is responsible for providing the director with a realistic assessment of the budget, including what resources are available and how they can be distributed across the various needs of the project. The producer then keeps a close eye on the expenditures of the film for the duration of the project. The producer also helps devise strategies to make maximum creative use of limited budgets. It's considered a high compliment to a producer for someone to say, "The producer made a $5,000 budget look like $500,000!" Producers select their own support staff, including the production manager, and help directors choose the rest of the production and postproduction team. Indeed, sometimes the producer is *the* original force behind a film project and brings together a writer and director with compatible sensibilities and styles to develop the film.

The **production manager** (P.M.; sometimes called the **line producer**) is the producer's right hand during the production process. While the producer has the bird's-eye view of the project and organizes the big picture, the production manager is responsible for the day-to-day operations of the film set and overseeing all budget expenditures. The P.M. manages the master schedule, ensuring that everything and everyone necessary for every shooting day will actually be on the set, on time. The P.M.'s job is formidable. P.M.s coordinate people, props, equipment, transportation, food, money, and locations. In many ways the production manager is the linchpin for the entire, logistical effort of film production. The P.M. helps the director and assistant director break down the script and is therefore acutely aware of the time, material, and personnel needs of the project. The P.M. then creates the shooting schedule and breakdown sheets from the shooting script with the assistant director (see Chapter 5).

Although each department is responsible for the safety issues in its own area, the producing team is ultimately responsible for the general oversight of safety and security concerns. If a project is large enough and includes risky elements, it is wise to add a **safety coordinator** to the team. On small shoots, this supervision falls to the producer and production manager.

Veteran film producer Christine Vachon truly puts the "independent" in the term "independent film" (**Figure 7-1**). Producing movies since the 1980s, her credits include some of the most groundbreaking, risky, innovative and influential movies of American independent cinema, including *Poison* (Haynes, 1991), *Kids* (Clark, 1995), *I Shot Andy Warhol* (Harron, 1996), *Happiness* (Solondz, 1998), *Boys Don't Cry* (Peirce, 1999), *Hedwig and the Angry Inch* (Mitchell, 2001), *One Hour Photo* (Romanek, 2002), *Far from Heaven* (Haynes, 2002), *What's Wrong with Virginia* (Black, 2010) just to name a few. Her company, Killer Films, continues to flourish even though most of the early independent film companies have disappeared. Vachon's success and longevity can be attributed to maintaining a relentless passion and sense of mission for small films that have something important to say and contribute to the art form. She has never wavered from this mission. Vachon has also authored two books that detail her experiences as a producer. The aphorisms that follow are excerpted from the list of personal maxims that open her second book, *A Killer Life,* and provide a good sense of her producing method and philosophy.

Enjoy the process.
But get out of the way.
The budget is not the aesthetic.
Never put in your own money.
OK, Sometimes it has to be your money.
(Money is overrated)
Identify talent and stick to it like glue.
Every little picture needs a big picture.
In the big picture, we need little pictures.

Less money = more control; more money = less control.
Find the intersection of an investor's courage and cash.
Do what you love; do it consistently.
Everything else will follow.
Every story behind a movie that gets made is a success story.
This is the best job in the world.
Christine Vachon (From *A Killer Life*, Simon & Schuster, 2006)

■ **Figure 7-1** Producer Christine Vachon of Killer Films (photo by Henny Garfunkel).

The Director and Assistant Director

The **director** is the creative driving force of a film project. The director is responsible for bringing the screenplay to the screen and maintaining an appropriate, consistent, and coherent stylistic approach. Despite the popular impression of the director as some sort of demigod, they are usually more like the captain of a ship. They oversee all creative activity on the film, and, working from their own vision as well as the suggestions of the other principal personnel, they make sure that everyone's efforts culminate into an effective and cohesive movie. To this end, the director is responsible for fostering creative input and inspiring enthusiasm and commitment among the cast and crew. Film is a collaborative art form; listen again to what Kathryn Bigelow said when she accepted her Oscar for Best Director in 2010: "I think the secret to directing is collaborating." More than any other team member, the director sets the tone for the production. If the tone is adversarial with the cast and crew, then the experience will be a terrible struggle, which often manifests on screen in the form of unremarkable or sloppy work. If the director has created a collaborative and encouraging environment, then it is astonishing how much great work can be accomplished in a short time with few resources. This is especially critical on low-budget shoots when you are not paying people for the hard work of making a movie.

The director is also the ultimate problem solver. During the course of any film production, there are countless puzzles to solve and endless questions to answer—for example, where do we set up the camera and why? What is the actor's motivation? How many setups are required to cover a scene? How long will each take be? From what direction should the light come? What are the color tonalities of the set? Which shirt should the lead wear? When do we move the camera and why? How does an actor move in the location?

in practice

For her first feature film, director Courtney Hunt set herself some formidable challenges. *Frozen River* (2008) tells the story of two women, one white and one Mohawk, who reluctantly become partners in crime. Compelled by their personal economic hardship, the women smuggle illegal immigrants from Canada into the United States by driving them across the frozen Saint Lawrence River and into Mohawk reservation territory where they elude the police. *Frozen River* was shot with a small crew on an extremely low budget. As Hunt tells it, "Everybody did two jobs and every job was crucial and everyone worked really hard." This is certainly not atypical of independent filmmaking; however, there was another challenge that was built right into the very premise of the film—the frozen river! In this film the harsh winter landscape along the New York/Quebec border and especially the titular frozen river are not mere backdrops; rather they carry critical narrative and metaphoric weight and this guaranteed extensive shooting in frigid conditions. With low-budget independent film wages and harsh shooting conditions, one of Hunt's principal tasks as a director was keeping everyone invested, engaged and involved, not just in their specific craft areas but in the project as a whole (**Figure 7-2**):

We had days that were subzero, we had days that were in the single digits and we had the occasional, terrifying day when it would fly up toward freezing and we'd worry about the ice melting. So, every day had it's own worry in terms of weather.

For me, it was just making sure that the story-telling involved the crew, the cast and myself. And that it was compelling enough to give us the courage to go outside and stay outside because there are tons of exteriors in this movie and tons of night exteriors, which can be just grueling. But everyone was committed to the story. They were behind Ray Eddy and her quest. They were behind Lila and her struggle in a very personal way, and that helped us get through.

Courtney Hunt (From "From Law School to Oscar: Courtney Hunt Talks *Frozen River*," by Mark Sells, *MovieMaker*, February 11, 2009)

■ **Figure 7-2** Director Courtney Hunt credits the hard work and dedication of her crew, who often worked in subfreezing temperatures, for helping her realize her award-winning, low-budget feature film *Frozen River* (2008).

■ **Figure 7-3** Whether you are film student or a cinema legend, the complex job of directing is essentially the same. Director Miles Adgate giving direction to actor Jarret Berenstein on the student film *Discovering* (2006, *left*), and director Jean-Luc Godard showing Jean Claude Brialy how he wants him to ride a bicycle in the film *Une Femme est Une Femme* (1961, *right*). (Godard photograph courtesy of Raymond Cauchetier-Paris.)

How do we revise the shot list if we're running out of time? The director's job sometimes can seem like nothing more than answering one long stream of questions and solving one creative puzzle after another (**Figure 7-3**). However, the director answers all of these questions because every one of them determines the expressive style and aesthetic approach of the film. Because of this, a director needs to be broadly knowledgeable in the process, techniques, and creative possibilities of all aspects of film production. Also, a director needs authority, and that authority comes not only from knowing what one is doing, but also from being very clear about everyone else's role in the creation of the film and respecting their contributions. It's equally common for directors to ask the questions. A director might ask a D.P., "I need this scene to feel claustrophobic, tight, suffocating; what lens do you suggest?" Or one might ask an art director, "This character is a rebellious teenager with a penchant for Goth; what do you think she'd have in her room?" With actors, the director enters a very special collaboration, which we will discuss in more detail later in this chapter and in Chapter 17. One final note: the director needs to always keep a level head and should not attempt or demand anything that compromises the safety of anyone on the production team, or anything that is in excess of the available resources, or anything that approaches an abuse of personnel, location, or equipment.

> *The function of the director is to lead.[...] if no one is leading the troops, the troops will become lethargic and disheartened very quickly because they are working for you and they are trying to service your vision. Unless they have some energetic connection to your vision, they end up being functional technicians.*
>
> **Mike Figgis (From *Digital Filmmaking*, Faber & Faber, 2007)**

The **assistant director** (A.D.) is to the director what the production manager is to the producer. The A.D. is responsible for the smooth operation of the set. This usually means communicating the director's instructions to the various technical departments (e.g., camera, art, and sound departments) and relating the crew's concerns back to the director. The A.D. makes sure that everyone on the set knows the order of camera setups and what is needed of each department. This leaves the director freer to work with the actors and to make creative decisions on the set. The A.D. works very closely with the P.M. The A.D. helps the director create the shooting script and then, with the P.M., breaks down the script to create a shot list and scene breakdowns (see Chapter 5). In scenes that involve many extras, the A.D. essentially blocks and directs their actions. On small films, the A.D. is often responsible for keeping track of scene coverage and continuity from shot to shot.

■ **Figure 7-4** The D.P. and A.C. are a tight unit. Here, D.P. Joe Foley lines up a shot while A.C. Loui J. LeRoy maintains focus with the aid of his own monitor on the set of John Daschbach's *Brief Reunion* (2011).

The Camera and Electric Departments

The **director of photography** (D.P.; also referred to as **cinematographer**) collaborates closely with the director on the visual interpretation of the script and the photographic look of the movie. This involves designing the lighting, choosing film stocks or video format, and devising expressive camera angles, compositions, exposures, and focus. The D.P. knows very well the storytelling capability of the image and is in charge of capturing it all on film or DV. The D.P. collaborates with the director during preproduction, and this collaboration continues into production and postproduction, where the D.P. often oversees final color corrections. Although the director has the final say, the D.P. should never hesitate to make creative suggestions if they believe it will enhance the movie. However, a D.P. should never make suggestions simply as an excuse to play with snazzy camera toys. A good D.P. knows that, in the end, making a movie is not about equipment, it's about visual storytelling. For more on the duties and contributions of the D.P., see Chapters 12, 13, 14 and 17. (**Figure 7-4**).

Whether on a professional or a student level, the trust and the creative energy generated as a result of the director and D.P. collaboration are vital to the success of a film. It is important for both people to nurture this relationship beginning in preproduction. The cinematographers Ellen Kuras and Michael Ballhaus described the importance of preproduction meetings with the director in this way:

> *I always, always value the time of the director before photography, because for me the film really gets made during those discussions—in my mind and in our minds. It creates a common language between me and the director to be able to understand the look and what the "third eye" is, in a way. What the vision of the film is.*
>
> **Ellen Kuras (From "Where the Girls Are," by Jennifer M. Wood,**
> ***MovieMaker*, Vol. 2, # 9)**

> *Every morning we met in his office. He explained the scenes to me and his ideas. It was like being in heaven for me. I made a shot list and tried my best to integrate all of the fantasy that he imagined. Francis made any changes he wanted and gave it to the storyboard artist. After that, it was like shooting the film by heart. I would watch him rehearse with the actors and figure out the angles we wanted the audience to see. We finished the movie on time and on budget.*
>
> **Michael Ballhaus on working with Francis Ford Coppola on the film *Dracula***
> **(From "A Conversation with Michael Ballhaus," *ASC Magazine*,**
> **November 20, 2006)**

Another key position in the camera department is the **assistant cameraperson**, or A.C. The A.C. is a camera and lens expert. They are responsible for the proper functioning of the camera, which includes setting it up, cleaning the gate, checking and pulling focus, and selecting filters and lenses (with the D.P.). They know with precise detail what various cameras and lenses are capable of, both technically and aesthetically. On low-budget shoots, the A.C. is responsible for loading and unloading the film as well as for keeping accurate camera logs. The acronym FAST has become the mantra for working A.C.s. FAST stands for the key camera settings that must be checked before each and every shot: *Focus*, *Aperture*, *Speed* (frames per second), and *Think*, meaning that an A.C. should take nothing for granted before the camera rolls. On most low-budget films, the D.P. handles the camera, but on large-budget films or projects that require multiple cameras, there is also the position of **camera operator**. A camera operator, an expert in composition and the technical implementation of shots, can collaborate with either the D.P. or the director in planning the execution of a particular shot.

As movie projects and budgets become larger, the camera department expands to meet the technical demands of the shoot and may include the additional support positions of gaffer and grip(s). The **gaffer** is the hands-on lighting person who implements the lighting designs of the D.P. The gaffer is in charge of the setup and proper (and safe) functioning of the lights. The gaffer is also responsible for getting the necessary electricity to the set. To ensure the safety of cast and crew, gaffers are almost always certified electricians. On large sets, gaffers will be in charge of their own department, the electrical department.

in practice

A good friend and colleague of mine was on the crew of Martin Scorsese's *The Last Temptation of Christ* (1988) and told me this story from the shoot in Morocco. *The Last Temptation of Christ* was shot on a remarkably small budget and tight schedule in general, and with a much smaller crew than is usual for a film of that scale. Leading up to the shoot for the crucifixion scene, Scorsese lost the original location, an elevated hilltop in the desert, because it was covered with snow! While the crew continued shooting other scenes, a new location was found, which the art department prepped, day and night, in only two days. As my friend remembers, "That the art department could prep that location in only two days was a miracle."

The location switch only made a tight schedule tighter and the crew had to move fast in order to get everything planned for that location, which included nearly a hundred shots and the crucial crucifixion scene. As my friend tells the story, "Because the sun set early behind the surrounding hills, we had limited hours for each shooting day so we had to work fast. We didn't even have time to break for lunch; we were eating on the run so that we could get all the shots in. This was a key scene in a film that Marty had been dreaming about for years and we were understaffed and had limited time. At one point, when we were moving up the hill to set up a shot, I looked over and saw Marty himself grab two magazine cases weighing about 70 pounds and climb up the hill with them to the next setup. For that moment, Marty Scorsese was doing the job of a P.A. to get the film done. I was impressed" (**Figure 7-5**).

■ **Figure 7-5** On a film set teamwork is crucial and everyone does what needs to be done to get the film in the can. The famous crucifixion scene from *The Last Temptation of Christ* (1988) required all available hands *(right)*. Time was so tight on this shoot that Scorsese himself schlepped equipment when necessary (pictured in the photo at left with D.P. Michael Ballhaus, *middle)* and A.C. Florian Ballhaus *(left)*.

Gaffers and D.P.s are supported by electrical and camera department grips, respectively. **Grips** are the muscle on a film set. They move lights, sets, and dollies. They are responsible for the actual physical placement of the lights on the set and for the safe use of all lighting equipment or any production elements they have set up or rigged. Grips are also in charge of the orderly staging and breakdown of the lighting gear. On *very* large films, the grips become their own department, overseen by the **key grip** who in turn answers to the D.P.; but on very small projects with small crews, practically everyone on the set doubles as a grip at one point or another.

The Art Department

The **production designer** is responsible for the look and design of the film as they pertain to locations, sets, costumes, and props. The production designer works in close collaboration with the director and makes creative suggestions about the interpretation of story and characters in terms of location choices, the visual design and dressing of sets, and specific props and costumes. The production designer and cinematographer work very closely because together they create the total visual environment and style of the film. The production designer is also responsible for all safety issues concerning sets, props, and locations.

■ **Figure 7-6** A special effects makeup artist does quick touchup work on the set of Matt Post's short film *Super Spree* (2011). (photo by Johnny Wolf.)

The larger the project and budget of a film, the larger the support team for the production designer becomes. Often the production designer designs the film, but the specific tasks are distributed among an **art director,** who supervises set construction and location details, **set decorator**, who dresses the set with objects, a **propmaster**, who locates and coordinates props, a **costume designer**, who finds or makes all costumes and maintains them for the duration of the film, and a **makeup and hair stylist** (Figure 7-6). On films that require set construction, the art director is also in charge of hiring and coordinating a team of **carpenters and painters.** Just a note on nomenclature: sometimes the designations "production designer" and "art director" are use interchangeably or collapsed together. If there is no "production designer" in the credits, then the art director fulfilled both roles, if you see both credits, then the duties were distributed as described here (see Chapter 6).

The Sound Department

The **sound recordist** (also called the **location sound mixer**) is the head of the sound department and is responsible for recording the best possible quality sound. A perpetual puzzle solver, the sound person chooses the appropriate microphone(s) and microphone placement for every scene that requires sound. They also monitor and maintain proper recording levels. Sound recordists are trained to listen to everything in the aural environment of the set, and they make technical decisions based on the acoustics of the space and the ambient sounds. They also need to be alert to unwanted sounds intruding on takes, like airplanes flying overhead or a refrigerator suddenly kicking on. The sound recordist often teams up with a **boom operator**, who is responsible for the proper use and actual placement of the microphone(s) for optimum quality (Figure 7-7). Sometimes this means planting a microphone on the talent or on the set; other times this means holding a boom pole, which suspends the microphone over the action. The boom operator position is extremely important on any film with extensive synchronized sound, because bad audio is as disastrous and irremediable as bad camera work. On bigger shoots there is also a third person, called the **cable wrangler**, who sets up the cables, holds a second boom when necessary, and wrangles the cable when the boom operator follows a moving shot. Chapter 16 describes the role of the sound team in more detail.

■ **Figure 7-7** The sound team. In its most common configuration, the sound team consists of a boom person *(left)* and a sound recordist *(right)*.

Keep in mind that these descriptions are a guide for very small films and student films, which generally do not involve major studios, distributors, lawyers, production office staff, and large technical crews, with dozens of people and budgets in the millions of dollars. There are many books on the market that define each film crew position in its full professional dimensions (see the Recommended Readings section at the back of this book).

Now that you have a sense for the essential production crew positions, remember that fitting the size of the crew to the scale of the project is important. Bear in mind the law of diminishing returns. You want just enough people to get the job done well, but not so many that you waste time and money on unnecessary bodies. As a colleague of mine once remarked about large production crews, more people creates a need for more people because you need extra people to manage and take care of all those people! When you work with small crews, people are required to double or sometimes triple up on duties. It is essential that no matter how you divide up the duties on a project, all crewmembers must know precisely what they are responsible for and what is expected of them.

Crew Meetings and Communication

To foster a professional, collaborative, and efficient environment, open and frequent communication is vital. The director/producer should hold regular crew meetings over the course of any project, no matter how small. Crew meetings are essential for conveying the creative vision of the project and everyone's specific role in bringing that vision to the screen. Meetings are also indispensable for organizing the general production schedule as well as everyone's individual schedules and duties. No one should show up at the set without knowing exactly what their job is or what the project is about. Finally, crew meetings are where people feel the progress and momentum of a project and where team motivation, connection, and collaboration are fostered. A cinematographer can't make suggestions about the aesthetics of lighting or composition if they never saw a finished script or sat down with the director to discuss the tone, mood, or meaning of the movie. A sound recordist needs to know what the locations and shot selections are like in order to bring the appropriate equipment to the set. An art director needs to be informed of their budget so that they know whether to buy, borrow, or make props and set pieces. The grips, like everyone else, needs to know the production schedule so that they can clear their calendar for the necessary shooting days. One of *the* most common reasons student films fail is that shooting days are

---

in practice

Here are a few examples of what types of projects are appropriate for small film crews and how small teams can be organized.

Three-Person Crew

Type of project. Very short films or exercises shot without sound (MOS). Very few locations using only available lighting and relatively little set dressing. Small cast.

Breakdown of duties. (person 1) co-producer, writer, director; (person 2) co-producer, P.M., cinematographer; (person 3) co-producer, art department, A.D., grip.

Five-Person Crew

Type of project. Short films involving very simple location sound recording. Few locations using limited lighting and set dressing. Small cast.

Breakdown of duties. (person 1) writer, director; (person 2) producer, P.M./A.D.; (person 3) cinematographer, A.C.; (person 4) art department and grip; (person 5) sound mixer, boom operator.

Eight-Person Crew

Type of project. Intermediate to advanced short films involving extensive sync sound, lighting, set design, and multiple locations.

Breakdown of duties. (person 1) writer, director; (person 2) producer; (person 3) P.M./A.D.; (person 4) cinematographer; (person 5) A.C. and grip; (person 6) art department and grip; (person 7) sound mixer; (person 8) boom operator.

Figure 7-8 A student film production crew meeting in progress. Crew meetings are essential for creative collaboration and logistical coordination.

scheduled without first meeting with the crew to determine their availability. The more your teammates know, the more they can do for the project and the more efficient the production process will be. (**Figure 7-8**).

It is always a good idea to include your crew in the initial script reading in order to allow cast and crew get to know each other. After previsualization, you should also schedule **technical read-throughs** with each department so that you can concentrate on the technical requirements of each area in isolation from the rest. Additionally, you should meet with your crew whenever there are major changes to the visualization, production requirements, locations, or production schedule. Obviously, communication is essential, but can you have too many meetings? Yes. You need to conduct efficient and informative meetings and not hold unnecessary ones just for the sake of meeting. You will respect people's time by not wasting it.

Being a Crewmember

When you are just starting out in filmmaking, it is imperative to crew on as many movies as you possibly can. You always learn an extraordinary amount on well-run productions and on poorly run productions alike. There is no substitute for on-set experience—being part of putting a movie together, watching other people at work, and witnessing the travails, struggles, successes, styles, and procedures of filmmaking firsthand is by far the quickest and most valuable learning you can attain.

As a crewmember yourself, it is essential that you endeavor to be as informed, skilled, and cooperative as possible. A great deal of time, money, energy, and hope is poured into making a movie, so reliability and resourcefulness from every crewperson is essential. Never forget that whatever your role on a film project, no matter how humble, in this business we build our reputations, professional relationships, and careers one film at a time. You must maintain a professional demeanor no matter what your role is. The film producer Cirri Nottage (*Girl Six*) once said to my film class that she always keeps her eye out for the person who excels at their job, even if it's a small job like photocopying and stapling script pages. "If that person is the best and most reliable script photocopier I've seen, then that person is going to be hired again and promoted, because that's the attitude I want on my film set." Initiative, effort, and energy pay off. If you show these traits, you will find yourself on a lot of film sets. Even if you're in school and taking your first film production class, the impression you make on your classmates follows you into the intermediate and advanced courses and beyond, into the professional world. This is how any creative community is developed. Often, the people you call on to help make your first films after graduation are those whom you trusted and collaborated with in school, and if you have proved yourself to be a trustworthy, energetic, and resourceful crew member, you can expect to get a few calls after graduation.

■ ON-CAMERA TALENT

Casting a film means finding the right people to play each of the various roles in your movie and securing their commitment to the project. The formality of this process varies widely depending on the scale of your film, but that doesn't mean you can ever be careless about casting. The success of small films and exercises, all the way up to big-budget features, depends enormously on the quality of the on-camera talent. The on-camera talent can determine the success of a film in two ways—through their performance skill and charisma and through their dedication to the project. Deficiency with either of these can likewise sink an otherwise admirable effort. There is a common adage that says that if a

You should be realistic about the scale of your project, your technical needs, and the spirit of the project when building your production team.

Too Few Team Members

When I was in film school, another student devised a short film that involved a perpetually moving camera. The scene was a small party and the camera mingled with the crowd and caught provocative snippets of dialogue as it entered into and left people's conversations—not unlike a Robert Altman approach to group scenes. It was a terrific idea, but the student filmmaker had only a three-person crew. Practically speaking, he needed a minimum of four people besides himself: one person on camera, one person pushing the dolly, one person holding the boom microphone, and one person on the sound recorder watching the levels carefully. So this director ended up pushing the dolly himself. He also pulled someone from the cast to hold the boom pole. The result was no surprise—unconvincing performances (because the director couldn't pay attention to performances), terrible sound (because the actor knew nothing about positioning a mike), and, even worse, a cast and crew who lost faith in the filmmaker's judgment and abilities.

Too Many Team Members

A few years ago, a friend of mine had some significant festival success with a lovely short film she made about traveling out west with her mother. She shot the film all by herself, over the course of the weeklong trip, with a Super-8mm camera. A professional producer liked her movie and offered to produce her next short film. My friend naturally took her up on the offer and wrote a delicate and poignant script about two neighbors who get stuck on a city rooftop and almost fall in love. With only one exterior location and only two principal actors, the script was designed to be easy to shoot so that she could really connect with her actors and get some memorable performances. Simple, right? Unfortunately, the very generous producer gave the project the red carpet treatment, and on the day of shooting a 12-person crew showed up—including two electricians (for a film using no artificial lighting!). My friend called me from the set, almost crying. She said that the overly large crew felt like a huge anchor and kept her from improvising and or even connecting in any intimate way with her cast—yet, she felt obligated to defer to all of these professionals who had made so many films and were there for free. She lost control of her own film. For example, her first idea was to simply handhold the camera, but when she saw dolly tracks being off-loaded and laid down, the camera being mounted on the boom arm, and a camera crew of four waiting for instructions, she felt obligated to go that way. The result was a film that looked like a million bucks yet felt stiff, overproduced, and lacked much of the director's individual spirit, which was so evident in her first film made with a crew of one.

role is well cast, then 90% of the director's work is done. Although this may be somewhat exaggerated for effect, there is truth in this statement. Without a good actor/character match, your film will never achieve its maximum potential power and resonance. This is not just an issue of experience and qualifications, it's a matter of fit and shared sensibilities for the role. For this reason, casting your film must be done thoughtfully, carefully, and with enough time to really find the best possible performer for each role.

Finding an Actor

When we think about actors in a film, we usually think about people who are trained in the craft, just as directors, cinematographers, and editors are trained in their fields. Trained actors bring a level of expertise to a project and work comfortably with the arcane process of filmmaking. But not all films require trained actors. For simple projects and film exercises, we often write a script for someone we know or we simply cast a friend (or a friend of a friend) (**Figure 7-9**).

This practice is fine. You certainly don't need to go through an elaborate audition process for a simple chase scene exercise, but you should be aware of a few pitfalls:

1. Never use one of your crewmembers as a player in the film. You diminish the size and therefore efficiency of your production team when you pull one of them out. A crew of four people that loses one to become a performer is diminished 25%. Usually this drastic trade-off becomes visible on screen in numerous ways.

■ **Figure 7-9** George Racz with his niece Panna, who was the inspiration for his short film *The Miracle* (see pages 21, 22 and 40). Panna was the obvious choice to play the lead role *(left)*. Ramin Bahrani auditioned more than 600 kids before settling on Alejandro Polanco for the lead in his feature film *Chop Shop* (2007) *(right)*.

2. Cast someone who has a reason to commit to the film. Filmmaking is arduous and time consuming. Actors and acting students have a reason to participate until the very end because it's important for them to gain movie credits and to have "tape," meaning performance samples. The better the project is, the better their "tape," so they have a strong incentive to perform well. However, a close friend who is an economics major might be *willing* to be in your movie, but after the first 10-hour production day your friend may start to lose interest. With midterms coming up and a job to maintain, suddenly the thought of sticking around for three more shooting days isn't so appealing. Frequently, really good friends find the limits of their friendship on film productions.

3. Think twice about casting family members. Family relations are often complex; add to that the stress and arduousness of the filmmaking process, and you're working with a volatile mixture. Besides, do you *really* think you can direct your mom?

4. The super funny guy at parties who does a spot-on perfect imitation of De Niro in *Taxi Driver* can suddenly seem less than convincing once you look at him through a camera lens. The context of a personal relationship is very different from that of a film. What's funny or brilliant among a group of pals kicking back on a Saturday night often doesn't cut it for a broader public.

Because off pitfalls like these, most films that are more involved, ambitious, advanced or costly will cast actors who are trained and committed to being in the movie.

Casting for type means casting someone because they seem naturally right for the part in some way, whether they look the part, or behave just like your character in real life, or have the same profession your character has. Casting for type can work well, especially if the person happens to also be a fine actor. **Nonactors** (people who have never seriously thought about acting before), don't necessarily have the skill to perform as anyone other than themselves, so casting for type is the only way to go. However, one should be careful that the nonactor doesn't suddenly change once the camera is turned on them. I once cast a real-life police officer, mostly because he volunteered to provide two real-life police uniforms for the film. The uniforms looked great, but the performance was another question. With the camera rolling, the officer was unable to keep a straight face. It didn't work so well to have a cop pull up on an emergency call with a silly grin on his face. Cut! You should always do a screen test before you commit nonactors to your movie. Here is what Abbas Kiarostami says about casting nonactors:

I sit and talk with them and turn on the camera without them knowing. After seven or eight minutes, once we've found our subject, I pretend to turn on the camera. If you see no difference between the moments before and after this flick of the switch, you know you have a good actor.

**Abbas Kiarostami (From "Four Golden Rules,"
interview by Paul Cronin, *The Guardian,* June 17, 2005)**

It often happens that a specific "real person" is the inspiration for a specific part; therefore, as a nonactor, this person is the perfect fit, so no additional casting is necessary or even recommended (see **Figure 7-9**, *left*). However, finding the "right" nonactor for a part already written can involve a long process. Gus Van Sant posted a casting call for his 2007 film *Paranoid Park* on Myspace, where ordinary high school kids would see it. His casting call listed the types he was seeking: "skaters, honor roll, cheerleaders, punks, drama kids, musicians, artists, student council, athletes, award winners, class skippers, photographers, band members, leaders, followers, shy kids, class clowns." Reportedly, nearly 3,000 Portland-area teenagers turned up for auditions, including Gabe Nevins, a nonactor who would become the film's star[1] (**Figure 7-10**).

That said, it takes a skilled director, and lots of patience, to get a great performance out of a nonactor. For most films, casting trained actors who have the ability to modulate their performance as needed and the experience to contribute ideas and insight to a character is important in order to get just what you need for your film. Even if your film has no dialogue, a good actor can bring a new interpretive energy and creative resources to the project.

Auditions

An **audition** is an organized process by which you schedule and work with a number of potential performers to determine their suitability to your film. The object of running an audition is to see if a performer is a good fit for the roles you have in the script and to see, to some extent, if you can work with the actors who are auditioning. Always remember that, especially for emerging directors, the actors are auditioning you as much as you are auditioning them. You must represent yourself and your project professionally and always treat actors with respect. The actor is one of your principal creative collaborators. If actors feel as though they will not be allowed to be creative or to collaborate, their interest in your project will certainly diminish.

Running a simple audition is not a terribly difficult task, but it must be well organized in order to convey a sense of your abilities and to assure the performers. You don't want a chaotic audition to be the actors' first impression of your capabilities, because they are sure to anticipate an equally chaotic shoot and will probably stay away. Here are the steps to running a smooth and productive audition:

1. *Put out an audition call for actors.* An audition call can be as basic as asking filmmakers and actors you know for recommendations (word of mouth) and hanging up fliers in a college acting department, or as broad as paying for advertising in trade journals or online (e.g., backstage.com, ReelACT.com, Castingnetworks.com Beakdownexpress.com, Craigslist.com). A public call for actors should have

■ **Figure 7-10** Gus Van Sant *(left)* posted his audition call for *Paranoid Park* (2007) on MySpace to attract local high school kids. From the overwhelming response he chose mostly nonactors for his cast, including lead Gabe Nivens *(center)*. Other cast members, like Taylor Momsen *(right)*, had some professional experience.

[1]"Filmmakers Find Fresh Talent on MySpace," Hugh Hart, www.wired.com, March 14, 2008.

Send headshots to: Nostromo Productions, 45 Lauriston St. Blixy, NV or e-mail to nostromo@mygama.com

"THE HAND-OFF" - CITY UNIVERSITY THESIS FILM

"The Hand-Off" is a ten minute film exploring the first time a child of divorced parents must travel from one house to another for shared custody exchange. Seeking: **Claire**, female lead (mid-thirties); **Gregg**, male lead (mid-thirties); **Ryan**, boy lead (9 yrs.). Shooting: June 2011. Non-Union, no pay. Meals, transportation and DVD copy provided. Send headshot/bio by April 5 to: Adela De La Vega, Dept. of Film, City University, City, State, zip or via email to Alavega@cityumail.edu

SHORT FILM "THE MUTE'S CONFESSION"

leads for short film. Liam (45-55)

■ **Figure 7-11** A casting call posted in a trade journal or online casting service needs to be brief but must include all pertinent information.

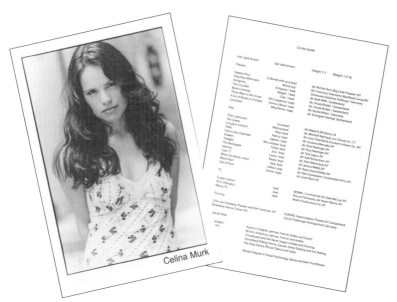

■ **Figure 7-12** A typical headshot and bio. Most serious actors have professional photographs taken for their headshots and will also submit a résumé listing their acting experience.

all of the basic information potential actors need in order to decide whether they are right for the part and how to contact the filmmaker (**Figure 7-11**). When an actor contacts you, a **headshot/bio** is the standard calling card. It usually consists of an 8-by-10-inch photograph on one side and a résumé on the other (**Figure 7-12**). Keep in mind, however, that when you open up your search to people with little or no acting experience, you might get a small photograph and a handwritten letter.

2. *Begin short listing.* Once you have received all of the headshot/bios and personal recommendations, you need to select who you are going to audition by reviewing their credentials and evaluating their photographs. It's tough to judge a person based on one photograph, but for the moment it's all you have. As you review the bios you make "yes," "maybe," and "no" piles. This is actually an illuminating process, because for the first time you are being asked to put a face to your screenplay characters. Occasionally you'll realize that you didn't know as much about your character as you thought. You'll also begin to see a certain flexibility in the character by noticing how they seem to change as you imagine each different face in the role. This is only the beginning of your encounter with the interpretation of your characters through the body and performance of an actor. The "yes" pile of performers, those who both look right for the part and have the performance background you are seeking, is your short list. But be advised—keep it short!

3. *Find an audition space.* To hold the audition, find a space that is large enough for all of the people you need at the audition and for the performers to stand, sit, move, and perform comfortably. The group attending the audition usually includes the director, the producer, and people to read lines with the actors. It is not a good idea to hold auditions in your home. Many potential actors will not go to a private residence to audition for an unknown director. It is also preferable to have a separate, comfortable waiting space to put the next-in-line actor. This is called the **green room**, a place where actors can relax, drink some water, and go over their lines. Incidentally, no one really knows why an actor's reception room is called the "green room," but the term has been part of the theater world since the 18th century.

4. *Decide on audition material.* It is important to be clear about what you want the actors to do in the audition. Obviously, you will need to have them perform a scene or two from your film so that you can see how each actor fits the role. Reading from script pages that actors are given minutes before the audition is called a **cold reading**. If a cold reading from the script involves dialogue with another person, then you need

to have someone of decent ability at the audition to read with all of the actors. Cold readings alone are sometimes not the greatest measure of an actor's abilities, so it's also good to have each actor present a monologue of their own choosing, something they have previously developed, to really give them an opportunity to show what they believe is their best, most prepared, and most convincing performance. Most trained actors have several monologues prepared and ready for auditions. But you need to tell them what sort of monologue they should bring so that *you* see what you need to see from them. A Shakespearean monologue? A modern monologue? Drama? Comedy? If you're doing a silent film with physical humor, maybe you don't want any words at all and need to see a short physical performance. I once made a film based on a series of adaptations of poetry by Pablo Neruda, which required the actors to speak stanzas of a poem to each other as if the lines were dialogue. So I asked the actors auditioning for me to bring in either some modern poetry or a modern monologue that they felt had poetic language. Once you have your short list and your audition space and you've decided on the material you want each performer to present, you're ready to schedule the audition.

5. *Supervise contact and scheduling.* Contact each performer and schedule enough time between auditions so that you can reflect and jot notes about what you saw. Do not schedule performers in so tightly that their auditions overlap and a waiting crowd starts to accumulate in your green room. When you contact each performer be clear about (a) where the audition is, (b) what you want the performer to do (i.e., modern monologue and cold read), and (c) how long the audition will last. Also be prepared to answer more detailed questions about the project.

6. *Run the audition.* A typical audition runs something like this: (a) As the actors wait their turns, give them the cold-read script pages to look over. (b) When you are ready, bring the actor into the audition room. Common courtesy is the rule. Greet the actor, introduce everyone in the room, and describe in more detail the project and the specific role. It's important to allow actors to relax and understand just what they're stepping into and who is watching them. (c) Give the actor an idea of your shooting schedule and when they need to be available. If there is an unworkable schedule conflict, then there is no need to waste their time, or yours, with an audition. Simply thank them for coming in and call the next person. (d) Have the actor perform the monologue they've prepared. If after this you are already sure that someone won't work in the role, then there is no need to waste time by keeping the person longer. Simply thank the actor for coming in and call the next person. If you like what the performer has done, then move on to the cold reading. (e) Give the actors any necessary context or background for the script pages they are reading and have them do the cold read. Remember, if the scene involves dialogue with another character, you need to have a person at the audition to read with the actor. If after the cold read it's clear that the actor won't work in the role, then simply express your thanks and call the next person. If they seem promising, then (f) work with the performer on the script pages and try to get a few adjustments and nuances in the performance. Have them try the scene with a different approach or tone. If the actor seems flexible and responds well to directing, then place them on the callback list (see later); (g) thank the actor for coming in and say that you'll be in touch. Once the person leaves, jot a few notes on your audition sheet and call in the next audition.

You should never prolong an audition that you know for certain isn't going well. It's not courteous to keep people working for you after you've already made up your mind, and it's a waste of your time, too. It's always best to politely thank them and let them go. The shortest audition I ever had ended just after the first handshake. I was casting for the role of Ray, a sweet, overly sensitive, and perpetually worried father of a 15-year-old daughter. One actor strode into the room, shook my hand, and, without allowing me to say one word, proceeded to tell me what he was going to do, in what order, and where he wanted us to sit for his monologue. He also announced that he preferred to do two monologues and skip the cold reading. I simply shook his hand again and thanked him for coming in. I explained that I didn't think he would work out and I didn't want to waste his time. He thanked me, turned on his heel, and left.

■ **Figure 7-13** Videotaping callbacks is a good strategy to see how a performer responds to the presence of a camera.

Callbacks

Callbacks are second auditions in which you look closely at all of your most promising candidates. Callbacks work primarily with the material of the script to really establish character/actor compatibility. It's common to send the entire script to your callback choices so that they can be more familiar with the material. Often, if a role involves a close relationship with another character, callbacks can involve pairing up performers to see what kind of chemistry exists between them. Although we generally don't videotape the first auditions, it's important to videotape the callbacks as a screen test (**Figure 7-13**). Some actors can perform wonderfully in front of people but stiffen up when they're on camera. This is especially true of nonactors. You need to know this before you commit to a performer. Also, when taping the callbacks make sure that you take many different angles and shots of the performances. Faces are important, but so is movement and voice. Take time to set up lights and microphones so that you get a high-quality recording. If you're shooting is from a single angle, way back in the corner of the room with lousy audio and dim lighting, the tape won't have enough information to help you make your final decisions.

Casting and Commitments

Based on your impression from the callbacks, you should be able to make your decisions and call your chosen actors to tell them you'd like to work with them on the film. Once you have thoroughly explored their availability and secured their commitment, you should inform the other callback actors that they were wonderful, but you decided to go with another performer. Of course, thank them for the time they gave auditioning for you. Actors are extremely valuable for a filmmaker. We need them to turn our literary characters into flesh-and-blood people. You should always be professional and respectful because, as I've mentioned, courtesy is important. Also, you never know when you might need that actor for a future project of yours, or for a colleague's film, and you want them to feel that they'd like to work with you someday.

Releases, Minors, and Unions

The shortest, simplest film, if done well, might play in festivals or be picked up for broadcasting. You never know, but you should be prepared for your film's potential success and public exposure. So it's important to obtain a talent release from each actor before shooting begins. A **talent release** (see www.voiceandvisionbook.com) is a legal document, signed before the cameras roll, simply stating that the performer gives you the right to use their image and voice in your film. Sometimes securing this right involves a fee, and sometimes actors work for free ("free" usually means, food, transportation, and a copy of the final film). The talent release protects you should the actor have a change of heart later on. As a student, I remember a classmate's film in which a fairly minor character felt, after the premiere screening, that the director made her "look fat" in the movie. She told the director that she didn't want him showing this film in public and that she'd sue him if he did. The director hadn't obtained a release and the actor's father was a prominent lawyer. Because he was unable to reshoot her scenes, the film ended up in the director's desk drawer.

If you are working with children as talent, it only stands to reason that you need to obtain a release from their legal guardian. Working with minors also requires you to organize your shoots around school schedules and the parents' or guardians' schedules, because they have a legal right to accompany their child to every film shoot. It is in your best interest to have someone to specifically look after the children on the set. Keeping track of a child on a film shoot is a full-time responsibility, and it's best done by the legal guardian.

Also, in general, you need to make special assurances for the safety and well-being of any child on the set. This means working shorter hours, allowing for regular breaks, and having plenty of healthy food and drinks. You may be able to persuade an adult actor to gut it out and stay an extra couple of hours to get those last shots, but when the going gets tough, kids usually need a nap! Before you proceed with any film involving children, check with your local or state film office: there are usually fairly strict legal requirements that you must know about.

Actors Unions

You'll notice in the call for talent (see Figure 7-11) that the ad clearly states that the call is for a nonunion film. There are two major unions that look after the interest of professional actors who have gained enough credits to become members. The union that most filmmakers encounter is the **Screen Actors Guild** (or **SAG**). SAG union actors generally work on union films (those that utilize union crews, union directors, etc.). However, exceptions are made for low-budget independent films and student films. SAG has developed a variety of contract agreements for student films, shorts, and ultra-low-budget projects. To use a SAG actor in your nonunion student film, you must enter into the SAG student film agreement. Generally speaking, this agreement protects the actor by making sure that certain baseline requirements are in place: (1) You must prove you own the copyright on the screenplay that you are shooting—in other words, you have the legal right to make this film. (2) If any money is made from this production (through festivals, broadcast, or other distribution), then the union actors are paid their minimum union wages before anyone else involved in the production is paid. (3) You must adhere to regulation scheduling, meal, and safety procedures and maintain accurate time sheets for each union performer. (4) You must provide proof that the production and the actors are adequately insured. These are just the basics to give you an idea of what it means to use a union actor and to enter into a SAG student contract or independent film contract. (For complete information about these contracts, go to www.SagIndie.org.)

■ WORKING WITH ACTORS I: BEFORE THE CAMERA ROLLS

The Actor as Creative Collaborator

Once you have assembled your cast, you will discover that there is a new energy that actors bring to the filmmaking process. Actors are creative collaborators whose job it is to bring a character off the page and into being. As such, they bring an interpretive energy that a smart director will acknowledge and cultivate. Starting from the callbacks, you are forming both your collaboration method as well as the final form of the characters in your film as you work and rework scenes, gathering from an actor their thoughts, reactions, and insights. This process continues until the last day of shooting. Broadly speaking, one of the principal jobs of a director is to guide actors to an understanding of their respective characters that is in line with the script and with the director's vision of the final film. However, based on the new insight, expertise, and energy of the performers, don't be afraid to allow your characters to evolve into something you might not have anticipated, as long as it remains appropriate for your story. It's not uncommon during rehearsals, and even during shooting, to rewrite lines and scenes to better fit a new concept of a character. Listen to director John Daschbach describe his collaborative rehearsal process during the making of his short film *Waking Dreams*, which you can see at www.voiceandvisionbook.com:

> *What I can say about the acting is that these two demonstrate the maxim (to which I heartily subscribe) that when it comes to actors, "90% of directing is casting." And I would add, the other 10% is having adequate rehearsal time. We shot the film in three days and we rehearsed for three days—a ratio which is not possible for feature films, but for shorts, it actually is and I would encourage as much rehearsal as possible. Our process consisted of the three of us sitting in a room and just going very slowly through the script scene by scene, line by line, and encouraging the actors to stop and ask questions, which they did often, whenever they didn't feel they quite understood*

■ **Figure 7-14** Rehearsals on Daschbach's *Waking Dreams* included close readings of the script to collaborate on scene and dialogue changes with his cast. A simple accommodation Daschbach made for actress Tina Holmes at her request was to change her character from a temp who nervously swigs coffee to one who nervously nibbles red licorice strings. Holmes felt this detail helped her better connect to her character.

a beat or a line. Sometimes I was able to adequately explain the intent; sometimes the other actor helped by explaining their perspective on the moment—what their character was playing/thinking; and sometimes it lead to a revision in the script where lines were cut, reordered, or replaced with something new—when one of us threw out an alternative line or beat that made the moment work better. In rehearsals, I always encourage the actors to feel free to suggest alternatives that they feel they can incorporate better into their character and what is happening dramatically at any given moment (Figure 7-14).

Rehearsals

Rehearsals are the time you spend in preproduction running through scenes in preparation for shooting. In general, some degree of rehearsing is always necessary. The length and depth of your rehearsal period depend greatly on the needs of the project and the availability of the cast (especially if they are not getting paid). There are no rules here. Some directors assiduously avoid a lengthy rehearsal period, thinking that it bleeds freshness out of a performance; others engage in long and detailed rehearsals in order to prepare and develop scenes thoroughly in preproduction. On short student films and low-budget independent films, rehearsals are generally not elaborate or lengthy; however, rehearsals of some sort, before the camera rolls, are a good idea. Not only do rehearsals allow for the integration of many new ideas, but they also can cut down on production time.

One process that is necessary for any film is a read-through. **A read-through** is a reading of the script by the actors, with all principal creative people in attendance. The read-through allows everyone involved to get to know each other, which is especially important for actors who will be performing together. Also, hearing the script read out loud, in front of people, illuminates any glaring problems with the script, like lines that simply don't work, plausibility problems, or character inconsistencies. It's common for the script to go through a solid rewrite after a read-through. A read-through is also a place where conceptual ideas—from characterization to visualization—are discussed so that all participants understand what the director is striving for. It's important for a director to be thoroughly prepared for the read-through. Everyone will want to understand the film and the director's vision for the film, so crewmembers, especially actors, will ask detailed questions.

Scene work rehearsals are a more detailed examination of specific scenes and aim to refine the interpretation of the drama. Scene work can include a close script analysis and scene run-throughs, in which dialogue, movement, and interactions are examined to develop—for the actors and often for the director, too—the nuances of characterization, motivation, dramatic context, emotional content, and scene dynamics. Scene work rehearsal also involves rough **blocking**, which is the coordination of the movements of the actors in the scene. More often than not this is done on a mock set, but if it can be done on the actual set, so much the better. As I mention in Chapter 5, scene work rehearsals can be important to the previsualization process because through working with the actors a director can better determine critical narrative moments, emotional pacing, and physical movement, which in turn suggests strategies for camera angles, edit points, and scene coverage in general. Generally, scene work is done with the director, the actors, and perhaps the A.D. If the rehearsal involves blocking, the cinematographer might be there too. Keep in mind that not every scene needs such thorough rehearsals; usually these are reserved for the more dramatically or physically complex scenes.

One final type of rehearsal is actually not part of preproduction but occurs during the production process. **On-set rehearsals** (or **on-set run-throughs**) are rehearsals during the preparation of the actual shooting on location (see Chapter 17). At this stage, on-set blocking rehearsals are mandatory; they are not only important for familiarizing the actors with the actual location, but they are also essential for the camera and sound departments to know exactly where lights, camera, microphones, and recording levels need to be in any given take. Most of the detailed analysis work should have been done before this point, but actors, directors, and cinematographers will invariably respond to the actual shooting environment and will want to make adjustments to their interpretations along the way.

Working with Trained Actors

It is not within the scope of this book to engage in a thorough discussion of the actor-director relationship and working method. This is one of the most complex collaborations in film, and like all complex relationships, methods and processes differ depending on the unique chemistry of the individuals involved. There are many, many books on the subject on the market, and some of them are good, so refer to the Recommended Readings section of this book for further study. That said, here are a few general and commonly shared thoughts on working with actors:

1. *Establish respect and trust.* The actor's job is to inhabit a role, to become someone they are not and be convincing at it. The public is very aware of actors and what actors do, in a way that exceeds the awareness of any other member off the filmmaking team, so an actor's ability to pull off the job is on display like no one else's—it's the actor's body, face, and voice. For this reason, the actor is especially vulnerable. The first job of a director is to establish trust and make an actor feel safe to experiment, make mistakes, and find their way as they explore a role. You must also demonstrate throughout the production that you know what you're doing so that the actor can trust that you'll make a good film from their good performance. Additionally, it is important that you show the actor—as with every other crewmember—that you respect and want their contribution. One of the most common ways that young filmmakers lose the trust of their cast is by concentrating exclusively on the technical aspects of the film. With money and time so limited and pressure so great on the set, it's easy to get pulled into devising camera angles, setting up lights, attending to location details and overlook the actors completely. Then once the shot is set up, you call the actors in and shout "Action!" and expect them to perform. To a large extent, a film crew needs to protect the director from technical tasks on the set; that way, the director's time can be devoted to getting the actor emotionally prepared for each shot (see page 375).

2. *Offer guidance, not commands.* It is important for actors to feel like they themselves can inhabit a role. If they can't "get there" in a way that makes sense to them, then they'll never be truly convincing. This is why line readings (i.e. the director performing the way a line should be delivered and asking the actor to mimic) never work. Actors need to be coaxed into the performance you are seeking in such a way that they "understand" your ideas and approach in the context of the character and themselves. How a director guides them to the right performance differs depending on who the director and actor are and the actor's training. In fact, it's not unusual for directors to find themselves employing different approaches for different actors on the same film!

However, the place to start during rehearsals is not quite so mysterious. Remember, you will have already engaged in a few script read-throughs, so you and your actors will have discussed the story and character to a certain extent. Start with a scene that is revealing of character—that way everyone will get a handle of the character right off the bat. Run the scene and see how it works. After the scene is done, simply discuss what worked, what didn't work, and explore why. Ask your actors why they made the choices they made and really listen to them. Suggest some performance adjustments based on your needs and their thoughts. Then, run the scene again. It should be better. Talk with them again about what worked, what didn't work, and why, and repeat as needed. With a little give and take, you'll get there. Always be as articulate as possible as to *why* you are seeking a particular approach or nuance. What it means to be a "trained actor" is that the performer has learned to modulate and adjust the performance according to the expressed needs of the director; however, if you can't convincingly articulate why you want something, then the actor may not ever be able to find it.

3. *Don't overdirect.* There are two issues around overdirecting. The first is doggedly insisting on a specific interpretation, which may not be possible for an actor. In these cases you need to be flexible and work with the particular abilities of the performer you have and devise another interpretation that works all around. The second kind of overdirecting means to drag an actor through unnecessary rehearsals, character analysis, trust exercises, emotional beat analysis, and so on and so on for simple scenes or moments. Sometimes all the "direction" you need to give is, "Put your coat on, grab your keys, and leave the room." There's no need to go through an intensive method acting emotional recall session for every little moment.

4. *Keep it fresh.* Related to the idea of overdirecting is the idea of overrehearsing. Many directors avoid rehearsing too much for fear that it bleeds the freshness out of the performance. One director I know does scene work rehearsal but asks the actors to only play at half the emotional level (fairly flat). Other directors will take their actors to the threshold of really nailing the scene and then they'll stop, saving the first dead-on performance for when the camera is rolling. Other directors don't directly rehearse scenes that are in the script but instead rehearse hypothetical scenes around (before and after) the actual written scene. There are no rules here (and plenty of superstitions) but the principle is important to note—don't bleed out the spontaneity of a performance by overworking a scene in rehearsal. (Figure 7-15.)

Working with Nonactors

As I mentioned earlier, a nonactor is usually cast for type, meaning that the performer is very close to who your character is in the film. Having the same age, background, jobs, preoccupations, and perspectives as the film's character, this nonactor is close to being the authentic person. So the first task of a director who is working with nonactors is to protect that authenticity. You must be careful not to squeeze the real person out; instead, you must bring the person out. Think of a nonactor as a source of character material, not someone who inhabits a character you've created. Of course, how to get naturalistic (or un-self-conscious) performances from a regular person when you stick a camera in their face is tricky and depends a lot on the specific person involved. Here are a few approaches to working with nonactors that are common among directors like Abbas Kiarostami, Ramin Bahrani, Gus Van Zant, and Lance Hammer, who all use nonactors extensively:

1. *Make sure your film idea is appropriate for nonactors.* Not all films are right for nonactors. If you're talking about a lead role, the film must, in some way, resonate with the real life of that person. If you want your written dialogue to be performed as-is or if you're on a very tight schedule, you may be better off with a trained actor.

■ **Figure 7-15** Although very similar in their naturalistic tone, *Frozen River* (2008, *top*) benefited from the deep experience of professional actors, including Melissa Leo *(left)* who received an Oscar nomination for her performance (with director Courtney Hunt), while Hammer's *Ballast* (2008, *bottom*) was well regarded for the authentic performances of its cast of nonactors, including JimMyron Ross *(left)* and Michael J. Smith Sr. *(right)*.

2. *Turn the camera on right away.* Put a camera on the nonactor immediately (throughout rehearsals) and keep it on them all the time. The more familiar a nonactor is with being in front of a camera (even a small video camera), the less self-conscious they will be when the actual shooting begins.

3. *Do not ask the nonactor to memorize written dialogue.* Asking a nonactor to memorize and then duplicate lines of dialogue from a preexisting script is contradictory to casting for type. Many directors who work with nonactors never even show them a script. Instead, outline in detail what the scene involves and tell them generally what they might say—as they rehearse the scene, the performer will use their own words to express themselves. This rehearsal process involves allowing the nonactor to play out the scene, with their speech, enough times that they essentially memorized their own words. Along the way, the director should be tweaking the scene based on any new ideas emerging from the performer as they negotiate the moments.

4. *Actions help, even small ones: .* Giving specific actions can create a context for the performance and makes delivering dialogue easier for a nonactor. Small actions that an actor does during a scene are called **business**. The more familiar your nonactors are with their '"business," the more comfortable they'll be performing in general. I had a student who used her eight- year-old brother for a scene between a teen-aged sister (played by a trained actor) and her little brother. The filmmaker's brother, a nonactor, just wasn't getting the hang of what he was supposed to say; he was self-conscious and was getting impatient. Then my student got a brilliant idea. She told him to play his favorite Xbox video game while he interacted with the sister. It worked. The boy was instantly comfortable and his dialogue came out smooth and natural. Also, the scene gained strength because the boy was doing what boys do, even when an older sister is trying to have a conversation with them. Business is important for trained actors as well.

5. *Don't overanalyze.* As mentioned previously, when directors talk with trained actors they often engage in metaphoric dialogue or analytical exploration to guide the actor to discover character motivation and nuances. Well, for the nonactor that sort of oblique process can be confusing. It's better to be direct with your direction. "Right here you're hurt because she's forgotten everything you've done for her." Then let the performers show you what they do when they're hurt and work from there.

6. *Maintain a flexible visual style and procedure.* If you're working with nonactors as leads, you cannot expect them to work within a rigid and standardized production process. Expecting them to hit specific marks—for example, where a light has been set up or where the focus will be right while they perform—is asking a lot. You need to devise a production process and style that allows for their comfort; otherwise all that lovely authenticity that prompted you to cast a nonactor will be squashed. Abbas Kiarostami offers us a good example. When he works with nonactors he doesn't use slates or scream "Action!" or "Cut!" For Kiarostami, this is contradictory to what you're after because you're essentially saying, "now start performing" and "now stop performing." But a nonactor isn't really performing. You want your nonactors to be themselves as much as possible. So Kiarostami just speaks to the actors, eases them into the moment, and when the scene is running he signals camera and sound with a gesture or a look to start rolling.

Working with Extras

If you write a script with a scene set in a crowded bar, you'll need to find people to play the crowd. If you write a scene in which your hero is the last person in a long line at an ATM cash machine, then you'll need people to make that line. If you need to shoot a scene in which a young professor is lecturing to a class of 20 students, then you'll need to find 20 willing people to sit in a classroom while you shoot. For each of these scenarios, you need extras. **Extras** are performers who have no lines or important actions in a film but who populate a scene and give it a sense of realism and authenticity. Extras are one detail that many novice filmmakers take for granted. Inexperienced filmmakers are so immersed in the big demands of a film—lead characters, locations, and equipment—that they often think that extras will just be there when needed; they think, extras have super small roles and no lines, so they must be easy to find, right? The fact is, being an extra requires a lot of time for very little payoff. Extras usually don't even get a credit in the film. It's *always* difficult to find people willing to stay on a set for hours and hours, doing very little, while you shoot your scene. So keep this in mind when you write your script. Small films on tight budgets should try to minimize the need for extras or find a clever alternate solution.

in practice

Finding Thousands of Extras

In his first short film, *Vive le Premier Mai* (1995), the French filmmaker Didier Rouget tells the sweet, simple story of a man who finds his true love, but then loses her in the crowd of a huge public demonstration, and finally, through a clever device, finds her again. Rouget set this film right in the middle of the traditional May 1 workers' demonstration in Paris in which tens of thousands of people march in the streets (**Figure 7-16**). Cameras are abundant, so no one noticed one more. His film involved a production crew of three and only two principal actors, but a cast of 40,000 extras! You can see this short film at http://didierrouget.com

■ **Figure 7-16** Emmanuel Salinger in Rouget's *Vive le Premier Mai* (1995). Rouget obtained 40,000 extras for free by setting the story of his short film during the traditional May 1 workers' demonstration in Paris.

Can't Find 10 Extras

Here is a cautionary tale. The producer on a recent student film project managed to acquire, for only a few hours, a very hard-to-get location, Grand Central Station in New York City. The film involved three shoeshine men talking and polishing the shoes of an elite business clientele. Everything was in place for the shoot except one thing, the 10 or so extras who would be playing the elite business clientele. The producer and director erroneously assumed that they could simply enlist passersby and offer them a free shoeshine if they'd be in the movie. But this was Grand Central Station, where everyone is in a hurry. What they discovered was that no one, not one person, was interested in sitting still for 10 minutes for a free shoeshine given by an actor playing a role, nor were they particularly interested in being on film.

Rather than scrap the entire shoot (and lose the time and location forever), the crew called up all of their friends and asked them to dress in suits and hurry down to Grand Central Station. A few hours later, about six friends showed up—many with less-than-convincing suits, several wearing sneakers, and most with haircuts that would not exactly cut it in a corporate boardroom. With time ticking away, the crew shot quickly and eliminated a lot of coverage. In the end they managed to get the basic footage they needed, but the clientele did not look much like they came from an elite business class; rather, they looked like a bunch of dressed-up college undergraduates, and the film lost an important component of its satire and irony.

The Contact Sheet

In the intense and creative environment of a movie production, the cast and crew become like a family for the duration of project. Communication is critical to keep this family involved, engaged, and informed. There is one very simple form that is essential for this necessary communication, the **contact sheet**. A contact sheet is a simple list of who is involved in the project, what their role is, and their contact information (phone and email). Keep in mind that your contact sheet also has value long after the film is completed. You may want to get back in touch with some of your extended filmmaking family when you make your next film. So save that contact sheet!

PART III TOOLS AND TECHNIQUES: PRODUCTION

The Film System

■ THE BASICS OF THE FILM SYSTEM

The essentials of the film system have changed very little since its invention in the 19th century. Film is a mechanical and photochemical motion picture system. It creates the illusion of motion through the rapid presentation of a series of sequential photographic images fixed to a flexible and transparent strip of cellulose. At a rate of 24 frames per second each image is projected onto a screen and held stationary long enough for the viewer to register the image before it is quickly replaced with the subsequent still image, which is again held for a fraction of a second, and so on and so on. The viewer perceives this rapid presentation of still images as motion through the perceptual phenomenon known as **short-range apparent motion.**[1] Simply put, when shown a rapidly changing series of sequential still images in which there is only slight difference from image to image, humans processes this visual stimuli with the same perceptual mechanism used in the visual processing of real motion. This mechanism transforms the series of still images into motion through the psychological and physiological interpolation of information between the still frames (**Figure 8-1**).

Essential to the perception of motion is that each still image must be held stationary for a fraction of a second and then rapidly replaced with the next stationary image. If we were to simply pull a strip of film smoothly in front of a projector's lamp, the result would be one long vertical blur. A movie projector must have the ability to move one frame into position, hold it steady while the lamp and lens project that image onto the screen, and then repeat this action with the next frame, and so on, at a precise and regular pace. This regular stop-and-start mechanical action, positioning and holding one frame at a time, is called **intermittent movement.** Both film cameras and film projectors have the same intermittent movement; cameras use it to record images and projectors use it to display images.

Frame Rate

Through a mechanical and photochemical process, the film camera creates 24 photographic exposures per second on a strip of flexible celluloid coated with a light-sensitive emulsion layer. These discrete photographic images are visible to the eye after a laboratory has processed the film. When these images are projected back at the same rate (24 fps) with a film projector, the audience perceives normal motion. Recording live events through a series of sequential still images at a rate of 24 frames per second (fps) uses 36 feet of film per minute in the 16mm film format (**Figure 8-2**) and 90 feet per minute in the 35mm format.

It is helpful to think of a film camera and a film projector as essentially the same mechanism, with the transmission of the image reversed. A film camera gathers light from the outside world, through its lens, and focuses that image

■ **Figure 8-1** The difference between still images in a strip of film is very slight.

[1]"The Myth of Persistence of Vision Revisited," Joseph and Barbara Anderson, *Journal of Film and Video,* Vol. 45, No. 1 (Spring 1993): 3-12.

16mm Footage & Running Time QUICK REFERENCE
16mm @ 24 fps = 36 feet / minute
1 foot = 40 frames
100 feet = 2 minutes 47 seconds
400 feet = 11 minutes 6 seconds

TIME	FOOTAGE	FEET	Min : Sec
1 sec.	24 frames	50	1 : 23
2 sec.	1 ft. 8 fr.		
3 sec.	1 ft. 32 fr.	100	2 : 46
4 sec.	2 ft. 16 fr.	150	4 : 10
5 sec.	3 ft.		
10 sec.	6 ft.	200	5 : 33
25 sec.	15 ft.	300	8 : 20
30 sec.	18 ft.		
50 sec.	30 ft.	400	11 : 06
1 min.	36 ft.		
5 min.	180 ft.	500	13 : 53
10 min.	360 ft.	800	22 : 13
15 min.	540 ft.		
20 min.	720 ft.	1000	27 : 46
25 min.	900 ft.	1200	33 : 20
30 min.	1080 ft.		

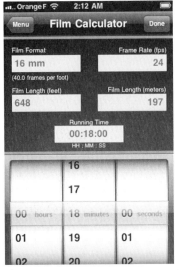

Figure 8-2 Quick reference footage chart for 16mm film running at 24 fps. Free footage calculator apps, like this one from Kodak *(bottom, left),* are easy to find online

onto the plane of the film to create the exposures. A film projector pushes light from within the apparatus, through the images and through a lens, to focus and project that image onto the surface plane of a movie screen. The intermittent motion for exposing and projecting the film therefore must be identical.

Twenty-four frames per second (24 fps) is the standard frame rate for all projectors and film cameras running at what is known as **sync speed** (Figure 8-3). While most projectors do not vary this frame rate, many film cameras are built with **variable-speed motors,** which allow them to alter the frame rate. We can, for example, shoot our film at 8 fps, 12 fps, or 72 fps. When we shoot at a frame rate faster than 24 fps, we get **slow motion** when we project at 24fps. The faster our camera's frame rate, the slower the motion will appear when projected. A movement that takes one second in real time, like a glass shattering on the floor, will take three seconds on screen when shot at 72 fps and four seconds if you shoot the glass breaking at 96 fps. Conversely, altering the camera's speed to frame rates below 24 fps (e.g., 12 fps or 8 fps) will create motion that appears sped up when projected. This is called **under-cranking,** and the slower the frame rate of the camera, the faster the motion appears when projected (Figure 8-4).

The extreme end of under-cranking is called **time lapse,** which occurs when one is taking exposures at frame rates as slow as 3 frames per *minute* or 1 frame per *minute.* A camera running at 1 frame per minute will record 24 minutes of activity in only 24 frames. When projected back at 24 fps, those 24 minutes will now happen in one second. With time lapse we can see movements that usually occur gradually over many minutes or hours, like the sun setting or storm clouds forming, in a matter of seconds (Figure 8-5).

Film and Sound

For all practical intents and purposes, film is a **double system sound** medium, which means that motion pictures shot on film needing synchronous sound recorded with the image must use a second apparatus to record the audio (see Chapter 15). So while the film camera records the image, a sound recording device records the audio separately to tape, flash memory, or a hard drive (Figure 8-6). This means that the images and the

24 frames = 1 second

■ **Figure 8-3** A 16mm filmstrip (actual size).

■ **Figure 8-4** In *2001: A Space Odyssey* (1968, *left*), the use of slow motion adds majesty to an evolutionary leap forward in intelligence. In *A Clockwork Orange* (1971, *right*), fast motion makes a caricature of the sexual act (both films by Stanley Kubrick).

■ **Figure 8-5** Time-lapse photography. Shooting at extremely slow frame rates lets you capture actions that take many minutes or hours to complete, as in this scene from Amiel's *Creation* (2009), which shows the complete decomposition of a bird in 22 seconds.

synchronous audio are separate and must, at some point later, be brought together. This process, know as **synching dailies,** is covered in detail on page 431. For now it is just important to note that, unlike DV cameras, which can record both image and sound with the same device and on the same material, film cameras do not record sound.

THE GENERIC FILM CAMERA

Even though there are many differences between cameras of different manufacturers and from model to model, the basic components and functions of all film cameras are essentially the same. Film camera technology is not especially mysterious or even terribly complex. Once you understand the basic mechanisms that all film cameras share, you can approach any specific camera with a reliable base of knowledge and with the confidence that you can figure out the

■ **Figure 8-6** Film is a double system sound medium. D.P. Rémon Fromont captures images with a film camera *(left),* while sound recordist Olivier Hespel *(right)* records audio on his digital recorder on location at the Sea of Galilee for *Zindeeq* (Kleifi, 2009).

particularities in no time at all. All film cameras have the following components: the **body,** the **gate,** the **movement,** the **drive mechanism/film transport,** a **viewing system,** and a **lens** (**Figure 8-7**). Here we'll look at each component in detail except the lens, which has its own chapter (see Chapter 10).

Body

The body of a film camera is a light-tight chamber in which film can be transported in complete darkness, exposed in a controlled manner, and then taken up in darkness. In many 16mm cameras, small rolls of film can be loaded directly into the body of the

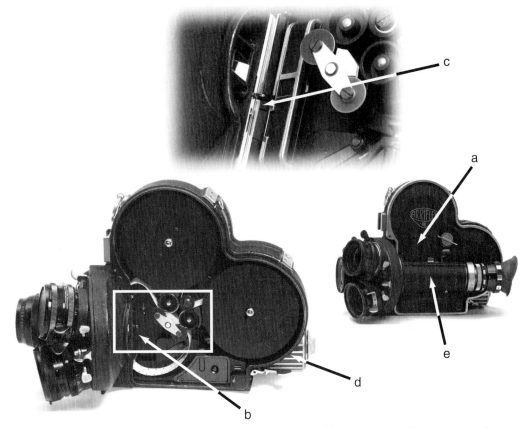

■ **Figure 8-7** The basic film camera: (a) body, (b) gate, (c) movement, (d) drive mechanism/film transport, and (e) viewing system.

camera; cameras that use longer rolls of film require a **film magazine** (**Figure 8-8**), which is essentially an extension of the light-tight camera body (see "Film Loads").

Gate

The only place where film stock is exposed to light is in the gate. The gate is composed of two plates. The **aperture plate,** located just behind the lens, has a rectangular opening called the **aperture opening.** The dimensions of this opening are the exact full-frame aspect ratio dimensions of the film format. In a standard 16mm camera, the aperture opening is 1.33:1. If you are shooting Super 16mm, the camera will be outfitted with a 1.66:1 aperture plate (**Figure 8-9**).

■ **Figure 8-8** The magazine. A lightproof extension of the camera body, the magazine permits the rapid reloading of film in a camera. Pictured here is an Aaton Xterá with a magazine for 400 foot film loads *(arrow)*.

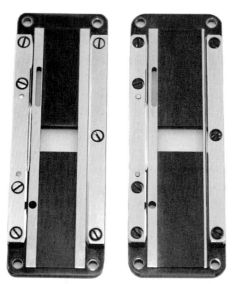

■ **Figure 8-9** A 1.33:1 aperture plate for regular 16mm filming *(left)* and a 1.66:1 Super 16 aperture plate *(right)*.

■ **Figure 8-10** The film plane. All film cameras have a marking on their bodies identifying exactly where the film is exposed to light. Camera-to-subject distance, for precise focusing, is measured from this exact spot.

■ **Figure 8-11** Carelessness during film loading can result in debris becoming lodged in the gate creating a permanent addition to the image; Woody Allen exploited this flaw to comedic effect in his film *What's Up, Tiger Lilly?* (1966).

The lens focuses all the light gathered from your scene right through this aperture opening, where it exposes (or tags) the film. The film is sandwiched between the aperture plate and the **pressure plate,** which applies constant, gentle pressure to assure that the film lies perfectly flat as it moves vertically through the gate. The light-sensitive emulsion side of the film faces the aperture and the base side of the film is against the pressure plate. The exact position of the film between these two plates is called the **film plane** (or **focal plane**) (**Figure 8-10**), and it is represented by the symbol φ, which is etched into the exterior body of the camera. Every frame of your film is exposed right here. The edges of the aperture plate become the edges of each frame. It is therefore essential that you keep your gate clean. An errant hair dancing in the aperture opening blocks light like a shadow puppet (**Figure 8-11**) and will become part of your image. On a film set, the camera operator should regularly "check the gate" (see page 372).

Movement: Claw and Shutter Mechanism

The claw and shutter work in concert with one another to precisely position and expose each and every frame of film (**Figure 8-12**). A strip of motion picture film is always perforated on one or both sides with **sprocket holes.** These sprocket holes allow the strip of film to be easily, accurately, and gently transported through the camera.

The claw is located on the edge of the aperture plate and is responsible for positioning the film in the gate and holding it steady during the exposure. As the camera runs, the claw moves up and down. On its way up, the claw is retracted into the aperture plate, but at the top of its arc, the claw reaches out and hooks a sprocket hole and pulls the film down, or advances the film, placing exactly one new frame into position in front

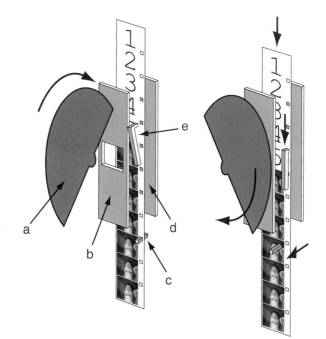

■ **Figure 8-12** The claw and shutter mechanism advances and exposes one frame of film at a time in the gate. Pictured are the shutter (a), aperture plate (b), registration pin (c), pressure plate (d), and claw (e).

of the aperture opening and holding it in place for exposure. The camera's **shutter** is a rotating half-disk located between the back of the lens and the aperture opening. When the 180° opening of the disk rotates in front of the gate, the film will be exposed; when the solid portion of the shutter spins into place, the film is protected from light.

As the claw advances the film one frame, the shutter rotates closed and blocks the light entering through the lens. Once the claw has positioned the new, unexposed frame of film steady in the gate, the shutter rotates open and allows the light to expose (or tag) the film, creating another frame. This is how the claw and shutter work in tandem: shutter closed, claw advances film; shutter open, claw holds film steady in the gate for exposure. At the standard transport speed this cycle occurs 24 times every second. That is to say, the claw and shutter mechanism create 24 frames per second. This cycle—shutter open, film stopped; shutter closed, film moves—is the intermittent movement essential to the film system.

Some cameras have an additional **registration pin** that skewers a sprocket hole to keep the frame extra steady in the gate. By securing two sprocket holes while a frame is being exposed, the film is held in place with much more stability and therefore a sharper, steadier image is exposed (Figure 8-13).

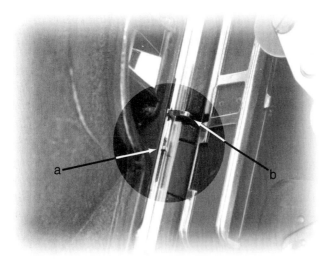

■ **Figure 8-13** The camera movement. A claw (a) advances a filmstrip one frame at a time, while a registration pin (b) holds the frame in place when it is being exposed to light.

Drive Mechanism and Film Transport

The camera's drive mechanism both provides power to run the film through the camera and governs the speed (frame rate) of the film. There are basically two types of motors: spring-wound and direct current (DC) electric (Figure 8-14). Cameras that use DC motors are powered by rechargeable NiCad battery belts or onboard battery packs.

Spring-wound cameras are powered by a large coiled spring much like the spring in a watch; the camera spring requires rewinding after each take. Each type of motor has its own advantages and disadvantages. In the case of spring-wound motors, one never has to worry about running out of batteries or forgetting to charge the battery beforehand. Batteries also lose their charge extremely fast under subfreezing conditions, whereas a spring-wind camera will always provide power, even in extreme weather. The limitation of spring-wound cameras is the relatively

■ **Figure 8-14** The two types of motors that run film and govern the frame rate in a camera: the Arri-S uses a DC battery belt *(left)* to power the camera, and the Filmo uses a spring-wound crank (right).

short running duration per wind. A single wind from a camera like the Bell & Howell Filmo or the Bolex will give you just under one minute of footage (depending on the age of the spring). Although this is much longer than the average shot in a conventional narrative film, filmmakers who plan to use long takes should opt for a DC motor, which will run as much footage per take as you want.

Another distinction of motors is their transport speed capabilities. **Constant-speed motors** run exclusively at 24 fps (sync speed). **Variable-speed motors** have the ability to run at a variety of transport speeds, giving the filmmaker a range of under-cranking or slow motion speeds to choose from (**Figure 8-15**).

■ **Figure 8-15** Frame rate selector for the Arri-BL. A variable-speed motor adds the capability to record an image at rates other than 24 fps. A constant-speed motor will only run film at 24 fps.

In Wong Kar-Wai's *In the Mood for Love* (2000), two couples move into an apartment building around the same time and the new neighbors, the Chows and the Chans, get to know each other. Before long Mr. Chow (Tony Leung Chiu Wai) and Mrs. Chan (Maggie Cheung) suspect that their spouses are having an affair with one another. Their close friendship and mutual sorrow bonds them intimately, but as their desire for each other grows, they struggle not to behave like their unfaithful spouses. Mr. Chow and Mrs. Chan are drawn inexorably to one another and the audience craves for these two to become lovers, but they will not yield. The tension and drama of their repressed desire is exquisitely protracted and stylized through the use of frequent slow motion sequences (**Figure 8-16**, *top*)

The final scene in *Women Without Men*, Shirin Neshat's 2009 film about the struggles of four woman during the 1953 coup d'état in Iran, shows one of the central characters, Munis (Shabnam Toloui), falling from a rooftop to the street below in extreme slow motion. During this stunning and greatly extended fall through the air, Munis calmly contemplates, in voice over, the nature of death and destiny. As the ground slowly gets closer and closer, her fall becomes not a plunge to death but a state of grace, and the slow-motion effect infuses this moment with a metaphysical dimension that speaks to the experiences of all four women represented in the film (**Figure 8-16**, *center*).

Darren Aronofsky's *Requiem for a Dream* follows four New Yorkers as each, in their own way, succumbs to the seductive and destructive influence of drugs: prescription and illegal. Whether following a middle-aged woman popping diet pills or a group of friends at a cocaine-fueled party,

■ **Figure 8-16** Wong's *In the Mood for Love* (2000) *(top)*, Neshat's *Women without Men* (2009) *(center)*, and Aronofsky's *Requiem for a Dream* (2000) *(bottom)*.

Aronofsky immerses the viewer into the warped, hyperdrive perspective of characters under the influence by accelerating actions through fast-motion (under-cranked) shots (**Figure 8-16**, *bottom*).

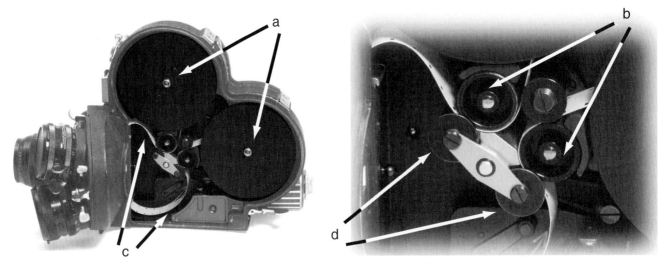

■ **Figure 8-17** Most of the mechanism inside a camera body is dedicated to transporting the film to and from the gate. Essential components include feed and takeup spindles (a), drive sprockets (b), the film loops (c), and guide rollers (d).

Shooting at sync speed (24 fps) is mandatory for scenes in which sync sound is needed; however, manipulating your camera's frame rate can be a powerfully expressive technique when used appropriately in shots not requiring sync.

Most of the other moving parts inside a camera are dedicated to transporting the film to and from the gate (**Figure 8-17**). They include the **feed and takeup spindles,** which feed the unexposed raw film stock into the gate and then take up the exposed footage. When the filmmaker is using larger loads of film, these spindles are located in the magazine. The **drive sprockets** (or drive rollers) are always rimmed with sprocket teeth to transport the film at a steady rate in concert with the intermittent movement of the claw and shutter. The rollers without sprockets are **guide rollers,** which guide the film onto the drive sprockets, ensuring smooth engagement with the film's sprocket holes. Film always travels in between the guide rollers and the drive sprockets.

One additional important element of the drive mechanism, which isn't exactly a physical component but rather an indispensable part of the transport system for both camera and projector, are the **loops** (short for **Latham's Loops**).[2] Loops are small bends of extra film located just above and below the gate. With the drive sprocket feeding film at a steady rate and the claw pulling, holding, and pulling the film, loops act as the shock absorbers of the whole transport system, providing some slack between these two movements, which ensures that the film does not tear in the course of all of this insistent activity. The size of the loops needs to be fairly exact. In some cameras, loops are created automatically by loop formers; in others they are created manually, with notches or etchings in the camera to aid the person loading the film to create the proper size loops. Although it is indeed maddening, **"losing your loop"** does not mean that you're ready for the nuthouse; it means that, usually as a result of improper loading, one or both loops shrink until the film is pulled taught between the movement of the claw and the drive sprocket. If you lose your loop the film jumps in the gate and sprocket holes can rip. When this happens, all shooting must stop while the camera is reloaded properly (see "Loading a Film Camera").

[2]Latham's Loops are named after Major Woodville Latham, who created the loops in order to shoot with and project long spools of film, rather than limit himself to the 20-second "living pictures" scenes in the enclosed kinetoscope boxes popular at the time (circa 1894). Latham needed longer lengths and projection because he wanted to cash in on showing boxing prizefights life sized! This proved to be one of the major innovations in the history of cinema.

Viewing System

All cameras have some sort of viewfinder that allows us to see and evaluate our framing before and during each take (**Figure 8-18**). Although there are a few different viewfinder systems, most recent cameras utilize a **reflex viewing system.** Reflex viewing means that we see the scene through the same lens with which we shoot the scene. In other words, the lens for our viewing is the same lens used for exposing the film. This requires that the light coming into the lens must be not only focused on the film plane but also diverted in some way to a **ground glass** or **fiberoptic viewfinder screen** for the camera operator to see. There are two systems commonly used for diverting this light from the lens to the viewing screen: the mirrored shutter and the beam splitter.

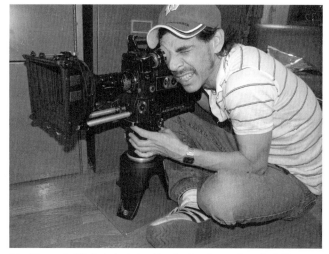

■ **Figure 8-18** A student checking the framing on the orientable viewfinder of an Arri-SRI.

The mirrored shutter system (**Figure 8-19**, a) utilizes the camera's rotating shutter to divert light to the ground glass viewfinder. The front side of the shutter is a mirror that reflects all of the light coming in from the lens to the viewfinder when the shutter is closed to the film. When the mirrored shutter rotates open to expose the film, all of the light entering from the lens hits the film plane and, for this instant, there is no image in the viewfinder. The mirrored shutter allows 100% of the light to expose your film half of the time and also diverts 100% of the light to your eye, but only half of the time, so there is a "flicker" while you view a scene as the camera is running. Once the camera stops rolling, the viewfinder stops in the closed position and you will have a bright and flickerless image to help you set up your next shot. Because the mirror lining on the shutter adds weight, these shutters are always butterfly shaped, meaning that the 180° opening is divided between two 90° wedges to more evenly distribute the centrifugal force as the shutter rotates.

The beam splitter system (**Figure 8-19**, b) works on a different principle. It uses a prism located between the lens and the film plane to divert a small percentage of the light to the viewfinder before it reaches the shutter or gate. The prism diverts around 20% of the light entering from the lens to the ground glass viewfinder screen, leaving 80% to expose the film. This makes for a flickerless viewing image, but one that is not as bright as with the mirrored shutter, especially when the camera is not running. Also, this obviously steals a bit of the incoming light away from the film, which means that some exposure compensation must be made because not all of the light from a scene is making it to the film emulsion.

Looking through the viewfinder, you usually see more than just the image on the ground glass viewing screen: you also see **finder markings,** which are etched or painted onto the viewing screen to help you compose your frame. There are many different finder markings depending on the camera and the anticipated use, but almost all viewfinders have **center crosshairs** marking the exact center of the frame and **frame edge brackets** (also called **camera aperture brackets**), which are four sharp corners, slightly smaller than the full area of the viewfinder. These brackets show you the exact parameters of your image frame (**Figure 8-20**).

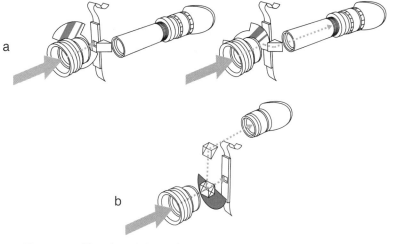

■ **Figure 8-19** The mirrored shutter viewing system (a) and the beam splitter viewing system (b).

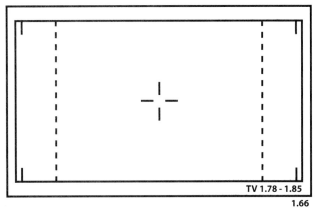

■ Figure 8-20 The viewfinder of a Super 16mm film camera. Finder markings in the viewfinder often include center cross hairs and frame-edge brackets for possible release format aspect ratios.

■ Figure 8-21 The Arri diopter at the end of the viewfinder, with a locking/unlocking ring (a), a focusing ring (b), and the eyecup (c).

One final important component of any viewing system is the **diopter,** found at the end of the viewfinder (**Figure 8-21**), just behind the eyepiece. The diopter is a simple lens that is focused on the viewfinding screen. Diopters must be adjusted for the specific vision of the person who is looking through the camera. Diopter adjustment allows people who normally wear glasses to go without them and to press their eye right up to the viewfinder to see the entire viewing screen clearly. It is important to remember to adjust the diopter before shooting, because the person before you may have adjusted it to a vision completely different than your own. In this case, every shot will appear soft, even though the lens is focused correctly.

The easiest way to set a diopter is to open up your aperture all the way, aim your camera at an uncluttered area, like a white wall, and de-focus the lens as much as possible. Next, loosen the locking screw on the diopter and rotate it until the finder markings (crosshairs and frame brackets) are sharp. You will also see the grain of the ground glass viewing screen get sharp; then retighten the locking screw.

■ LOADING A FILM CAMERA

The path that the film takes from the feed reel to the takeup reel is called the **threading pattern** (**Figure 8-22**). Every film camera model has a unique pattern, but the basic transport elements are common to almost every camera you will encounter, whether you are using a film magazine or loading small 100-foot spools directly in the body of the camera. Even cameras that offer automatic threading are not radically different from those requiring manual loading. Film always travels the same basic route inside the camera:

1. The unexposed raw film stock (core or spool) travels from the feed spindle and then …
2. passes between the feed sprocket roller and guide, and next it …
3. forms into the first loop and …
4. then passes through the gate (between pressure plate and aperture plate), emulsion side facing the aperture opening, and next it …
5. forms the second loop before …
6. passing between the takeup sprocket roller and guide, after which …
7. it is taken up by the takeup spindle (fitted with a core or spool).

Manual load cameras require you to thread the film through each mechanism, which often means separating the guide rollers from the drive sprockets, and the pressure plate from the aperture plate, to thread the film in between. It is essential to secure the film in its path by closing the guide rollers and pressure plate after you thread each mechanism, or the film can jump out of the threading path, rip, lose its loop, or wobble inside the gate. **Automatic threading** cameras simply require you to engage the automatic guide mechanism, trim the head end of the film, and feed it between the first sprocket and guide roller. Even though the threading and even the loop formation are done automatically, you should be familiar with the threading pattern of the camera in case something goes wrong.

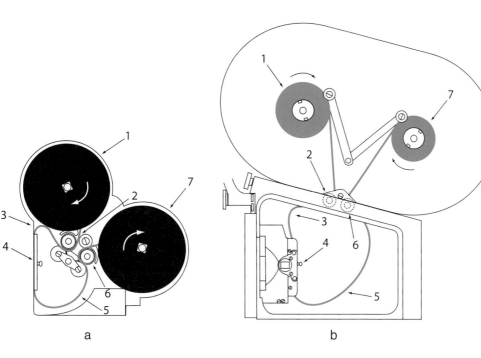

a   b

Film Loads

Film stocks for 16mm cameras most commonly come in two configurations for camera loading: **100-foot daylight-loading spools** and **400-foot magazine cores** (**Figure 8-23**). Be aware that not all cameras use both loads. You must know the film capacity of your camera before you buy your film.

100-Foot Daylight-Loading Spools

A 100-foot daylight-loading spool at normal sync speed will give you around two minutes and 45 seconds of footage. The 100-foot spools are very compact and are designed to be loaded inside the body of a camera without the need for complete darkness. You may load a daylight spool in subdued light without ruining the film. The film stock is wound around a solid, black spool that completely and snugly covers the sides so that light cannot

■ **Figure 8-23** Film loads: 16mm film is commonly sold in 400-foot core loads (that require loading inside a lightproof changing bag) and 100-foot daylight-loading spools (that allow loading in the light).

enter from the edges and expose the film. The top layer of film is obviously exposed to light during loading, but being opaque, these first layers of film protect the under layers around which they are wrapped, so the bulk of the film load is not exposed to light. When unloading a daylight spool in the open, the tail layers are also exposed. This is important to remember if you have vital footage all the way to the last frames of the film—known as **critical ends.** You will probably not want to sacrifice the ends to light, so you will need to unload your footage in complete darkness (see "Loading a Mag in a Changing Bag"). Film manufacturers know that a few feet at the head and tail of a 100-foot spool will be exposed, so there is always slightly more than 100 feet of footage on each roll to compensate.

When loading a 100-foot daylight spool, you need to have another, empty 100-foot spool for takeup. Usually, the previous feed spool, now empty after shooting, becomes the takeup spool for the next load of film. To attach film to the takeup spool, fold over and sharply crease three frames into the head end of the film (about an inch) (**Figure 8-24**). Slip the entire doubled end into the cutout slot in the hub of the spool and wind the film around itself a few revolutions

■ **Figure 8-24** To attach film to a daylight-loading spool, simply bend three frames and then insert them in the slot at the hub of the spool.

so that there is no possibility of the film slipping out of the hub. Then you can put the spool on the takeup post. Never use tape to attach film to a spool.

400-Foot Cores

Longer loads of 16mm film commonly come as 400 feet of film tightly wound around a 2-inch plastic core. At 24 fps, a 400-foot load will provide around 11 minutes of footage. The 400-foot cores are always loaded in camera magazines, and since there is no protection from accidental exposure to light, they require loading in complete darkness.

Camera Magazines

A **camera magazine** (**mag** for short) is a light-tight chamber that can be preloaded and easily attaches to and detaches from the body of the camera. There are basically two types of magazines: the displacement magazine and the coaxial magazine (**Figure 8-25**). The **displacement magazine**, occasionally called "mouse ears," places the feed and takeup sides on a single plane and shifts the film from the front (feed side) to the back (takeup side) of the magazine. Also, the feed and takeup are often housed within the same compartment, which requires that the entire film-loading process be completed in total darkness. In **coaxial magazines** the feed and takeup sides are parallel, side-by-side, and the film shifts from the left to the right side during shooting. Feed and takeup sides are in different compartments, so it's only necessary to load the feed side in darkness. Once the feed side compartment is locked shut, the rest of the threading process can be done in the light, including attaching the film to the takeup core. The other advantage to the coaxial design is its relative compactness compared with displacement mags.

All magazines also have **guide rollers,** which help the film feed smoothly and take up cleanly and sometimes serve as a footage counter. Without these rollers, the film runs the risk of rubbing the sides of the magazine. Finally, all magazines have posts for

a   b   c   d

■ **Figure 8-25** Coaxial *(left)* and displacement *(right)* magazines. In the illustration we can see a guide roller (a) and a core adaptor (b) in the coaxial mag and a guide roller (c) and a collapsible core (d) in the displacement mag.

the feed and takeup reels, but usually they are simply spindles that do not accommodate the standard 2-inch core. Many magazines require the use of **core adaptors,** which lock onto the spindles, before you load the film. Core adaptors must stay inside the magazine for reuse when unloading film and must not be removed with the film and accidentally sent to the lab. A mag with only one core adaptor is useless.

Not all cameras accommodate the use of magazines (e.g., Bell & Howell Filmo, Canon Scoopic); conversely, not all cameras allow 100-foot spools to be loaded inside the body of the camera (e.g., Arri-BL, Arri-SR). There are, of course, cameras that will accommodate both film loads (Arri-S, Bolex). The mags for cameras that accept only 400-foot core loads have the drive sprockets built right into the magazine rather than the camera body. In fact, the Arri-SR coaxial magazine (**Figure 8-26**) contains drive sprockets and the pressure plate. One of the great benefits of using magazines, besides the longer film rolls, is that they allow for the preloading and quick changing of magazines during the shoot.

■ **Figure 8-26** Arri-SR coaxial magazine. The integrated pressure plate (a) makes changing preloaded magazines quick and easy.

Does all of this have any bearing on the creative aspects of your film? Yes. The film capacity of the camera and even the type of magazine can have some effect on the visual conception of your movie. While allowing for longer loads of film (and very long takes), cameras that use displacement magazines are generally large and cumbersome and limit your mobility and ability to shoot in very confined spaces, like a car. Cameras that use only 100-foot internal loads are compact and allow you great flexibility in camera placement and angles, but, of course, they have a limited film capacity per load. I once had a student who tried to shoot a film in one of New York City's last remaining telephone booths with an Arri-BL (a bulky 16mm camera with a displacement mag). He was simply not able to fit the camera inside the booth and get the focus he needed. So again, you need to be aware of the requirements of your project as you consider the features of available film cameras.

Loading a Mag in a Changing Bag
Because there is nothing protecting the film on a 400-foot core from being accidentally exposed to light, magazines must be loaded in absolute darkness. We could use a darkroom for this, but more often loading is done on the set inside a **changing bag** (also called **dark bag**). A changing bag is simply a large, lightproof bag with a double zipper opening at the base and sleeves on the other end that enable the camera loader access to the inside of the bag without leaking in light (**Figure 8-27**).

Here is the process for loading a magazine in a changing bag:
1. Clean the inside of the changing bag. Hair, dust, and bits of film left in the bag by the previous user can easily get inside the magazine and wind up in the camera gate.
2. Put everything you need to load the magazine inside the bag. This includes the magazine (already opened and with core adaptors in place), the takeup core (if you're using a single-chamber magazine), and, of course, the can of film. You

■ **Figure 8-27** 400-foot cores require loading inside a lightproof changing bag. This is a critical procedure that takes a lot of concentration.

should remove the fabric tape from around the can before you put it into the bag, but be careful not to jostle the can open when closing the bag and inserting your arms.

3. Place your arms inside the changing bag, pulling the sleeves up to your elbows to avoid light leaks, open the can of film, and remove the film from its plastic bag. You will notice that the end of the film is taped down with a small strip of paper tape.

4. Remove the tape from the film and stick it to the inside of the film can lid. It is important that you do not let this piece of tape simply float around inside the bag. If it sticks onto your film, it will jam the magazine. You can also reuse this tape to secure your exposed film after you unload it from the magazine later.

5. Feed the film through the feed slot (or through the feed rollers). Now you can put the core onto the feed spindle (with core adaptor), but be careful. You should gently push on the plastic core to get the film onto the post. *Do not* push on the film itself, because the film could "dish," meaning a portion of film pushes away from the rest of the roll and unspools.

6. Put the feed guide roller into position against the edge of the roll of film.

7. If you're loading a coaxial magazine, you can close and lock the feed side door and remove the magazine to finish loading.

8. If you're using a single-chamber displacement mag, then you'll start to wish for Superman's x-ray vision while you (a) create the proper loop (by measuring to notches on the magazine by feel), (b) thread the film through the takeup opening in the magazine, (c) attach the film to the 2-inch takeup core, and (d) put the core on the takeup spindle all by feel and within the changing bag.

9. Engage the takeup guide roller and close the door.

You are now free to take the magazine out and secure it to the camera.

To attach the film to the takeup core, fold and crease the tip of the film over itself by half a frame and slip this thicker end into the core slot, with the film wrapping around the core in the same direction as the slot. Then wind the film several revolutions to ensure that the film will not slip out of the core slot (**Figure 8-28**).

After the film is securely attached to the core, you may gently push the plastic core onto the takeup spindle (with core adaptor). Never use tape to attach film to the takeup core. Also, although it may seem like a more secure fit, do not wrap the film *against* the direction of the core slot. This will create a slight lump that will only become more pronounced as the core gathers more and more film. This lump can create roller noise and even scrape against the inside of the magazine causing all sorts of trouble.

Miscellaneous Tips for Loading Film

1. Practice, practice, practice. Film is expensive, and properly loading your camera is absolutely crucial. So before you load real film stock, you should always practice loading a camera or magazine with a **dummy roll** (junk film) many times, first in the light and then inside a changing bag, to get familiar with the threading pattern, loop size, and the "feel" of loading that specific camera.

2. Check out your camera. Before you take your camera away from the rental house or checkout facility, run a few feet of dummy film through with the camera door open to make sure it's running smoothly. A maladjusted claw or mistimed drive sprocket can cause you to repeatedly lose your loop.

3. Clean your camera and magazine compartments (**Figure 8-29**). You may certainly use canned air to clean your magazine of dust, but is not advisable to use compressed air to clean the inside of a camera because this can force dust into the gate and the back of the lens.

■ **Figure 8-28** Attaching film to a takeup core.

■ **Figure 8-29** It is always a good idea to brush the inside of a magazine clean out dust, film chips, or fibers *(left)*. Likewise, taping the door of the magazine (or the camera body) safeguards your footage against possible light leaks *(right)*.

Cleaning a camera is best done with a white, soft bristle brush. White bristles are used in case the brush loses a hair; you will easily see a white hair in the black interior of the camera body.

4. Tape all of the seams around the door. Not only will this prevent light from leaking into the chamber, but it also is a visual reminder to everyone on the set that there is film inside the camera, so do not open it up!

5. Always have extra takeup cores or spools in case the previous user did not leave one inside the camera. You cannot use the camera without a takeup.

6. Do not hassle the camera loader! Hovering around the person loading the film, trying to get them to move faster, only increases their anxiety and is seriously counterproductive. Let the loader do the job calmly and carefully.

Removing Exposed Film and Splitting Cores

As you are shooting, when the 400-foot core runs out, the D.P. announces, "Roll out," and the magazine on the camera is changed with a fresh preloaded one. The exposed film is now completely on the takeup core and must be carefully removed. Keep in mind that your exposed film is the most precious item on the movie set; it contains the results of all of the hard work and long hours of the cast and crew, so take special care when unloading a magazine. The magazine is unloaded in a changing bag (that also contains the plastic film bag and can). When you open the magazine, feel the edges of the film to make sure that it has taken up smoothly. The exposed film will not be wound as tightly as the unexposed stock you loaded, so make sure that you do not pull the film up by the edges or it will dish. Removing an exposed core usually involves first removing the film with the core adaptor and then removing the core adaptor from the core. It's easy to forget this and inadvertently send the core adaptor to the lab—which is a costly mistake. After you've safely done this you can put the film in the bag, the bag in the can, and remove the can. Tape all around the edge to secure the lid shut, and label the can (see page 373 for proper film can labeling).

In cases where you have not used all of your film—say you've only exposed 200 feet out of 400—you can **split the core.** Splitting a core means breaking the film at the loops (which are outside the magazine) and unloading it twice. First unload the exposed footage in the takeup side, tape the can shut and label the can, then unload the feed side, tape up the can, and label that can with the amount of unexposed footage left on the core, the type of film, and the words "**short ends.**" This film can be used another day.

■ FILM STOCKS AND PROCESSING

Anatomy of Raw Film Stock

There are two major types of film stocks: **camera film** and **print film.** Print film is used in the laboratory to make the various prints during the postproduction process. Camera film, the focus of this section, is the **raw film stock** that is loaded into a filmmaker's camera.

Motion picture film stock is basically a long strip of strong and flexible material called the **base** that has been coated with a photosensitive substance called the **emulsion** (**Figure 8-30**). As the vehicle for the photographic image, the film base must not only be strong but must also be optically transparent without any imperfections that might distort the image. Film base for camera films is commonly made from **cellulose triacetate,** which replaced the highly flammable and archivally unsound cellulose nitrate around 1950. The base is between 125 and 130 micrometers thick (around five-thousandths of an inch).

The optically clear base is evenly coated with the light-sensitive component of the film stock, the emulsion. **Emulsion** consists of a layer of microscopic, randomly but evenly distributed, **silver halide crystals** suspended in gelatin and bound to the base with an adhesive layer called the **substratum** or **subbing layer.** The silver halide crystals are highly sensitive to light and are the element that actually creates the photographic image. Black-and-white film, as seen in **Figure 8-30**, has only one layer of emulsion, whereas color film has three layers of emulsion (see **Figure 8-36**). Film that has not been exposed to light is called **raw stock.**

On the other side of the base is a flat black coating called the **antihalation backing.** This black layer is light absorbent and keeps light, which is passing through the emulsion and then through the base with each exposure, from reflecting back and reexposing the emulsion from behind.

All motion picture film is perforated down one or both edges with **sprocket holes** (also called **perfs**) that allows the camera to gently and accurately advance the film, one frame at a time, through the gate, to create each exposure. Also along the edge of the film are **latent image edge code numbers,** which are imprinted at the time of manufacture. Edge code numbers are a sequential series of numbers along the edge of the film that assign a unique and specific identification number to every frame in the roll. In 16mm film, the edge code numbers are printed every 20 frames (every 6 inches) (**Figure 8-31**).

To the left of the edge code number is a small black dot indicating the **zero frame,** which means the frame identified by that number—for example, •KM48 1347 3556. Then each frame toward the tail end of the roll is that number plus one frame (… 3556 + 1), two frames (…3556 + 2), three frames (…3556 + 3), four frames (…3556 + 4), and so on, until after (…3556 + 19) the next imprinted number switches over one digit (•KM48 1347 3557). The ability to identify and find each and every frame is important throughout the workflow of a project shot on film, especially when we need to identify exact edit point frames, should we wish to go back to our original negative in order to finish our project as a film print (see Chapter 19). These numbers are called *latent image* edge code numbers because they are imprinted onto the film with light and are not visible until after the film is processed. All contemporary

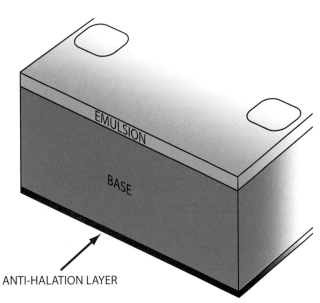

EMULSION

BASE

ANTI-HALATION LAYER

■ **Figure 8-30** A typical black-and-white negative film stock is composed of a light-sensitive emulsion layer containing silver halide crystals, a base, and an antihalation coating.

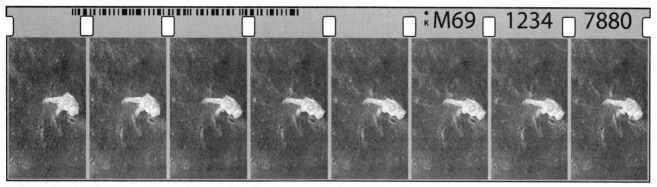

■ **Figure 8-31** Edge code numbers and barcode identification are standard on all film stocks, providing every frame a specific and unique number that ensures precise identification of edit points.

film stocks also have a barcode imprint that contains exactly the same edge code information but is machine readable. Kodak introduced the technology as "Keykode" and Fuji's version is called "MR-code." This system allows for rapid identification of frames and edit points and is helpful for maintaining a frame-accurate database throughout the postproduction process (film transfer and cutting).

Film Processing Basics

When the silver halide crystals are struck by light (actually light photons) there is a chemical reaction to that energy on the atomic level that corresponds to the intensity of the light. The greater the light intensity, the greater the chemical reaction, meaning the more silver halide grains are **exposed** to light, or "**tagged.**" This is an **exposure,** and when an exposure is taken on one frame of film, essentially what is created is a precise chemical record of the light intensities reflecting off your scene at that moment. A film camera takes 24 exposures every second. At this point, the emulsion has what is called a **latent image,** meaning that although the silver halide crystals have become chemically activated, there is not yet any visible change to the crystals. It requires additional chemical processing to produce a visible change. A latent image is an exposure that has not yet been developed, and at this point it is very unstable, which is why you should send your film to the lab as quickly as possible.

At the laboratory, the first step in processing film is to remove the black antihalation backing. Then the exposed film goes through the liquid **developing agent,** and those areas that were tagged with light turn into pure **metallic silver particles,** whereas those grains that were not exposed remain as silver halide.

Next the film is run through a **stop bath,** to arrest the developing process at precisely the proper moment, and then through a fixing bath (Figure 8-32). The **fixer** removes all of the unexposed silver halide particles, leaving behind (and fixing to the base) masses of opaque silver particles in varying degrees of density, which correspond to the various levels of light exposure. A bright area of the image, which exposed many crystals, will be very dense, whereas a low light area would have exposed only a few crystals and therefore will have a thinner silver particle density. An area that corresponds to a black part of the image will have exposed no crystals and will therefore have no silver particle density at all.

After the development process what we are left with is a **photographic negative**—a perfect record of the scene, in silver particle densities, which is the inverse

■ **Figure 8-32** During processing, film stock is run along rollers that dip it in various chemical baths.

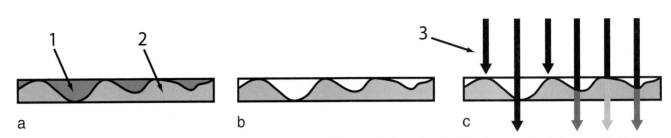

■ **Figure 8-33** When film is exposed to light (a), some of the silver halide crystals change into metallic silver according to the amount of light they received (2), while unaffected crystals remain in their silver halide form (1). During the processing of negative film, the unaffected crystals are removed (b), leaving behind various densities of metallic silver. Areas with heavy silver density block light (3) and areas with little or no silver particles allow light to pass through.

of the actual light values. Imagine projecting this image, pushing light through this strip of film. The area corresponding to black, with no silver density, would be transparent, with only the clear base between the lamp and the screen, allowing the projector light to pass directly through. The area corresponding to a white detail in the scene would have built up a very dense and opaque mass of silver particles, allowing no light to pass through and would therefore appear black on the screen. Any density in between would be a shade of gray, with the inverse relationship to the actual brightness of the photographed detail (Figures 8-33).

Identifying Film Stocks

We have discussed the basics of all film stocks, but obviously there is more to it than this. All camera film stocks are further identified and ultimately chosen according to five major characteristics:

1. Color or black and white
2. Negative or reversal
3. Film speed (also called the exposure index, or EI)
4. Color temperature balance
5. Gauge/format

Let's take a closer look at each category (Figures 8-34).

Color or Black and White

Obviously, this is a choice between film that renders images as tones of the grayscale (black and white) and films that duplicate the colors of the visible light spectrum as they appear in your scene (color film). As of the writing of this book, Kodak offers eight different color film stocks but only two different black-and-white stocks for 16mm production. It is clear that black-and-white film is receiving no research and development attention because very few people opt to make black-and-white movies these days—and for those who do, removing the color component is easily done in digital postproduction (Figure 8-35).

The basic construction of color film is similar to that for black-and-white film stock—emulsion, subbing layer, base, and anti-halation backing—but there is one significant difference. Color film contains three layers of light-sensitive emulsion instead of one. Because every color in the visible spectrum is made up of some combination of the three primary colors of light—red, green, and blue—each of the three layers is sensitive to one of these primary hues.

The first layer is sensitive to blue light, the second layer is sensitive to green light, and the final layer is sensitive to red light. This three-layered emulsion is called **color tripak** (Figure 8-36). Also, because all silver halide emulsions are sensitive to the blue

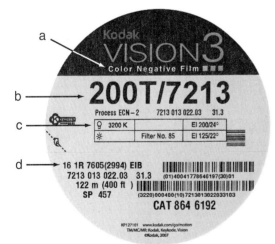

■ **Figure 8-34** A film can will always have the following information: whether it is color or black and white, negative or reversal (a), the Exposure Index (b), a color temperature rating (c), and the gauge (d).

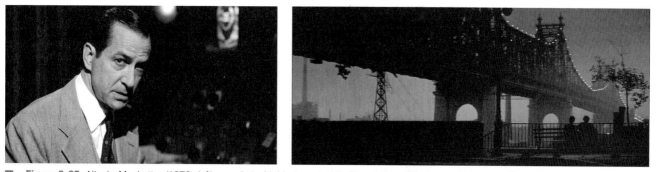

■ **Figure 8-35** Allen's *Manhattan* (1979, *left*) was shot with black-and-white film stock, unlike many contemporary films released in black and white, like Clooney's *Good Night, and Good Luck* (2005, *right*), which are shot on color stock and desaturated in post.

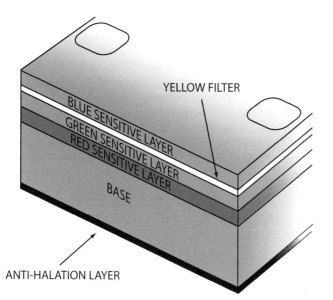

■ **Figure 8-36** The composition of a color film stock includes three emulsion layers, each one sensitive to a primary color. The color dyes that form the image in negative film are the complementary, or opposite, of the emulsion sensitivity. In the blue-sensitive layer the dye is yellow, in the green layer it is magenta, and in the red layer it is cyan.

range of the light spectrum, there is an additional yellow filter coating between the first blue layer and the other two emulsion layers. This yellow filter absorbs all blue light before it reaches the green and red emulsions.

Because silver halide photochemistry is exclusively a black-and-white process, color film additionally incorporates **color dye couplers** into the emulsion gelatin along with the silver halide crystals. **Color dye couplers** are grains containing color dye that cluster around the exposed metallic silver sites. During the development process, the couplers release their dye in relation to the density of the exposed silver grains. The greater the density, the more dye couplers bunch up and the more saturated the color will appear. The color dyes that form the image in negative film are the complement, or opposite, of the actual color in the scene. Specifically, the dye couplers used in the blue-sensitive layers are yellow, the dye couplers used in the green layers are magenta, and the dye couplers used in the red layers are cyan (**Figure 8-37**).

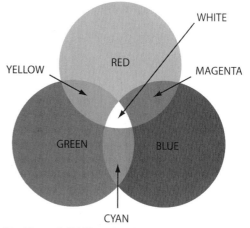

■ **Figure 8-37** The color wheel shows at a glance the three primary colors of light, red, green, and blue, and their respective complementary colors directly opposite, which are cyan, magenta, and yellow. See the color insert.

In Zhang Yimou's *Hero* (2002), various episodes narrated by Nameless (Jet Li) are clearly demarcated by their use of color and reflect the mythic storytelling style of both the character and the film itself. Details in the costumes, set design, and lighting are carefully controlled to reflect a unified and vividly stylized tone without ascribing a specific psychological state or metaphoric association to the use of a particular color (**Figure 8-38**). Zhang and his D.P., Christopher Doyle, alternately shot Kodak and Fuji stocks to achieve the specific effect they needed to push color film to the spectacular limits seen in these scenes from *Hero*. Here are some thoughts on the use of color from Doyle's personal journal while making *Hero*:

> *The same story is told in a number of ways, a slightly different version each time that is as much a response to as a compounding of the story that came before. Each elaboration has a color system of its own—white, red, blue, and green are the colors we have settled on. Some will give (and have given) complex explanations for what those colors do or mean, but for me the choices have come as much out of personal taste and convenience as any concept of color or theory of Art.*

> *Like the West from Aristotle until Newton, Chinese conceptual systems associate color with elements, objects, parts of the body, and sounds ...*

> *As far as I'm concerned, these colors are nothing more or less than what they are.*

Red

> *Red is primary in the Chinese world. Red demands. Red takes all in. The red in Hero can't be Raise the Red Lantern red. It has to have a touch more blue so it will relate better to the blue part of the film. It also has to be*

Figure 8-38 Scenes from Zhang's *Hero*. See the color insert.

> *softened but not polluted by our Hu Yang leaves, which are so yellow and light. Our red can't touch the green that is the past (and maybe dreamed) section. It has to be the red of a hero, a red of decisiveness in the face of moral quandary. It has to mean resolve.*

Blue

> *Transparent. Lots of sky. Unreal. Make it beautiful, like a concept. As thin as watercolor. Lots of high-speed. Movement follows story—as little as possible at beginning of the section, then more evident movement.*

(From *R34G38B25*, by Christopher Doyle, Gingko Press, 2004)

Negative or Reversal

When **negative film** is developed, the values of light and color are represented in inverse relationship to the actual scene photographed. Light areas are dark and colors are represented by their complement. Camera original negative film is not useful as is and must be printed onto another strip of film or transferred to DV in order to reverse the image so we can see what we've captured. **Reversal film** creates positive images—images with the same light and color values of the actual scene—right on the camera original film (**Figure 8-39**).

Reversal films are designed to go directly from camera, to the editing bench, to projection, without the need for additional prints or transfers. In the mid-20th century, 16mm reversal

Figure 8-39 Reversal film stocks render positive images, just like our subject *(left)*. Negative stocks render a negative image, the exact opposite in terms of brightness and color *(right)*, and need to be printed or transferred to DV to create a positive image.

film was the standard format for television news crews. They could shoot a breaking story, like a building fire, on reversal film, get the film to the lab for processing, and get the footage back to the station, cut it, and put it on the air within a few hours, after which they would probably never use it again. There was no need for additional prints (costing additional money). But in the late 1970s, when video technology completely replaced film for all news gathering, the market for reversal film dwindled to a trickle. Kodak offers only two reversal film stocks in 16mm, one color and one black and white, and they are generally regarded as having the least finesse of all of the films in the catalog. These days, reversal film is considered a specialty item, but enough students still use it to warrant a brief explanation.

The makeup of reversal film emulsion is essentially the same as that of negative film. The difference really comes in the processing. You already understand that the silver halide crystals that have been exposed to light develop into metallic silver of various densities. However, instead of the unexposed silver halide grains being washed away in the fixing process, reversal film undergoes a **bleach process** that washes away the *exposed silver grains* and leaves behind the *unexposed* crystals, which form densities exactly the opposite of negative film—that is to say, densities that correspond positively to the original light values (Figure 8-40).

A white area in the frame, which exposed a lot of silver halide crystals, would have all of those crystals washed away: no crystals means total transparency. A black area, which exposed no grains, would have nothing washed away and therefore would have a deep density of unexposed silver halide, and so on. The unexposed silver halide left behind is then uniformly reexposed under an even and consistent light in a process called **fogging,** and then it is developed a second time to transform all of the remaining silver halide crystals into opaque metallic silver. Finally, the film is fixed in a chemical bath. The result is an image that retains the original light values of the scene, forming a positive image.

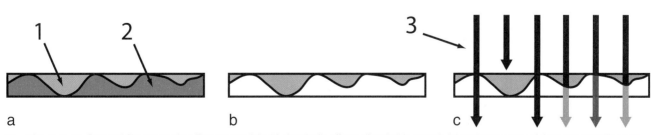

Figure 8-40 Reversal film processing. Exposure to light (a) chemically affects silver halide crystals (1) and turns some of them into metallic silver (2). The exposed metallic silver is removed (b) leaving the unexposed crystals behind, which are then reexposed and processed turning them into metallic silver. This creates a positive image when developed and projected (c). Areas with heavy density block light and areas with little or no silver particles allow light to pass through (3).

The exposure index scale (EI) corresponds exactly to that of the American Standards Association (ASA) scale, which is used for still photography film stocks, and to the International Standards Association (ISO) scale. Although different light meters will label the film sensitivity setting with different indexes, they are all the same scale (**Figure 8-41**).

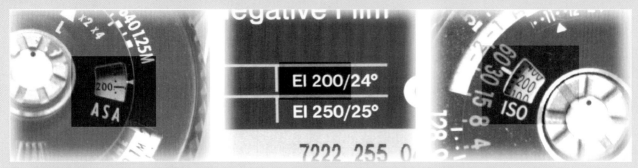

■ **Figure 8-41** An older incident light meter with an ASA scale *(left)*, a new box of film with the EI scale *(center)*, and a newer incident light meter with an ISO scale *(right)*. All of these film sensitivity scales are analogous and are found on many film-related pieces of equipment.

Reversal color film additionally renders the original colors of the scene as a positive image and therefore incorporates primary color dye couplers that match the color sensitivity of each emulsion layer: blue dye coupler for the blue sensitive layer, green dye coupler for the green layer, and red dye coupler for the red layer.

Film Speed (EI)

The sensitivity of a specific film stock to light is referred to generally as the **film speed**, and each individual film stock has a specific **exposure index** (or **EI**) that gives us a relative indication of how that stock responds to light. Film stocks that require a lot of light to make an exposure, like EI 50 film, are called **slow films,** and stocks that can register an image in low-light situations, like EI 500 films, are called **fast film** stocks. The higher the EI number, the faster the film and vice versa.

Some common film speeds for color film stocks, in order of increasing sensitivity to light, are EI 50, EI 64, EI 100, EI 200, EI 400, EI 250, and EI 500. A doubling of the EI number represents a doubling of the emulsion sensitivity, so EI 200 film is twice as fast (twice as sensitive to light) as EI 100, meaning that EI 200 requires only half as much light to make the same exposure.

However, although it is true that using fast film makes production easier in many ways by allowing you to reduce the amount of lighting units you need to light a scene or even to go without artificial light altogether, there is a trade-off. What makes film more or less sensitive to light is the size of the silver halide crystals in the emulsion. Larger silver halide grains are more sensitive to light, so faster film uses larger grains. However, the grains also become more visible, so fast film appears grainier when projected or transferred to DV.

Fast film also is more contrasty, meaning that it reproduces fewer shades of color and brightness. Fast films tend to lose detail in bright and dark areas and have fewer subtleties in shading overall. Slow film, by contrast, has a much finer grain structure and reproduces an astonishing amount of subtlety in color and gray tones in the image, allowing a cinematographer an enormous amount of control over image details. Slower films also transfer excellently to DV, revealing very little grain.

Until recently, silver halide grains have always been cubic crystals, but advancements by Kodak have created the **T-grain,** an evenly sized, flat crystal (**Figure 8-42**). The T-grain has transformed motion picture imaging by increasing the sensitivity of each grain by creating a larger surface area yet maintaining a fine grain structure because the grains lay flat and slightly overlap, kind of like spreading out a deck of playing cards on a table. Fuji film has its own version of this crystal structure, called Σ grain. With T-grain and Σ grain, we are able to purchase relatively fast film stocks (e.g., EI 200 or EI 320) and maintain good contrast and a fine grain look. These film stocks also transfer exceptionally well to DV.

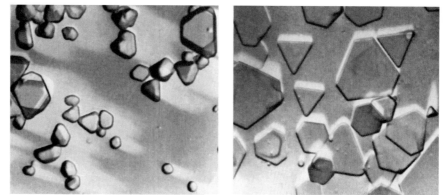

■ **Figure 8-42** Earlier film stocks had cubic-shaped crystals *(left)*, but later developments resulted in the creation of the T-grain crystal *(right)*, providing greater sensitivity while maintaining a fine grain structure.

 in practice

As with almost every element of film production where you are given a variety of options, there is no film speed that is inherently "better" or "worse"—there is only the "right" film speed for how you want your film to look and how you need to work. These choices are ideally aesthetic, but practical considerations are often a major factor.

The Look

In Darren Aronofsky's *Pi* (1998), mathematician Maximillian Cohen searches for a numerical pattern that will allow him to predict fluctuations in the stock market. As he gets closer to uncovering this code, he realizes that he's onto something much larger. However, Max is relentlessly pursued by both a Wall Street investment group eager to use his knowledge for profit and a Hasidic sect whose members believe the code is the secret name of God, and his life and mental stability are thrown into turmoil.

The film is told from Max's perspective. His search has turned him into an obsessive-compulsive paranoiac

who mistrusts anyone and fears physical contact. Director Aronofsky and director of photography Matthew Libatique chose a highly stylized visual design to represent this character's warped view of the world. This chaotic, paranoid view was accomplished by shooting most of the film in Tri-X reversal film, which renders a grainy, high-contrast image (manipulated further in postproduction to increase this contrast even more). In the scenes in **Figure 8-43** *(right)*, the images are quite hard edged, made up of only pure blacks and pure whites, with very few shades of gray, as if Max's perception is so warped by his obsessive search for the code that he simply cannot see the world as it really is. There are times, however, when Max is at peace and temporarily out of danger. To mark this change in Max's state of mind, these scenes are shot with Plus-X reversal film, which has a wider latitude and lower contrast than Tri-X. In the scenes of relative calm, Max and his surroundings are rendered in a more subtle, soft, and realistic way, with a wider range of grays clearly visible. The dichotomy between the look of these two stocks is further emphasized by their content: the organic order

■ **Figure 8-43** The paranoid world of mathematician Max (in Aronofsky's *Pi*, 1998) is divided between moments of peace *(left)*, shot with lower contrast Plus-X stock, and periods of anxiety *(right)*, shot with higher contrast, grainier Tri-X reversal stock.

of Nature (i.e., the tree branch Max observes when he is at peace) and the inorganic order of numbers (i.e., the computer screens in his apartment).

The Look and Practical Considerations

In George Racz' student shorts—*The Miracle* (see pages 22 and 40) and the two other films in his trilogy on childhood *TheFishMiracleSky*—his central idea was to vividly represent the colorful and magical perspective of a little girl (**Figure 8-44**). As George himself tells it:

This film is about childhood, where colorful dreamlike images mix with reality. I conferred closely with my D.P. Timothy about the best film stock to use, one which could represent the brilliant colors of the little girl's environment, especially the colors of her red dress, blue leggings, and her room and toys. But we also didn't have very much light for the interior scenes so we needed to go with a high-speed film. We shot a few tests and we felt that 7229 (Kodak Vision 2 Expression, 500T Color Neg Film) gave us the most saturated colors for the speed we needed in the interiors, and then we used the medium speed 7205 (Kodak Vision 2, 250D Color Neg Film) for most exteriors. One entire film, Closer to the Sky, was shot outside in the bright sun, so we decided to use 7201 (Kodak Vision 2, 50D Color Neg Film), a slow-speed and very fine grained film stock.

■ **Figure 8-44** In George Racz' *The Miracle* (2006), special attention was put into selecting a stock that would render the little girl's environment, toys, and clothing as colorfully as possible. See the color insert.

The Practical Choice

Practical considerations are another factor in choosing the right EI. Recently, a student group in my class made a short film inside St. Patrick's Cathedral in New York City. The stained-glass windows allow very little sunlight into the church, and the students were not allowed to bring in any lights. They had no choice but to select a very fast film stock and take all their shots around the offertory candles and spotlighted statues. The look of that film was dark, but this worked wonderfully because, well, it made the viewers feel like they were in a dark cathedral.

Color Temperature Balance

Different sources of light favor different areas of the light spectrum. For example, the sun is a relatively blue light, while the 60-watt incandescent bulb in your desk lamp has a warm, amber hue. The specific hue of a light source is called its **color temperature.** Color temperature is measured by the Kelvin scale, which was devised by Lord William Kelvin in the late 1800s. Lord Kelvin discovered that if he heated a block of black carbon until it was white hot, its glow duplicated all of the colors in the visible light spectrum one by one as the heat went up, so he measured the temperature of the carbon at each color stage. The hotter the black body got, the bluer the color turned, and the lower the temperature was, the redder the color of the heated carbon. Color temperature has nothing to do with the actual heat of any light; instead, the color temperatures ascribed to different light sources in degrees Kelvin (°K) are simply based on matching the colors between a light's hue and Lord Kelvin's block of heated carbon.

If we look at a blank sheet of paper it appears white to us, both under the sun or on the desk, because the human eye automatically compensates for the difference in color temperatures, but film stock cannot change its sensitivity to color like this. As a way of compensating, film stocks come balanced for the two most common lighting situations under which we shoot: **daylight (5,600°K),** which favors a distinctly cool, blue hue, and **tungsten (3,200°K),** the color temperature of commonly used movie lights, which are quite warm and amber in tint. What it means to balance a film stock to color temperature is to manipulate emulsion sensitivity so that the light source appears to be simply white.

Daylight-balanced film emulsion is manufactured such that the blue emulsion layer is slightly less light sensitive than are the other two layers, and **tungsten-balanced** film is made with a less sensitive red emulsion layer.

Color temperatures of common light sources.	
Cooler (Bluer)	
Sun (overcast sky)	8000°K
Daylight (average midday)	5600°K–6000°K
HMI movie light	5600°K
Tungsten movie light	3200°K
Halogen light	3000°K
60-watt household incandescent	2900°K
Sunrise/sunset	2500°K
Candle flame	1800°K
Warmer (Redder)	

In general, we choose the film stock for our specific shooting situation. If we are shooting outdoors, we choose daylight-balanced film, and if we shoot inside under tungsten movie lights, we choose tungsten film. However, things rarely work out this neatly. What if your film involves some exterior locations and some interior scenes under movie lights? For those times when we are forced to shoot film in situations for which the film is not balanced, we can compensate by using **color conversion filters** (Figure 8-45) in front of the lens to alter the incoming light to match the balance of the film.

If we shoot with tungsten-balanced film under daylight conditions, the image will appear extremely blue, but placing the standard **Wratten #85** amber filter in front of the lens converts the incoming light to 3,200°K. Conversely, if we shoot daylight film under tungsten movie lights, the image will have an overall amber wash to it. By using a **Wratten #80A** blue filter, we convert the tungsten light entering the lens to 5,600°K.

When cinematographers have to select one film stock for shooting under different light sources, they will almost always choose tungsten film and convert with an #85 filter for shooting outdoors. This is because color filters work by absorbing certain colors of the light spectrum, which also means that they cut down on the total amount of light entering the lens. In other words, when you place a filter on a lens, you lose light. With an #85 filter we lose two-thirds of a stop, but with an 80A filter we lose two full stops of light. Losing two-thirds of a stop of exposure when you're going outdoors is not a big deal because the sun is usually brighter than most tungsten setups anyway. But losing two stops when your source changes from the sun, which is a high-intensity source, to the relatively low intensity of tungsten lights is usually too great a loss. Color conversion filters are so common in film production that color film labels often indicate a specific adjustment to the EI number when these filters are in use, so that you can easily compensate for the loss of light. For example,

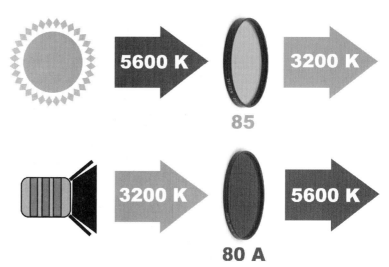

■ **Figure 8-45** Color conversion filters. Two of the most commonly used filters are the 85 (amber), which turns 5,600°K daylight into 3,200°K tungsten light, and the 80A (bluish), which turns 3,200°K tungsten into 5,600°K daylight. See the color insert.

Kodak Vision3 7213 is a tungsten-balanced film with a normal EI 200, but the label tells us that if we shoot under daylight with an #85 filter, the new EI will be 125 (see **Figure 8-34**). In other words, we compensate for losing two-thirds of a stop of light by saying the film is less sensitive and needs more light to achieve a given exposure.

Gauge/Format

A film **gauge** refers to the actual width of the film stock. There are currently only four gauges of film stock manufactured for film production use: 8mm, 16mm, 35mm, and 65mm. The term **format,** however, refers to both the width of the negative filmstrip and the dimensions of the exposed frame. There can be several formats on the same gauge film. For example, 16mm gauge film is used for both standard 16mm format and Super 16mm film production format, which has a larger image area. Because Super 8mm film is hard to find and harder to get processed and 65mm film (used for 70mm projection format) is used for large scale, big-budget Hollywood epics and Omnimax productions, I'll restrict my discussion to 16mm and 35mm film formats, which are the most commonly used production formats.

There is no difference in the actual emulsion used for 16mm and 35mm film of the same type. However, the larger the film format is, the better the quality of the overall recorded image. A regular 16mm frame measures 0.404″ × 0.295″, super 16 is 0.493″ × 0.295″, and a full frame of 35mm film is 0.864″ × 0.630″. The larger the exposure area of an image, the greater the clarity will be in rendering fine details and subtle shades. This is called a format's **resolving power,** and the fact that 35mm has four times the picture area of standard 16mm is the reason it has greater resolving power and higher quality when transferred to DV (standard definition [SD]or high definition [HD]).

Another reason larger film formats look better than smaller ones is the magnification necessary for projection. Smaller gauge film requires much more magnification when projected, which also includes the magnification of grain and image imperfections. Projecting full frame 35mm film onto a modest theatrical screen around 20′ × 30′ requires it to be magnified around 158,000 times, but standard 16mm film projected to the same dimensions is magnified 726,000 times. This is one reason why 35mm and 70mm have become the theatrical release standards.

Aspect Ratio

One other major element of a film's format is its aspect ratio (**Figure 8-46**). In Chapter 3 we discussed aspect ratio as the shape of your compositional canvas, whose dimensions are expressed as a ratio of the width of the frame to its height. But in film

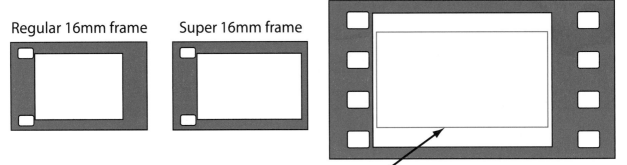

■ **Figure 8-46** The 16mm formats include the standard 1.33:1 aspect ratio *(left)* and Super 16, with a 1.66:1 aspect ratio *(center)*; 35mm films *(right)* are projected at a 1.85:1 theatrical aspect ratio, effectively discarding some of the top and the bottom of the frame in the process.

there are two aspect ratios that we need to consider: full frame aspect ratio and projection aspect ratio. **Full frame** aspect ratio is the actual dimensions of the frame created by the aperture opening in the gate. The aspect ratios of a full frame of 16mm film and 35mm film are identical, 1.33:1. This is referred to as **academy aperture.** Incidentally, this is the same aspect ratio for a frame of the old standard NTSC TV signal (4 × 3), which, in its early development was designed to be compatible with the movies of the time. However, in the 1950s, when color TV entered the market, the film industry felt the need to compete with the TV industry for viewers. After much experimentation with various frame widths, the industry eventually settled on 1.85:1 as the standard aspect ratio for theatrical presentation[3] (see pages 48–49). This aspect ratio is much wider and was developed to provide a unique visual experience, one that couldn't be duplicated on TV and therefore would encourage viewers to keep going to theaters. This change in aspect ratio, however, does not alter the actual size of the full 35mm camera frame, only the portion of that frame that is projected. The wider format is accomplished through masking, which involves using a projector gate that cuts off the top and bottom of the full frame to the 1.85:1 proportions. This is common practice in commercial film production, so the final projection aperture must be anticipated when shooting. This is accomplished with the finder markings in the viewfinder of a 35mm camera; the markings indicate, through shading, the exact 1.85:1 frame that will be projected and thus aid in framing and composition (Figure 8-47).

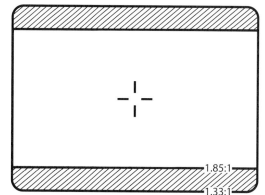

■ **Figure 8-47** The ground glass in a viewfinder usually has some markings to aid in the composition of a frame. Ground glasses come in literally hundreds of aspect ratio combinations (pictured: a 35mm ground glass masking the full frame negative to a 1.85:1 aspect ratio).

Because we cannot spare any of the area of the smaller frame, 16mm film is often shot and viewed in its 1.33:1 aspect ratio; however, standard 16mm can be a problem when transferring to any format other than NTSC video (which is all but obsolete). Most filmmakers who want to take advantage of the image quality of film and the lighter, much more affordable 16mm gauge, and who have the intention to later transfer the negative to 35mm (for theatrical release) or HD video in the 16:9 aspect ratio, will more often use the Super 16mm format. **Super 16** was invented by the Swedish filmmaker Rune Ericson in 1961 as a way to use 16mm gauge film to inexpensively produce films for theatrical release. The aspect ratio for Super 16 is 1.66:1 — that is, the same as standard European 35mm theatrical projection. To create the 1.66:1 dimension, Super 16 uses a gate that is a little bit wider than standard 16mm, which also creates a slightly larger picture area (see Figure 8-46).

This aspect ratio is closer to American theatrical projection (1.85:1), so the transfer, or blowup, from Super 16 to 35mm, is *much* more compatible than from standard 16mm. The transfer from Super 16 to the 16 × 9 (or 1.78:1) digital video formats is nearly perfect. With home televisions exclusively employing the 16 × 9 format, people are rapidly modifying standard 16mm cameras to shoot Super 16 (but not all 16mm cameras do this). In terms of theatrically released films, many low-budget and independent films continue to be shot on Super 16 and are later blown up to 35mm for release, not only because it costs less than 35mm as a production format but also because the grittier look resulting from the blowup process contributes a particular edgy aesthetic. It's important to remember that Super 16 is an acquisition format only. There are no Super 16 projectors. Shooting Super 16 necessarily means that you must transfer to either SD or HD video, or to 35mm to exhibit the movie.

---

[3]For a fascinating discussion of the history of projection aspect ratios and the American film industry, see *Widescreen Cinema,* by John Belton, Harvard University Press, Cambridge, MA, 1992.

According to D.P. Maryse Alberti, she and director Darren Aronofsky briefly considered the idea of shooting *The Wrestler* on HD but decided on Super 16 because the grain and contrast of the film stock was best for telling the story of Randy "The Ram" Robinson (Mickey Rourke), an aging wrestler trying to piece his life together after a heart attack. According to Kodak's "Focus on Film," Alberti shot with two film stocks, both rated EI 500, and often pushed them several stops. "[…]Darren and I agreed that film was the right medium for this story. It's a different look that feels right for the emotional tone. The decision to shoot in Super 16mm format was partially based on a modest budget, but mainly it's a bit of an edgier look that we felt was right." The subsequent blowup to 35mm for release preserved the gritty texture and realism they were after (**Figure 8-48**, *top*).

Most of Meirelles and Lund's *City of God* was shot by D.P. César Charlone on Super 16 for much the same reason. The look of the film reflected the energy and rawness of the tough Rio slums and the street gangs they were depicting, while the lighter cameras allowed for handheld mobility. However, the intricately detailed long shots of the favelas required extra resolution, so for these the filmmakers switched to 35mm for its ability to render fine detail (**Figure 8-48**, *center*).

Stephen Frears's film *The Queen* also mixed Super 16 and 35mm film stocks but did so for different reasons—Frears and D.P. Alffonso Beato used the unique characteristics of each film stock for character development. *The Queen* follows the reactions and actions of Her Majesty Elizabeth II, the newly elected Prime Minister Tony Blair, and the British public in the weeks following the death of Princess Diana. The filmmakers decided that Blair, the populist Labor Party prime minister, would be more appropriately

■ **Figure 8-48** *The Wrestler* (2008, *top*) was shot entirely on Super 16 for its grain and gritty look. *City of God* (2002, *center*) mixed Super 16 and 35mm stock depending on the resolution required. *The Queen* (2006, *bottom*) also mixed film gauges; Super 16 for the scenes involving Prime Minister Blair and 35mm for scenes with Her Royal Highness the Queen.

shot on rugged Super 16, whereas the exquisitely fine grain, nuance, and detail of the 35mm film image would better reflect the world of the Royal Family and Queen Elizabeth II herself. (**Figure 8-48**, *bottom*).

The Digital Video System

While the basic film system has remained virtually unchanged in well over 100 years, the video system seems to be in a perpetual state of rapid evolution. New video formats are introduced almost yearly, and swift technological obsolescence is the rule rather than the exception. Lucky for us, with each technological generation the trend is toward broader access to an electronic image that is sharper, richer, and increasingly responsive to the subtleties of light and shadow. A good example is the speedy expansion of high-definition video from a highly expensive professional format to one that in only a few years has become available at all budget levels of video equipment. Unfortunately however, the world of video engineers, corporations, and government committees have not managed to coordinate their efforts to establish a single national video standard, let alone a world-wide standard. With enormous profits on the line, corporate rivals and nations are all racing to develop their own superior system in the hope that theirs will become the new standard. Current count reveals dozens of major digital video formats, many of them in high definition and most of which also offer multiple frame rates and aspect ratios. These days the world of video production can seem like a technological tar pit for emerging filmmakers and veterans alike.

To maintain some degree of organizational clarity, it is important to carefully consider this slippery word, "format." In the world of video, format can mean a number of things, and these fall into three broad categories:
1. **Display formats** are a set of specifications for how video is broadcast, received, and displayed and are reflected in the set of nationally mandated digital television broadcast standards, which were devised by the Advanced Television Systems Committee (ATSC, discussed later in the chapter). Digital Cinema has a separate set of format specifications, which specifically address digital theatrical projection (see page 407).
2. **Recording formats** determine the way a particular system (camera, Blu-ray, etc.) encodes and records video. Recording formats consist of several technical specifications including resolution, aspect ratio, data rate, and encoding system (sampling/compression), Recording formats divide up roughly by manufacturer (page 217).
3. **Media Formats.** The physical media on which video data are recorded are often referred to as a format. MiniDV, HDCam and DVCPro HD are popular tape formats. P2 and SxS are common file based media formats (see page 208). These formats are very closely associated with record formats and also divide up by manufacturer.
4. **Audio/video codecs** are not technically formats, but they are so integral to the process of working with, within, and across formats (in recording, editing, and transmission) that a filmmaker must be able to identify them and understand their function. Because codecs are utilized both in display formats and recording formats, they are frequently and inaccurately referred to as formats (page 216).

In the United States there are 18 broadcast television display formats, with many more around the world; 9 or 10 major recording formats, which change all the time; and dozens of audio and video codecs, which are also constantly evolving. Obviously it would be folly to try to cover them all in detail. But in the world of digital video, knowing some technical information is imperative in order to make informed creative choices and to have a smooth creative and technical process from preproduction to distribution. This chapter explores all three of these categories in a general way, to demystify the basic technology of video and to explain some of the terms, specifications, and concepts that are essential to you in your capacity as a filmmaker. Beyond the information in this chapter, you will find a list of related websites in the Web Resources section at the back of the book, which you can visit to find more details and stay up to date with the most recent changes, facts, and statistics.

■ BROADCAST STANDARDS

In 1941 a group of television engineers and government policy makers established the standards for creating and broadcasting black-and-white television in the United States. The **National Television Standards Committee (NTSC)** addressed various technical specifications for image reproduction and reception, ensuring compatibility between every television camera and TV set across the country and with those of any other nation that shared the NTSC system. In the early 1950s the NTSC changed these standards slightly to accommodate the addition of color to the television signal. NTSC broadcast standards were devised in the analog video era; however, around the turn of the century film and video production was manifestly transformed by the digital revolution. **Analog video** (and audio) means that the creation, recording, playback, and distribution of the video/audio signal are accomplished on videotape via fluctuations in electronic voltage recorded on magnetic particles, which are, respectively, analogous to the original light values of the image and the acoustic waves of the audio. **Digital video (DV)**[1] and audio, on the other hand, create, record, and disseminate video and audio by transforming light values and acoustic energy into binary code, or a series of ones and zeros. There are numerous advantages to digital media: including superior resolution, greater flexibility for creative manipulation, and the ability to make copies with no generational loss. In addition, the advent of digital video precipitated another revolution by delivering high-definition (HD) video formats in addition to the standard-definition (SD) format. And so with the digital revolution came a reappraisal of broadcast standards.

In 2009 the NTSC was phased out as the government mandated a switchover to an all-digital broadcast system with a new set of standards devised by a new consortium of engineers, telecommunications companies, and government policy makers called the **Advanced Television Systems Committee (ATSC)**. These new **video display standards**, like their predecessor, ensure compatibility between image recording and display processes in the digital domain and across all nations that adopt the standard (including the United States, Mexico, Canada, South Korea, and other countries in central America, the Caribbean, and Asia Pacific). Analog video is now a historical artifact and DV is the standard; however, the legacy of NTSC still remains with us in many forms, primarily the ATSC formats for standard-definition video are adapted from the old NTSC standards, partly to ensure backward compatibility.

Although ATSC broadcast standards incorporate volumes of arcane technical requirements, for our purposes **broadcast standards** refers to four primary details of the video image: (1) frame rate, (2) scanning method, (3) aspect ratio, and (4) resolution. Figure 9-1 lists the eighteen digital video format standards supported by the ATSC broadcast system. Six of these are **high-definition (HD)** formats and the rest are **standard-definition (SD)**. It is important to understand the ATSC standards because every time you pick up a DV camera to shoot your movie, you are faced with a menu of shooting options. Should you shoot in HD or in SD? Some cameras allow you to shoot at 60i, 60p, 30p, or even 24p. Should you choose

ATSC Digital Television Standard Video Formats				
Resolution		Aspect Ratio	Frame rate	
Vertical lines	Horizontal pixels		Progressive (p)	Interlaced (i)
HD 1080	1920	16:9	24 / 23.976 30 / 29.97	30 (60i fields/sec) 29.97 (59.94i fields/sec)
HD 720	1280	16:9	24 / 23.976 30 / 29.97 60 / 59.94	
SD 480	704	16:9 , 4:3	24 / 23.976 30 / 29.97 60 / 59.94	30 (60i fields/sec) 29.97 (59.94i fields/sec)
SD 480	640	4:3	24 / 23.976 30 / 29.97 60 / 59.94	30 (60i fields/sec) 29.97 (59.94i fields/sec)

Source : ATSC

■ Figure 9-1 The ATSC digital television standards support 18 different DV formats.

[1]In this book the term "digital video" (DV) encompasses both standard-definition (SD) and high-definition (HD) formats. Occasionally you will hear people use DV as a synonym for SD video.

the 4:3 aspect ratio or 16:9? Remember, the standards are not just for broadcast display, but for the capturing of images as well.

Frame Rate and Scanning

Film and video share the process of recording a scene as a series of still images and then replaying those images in rapid succession to create the illusion of motion. While film runs at a frame rate of 24 frames per second (fps), DV runs at a frame rate of 30 fps[2] (60 fps in some progressive modes). The major difference, however, is *how* those images are created and then played back. Film accomplishes this through a mechanical and photochemical process, but DV uses an electronic process known as **scanning**, and there are two types of scanning: interlaced (i) and progressive (p).

Interlaced Scanning

As with film, the creation of the image begins with the lens gathering light from the scene and focusing it on the image plane. In video, this is called the **sensor** (or **imager)**, and it is the surface of a CCD chip (or CMOS [complementary metal oxide semiconductor] chip). A **CCD chip** (for charged coupled device) is a solid-state sensor (measuring either ¼″, ⅓″, ½″, or ⅔″ across) composed of hundreds of thousands to millions of light-sensitive photodiodes called **pixels** (short for **picture elements**), which are linked together (coupled) and aligned in tight horizontal rows (Figure 9-2). When these pixels, which are actually tiny capacitors, are struck by the incoming light, they build up an electronic charge that corresponds to the light intensity hitting *that* particular spot. So all at once, the image is created on the face of the CCD. The CCD then **outputs** or **reads out** this pixel specific voltage information in two different ways, depending on the format you've chosen. In the case of **interlaced scanning**, the chip first outputs the odd-numbered horizontal pixel lines (1, 3, 5, 7, etc.), one at a time, from the top to the bottom, creating a half-resolution image that is called a **field** of video. Then, the scan process returns to the top of the frame to output the even-numbered rows (2, 4, 6, etc.), from the top to the bottom, to fill in the rest of the information with a second field of video. These two fields of video are interlaced to make up one full **frame** (Figure 9-3). All this electronic information (visual and scanning) is then converted into digital data for storage on the record media (and sent to a monitor). During playback, the receiver/monitor duplicates the exact same interlaced process, line for line, field for field, and frame for frame, in perfect synchronization with the scanning used to record the image only in reverse. Now, the digital information is converted back into electrical voltage, which is then translated into light values (an image) as the electrical voltage causes the horizontal rows of pixels in a monitor to glow at the same scanning rate. In a plasma display, these pixels are colored fluorescent cells, and in an LCD monitor they are tiny LCD crystals.

When you see the scanning rate of 60i in the ATSC table above ("i" for interlaced), it means 60 fields of video information interlaced per second for a frame rate of 30 frames per second. Interlaced scanning was developed as the standard scanning method for the old NTSC video system because it created a "flickerless" image as the rapid interlacing "refreshes" the image twice as fast as the equivalent progressive scan. It has remained in the ATSC standards both to ensure backward compatibility and as a way to deliver high-quality content at reduced signal bandwidth.

Progressive Scanning

Progressive scanning differs from interlaced scanning in that one frame is not made up of two interlaced fields (odds lines first, then even lines); instead, with progressive scanning both the imager and display are synchronized to scan a full frame of video (all horizontal

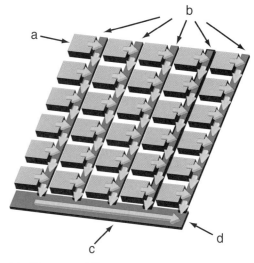

■ **Figure 9-2** CCD chip. Individual pixels (a) collect brightness information and feed a corresponding charge down vertical registers (b), which carry them to a horizontal register (c). The raw video signal (d) is then fed to an output amplifier. The pixels are read one row at a time at the horizontal charge transfer area; once the information is collected, the row above gets transferred one row down to be collected. The charges in the rows are therefore "coupled" to one another.

[2]Video frame rates can be expressed as frames per second or Hertz. So 30 fps can also be 30 Hz. Also, see "More on Frame Rates" later for more details.

field a   field b

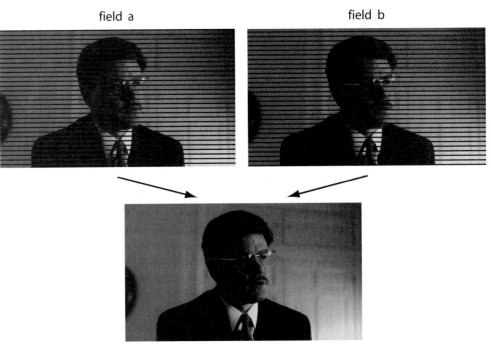

1 interlaced frame

■ **Figure 9-3** Interlaced video. A single frame is created by scanning two alternate fields; first, the odd lines are scanned, from top to bottom, then the even lines are scanned, creating the second field.

■ **Figure 9-4** Progressive scanning draws a full frame of video, from top to bottom, with each pass.

lines in order 1, 2, 3, 4, etc.) from top to bottom at a rate of 30 fps (or 60 fps as with the 720p format). There are no fields, just complete frames (Figure 9-4). Progressive scanning formats are written as 30p and 60p ("p" for progressive). Although progressive scanning requires more bandwidth space than interlaced video at the same frame rate, the resolution of progressive scanning is visibly superior to interlaced scanning. However, some people maintain that interlaced scanning is superior for content that has a lot of fast motion, like sports.

One serious problem occurs when you try to view an interlaced image on a progressive scan display (which includes computer monitors). The process of the progressive scanning pattern will present the two interlaced fields slightly offset, which is especially noticeable with objects in motion (or during camera movements), and this creates a **combing** artifact along edges in the image (Figure 9-5). In these cases, the interlaced scanned video should undergo a process known as "de-interlacing" before it is displayed on progressive scan monitors.

The 24p Frame Rate

The 24p frame rate refers to a video signal with a progressive scan frame rate of 24 frames per second. Sound familiar? The 24p video format was developed specifically to be compatible with and to duplicate the look of motion picture film by recording motion in 24 rather than 30 discrete still images per second, thus replicating some of the motion artifacts of film and giving it a so called "film look" even when played back on 60i video monitors (Figure 9-6). At resolutions of 1080 or 720, 24p is considered a high-definition format, and when displayed on a system capable of 24p HD (usually

■ **Figure 9-5** When interlaced video is shown on progressing displays, a "combing" artifact occurs at the edges of moving objects caused by the displaced scan lines (notice that the stationary objects do not show any combing).

professional projection and not home flat-screen displays) can approximate the look of film. Many short and feature films are shot in 1080/24p HD and then, taking advantage of the simple one-to-one frame correspondence, transferred to film for theatrical distribution (**Figure 9-7**). The 24p frame rate is also an option on standard-definition DV cameras. Even though standard-definition 24p does not have nearly the resolution of 24p HD, 35mm, or even 16mm film, nonetheless, this hasn't stopped filmmakers from using this extremely inexpensive, accessible, and mobile format for shooting and then later transferring and releasing on film (**Figure 9-8**). Some people really like the 24p look; others are not as convinced. My recommendation is to do some tests and see if you like it. As with all technical choices, it all boils down to which look is best for the project? Which quality will help you tell your story better?

■ **Figure 9-6** The 24p shooting mode is available on most HD cameras from the ultra-high-end ($65,000+) rigs, like this Sony Cine-Alta F23 *(left)*, to cameras in more affordable price ranges, like the Panasonic AG-HVX200A *(right)*.

Although it is fairly simple to understand how we can transfer 24p video (SD or HD) to film for distribution (frame by frame), one might ask how we can view a video shot at 24 progressive frames per second on a 60i (30 fps) monitor, which is the most common display format. The answer is, the same way we are able to watch a film shot at 24 fps on television. The very common transfer process from a 24 fps system to a 30 fps system is called 2:3 pulldown and is explained in detail in Chapter 19.

More on Frame Rates (29.97, 59.94, and 23.976)
In the ATSC Video Format Standards table (see **Figure 9-1**), you'll notice that there are whole number frame rates supported, like 30fps (60i), 60p, 30p, and 24p. However, there are also frame rates listed, which are ever so slightly slower than their whole number counterparts, namely 59.94, 29.97, and 23.976. So what are these?

■ **Figure 9-7** Shooting at 24p for theatrical release is available on high-end video cameras, like the RED used to shoot Soderbergh's *The Informant!* (2009, *left*), as well as consumer models, like the Canon XH-A1, which, because of its small size, was used to shoot much of the action in Nevildine and Taylor's *Crank! High Voltage* (2009, *right*).

■ **Figure 9-8** Von Trier's *Dancer in the Dark* (2004, *left*) was shot in SD MiniDV at 24p with the Sony PD-150 *(right)*.

These slowed-down frame rates (0.1% slower) are legacies of the old NTSC system, which remain with us in order to stay compatible with SD format standards (which were derived from the NTSC system). Here's a little history. Before the advent of color TV, the original NTSC black-and-white video signal was a nice and neat 30 fps. In the early 1950s, NTSC developed the standards for color television and in an effort to make color television compatible with all preexisting monochrome receivers; NTSC super-imposed the color component on top of the existing black-and-white signal along a subcarrier frequency (3.58 MHz) rather than create a whole new, fully integrated signal. This ensured that even though a program was broadcast in color, viewers who owned black-and-white TV sets could still receive the signal. However, this approach required a few sacrifices, the most important being literally slowing down the frame rate such that the 30 fps signal (60 integrated fields per second) was actually 29.97 fps (59.94 integrated fields per second). Therefore, when we are talking about video production purposes, the rate 60i (perhaps the most widely used) is actually 59.94 fields per second (29.97 frames per second). The 24p frame rate is actually 23.976, to provide a much easier conversion to the SD frame rates. (It should be noted that 30p is a little used frame rate for filmmakers). Most video cameras in fact shoot in these slowed-down frame rates, even if the frame rate options menu lists the rounded numbers. Ultimately, what this means for filmmakers is that we have to anticipate how our movie will be distributed in order to choose a production frame rate that will cause us the fewest headaches in postproduction. This issue of moving from production format, to editing format, to distribution format is called **workflow,** and we discuss it in much more detail in Chapter 19. But for the purposes of this chapter, what is important to keep in mind is that if you intend your project to be screened via an SD format (i.e., SD broadcast or DVDs), then at some point you will be working with these slightly slower frame rates.

Aspect Ratio

The aspect ratio of a video frame is the dimensional relationship between the height and the length of a frame of video (see page 48 for more on aspect ratios). The ATSC format standard supports two aspect ratios natively, 16:9 and 4:3. All ATSC high-definition formats have an aspect ratio of 16:9 and in terms of common industry practice (rather than government standards) 16:9 has become the standard shooting aspect ratio for the majority of newly produced shows whether in HD or SD. The 4:3 aspect ratio is another holdover from the old NTSC standards and also happens to have practically the same dimension as the first established motion picture aspect ratio of 1.37:1, called Academy ratio. Academy ratio was the theatrical film standard before the introduction of widescreen theatrical release in 1953.

■ **Figure 9-9** A 4:3 signal viewed on a widescreen television is displayed with the use of black or gray bars on the sides of the screen, a practice called "pillar-boxing."

Although a large quantity of material is still being broadcast in 4:3, practically all flat-screen video monitors are manufactured to accommodate the 16:9 format. What this means is that vertical edges of the video display are masked in a process is called pillar-boxing for broadcasts that are in 4:3 (**Figure 9-9**).

Resolution

Whenever there is an evaluation of video image quality, you will hear the term "resolution." **Resolution** generally refers to the ability to reproduce visual detail: sharpness of line, subtlety and degrees of luminance, and accuracy of color. Video resolution is affected by many factors in addition to the format scanning system; these include lens quality, the number of imager pixels, sampling bit rates, chroma subsampling, and data compression (all explained later). In this section we're looking specifically at **ATSC format resolution,** which is determined primarily by the number of pixels, and the more pixels one has to create the image, the more detail, smoothness of curve, and nuance of shade and color can be rendered (**Figure 9-10**). We can determine the pixel resolution of a given format by multiplying the vertical lines by the horizontal pixels. The standard-definition DV resolution that most resembles the old NTSC format is SD 704 × 480; it contains a little more than 338,000 pixels with which to define the image, whereas the two high-definition resolutions, 720p and 1080i, provide for 921,600 and 2,073,600 pixels per frame, respectively; this represents a much greater resolution capacity (more detailed visual information). HD looks much better—this is no surprise—but by exclusively considering this measure, one would wonder why anyone would use 720p HD, which has only half the pixel count as 1080i. This is where scanning frame rates enters into the resolution question. 1080i has twice as many total pixels, but the fact that it is an interlaced signal means that each field contains only half those lines (540) and the frame rate is 30 fps. On the other hand, 720p, with its progressive scanning, presents twice the number of frames per second (60 as opposed to 30). So in the final calculation, 720p utilizes somewhere around 56 million pixels per second, while

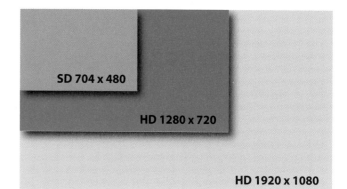

■ **Figure 9-10** The resolution of DV formats can be roughly determined by multiplying the horizontal and vertical pixels. This illustration shows the relative resolution capabilities based on pixel count.

■ **Figure 9-11** The resolution of HD allows for richer colors, more information in shadow areas, and, as shown here, much finer detail reproduction. In this frame, the individual hairs on Maximus' (Russell Crowe) fur cape are visible in HD *(left)* but fuzzy on SD (right). (Still from Scott's *Gladiator*, 2000.)

1080i utilizes somewhere around 62 million pixels per second.[3] In these terms, the resolution difference isn't so great, and this is why most people cannot tell the difference between the two HD formats.

It is important to understand that HD is a complete system of image creation and exhibition. To realize the improved resolution of HD, you not only need to shoot on HD but you also must display that image on an HD-capable monitor or projector. Shooting HD but displaying the footage on an SD monitor will reduce the quality of your original image to—you guessed it—480 lines of vertical resolution. Conversely, if your footage originated in an SD format, displaying it on an HD monitor will not increase the resolution quality. Footage originating on HD will also retain all of its visual resolution when it is transferred to film, a practice that is common for theatrically released motion pictures (**Figure 9-11**).

Color Encoding

The element of the video image that determines image brightness (shades of black and white) is called the **luminance** signal (also written as Y). The color component of the video signal is referred to as **chrominance** (also written as C, or chroma). Chrominance is made up of **hue**, which determines the tint of a particular color, and **saturation**, which determines the intensity of the colors. To achieve a color image, the video signal is divided into **the three primary colors of light: red, green, and blue (RGB)** and an accurate color blend is created through the additive process of mixing these three primary colors with the brightness information. In most midlevel and high-end video cameras, there are three CCD chips that are used to record the light intensities of each primary color (see **Figure 9-30**). In flat-screen displays, each pixel is made up of three separate, individually controlled cells (or subpixels) for each color, and these cells glow according to voltage fluctuations during the scanning process (**Figure 9-12**).

■ **Figure 9-12** Just like camera sensors, color flat-screen displays (LCD or plasma) are made up of millions of pixels. Each individual pixel contains red, green, and blue subpixels (outlined). (See the color insert).

[3]Note that **720p**: 921,600 pxls/frame × 60fps = 55,656,000 pxls/sec; **1080i**: 2,073,600 pxls/frame × 30fps = 62,208,000 pxls/sec.

A Final Note on ATSC Standards

You should be aware that the ATSC standards are voluntary, meaning the broadcaster may choose which formats it wishes to broadcast (no one broadcasts all formats). The trade-off is quality for quantity. The amount of bandwidth space it takes to carry an HD signal can carry multiple SD channels (called **multicasting**) or additional data information or services. Media companies who broadcast in HD only use one of the two HD formats. There are other companies that broadcast several channels entirely with SD, and still others that offer an SD channel and an HD channel. Additionally, the electronics companies who build flat-screen receivers can choose which resolutions they wish to support natively. Almost all receivers are built in the 16:9 aspect ratio, but some receivers natively support 720p HD (cheaper), while others natively support 1080i HD (slightly higher image quality). There is no difference in picture quality when it comes to displaying SD broadcasts, and both receivers can, of course, display both HD broadcasts in 720p and 1080i. However, it requires some signal conversion (called **scaling**) to display the SD or HD signal that is not native to the receiver. Scaling a 720p signal to display on a native 1080i monitor is called **up-conversion** and requires no loss in quality. Scaling 1080i signal to display on a native 720p display is called **down-conversion** and necessitates a nearly imperceptible loss in resolution. There is much debate on the blogosphere concerning whether the quality difference is noticeable, but I'll leave you to research that question on your own.

in practice

WHAT IS 1080p60?

Many flat-screen monitors offer a 1080p60 resolution, which is the highest HD format resolution currently available; 1080p60 has the ultrahigh pixel resolution of 1080i, the smoothness of progressive scan playback, and twice as much picture information as 1080i. Remember, 1080i has a frame rate of 60i, or 60 *interlaced fields*, which equals 30 frames per second; 1080p60, on the other hand, runs at 60 progressive frames per second. You'll note that 1080p60 is *not* a broadcast standard format (it is too large a signal for the available bandwidth). But 1080p is a HD resolution for Blu-ray discs (as well as the resolution for many video game consoles). The 1080p60 receivers are becoming very popular because there is never any down-conversion of quality. They can display any signal at full resolution.

Other Broadcast Standards

As mentioned earlier, ATSC video standards ensure system compatibility in any country that uses it. Unfortunately, there is not a single global digital broadcast standard, there are four. Other digital television standards around the world are **DVB-T** (Digital Video Broadcasting-Terrestrial), which is used throughout western and eastern Europe, Russia, Australia, and many nations throughout Asia and Africa; **ISDB-T** (Integrated Services Digital Broadcasting-Terrestrial), used in Japan, Brazil, and most of South America; and **DTMB** (Digital Terrestrial Multimedia Broadcast), used by China and Hong Kong. As of the writing of this edition, global digital television standards were still in the process of being fully adopted by many nations. The target date for the complete global transition from analog to some form of digital broadcast is 2020. Just as the ATSC standards are based for backward compatibility with the old NTSC standards and easy down-conversion from HD to SD resolutions, so too is DVB-T based on the widespread former European analog standards **PAL** (Phase Alternate Line) and **SECAM** (Séquential Couleur Avec Mémoire). The primary differences between NTSC and PAL or SECAM video formats are frame rate and the number of horizontal lines. Both PAL and SECAM contain 625 horizontal lines (producing superior resolution to NTSC's 525 lines) and they have a frame rate of 25 frames per second (which allows for much easier film-to-tape conversions). This frame rate is exact and there are no "slowed-down" frame rates as there are with NTSC. The new DVB-T standards are based on 25fps frame rates including 50i and 25p for HD transmissions. Many professional cameras have the capacity to switch formats (NTSC, ATSC, PAL, and SECAM), and on them you will find these frame rates as options. However, unless you intend to broadcast exclusively in the European Union or other DVB-T countries, stick with

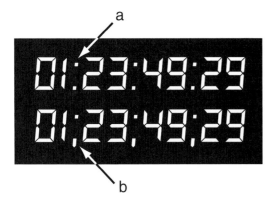

a

b

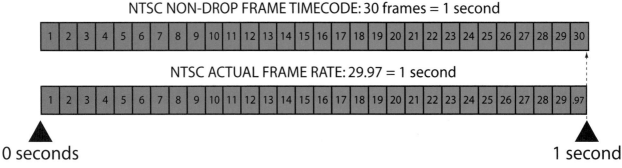

■ **Figure 9-13** Timecode assigns a specific number to every video frame according to a format based on hours, minutes, seconds, and frames. Broadcast video uses only "drop frame" timecode, easily identified by its use of semicolons (b), because it is time accurate. Some applications still provide the option to use "nondrop-frame" timecode, which uses colons as separators (a).

the ATSC standards. If you are an American filmmaker who plans to submit your projects to European festivals, you'll need to ask what the format specifications are. You may have to transcode your project to a 25fps compatible system—and that takes time.

Timecode

The system in video by which every frame is assigned a specific and unique number is called **timecode (TC)**. Recorded right along with the video data for each and every frame is an electronic number with four fields hours:minutes:seconds:frames. This numbering system is vital to the workflow of every video project. We use timecode to quickly log, reference, or locate specific frames; to calculate the length of shots, scenes, and entire projects; to maintain audio and video synchronization; to ensure frame-accurate edits; to calculate trims and transitions in editing; and more. In short, timecode is the way we keep track of the frame-by-frame timing of every element, in every stage of a project. All DV cameras have timecode, but some offer a choice of two different flavors: drop-frame timecode and nondrop-frame timecode (Figure 9-13). Why do we have two ways to count frames? Well, it goes back to that blasted slowing down of the frame rate in NTSC video from 30fps to 29.97 fps, and it's still with us. Grrrrrr.

Nondrop-frame timecode is simple to understand but is less frequently used. **Nondrop-frame TC** simply counts frames according to the original black-and-white video frame rate, assigning a new number to each video frame at a consistent rate of 30 frames per second. But as we discussed previously, the true frame rate of video is slightly slower: 29.97 fps. So simply allocating frame numbers to frames 1 to 30 to video that is actually running at 29.97 frames per second means that what we are calling 1 second (30 frames) is in real time 1 second and a fraction—because 1 second should have turned after 29.97. In essence, nondrop-frame timecode isn't reflecting real time; it is simply counting frames, so we end up accumulating slightly more frame numbers than actual frames per second (30 numbers/second versus 29.97 actual frames/second) (Figure 9-14).

Because it takes a fraction of a second longer to count off 30 frames, the difference between nondrop-frame TC counting time and true video running time is 1.8 frames per minute. That may not seem like much, but when nondrop-frame TC counts off 1 hour of time in a program—which looks like this: 01:00:00:00—it would ostensibly have "counted" 108,000 frames. However, in true NTSC running time there are only 107,892 frames of video in an hour-long program.[4] The discrepancy between constant 30 fps counting and

NTSC NON-DROP FRAME TIMECODE: 30 frames = 1 second

| 1 | 2 | 3 | 4 | 5 | 6 | 7 | 8 | 9 | 10 | 11 | 12 | 13 | 14 | 15 | 16 | 17 | 18 | 19 | 20 | 21 | 22 | 23 | 24 | 25 | 26 | 27 | 28 | 29 | 30 |

NTSC ACTUAL FRAME RATE: 29.97 = 1 second

| 1 | 2 | 3 | 4 | 5 | 6 | 7 | 8 | 9 | 10 | 11 | 12 | 13 | 14 | 15 | 16 | 17 | 18 | 19 | 20 | 21 | 22 | 23 | 24 | 25 | 26 | 27 | 28 | 29 | .97 |

0 seconds

1 second

■ **Figure 9-14** After exactly one second, nondrop-frame timecode displays that 30 frames have been screened. In fact, NTSC video runs at 29.97 and not 30 frames per second. Drop-frame timecode accommodates for this discrepancy by selectively skipping numbers, not frames, so that the time displayed matches the actual time elapsed.

[4]430 frames/second × 60 seconds × 60 minutes = 108,000 frames, but in reality the counting should reflect 29.97 frames/second × 60 seconds × 60 minutes = 107,892 frames.

true 29.97 video time after 1 hour is 108 frames, or 3 seconds and 18 frames. By using nondrop-frame timecode, when the timecode numbers display 1 hour (01:00:00:00) your video will in fact be shorter by 3 seconds and 18 frames (00:59:26:12). That may not seem like such a big deal, but in broadcast television, where programs and commercials must conform to frame-accurate timing, it is crucial to have a precise frame count.

Nondrop-frame timecode is usable when you are shooting and editing HD footage that will remain in the HD realm (or PAL). But any program that you anticipate distributing in SD formats (like SD broadcast and DVDs) should use nondrop-frame timecode. For all SD DV applications, **drop-frame timecode** is the standard and default method for counting and addressing frames with ID numbers. Drop-frame timecode does not actually drop any video frames, but it does skip over some timecode numbers from time to time in order to adjust the frame count to accurately reflect the true 29.97 fps of SD video. To be precise, the drop-frame TC system skips over the :00 and :01 frame numbers once every minute, except for the 10th minute. Here is how the TC numbers change at each minute of footage (except for every 10th minute): 00;09;26;28, 00;09;26;29, 00;09;27;02, 00;09;27;03. This method compensates for the slowed-down video frame rate and, in the end, is completely frame accurate. After an hour of drop-frame timecode counting, we will arrive at TC 01;00;00;00 for exactly 1 hour of video footage.

in practice

■ WHEN TO USE WHICH DV FORMAT?

It's common to find DV cameras that gives you the option to shoot in 60i, 24p, or 30p, in either SD or HD resolutions. So how do you choose? When do you shoot in each format? It all depends on what your finishing format will be and how you plan to distribute your movie:

- **Shoot** everything in 16:9 aspect ratio unless you have a very specific aesthetic reason for using 4:3.
- **Shoot SD 60i** when you anticipate distributing on standard 60i video (broadcasting SD DV or DVD distribution) and don't need or want the so-called film look of 24p. This is also a good option if you plan to stream your film as compressed video on the web.
- **Shoot 24p** when you plan to finish and distribute on film or D-Cinema (see page 406). The one-to-one frame correspondence makes the transfer much easier. Also, shoot 24p if

you like the unique visual quality of the format when the project is finished and displayed on standard 60i video. In either case, the HD 24p (720/24p or 1080/24p) will always give you better quality than SD 24p.

- **Shoot HD (720/60p or 1080/60i)** if you plan to broadcast as an HD signal or screen on HD-ready equipment. The superior resolution, the ability of HD to handle subtle lighting, and the overall superiority of HD equipment (lenses, encoders, etc.) make this a good format even if you plan to distribute your work in standard definition. In other words, if you've got HD, use it and down-convert to SD when necessary. In general, 1080/60i is the more popular and flexible of the two HD formats.
- **Ignore 30p.** To some extent, 30p is a format that is there because the engineers could put it there. There is no advantage to shooting 30p for most applications related to narrative filmmaking.

■ DIGITAL VIDEO CAMCORDERS AND FORMATS

Historically, analog video cameras have broken down into neat categories. Professional cameras were big, expensive, well made, and produced high-quality video, whereas consumer cameras were small, inexpensive, had an inferior image, but above all were easy to use. Then came digital video and everything changed. Now small, affordable cameras are delivering extremely high-quality footage, so much so that the "pros" use them extensively. Only a few years ago true high definition was only available on cameras costing $60,000 or more; today HD is available in all price ranges, and this trend is quickly making standard-definition video redundant. It is now easy to find cameras capable of excellent high-definition video with very good lenses and high-end user functions for around $5,000! It seems downright inappropriate to call a camera that is capable of shooting high-definition 1080i, 790p, *and* 24p in the 16:9 aspect ratio a "consumer" camera. Some people use the term "prosumer" for this phenomenon, and you'll also hear these cameras called "midlevel" or "industrial" cameras. In any case, this range of high-quality yet affordable camcorders, which are too complex for the average consumer, are perfect when a polished and controlled look is important, but a full-blown, high-end, professional rig would be overkill. Whichever term you use, suffice it to say that the line dividing professional-quality gear and nonprofessional access is fading. Price tags on high-quality equipment are so low that virtually anybody can create HD broadcast quality projects on video. Sure, there will always be a line of high-end professional cameras so technologically advanced and tricked out that buying one requires a second mortgage (see page 217), just as there will always be a line of super cheap consumer cameras that do everything easily but nothing particularly well, but the range of cameras between those two poles are getting better and more affordable.

The Basic DV Camcorder: Exterior

The standard form of the video camera for location field production is the **camcorder**, which simply means that the camera and recording device are built into the same unit. Just like film camera, most DV camcorders contain the same basic components and essential functions (**Figure 9-15**).

The Body

Video is a single-system sound format, which means that the body of a video camera contains all of the electronic circuitry to gather and record both audio and video. Generally there are two types of camcorder bodies: shoulder-mount cameras and palm camcorders. Shoulder-mount camcorders tend to be found on the high-end professional range, where cameras are heavier. A shoulder-mounting camera allows for very stable handheld shots,

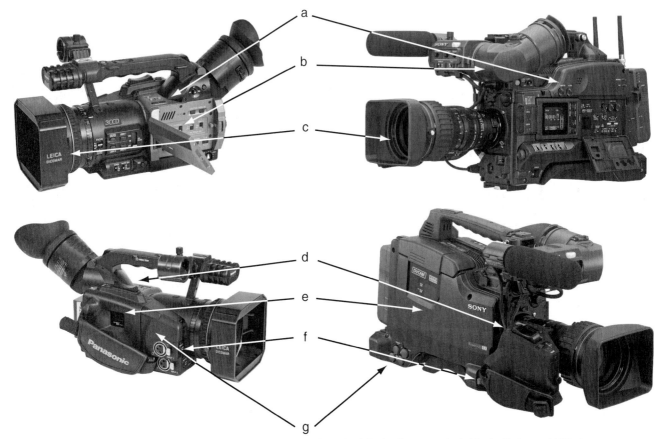

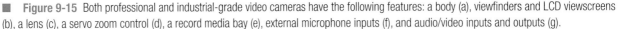

■ **Figure 9-15** Both professional and industrial-grade video cameras have the following features: a body (a), viewfinders and LCD viewscreens (b), a lens (c), a servo zoom control (d), a record media bay (e), external microphone inputs (f), and audio/video inputs and outputs (g).

while the ultralight palm cameras are more difficult to keep steady without a tripod or stabilizing rig. However, shoulder-mount cameras are also more obvious than are the smaller palm-held camcorders. They announce loudly, "Professional camera here! Broadcast!" Many filmmakers find that the unobtrusiveness and mobility of the smaller camera make them beneficial in certain situations for a sense of spontaneity, dynamic camera styles, or simply a degree of comfort. One type of camcorder body is not inherently better than the other, but the difference in size and weight does have an impact on what you are able to do with the camera and so should be considered with your visual approach.

in practice

After shooting the epilogue to his 1997 film *A Taste of Cherry*, director Abbas Kiarostami was told that the lab had ruined this portion of the film. He could not reshoot because the most beautiful part of the spring season (essential for the story) had already passed and he couldn't wait a full year to get these images again. So to finish the movie, Kiarostami simply used the footage from a small video camera that had been on the set shooting a "behind the scenes" documentary. The epilogue to *A Taste of Cherry*, as is the case with most Kiarostami films, includes many nonactors. "What dramatically distinguished the performance of the video camera from that of the 35mm camera was the reaction of the simple people who behaved so naturally and spontaneously in front of it. This is something I've always striven to achieve during my 30 year career." In trying to get natural performances from nonactors with large, bulky 35mm film cameras, Kiarostami eliminated as many distractions as possible by paring down his equipment and crew to

the bare minimum. "However, when I said 'action,' there was action but it was artificial. . . . There is lighting, tracking, booms, and so on, all of these things keep them from giving a natural performance. . . . [People] know there is nothing natural on the other side off the camera, so why should they be?" But when Kiarostami started to use a small DV camera he discovered something different, "freedom." Nonactors responded with naturalness and spontaneity and Kiarostami was delivered from the large production crews and extra equipment necessary for a 35mm production. "This camera gives the filmmaker an opportunity for experimenting without fear of losing the essential. It's a liberty for a filmmaker." Kiarostami made his next two films exclusively on small format DV. "It would have been impossible to shoot a film like *Ten* without a digital [video] camera" (**Figure 9-16**).

(From *10 on Ten*, by Abbas Kiarostami, 2004)

■ **Figure 9-16** Abbas Kiarostami achieved a high level of spontaneity and naturalness from his actors by using small, consumer-grade DV cameras in *A Taste of Cherry* (1997, *left*) and *Ten* (2002, *right*).

Viewfinders and LCD Viewscreens

The **viewfinder** allows you a close and glare-free look at the video image. The viewfinder is usually a small black-and-white monitor seen through a diopter, but color viewfinders are being used more and more. Just as with a film camera, there is a diopter adjustment that focuses a lens on the tiny viewfinder video screen; the adjustment should be set for the camera operator's eye.

■ **Figure 9-18** Some video camera makers outsource their lenses to well-known lens manufacturers. Pictured here is a Leica Dicomar lens on a Panasonic DVX100A camcorder.

■ **Figure 9-17** An LCD monitor hood keeps sunlight from washing out the LCD screen when shooting at sunny locations.

Most DV cameras also have a flip-open **LCD viewscreen** to monitor your video. These screens are not as accurate as the viewfinder because changes in the viewing angle seriously alter the color and brightness of the image, as does the amount of glare the LCD screen catches from the ambient light. When shooting outdoors, an LCD monitor hood is essential for keeping sun glare from washing out the screen (Figure 9-17). As a focusing aid, many cameras offer **focus assist,** which magnifies a portion of your image allowing you to find critical focus with the LCD monitor. It is also important to note that the LCD screen quickly eats up battery power. However, viewscreens are invaluable as a composition aid when you want to shoot from angles or create camera moves that make using the viewfinder difficult.

The Lens

The function of the lens is to gather the light reflecting off your scene and focus it onto the CCD chips. In other words, everything visual goes through the lens, so quality is important. A poor-quality lens will give you a poor-quality image. Lens quality is a major detail that separates consumer camcorders from those intended for professional applications. Lucky for us, the dramatic improvement of video resolution and imaging devices has been paralleled by an evolution in optical quality in order to realize the new resolution potential. Many video camera manufacturers capitalize on these advancements by outsourcing the manufacturing of their lenses to highly respected specialists, like Carl Zeiss and Leica (Figure 9-18).

■ **Figure 9-19** The Panasonic AG-AF100 camera includes a large 4/3 type sensor and a lens mount capable of accepting a wide range of lenses from the micro 4/3 SLR lens system.

The majority of midlevel and professional camcorders come with a zoom lens, which means that the lens has a range of focal lengths. This is usually sufficient for most situations. The zoom range of any specific lens is expressed in its magnification ability. The degree of magnification increases 10 times over its full range with a 10× (or 10:1) lens, 16 times with a 16× lens, and 20 times with a 20× lens. The larger the magnification ratio, the greater the magnification power of the lens. There are some camera systems that offer interchangeable lenses; for example, almost all of the ultra-high-end rigs for Digital Cinema (like the RED and Sony CineAlta) are equipped with a PL lens mount that is standard for 35mm photography so they can take advantage of a wide range of zoom and prime lenses (see page 226). However, there are a few midpriced cameras that also provide for interchangeable lenses (Figure 9-19). Consumer cameras under $1,000 generally come with a single, unchangeable lens that is made with plastic or extremely low-quality glass elements. Plastic lenses are lighter and cheaper, but they are less sharp and often result in an image of lower resolution than the format is capable of producing. This is one reason why SD footage from a professional rig can look better than HD footage from a consumer camera.

The basic optical functions and compositional attributes of a lens are common to both film and video and are so important to the creative dimension of filmmaking that I have devoted an entire chapter specifically to this topic (see Chapter 10).

Servo Zoom Control

Accompanying the video zoom lens is the ubiquitous **servo zoom control**, which enables you to glide through the zoom range, from wide angle to telephoto, with the touch of a button (**Figure 9-20**). The servo zoom mechanism is usually a "rocker switch," but not all rocker switches are created equal and this is another area that separates the professional cameras from the cheapos.

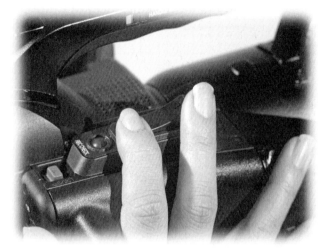

■ **Figure 9-20** The servo zoom rocker-switch allows the camera op to glide through the entire range of focal lengths available on the lens. High-end cameras provide a speed adjustment to this switch, allowing greater control.

The speed of a good-quality servo zoom is pressure sensitive. The further you depress the mechanism, the faster the zoom, and the lighter you touch the button, the slower the zoom. This enables a camera operator not only to control the rate of a zoom, but also to taper it at the beginning and end. Consumer cameras tend to have only one zoom speed, which lurches on and clunks off when you start and stop.

It's also important to note that there are two types of zooms, optical zooms and digital zooms, and they are not even remotely the same, even though the rocker switch controls them both. An **optical zoom** adjusts the central lens element to magnify or de-magnify the scene being shot. Although the composition and perspective of the image changes, the resolution of the video image remains the same. The optical zoom on most DV cameras falls between the 10× magnification range and 20× magnification range. A **digital zoom**, on the other hand is essentially an in-camera digital special effect in which the circuitry in the camera magnifies the captured video signal by selecting the central pixels and blowing them up (**Figure 9-21**). The loss of resolution quality is rapid and significant with digital zooms. Cameras that advertise a 100×, 200×, 300×, or more (!) zoom range combine the two types of zooms. Once the rocker switch reaches the telephoto limits of the optical zoom range, the digital zoom (very obviously) kicks in. As the digital zoom enlarges the image, individual pixels become visible and video noise rakes the image. Many of the better-quality cameras

■ **Figure 9-21** A digital zoom can greatly augment the size of a subject in the frame, but the resulting image *(right)* shows severe resolution compromises compared to the far end of the optical zoom range *(left)*.

allow you to turn the digital zoom off, and many professional cameras don't even bother with digital zooms because of the extreme compromises to the image. Most filmmakers would agree that the digital zoom has limited applications; however, I did have a student effectively use the extreme end of a digital zoom to create the sense that a surveillance camera was observing an illicit encounter between two people. So think of it as another visual tool in your creative toolbox, albeit seldom used.

Media Bay

The **media bay** is where the video signal is recorded. Historically speaking, this part of the camcorder has been referred to as the video tape recorder (VTR) because magnetic tape was the universal recording format for all video systems since the earliest days of the recorded electronic image. However, as a shooting medium, the video tape cassette is on its way toward obsolescence as solid-state memory cards like P2, SxS, and SDHC are incorporated into every newly released camera. Nonetheless, there are still so many great cameras in circulation that use videotape that we can't close the book on this format quite yet.[5] Because of their compact size and high quality, MiniDV tape cassettes are frequently used on consumer and midlevel cameras. Professional cameras use larger cassettes devised for a specific recording format (DVCPRO, DVCAM, etc.) (Figure 9-22).

The amount of data involved in video recording is enormous compared with that for audio recording. For one hour of standard-definition DV footage, a MiniDV cassette must record approximately 12 gigabytes of data on magnetic tape that is ¼ inch wide and a little more than 200 feet long. One rule for recording anything on metal oxide tape stock is that the faster the tape speed is, the more information you can store. However, rather than actually move the tape fast, over stationary heads (which would take up an absurd amount of tape), video and audio data are laid down onto the metal oxide surface by two **write heads**, which are mounted on a spinning drum. The movement of the heads greatly increases the "effective" tape speed without using up more tape.

Although the actual tape speed of MiniDV is only 18.9 mm per second, the two write heads are spinning at a speed of 9,000 rpm *against* the direction of the tape and can therefore lay down all of the data necessary for high-resolution image and audio. In addition, the record heads are mounted on the spinning drum at an angle, so that the data are written along diagonal tracks, called **helical scanning**, giving the heads even more recording space on the tape (Figure 9-23). All videotape formats use this method, even though actual tape speeds from format to format differ. All of the video, audio, and auxiliary system data (i.e., timecode) are written in discrete diagonal tracks between 10 and 15 microns wide. The data for *one frame* are written in five revolutions of the two write heads, which lay down 10 tracks of data the total width of which is only 100 microns, or about the width of a human hair!

■ **Figure 9-22** Although consumer-grade, tape-based camcorders use MiniDV tape, there are many other formats including DVC-PRO, DVC-PROHD, and HDCAM.

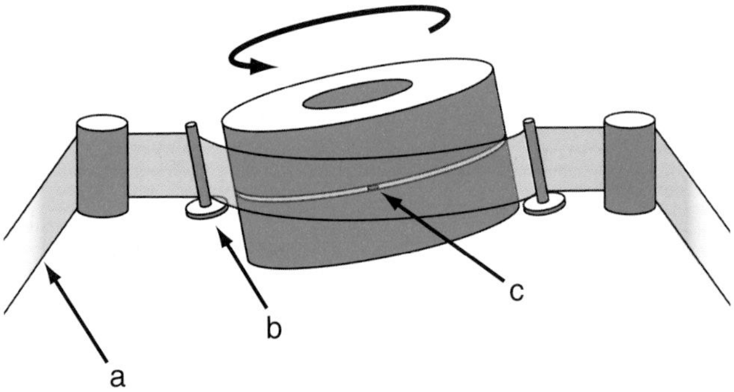

■ **Figure 9-23** When a cassette is inserted into a video camera, the tape (a) is pulled from the casing and it is wrapped around a spinning drum and against the write heads inside (c). Because the drum writes the information using a helical scan, the tape is set at an angle using slant pins (b).

---

[5]Although fading out as a shooting medium, video tape remains the predominant format for project mastering and archiving (see Cht. 24).

As remarkable as it is, the DV cassette format has several disadvantages. The first is the "linearity problem," meaning that to move around to different areas of the tape you need to fast forward and rewind, which takes time. Second, a VTR contains numerous moving parts (springs, cogs, wheels, capstans, flying heads, etc.), and moving parts need care and cleaning and eventually break. Finally, the tape stock itself is susceptible to damage from humidity, dust, and heat. With so much data being written on such a small area, even the slightest damage to the magnetic tape surface can result in **dropouts**, data loss on the tape, which shows up as pixel areas in the image with missing video information.

It is for these reasons, as well as the ability to access footage instantaneously for editing, that tape formats have given way to memory cards, which are a solid-state, file-based recording technology. Unfortunately, there is no single memory card standard; instead each video format favors a different card depending on the manufacturer. Three common memory cards are the **P2** card (from Panasonic's line of DVCPRO HD cameras), the **SxS** cards (Sony's XDCAM line), and **Secure Digital** cards (**SDHC**: up to 32 GB and **SDXC**: over 32 GB) (Figure 9-24). HD video requires vast amounts of storage space, so memory cards are compared (and priced) by their storage capacity, and that, of course, depends on the size of the card (32 GB, 64 GB, etc.) as well as the video data rate of the shooting format (see page 219).

Solid-state memory cards are referred to as **file-based media**, because each camera take is saved as a discrete digital file. File-based recording offers the convenience of instantaneous random-access data retrieval. In the field you can see thumbnail images of every scene you've recorded, which allows you to see, at a glance, your script coverage. Footage recorded on any of these formats is immediately available for editing without the need to capture in real time, as is necessary with tape. Memory cards can also be off-loaded to portable hard drives in the field, allowing you to reuse them again and again (see page 374).

External Microphone Inputs

External microphone inputs are especially important for narrative film production. The **onboard microphones** that come with many camcorders are insufficient for most filmmaking applications where we need to acquire optimum quality audio through careful microphone placement. The microphone input connection is another line demarcating professional/midlevel grade equipment, which is suitable for narrative production, from consumer cameras, which are often inadequately equipped for serious projects.

All professional microphones use the three-pronged XLR connector. The advantages of this connector are a secure connection and balanced audio, which means that the cable is grounded and shielded from interference. Many consumer cameras, however, come with a ⅛″ miniplug connector for external microphone input. The primary shortcoming of this

■ **Figure 9-24** File-based recording on solid-state memory cards, like the P2 card (Panasonic, *left*) and SxS card (Sony, *right*), offer many advantages over tape and are now the standard.

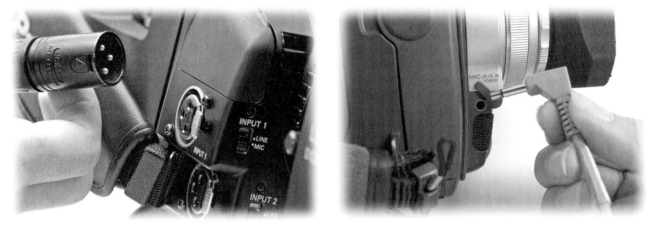

■ **Figure 9-25** Although higher-end camcorders come with XLR inputs for professional microphones *(left)*, consumer cameras often only have ⅛"
connectors *(right)*, which are prone to interference and offer poor quality in the long run.

connector is its flimsiness. The miniplug easily breaks under the rigors of field production. The other shortcoming of the ⅛" minijack is that it is not a balanced audio connection and is highly susceptible to interference (**Figure 9-25**) (see Chapter 15).

Audio and Video, In and Out

There are four common in and out (**I/O**) connectors on camcorders for moving digital video—primarily out of the camera to an external device. On professional and midlevel camcorders you'll usually find a **FireWire** connector (also called **IEEE 1394**), the **HDMI** (High-Definition Multimedia Interface) connector, and **USB (2.0 and 3.0)**. These cables send digital data from the camera to a field monitor or to your editing system for logging and transfer. Professional cameras also come equipped with **SDI/HD-SDI** output (**Serial Digital Interface**), which uses the tried and true, locking **BNC connector** (**Figure 9-26**). This interface can output uncompressed video (SD or HD) to a high-capacity hard drive (HHD) or solid-state (SSD) video recorder for recording footage as you shoot (depending on your camera), thus simultaneously creating a backup or bypassing the onboard record media all together. Many camcorders still have a standard analog NTSC **composite video and audio** output for viewing footage on a regular NTSC monitor or transferring to an analog format. On consumer and midlevel cameras, these line signal connectors are usually the standard **RCA plug**. The RCA plug is also used for audio **line signal** I/O, but on professional gear the sturdier and more secure **XLR connector** is used for both line audio and microphone audio (see Chapter 16). Every camcorder has its own audio and video I/O configuration; always check your camcorder's specific hardware.

■ **Figure 9-26** I/O connectors on midlevel video camcorders usually include S-video (a), RCA (b), and 4-pin FireWire connectors (c). Professional video cameras additionally have the sturdy XLR (d), BNC (e), and 6-pin FireWire connectors (f) HDMI connectors (not pictured) are becoming standard on most cameras.

Component and Composite Analog Video

Composite video simply means that all of the elements that make up the video signal, luminance (Y) and chrominance (C) are encoded together and transmitted via a single wire, like an RCA or BNC cable. However, on some equipment you will find an **S-video connector** (**super-video**). S-Video is a four-pin analog component video connector. **Component video** (or **Y/C video**) keeps the chrominance and luminance components of the signal separate for a superior image. You can only realize this extra quality if both your playback and monitor have S-video connectors and capabilities. Other flavors of component video include **R, G, B,** and **YPbPr** (**YCbCr**), which also keep the various chroma and luminance signals discreet. All of these, however, are analog signals and in a world rapidly dominated by digital technology, these are more often than not eschewed for the broadly compatible and compact HDMI connection.

Common Audio And Video Connectors For Dv Camcorders (Figure 9-27)

a. ⅛" mini (line audio and microphone audio with adaptor)
b. XLR (microphone audio and line audio if switchable)
c. BNC (composite video [SDI] and uncompressed HD [HD-SDI])
d. S-Video (component analog video)
e. RCA (line audio and composite analog video)
f. FireWire 4 pin (audio, video, and auxiliary data)
g. FireWire 6 pin (audio, video, and auxiliary data)
h. HDMI (audio, video, and auxiliary data)
i. USB 2.0 (audio, video, and auxiliary data)

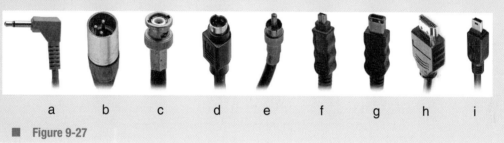

a   b   c   d   e   f   g   h   i

■ Figure 9-27

DC Power

Video cameras run on DC power provided by **onboard batteries** or via an adaptor that transforms the unstable AC power coming from the wall outlet into steadier DC current. Despite the unlimited power supply of an AC adaptor, most shooters only use batteries, preferring the freedom of not being tethered by a chord to the wall (Figure 9-28). I just need to mention one detail that should be obvious but is all too often overlooked. Batteries need to be charged to work—and it takes time to charge them. I have seen so many student shoots abandoned because no one remembered to charge the darn batteries, and it breaks my heart every time.

Camera Function Menus and Switches

Depending on the make and model of your camera, many camera functions and options are embedded inside a menu that can be accessed through buttons and viewed on the LCD viewscreen; some regularly used functions are located as switches, buttons, or wheels on the outside of the camera body (Figure 9-29). You must consult your camera's manual to find out how to navigate all the camera's menus and control the functions you require on your shoot, and you should do this long before you get on the set. With shooting options rapidly multiplying, camera function menus are getting longer and more labyrinthine with each generation, so this is critical preproduction research.

One very important measure of a camera's capability to function as an expressive tool for the visual storyteller is the capacity for manual control of certain critical functions, namely

■ **Figure 9-28** Video cameras run on batteries available in a variety of sizes and power capacities.

focus, exposure, white balance, and audio. Video cameras are designed by engineers and business people, not artists, and the **auto functions** on a DV camera (auto focus, auto exposure, auto white balance, and auto sound levels) are designed to give the user easily obtained, generally acceptable results. Point-and-shoot simplicity is what most home video shooters are looking for to record their kid's birthday party, and some can also be useful in a fast and unpredictable documentary situation; but if you are telling a story with images, something that you want to show to an audience, to move people, to communicate ideas and emotions, you need to be able to control all the elements that are part of your expressive and aesthetic palette. Focus, exposure, color, and sound are central creative elements in filmmaking and each offers a range of expressive possibilities. To leave these creative decisions up to a machine is to give away your voice. All professional video cameras allow for manual control of all of these functions by the camera operator. The better the camera, the more precise and detailed that control will be. Cameras that do not allow us to set our own focus, sound levels, exposure, or white balance (usually the cheapest consumer cameras) severely limit us in terms of craft and are therefore less useful. All professional and most midlevel camcorders give us the option of **auto functions** or **manual override** for these critical functions, and you should immediately learn how to take control of your own image by turning off the auto functions in favor of manually controlling your shots. We will look closer at how to use manual focus, exposure, white balance, and audio in the sections dedicated to these functions.

The Basic DV Camcorder: Interior

DV camcorders essentially turn light into data. The best way to understand the interior workings of a basic, three-CCD chip DV camcorder is to follow the progress of an image, which begins as light entering the lens and emerges as a stream of data recorded onto a memory card or tape (**Figure 9-30**).

■ **Figure 9-29** Some video camera functions are embedded inside menus accessible on the LCD screen *(left)*, while other, more commonly used features (like the manual overrides for focus and iris) are found on the camera's body *(right)*.

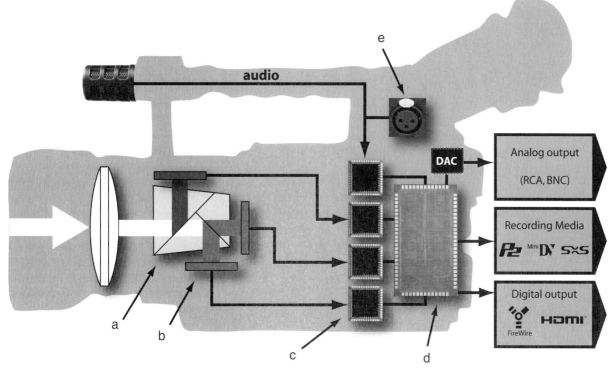

audio

Figure 9-30 A three-chip video camera produces an image by first dividing the light entering the lens into primary colors with a prism block (a), which are read by three CCD chips (b), their signal outputs are converted into digital data by an ADC (c), and they are processed by the DSP (d), ultimately outputting the data to the record media. Audio inputs (e) have their own ADC as well. See the color insert.

The Prism Block

The light gathered from the lens first passes through the **prism block**, located just behind the lens; this splits the image into the **three primary colors of light**: **red**, **green**, and **blue** (**RGB**). These three images, identical except for their color, are reflected onto the faceplates of three image sensors (CCDs or CMOS), which register the relative light intensities and create a separate video signal for each color. Cameras with only one image sensor utilize a **Bayer Pattern Filter** which uses color filters in a mosaic pattern to separate the incoming light into R,G,B creating color separation on a single chip by striking individual pixels with one discrete color signal - either red, green or blue.

Sensors

The **video sensor** (or **imager**) is an image plane made up of tightly packed rows of photosensitive **pixels** (photodiodes actually) that capture light and convert the specific light values on each pixel into fluctuations in voltage. In the case of CCD chips, these rows are linked (coupled) and the electronic information built up in every photosensitive cell is regularly and repeatedly "read," or transferred to an output register as an analog signal row-by-row, top-to-bottom, according to the system's scanning pattern (60i, 24p, 60p, etc.) (see page 195,196). It is an analog signal at this point because the voltage fluctuations are analogous to the various intensities of light in the actual scene.

Consumer cameras usually have a single, small CCD chip measuring ⅛" or ¼", but most midlevel and professional camcorders utilize three larger chips commonly measuring ⅓", ½", or ⅔". The larger the chip, the larger the imaging area and therefore the greater its resolution capability, and using three sensors also provides better image quality (**Figure 9-31**). (also see box on page 215.)

For your imager to reproduce colors accurately, you must take care to **white balance** your camera each time you change location or lighting conditions.

Figure 9-31 Most HD cameras have CCD chips in the 6:9 format. Pictured is a ⅔-inch CCD image sensor. (Photo courtesy of sphl.)

White balancing means adjusting the imager's color circuitry to match the color temperature of the light source (see page 188 for color temperature). On nearly every DV camera there are two easily accessible color temperature presets, one for daylight color temperature (5,600°K) and one for tungsten light (3,200°K). In addition, many cameras provide a way to manually set your white balance, which is more accurate than a factory preset. Setting white balance is accomplished by filling your frame with something white and matte (like a white card or sheet of paper) that is lit with representative light, and then engaging the manual white balance button (◣■◢). Whether the white card is reflecting the bluish tint of daylight or the amber tint of tungsten bulbs or the greenish hue of fluorescent lights, the camera adjusts the R, G, and B chip sensitivity levels until that card is rendered "white." When you release the manual white balance button, the adjustment is locked in. On many cameras you can also assign these manually

■ **Figure 9-32** White balancing. All video cameras have a way to balance the image sensors to a variety of color temperatures. For manual white balancing you must first switch off the auto white balance function (a). A user can manually set color temperature balance for each scene (b) or recall daylight and tungsten presets (c).

determined white balance settings to user preset buttons (Figure 9-32). White balancing must be done every time your lighting source changes.

Analog-to-Digital Converters
After each CCD converts the light values into voltage, it sends this analog electronic signal to separate **analog-to-digital converters** (ADC) where it is transformed into digital data, meaning binary code (a series of 1s and 0s).[6] The process of transforming analog information into digital data is called **quantizing** and requires the ADC to regularly **sample** the constantly flowing stream of voltage information from each pixel to ascribe discrete digital values. The more times the ADC samples the analog information, the better the resolution and image detail will be (Figure 9-33). ADC sampling rates are referred to as **bit rates**, and camera systems capable of higher bit rates convert more of the original signal information into digital data and therefore deliver superior quality. Most standard-definition DV ADCs have an 8-bit or 10-bit sampling rate, and HD cameras are capable of 10-bit, 12-bit, or even 14-bit sampling rates.

■ **Figure 9-33** ADC sampling rates determine the amount of information processed and the resolution of the image. The extremely low 2-bit sample rate used in the now defunct Fisher Price Pixelvision format (*left,* from Almereyda's *The Rocking-Horse Winner,* 1997) produced low-resolution video with prominent aliasing artifacts. The MiniDV format (*right,* from Harrison's *November,* 2004) has an 8-bit rate that produces a polished standard-definition image.

The Digital Signal Processor
Once the ADCs have sampled the analog signal from the CCDs and crunched the numbers, the raw digital video and audio data are sent to the **digital signal processor** (**DSP**) to create the final, digital image. The DSP is the most complex part of the entire digital video

[6]Just as each CCD chip has its own ADC, so, too, does the audio input signal, which also needs to be converted from an analog electronic signal into digital data.

in practice

■ CCD AND CMOS COMPARISON

For many years, the CCD sensor was the only imager used in digital video. This is changing as the **CMOS** (complementary metal oxide semiconductor) sensor becomes incorporated into more and more video cameras. Both imagers initially do the same thing—convert the light, striking millions of pixels packed onto an image plane, into electrons. But that is where the similarities end. The CCD employs a **global shutter**, meaning all the pixels are exposed to light at the same moment and register a complete image. This image is then "read out" or outputted line by line across the coupled pixels to a transfer area where it is converted into amplified voltage and sent off-chip to the ADC where this analog signal is converted into digital data. After this, the CCD registers another complete frame and repeats the process again and again at your chosen frame rate. A CMOS imager, on the other hand, contains all the circuitry necessary for converting light values into voltage and then into digital data in each and every pixel (**Figure 9-34**). Cameras that use CMOS sensors do not need an ADC because each pixel processes its own electron charge and directly outputs a digital signal. However, rather than expose and then "read out" a complete frame, CMOS sensors have a **rolling shutter**, which exposes and reads out one line of pixels at a time (from top to bottom). In other words, a CCD registers a complete frame and then outputs that frame line by line, whereas a CMOS sensor exposes and outputs one line at a time eventually creating the complete frame. The rolling shutter, which is

■ **Figure 9-34** The CMOS sensor from the Arri Alexa HD camera is the same size as a 35mm film frame.

unique to CMOS imagers, is responsible for several characteristic artifacts, most infamously the **"jello" artifact** (also called **skew**), which occurs when there is horizontal movement, especially quick panning. With horizontal movement, it is possible for the top part of an object to be registered in one area of the frame, the middle scanned slightly later, and the bottom part registered even further along. The result is that vertical lines can appear slanted during the pan, and complex movement produces a wobbly, jello undulation in objects that should be stationary. Although CCDs are immune to the rubber artifact, they have their own peculiar artifacts, most notably the common **vertical smear** effect, where bright points of light smear vertically across the image. In any case, these are the imagers we currently have to work with, and happily they're getting better and better with each generation.

system and works with algorithms specific to the camera's format (DVCPRO HD, XDCAM, AVCHD, etc.). Primarily, the DSP combines the image information from the three ADCs and determines the brightness and color value of every pixel in every frame of video to create the full-color image, along with incorporating the audio signal. However, at this point, these uncompressed DV images contain an enormous amount of data, something on the order of 25 MB/sec (94 GB/hr) for SD video; 1080i HD video, being more than five times that size, generates around 150 MB/sec—that's 556 gigabytes/hr! At that rate we would fill up a 64-GB memory card in about six minutes! This is simply way too much data to move around and store. So when processing raw video information, the DSP is forced to reduce the amount of data it sends to the recording media; on the other hand, this reduction of data cannot be accomplished at the expense of too much resolution quality. To this end, the DSP uses highly complex, format-specific algorithms to reduce data in two ways, **compression** and **color depth sampling**, and both have a significant impact on image quality.

Compression and Color Subsampling

In the world of digital video there is a saying: "Speed, size, quality—pick two." This is the critical juggling act of all video formats—how to reduce the size of the image data while maintaining as much quality as possible. If you compress too much, the image quality suffers,

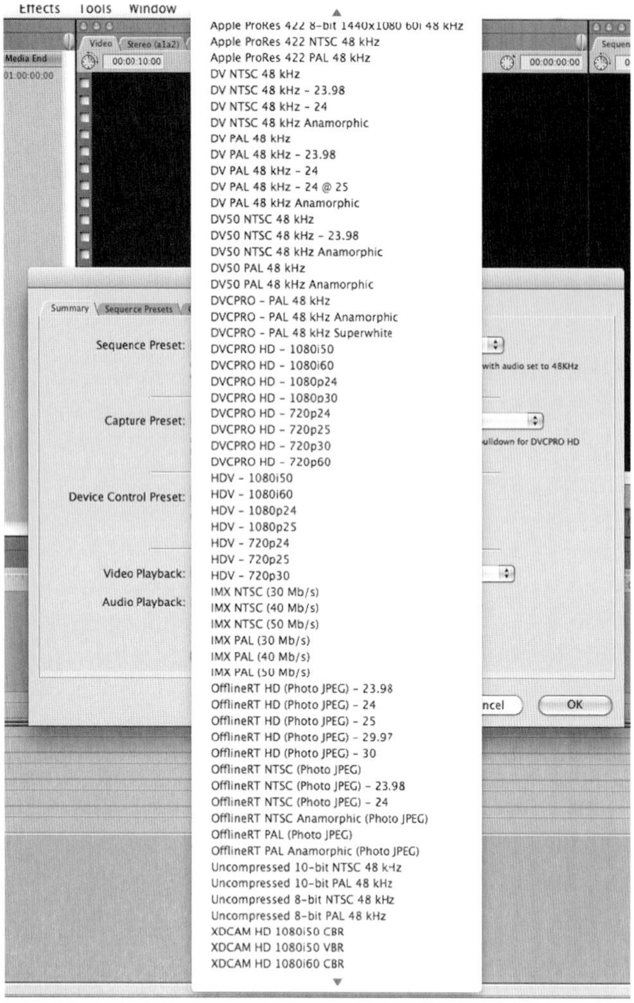

Effects Tools Window

Media End
01:00:00:00

Video Stereo (a1a2)
00:00:10:00

Apple ProRes 422 8-bit 1440x1080 60i 48 kHz
Apple ProRes 422 NTSC 48 kHz
Apple ProRes 422 PAL 48 kHz
DV NTSC 48 kHz
DV NTSC 48 kHz – 23.98
DV NTSC 48 kHz – 24
DV NTSC 48 kHz Anamorphic
DV PAL 48 kHz
DV PAL 48 kHz – 23.98
DV PAL 48 kHz – 24
DV PAL 48 kHz – 24 @ 25
DV PAL 48 kHz Anamorphic
DV50 NTSC 48 kHz
DV50 NTSC 48 kHz – 23.98
DV50 NTSC 48 kHz Anamorphic
DV50 PAL 48 kHz
DV50 PAL 48 kHz Anamorphic
DVCPRO – PAL 48 kHz
DVCPRO – PAL 48 kHz Anamorphic
DVCPRO – PAL 48 kHz Superwhite
DVCPRO HD – 1080i50
DVCPRO HD – 1080i60
DVCPRO HD – 1080p24
DVCPRO HD – 1080p30
DVCPRO HD – 720p24
DVCPRO HD – 720p25
DVCPRO HD – 720p30
DVCPRO HD – 720p60
HDV – 1080i50
HDV – 1080i60
HDV – 1080p24
HDV – 1080p25
HDV – 720p24
HDV – 720p25
HDV – 720p30
IMX NTSC (30 Mb/s)
IMX NTSC (40 Mb/s)
IMX NTSC (50 Mb/s)
IMX PAL (30 Mb/s)
IMX PAL (40 Mb/s)
IMX PAL (50 Mb/s)
OfflineRT HD (Photo JPEG) – 23.98
OfflineRT HD (Photo JPEG) – 24
OfflineRT HD (Photo JPEG) – 25
OfflineRT HD (Photo JPEG) – 29.97
OfflineRT HD (Photo JPEG) – 30
OfflineRT NTSC (Photo JPEG)
OfflineRT NTSC (Photo JPEG) – 23.98
OfflineRT NTSC (Photo JPEG) – 24
OfflineRT NTSC Anamorphic (Photo JPEG)
OfflineRT PAL (Photo JPEG)
OfflineRT PAL Anamorphic (Photo JPEG)
Uncompressed 10-bit NTSC 48 kHz
Uncompressed 10-bit PAL 48 kHz
Uncompressed 8-bit NTSC 48 kHz
Uncompressed 8-bit PAL 48 kHz
XDCAM HD 1080i50 CBR
XDCAM HD 1080i50 VBR
XDCAM HD 1080i60 CBR

Summary / Sequence Presets

Sequence Preset:

Capture Preset:

Device Control Preset:

Video Playback:
Audio Playback:

Sequen
00:00:00:00

with audio set to 48KHz

ulldown for DVCPRO HD

ncel OK

■ **Figure 9-35** This user preference menu in Final Cut Pro reveals just how many format/codec variations exist these days. The list extends beyond the top and bottom of this screen grab.

if you don't compress enough, the files are too big and too slow to work with. **Compression** is the method of reducing the amount of data flowing from the ADC by discarding visual detail that is either imperceptible to the human eye or redundant. The programs that perform this compression are called **codecs** (for compression/decompression). There are multiple **standard codecs** in the world of digital video (i.e., JPEG, MPEG-2, MPEG-4, H.264/AVC), with new ones being introduced regularly. However, when we're talking about video camera encoding, each manufacturer relies on a **proprietary codec**, meaning it is specific to that particular camera format. To ensure compatibility, however, most proprietary codecs are based on one of the standard codecs. For example, Panasonic's format utilizes the AVC-Intra codec, which is based on and compatible with the H.264/MPEG-4 AVC standard (the codec used in Blu-ray). Sony uses a codec called MPEG-2 Long GoP, and RED camera system uses its own REDCODE RAW codec, which is a variant of JPEG2000. To make matters even more confusing, Panasonic and Sony collaborated on a recent HD format called AVCHD (which uses the standard H.264/MPEG-4), and now other camera manufacturers like JVC use this technology. As you can imagine, there is constant negotiation with the most popular editing systems (i.e., AVID and Final Cut Pro) to support these compression schemes, which, thankfully, they usually do (Figure 9-35). Recording formats and their proprietary codecs are numerous and constantly changing, so rather than look at them specifically, we'll simply look at the essential principles of compression, especially as they pertain to the DSP and image quality. Understanding some basics about compression is important because it has a bearing on choosing a shooting format, your anticipated workflow, and, ultimately, on what we see on the screen.

One priority for compression algorithms is to remove redundant information. **Redundant information** is the data for visual details that are repeated, from pixel to pixel and frame after frame. In video there is a lot of redundant color and brightness information. For example, say we have a close-up shot of a green lizard crawling across a red tabletop. The pixels along the path of the lizard change from red to green as the lizard passes, but the rest of the frame remains exactly the same frame after frame—red. It would take a great deal of space to re-record all of the common and repeated luminance and chrominance values for every pixel in every frame. In standard DV resolution (720 × 480), we would need to re-record the same numeric value for "red" 345,600 times (minus the 200 pixels or so for the lizard) for every single frame. For 1080i, HD we would need to re-record the same repeated "red" values 2,073,600 every frame (again minus the lizard pixels). The codec, instead, reduces all of this common information to a smaller file size by recording the numeric value for "red" once and then indicating that every other pixel in each subsequent frame (except for the lizard pixels) is "just like that first one." The rest of the information is then tossed out. Later, when we play back that image, the codec **decompresses** that information by reconstructing the data through duplication of that one saved numeric value for the "red" areas of the frame. It may not be exactly the original data making that image of a lizard crawling over a red table, but codecs work so well that it looks just like the original.

Another compression strategy is to discard visual information that cannot be perceived by the human eye, like many of those billions of colors and indiscernibly subtle nuances in tonal shades. Why move it and store it if you can't even see it? This is the visual equivalent of tossing out the audio frequencies, like those of dog whistles, which the human ear can't hear anyway. **Chroma subsampling** is one way compression algorithms eliminate color data that may not even be perceptible in order to save space. Color sampling is the number of times **brightness (luminance)** and **color (chroma)** information is measured and translated into data by the DSP algorithms. It is expressed as a ratio of luminance sampling to blue sampling to red sampling. The information for green is not sampled because it can be interpolated given the data for luminance, blue and red. Color sampling is done by looking at and averaging out blocks of four pixels rather than every pixel, which already saves space. Because the human eye is capable of perceiving very subtle variations in brightness shades but relatively fewer shifts in color tonalities, all DV formats sample 100% of the luminance information, but much less blue and red information. A full sample is represented with the integer 4, so a color sampling ratio of 4:4:4 would mean that all luminance data, blue and red colors, are sampled equally and fully. However, standard-definition color sampling comes in at 4:1:1, which means that the color components are sampled only once for every four luminance samples. The resulting image, even after losing three-quarters of the color information, is surprisingly good. Most HD formats, on the other hand, have a color sampling rate of 4:2:2. The extra color information takes up much more space, but the quality is clearly superior—which is partly what puts the high definition in HD (also see "The Ultra High End", later).

Discarding imperceptible data and redundant data is called **lossy compression**, because the original data is gone for good. DV codecs can reduce video information by 70% to 80%, but there is clearly a limit to the amount of lossy compression we can employ before we see a degeneration of picture quality. In general, the less compression employed, the better the image, but many other factors bear on image quality, so this is not a hard-and-fast rule. For example, HD video formats have greater compression ratios than SD, but with progressive scanning and the increased pixel count, HD more than makes up for the larger data loss.

There is another type of compression, called **lossless compression**, which warrants mentioning in order to avoid confusion. **Lossless compression** is a kind of compression in which no data is lost at all. This is the sort of compression used for "zip" or "stuffit" computer files, in which the original data is compressed into smaller data codes, or "tokens," and then exactly reconstructed upon decompression for a perfect copy of the original. But lossless compression isn't used in digital video codecs—yet!

Recording formats roughly divide up by manufacturer and are made up of the following specifications: **shooting mode** (SD, HD), **resolution capability** (480, 720p, 1080i pixel count), frame rate options (60i, 60p, 30p, 24p), **compression codec type** (usually proprietary and includes **color sampling** rates), and **record media type** (P2, SDHC, SxS). You should always research these specs to ensure compatibility between the camera recording format and your edit system before you start to shoot. (For a list of common recording formats, go to www.voiceandvisionbook.com.)

The Ultra High End: Uncompressed, 2K, and 4K

Digital video, even HD, is almost always recorded compressed, transmitted compressed, and then decompressed for display. As I mentioned previously, some professional DV cameras allow you to bypass the native format compression by sending the 8-bit (or 10-bit) uncompressed signal out via the **SDI/HD-SDI** output to a high-capacity hard drive. However, several ultra-high-end systems, like the Sony CineAlta, Panasonic Varicam, Arri Alexa, Aaton Penelope Δ, and RED, natively record full resolution, 12-bit *uncompressed* video with chroma sampling at 4:4:4, creating an image

■ **Figure 9-36** Among the ultra-high-end D-Cinema cameras available, the relatively affordable RED ONE has proven popular with independent filmmakers. Pictured is D.P. Jonathon Narducci on the set of Sluser's *Path Lights* (2009).

quality and light sensitivity matching 35mm negative film (**Figure 9-36**). These cameras also shoot at resolutions that greatly exceed the ATSC standard resolutions listed at the beginning of this chapter. These formats are known as **2K** (2048x1080) and **4K** (4096 × 2304), named after the rough number of horizontal pixels (**Figure 9-37**). So what's all that resolution for? These ultra-large resolutions do not conform to the ATSC standards because they're not intended for HDTV broadcast; instead these massive resolutions are used for large screen theatrical projection. Clearly, this much nuanced light sensitivity and image detail is welcome when you are shooting on video with the intention of transferring to 35mm film for theatrical release. These resolutions are also used for release to **Digital Cinema** (**D-Cinema**), which is a high-resolution digital theatrical projection format established by the **Digital Cinema Initiative** (**DCI**) (see page 407). Both 35mm and D-Cinema frame rates are 24 fps, which is why shooting is always done at the 24p frame rate (**Figure 9-38**).The data rates for these formats are enormous and because of the extreme memory requirements of shooting uncompressed 2K or 4K formats, these systems always record direct to high capacity, removable hard drive "magazines."

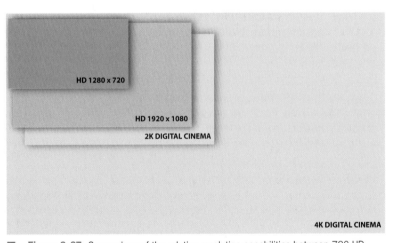

HD 1280 x 720

HD 1920 x 1080

2K DIGITAL CINEMA

4K DIGITAL CINEMA

■ **Figure 9-37** Comparison of the relative resolution capabilities between 720 HD, 1080 HD, 2K, and 4K formats based on pixel count.

As you might imagine, the imagers for these cameras are of exceptionally high quality and are *large*. Some systems utilize three ⅔″ CCDs, while others have a single, huge sensor (CCD or CMOS) the size of a 35mm negative frame. These systems also take advantage of the large image plane and PL lens mounts to allow for the use of high-quality 35mm photography lenses, which give the same depth of field and visual perspective as 35mm film. It should be noted that these cameras usually also provide the options for shooting compressed HD video at 4:2:2 for projects that can benefit from the enhanced optical qualities but that may not be bound for large-scale theatrical release.

■ **Figure 9-38** Lucas's *Star Wars Episode II: Attack of the Clones* (2002) was the first major commercial motion picture to be shot entirely on HD 24p and exhibited digitally.

If you've read the chapter up to this point, you probably understand that the truest thing one can say about digital video is that it's constantly evolving, improving, and changing. Do not expect things to ever settle down to some sort of manageable stasis. If you've finished your script and are ready to start shooting, just jump in, use whatever technology is available to you at the time, and make your movie. Don't wait for "the next great thing" because there will always be another "next great thing" around the corner. Your production technology *will be exceeded* in a few years. So what? You will have your movie and you will be ready to make your next one with the new formats—like maybe one of the ones described in the accompanying box.

■ DATA RATE

Throughout your workflow you'll need to be aware of the data rate for your particular format. This determines, among other things, the amount of storage space you'll need for your project (in production and postproduction). Format data rates are determined by a number of factors including whether you're shooting SD, HD, or uncompressed; the resolution format (480, 720, 1080, 2K, 4K); the frame rate (60i, 24p); and the specific quantizing and compression factors of the record format (DVCPRO-HD, XDCAM-HD, AVCHD). It's a very good thing that **data rate calculators** are easy to find for free. There are many calculators you can download (as software or as an iPhone app) that include virtually every shooting format and codec available, like this calculator provided by AJA Video systems for free (**Figure 9-39**).

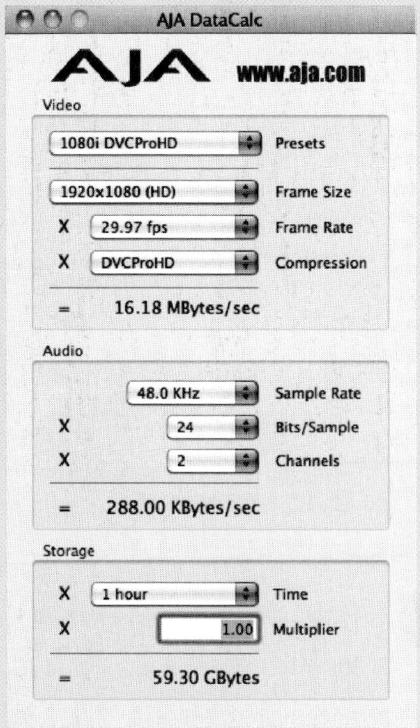

■ **Figure 9-39** Format data rate calculators, like this free one from AJA Systems, are a handy for calculating data storage needs.

■ RECENT DEVELOPMENTS IN DIGITAL SHOOTING

That "movie mode" hidden in the menu system of your new DSLR? It's not just a novelty feature. It's nothing short of a revolutionary, democratizing, disruptive moviemaking technology, as important as the invention of color film, 16mm, or HDTV.
Ryan Coo (From *The DSLR Cinematography Guide*, http://nofilmschool.com/dslr)

DSLR cinematography is not an emerging format. It is here, and it will surely get better (**Figure 9-40** *top*). High-end digital SLR cameras (like Canon's EOS series or Nikon's D series) are designed with an extra large format, pixel-packed CMOS sensor, which takes high-resolution photographs that approach 35mm film. But in "movie-mode" that CMOS sensor can reel off 1920 × 1080 images at 24 frames per second! There are a number of confluent factors that have made DSLR cinematography a very popular video production format: (1) the increase of SD card storage capacity and the drop in price, (2) the fact that you can use the entire range of high-quality interchangeable lenses for your camera system, (3) easy access to many ISO sensitivity options, (4) cameras that cost in the hundreds of dollars rather than thousands of dollars, and (5) the lightweight, and compact, body. But there are downsides to DSLR video shooting. These cameras are designed for still photography, so shooting hours of motion picture footage can take a heavy toll. According to Ryan Coo, "… no matter which DSLR you buy, you're likely to have overheating problems […] after several minutes of continuous shooting." Overheating results in noisy images or total camera shutdown. Another issue is that the extra large CMOS chip with its rolling shutter makes it particularly susceptible to the skew and "jello" motion artifacts when you move the camera. It's a bit dubious to say to a filmmaker, "Well, just don't use any pans." Also, the shape and size of a DSLR camera, while perfect for still photography, is awkward for creating smooth camera moves and pulling focus, so some sort of stabilizing rig is neces-

sary when shooting without a tripod. Often, these rigs can be more expensive than the camera itself. Finally, transferring footage into an editing system usually requires some form of transcoding (which can be tricky but is getting easier all the time). Despite these limitations, filmmakers are making great use of this highly affordable shooting format (**Figure 9-41**).

The year 2010 began with the release of the mega-million dollar 3D production of *Avatar*, and a few months later a consumer-level 3D camcorder emerged! (**Figure 9-40** *bottom*). 3D cinematography is nothing new; it was first introduced in the 1950s and is regularly reintroduced (and improved) with each subsequent decade. There is a lot of debate as to what we are witnessing now, after the first decade of the 21st century. Some say that 3D digital video represents a "revolution" that will change filmmaking as we know it and make two-dimensional cinematography totally obsolete. Others claim that this is just another cycle in the nostalgia craze for a movie-making gimmick. My opinion is that 3D is here to stay and it's likely to improve rapidly (especially by eliminating the special viewing glasses). But this format will settle into its own mass market niche, becoming a regular offering but sharing the screens with traditionally made films. There is no doubt that 3D is an exciting addition to the filmmaker's visual arsenal, and if we have it at our disposal, we should conceive of stories, scenes, and images in ways that benefit from the new quality of depth perception. However, all of the traditional 2D principles of lighting, composition, exposure, mise-en-scène, and editing still apply to 3D film—not to mention the principles of writing and directing good stories. More specifically, object overlapping and compositional planes, z-axis and receding horizontal lines, diminishing perspective, depth of field, and light and shadow ratios (see page 49) have the same compositional effect whether you're shooting 2D or 3D. So if we're witnessing a revolution, it remains primarily one of equipment and exhibition and less one involving the artistic craft of creating compelling and expressive images.

■ **Figure 9-40** Recent developments in digital filmmaking: shooting with DSLR cameras, like the Canon 5D (pictured on a support rig from Red Rock) *(top)* and consumer-level 3D camcorders, like the Panasonic AG-3DA1 *(bottom)*.

■ **Figure 9-41** Shot entirely on a Canon 7D DSLR, director Lena Durham's feature film *Tiny Furniture* (2010) was a festival hit.

The Lens

chapter 10

■ THE CAMERA LENS

The lens of a camera is often likened to the human eye—in fact, many people have announced that "the lens is the eye of the camera." This is true, in that light enters through and is controlled by the lens and ultimately this light registers an image. However, there are many things that human eyes and human psychology of perception do automatically, which, on a lens, must be accomplished manually. Framing, focusing, and exposure are activities we rarely consciously think about with respect to the function of our eyes, but on a lens, which relies on us to deliberately set each of these functions, we are presented with a range of possibilities. Every lens-related variable offers not just a function, but also an array of creative choices. These choices are, in fact, part of the creative potential of any lens and part of the aesthetic palette of a filmmaker. Often there is no absolute "right" setting; rather, you must find the appropriate setting for what you want to express. In film or video production, registering an image is not done in the blink of an eye. Focus doesn't just happen; we must ask, "Where do we want our focus to be?" There is more to creating a powerful image than simply allowing enough light to see the subject clearly. We get to decide how much light we want and exactly how bright or dark, clear or obscured our subject will appear. On every shot we must decide, from a wide range of possibilities, the size of the subject and the visual perspective within the frame. Knowing how lenses work will help you choose the right lens and settings to express exactly what you need them to say to your audience. It is helpful to remember that the lens is much more than just the eye of the camera: it becomes the eyes of your audience.

Whether you are shooting on digital video, 16mm film, or 35mm film, the basic construction and function of the camera lens are the same. All light entering the camera comes in through the lens, and this light must be carefully controlled in order to achieve a usable and expressive image.

Broadly speaking, lenses are a series of polished glass sections called **lens elements.** These elements are held parallel to each other in a light-tight housing called the **barrel,** or **lens housing.** The function of these glass elements is to gather the light reflecting off a scene and, through optical refraction, direct that light precisely onto the camera's focal plane. The **focal plane** (also called **film plane**) of a film camera is the emulsion of the film, and every film camera has an external marking that indicates precisely where the film is located. The film plane marking looks like this: ϕ. The focal plane of a video camera is the **faceplate** of the CCD chip. In video cameras with three chips, there are three focal planes, all calibrated to exactly the same distance from the last element of the lens. The lens gathers light reflecting off a three-dimensional scene and projects it as a two-dimensional image onto the focal plane. The image registered on the focal plane is both reversed and flipped (**Figure 10-1**). This flipping of the image occurs at the exact optical center of the lens and is later reversed in the projection (film) or scanning process (video).

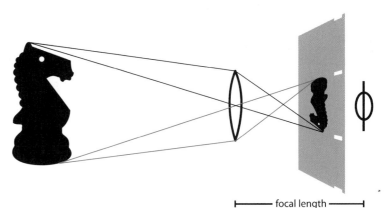

focal length

■ **Figure 10-1** Simple image formation by a lens. A lens gathers incoming light and focuses it on the film plane. At the optical center, the image is not only flipped, but also reversed.

The type, placement, and number of glass elements in any given lens vary widely depending on the function, quality, and perspective attributes of the lens. There are many lenses to choose from, so understanding lenses in general will help you pick the right one to create the image you want.

Focal Length

The **focal length** of a lens determines the degree of magnification or de-magnification of the scene being shot. Different lenses offer different focal lengths. Focal length is determined by the distance between the **optical center** of the lens (the point at which the image flips) and the focal plane, ϕ. This distance is usually measured in millimeters (25mm, 75mm, 150mm, etc.), although older lenses may be marked in inches. The focal length of a lens affects both the image size within the frame and the **angle of view**, which means how much of the scene the lens takes in horizontally (x-axis) and vertically (y-axis).

The longer the focal length, the more the subject is magnified and appears larger and closer to the camera. The shorter the focal length, the smaller the subject is and the farther away objects appear. More specifically, if you double the number of millimeters (say from 50mm to 100mm), you will double the size of the subject in the frame. Also, the longer the focal length, the narrower the angle of view becomes and vice versa. There are three broad focal length classifications for lenses: **wide angle** (short lenses), **normal** (medium lenses), and **telephoto** (long lenses) (Figure 10-2).

A **normal lens** approximates the same perspective and image size that the human eye would see if one were to stand in the same spot as the camera (not including peripheral vision). Although this sounds like a fairly nonscientific description of a normal lens, human visual perspective is indeed the intended reference point. The actual focal length of a normal lens is primarily determined by the size of the imaging format you are using. For the 16mm film format, the focal length for a normal lens is 25mm. For the 35mm film format, a normal lens is 50mm. In video, the normal lens length for a ⅔″ CCD is 20mm, for a ½″ CCD it is 15mm, for a ⅓″ CCD it is 11mm, and for a ¼″ CCD it is 8mm. As you can see, the larger the area of the imaging device, the longer the focal length is for a normal lens.

Wide-angle lenses are those with focal lengths shorter than normal lenses. Wide-angle lenses reduce the size of the image and broaden the angle of view, compared to the perspective of the human eye. In the 16mm film format, a 15mm lens is considered slightly wide angle, a 10mm lens is wide angle, and an 8mm lens very wide angle. An extreme wide-angle lens, with an angle of view greater than 180°(!), is also called a fisheye lens.

Given the small size of most consumer and "prosumer" video imaging devices, which makes for a very short normal lens, it's difficult to find a video camera with an extreme wide-angle end to their lens. However, most camera manufacturers offer a wide-angle lens attachment as an optional purchase. This is, in effect, another lens that attaches to the camera's existing lens and allows for extreme wide-angle shots.

Lenses that have a longer focal length than normal and that enlarge the size of the image and narrow the angle of view are called **telephoto lenses.** In the 16mm film format, a 75mm lens is slightly telephoto, a 120mm lens is telephoto, and a 250mm lens is very telephoto. The exact focal length of a lens can be found etched into the front of the lens barrel.

■ **Figure 10-2** Prime lenses have a fixed focal length, and can be easily identified by reading the engravings on their barrels.

Lens Perspective

Perspective is one of the most important considerations when we think about framing and composition. Perspective is essentially a combination of the angle of view, in terms of both the **horizontal dimension** (**x-axis**) and the **vertical dimension** of the frame (**y-axis**), and the depth relationship (near versus far) between objects. This **depth dimension** is the **z-axis**, and because a film image is two dimensional, the sense of depth is an illusion created by the composition of the frame. We have already discussed creating deep frames and flat frames through mise-en-scène in Chapter 3 ("Shot Composition and the Graphic Qualities of the Frame"), but how does lens choice actually affect perspective?

When we set up a shot, we often first consider the size of the framing (e.g., long shot, medium shot, close-up), which determines the size of the subject in the frame. How we achieve that specific framing (say a medium shot) can be accomplished with any number of different lenses, and this choice has a profound effect on all the perspective dimensions in the frame.

X-axis and Y-axis Field of View

There are two ways to affect the size of a subject in the frame. The first is to change the camera-to-subject distance—moving the camera itself closer or farther from the subject. The other is to alter the magnification of the scene by changing the focal length of the lens you use. There are significant compositional differences between these two options. First, let's consider the x-axis and y-axis differences. When you change only the camera-to-subject distance, the subject indeed gets larger or smaller, but you maintain the same horizontal (x-axis) and vertical (y-axis) vista - called the **field of view** (or **angle of view**). However, leaving the camera stationary and changing focal length (longer or shorter) to change the size of the subject in the frame alters the field of view, narrower or wider. This significantly changes the amount of background information contained in the frame. Compare the two long shot examples (photos b and b1) from Figure 10-3. The subjects in both shots are nearly identical in size, and the horizontal center of both frames is the same (no left-to-right angle adjustment); however, the shot taken with the wide-angle lens and camera moved closer (shot b1) includes the two women talking (to the left of the frame), and the shot taken by leaving the camera stationary and using a longer focal length (shot b) has narrowed the field of view to exclude them. Notice also how much more we see of the space above and below the two subjects in the wide angle/close camera frame (shot b1).

Y-axis and Depth

The other perspective dimension that is important to consider is that of the perception of depth, or relative distances of objects along the z-axis. A normal lens replicates the same perception of depth that our eyes see. For example, if we use a normal lens to frame a subject in a medium shot with another object five feet behind, that object will indeed seem like it is five feet behind the subject in the shot.

Wide-angle lenses tend to exaggerate the depth along the z-axis, especially when close to the subject. The space between objects appears to be greater because of the relative distances between the camera and the objects along the z-axis. For example, look at the three images taken with a wide-angle lens and moving the camera (Figure 10-3, a1, b1, and c1). The two subjects are, in reality, about six feet apart and the z-axis perspective in shot a1 doesn't seem exaggerated; but as we move closer with the wide-angle lens (b1 and c1), the distance between them seems to grow wider and wider. This is because the distance between the subjects, relative to the distance of the camera to the foreground subject, becomes greater. Put another way, the distance between the camera and foreground subject is much shorter than the distance between that subject and the background objects (background guy and other pillars). In shot c1, the camera is only about a foot and a half away from the guy in the foreground, making the distance between the subjects four times greater, causing these objects to appear far from each other. The more

☞ ■ **Figure 10-3** Changing focal length versus moving the camera to achieve a specific shot size has a significant impact on the field of view and the perspective of the image *(left)*. Three frames from a stationary camera (wide angle (a); normal (b); telephoto (c), *left*). Three frames taken by moving the camera (all wide angle) *(right)*. (See this as a high resolution and interactive example online.)

wide angle our lens, the more it will exaggerate depth in this way. Wide-angle lenses are often used to exaggerate, for example, the space between a person (near foreground) and a destination (background), to stress the idea that they have a long way ahead of them before reaching their destination.

The converse is true for telephoto lenses, which have the effect of compressing space along the z-axis. Look at the shots a, b, and c in **Figure 10-3** as we increase the magnification (the focal length) of the scene from the stationary camera. As the focal length increases, it appears as if the depth distance between the two subjects (and pillars) collapses. The more telephoto the lens, the more compressed the z-axis distance. We have all seen shots of a character walking among the crowds on a city sidewalk. It looks as though there is no space at all between all these people; the crowd looks like it's packed so dense that it seems they are practically walking on top of each other. This is accomplished with a very long lens, shooting from a long distance, with the depth compression effect suggesting a feeling of claustrophobia and congestion.

Now compare shots b with b1, and c with c1 in **Figure 10-3**. Even though the shots are more or less the same size (long shot and medium shot, respectively) there is a big difference in the perception of horizontal, vertical field of view and the perspective of depth, creating an entirely different look and feel to the shots. The famous dolly/zoom from Martin Scorsese's *Goodfellas* (1990) perfectly illustrates this lens phenomenon in one single shot (**Figure 10-4**). A **dolly/zoom shot** involves changing the camera-to-subject distance with a dolly while simultaneously changing the focal length to maintain the same framing. In the case of the *Goodfellas* diner scene, the dolly was pulled away from the subjects while the focal length was adjusted increasingly telephoto to maintain

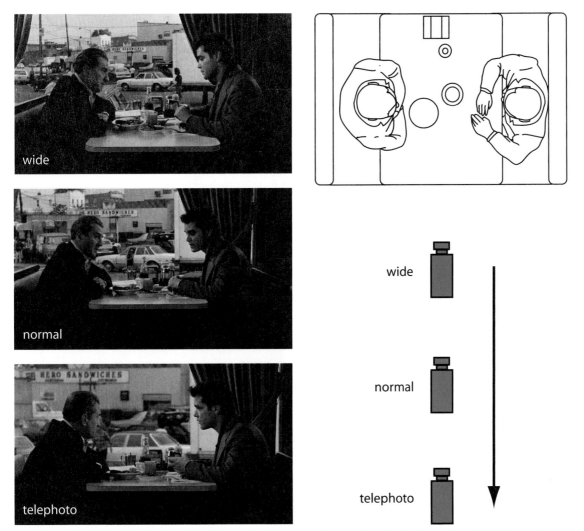

■ **Figure 10-4** This single shot from *Goodfellas* used a dolly move and a zoom lens to simultaneously pull back from and zoom in to a conversation between Jimmy (Robert De Niro) and Henry (Ray Liotta). This technique effectively keeps the subjects the same size in the frame but creates substantial spatial distortion in the background, which, in this case, vividly reflects Henry's unsettled mental state.

in practice

Understanding how the perception of depth can be manipulated with lenses is certainly vital to creating dynamic compositions, but one must also understand the narrative context of the scene or shot in order to utilize their expressive potential in appropriate ways.

Terry Gilliam is known for being a "short lens director" for his frequent use of wide-angle lenses, which is an essential part of his unique visual sensibility. In general he is keen on exposing as much of the location and art direction as possible, and wide lenses are the best option for this, given their wide field of view and deep focus capabilities. However, sometimes Gilliam will pull out an extra wide-angle lens to infuse a scene with a very particular emotion. In *The Fisher King* (1991) (photographed by Roger

Pratt), the protagonist Jack Lucas, in an effort to heal his comatose friend Parry, attempts to steal what Parry believes to be the true "holy grail." In fact, the object is merely a worthless trophy cup in a rich person's house. In the scene in which Jack, who is clearly not an experienced thief, must climb a rope to get onto the roof of the rich man's "castle," Gilliam uses an extreme wide-angle lens from above and below to exaggerate the sense of height and depth and therefore the sense of mortal danger. These shots convey a strong sense of vertigo, which Jack himself must be feeling—since it looks like it's is a long, long way to the pavement should he fall.

Similarly in Steven Zaillian's *Searching for Bobby Fischer* (1993) (cinematography by Conrad Hall), in the climactic scene in which the protagonist Josh plays a fearsome opponent in a children's chess tournament, a wide-angle lens is used to exaggerate the space that Josh must walk in order to reach the chess table. The wide-angle of view also reveals a gauntlet of other players watching his progress to the head table. His apprehension and nervousness in the scene is conveyed by the wide angle lens because it feels to the viewer (as it must to him) that this is the longest walk of his life (**Figure 10-5**).

On the other end of the scale are telephoto lenses, which are used to collapse space. Ramin Bahrani calls *Man Push Cart* (2005) a "long lens" film, meaning that it was shot primarily with telephoto focal lengths. *Man Push Cart* is the story of Ahmad, a Pakistani immigrant in New York City who is trying to start a new life for himself and his son. His main hope for survival is the tiny food cart that he rents. By shooting with a telephoto lens, Bahrani and cinematographer Michael Simmonds were able to create an overall sense of the packed and claustrophobic environment of New York City. The telephoto lens is used to particularly harrowing advantage in the scenes in which Ahmad pulls his food cart along the roadside to get to his spot early in the morning. The dangers of his morning routine are viscerally communicated in these scenes, which are shot with a telephoto lens from some distance, greatly compressing the space between Ahmad and the huge trucks bearing down on him from all sides.

■ **Figure 10-5** Perspective can be manipulated for dramatic effect by carefully selecting the focal length of your lens. Wide-angle lens shots from Gilliam's *The Fisher King* (1991, *top left*) and Zaillian's *Searching for Bobby Fischer* (1993, *top right*) and two shots taken with a telephoto lens from Bahrani's *Man Push Cart* (2005, *bottom*).

the same subject size. The result is that the background loses some of its horizontal and vertical field of view (notice the cars and buildings) and it also appears to be drawing closer and closer to the subjects.

Prime and Zoom Lenses

Lenses that have one fixed focal length are called **prime lenses.** These lenses are very common in film production. Many cinematographers favor prime lenses because their simple design allows them to be made with few glass lens elements, which means that there is less chance for loss of light or lens aberrations to occur (see "Lens Speed" section). However, if you are using primes lenses and decide to change the focal length of a lens from one shot to the next (say change from a 25mm lens to a 120mm lens in order to get in closer to the subject without moving he camera), then you need to change your lens. With prime lenses, you need to change the lens every time you want a new focal length. For this reason, many 16mm cameras are built with a rotating turret (**Figure 10-6**). This turret has three lens mounts and will accommodate three prime lenses of various focal lengths. The three lenses mounted on a lens turret usually consist of one normal lens, one telephoto lens, and one wide-angle lens. Turrets allow you to switch between lenses by simply rotating and positioning the desired lens in front of the gate. **Zoom lenses**, which are also referred to as **variable focal length lenses**, offer precisely that—a continuous range of focal lengths in one lens housing. Zoom lenses are constructed with movable lens elements that slide forward and backward to physically shift the optical center and therefore change the focal length of the lens. **Zooming in** means adjusting the optical center away from the focal plane and therefore increasing the magnification power of the lens (telephoto), and **zooming out** means adjusting the optical center back toward the focal plane, causing the image to become more wide angle. Zooming is accomplished with the adjustable **zoom ring**, calibrated in millimeters, which allows the filmmaker to manually set the desired focal length. Some zoom lenses, primarily on video cameras, utilize a servo zoom motor, so that you can glide from one focal length to another smoothly during a shot (**Figures 10-7** and **10-8**).

■ **Figure 10-6** Switching between prime lenses is a simple task when they are mounted on a rotating turret, like the lenses on the Arri-S.

Different zoom lenses offer a different range of focal lengths, and this range is often stated as a ratio (etched into the lens barrel). A 12:1 zoom lens (also stated 12×) is one that increases the focal length 12 times over its full range, and a 10:1 (10×) has a focal length range that increases 10 times. However, the specific range can vary; a 10:1 zoom lens could go from 10mm to 100mm or from 12mm to 120mm. The millimeter range is found on the zoom ring itself (**Figure 10-9**).

Zoom lenses are wonderfully convenient, as they can offer a wide range of focal lengths in one lens; however, there can be trade-offs for this convenience. It requires many more glass elements to make a zoom lens as compared to a prime lens, so zoom lenses are prone to light loss (see "Lens Speed" section) and optical aberrations. Nevertheless, current research and development trends are producing high-quality zoom lenses that are being used by cinematographers who shoot 35mm film for theatrical distribution. Conversely, given the increases in digital video resolution, it's not unusual to see high-end HD cameras fitted with prime lenses in order to achieve maximum image clarity. In fact, there are currently several midlevel DV cameras on the market designed to take prime lenses (see **Figure 9-20**).

■ **Figure 10-7** Zoom lenses have variable focal lengths and provide great flexibility during shooting at the cost of some quality; they are widely available for film cameras *(top)* and standard on video camcorders *(bottom)*.

Focus

We all have some sense for what focus is. Images that appear fuzzy and indistinct are "out of focus" and images that are sharply defined and clear are "in focus." But to be more precise about it, **focus** can be generally defined as when a point of light reflecting off the subject is registered as a point of light on the focal plane. The **focus ring** on a lens brings a subject into focus by very precisely moving the front element of the lens forward and backward in relation to the focal plane, which is why the focus ring is always found at the front of the lens.

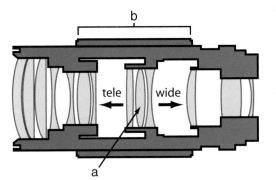

■ **Figure 10-8** A zoom lens changes focal length by shifting the position of the internal optical center elements (a) by adjusting the zoom ring (b).

■ **Figure 10-9** The focusing ring on a lens has a series of distances engraved in both feet and meters, which are aligned to a witness mark (a) as a reference point. Etched into the zoom ring are the focal length settings in millimeters (b).

What you are adjusting when you move the front lens element is called the **focus point**, or **plane of critical focus**—that is, the precise distance in front of the camera, from the focal plane φ, which will be in sharp focus. If you set the focus ring for 5 feet, objects 5 feet from the focal plane will be rendered sharply on the film, and if you set the focus ring to 20 feet, objects 20 feet from the focal plane will be in focus, and so on. Turning the focus ring counter-clockwise moves the plane of critical focus, along the z-axis, away from the camera and vice versa. The range of distances that you find on the focus ring scale will be from the closest to the farthest an object can be and still be brought into focus. This range usually falls somewhere between 3 feet to infinity, which is represented on the focus ring scale with the symbol ∞. The focus adjustment scale is etched on the focus ring and is often in both meters and feet. Be careful not to mix up these scales. Setting the focus is done by turning the focus ring until the distance you want is lined up against a **witness mark**, which is a line etched into a nonmovable part of the lens barrel (Figure 10-9).

When shooting video we can see the actual image that is being registered on the CCD chip, either through the viewfinder or through a larger field monitor, so focusing is usually done by eye. Some video camcorders offer a **focus assist** function, which enlarges a portion of the image to help you find critical focus. In film, we do not see the image being registered on the film; also, as we discussed, many film viewfinder systems involve either a loss of light, a flicker, or a different viewing lens altogether (non-reflex). For this reason, measuring the distance from the focal plane φ to the subject with a tape measure is common practice on film shoots (Figure 10-12). Focus has another dimension called depth of field, which will be covered in detail later in this chapter.

Is there a creative and expressive dimension to focus? Absolutely. What you decide to presented in sharp focus and what you decide should not be in focus can have a huge impact on the narrative content and emotional power of your shots. This scene from the Coen Brothers' film *No Country for Old Men* (**Figure 10-10**, *left*) shows Anton Chigurh *(background)* after he has been apprehended by a west Texas sheriff's deputy *(foreground)*. This is only the second scene in the film and the Coens have been careful not to show us Anton's face yet, so the precise placement of focus on the deputy, who is simply making a phone call, effectively keeps Anton a mystery—though we *can* see enough of him to know he's maneuvering his

■ **Figure 10-10** Focus is carefully controlled to first conceal and then reveal the disturbing features of killer Anton Chigurh (Xavier Bardem) at just the right moment in *No Country for Old Men* (Coen Brothers, 2007).

handcuffs from behind his back to his front and approaching the unaware deputy. Even though we do not know who this character is yet, the choice to obscure his face by keeping him out of focus during this action builds enormous tension, foreboding, and malevolence, so we are not entirely surprised that Anton throttles the deputy with the handcuffs the moment he hangs up the phone. It is not until Anton is well on is way to strangling the deputy to death that we get the first, sharp focus look at the face of Anton Chigurh—the face of a psychopathic killer (**Figure 10-10**, *right*).

■ Figure 10-11 In this scene from Alfredson's *Let the Right One In* (2008), maintaining sharp focus exclusively on Oskar's tormentors places us in Oskar's (Kåre Hedebrant) point of view.

In Tomas Alfredson's film *Let the Right One In*, focus point placement is carefully controlled throughout the film to put us in the main character's point of view (**Figure 10-11**). In this scene, Oskar (foreground with back to us) is in class and is answering a question correctly and quite precociously. Oskar is clearly the central character here, but notice that the sharp focus is placed on the two boys to the left and right of Oskar, as they glare at him. These boys are school bullies who tease Oskar mercilessly. By maintaining the focus on Oskar's tormentors (we never see Oskar's face in this scene), this shot effectively places us in Oskar's point of view; even though he's speaking to the man at the front of the classroom, his mental focus is on the bullies because he knows he has called attention to himself and will now likely be punished for it.

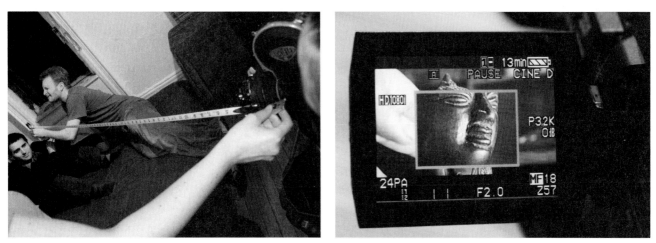

■ Figure 10-12 Camera-to-subject distance is measured from the film plane engraving, found on all film cameras, to the subject *(left)*. To aid with critical focus, some video cameras offer a focus assist function, which magnifies a portion of the scene *(right)*.

Pulling Focus

Usually, focus is something you set and leave for the duration of a shot. However, there are times when you may need to change the plane of critical focus during a take, while the camera is running. This is called **pulling focus** and it is common practice in film production. The person who does the actual adjustments to the focus ring is called the **focus puller**. There are two kinds of focus pulling. **Rack focus** means shifting the plane of critical focus between two static subjects along the z-axis. For example, in this shot from Tim Burton's 1994 film *Ed Wood* (**Figure 10-13**), the focus begins on the background subject Dolores, Ed's girlfriend, as she looks through her closet. When she wonders out loud where her lost angora sweater is, a precisely timed rack focus shifts the visual emphasis to the foreground, and to Ed's knowing reaction, providing a humorous punch line for the scene

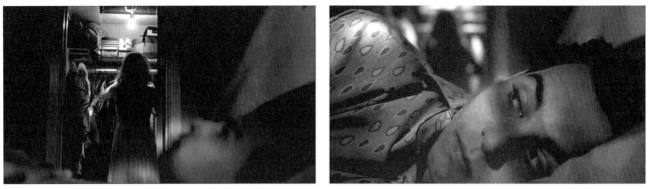

■ **Figure 10-13** A perfectly timed rack focus provides humorous punctuation to this scene between Ed (Johnny Depp) and his girlfriend Dolores (Sarah Jessica Parker) in Burton's *Ed Wood* (1994).

because we know he has been secretly wearing his girlfriend's clothes. In these cases, you must find each focus point ahead of time and mark them—either on the focus ring of the lens with paper tape or on a follow focus ring if you have one (**Figure 10-14**); this allows you to rack focus smoothly and precisely without hunting for focus.

Another type of focus pulling is called **follow focus.** Follow focus is used when your subject is moving along the z-axis either closer to or farther away from the camera, and you must adjust the plane of critical focus to follow your subject's progress. For example, let's say we have a shot in which a subject begins 30 feet away from the camera, then moves to 20 feet away, and finally comes to a rest 10 feet from the focal plane. In this case we need to set marks for both the actor and the focus puller. **Setting marks** means that we place precise markers on the ground for the actor to hit during the course of their movement. You can use tape if the ground is not seen in the shot, but if it is seen, then you need to use something that will not be too obvious, like leaves or twigs. In any case, these marks are set at precise distances. Then, during the take, the focus puller keeps the subject in focus by smoothly following them with the plane of critical focus—hitting the same feet markings on the focus ring when the subject reaches each mark. Follow focus should be done in one smooth movement, not in choppy adjustments, and can require a few rehearsals to get just right (**Figure 10-15**). (Go to the companion website for video examples of rack and follow focus).

■ **Figure 10-14** A follow focus device *(left)* allows you to mark predetermined focus points for easy focus pulling. If you don't have this device, using paper tape on the barrel of a lens *(right)* can accomplish the same thing.

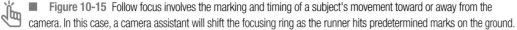

30 ft   20 ft   10 ft

■ **Figure 10-15** Follow focus involves the marking and timing of a subject's movement toward or away from the camera. In this case, a camera assistant will shift the focusing ring as the runner hits predetermined marks on the ground.

Aperture

Another adjustable ring found on all lenses used for film production and on all professional video lenses is the **aperture ring** (or **f-stop ring**). The aperture ring controls a slender disk, a diaphragm, inside the lens called **the iris**, which is made up of flat, matte black, metal blades. These blades overlap in such a way that they create an opening that is nearly circular. This opening is called **the aperture** and all light gathered by the lens must pass through the aperture before it is registered on the film plane or imaging device. By adjusting the aperture ring, the iris either opens (creating a larger aperture opening) to allow more light or closes (smaller aperture opening) to allow less light to reach the film or CCD chip. The size of the aperture opening is calibrated to a scale called the **f-stop scale**, which is etched into the aperture ring.

The F-stop Scale: f/1.4, f/2, f/2.8, f/4, f/5.6, f/8, f/11, f/16, f/22

At first, f-stops can be a little confusing because the smaller the f-stop number, the larger the aperture opening is and the more light is allowed to reach the imaging device. Conversely, the smaller the f-stop number, the larger the aperture opening is and the more light is allowed through the lens. So f/2 lets in more light than f/11. This inversion occurs because the f-stop scale is arrived at by dividing the focal length by the diameter of the aperture opening (**Figure 10-16**). As a filmmaker you don't need to worry too much about *how* this scale was derived; you do, however, need to understand the relationship between this scale and how it corresponds to the amount of light passing through the lens and exposing your film.

Each number on the scale is called a **stop.** We say, there is one stop between f/4 and f/5.6 and two stops between f/4 and f/2. The difference of one stop has the effect of doubling or halving the amount of light allowed to pass. Expanding the aperture (smaller numbers) is called **"opening up."** Reducing the size of the aperture (bigger numbers) is called **"closing down"** or **"stopping down."** Opening up to f/4 from f/5.6 allows in twice as much light. Closing the aperture to f/2.8 from f/2 cuts the light in half. Each stop, open or closed, doubles or halves the previous number, so that if we open up one stop we double the light (×2); if we open up another stop it is doubled again 2 × 2 (four times more light); if we open up a third stop we get 2 × 2 × 2 (eight times more light), and so on (**Figure 10-17**).

Iris

The iris is actually a simple device, but it plays an enormous role in film production. Obviously the simplest application of the iris is to control the amount of light

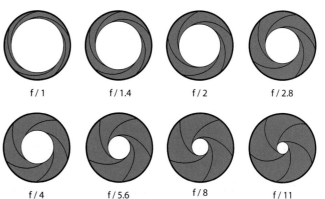

f/1   f/1.4   f/2   f/2.8

f/4   f/5.6   f/8   f/11

■ **Figure 10-16** As the f-stop number grows larger, the aperture opening grows smaller, and vice versa.

■ **Figure 10-17** Both film and high-end video lenses have engraved aperture f-stops for precise control over the incoming light.

exposing the film, or striking the CCD, in order to give us an "acceptable" image. Allow too much light through the lens and we will have a washed out, overexposed image; block too much light and we will have a dark, underexposed image. This is why it is easy to believe that there is one "right" exposure for a scene, but nothing could be further from the truth. The interrelationship between the illumination intensities of a given scene and the selection of your f-stop is a central factor in determining the look, tone, mood, and visual content of each and every shot. For any given scene, there may be a range of f-stops that will give us an "acceptable" image, but each different setting can inflect the image in various ways. With more than one option, the decision always boils down to the questions: What do you want to communicate with this shot, and which f-stop will create the image that best expresses your idea? In fact, understanding apertures and exposures is so essential to the filmmaker's creative palette that I have dedicated two chapters later in the book to this topic. (See Chapters 12 and 14.)

Lens Speed

The ability of a lens to gather light is determined by the largest possible f-stop of that particular lens. We refer to this ability as **lens speed.** A **fast lens** can open up to allow more light than a **slow lens.** The larger the maximum aperture can be, the faster the lens is. What limits the ability of a lens to gather light are the optics—the number and quality of the glass elements. For this reason, it is usually the case that wide-angle lenses are faster than telephoto lenses (they use fewer elements). A lens with a maximum aperture of f/1.4 is a very fast lens and can register a readable image with very little light. Zoom lenses tend to be much slower, as their construction requires many more elements. A lens speed of only f/3.5 is not uncommon for a zoom lens. The maximum f-stop number is usually etched into the front of the lens barrel and can sometimes fall between the usual numbers found on an f-stop scale.

T-stops

As we have seen, the f-stop scale is devised through a mathematical formula. This formula, however, assumes a lens with perfect optics; meaning that 100% of the light is transmitted through the lens without any light loss. In effect, f-stops are a theoretical number because no lens has absolutely perfect optics. This can present an inaccuracy in exposure, as many lenses lose quite a bit of light, some as much as one full stop! To remedy this, some lenses show T-stops instead of, or in addition to, f-stops. **T-stops** (short for transmission stops) are f-stops that have been adjusted to take into account the amount of light that is lost, dissipated, or absorbed by that particular lens. T-stops are simply more accurate f-stops. If a lens has T-stops, they will always be found on the aperture ring in red (f-stops are in white). Using T-stops is simple and more accurate. After you determine your exposure (shown as f-stops on your light meter), simply set the T-stop scale instead. High-quality prime lenses lose so little light that T-stops are not necessary. Zoom lenses, however, utilize many more lens elements and can lose as much as one-third to a full stop before the light finally reaches the focal plane.

■ DEPTH OF FIELD

As we discussed earlier, the point at which the lens focus is actually set, and there can be only one setting, is called the plane of critical focus. However, when we look at an actual photographed image, we notice that there is always an area, both in front of and behind this plane of focus, that also appears to be in focus. This range of apparent focus along the z-axis is called the **depth of field** (DOF). The relative depth or shallowness of this area is not fixed. It can be as shallow as a few inches or as deep as infinity (!) depending on a number of variables. Because our eye cannot see the depth of field being registered on the film, it is important to have some way to predict how deep this range will be in order for us to truly know what our final image will look like. Also, what is especially important is that this range can, to a certain extent, be controlled. As with every other controllable variable associated with the lens, depth of field can and should be manipulated in order to serve the content and visual style of your movie (see Figure 3-11 in Chapter 3).

Creating a frame with a **shallow depth of field** makes your subject stand out from the environment and gain prominence in the frame, because objects both in front of and behind the subject are out of focus and indistinct. Adopting a **deep depth of field** increases the amount of information we see along the z-axis and therefore you gain environmental detail that can inflect the mood of the scene and the narrative content. Learning to control depth of field and use it creatively is a big step toward harnessing the aesthetic power of a lens for your needs (Figure 10-18). There is a practical dimension to DOF as well. If, for example, you have a lot of character movement away from and toward the camera, you might think about using a deep depth of field to keep your subject in focus without having to resort to complex focus pulling.

Controlling Depth of Field

The primary factor in determining depth of field is the size of the image format. The smaller the format, the deeper the depth of field tends to be. It is easier to get a deep DOF in 16mm film than it is in 35mm film. And consumer video cameras, with very small CCD chips, tend to have very deep depths of field. However, as one of the controllable variables, production format is not especially flexible because it is usually chosen for reasons more pressing than its depth of field potential. There are three other variables that determine the actual range of DOF over which we have some control:

■ *The aperture opening.* The larger the aperture opening (smaller f-stop numbers), the shallower the DOF will be, and the smaller the aperture opening (larger f-stop numbers), the deeper the DOF will be. That is why scenes shot in very low light situations have such a shallow depth of field that we sometimes can see an eye in focus, but the ear, just a few inches back, is out of focus. Conversely, scenes shot in brightly lit environments can have a DOF so deep that it appears that everything in the background, as far as we can see, is in focus.

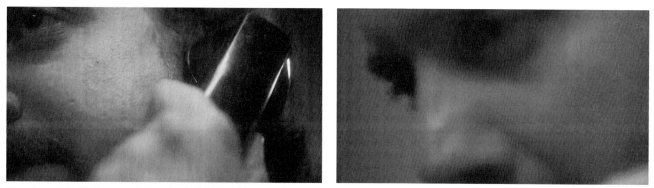

■ **Figure 10-18** The very shallow depth of field in this scene from Payne's *Sideways* (2004) causes Miles (Paul Giamatti) to fall in and out of focus, reflecting his inebriated state when he places an ill-advised call to his ex-wife.

- *The focal length of the lens.* The longer the focal length of the lens, the shallower the DOF will be, and the shorter our lens, the deeper our depth of field will be. Wide-angle lenses create deeper depth of field than telephoto lenses.
- *The focus point setting (distance of the critical plane of focus).* The closer to the camera the focus setting, the shallower the depth of field will be, and the farther away we place the plane of critical focus, the deeper the DOF will be.

To predict what the DOF for any shot will be, filmmakers consult standard DOF tables like those found in the *American Cinematographer Manual* or online (see the box below). These tables are very simple to read and will tell you exactly what in your frame will appear to be in focus—so there will be no surprises when you get the film back from the lab. It is then up to you to use this information to creative advantage. Figure 10-19 shows two DOF tables. You will notice that the four variables we discussed for controlling the depth of field are part of the calculation. First, these are for the 16mm film format (other formats, like 35mm film require different tables). Each table is for a specific focal length lens (located at

Lens Focal Length: **25mm**						**DOF table: 16mm Film Format**									CoC = .015mm (.0005")	
focus distance (feet)	f/1.4		f/2		f/2.8		f/4		f/5.6		f/8		f/11		f/16	
	Near	Far	Near	Far	Near	Far	Near	Far	Near	Far	Near	Far	Near	Far	Near	Far
2	1' 11.5"	2' 0.5"	1' 11.3"	2' 0.7"	1' 11.1"	2' 1"	1' 10.7"	2' 1.4"	1' 10.2"	2' 2.1"	1' 9.6"	2' 3"	1' 8.7"	2' 4.5"	1' 7.6"	2' 6.9"
4	3' 10.1"	4' 2"	3' 9.4"	4' 2.9"	3' 8.4"	4' 4.2"	3' 7.1"	4' 6.2"	3' 5.3"	4' 9.3"	3' 3"	5' 2.3"	3' 0.2"	5' 11"	2' 8.9"	7' 4.7"
6	5' 7.8"	6' 4.7"	5' 6.3"	6' 6.8"	5' 4.1"	6' 10"	5' 1.4"	7' 3.1"	4' 9.8"	7' 11.4"	4' 5.5"	9' 2.1"	4' 0.3"	11' 9"	3' 6.5"	19' 6"
8	7' 4.7"	8' 8.6"	7' 2"	9' 0.6"	6' 10.5"	9' 6.8"	6' 5.9"	10' 5"	6' 0.3"	11' 11"	5' 5.6"	14'11"	4' 10"	23' 3"	4' 1.8"	109'
10	9' 0.8"	11' 2"	8' 8.8"	11' 8"	8' 3.6"	12' 7"	7' 9"	14' 1"	7' 11"	17'	6' 3.9"	23' 10"	5' 5.9"	56'	4' 7.5"	∞
12	10' 8"	13' 8"	10' 3"	14' 6"	9' 7.5"	15' 11"	8' 10.8"	18' 5"	8' 0.4"	23' 8"	7' 0.8"	39' 8"	6' 0.5"	880'	5' 0.1"	∞
14	12' 3"	16' 4"	11' 8"	17' 7"	10' 10"	19' 8"	9' 11.4"	23' 7"	8' 10.6"	33'	7' 8.6"	75'	6' 6.1"	∞	5' 3.9"	∞
16	13' 9"	19' 2"	13'	20' 10"	12'	23' 10"	10' 11"	29' 11"	9' 7.8"	46' 11"	8' 3.4"	234'	6' 10.9"	∞	5' 7.1"	∞
18	15' 2"	22' 1"	14' 3"	24' 5"	13' 2"	28' 7"	11' 10"	37' 10"	10' 4"	70'	8' 9.4"	∞	7' 3"	∞	5' 9.7"	∞
20	16' 7"	25' 2"	15' 6"	28' 3"	14' 2"	34'	12' 8"	47' 11"	11'	114'	9' 2.8"	∞	7' 6.6"	∞	6'	∞
30	22' 11"	43' 5"	20' 10"	53'	18' 6"	79'	16'	241'	13' 5"	∞	10' 11"	∞	8' 7.6"	∞	6' 8"	∞
40	28' 4"	68'	25' 3"	96'	21' 11"	230'	18' 5"	∞	15' 1"	∞	12'	∞	9' 3.5"	∞	7' 0.6"	∞
50	33'	103'	28' 11"	185'	24' 7"	∞	20' 4"	∞	16' 4"	∞	12' 9"	∞	9' 8.9"	∞	7' 3.7"	∞
∞	97'	∞	68'	∞	48' 5"	∞	34' 3"	∞	24' 3"	∞	17' 2"	∞	12' 2"	∞	8' 7.5"	∞

Lens Focal Length: **100mm**						**DOF table: 16mm Film Format**									CoC = .015mm (.0005")	
focus distance (feet)	f/1.4		f/2		f/2.8		f/4		f/5.6		f/8		f/11		f/16	
	Near	Far	Near	Far	Near	Far	Near	Far	Near	Far	Near	Far	Near	Far	Near	Far
7	6' 11.6"	7' 0.4"	6' 11.5"	7' 0.5"	6' 11.3"	7' 0.7"	6' 11"	7' 1"	6' 10.6"	7' 1.5"	6' 10"	7' 2.1"	6' 9.2"	7' 3"	6' 8.1"	7' 4.3"
8	7' 11.5"	8' 0.5"	7' 11.3"	8' 0.7"	7' 11.1"	8' 1"	7' 10.7"	8' 1.4"	7' 10.1"	8' 1.9"	7' 9.4"	8' 2.8"	7' 8.3"	8' 4"	7' 6.9"	8' 5.7"
10	9' 11.3"	10' 1"	9' 10.9"	10' 1"	9' 10.5"	10' 2"	9' 9.9"	10' 2"	9' 9.1"	10' 3"	9' 7.9"	10' 4"	9' 6.3"	10' 6"	9' 4.1"	10' 9"
12	11' 11"	12' 1"	11' 11"	12' 2"	11' 10"	12' 2"	11' 9"	12' 3"	11' 8"	12' 5"	11' 6"	12' 6"	11' 4"	12' 9"	11' 1"	13' 1"
14	13' 11"	14' 2"	13' 10"	14' 2"	13' 9"	14' 3"	13' 8"	14' 4"	13' 6"	14' 6"	13' 4"	14' 9"	13' 1"	15' 1"	12' 9"	15' 7"
16	15' 10"	16' 2"	15' 9"	16' 3"	15' 8"	16' 4"	15' 7"	16' 6"	15' 5"	16' 8"	15' 2"	17'	14' 10"	17' 5"	14' 4"	18' 1"
18	17' 10"	18' 3"	17' 9"	18' 4"	17' 7"	18' 5"	17' 5"	18' 7"	17' 3"	18' 10"	16' 11"	19' 3"	16' 6"	19' 10"	15' 11"	20' 8"
20	19' 9"	20' 3"	19' 8"	20' 4"	19' 6"	20' 6"	19' 4"	20' 9"	19'	21' 1"	18' 8"	21' 7"	18' 2"	22' 3"	17' 6"	23' 4"
30	29' 5"	30' 7"	29' 3"	30' 10"	28' 11"	31' 2"	28' 6"	31' 9"	27' 10"	32' 6"	27' 1"	33' 8"	26'	35' 5"	24' 8"	38' 4"
40	39'	41' 1"	38' 7"	41' 6"	38' 1"	42' 2"	37' 4"	43' 2"	36' 3"	44' 7"	34' 11"	46' 10"	33' 2"	50'	31'	56'
50	48' 5"	52'	47' 10"	52'	47'	53'	45' 10"	55'	44' 4"	57'	42' 4"	61'	39' 9"	67'	36' 8"	79'
75	72'	79'	70'	80'	68'	83'	66'	87'	63'	93'	59'	103'	54'	122'	48' 6"	165'
100	94'	107'	92'	110'	89'	115'	85'	122'	80'	135'	73'	157'	66'	206'	58'	369'
∞	1547'	∞	1094'	∞	774'	∞	547'	∞	387'	∞	274'	∞	194'	∞	137'	∞

■ **Figure 10-19** DOF tables for 25mm and 100mm lenses (16mm film format). Depth of field tables are essential on location for determining which areas of the frame are in or out of focus. (Downloadable DOF tables for 16mm format can be found at www.voiceandvisionbook.com or DOF Masters.com.)

the top, left of the chart). The two here are for the 25mm and 100mm lenses. The lens focus distance is located on the left vertical column, and the f-stop settings are on the top, horizontal column. Let's see how to read these very simple tables.

Look at the DOF table for the 25mm lens (normal lens). If we are focused at 16 feet with an aperture of f/2.8, we can see that the DOF range is 12' to 23' 10". All objects between these points will appear to be in focus even though your actual plane of critical focus is 16 feet. The range of apparent focus along the z-axis is therefore 11' 10". Now read across and along the f-stop scale for the same focus point (16 feet) and you will see the DOF get deeper as the aperture gets smaller, and as the aperture opens up, the DOF gets shallower. Now, read down the various lens focus distances for f/2.8 and you will notice that the DOF gets shallower the closer the focus point is, and deeper the farther the focus is set.

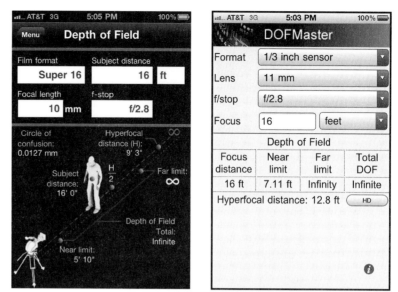

Figure 10-20 Many DOF calculators are available online and as apps for smartphones. Some are free, like this Kodak iPhone app *(left),* others charge a nominal fee, like the highly versatile DOF Master app *(right),* which calculates DOF for all film and video formats.

Now look at the table for the 100mm lens (telephoto) and compare the same settings (focus at 16 feet and aperture at f/2.8). The DOF is 15' 8" to 16' 4". The range is only 8 inches—much shallower. Now, go to Figure 10-20 and look at the DOF calculation on the Kodak smartphone app *(left);* you'll see the same settings (focus at 16 feet and aperture at f/2.8), but this time calculated for a 10mm lens. Now, with the wide angles lens, the DOF range is from 5' 10" to infinity!

Getting back to our examples for setting focus for narrative and emotional impact (Figures 10-10 and 10-11 on page 228-229), you now understand that it's not just a matter of where you set your focus ring, but you must also understand just how deep the focus range is in order to accurately achieve the shot you want. Using a wide-angle lens and lots of light (small aperture) might have brought Anton Chigurh into the DOF range and the character would have lost much of his menace and mystery. A DOF only a few feet deeper would have brought Oskar and other children into sharp focus; we would likely not have even noticed the bullies, and the shot would have lost its tension and meaning.

DEPTH OF FIELD CALCULATION TOOLS

To predict what the DOF for any shot will be, filmmakers consult standard DOF tables like those found in the *American Cinematographer Manual.* You'll also find a set of DOF tables for the 16mm format at www.voiceandvisionbook.com. Additionally, you can easily generate and print out DOF tables for any film or video format at www.dofmaster.com. The DOFMaster website also offers a DOF calculator where you enter in the four DOF variables mentioned earlier and it will instantly calculate your precise DOF range. Panavision has the same DOF calculator tool at www.panavision.com/tools.php. Additionally, there are a number of smartphone apps that allow you to calculate DOF in the field, including the free *Kodak Cinema Tools* app, which only calculates DOF for film formats. There are a number of DOF apps you can download for a nominal price that work for all film and digital video formats. Two of these are the *DOFMaster* app and David Eubank's *PCam Film+Digital Calculator* (**Figure 10-20**).

in practice

The 1/3–2/3 Rule

You may have noticed while you were reading the DOF tables that there seems to be more of the range of apparent focus behind the actual focus setting than in front of it. This is always the case. The **1/3–2/3 rule** for DOF tells us that two-thirds of the depth range along the z-axis is behind the focus point and one-third is in front (**Figure 10-21**). This is an important principle to consider when you are trying to move objects into and out of the range of apparent focus (see the In Practice box, "Working with DOF").

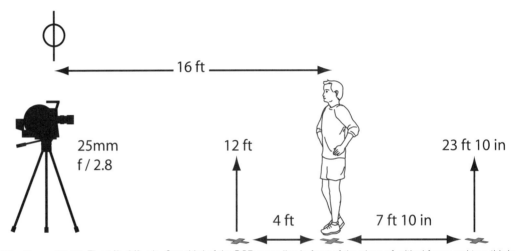

25mm
f / 2.8

16 ft

12 ft

23 ft 10 in

4 ft

7 ft 10 in

■ **Figure 10-21** The 1/3–2/3 rule. One-third of the DOF range lies in front of the plane of critical focus and two-thirds behind it.

in practice

■ WORKING WITH DOF

In a final project for an intermediate film production class, Gisela M. ended her film with a shot for which depth of field was a critical element of telling her revenge fantasy story:

> *Joey is a materialistic cad who leaves his sweet girlfriend for a woman who makes very good money. But Joey is quickly dumped when the woman finds out that he has no money himself. In the last scene we see a rejected Joey riding a train, on his way back to reconnect with his girlfriend—but he's out of luck.*

Here is our essential train shot. The train is moderately full; we see Joey in a medium close-up shot, sitting alone and gazing out the window. Passengers in front of him (foreground) and behind him (background) are engrossed in their newspapers. The guy sitting right behind Joey turns the page and we see a photograph of Joey's smiling girlfriend under the headline "Bronx Woman Wins 10 Mil. Jackpot" right behind Joey's head. **Figure 10-22** is a storyboard of the frame Gisela was after and an overhead diagram of the setup for this train shot.

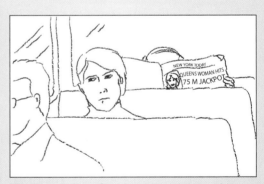

■ **Figure 10-22** Gisela's storyboard shows what must be seen clearly in the frame: Joey's face looking out the train window and the newspaper headline directly behind him.

Obviously, it is essential for the audience to read the headline. The fact that Joey's girlfriend has struck it rich and that Joey will likely never get her back provides the central irony of the film. Also, this shot allows our audience to know more than the character. We see that his scheming has backfired on him and we can predict the final encounter with the girlfriend, so it's not necessary to show it. This one shot contains both narrative information and the humorous tone of a well-timed punch line.

Here is Gisela's technical information: she was shooting on 16mm film and to get a nice medium close-up on Joey, along with a dynamic composition, including foreground, midground, and background, she used an 85mm lens with the camera set up 15 feet away from Joey. The newspaper headline was 3 feet behind Joey's head, 18 feet from the film plane. Given the intensity of the light in the train car, Gisela set the f/stop at f.11.

Everything seems fine and a careless filmmaker would simply focus on the face of our subject Joey (set focus to 15 feet) and just take the shot as is. However, when the footage returns from the lab, they would discover, too late, that the news photo and headline are out of focus and cannot be read. By simply consulting a DOF chart, the filmmaker would have seen that, given the variables (85mm lens, f.11, focus at 15 feet), the DOF range was 13' 7" to 16' 9", not deep enough to include the newspaper.

However, Gisela was a careful filmmaker and she checked the DOF chart and knew she needed to make an adjustment. But which one? Which variable should she choose to obtain the depth of field necessary to see Joey and read the newspaper, to deliver the ironic punch line to resolve the story! Let's look at her options (**Figure 10-23**):

■ *Changing the lens.*
If Gisela were to change the lens focal length to 65mm, with all other things remaining the same, her DOF would deepen to a range of 12' 8" to

18' 4". That's great; the newspaper is now in focus—but wait: all things have not remained the same. Changing a lens affects many other aspects of her frame besides DOF. First, with the shorter focal length lens we might not be able to read the newspaper anymore, even if it is in focus, because it appears too far away. Second, Joey is now smaller in the frame and the extras in the foreground take on greater, and maybe excessive, prominence. Also, Gisela's field of view is wider, maybe wide enough to see things she wanted to keep outside the frame, like a light stand or a microphone. Obviously, changing the focal length will require other adjustments: move some lights, shift the extras around, and maybe it's even necessary to move the camera closer to Joey and the newspaper. But wait! We know that a closer camera-to-subject distance will *decrease* DOF and Gisela will lose much of the depth of field she just gained. There's got to be an easier way.

■ *Adjusting the aperture variable.*
If it's possible to add more light, then Gisela can leave her focal length and camera-to-subject distance as it is and simply close the aperture down. Doubling the intensity of the light means she can shoot at f/16. Consulting the charts shows that at that f-stop her DOF is 13' to 17' 5". Not quite deep enough. According to the charts, she needs to get to f/22 (even smaller) before the depth of field deepens to 12' 5" to 19'. Shooting at f/22 would mean that everything she needs will be in focus and she gets to keep the framing she had in mind. However, adding *four times* the light isn't always that easy; in fact, on a very low-budget shoot, like Gisela's, there was no way to quadruple the amount of light. So what else?

■ *Adjusting the plane of focus.*
So Gisela couldn't add any light at all and she didn't want to change lenses: what now? Should she rethink the shot completely? Not necessarily. Remember that one-third of the DOF is in front of the plane of focus and two-thirds is behind! Also remember that adjusting the plane of critical focus farther from the film plane actually *deepens* the DOF. Obviously, there is no reason to have the plane of critical focus exactly on our subject Joey as long as he falls within the DOF range. So Gisela simply adjusted her focus ring to 16 feet and her DOF shifted back toward the newspaper and deepened slightly to 14' 3" to 18' 1". The newspaper is now readable and Joey falls within the near end of the DOF range.

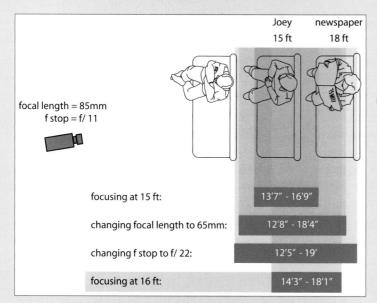

Joey — 15 ft newspaper — 18 ft

focal length = 85mm
f stop = f/ 11

focusing at 15 ft: 13'7" - 16'9"

changing focal length to 65mm: 12'8" - 18'4"

changing f stop to f/ 22: 12'5" - 19'

focusing at 16 ft: 14'3" - 18'1"

■ **Figure 10-23** After some research, Gisela found the right combination of aperture, camera-to subject-distance, and focal length to create the shot exactly the way her story needed it. (see this as an interactive figure online.)

Circle of Confusion

As we have discussed, depth of field is a phenomenon of *apparent* focus along the z-axis range, but let's look a little closer. Focus, as we have defined it, is achieved when a point of light coming off our subject is registered as a point of light on the focal plane and we know that there is only one setting that will be truly in focus (i.e., setting the focus ring to 16 feet). This means that the light points emanating from the area in front of and behind the plane of critical focus are not registered as a points; rather, they begin to spread larger and larger and get fuzzier the farther away their origin is from the focus setting point. However, neither the human eye, nor film stocks, nor CCD chips can distinguish between very small degrees of unsharpness. There is an acceptable size range to which a point of light can spread (be technically out of focus) and still *appear* to be in focus. For 16mm film, a point of light can spread to a diameter of .015mm or 0.0005″ (that's five ten-thousandths of an inch) on the film, and our eye will see it as in focus. Beyond that, the image starts to appear fuzzy. This measurement of acceptable diameter, which creates the appearance of focus, is called the **circle of confusion (the CoC).** You can find the CoC for the shooting format on any DOF table (see **Figure 10-19**). Every format size has its own acceptable CoC measurement. For 35mm film format, the CoC is 0.001″. In video, the CoC for a ¼″ CCD is 0.008mm, for a ⅓″ CCD it is 0.011 and for a ½″ CCD it is 0.016mm.

■ LENS CONSIDERATIONS ON DV

Although all of the principles of optics apply equally to film and DV lenses, there are a few special details concerning lenses that must be considered when shooting on DV.

DOF and DV

Using DOF tables or a DOF calculator is standard practice in film production because film camera viewfinders are not clear enough to really *see* your range of apparent focus. Because film is projected many times larger than the original frame, absolute accuracy is essential. However, DOF tables are rarely used in video production for two reasons. First, when DOF is absolutely critical to a video project, there is usually a production field monitor on the set for reference (see page 264). This monitor is many times larger than the viewfinder and allows one to see DOF fairly clearly. Also, it was always assumed that video was a small-screen TV medium, so who could tell DOF to the inch anyway? That, of course, is changing as home TVs are growing bigger every month, and more and more films originating on DV (SD and HD) find their way into theaters and are projected as big as any 35mm film.

Most consumer and midlevel digital video cameras have very small CCD chips; ¼″, ⅓″, and ⅔″ chips are most common. Small imaging devices, as we have discussed, produce deeper depth of field. One of the main complaints of D.P.s using video is that the DOF is too deep. There are a number of remedies for this if you want to achieve a shallow depth of field. Most of these strategies involve staying at the widest aperture possible by either keeping the lighting intensity low or, if you cannot control the illumination of the scene (e.g., a sunny exterior shoot), utilizing the camera's built-in **neutral density** filters to block light or using the **electronic shutter control** to reduce the light entering the camera. Either way, reducing the light will force your aperture to open up and your DOF will narrow.

> *One of the characteristics of digital cameras that I particularly like is that they have such deep focus. With most film cameras the depth of field is limited, and so focus becomes crucial in respect of the actor's movement, since it's so important that the character is always in focus. Most digital cameras, though—certainly when they're on their wide angle mode—have such depth of field that you don't really have to worry about focus.*
>
> **Mike Figgis (From *Digital Filmmaking*, Faber and Faber, 2005)**

If you are shooting on DV and wish for your project to have shallow DOF throughout, then you might consider using a **35mm lens adapter kit** for DV cameras. Most 35mm lens adapters consist of a lens mount that utilizes standard 35mm lenses that focus the light from the scene onto a vibrating ground glass screen positioned in front of the existing video camera lens (**Figure 10-24**). The video camera essentially shoots the image, which has the dimensions of a 35mm film frame, off the ground glass screen. Given the size of the imaging frame and the length of the lenses (interchangeable), you effectively achieve, on video, the same perspective and DOF possibilities as the 35mm film format. The downside to lens adapters is that they make a mobile video camera much more cumbersome and conspicuous.

Focusing a Zoom Lens

Because depth of field becomes narrower as we move toward the telephoto end of a zoom lens, it is possible to have an image perfectly in focus with a wide-angle setting, and simply changing the focal length will throw the subject out of focus. The proper way to assure that focus will be maintained throughout the zoom range of a lens is to find your focus at the extreme telephoto end of the range, then pull out to the focal length you want. Going from telephoto to more wide angle will only increase your DOF and the subject will remain in focus. This is especially important to know if you are shooting on the fly—as in many documentary situations. The procedure for focusing a zoom is this: First zoom all the way into the subject you want to have in focus (for example, the eyes of your talent). Adjust your focus until the image is sharp. Now zoom out and find your initial frame. The subject will now remain in focus for the entire zoom range. This is called **presetting focus.**

Video Lenses and Automatic Functions

Unlike film cameras, which oblige us to choose focus and aperture settings manually, most DV cameras provide an automatic setting option for both of these functions. As I mention throughout this book, it is preferable to turn off all automatic functions in your camcorder. Manual settings ensure that the filmmaker is in control of all variables and therefore in control of how their film looks. Remember, choosing your focus is a creative and aesthetic decision: Why would we want to hand that important decision to a machine, with no aesthetic judgment at all? By using automatic focus and exposure, your film cannot help but look like every other film using auto functions.

All professional video cameras employ lenses with focus, f-stop, and zoom rings etched with their respective scales. However, many consumer and industrial DV cameras place some or all of that information within menus. It is important for you to familiarize yourself with these functions and figure out how to access all manual modes for your particular camera before you are on the set and shooting your project (**Figure 10-25**).

■ **Figure 10-24** Lens adaptors, like the Letus Elite *(top),* allow DV camcorders to take advantage of a large range of high-quality 35mm lenses. Filmlike shallow DOF, as in this shot from *Kiarra's Escape (bottom),* is easily achievable on video with the use of a lens adaptor. (video examples of a scene shot with and without a lens adaptor are at the companion website.)

■ **Figure 10-25** Most video cameras have a way of switching from automatic to manual focusing, an important feature for maintaining complete control over the way your images are recorded.

■ **Figure 10-26** Video cameras set to auto focus have trouble deciding where to focus in situations with multiple planes. Switching to manual focusing solves this problem, letting the users set the focus according to their needs.

One significant problem with the **auto focus** function is that it favors objects in the center of the frame—which might not be appropriate for the composition you want—and it tends to shift focus in the middle of a shot when anything moves across the foreground of the frame. Let's say we have a composition in which your subject is tucked over to the right of the frame, with a forest behind her. It's likely that the camera will choose to set focus automatically for that which is in the middle, the forest, leaving the subject fuzzy. Auto focus is also easily confused by images with multiple planes. For example, let's say we wish to shoot a character who is 10 feet behind a chain-link fence. The auto focus will likely select for the fence in the foreground, especially if your subject is slightly off center. Quite often, auto focus mechanisms will go crazy in a situation like this, shifting arbitrarily from the fence to the character and back to the fence, searching for focus but never quite settling on it (**Figure 10-26**).

A common procedure for setting video focus is to zoom in to what you want to be in focus. Allow the auto focus to choose its setting and then flip into **manual mode.** Now when you pull back and readjust your frame, with the subject to one side, the camera will hold your focus point. Also, if a car should pass through in the foreground, your camera will not try to change the focus setting.

Camera Support

It doesn't matter if you are shooting on film or video. Deciding if your camera should move during a shot, and how you want the camera to move are as important to the tone, style, and meaning of your film as the lighting, locations, costumes, or any other creative element. Whether you're panning, tracking, following, or craning, choosing the appropriate camera support is vital. You need to understand the equipment you have available to you and the expressive potential each piece of gear allows so that you can achieve the aesthetic approach you want.

For example, let's say during previsualization you and the D.P. decided that your film would best be told as a series of meticulously lit and composed static compositions, where the camera barely moves, as in *Café Lumière* by Hou Hsiao-Hsien (cinematography by Ping Bing Lee); or perhaps you conceived the visual style of your film to be similar to Gus Van Sant's *Elephant* (shot by Harris Savides), with extremely long takes that smoothly follow characters down corridors, through doors, and from inside to outside; or perhaps you want to invoke hard realism through a restlessly moving, seeking, edgy camera, as we see in a film like *The Hurt Locker* by Kathryn Bigelow and D.P. Barry Ackroyd (Figure 11-1).

All three of these choices were perfectly suited to the content and concept of each film, and each one required a different kind of camera support. You need to ask, what will allow me to achieve the particular look I'm after? And, of course: Do I have or can I afford what I need to achieve that look? The way you support your camera is central to achieving the visual style you're seeking. Let's take a look at some options.

■ THE HANDHELD CAMERA

The cheapest and most readily available method of camera support is the human body. "Going handheld" means using your hands and arms for holding small and lightweight cameras (small DV cameras and film cameras like the Arri-S or Bolex) or carrying the camera on your shoulder and bracing it with your arm (large DV cameras and film cameras like the Arri-SR). Most video field production cameras are designed for easy handholding (Figure 11-2), as are most 16mm film cameras, but some, like the Arri-BL, are very heavy and awkward. Only very few 35mm film cameras are designed for handholding and even with those that are, handholding can be a challenge.

■ **Figure 11-1** A stationary camera and long takes matches the contemplative tone of Hou's *Café Lumière* (2003, *top*). In Van Sant's *Elephant* (2003, *center*) much of the film is shot with a smoothly gliding camera, inescapably leading us to a tragic end. Bigelow's *Hurt Locker* (2008, *bottom*) uses handheld cameras to reflect the danger and nervous tension experienced by an Army bomb disposal squad in Iraq.

Handholding always introduces some human instability in the image, because the camera reflects the human movements of the operator. No matter how steady the camera operator is, a handheld camera is never as stable as one mounted on a tripod; nor should it be. The movement obtained with a handheld camera

■ **Figure 11-2** Handholding a camera can be fairly easy when using a small DV camcorder (*left,* filmmaker Diana Logreida with a Panasonic DVX-100), but it is more physically demanding with larger film or video cameras (*right,* cinematographer Rain Li with an Arriflex 435).

has an aesthetic quality that recalls the documentary style of Direct Cinema, and this quality has been used to great effect to add a sense of immediacy, spontaneity, and direct involvement in numerous narrative films, including *4 Months, 3 Weeks and 2 Days* by Cristian Mungiu; *Eternal Sunshine of the Spotless Mind,* by Michel Gondry; and *La Promesse,* by the Dardenne Brothers. All of these films were shot entirely or mostly with a handheld camera.

Using a handheld camera is not as easy as simply slinging a camera on your shoulder and shooting. We've all seen plenty of home movie footage that's so jittery that watching it makes us nauseous. Techniques for handheld shots require practiced skills and a great deal of body control and strength to keep from looking haphazard or sloppy. In many ways, the small, ultralight DV cameras are more difficult to control because the weight of a camera, especially when mounted on a shoulder, provides some stability. If you decide to go handheld, your movements should be as controlled as possible. Don't worry that it will look like a tripod shot; it won't. It will look handheld. If what you're after are super smooth moves and rock-steady compositions, then don't go handheld in hopes that no one will notice the human movements; they will. Controlled imperfection is the aesthetic point.

Here are a few tips for shooting with a handheld camera:
- Camera movement comes from the body, not just the hands. Use your entire body—feet, legs, torso, arms, and hands—to perform a camera move.
- Keep your knees bent and loose, like a skier, for shock absorption.
- Stay toward the wide-angle end of the lens. A telephoto lens only magnifies the jitter and instability of the frame. Use wider-angle lenses and move in close for tight shots and out for longer shots.
- Breathing should be long and steady. Don't hold your breath or you will find the need to gasp for air in the middle of a shot, causing an inevitable jerk of the frame.
- Don't hold the camera rigid. Rhythm, grace, and controlled movement are key.
- Take advantage of the pivoting LCD screen and the light weight of palm-held camcorders to go beyond eye-level shots. These cameras allow you to see your compositions even when the camera is dangling low from your arm or held aloft far over your head.
- Practice, practice, practice. Like any other creative skill, you get better at handholding a camera by doing it over and over again. Great cinematographers who are skilled at handheld technique, like Ellen Kuras, Christopher Doyle, Anthony Dod Mantle, Maryse Alberti, and Thomas Mauch, are great because they've handled a camera nearly as often as a great pianist has touched the piano keys or a tennis pro has swung a racket. No great skill is acquired without effort, learning, and practice.

■ **Figure 11-3** The tripod has been used since the early history of filmmaking, as seen in Vertov's seminal film *Man with a Movie Camera* (1929).

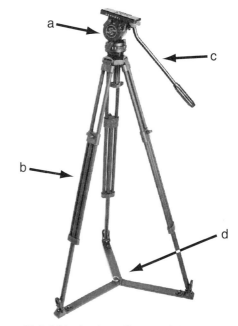

■ **Figure 11-4** A tripod system will commonly have a head (a), extendable legs (b), a pan handle (c), and a spreader (d).

■ THE TRIPOD

Tripods are perhaps the most common form of camera support. Their design has remained essentially unchanged since the earliest years of cinema (Figure 11-3). Tripods are a three-legged support designed to both hold the camera steady for precise subject framing and to allow for fluid pans, tilts, and compound moves. Professional tripods are especially adjustable, allowing a filmmaker to frame and maneuver with a precision and fluidity not possible with a handheld camera.

A tripod can be broken down into two major components: the head and the legs (also called sticks). Some less expensive tripods are constructed with the head and legs in one unit, but the most flexible tripods are those that are designed as systems, so that each component is separate and interchangeable to fit a variety of production situations (Figure 11-4).

Tripod Head

In terms of movement precision, the most important component of any tripod is the **head**. The tripod head is where the camera is mounted and is the component that swivels left and right for panning, and up and down for

■ **Figure 11-5** Picking the right tripod for the job. For smooth, controlled camera moves and even for safety's sake, the tripod should match the weight rating of the camera being used.

tilting. The quality of the head greatly affects the smoothness of the camera moves. Tripod heads also come in different sizes to accommodate various camera weights. A small head, like the Cartoni C-10, are designed specifically for small cameras (Figure 11-5). Larger heads, like the Miller DS60, are built to accommodate the bulk of large video camcorders and heavy film cameras weighing up to 65 pounds.

An important factor determining the quality of the tripod's panning and tilting abilities is the **resistance mechanism**. Smooth moves with a tripod are accomplished by adjusting the resistance of the tripod head against the weight of the camera and the speed of the move. A very slow pan, for example, is smoothest with heavy drag on the pan mechanism. The two types of resistance mechanisms you're likely to come across for

DV and 16mm film production are **fluid heads** and **friction heads**. Fluid heads use pressurized hydraulic fluid to provide the adjustable drag necessary for smooth camera moves. Friction heads use the surface friction between internal plates, sometimes lined with cork, to create movement resistance. Fluid heads are more expensive but they also give you much more precise and varied adjustments to facilitate your camera move, and they generally have a smoother and more even action throughout the panning and tilting range.

There are several features on a tripod head that are common to all professional tripods, and you should locate these right away (Figure 11-6):

1. **Pan and tilt locks** completely lock down the mechanism, keeping the tripod from pivoting at all. The most important lock for you to locate is the tilt lock. If your camera is slightly unbalanced on the tripod (because the magazine load has shifted from the front to the back during the shoot or from the addition of a heavy battery), this will cause the camera to tilt forward or backward all the way. If unattended, the whole thing can eventually pitch all the way over, sending the camera crashing to the ground. The standard procedure to avoid this catastrophe is to tighten the tilt lock between takes and never leave the tripod and camera unattended.

2. **Pan and tilt dampers** adjust the amount of resistance for their respective movements. Generally speaking, the more slowly you wish to execute a move, the more resistance you want, and vice versa. This assures smoother motion and greater control.

3. **The pan handle** is used to control the movements of the camera. On good tripods, the angle of the pan handle can be adjusted for various tripod heights and personal comfort. Many tripods allow you to mount the pan handle on the left or right, depending on whether you are right- or left-handed. Take the time to adjust the handle for maximum comfort and control. The important cautionary note here is that you should never carry a tripod by the pan handle. Pan handles are usually made of lightweight aluminum and the adjustment threads can easily strip or they could simply break off.

4. The **head mount** is at the base of the tripod head and is where the head mounts to the tripod legs. With modular tripod systems, the head can be used with a variety of sticks offering a broad range of heights. Most quality tripods have claw ball or ball-and-socket mounts, which can be loosened to freely adjust the angle of the tripod head in any direction to achieve a level base no matter where the tripod is standing. It is much easier to level a tripod by using this adjustment than by varying the lengths of the three legs. Tripods with adjustable heads also usually have a bubble leveler to assist in leveling of the head.

5. Finally, all tripod heads have a **camera mounting plate** where the camera is attached to the tripod head. Cameras are secured to the mounting plate with a threaded mounting screw. Most film cameras and professional DV cameras use a ⅜" mounting screw, and small DV cameras use a smaller ¼" mounting screw. Make sure the mounting screw matches the threads on the underside of the camera.

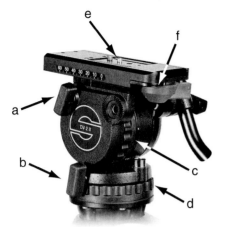

■ **Figure 11-6** A professional fluid head has a tilt lock (a), a pan lock (b), tension adjustments for the tilt and pan controls (c, d), a base plate for the camera (e), and a quick release lock for the base plate (f).

You might be wondering why I mention a tiny detail like the size of the camera mounting screw. As I've mentioned before, in film production every little detail is crucial. I have had more than a few students go on location with tripod heads that had the wrong-sized mounting screw. These students often were shooting on MiniDV, but wanted to use a larger tripod or dolly system generally used for 16mm cameras without stopping to think that they also needed a different mounting screw. These students arrived on location with everything in place—crew, cast, costumes, locations—but had no way to secure the camera on the tripod. In one case they gaffer-taped the camera to the tripod head, which was not only unsteady but also nearly destroyed the delicate camera. Then, they had to untape and retape it every time they needed to change their cassette. In another case the director simply decided to go handheld, and the dolly they had rented sat on the sidelines, unused. Unfortunately, the handheld look was not the aesthetic approach they were after at all. In both cases the look of each project was seriously compromised, all on account of one lil' ol' screw!

It's also important to note that many tripods have adjustable and quick-release mounting plates. An adjustable mounting plate will slide slightly forward and backward on the head. This allows the camera operator to precisely balance the camera on the tripod. Ideally, you should be able to take your hands off the camera, without the tilt lock engaged or any drag on the mechanism, and the camera will remain level. This way, the operator doesn't fight gravity while executing a camera move. The quick-release function allows you to pop the camera on and off the head of the tripod quickly, which makes moving the tripod and camera from one location to another much faster. You should never carry the tripod around with a camera attached. Quick release also lets you quickly remove the camera from the tripod to go handheld and then pop it back on again for tripod shots.

Tripod Legs

The **legs** (or **sticks**) of a tripod are adjustable so that the tripod height, and therefore the camera height, can be easily changed from shot to shot. Also, because the legs are independently adjustable, they provide a firm footing on uneven terrain, like a hillside or on stairs (Figure 11-7). Some tripod systems offer legs in three different heights, on which the same head can be used interchangeably. Typical **standard legs** position the camera between three feet and six feet. Some standard legs are two-stage legs, which means that they have additional length for extension and offer even higher angles. For shots lower than three feet we often use **baby legs**, which have a height range from one foot to about three feet (Figure 11-8). Lower than baby legs is a **high-hat**, which is a fixed metal head mount, usually attached to a plywood board. In addition to being the lowest base for a camera, a high-hat can also be attached with clamps in areas where a tripod cannot be used (Figure 11-9).

Figure 11-7 The individually extendable legs of a tripod make it possible to get stable support on uneven surfaces, such as a staircase.

On many professional tripods, the legs are allowed to open out freely to any width for a stable base of support. To keep the legs from completely sliding out from under the camera, a **spreader** is often used. Some tripods have a built-in spreader, while others require a separate unit. The feet of some tripod sticks have spikes that can be pushed into the ground in exterior locations, but these spikes will obviously slip on hard surfaces or destroy wooden floors, so you must use a spreader in these situations.

Tripods have remained the single most essential camera support throughout the history of cinema because they are inexpensive, extremely mobile, and give a filmmaker great control and a wide variety of camera angles and fluid camera movements.

Figure 11-8 Yasujiro Ozu's longtime collaborator, cinematographer Yuharu Atsuta, demonstrates a quintessential element of the Ozu style: the "tatami" shot, made possible through the use of a baby-legs tripod.

Figure 11-9 A hi-hat allows the camera to be placed close to the ground or attached to other surfaces with the use of clamps, as pictured.

■ **Figure 11-10** A doorway dolly *(left)*. Inflatable wheels allow for a smooth transit and do not require tracks. A spider dolly, capable of crablike lateral moves *(right)*.

■ **Figure 11-11** Dollies that use tracks can create extremely smooth moving shots, even over rough terrain, but their setup is a time- and labor-intensive endeavor.

■ **Figure 11-12** Innovator Garret Brown operating his Steadicam system in one of the first films to use it, Kubrick's *The Shining* (1980).

■ THE DOLLY

A **dolly** is a camera support on wheels that is used when your shot requires a dynamic move (when the camera itself moves through space) and you want it to be smoother and more controlled than what you can achieve with a handheld camera. Many types of dollies are available, from expensive to inexpensive and extremely heavy to relatively portable. Some dollies move on soft, inflated rubber tires and require a smooth, even floor (**Figure 11-10**). Other dollies run on tracks that are laid out in straight or curved sections along the desired path of the camera movement.

Laying dolly track creates extremely smooth camera moves, but it is a time- and labor-intensive task that requires the careful placement of wooden shims to even out the dolly's movement. For this reason, students often think twice about using dollies on tracks. Professional dollies provide a post for you to mount your fluid head so that you can execute smooth pans and tilts while the camera is being moved around; inexpensive dollies require that you mount the entire tripod on the base, which is substantially less stable. There is no doubt: dynamic moves with dollies are wonderful, but you need to be aware that using a dolly can be a time-consuming addition to your production schedule (**Figure 11-11**).

■ STABILIZING ARM SYSTEMS

Invented by cinematographer Garrett Brown (**Figure 11-12**) and introduced in the early 1970s, the **Steadicam** stabilizing system completely won over the film world when it was used successfully in films like *Rocky* (1976), *Marathon Man* (1976), and *The Shining* (1980). It has since become a standard tool on large-budget productions.

The Steadicam is basically an articulated arm incorporating a complex system of counterweights and springs to minimize gravitational forces and absorb any shock. On one end of the arm is a camera mount and at the other end is a vest that the camera operator wears to carry the weight of the entire apparatus. Combining the mobility and ease of use of a handheld camera with the smooth and controlled movements of a dolly, the Steadicam system allows the operator to move, walk, or run with the camera through space, in any direction, while the articulated arm maintains a steady and easily controlled frame. The downside to Steadicam systems for students and low-budget filmmakers has always been the cost and complexity of the system. However, since the advent of lightweight DV and HD cameras, we've experienced the emergence of a whole range of far less expensive and less cumbersome stabilizing arms (Figure 11-13).

DV stabilizing systems are ultra-lightweight handheld units that use a simple system of counterweights to smooth out the movements of the operator as they move with the camera through space. With a little practice, you can get wonderfully smooth tracks, dollies, and arcs with these systems. The only limitation is that they are designed specifically for lightweight DV camcorders so they can't be used for 16mm film productions, where the cameras are heavier.

■ JERRY-RIGGED OR IMPROVISED SUPPORT SYSTEMS

As the saying goes, necessity is the mother of invention, and many people throughout the history of cinema have used their ingenuity to achieve their ends with minimal resources. The cost and complexity of dollies and Steadicam systems have given rise to many wonderful improvised methods for achieving more or less smooth, dynamic camera moves. One of the most common dolly-like devices is a wheelchair (Figure 11-14). The cinematographer simply sits in the wheelchair and is pushed. Obviously this requires relatively smooth surfaces and a stable hand, but this simple solution has been used by countless students and also by great filmmakers, from Godard to Gondry.

For his *Evil Dead* films, director Sam Raimi and D.P. Tim Philo invented the "shakey-cam," which was an ultra-inexpensive stabilizing system made by mounting a film camera in the middle of a long wooden board (Figure 11-15). With two grips holding the board on each end, they could run, lift, lower, or tilt the suspended camera, and the board itself absorbed all the shocks. The framing isn't terribly accurate, but the moves, reflecting the point of view of a demon as it rushes through the woods, are exceptionally dynamic and sufficiently demonic. So impressed were the Coen Brothers with this jerry-rigged system that they used it themselves in *Blood Simple* and *Raising Arizona*.

For one scene in *The Celebration (Festen)* (1998), Thomas Vinterberg and D.P. Anthony Dod Mantle simply secured an ultra-lightweight DV camera to the end of a long microphone boom pole and swung it around the room to move the camera in a spiral from ceiling height to eye level.

Even if the shot does not involve a moving camera, there are times when a camera operator needs to improvise camera support to get just the right angle Figure 11-16.

■ **Figure 11-13** The emergence of DV as a viable filmmaking format has prompted the creation of lighter, cheaper stabilizing systems, like this Glidecam being used for a moving shot.

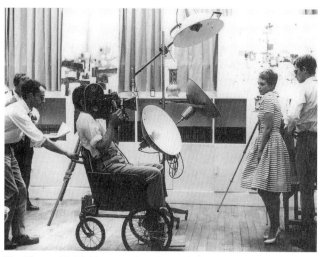

■ **Figure 11-14** New wave icon Jean-Luc Godard is seen here pushing cinematographer Raoul Coutard in a wheelchair for a moving shot during the filming of *Breathless* (1960). (Copyright Raymond Cauchetier—Paris.)

■ **Figure 11-15** Raimi's use of a long wooden board as a camera support made it possible to execute a dynamic shot in his film *The Evil Dead* (1981).

■ **Figure 11-16** Mike Figgis using whatever is handy for a camera mount (*top,* on the set of *Miss Julie,* 1999). Director Miles Adgate and D.P. Nick Vega on the set of *Kiarra's Escape* using sandbags to stabilize the camera *(bottom).*

The stories of improvised dynamic camera moves and jerry-rigged camera supports are endless, because in the final analysis it doesn't really matter how you arrive at a specific effect (makeshift device or expensive equipment rental), all that matters is what it looks like when the film comes back from the lab. The fact that he used a simple wheelchair dolly did not keep Godard's film *Breathless* from being one of the most important films in the history of cinema.

in practice

Barry Lyndon

Stanley Kubrick's study of the 18th-century English aristocracy, *Barry Lyndon* (1975), tells the story of Redmond Barry, a relentless and ambitious social climber who attains a name and position among the nobility by marrying the rich widow Lady Lyndon. Photographed by D.P. John Alcott, much of the film is shot in steady, carefully composed frames, with the camera planted firmly on a tripod, a choice that perfectly reflects the strict and rigid social codes of conduct of aristocratic culture. Even the duels are photographed with poise and containment, which adds to the genteel restraint and cold ritualization of the violence. Late in the film, however, after Barry has spent vast amounts of effort and money to be accepted into the aristocracy, he holds a music recital in his home and invites the elite of the society. In this scene (**Figure 11-17**), his stepson, incensed that a lowly soldier has married his mother and obtained the family fortune and title, reveals Barry Lyndon's true origins by bringing Barry's real son into

■ **Figure 11-17** When Barry (Ryan O'Neal) attempts to punish his stepson's (Leon Vitali) transgression in Kubrick's *Barry Lyndon,* the camera's handholding adds a visceral feel to the emotional eruption of violence *(left).* Later on, when Barry duels with him, the camera's stability reflects the more civilized nature of ritualized violence in the 18th century *(right).*

■ **Figure 11-18** A 360° pan takes us from Maggie's (Glenn Close) imagined reality to the sad truth: she's actually mourning the loss of her daughter (Dakota Fanning) (from Garcia's *Nine Lives*).

the salon. Barry erupts with anger and humiliation and physically attacks his stepson. Suddenly the camera work becomes a raw, unfettered handheld style—reflecting the deep impulsive rage Barry is expressing. These actions are not proscribed by culture anymore; they emerge from an animal instinct, and the camera style telegraphs the uncontrollability of this violence. The contrast with the controlled style of the rest of the film makes this an even more powerful moment, as we are certain that Barry has, in one rash moment, revealed his true nature and undone everything he has worked so hard to accomplish.

Nine Lives

In "Maggie" the final episode of Rodrigo García's film *Nine Lives* (2005), a mother and her 8-year-old daughter, Maria, visit a grave in a large cemetery. They talk and play; at one point Maggie scolds her daughter for stepping on graves and later keeps a lookout as the little girl takes a pee behind a tree. On a blanket they've laid out in front of a grave, they share some grapes, clearly a favorite fruit of the little girl, and they play patty-cake. It's all very casual and remarkably free from the pathos and gloom usually associated with cemeteries. But, in the middle of the patty-cake game, Maggie breaks down in a sudden moment of grief. She tells Maria "I'm tired," and lays her head on her little girl's lap to sleep (**Figure 11-18**).

At that moment, the camera begins a long, slow pan, away from the pair by the tombstone and across the beautiful, tree-filled, cemetery. The camera is mounted on a stabilizing arm, so the move feels as if it is gliding, floating across the cemetery. The pan covers a full 360 degrees, and when it returns to the tombstone, Maggie is now alone and folding the blanket to leave. The pan, which lasted only 30 seconds, creates a time ellipsis; clearly an hour or so has passed. After Maggie folds the blanket, she lays the grapes on the tombstone. The camera move not only traverses the space of the cemetery but it also initiates a complete perception shift for the audience. What we understood to be true, a mother and daughter's visit to the grave of a long-dead relative, is in fact revealed to be a grieving mother's visit to the grave of her daughter. Her imagination brought back memories of her little girl so vividly that the daughter took on real flesh and blood beside her. One could say that the camera move serves as a psychological transition, beginning in Maggie's fantasy and ending in reality. *Nine Lives* was shot by Xavier Pérez Grobet, and his perfectly placed camera move completely flips our perspective on the story.

The Hurt Locker

Very few films in recent memory have injected as much tension, anxiety, and second-by-second suspense in so many scenes as Kathryn Bigelow's *The Hurt Locker* (2009), which follows the final weeks in the rotation of an elite bomb disposal squad in Iraq. People frequently use words like "excruciating" and "unbearable" to describe this film, and often you'll

hear, "makes you feel like you're there." This "feeling" is largely a result of D.P. Barry Ackroyd and his camera operators who shot the preponderance of the film with handheld cameras, frequently multiple cameras. Handheld camera work is often associated with a documentary aesthetic; it feels as if "you are there" because the visual approach is that of a nonfiction film objectively recording real events. But this is not the way Bigelow and Ackroyd employ a handheld camera. Their camera technique is highly subjective. The camera relentlessly and anxiously pans, searches, scans, focuses and refocuses, putting us directly into the consciousness of these men as they carry out their horrifically dangerous missions in broad daylight and in plain sight of an unknowable public. Surrounded by onlookers, it's impossible to know who is friendly, who is an enemy, who is the bomb maker, who has a gun? The visual approach encourages the viewer to experience what it's like to monitor 360 degrees of hostile territory, searching for clues, watching for signs, keeping tabs on everyone. The palpable danger of the situation is occasionally punctuated by shocking reverse angle subjective shots. Suddenly, someone is watching them! Who is it? Friend of foe? More than a few times one thinks an onlooker is surely out to kill them, or maybe this person is the bomb maker. We jump to these conclusions without any real evidence—does a video camera constitute a mortal threat? Three men whispering to each other? The wave of a hand? A cell phone? These are guesses born of the danger we're feeling because the camera movement plunges us into the subjectivity of a fearful and adrenalized state of mind; jittery, nervous, hyperalert, hypervigilant, very human—you can almost sense a racing pulse in the camera movements (**Figure 11-19**). And then a bomb will detonate, and time stands still—the moment becomes vertical. The largest actions (an enormous explosion of flame) and smallest details (sand lifting off the ground) are registered in extreme slow motion and a rock steady, stabilized camera. In contrast with the frenetic motion of the moments before the blast, this abrupt shift plunges us into another altered and extreme psychological state, one that is even closer to death.

■ **Figure 11-19** Friend of foe? The nervously searching handheld cameras in Bigelow's *The Hurt Locker* reflect the apprehensive state of mind of soldiers in hostile and dangerously exposed circumstances.

■ AESTHETIC AND PRACTICAL CONSIDERATIONS

The camera support you choose ultimately should help you achieve the look and style you need to tell your story. From the super controlled fluidity of a dolly, to the edgy movement of the handheld camera, to the pivot moves of a tripod, different supports offer different "feels." There is no system that is better or worse—there is only what is appropriate for the conception of your film. Even within a single film, there may be some scenes that conceptually work best with a handheld camera, and others that require the stability of a tripod. But, of course, choosing the right support to move your camera is more than simply a matter of style for style's sake. Whether you handhold a camera, put it on a tripod, or wheel it around on a dolly, both the movement of the camera and the fashion in which it moves must be motivated by the story you're telling. You need to ask yourself: Why move the camera? Why move the camera now? Why move the camera in this fashion? (See page 62) (For a video comparison between a camera move achieved by hand holding, a tripod, and a stabilizing arm, go to the Voice & Vision companion website).

Always practice moves before you run tape or film. Rehearsals and blocking on the set are not just for the actors; they are also for the camera. The director of photography must know before the camera rolls how to execute a move in relation to the action in the scene. Performing a good camera move, especially combination moves, takes a few rehearsals to get just right.

You should always have a sense for where any camera move begins and ends. Moving the frame means constantly reframing your shot. It is very important to know in advance where your move begins and precisely where it ends and what pace and path you will take to accomplish the move so that you can be accurate with the composition and mise-en-scène from the beginning to the end. A common problem with inexperienced filmmakers is that they begin a camera move without knowing exactly where they are going, and they wind up fishing around for a place to land, making the move look sloppy.

Camera moves versus camera adjustments. Whether you're executing a pan, tilt, dolly, or track, a camera move is a clear and substantial alteration of the subject or composition. A **camera adjustment (or reframe)**, on the other hand, is a slight shifting of a frame to maintain your composition on a person or object that is moving only a little. For example, if we frame a character in a medium close-up while they speak to someone off screen, the actor may shift from one foot to the other or take a step forward or back, or even just shift their gaze from screen right to screen left. Each one of these changes requires a minor adjustment of the frame to maintain a balanced MCU composition. The person operating the camera needs to have a keen sense for the emotional content of the script, the rhythm of the performance, and the body language of the actor to anticipate these little movements and adjust accordingly. For this type of adjustment, we say that the camera is "breathing with the subject." Camera adjustments are practically invisible to the audience, but you can spot them by looking, not at the main subject of a shot, but at the edges of the frame. You'll see objects in the background moving in and out of the frame as the camera adjusts to maintain a steady composition on the primary subject (Figure 11-20).

■ **Figure 11-20** Small camera reframes are employed to maintain a consistent composition of the subject within the frame. In this shot from the Coen Brothers' *No Country for Old Men* (2007), looking room is maintained by a slight camera adjustment to the right when Llewelyn Moss (Josh Brolin) leans slightly to reach the telephone.

Practical considerations need to be considered in deciding on one or another camera support. To begin, moving the camera always adds production time because there are more technical details, like losing focus and camera bobble, that can go wrong, requiring multiple takes. Using a dolly requires more time for camera and subject choreography and for laying down tracks (when necessary), not to mention the addition of dolly grips to your crew. Some camera support systems, like professional dollies and Steadicam systems, are relatively expensive and are a major budget item if you need them every day. And many professional dollies are so heavy that you need to rent a van to transport them. In the final analysis, you must be realistic about what practical ramifications there might be with any piece of equipment. You don't want to commit to a major piece of gear only to have it slow you down so much that you don't get your film done.

Basics of Exposure

Photography is first and foremost a record of light. You are alone behind the camera, doubling as artist and scientist, hoping that your light—and it is your light—will bring it all to life.

Tom McDonough (From *Light Years: Confessions of a Cinematographer*, Grove Press, New York, 1987)

This quote by cinematographer and writer Tom McDonough neatly sums up the split personality of the cinematographer's art ... or is it craft ... or is it science? The truth is, getting just the right image for the story you are trying to tell, for the mood you want to create, for the connection you're trying to make with the audience, requires the instincts and sensitivity of an artist, the discipline of a craftsman, and the research of a scientist. In other words, when we create the film image, we need to know aesthetically what we want and technically how to achieve that. Here and in the next chapter we will look at all of the basic technical factors of exposures and lighting so that you can tell your story with visual eloquence and impact (**Figure 12-1**).

■ ELEMENTS OF EXPOSURE

What does it mean to get an exposure? It's all about light: how much of it is bouncing off your scene, into your lens, and tagging your imaging device. But how do we control exposures? How can we assure that the image we imagine in our heads is the one that will make it onto the film or CCD chip? Whether you are shooting film or DV, *every* exposure you make involves an intricate interrelationship between all of the variables that produce, transmit, control, transform, or record light. Here are the primary elements along the path, beginning at the light source and ending at the imaging device:

1. *The light source.* Whether you are shooting under the sun or with artificial lights or a mixture of both, the aesthetic and technical properties of your lighting source have the biggest impact on the look of your image. Of central importance for exposure control specifically is the intensity of light, meaning how much light is falling onto your scene.

2. *The scene.* What are the visual dynamics of your scene? Or more specifically, what are the physical properties of the space, the reflectivity of the objects, the volume of the area, the colors and shadows, and movement? All these need to be considered when lighting and creating an exposure.

3. *Filters.* Lens filters are often employed in film production to alter the quality, color, or intensity of the light entering the camera. We don't always use filters, but when we do, they affect many of the other exposure elements.

4. *The lens and aperture.* As we mentioned in Chapter 10, all of the light exposing your imaging device passes through the lens. Lens optics plays a primary role in forming the composition (wide angle, telephoto, etc.), but it is the lens

■ **Figure 12-1** Haneke's *The White Ribbon* (2009) is a close study of innocence and evil photographed in shades of black and white by D.P. Christian Berger. Often shooting with only available light, exposures needed to be absolutely precise for a film in which light and shadow carry emotional and metaphoric weight. In this somber frame, a farmer (Branko Samarovski) regards his wife's body following her mysterious death; notice the wide range of light values from bright white to inky black.

aperture that determines the amount of light that is allowed to pass through to tag the film or CCDs. Aperture control is one of our most flexible variables for creating the best exposure for each image.

5. *Speed and shutter.* The camera's frame rate and the size of our shutter constitute the shutter speed, which determines the duration of each exposure. Shutter isn't a concern only of people shooting film: most DV cameras have an electronic equivalent that equally has an impact on both image quality and exposures.

6. *Imaging device.* Whether you're using film stocks or CCDs, understanding and factoring in your imaging device's particular and unique sensitivity and response to light is essential in getting the shot down the way you want it.

The ultimate factor is, of course, your creative needs: what you want the audience to see and how you want them to see it. It's easy enough to arrive at a "proper" exposure, but your primary task as a filmmaker is to find the "best" exposure for what you want to express. When determining the exposure for any given scene, we are faced with not one solution, but with a range of options, which can involve manipulating any or all of the other exposure factors.

Although the *basic* elements for creating exposures are the same for film and digital video, the method by which we determine proper exposure for each is very different. What makes film and DV so different is the simple fact that we can actually see the image being recorded in DV. Shooting on film, we can only predict what we're doing, because the image you see in the viewfinder is not exactly what is on the film, in terms of exposures. The actual image itself is not revealed to us until the film lab has done its work. However, determining the exposure you need follows a reliable process, because the factors are precisely controllable and measurable and the science is tried and true. The main tool for determining exposures when shooting on film is the light meter.

■ THE LIGHT METER IN FILM

The light meter is like a third eye because it allows us to "see" a scene the way your film stock is "seeing" it. A **light meter** is a small calculator that accurately measures the light intensity values of a scene and then calculates a "proper" exposure taking into account the exposure variables of the shooting situation. The final exposure suggestion of a light meter is a recommended f-stop. Always keep in mind, however, that the calculations of a light meter are only the starting point for a filmmaker deciding on a "best" exposure (Figure 12-2).

Every light meter works with the same set of variables in essentially the same sequence to arrive at an exposure calculation:

1. *Film speed.* The exposure index (EI) for your film stock is the very first variable to set on your light meter. For the meter to accurately calculate exposures, it needs to know the sensitivity of your film to light. (For more information on EI, see page 186.)

2. *Intensity of light.* All light meters utilize a light-sensitive photocell (either selenium or

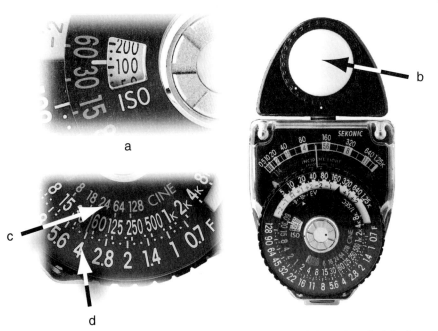

a

c

d

b

■ **Figure 12-2** Incident light meters, like this the Sekonic L-398, will always have the following features: an Exposure Index indicator (a), a photosphere to sample the light falling on the scene (b), a shutter speed/frames per second scale (c), and an f-stop scale (d).

cadmium sulfide cells) that responds to the amount of light entering the meter and generates a light intensity reading via a floating needle or digital readout. There are two methods for reading light intensity. The most common for film production is to read the light *falling on* a scene, which is known as **incident light**. The unit of measure for incident light is **footcandles**. One footcandle is equal to the light generated by an "international standard candle" one foot away from the center of the flame. If this scale of measure sounds a bit, well, arbitrary, just remember that the inch was derived from the width of someone's "average" thumb. The other method is to measure the light *reflecting off* a scene, which is known as **reflected light**. The unit of measure for reflected light is **footlamberts**. Measuring the light that is bouncing off a scene (or an object), known as the **reflectance value** or just **reflectance**, takes into account the light absorption qualities of objects (see the "**What is Middle Gray?**" box). So a footlambert reading therefore measures only the percentage of the incident light being reflected off a surface. Incident and reflected light readings are taken by two different meters called, respectively, an **incident light meter** and a **reflected light meter**. We will look closer at the uses of and distinctions between these two meters later.

3. *Shutter speed.* Once we factor the sensitivity of the film stock and determine how much light is illuminating the scene, we next need to figure in our **shutter speed**, which is the amount of time a single frame is exposed to light. Shutter speed in film production is far more constant than in still photography, changing only when we attempt a special effect. Two variables determine the shutter speed of a film camera: the angle of the shutter opening, which rarely changes from the standard 180° (see page 169), and the film transport speed. Given that the standard frame rate for 16mm sync speed is 24 frames per second, and each frame is only exposed to light by the rotating 180° shutter for half that time, the shutter speed for each exposure is calculated: $\frac{1}{24} \times \frac{1}{2} = \frac{1}{48}$ of a second. *The shutter speed for film running at standard 24 fps is $\frac{1}{48}$ of a second (often rounded off to $\frac{1}{50}$ of a second).* Changing transport speed, therefore, changes the shutter speed. For example, if we want to shoot a scene in slow motion, we need to speed up the frame rate of the camera to, say, 48 frames per second, which means each frame would stay in the gate half as long ($\frac{1}{48} \times \frac{1}{2}$), which gives us a shutter speed of $\frac{1}{96}$ of a second. Because filmmakers alter shutter speed with some frequency, light meters used in film production have a **cine scale**, which shows a range of shutter speeds calculated for different frame rates. Only a few 16mm cameras also allow you to adjust the shutter angle open or closed, which would then require a recalculation of shutter speed, so this is much rarer.

4. *F-stop (aperture opening).* The final step in determining an exposure, and the endpoint for the calculations of the light meter, is the f-stop setting. After all of the other variables are entered into the light meter, the calculations tell us at what f-stop we should set our aperture ring in order to get a "proper" exposure for that reading.

Calculating Exposure

Using a light meter to determine the f-stop setting for a particular spot in the scene is called, **taking a reading**. If your scene is lit evenly throughout, then one reading will do, but very often scenes are made up of areas with different light intensities that would yield different exposure readings. In these cases the "correct" exposure determined through one reading at a single spot might yield an *acceptable* result, but perhaps not the best or most expressive exposure. To truly control the visual impact of your images, you should take multiple readings to determine how your film stock sees the variation of exposures in your scene, and then make a creative choice given the range of possibilities. Let's look at a simple example.

You are shooting a scene with two subjects in the frame. One subject is standing in the shade and the other is standing in the sun (**Figure 12-3**). You get a reading of f/16 in the sun, but when you take a reading in the shade you get f/5.6. So where do you set your

f/ 16   f/ 5.6   f/ 8 - f/ 11

 ■ **Figure 12-3** A common situation shooting outdoors on a sunny day. Exposing for the sunny side, at f/16, underexposes the subject in the shade. Exposing for the shade, at f/5.6, overexposes the subject in the sunny side. A compromise exposure, between f/8 and f/11, can be used if both subjects are to be seen with detail.

f-stop? Which reading is "right"? The truth is, neither reading is right or wrong. If you set your camera f-stop to f/5.6 in order to expose the shade correctly, then the subject in the sun will be three stops overexposed, and if you set your f-stop ring to f/16, then the man in the shade will be three stops underexposed, but the bright side will be correctly exposed. You could split the difference and set the exposure between f/8 and f/11, in which case one person will be 1.5 stops overexposed and the other will be 1.5 stops underexposed — a little compromise both ways. All three options are technically "correct," so now you need to ask yourself: What do I want this image to express? What is the mood of the scene, the style of the film? What do I want to show the audience, or hide from them? Do I need to show the guy in the shade? Does it matter if the man in the sun is bright? In short, exposures are such an important creative element of your film that they should not be left up to the indifferent calculations of a light meter. Instead, choosing the right exposure is a creative decision determined by the filmmaker, who also considers the other important exposure variables, like the specific visual approach necessary to tell the story. We will revisit this issue of exposure control in detail in the next chapter.

in practice

Deciding on the best exposure for any scene is a critical creative decision that can have tremendous impact on the meaning and emotional tone of a scene. Sometimes, the right f-stop is not necessarily the one that gives a "correct" exposure of the subject. Sometimes over or under exposure tells a better story (**Figure 12-4**).

The first shot (*top frame*) shows a crucial moment from Paul Thomas Anderson's 2007 film, *There Will Be Blood*. Oil prospector Daniel Plainview (Daniel Day-Lewis) is just coming into some serious profit when he is visited by a man claiming to be his long-lost brother Henry. At first Daniel is thrilled to discover that he has kin, but later he begins to doubt Henry's stories of their past. This moment on the beach is where Daniel realizes for certain that this man is an imposter. The shot is not unlike **Figure 12-3** with one man in the sun and the other in the shade, but Anderson and D.P. Robert Elswit

decided to expose for Daniel and allow "Henry" to fall into deep underexposure. The exposure not only isolates Daniel and draws the viewers' attention to him as he realizes that he's being deceived, but the similar body positions and extreme contrast of the two figures bring to mind a man and his shadow. By rendering "Henry" as Daniel's shadow, Anderson has in effect created a visual metaphor for Daniel's inner demons and indeed from this moment on we witness his inexorable descent into fury, madness, and violence.

Latent violence is also the undercurrent in the next shot (*center frame*) from the Cohen Brothers' *No Country for Old Men* (2007). In this scene the psychopathic killer Anton Chigurh (Javier Bardem), who has already left behind him a collection of corpses in his search for pilfered money, has arrived at the hideout of Carla Jean, the wife of the man who took the money. We already know that Chigurh can kill easily, or he can just as easily let people go. But we don't know which Chigurh is in the room with Carla Jean as she tries to reason with him to spare her life. The Coens (and D.P. Roger Deakins) chose to place Chigurh in the shadows in a corner of the room. The decision to expose for the bright areas of the room (see his hands in the sun) and allow Chigurh's face to fall several stops into underexposure heightens the tension of the scene because it keeps his features difficult to make out and his intentions inscrutable.

In Mike Nichols' *The Graduate* (1967) (*bottom frame*), Benjamin Braddock has just graduated from college and he's already unsure and worried about his future. This premature midlife crisis manifests itself in two ways. He lazily hangs out in the family pool all day long and he begins an illicit sexual affair with his father's partner's wife, the much older and more experienced Mrs. Robinson (Anne Bancroft). At one point Mr. and Mrs. Robinson come over to his house for a friendly visit while Benjamin is floating on an inflatable pool mattress. When Mrs. Robinson says hello to him, he looks up at her and what he sees is blinding and colorless. The extreme overexposure of Mrs. Robinson's face mimics both the bright glare of sunlight behind her as well as Benjamin's totally confused and blown-out state of mind in this phase of his life.

■ **Figure 12-4** Precise and expressive exposure choices: Anderson's *There Will be Blood* (top), Coen Brothers' *No Country for Old Men* (center), and Nichols' *The Graduate* (bottom).

The Incident Light Meter

The **incident light meter** is the most common and versatile meter used in film production (see **Figure 12-2**). It measures the intensity of light falling on a scene. This meter is simple to use and gives a consistent reading from shot to shot. All incident meters have a half-globe light diffuser, called a **photosphere** (also called a **lumisphere**), which fits over the photosensitive cell. The photosphere, held near the subject and pointed toward the camera, gathers the light falling on the subject from the front and sides and averages out these light intensities to arrive at an overall incident light intensity reading (**Figure 12-5**).

The final exposure reading of an incident light meter is derived from the exposure calculation specifically for the middle gray tone. In other words, the f-stop suggestion of an incident meter ensures that, given the intensity of the light falling on that part of the scene, objects with a luminance value of 18% (middle gray) will be exposed correctly (i.e., will be rendered exactly as middle gray on the film) (see the box, "What Is Middle Gray?"). It then will follow that objects that are lighter and darker (more or less reflective) will appear

■ **Figure 12-5** An incident light meter should be positioned at the subject with the photosphere pointing toward the lens of the camera.

in practice

What Is Middle Gray?

Let's say we have three articles of clothing hanging out on a laundry line to dry: a black towel, a gray T-shirt, and a pair of white jeans (**Figure 12-6**). All three are being lit by the same light source, the sun, but each one reflects a different amount of the incident light back to the camera. The black towel reflects very little, about 4% of the light, which is why it looks black on film. The white jeans reflect a lot, about 96%, and so exposes the film much more, and the gray T-shirt is somewhere in between, reflecting about 25% of the incident light. Each article of clothing has a different **reflectance value.** Understanding reflectance values is important to understanding how light meters work and in calculating how objects will appear on screen.

■ **Figure 12-6** The amount of light a subject reflects is called its "reflectance value." The white jeans reflect 96% of the light they receive, the black towel reflects only 4%, and the gray T-shirt is somewhere in between these two; it reflects about 25%.

The photographer Ansel Adams developed a scale of gray tones, known as the **zone system**, by dividing up the shades of gray, from black to white, into eleven steps, or zones of luminance (**Figure 12-7**). Each luminance zone represents a halving or doubling of the brightness (or the reflectance value). For example, zone VI is half as bright as zone VII, and zone IV is twice as bright as zone III. Yes, Adams created the scale so that it would correspond with the way the aperture in a lens halves and doubles light. If we look at the preceding example of the laundry, we can see that the black towel falls closest to zone I, the gray T-shirt falls around zone VI (five zones or stops brighter than the towel), and the white jeans falls in zone IX (three zones or stops brighter than the sweatshirt).

The most important zone for us to consider in order to understand how light meters work is the one right smack in the middle, between pure black and pure white. *Zone V has a reflectance value of 18%** and is also known simply as **middle gray**. (According to Blain Brown in his book *Cinematography*, the true reflectance of middle gray is 17.5%, but it is always rounded off to 18%.) All light meters, incident or reflected, are calibrated to the middle gray tone, although in very different ways.

*Reflectance percentages follow a logarithmic progression, not an arithmetic progression, which is why middle gray is 18% and not 50%.

0	I	II	III	IV	V	VI	VII	VIII	IX	X
3.5%	4.5%	6%	9%	12.5%	18%	25%	35%	50%	70%	100%

Black velvet	2%	Midgray	18%	Caucasian face	36%
Black face	10%			Light grays	70%
Green leaves	14%			Off-whites	80%
Brown face	16%			White chalk	96%

■ **Figure 12-7** Ansel Adams' Zone System uses a grayscale divided into eleven steps or "zones." These zones can be used to assign an exposure to a subject according to predetermined reflectance values (percentages from Blain Brown's *Cinematography*, Focal Press, 2002).

exactly as they should relative to the middle gray tone, thus duplicating the actual range of brightness values in the scene. In the case of our laundry photo (see **Figure 12-6**), because everything was equally lit by the same source, a single incident meter reading assured that the inherent brightness values of each article of clothing would be rendered correctly by following the light meter's f-stop calculation for exposing middle gray correctly. It doesn't matter if the meter reading was f/4, f/5.6, or f/16; by setting the camera aperture to the f-stop appropriate for the light intensity, which is what the light meter tells us, middle gray and all of the other tones will be rendered correctly. This consistent standard for the exposure calculation assures uniformity from reading to reading. It is often said about incident meters that middle gray is "built in," which means you don't literally

f / 16   f/ 5.6   f/ 8 - f/ 11

■ **Figure 12-8** Exposing for middle gray in the sunny areas will underexpose the shaded areas (*left frame,* f/16), while exposing for middle gray in the shaded areas will overexpose the sunny areas (**middle frame,** f/5.6). A compromise exposure will slightly overexpose the sunny areas and underexpose the shaded areas (*right frame,* f/8). Note the effects of exposure change on the middle gray cards (which are all exactly the same shade of gray).

need a middle gray tone in the scene for the meter to make the proper calculation and for the rest of the luminance values in the scene to fall where they would naturally.

But what about a scene in which there is more than one light intensity level? In the scene in **Figure 12-8**, the young man is standing such that half of him is in the sun and the other half is in the shade. The two readings, sunny side (f/16) and shade side (f/5.6), were taken with an incident meter. If the camera f-stop is set for the bright side of the subject (*left*), the middle gray card in the sun is exposed correctly and the luminance of the other objects in the sun (i.e., shirt, jean jacket, background) is rendered appropriately, but the shade side is underexposed. Conversely, when the f-stop is set for the shade side (*middle*), the middle gray card in the shadow is exposed correctly, along with everything else in the shadows, but the sunny side is now overexposed. Splitting the difference and setting the f-stop in between (*right*) will cause each side to be slightly overexposed and slightly underexposed, respectively. The choice is yours.

The Reflected Light Meter and Spot Meter

A **reflected light meter** (also called an **averaging meter**) measures the intensity of light reflecting off a scene. A general-purpose reflected light meter has a wide angle of acceptance, which means it measures the reflected light intensity from a fairly wide area, around 45 degrees. A reflected light meter, held near the camera and *pointed at* the scene, averages out all of the various light intensities bouncing off the objects in the scene, toward the lens. It then assumes that the average reflectance of any scene is middle gray, which may or may not be the case, and gives you an f-stop suggestion for middle gray. However, because these meters always assume a reflectance value of middle gray (18%) for every scene, no matter what, they can be easily fooled. For example, let's say you're shooting a polar bear in the snow. The overall brightness of this scene is close to pure white, but a reflected light meter will suggest an f-stop to render this scene middle gray. This obviously is not the correct exposure. The same problem exists if we bring the meter in closer, to measure specific objects; for example, if we take a reading off a black jacket, the f-stop calculation will give us the aperture to render that jacket as middle gray.

To assure proper tonality in the scene, reflected meter readings are often literally taken off a middle gray card (**Figure 12-9**). This way the reading will give the proper f-stop to render that middle gray card, middle gray, and objects lighter or darker will then be

■ **Figure 12-9** Taking a reflected light reading off a middle gray card ensures we will set the aperture for proper tonality, as if we had taken a reading with an incident light meter.

■ Figure 12-10 Use a reflected light meter to get an exposure reading for objects that emit light, as in this shot of a video monitor from *FearFall* (2000).

rendered in proper relationship to middle gray. In effect, we're back to the way an incident meter functions, but an incident meter is much easier to use. It's not hard to see why incident meters are preferred and standard for general exposure calculations.

Reflected light meters, however, are useful when photographing objects that are themselves a source of illumination—when you need to ascertain the light intensity of an object that is emitting light, as opposed to the light falling on it—for example, if we are shooting a television set (Figure 12-10), the neon lights of a Las Vegas casino, or the glow of a frosted windowpane.

One important variation on a reflected meter is the spot meter, which is commonly used on film sets. A **spot meter** is a reflected light meter with a zoom lens and a very narrow and precise angle of acceptance, usually

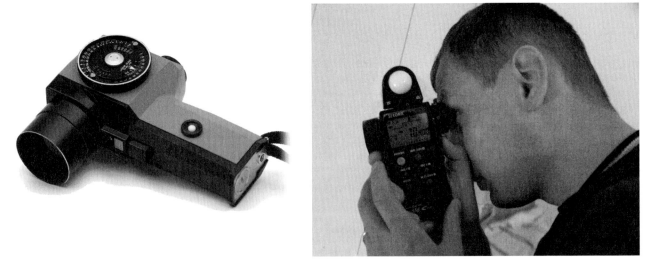

■ Figure 12-11 A spot meter is a reflected light meter with an extremely narrow angle of incidence, allowing for precise readings far from the subject. Shown here are a Pentax spot meter *(left)* and a Sekonic combination incident/spot meter *(right)*.

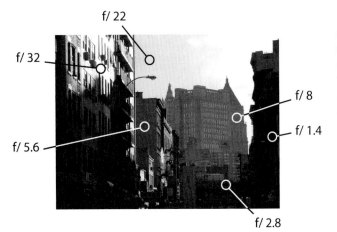

f/ 22
f/ 32
f/ 8
f/ 1.4
f/ 5.6
f/ 2.8

■ Figure 12-12 Taking readings from subjects far away from the camera is an easy task with a spot meter, but the readings have to be interpreted before setting the f-stop. Setting the aperture for the sky at f/22, for instance, will darken it to middle gray and underexpose everything else. Can you tell what f-stop was chosen to record this image?

around 1° (Figure 12-11). A spot meter can pinpoint a small area from a distance. This is useful in measuring a variety of areas to determine the different light reflectance values of various objects in a single scene. It also allows us to take meter readings of areas that are not easily accessible. For example, we can take multiple readings of a city skyline, where some buildings are lit by bright sunlight and others fall into the shadows, from one location. Using a spot meter we can get a very accurate assessment of the relative exposure values of each area from our one setup on the sidewalk (Figure 12-12).

Being a reflected light meter, however, a spot meter reading still needs to be interpreted, because it calculates an exposure to render that area middle gray, whether it's a white table cloth or a deep, black shadow. However, unlike an averaging reflected meter, the precision of the spot meter allows for easier interpretation. Let's say you

■ THE BRIGHTNESS OF OBJECTS ON SCREEN

Keep in mind that the reflectance value of an object does not change. That gray T-shirt in **Figure 12-6** always reflects 25% of the incident light. But it can appear more or less bright on screen. The brightness of an object as it appears on screen is determined by three factors with which you are now familiar:

1. Intensity of the incident light (variable)
2. Reflectance of the object (fixed)
3. Lens f-stop setting (variable)

We will explore this exposure interrelationship more in Chapter 14.

meter a precise area in the frame that is clearly white and the spot meter gives you a reading of f/16. You know that the reading tells you where to set your f-stop to expose that white area as middle gray. It's not right, but you also can see from a zone system chart (see page 258) that the white zone is four zones, or stops, brighter (i.e., the iris should be more open) than middle gray, so you simply open up four stops from f/16, which is f/4, and that will give you not only a correctly exposed white area in the frame but also, since this f/4 is the correct f-stop, all of the other luminance values will fall correctly into place as well. This is clearly illustrated with the shift in middle gray cards in **Figure 12-8**.

■ METERING FOR DIGITAL VIDEO (SD AND HD)

Metering for DV is quite a different matter, for two reasons. The first is that we can see our final image on a monitor and the second is that all DV cameras come with built-in through-the-lens meters, so handheld light meters are never used. A **through-the-lens meter** (TTL) is a reflected light meter that calculates the aperture setting by averaging out the light from a scene *after* it has entered the lens. That means that it also takes into account any filters you may be using in front of the lens. The fact that the meter is built in means that it is already calibrated with all of the exposure variables we must enter in manually on a film light meter, like the sensitivity of the CCD chips to light and the frame rate of video.

The range of acceptance on a DV camcorder light meter varies from model to model, and it is vital that you understand how your specific camera "reads" the scene. Some models take an average of the entire frame, and others take an average reading from a smaller portion of the middle of the frame, assuming that your subject will be framed in the middle of the composition. It is also essential to know that, because the meter is located right behind the lens, you can use the zoom capabilities of the lens to turn the TTL meter into a spot meter. Zooming in greatly narrows the angle of acceptance of the meter and allows you to read light values off very circumscribed areas and specific objects.

Exposure Control and DV

Just as we discussed with film exposures, there is not one single "correct" exposure in DV production either. There is a range of possible exposures from which creative filmmakers must choose in order to achieve the mood, style, and visual meaning they are after. The built-in meter on all DV cameras can trigger an **auto iris** function (also called **auto exposure**), which will take the average meter reading for your scene and automatically set the camera's aperture. However, exposure control is such a crucial area of aesthetic impact that any serious filmmaker will recognize the folly of relinquishing this important decision to an impassive machine with an automatic function designed to create an *acceptable* image instead of a truly *expressive* one. You should never let the camera select the look of your images for you, especially because the auto exposure mechanism of a DV camera can easily be fooled. Here are three common situations in which auto iris will backfire:

1. *Center averaging.* As we mentioned before, most TTL meters average out the exposure values at the center of the frame, assuming that your subject will always be at the center. But what if your subject isn't in the center? Perhaps the composition you want puts the subject at the edge of the frame. In cases like this, the auto iris can easily choose an unacceptable exposure (**Figure 12-13**).

■ **Figure 12-13** Auto iris functions often give priority to the center of the frame. As a result, if the subject is placed off-center, the camera's light meter will not read it properly. In this example, the sunlit traffic in the background is exposed properly, but our subject is underexposed.

2. *Extreme backgrounds.* Auto iris functions are often confused by extreme backlighting or dark backgrounds and will average in portions of the frame that are clearly not average. For example, an actor standing in front of a bright window will cause the auto iris to close down to compensate for the increased exposure value, thus underexposing the subject. Conversely, an actor standing in front of a blackboard will cause the iris to open up and potentially overexpose the subject.

3. *Temporary brightness shifts.* Another common situation that confuses the auto exposure function occurs when a bright object enters the frame during a shot, triggering an adjustment in the exposure during a take. For example, say we're shooting a subject in a dark shirt, standing in a shady area, and during the shot a passerby in a bright white T-shirt crosses in front of him. The in-camera meter will detect the bright object and trigger the auto iris to quickly close down, to maintain that "average" exposure (Figure 12-14). When the passerby leaves the frame the auto iris will respond to the new average light value and open up again. The same spasmodic iris opening and closing phenomenon also happens if we pan across a scene with various light and dark areas.

So the first thing you must do is find out how to turn off the auto iris function. Look for the **manual aperture override** (also called manual exposure) function on your camera and do it. All professional and industrial-grade DV cameras and many (but not all) consumer cameras have manual override capabilities. However, only high-end professional cameras have iris rings that are calibrated in f-stops and actually have the f-stop scale etched on the iris ring. Many cameras, including some very fine industrial DV camcorders, display a quasi-f-stop scale on their LCD screen or viewfinder. Consumer cameras often have no scale at all, requiring you to judge exposure by eye (Figure 12-15).

Manual Exposure Control
Determining your "best" exposure with a DV camcorder requires using a combination of the zoom lens, the in-camera meter, the auto iris, and the manual override functions (Figure 12-16).

■ **Figure 12-14** The sudden appearance of a bright object in the frame will trigger the auto iris function to adjust the exposure in midshot to compensate, only to change it again after the object leaves the frame.

Here are the standard steps for finding your exposure:

1. Decide which part of the frame you would like exposed correctly. This is an aesthetic decision based on the composition, mood, and story.
2. With the camera on auto iris, zoom in tightly to that portion of the composition, preferably so that it fills the frame, and let the auto iris select its "correct" exposure for that small portion of the total scene.
3. Turn off the auto iris by switching to manual override. This will lock in that exposure.
4. Zoom out and compose your shot. It doesn't matter where in the frame you place your subject, or how bright the background is, or what might pass in front of the lens during the take: that exposure is locked in and will not change.
5. Finally, tweak the manual iris to finesse the exposure by looking at the final result in your viewfinder or, preferably, on a high-quality field monitor.

■ **Figure 12-15** Although professional video cameras have f-stop numbers etched on the lens, some camcorders that allow for manual exposure display f-stops on their LCDs.

Keep in mind that you can zoom in to any portion of the scene and lock in the exposure there to check out the effect of various apertures. This will give you a clear sense for the range of light values and exposure possibilities within your scene. Metering for film and video are similar in this regard. Multiple readings will give you a better understanding of the range of exposure possibilities that you can choose from.

■ **Figure 12-16** Setting exposures manually with a camcorder. Zoom in so that the subject fills the frame and the auto iris finds a good exposure. Then switch to manual override to "lock in" that setting. Now our subject will remain correctly exposed no matter how we frame the shot. (Go to www.voiceandvisionbook.com to see a video of this process.)

in practice

Determining your "correct" exposure on DV, as with film, is a matter of finding the right aesthetic choice for the narrative content of your scene and the overall look of the film. The frames in **Figure 12-17** prove that one need not be timid with digital video, even standard definition. These are great examples of fearless cinematographers using consumer-grade camcorders and pushing DV exposures to their expressive limits.

The first frame (*top*) is from *Personal Velocity: Three Portraits* (2002), directed by Rebecca Miller and shot by Ellen Kuras on consumer SD video. The color palette for the character Delia, shown standing next to a window, are warm, golden tones, but Delia is a woman whose life is falling apart after she leaves her abusive husband. It's a desperate, messy, and extreme situation, and this "feeling" is wonderfully conveyed in Kuras' extreme cinematography, where she often allows Delia's blonde hair to overexpose, looking as if it's practically ignited.

Director Zhang Ke Jia's 2006 film *Still Life* follows a nurse who is looking for her estranged husband and a laborer who is searching for his wife who left him long ago. These journeys take us into and

around the small town of Fengjie, which is slowly being submerged under water as part of the Three Gorges Dam project. Zhang and D.P. Nelson Yu Lik-Wai shot in real locations in the doomed town and along the dam construction site with a consumer-grade HDV camera. The film is filled with stunning, metaphoric tableaux juxtaposing the natural and the industrial, the old and the new, growth and decay, and especially the fragility of humans against the severity of manmade structures. This particular shot (*center*), where the nurse Sehn Hong (Tao Zhao) is standing before a concrete opening that frames the old village, challenges assumptions of interior and exterior space in a landscape which is in total mutation. Although shots like this, with its wide exposure range, pose great challenges for DV shooting, they also offer imagery rich with visual metaphor and allegorical weight for those who dare to create such compositions.

The final frame (*bottom*), from Thomas Vinterberg's 1998 film *The Celebration*, is at another extreme. Exploiting DV's sensitivity to light, D.P. Anthony Dod Mantle shot an entire scene exclusively illuminated by the flame of a cigarette lighter. The context for the scene is a young man who encounters the ghost of his dead sister, whom he adored, during a particularly harrowing and revelatory family celebration. Many people will tell you that you can't underexpose DV like this—"there is too much noise in the image, the blacks are murky," they'll tell you. But all of those characteristics of underexposed DV created a devastating moment in *The Celebration*— haunting, surreal, and affectionate all at the same time—because they were *right* for the scene.

Figure 12-17 Expressive uses of exposure on DV. Miller's *Personal Velocity* (*top*) was shot in SD video. Zhang's *Still Life* (*center*) used the HDV format. *The Celebration* by Vinterberg (*bottom*) was an early feature film shot on consumer format SD.

All three D.P.s not only capitalized on the unique qualities of the DV image, they also understood the freedom that DV technology provides and they took that freedom to the nth degree.

Using Field Monitors

Unfortunately, it is not uncommon for filmmakers shooting on DV to be happy with what they're seeing on their little LCD screens as they shoot, but when reviewing the footage later, on a professional monitor, they find the exposures are markedly different and to cry out, "But it didn't look that way when I was shooting it!" The fact that we can see the video image as we shoot can be a great help in evaluating and choosing exposures, but filmmakers must be confident that what they are viewing in terms of brightness, color, and contrast, while they shoot, is an accurate representation of what is actually being recorded by the camera. The flip-out LCD screens on most DV camcorders cannot be accurately calibrated for critical judgments, which is why they are considered primarily a composition tool, but not a reliable image evaluation instrument. Many DV filmmakers claim that the tiny CRT viewfinder is more accurate for determining exposures and, especially, focus. In many situations, simply white balancing your camera correctly along with careful attention to exposure levels will yield acceptable results. Digital video is also flexible enough that minor image adjustments can be made successfully in postproduction. However, when absolute precision is imperative, most filmmakers will also use a high-quality **portable field monitor** that is attached to the video output of the camera (Figure 12-18). The color, brightness, and contrast settings for any field monitor, however, must be set to a standard in order to ensure that what we are seeing is indeed what we are getting. All professional and some industrial-level DV cameras generate a video test pattern called **NTSC split field color bars**, which are used to calibrate field production monitors (Figure 12-19). NTSC color bars are a standardized set of colored stripes and squares that allow you to easily calibrate your monitor's adjustable settings for brightness (luminance), contrast, hue (tint), and saturation (color level) to ensure faithful display of the images being recorded. (Instructions for calibrating monitors with color bars are at www.voiceandvisionbook.com.) Unfortunately, not all cameras generate standard colors bars. Some industrial grade DV cameras only generate nonstandard full-field color bars, which are not really that helpful because they rely too much on a subjective understanding of what colors should look like and provide no feature for calibrating brightness and contrast. Even more difficult, many DV cameras don't generate color bars at all. In these cases you need to improvise. Some people hook up a small, portable color bar generator to calibrate their monitor and others record NTSC color bars on a DV tape that they carry with them in the field to play through the camera. It's not the most accurate method, but it's better than nothing.

In addition to calibrating your monitor, you also need to take care to protect the monitor screen from the sun or movie lights, which can wash out the image. LCD flip-screen viewfinders are especially vulnerable to being washed out by ambient light; also, viewing LCD screens at a slightly oblique angle can cause dramatic shifts in color, contrast, and brightness. **Monitor sunshades** (also called **hoods**) are often used in the field to avoid these problems.

Zebras

Another exposure aid found on many cameras is **zebra stripes** (or **zebras**). Zebras are thin, slanted black stripes that show up in the hot spots in your image and can be seen in the viewfinder, but they are not recorded or even visible on an external monitor hooked into the video output. Zebra stripes tell you when a bright area in your image has reached the limits of proper exposure and is in danger of being overexposed. The two most common luminance settings for zebras are **100% white** and **70% white** (sometimes **80% white**). Some cameras allow you to switch between the two.

The **100% white** (or **100 IRE**) setting is considered the absolute upper range of brightness for a video exposure, beyond which your whites "clip" or "burn out," meaning that you've completely lost all detail in that area. When 100% stripes begin to appear in the white areas of the frame, you know you've reached the limits and do not want to open up your aperture any more. For example, let's say we are shooting a subject leaning against a white car and

Figure 12-18 A high-quality field monitor makes the job of maintaining precise focus and exposures much easier than using the inaccurate LCD flip screen found on most camcorders.

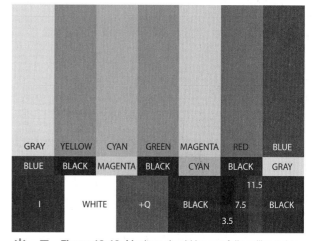

Figure 12-19 Monitors should be carefully calibrated to color bars for luminance, contrast, hue, and saturation, providing an accurate rendition of the video signal from the camera. See the color insert and companion website.

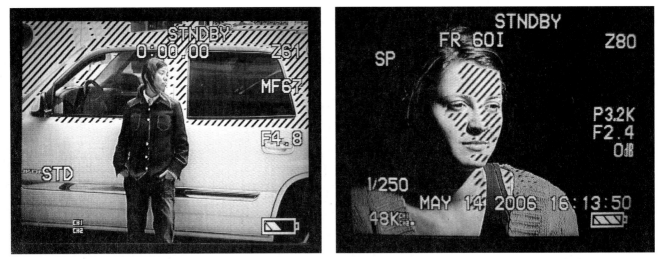

we want that car to gleam nice and bright. The DV camera's auto exposure will see a very bright object dominate the frame and will try to expose the white car closer to a middle gray tone. This won't be acceptable. So we go into manual override and open up the iris to the point when zebra stripes show, and then we close down just enough that they begin to disappear. Now that white car is properly white. The benefit of using the zebras is that they give you the only absolute measure of brightness in your image. Monitors might be slightly off, even after calibration, but zebras will show up at 100% white no matter how you've calibrated the monitor (**Figure 12-20**).

Some cameras allow you to calibrate zebra stripes to **70%** or **80% white**, which is considered the upper limit of "proper" exposure for Caucasian skin tone. These zebras start to show at 70% white and then disappear around 90%. The logic here is based on the assumption that Caucasian skin is properly exposed around 70% to 80%. When shooting the face of a "Caucasian" subject, you should see zebras in the highlights of the face, like the cheekbones and the forehead. The limitations of 70% zebras should be fairly obvious. Are all Caucasian skin tones alike? Surely not. And what about all of those other skin tones we might want to shoot? In addition, there are many situations where we don't want to use an exposure standard that makes our people look like they're being taped for the evening news. So 70%/80% stripes—if you use them at all—should be considered only as an exposure guide and never as an absolute.

Other DV Exposure Factors

Electronic gain is one way many DV cameras deal with low-light situations. **Gain** is an electronic amplification of the video signal coming from the CCD chips, increasing the sensitivity of the imaging system to light. Gain is considered an exposure adjustment of last resort, to be employed when we absolutely need to get the shot, but there simply isn't enough light for a decent exposure. Hit the gain switch and suddenly the image appears much brighter. Gain, however, also involves serious compromises to image resolution and contrast and increases **video noise**, which is unwanted electronic aberrations and artifacts. Most cameras offer three preset gain settings: 0 dB for low gain, 9 dB for medium gain, and 18 db for high gain. Some cameras have the option for even more gain than this. Obviously, though, the noise level increases as the gain level increases. Some cameras also have an automatic gain adjustment, which, like most auto functions, should immediately be turned off in favor of the manual settings. Gain requires such serious image compromises that most people stay away from it except under extreme circumstances. That said, gain does have a "look" of sorts that could work well for certain scenes as an aesthetic choice. You never know, so tuck it away into your visual toolbox (**Figure 12-21**).

Just because DV cameras don't have a physically rotating 180° shutter like a film camera doesn't mean they don't have a shutter of sorts. DV cameras have an **electronic shutter** that determines the amount of time each frame of video is exposed. The normal shutter speed for video is $\frac{1}{60}$ of a second, but shutters can be manually adjusted over a range. Setting the shutter to slower speeds, like $\frac{1}{16}$ of a second, creates longer exposures, allowing more light to fall on the CCD chips and causing movement smears in each frame (**Figure 12-22**).

Setting the shutter to faster speeds, like $\frac{1}{4000}$ of a second (some cameras have the capability of shooting at $\frac{1}{15,000}$ of a second!), creates sharper, crisper images as the speed increases. Fast shutter speeds are great for shots you intend to manipulate, in postproduction, into slow motion because there is no blur in the individual frames. However, when you play back fast shutter speed shots at the normal frame rate, the image can have a staccato or stroboscopic

■ **Figure 12-21** DV cameras can shoot in extreme low-light situations through the use of the gain function, sacrificing resolution and adding video noise in the process.

effect, which becomes more noticeable as your shutter speed increases. Just as with the slow shutter speed effect, this, too, can be a desirable aesthetic choice when used appropriately. Keep in mind that the faster your shutter speed, the less light hits your CCD. Ultrafast shutter speeds require a lot of light to create an acceptable exposure.

■ **Figure 12-22** A slow shutter setting smears the image (*left*), whereas a fast shutter captures even fast action without any blurriness (*right*).

CHAPTER 13

Basic Lighting for Film and DV

Movie lighting is an art form in which the interplay of light, shadows, color, and movement serve as fundamental expressive elements in the telling of a story. Whether you are shooting on film or video, using only sunlight or using 20 movie lights, with lighting designed for a realistic style or a stylized look, it all comes down to finding a lighting scheme that is appropriate for this scene, at this moment, in this story. Like all art forms, there is really only one absolute rule to dramatic lighting—make it work. If you can justify the lighting design of a scene within the overall intentions of the project, then do it. However, as with all art forms, "making it work" also means having the skill and control to actually pull "it" off. With lighting, the more knowledge you acquire about the history, conventions, and approaches of dramatic lighting and the more control you develop over the materials, tools, and techniques of the craft, the more successfully you will achieve your vision. To gain this sort of control you must start with a solid foundation, which means knowing what tools you have at your disposal and how those tools work. It also means knowing some basic principles of light and lighting. Principles, unlike rules, can be applied creatively, used to improvise, and serve as the foundation for creative exploration and expression. As the great cinematographer Maryse Alberti tells us, "You have to master your tools and stay in the creative zone. It begins with knowing what you want your images to look like and why."

A thorough understanding of lighting principles is especially important to student and independent filmmakers, who are typically making films on a tight budget and time schedule. Lighting is the most time-consuming and labor-intensive process in making movies. It takes muscle and many hours to get lighting gear onto a set, into position for shooting, broken down afterward, and loaded back onto the truck. Hollywood films look like Hollywood films because they have all the time, money, and manpower they need for elaborate lighting schemes and setups. But just as with every other element of a filmmaker's art, money and size don't necessarily translate into a good or successful film. Ingenuity, imagination, and a practiced eye are your primary resources for using light to tell your story with visual eloquence and impact. If you really want to learn about lighting, stay away from the Hollywood blockbusters, which have an army of grips, gaffers, and electricians and several five-ton grip trucks filled to the brim with state-of-the-art lighting and grip equipment. Not only can these films make you feel that your resources are insufficient, but in fact, this surfeit of resources often proves to be an encumbrance that threatens to supersede the creative impulse with logistics and pure technical procedure for its own sake. Anyone who goes to the movies on a regular basis sees many films that were made with virtually limitless access to lighting gear and labor but that nonetheless feel lifeless. This feeling comes, in no small measure, from the lighting approach itself, which, for all of its professionalism, often is simply big, blunt, and overproduced rather than uniquely expressive.

Both film students and independent filmmakers should look instead at the filmmakers who have made great movies with very little—whether out of necessity or by choice—and who have conceived of simple, elegant, and expressive lighting designs. For example, look at the brilliantly innovative films from the French New Wave like *Masculin/Féminin* (Godard/Kurant); the New German Cinema movement like *Ali: Fear Eats the Soul* (Fassbinder/Jürges); the more recent American Independent and European films like *Personal Velocity* (Miller/Kuras), *Leaving Las Vegas* (Figgis/Quinn), and *Nanette et Boni* (Denis/Godard); and, of course, the fearless lighting of recent Asian films like *Chungking Express* (KarWai/

■ **Figure 13-1** Expressive and innovative lighting with modest resources. Top row: *(left)* Godard's *Masculin/Feminin* (1966), *(middle)* Miller's *Personal Velocity* (2002), *(right)* Wong's *Chungking Express* (1994). Bottom row: *(left)* Figgis' *Leaving Las Vegas* (1995), *(middle)* Denis' *Nenette et Boni* (1996), *(right)* Fassbinder's *Ali: Fear Eats the Soul* (1974).

Doyle) (Figure 13-1). These pictures all had relatively modest lighting resources but used them with a profound understanding of artistry and technique, which can teach us far more about lighting, camerawork, and storytelling than the latest $150 million Hollywood production.

The great cinematographer Néstor Almendros made a critically important point when talking about his work lighting and shooting Eric Rohmer's *La Collectionneuse* (1966). In his interview for the book *Masters of Light* (by Dennis Schaefer and Larry Salvato), Almendros talks about his naturalistic lighting approach, working with Rohmer, and how few lights and crew they discovered they actually needed to make the film: "[We] realized that most technicians had been bull***ing, you know, and inventing uses for enormous amounts of light to justify their importance, to justify their salaries and to make themselves look like someone who knows a secret, when there is technically very little to know."

■ THE FUNDAMENTAL OBJECTIVES OF LIGHTING

Whether we are lighting with a grip truck filled with movie lights, a small portable lighting kit, or just the sun, there are five fundamental objectives to lighting any scene: (1) exposure and visibility, (2) depth and dimension, (3) narrative emphasis (4) tone and mood (5) consistency. The most rudimentary and utilitarian function of movie lighting is *exposure and visibility*, ensuring a scene will register on our imaging medium and a viewer can see details. However, anyone can blast thousands of watts of light at a scene and guarantee that the viewer will see absolutely everything! Expressive lighting, on the other hand, involves lighting for the dramatic needs of the scene. This means manipulating light sources, shadows, and colors to create the visual look appropriate for your scene and story. As we mentioned on page 51, lighting angles and shadows are significant factors in creating or minimizing *depth and dimension* within a shot, and this contributes significantly to the composition of the frame. Additionally, we must consider how our lighting scheme works to compliment the *visual narrative emphasis* that may be required in a scene. For example, lighting to reveal some details clearly while perhaps concealing others; or to create areas of greater and lesser prominence within a shot; or lighting to create visual relationships between characters or maybe characters with their environment. These aspects of lighting function in tandem with shot composition and set design to give emphasis to visual information and to guide the viewer's attention. Very closely related to this is the fourth objective of lighting, to establish a particular (and appropriate) *emotional tone or mood* for a scene. The inclusion or elimination of shadows, the range of colors in a scene, the hardness or softness of the light, the direction from which lights come: all of these lighting choices, when conceived intelligently from the content of the script, can have a profound impact on the emotional tone that will be communicated to an audience. The way we use, control, and manipulate our sources of light to create narrative and emotional emphasis plays an enormous role in the overall visual style of the cinematography and therefore the film. That style can be naturalistic or stylized (I explore these concepts in detail in Chapter 14). Finally, with so many possible lighting variables available every time we set up a new scene, we need to be vigilant that our lighting schemes *remain consistent* from shot to shot and scene to scene so that the finished film has a unified visual style (even if specific lighting details change to reflect tonal shifts in the story). If we light each shot without considering the larger canvas we run the risk of creating shots that look fine on their own, but will not edit next to other shots (lighting continuity) or scenes which break the emotional tone of the film.

Figure 13-2 An 18,000-watt HMI on location *(top)* and a flashlight in *The Blair Witch Project* (1999) *(bottom)*. Usable artificial lights come in many sizes.

■ THE FUNDAMENTAL SOURCES OF LIGHT

Anything that gives off light, from the blazing midday sun to a candle, can be used as a lighting source in a scene. **Natural light** is a term meaning a light source coming from nature, a source that is not artificial. Usually we mean the sun when we talk about natural light, but the term also applies to light that comes from nonelectric sources, whether or not they are indeed naturally occurring, like campfires, candles, and fireplaces. If your scene included flashes from lightning bolts, that, too, would be a natural light source. **Artificial light** is any light source that generates light though electricity. Artificial lights can be as big as a 50,000-watt movie light or as small as a flashlight (**Figure 13-2**).

The term **available light** refers to light sources that ordinarily exist in any given location. For example, if we walk into a grocery store with our camera and simply shoot by the light of the fluorescent fixtures overhead or if we shoot in a bedroom illuminated only by the sun streaming in from a window, we are shooting with available light. And, as you might suspect, **mixed lighting** refers to combining available sources and artificial lights to achieve the look we're after. It's very common to use the sun as one light source and artificial lights another (**Figure 13-3**).

Very often natural or available light sources are not powerful enough to create an exposure, but we nonetheless want the audience to feel like that particular source is illuminating the scene. For example, a character is watching TV and we want the audience to believe that the glow from the screen is the only light illuminating her face, but the glow from a TV (or candle, or fireplace, or 25-watt reading lamp, etc.) is almost never strong enough to get a good exposure, especially if your character is some distance away. In this sort of situation we bring in an artificial light to duplicate the color, quality, and direction of the ostensible light source, but at a higher intensity (**Figure 13-4**). While this light obviously remains off screen, the ostensible source is often shown in the scene (see the "Specials and Practicals" section).

This strategy of using movie lights to duplicate where light would logically be emanating from is called **motivated lighting**. Motivated lighting is a central strategy for creating naturalistic lighting designs (see page 318).

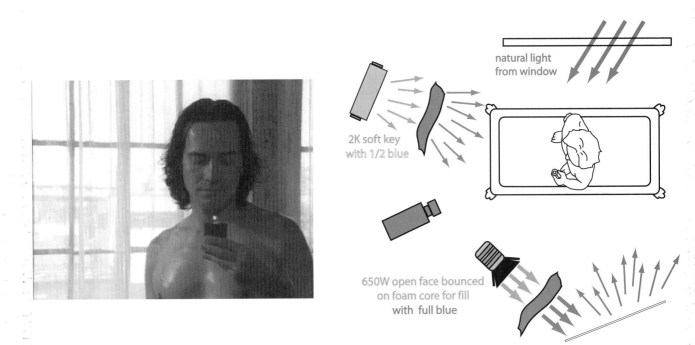

■ **Figure 13-3** In this scene, from Katherine Hurbis-Cherrier's *Ode to a Bar of Soap* (1998), mixed lighting (artificial and sunlight) has been balanced for color temperature and quality. See the color insert.

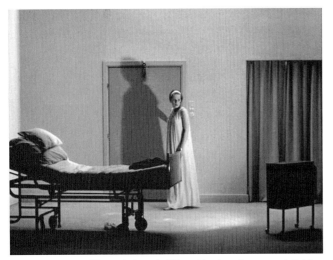

■ **Figure 13-4** The real glow of a TV could not produce enough light for an exposure, so its output was amplified with the use of a movie light in Ingmar Bergman's *Persona* (1966).

■ THREE ESSENTIAL PROPERTIES OF LIGHT

Light sources don't simply give off generic light: every light source emits a light that has specific characteristics that contribute to the look of your scene. Three of the basic properties of light that give any light source its distinctive character are **intensity, hard versus soft**, and **color temperature**.

Intensity

Light **intensity** is the strength of the light emitted by a source and, as we mentioned earlier, is measured by a light meter in footcandles. Direct sunlight is obviously a very intense source of light, although the actual intensity changes depending on its angle at various times of day. With artificial light, intensity depends on the **wattage of the lamp** used (500 watts, 1,000 watts, etc.) and on the **reflector system**. When we speak of lamp wattage we use the symbol "K" to stand in for "thousand."

So a 1,000-watt light is called a 1K and a 2,000-watt light is called a 2K. (Do not get this K mixed up with the "K" symbol used for degrees Kelvin, when referring to color temperatures.) A very common movie light is a 1K Fresnel with a color temperature of 3,200°K.

Some lighting instruments have a **specular reflector system**. A specular reflector system uses a highly polished, mirror-like surface to reflect the light from the lamp and is very efficient in maintaining the intensity of the lamp wattage. Other instruments use a **diffuse reflector system** to soften the light, and this cuts down the intensity (**Figure 13-5**). In addition, some lighting units employ a lens in front of the lamp to help control the directionality of the beam, but this, too, cuts down the intensity of the light.

The intensity of incident light on your scene is also greatly affected by the lighting unit-to-subject distance. The farther away an instrument is placed from the subject, the weaker

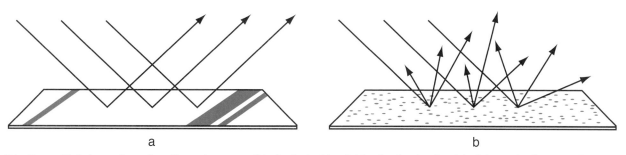

■ **Figure 13-5** A specular surface, like a mirror or a polished reflector (a) maintains the directionality of the light rays it reflects. A diffused surface (b), like foam core or a matte reflector, scatters the light rays, changing the quality of the light from hard to soft.

the light is falling on the scene. This diminishing intensity as the unit is moved away follows the **inverse square law**, which says that the intensity of light falls off by the square of the distance from the subject (**Figure 13-6**).

Obviously the converse applies when you bring a light in closer, to increase its intensity on the subject. If the inverse square law seems like a lot of calculation to do on the set, you can simply apply this rule of thumb: if you double the distance between the lighting unit and your subject, say from 10 feet to 20 feet, the strength of the light will fall off four times and will be only one-fourth the intensity compared to the original position. If you halve the distance between the subject and the lighting unit, you will increase the light intensity four times from the original position.

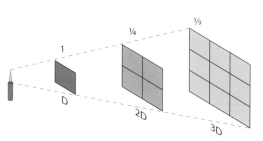

■ **Figure 13-6** The inverse square law. Doubling the distance from the light source to our subject means that the illumination is spread over four times the area and is therefore only one fourth the intensity.

Hard versus Soft

The lamps for the most commonly used film lights involve a wire filament, enclosed in a glass bulb, surrounded by a vacuum of inert gases, heated to the point where it glows white hot. That glowing filament becomes the **point source** of the lamp's illumination, creating a highly directional beam. Light that travels directly from a lamp to the subject is referred to as a **hard light** or **directional light**, because the light rays, which travel straight and parallel to each other, all fall on the subject from a single angle, causing sharp shadows and bright highlight areas. Lighting instruments with specular reflector systems preserve this hardness because a specular surface, like a mirror, redirects the light rays yet maintains their direct and parallel path. Units that do not illuminate directly from the lamp but instead reflect the light off an unpolished, white surface emit a **diffused** or **soft light**. The unpolished surface scatters the light rays in a variety of angles, disturbing their parallel paths (**Figure 13-7**).

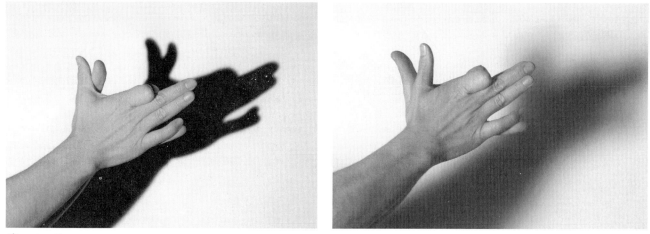

■ **Figure 13-7** Hard light creates sharp shadows *(left)* because the light beams maintain their parallel direction. Soft light *(right)* creates diffused shadows because the scattered light beams reach the subject from many directions.

■ **Figure 13-8** Hard light can be softened (diffused) by applying diffusion material in front of it *(left)* or by bouncing it off a white surface, like foam core *(right)*.

■ **Figure 13-9** The decision to use hard or soft light depends on the aesthetic needs of your film. Although both of these shots use a low-key lighting approach, S. Coppola's *Lost in Translation* (2003, *left*) uses soft light, while Boe's *Reconstruction* (2003, *right*) uses hard light, which explains their radically different look and feel.

Diffused light rays do not hit the subject from the same angle and therefore create softer shadows and smoother highlights. This sort of lighting instrument is called a soft light. It's important to note that the larger the area of the diffused bounce surface is, the softer the light will be.

Understanding this principle, you can see that it is not difficult to soften the light from a hard lighting instrument by simply bouncing it off any diffused surface, like a white wall or a white bounce board. You can also soften light from a hard lighting unit by placing **diffusion media** in front of the beam (**Figure 13-8**). Diffusion media scatters the light rays in a way similar to that achieved by bouncing light off a diffusing surface (see "Altering Light with Gels" section). Be aware, however, that diffusing light either way decreases its intensity. It's also important to understand that the terms "hard" and "soft" describe a characteristic of light and should not be viewed as a value judgment. One is not better than the other. As with so many other things, the appropriate choice is based primarily on applying the appropriate aesthetic choice for the content of your story (**Figure 13-9**).

Color Temperature

As mentioned in the chapter on film stocks, different sources of light favor different areas of the light spectrum, and the tonality that a light favors is called its **color temperature** (see page 188). Color temperature is measured by the Kelvin scale. In discussing film color sensitivity, we already mentioned that average daylight is 5,600°K (quite blue), but the sun can change color temperature dramatically over the course of the day; the late afternoon sun can dip to around 4,000°K, and dawn and dusk can be as warm as 2,000°K.

The most common artificial lighting instruments for medium-scale film and DV production are **tungsten lights** (tungsten-halogen) (also called **quartz lights**), which have a color temperature of 3,200°K (quite warm). Tungsten lights are efficient and powerful for their wattage, but they burn hot and so require ventilation and careful handling. Another kind of light commonly used in bigger budget productions is the **HMI** (hydrargyrum medium-arc iodide). HMIs are designed to emit a light that matches daylight color temperature, 5,600°K. HMIs are very efficient lights and burn cooler than tungsten lights, but they require a heavy power ballast in addition to the lighting unit itself. This additional encumbrance along with a higher rental price make the HMI primarily a professional lighting unit (**Figure 13-10**).

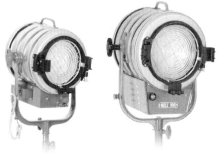

■ **Figure 13-10** Lighting units are designed in either Tungsten *(left)* or daylight color temperatures, also called HMI's *(right)* to make the balancing of mixed lighting easier.

■ CAMERA FILTERS AND LIGHTING GELS

Camera filters and gels are used to change, in some essential way, the quality of light in a scene. The fundamental difference between the two is that **gels** (short for gelatin) are sheets of dyed plastic material that are used in front of a lighting unit (or in a window) to alter the quality of that particular light source *before* it falls on the scene. **Camera filters**, on the other hand, are glass or hard plastic elements mounted in front of the camera lens to change the quality of the light, from all sources, entering the camera.

■ **Figure 13-11** Matte boxes are useful to block out unwanted light from the lens and can come equipped with filter holders.

Altering Light with Filters

Camera filters are mounted in front of a lens in two ways: they either screw directly onto the front of the lens or are held in a matte box. Filters that mount directly onto the lens are usually glass filters inside a mounting ring. These filters come in a wide variety of sizes to match the diameter and mounting threads of various lenses. **Matte boxes** attach to the front of the camera and extend out from the lens to keep unwanted light from glancing off the lens. They usually also have filter holders and slots for holding several rectangular glass or plastic filters (**Figure 13-11**). Different matte boxes are designed to hold specific filter sizes (i.e., 2 × 2, 3 × 3, or 4 × 4). Make sure that you have the proper size filter for your particular matte box.

There are literally hundreds of different filters on the market that accomplish a wide range of different effects. Camera filters break down into four broad categories of usage: **color correction, exposure control, special effects,** and **black-and-white photography**. I have already discussed the two most common color correction filters for film shooting, the Wratten #80A and #85, in the chapter on film stocks (see page 189). It's not possible to cover every filter available, but the following sections cover a few of the most common and indispensable filters for filmmaking.

Neutral Density Filters

Neutral density filters (or ND filters) are gray tinted filters that simply cut down the amount of light entering the lens (**Figure 13-12**). ND filters are exposure control filters and do not affect color at all. An ND 0.3 filter cuts the amount of incoming light in half, or one full

Figure 13-12 Neutral density filters cut the amount of light entering the lens without changing its color. ND 0.3 *(left)* reduces light by one stop and ND 0.6 *(right)* cuts the light by two stops.

Figure 13-13 Many video cameras come equipped with built-in neutral density filters.

Figure 13-14 Diffusion filters are used to soften the image while maintaining sharp focus. Notice in this shot, from Sluser's *Path Lights* (2009), the glow on the metal highlights and hair and the softness added to Bobby's (John Hawkes) face. See the color insert.

stop; an ND 0.6 cuts down two stops, and an ND 0.9 cuts down three stops. Obviously, the ND filter is useful if you find yourself shooting with a fast film stock on a sunny day; but more frequently, this filter is used when you want to decrease your depth of field without changing your lens, lighting, or composition. By adding ND filters you are forced to compensate for exposure by opening up your aperture, thus decreasing the depth of field. This is especially important when shooting DV where, because of the small size of the image sensor, the depth of field is generally very deep. Many DV cameras have ND filters built in and accessible either through menus or on a filter wheel (**Figure 13-13**).

Diffusion Filters

Diffusion filters are special-effect filters used to soften an image while maintaining sharpness of focus. Exactly how and how much they soften the image is different depending on whether the filter uses a white or black diffusion effect and on the degree of diffusion. **White diffusion** creates a soft haze, from the subtle refracting of white highlights, and **black diffusion** softens the image by delicately flaring the dark, shadow areas of the image. The degree of diffusion is designated by a scale beginning with fractions, ⅛, ¼, and ½ diffusion, and then going from 1 to 5 diffusion. The ⅛, ¼, and ½ diffusion filters show the least amount of diffusion and are not really considered a special effect; the diffusion is barely noticeable except that it slightly smoothes out areas with fine, sharp lines, like skin wrinkles. Many shooters feel that the DV image can be excessively harsh and will routinely use a very light, black diffusion (⅛ or ¼) to slightly soften the image's "electronic" edge. At 1 and 2 diffusion levels, you will begin to clearly see softer edges on everything and the subtle flaring of white or black areas (**Figure 13-14**). By the time you reach a 5 diffusion filter, the soft image becomes a hazy one, creating an overt "dreamy" or "romantic" effect whose use requires very legitimate narrative motivation.

Polarizing Filters

When light reflects off shiny surfaces, specifically nonmetallic surfaces like glass or water, it scatters and vibrates in many directions causing glare. A **polarizing filter** (or **pola filter**) is used to block light rays that are not parallel when entering the lens. The primary use of a polarizing filter is to reduce or eliminate the obstructing glare and reflections coming off transparent surfaces like glass and water. A polarizing filter is made of two glass elements: one is fixed and one rotates. Each element is manufactured with parallel rows of glass grain, similar to partially opened Venetian blinds. These striated rows block light that is off axis (**Figure 13-16**), allowing only light waves that are parallel to one another to pass through the filter. By rotating these layered, parallel grains, a polarizing filter creates an adjustable grid that progressively blocks scattered light (horizontally and vertically) from a selectively wider or narrower axis. Polarizers offer a great amount of creative control because you can easily see, as you rotate the filter, exactly how much glare and reflection you are eliminating (**Figure 13-17**). Be careful, however; polarizing filters work

It's not uncommon to find cinematographers who make their own diffusion filters by stretching very fine silk stockings over filter frames, to create a customized diffusion effect. Different cinematographers swear by different brands and grades of hosiery but, anecdotally speaking, it seems that French stockings are preferred. When shooting the black-and-white portions of his film *Wings of Desire* (1987), Wim Wenders had the A.C. try a number of diffusion filters from high-end professional brands, but he was not satisfied with any of their looks. Exasperated, he turned to his D.P., the legendary French cinematographer Henri Alekan, who pulled out of his filter box an old wood-framed black diffusion filter he made in the 1930s with his grandmother's silk stockings. For Wenders the unique visual quality of this filter, that had been handmade some 50 years earlier, was perfect, and they used it.

Wings of Desire is acknowledged as being one of the most visually stunning films of all time—thanks to Henri Alekan's grandmother (**Figure 13-15**).

■ **Figure 13-15** Cinematographer Henri Alekan is said to have used a special filter made from his grandmother's silk stockings on Wenders' *Wings of Desire* (1987).

so well that it is possible to "dial out" all glare, thereby making it seem like there is no glass in a window at all (**Figure 13-18**).

Because much of the light that comes from the clear blue part of the sky is reflected light (haze), polarizers are also handy for darkening blue skies to make cloud formations stand out vividly. For this use, the angle of the sun to the filter is important. Darkening blue skies works best with the sun at a 90° angle to the filter, but the technique will not work at all if the sun is along a 180° axis directly in front of or behind the filter. A polarizer does not alter the color tonalities of your scene; however, it does take a toll on exposure. Most polas require a compensation of 1.5 to 2 stops. Also remember that polarizers work through the precise angles between the light and filter elements, so moving the camera by panning or tracking can visibly change the polarizing effect.

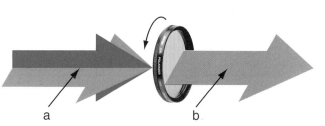

a   b

■ **Figure 13-16** When shooting shiny, transparent surfaces, the reflected and direct light travel together toward the lens (a). To "catch" reflected light, the pola is rotated until it blocks the off axis light rays, so that only direct light (b) passes through.

■ **Figure 13-17** The pola filter at work. Glare on the window makes it difficult to see through it *(left)*. Turning the polarizing filter shows the gradual reduction of the light glancing off the window's surface *(middle)*. At its most effective angle, the pola can almost completely eliminate glare *(right)*.

■ **Figure 13-18** Sometimes reflections can be used as a narrative device, as Wenders did on *Wings of Desire* during the introduction of the angel Cassiel (Otto Sander). The bright neon lights that conceal his presence hint at his ethereal nature.

Graduated Filters

All of the filters discussed so far have an effect on the entire image. **Graduated filters** (**grads**), on the other hand, gradually introduce a filter effect into only a portion of the frame, leaving the rest of the frame unaffected. A graduated ND filter, for example, will incorporate a noticeable ND 0.9 at the top of the frame, to darken the sky, but the ND effect will taper off and disappear by the center of the frame, leaving the bottom half of the image completely unchanged. Graduated ND filters are popular because they reduce the contrast range in an image that might include, say, a bright sky and a shaded area on the ground (**Figure 13-19**). Graduated color filters are also popular, especially those that affect the color of the sky; examples include the sunset grad filter, which warms up the sky with an amber tint, and the blue grad filter, which deepens blue skies. Color graduated filters need to be used with some caution, as they are not the most subtle effects you can apply to your image. The effect can be quite noticeable if you fail to conceal the transition area in some compositional element in the scene—for example, placing the transition area in the tree line between the sky and the ground. Camera movement can also reveal the use of this filter.

■ **Figure 13-19** Grad filters gradually introduce a filter effect into a portion of the frame. Shown are *(from left to right)* ND 0.9 grad., ND 0.6 grad., and ND 0.3 grad.

Just as with all craft aspects of film production, when properly used, camera filters can be a powerful tool to refine the look of your film and establish the precise tone or emotional impression you want for your story (**Figure 13-20**). When unjustified or clumsily employed, however, filters make your footage look downright cheesy. When using camera filters always ask yourself why you've chosen a particular filter, what that filter helps you show or express, and then approach its use with some restraint at first.

Filters and DV Cameras

Not all filters that were made for film cameras work with DV camcorders. The nature of CCD registration, digital resolution, and even DV's inherently deep depth of field can interact poorly with filters made specifically for film cameras, causing unexpected results. Fortunately, many companies are

■ **Figure 13-20** In Fassbinder's *Veronika Voss* (1982), the dazzling world of celebrated actress Veronika (Rosel Zech) is underlined by the exuberant use of a star filter effect.

now manufacturing filter systems with small-format DV in mind. In any case, always try out your filters by taking some test footage before you employ them on the set.

Altering Light with Gels

While filters are mounted in front of the cameras lens and so affect all sources of light, gels, on the other hand, are positioned in front of a specific light source to change the color or quality of that particular light's output before it falls on the scene. There are several different manufacturers of lighting gels offering literally hundreds of different colors, shades, and effects to choose from (Figure 13-21). Aside from those designed to create colors, there are also a few utility gels that are absolutely indispensable for the creative filmmaker.

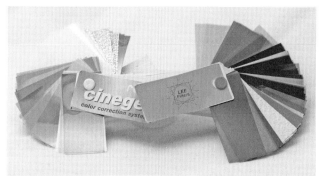

■ **Figure 13-21** Gels come in hundreds of colors and intensities, including color correcting, neutral density, and diffusion media. See the color insert.

Color Conversion Gels

Color conversion gels are used to change the color temperature of a light source, and they come in two basic flavors: **CTO**, for *color temperature orange,* and **CTB**, for *color temperature blue* (Figure 13-22). Similar to the Wratten #85 camera filter, CTO gels convert daylight (5,600°K) into tungsten color temperature light (3,200°K). CTO gels come in a variety of shades that allow fairly precise control over the change in the color temperature.

Full CTO converts 5,600°K light directly into 3,200°K, but ½ CTO converts 5,600°K daylight to 3,800°K (a little bluer) and ¼ CTO converts 5,600°K daylight to 4,500°K (even bluer). These gels allow the cinematographer a high degree of control in shifting the color tonalities of light sources.

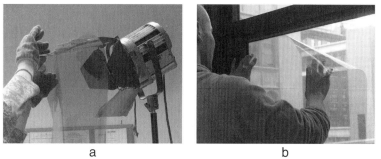

a   b

■ **Figure 13-22** CTO and CTB gels are used to correct the color temperature of a light source. CTBs are placed on movie lights to make them "daylight," and CTOs are placed on windows to make them "tungsten." See the color insert.

CTB gels convert a tungsten light source to daylight color temperature and are mostly used directly in front of lighting units. **Full blue** converts 3,200°K light into 5,600°K, but CTB also comes in various conversion degrees. For example, ½ CTB converts 3,200°K to 4,100°K (a little warmer) and ¼ CTB converts tungsten to 3,500°K (even warmer).

Color Conversion Gels and Mixed-Lighting Situations

Whether you are shooting film or digital video, CTO and CTB gels are indispensable for situations in which you have lighting sources with different color temperatures in one location (Figure 13-23). Let's say we have a situation in which we are lighting our subject with tungsten light (3,200°K) but we also have a window with daylight streaming in (5,600°K), visible in the background of the shot. If our camcorder (or film stock) is balanced for daylight, the subject will look as orange as a carrot; conversely, if we are balanced for tungsten, the window light will turn an unnatural blue. What to do? There are two ways we can balance the lighting in this situation.

We can cover the window with CTO gel and white balance the DV camera to tungsten light (or shoot with tungsten-balanced film), as now all lighting sources are tungsten color temperature. The difficulty with this approach is that it's not so easy to cover a window with gel, especially large windows. Lining windows requires that you carefully tape the gel to the window frame, making sure that there are no wrinkles that will refract light and reveal the gel. It can certainly be done, but it takes a little time and practice.

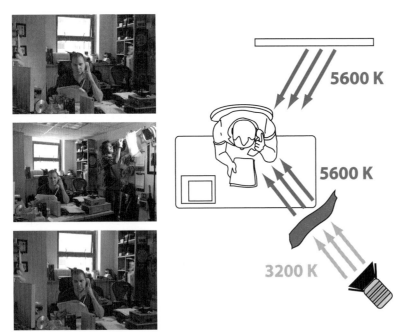

The other option would be to cover your tungsten lights with CTB gel and white balance your DV camera to daylight (or shoot with daylight-balanced film or tungsten film with a Wratten #85 filter), because all lighting sources are now daylight color temperature. Although putting a gel in front of a light is easier, there are drawbacks to this approach, too. On a super bright day you might not want to sacrifice any of your tungsten light's intensity, because doing so creates greater contrast between the tungsten areas and the bright sunlight areas. Both solutions work, so choosing one depends on your specific situation. The principle to remember is to use gels to change the color temperature of one source to match the other. Keep in mind that anytime you put a gel in front of a light source you reduce the intensity of that light somewhat. Full CTB reduces intensity around two stops and full CTO cuts the light by about ⅔ stop (actual light loss depends on the distance between the unit and the gel).

■ **Figure 13-23** Shooting with daylight film (or DV balanced for daylight) matches the sunlight coming through the window but records tungsten light as excessively orange (A). Placing a CTB gel over the tungsten unit changes it to daylight (B), matching the color temperature of all sources (C). See the color insert.

Also, remember that ½ and ¼ color conversion allows you to truly control the color. Let's say the image you are shooting is a winter scene and you want it to feel like it's cold outside but warm inside the house. You might choose only a ½ blue gel for the interior lights, which would convert them only partially to daylight, maintaining the warmth of your interior sources.

Neutral Density Gels

Just as with ND filters, **neutral density gels** are gray and do not affect the color of a light source: they simply cut down its intensity (**Figure 13-24**). ND 0.3 cuts intensity by one stop; ND 0.6, by two stops; and ND 0.9, by three stops. Because these gels are very often used in windows to moderate the intensity of light pouring into interior scenes, you will often find ND mixed with CTO in a single gel. A CTO ND 0.6, for example, will change the color temperature of the daylight to 3,200°K and will reduce the intensity of the window 2⅔ stops (2 stops for the ND and ⅔ stop for the CTO).

■ **Figure 13-24** Neutral density gels work like their glass counterparts, cutting the intensity of light without changing its quality or color. Pictured are ND 0.6 *(left)* and ND 0.3 *(right)*.

Diffusion Media

Diffusion media are used to soften the output of a hard light source (e.g., open face or Fresnel light). Using diffusion instead of bringing along a genuine soft light unit to the location is often more practical, because soft lights tend to be large and bulky (explained later). Diffusion can be used as a single layer or doubled or tripled to increasingly soften the light. Although softer light is very flattering, especially for lighting faces, the trade-offs are that diffusion can cut light intensity drastically and the spill of diffused light is harder to control with barndoors or flags. Diffusion is not called a gel because there are many different kinds of diffusion, made from a variety of materials, that determine the degree and texture of the diffusion. Tough spun (made of spun glass), tough frost, grid cloth, and tough opal are some common diffusion materials. The designation "**tough**" on any gel indicates that it is heat resistant and can be placed on barndoors—with caution (see page 393) (**Figure 13-25**).

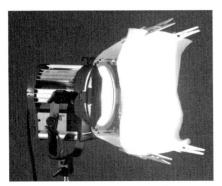

■ **Figure 13-25** A layer of tough frost attached to barndoors to create a softer light from this Fresnel.

■ **Figure 13-26** The overhead lighting used in Coppola's *The Godfather* (1972) created deep shadows over Vito Corleone's (Marlon Brando) eyes, adding an inscrutable quality to his character. In Welles' *Mr. Arkadin* (1955), a light placed low on the ground throws an ominous shadow as a murderer gets away.

■ LIGHT AND DIRECTIONALITY

When we devise our lighting strategy, among our most fundamental considerations, along with the qualities of light, is the question of directionality. Where is this light coming from? Even if we are simply shooting a film with one actor in a park with no artificial lights, by positioning the actor to face one way or another, in order to have the sun fall in a specific way on our subject, we are in fact controlling the directionality of our light source—we are lighting.

It is crucial to know that the visual emphasis and dramatic potential of lights change significantly given their placement in relation to the illuminated object. The placement of the lighting unit not only determines the directionality of the light source but also the direction and length of the shadows. By gaining control of light and shadow you gain control over the motion picture's most powerful elements for creating depth, texture, mood, tone, and even character and narrative meaning in your frame (Figure 13-26).

It is always helpful to remember that the range of light placement options is three dimensional. We can place our lights anywhere in the imaginary globe that surrounds our subject: in front, behind, along the side, high above, below, near, far—any angle, any distance, as long as the lights stay out of the frame of the shot (although this, too, is not an absolute rule). As a point of reference, here are a few basic light angles that depict a single, hard light source at the camera's level. Remember, don't just look at the direction of the light but at the throw of shadows as well (Figure 13-27).

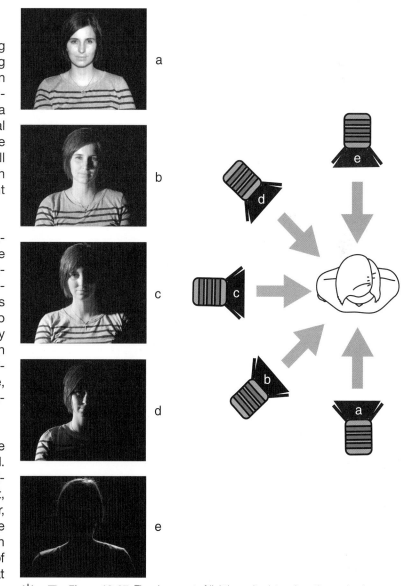

■ **Figure 13-27** The placement of lighting units determines the angle of illumination and the angle at which shadows fall. Pictured are five standard angles along the same horizontal plane: (a) frontal, (b) ¾ front, (c) side, (d) ¾ back, and (e) back (rim light). (Go to www.voiceandvisionbook.com to see this figure in high resolution.)

■ **Figure 13-28** The vertical angle of a lighting unit can dramatically change the look of a subject. Pictured are a high-angle frontal *(left)* and a low-angle frontal *(right)*.

1. **Frontal light** is illumination that comes essentially from the angle of the camera. Because the light rays duplicate the camera's angle of vision, most of the shadows are not visible to the lens as they fall straight back. Frontal light has a flat look resulting from the absence of visible shadows.

2. Move the light along an arc, away from the camera, and shadows start to appear and get more prominent as the light moves farther from the camera position. A ¾ **frontal light** is a lighting unit that is positioned 45° from the camera. Notice how the shadows cast by this light are at 45° angles. This light position is often also raised vertically by 45° as well.

3. Move this light another 45° away from the camera so that it is now positioned at a 90°-angle from the camera and we have a **sidelight**. This light comes directly from the side of the subject and has the effect of dividing the illuminated object in half, one side lit and the other in shadows. Sidelight maximizes shadows and therefore texture as well.

4. Moving this light another 45° away from the camera, we have a ¾ **backlight**. The area that this position lights is mostly hidden from the camera, but we do see bright highlights on the top and side edges of the subject. Notice how this angle causes the light to illuminate the shoulder and hair and cuts the light side of the figure out from the background while allowing the other side to blend into the shadows. This placement for a backlight is so common that it even has its own nickname, a **kicker**. This light is also commonly raised vertically by 45° as well to catch slightly more of the hair and shoulders.

5. Finally, move this light another 45° from the camera and the light is now 180° across from the camera, illuminating the subject's back. The camera can see only a small sliver of illumination around the top of our subject, as the front falls completely into shadow. This light is commonly called a **rim** light.

In addition to the horizontal angles, you need to also consider the dramatic changes in shadow and mood as you adjust the lighting unit's **height** (or **vertical angle**) from **high angle** to **low angle** (Figure 13-28).

■ FUNDAMENTAL LIGHTING SETUPS AND PRINCIPLES

Like all other art forms, lighting for film requires creativity, craft, experimentation, and experience. When you first start out, movie lighting can seem somewhat mysterious and tremendously time consuming. Simply answering the most basic questions (Where do I physically place the lights with respect to the subject and camera? What quality of light—intensity, hard, soft, etc.—should I use? How does this one light work in combination with the other lights?) can seem intricate and arbitrary. But with a little bit of book research, some hands-on experience, and by listening to the stories of other filmmakers who faced similar lighting challenges, you will quickly develop a repertoire of lighting approaches, styles, and techniques that you can confidently draw upon and build upon from one film to the next. What follows is a discussion of the most commonly used lights in the craft (Figure 13-30).

in practice

Always keep in mind that you are not on your own when it comes to devising lighting strategies to tell your story. The works and accomplishments of generations of cinematographers are only a DVD rental away for you to study and learn from. Henri Alekan, Gregg Toland, James Wong Howe, and Karl Freund are four of the early masters of light whose work is more available now than ever before (**Figure 13-29**). Their methods and tools were often much simpler than those used today, but their imagination, ingenuity, and understanding of light itself is unparalleled. The images are veritable and valuable textbooks on lighting. Over the years the old lions of dramatic film lighting like these (who themselves drew from previous generations of masters of photography, theater, and painting) developed a body of fundamental lighting setups that are used, in some combination, in most film lighting situations today. The basic setups represent the building blocks of the cinematographer's craft. Knowing these fundamental setups, which combine directionality, quality of light, and function, will help you

to understand how to create certain dramatic visual effects and will also help you determine an answer to the most basic question: Where do I put this light? All smart cinematographers learn from the giants who came before them, even the great Michael Ballhaus who worked with directors like Fassbinder, Scorsese, Coppola, and Redford, to name just a few.

> *[I] saw a lot of movies. I saw some films 10 to 15 times. My heroes were the French and Italian directors and cinematographers who were experimenting with film noir at the time (the early 1960s). Later, I learned a lot from Sven Nykvist (ASC) by watching his films. I saw every movie that he shot. I learned so much from just watching how he photographed faces and eyes. I have watched his Bergman movies many times. They are fantastic.*
> **Michael Ballhaus (From "A Conversation with Michael Ballhaus," November 20, 2006, www.theasc.com)**

■ **Figure 13-29** Four masters of light and shadow to learn from: *(clockwise from top left)* Henri Alekan (from Cocteau's *Beauty and the Beast*, 1946), James Wong Howe (from Mackendrick's *Sweet Smell of Success*, 1957), Greg Toland (from Welles's *Citizen Kane*, 1941), and Karl Freund (from Murnau's *The Last Laugh*, 1924)

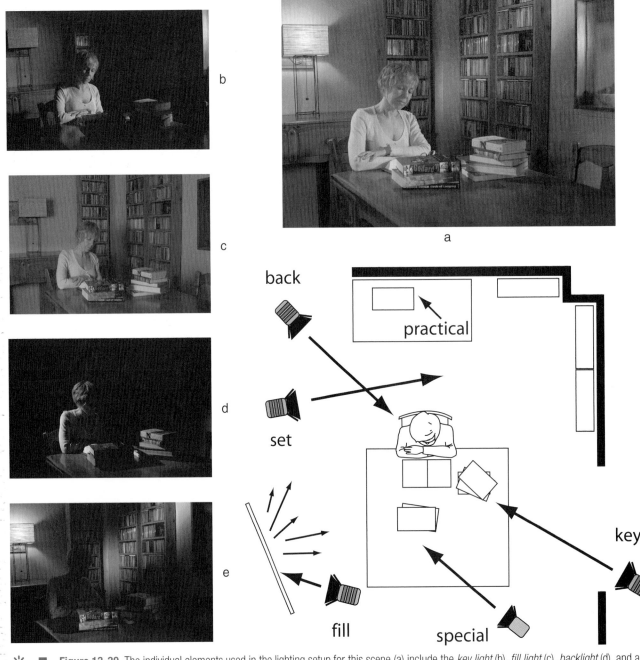

👆 ■ **Figure 13-30** The individual elements used in the lighting setup for this scene (a) include the *key light* (b), *fill light* (c), *backlight* (d), and a *set light* focused on the shelves (e). There are two other lights as well: a small *special* light on the books and a lamp *practical* (e). Notice that the lamp is not powerful enough to serve as a backlight, but it provides the motivation for the backlight (d). (Go to www.voiceandvisionbook.com to see this figure in high resolution and color.)

Key Light

The key light is the primary source of illumination in your scene (Figure 13-30, B). For scenes in which a realistic or naturalistic look is needed, the key light should be a **motivated light source**, which means that when positioning this light we must consider the ostensible and logical source within the scene for that illumination. It might be that we actually use the sun streaming into a window for our key light, or we may use an artificial light to simulate the sun streaming into the window in a naturalistic way. We might place our key light at a high angle to simulate an overhead street lamp on a dark night, or as a sidelight to simulate a reading lamp on a desk, or at a low angle to simulate the glow from a fireplace. In all of these cases, the placement of the key light is motivated by the ostensible source, visible in the frame or not, and its logical throw. Obviously, the key light can be placed anywhere. In cases where a pool of light creates a silhouette, the key light doesn't even fall on our subject (Figure 13-31). Usually, the key light is a hard and bright light source, but certainly not always. It's not uncommon to see soft keys being used in films.

Fill Light

As you can see in the directionality examples (see Figure 13-27), a hard light (like most key lights) casts sharp and dark shadows. When lighting people, this means nose and chin shadows and sunken eyes. A **fill light** is a soft light that is positioned to fill in the shadows created by the key light (Figure 13-30, C). Using a fill light is not mandatory, but it is commonly used in most lighting setups. The reason that fill lights are soft lights is that it would be counterproductive if the light we use for filling in shadows itself created additional shadows.

■ **Figure 13-31** Careful placement of the key light off the subject in Laughton's *The Night of the Hunter* (1955) effectively reverses the conventional association of light with good and darkness with evil by silhouetting righteous Rachel (Lillian Gish) while illuminating evil preacher Harry (Robert Mitchum).

There are two schools of thought concerning the placement of fill lights. One states that the fill light should be placed opposite the key light, which makes sense, given that it has to fill in the shadows that fall exactly opposite the illuminated area. Other people prefer to place their fill light as close to the lens as possible, creating a soft frontal light. This way, despite it being a soft light, if the fill casts any shadows, they fall straight back and out of view of the camera. Both methods work well, so experiment with this yourself and see which works best in your situation.

The degree to which you decide to fill in those shadows varies depending on the look you are after. You can choose to keep shadows quite dark, but fill in just enough to see some detail in the shadows, or you could almost completely fill the shadows with soft illumination, flattening out the image to create a bright scene in which everything is visible. The critical factor in determining the density of the shadows is the intensity of the fill light. The stronger the fill light, the less prominent the shadows will be (see the "Lighting Ratios" section).

Fill lights are not generally considered as motivated light sources, although when you're going for a realistic look, you do need to be aware of unnatural fill. For example, if we're shooting a scene in which two characters are talking in front of an idling car in the middle of the night, with the main and only source of illumination ostensibly being the car headlights (key light), you can get away with some very light fill to boost the exposure on the shadow side of the face, because it could be mimicking the way the human eye adjusts in dark conditions. But excessive fill in this situation would look as if the light was coming from an off-camera artificial lighting unit being used by a film crew to light the scene.

Backlight

A **backlight** is a light that separates the subject from the background by positioning a somewhat lower intensity hard to semi-soft light at a high angle and behind the subject. This creates, along the edge of the subject, a rim of light that clearly traces the edges of the figure and helps create depth in the frame (Figure 13-30, D). When lighting people, this light is often a ¾ backlight (or kicker), positioned opposite the key, which illuminates the hair and shoulders of the subject. Obviously the color of the subject's hair is a factor in determining the intensity of the backlight. Blonde hair tends to thin out and create a halo when intense backlights are used.

Backlights are notoriously easy to overuse. Overly intense backlight coming from seemingly nowhere will give your shot a highly artificial feeling. Automatically employing a ¾ backlight opposite the key can quickly make an image seem generic. For this reason, a backlight should be considered a motivated light source that needs some logical source, whether it's an existing overhead light, the sun behind the character, a neon sign in the background, or a wall sconce over the subject's shoulder.

Backlights are especially helpful when shooting very dark objects that absorb light. An object with low reflectivity, like a black curtain or dark wood bar counter, cannot be adequately lit by pouring light onto it because it simply will not reflect the light back. Instead, a backlight, glancing off the edges of the dark object, will create a rim of illumination that will define and highlight the object's dimensions.

Tim Burton's film *Ed Wood* is a good example of the creative use of the basic lighting positions. The lighting design of the film, which was shot by Stefan Czapsky, clearly references the lighting of the B-movie horror genre of the 1950s, but it also manages to appear substantially more polished and expressive. Burton is obviously not making a straight up B-movie; instead, he is telling a poignant, tragic, and at times hilarious story of Ed Wood (Johnny Depp) and Bela Lugosi (Martin Landau), the alienation they experience, and the community of supportive misfits, loners, and outcasts they forge through making movies. Just like the screenplay, the lighting style is at one and the same time humorous, camp, and touching (**Figure 13-32**).

■ **Figure 13-32** Three expressive lighting examples from Burton's *Ed Wood* (1994), which make dramatic use of a soft fill light *(top)*; a low angle, hard key light *(center)*; and hard backlight motivated by visible practicals *(bottom)*.

- *Fill light.* In the top still, Ed takes his new true love Kathy (Patricia Arquette) out on their first date to a carnival and, naturally, they take a turn through Ed's favorite carnival ride, the "Spook House." In the middle of the ride it breaks down and they're stuck. All of the lights that have been swirling around them stop, and the couple is lit only by soft, low-intensity fill and hard backlights. The lighting creates a calm, flat, and honest tone. Ed takes this opportunity to tell Kathy that he likes her a lot *and* that he likes to wear women's clothing, hoping that she'll be okay with all of it. Kathy thinks a moment and then says, "Okay." At that moment the Spook House ride comes alive again, complete with swirling lights.

- *Key light.* Bela *(center still)* is lit with a very low angle, hard key light, making him look especially ghoulish. This is typical of the excessive lighting approach of B-movie horror films; however, the content of the scene is anything but campy. Bela is broke, addicted to drugs, and completely at the end of his tether; he is holding a gun while Ed is trying to keep him from committing suicide. The lighting here creates a profoundly unnerving ironic tension between a genre style that we can't take seriously and desperate human emotions that we must.

- *Backlight.* All of the light *(bottom still)* in this beautifully designed shot is motivated. The key light comes from the candle (augmented) on the bar counter under Ed, and the backlight is designed to appear to be coming from the chandeliers hanging in the background (also augmented). Notice the important function the backlights serve in illuminating the curves of the bar countertop, Ed's cigarette smoke, and glass ashtrays. Dark objects and transparent material (glass, smoke, water) are difficult to light from the front. Backlighting that glances off the surface creates a gleam that defines the dimensions of the object while keeping the overall look of the scene dark—the way a dimly lit bar should look.

Set Lights

Set lights are used to light the larger area of the set: the architecture, furniture, set dressing, etc. (Figure 13-30, E). The angle and intensity of set lights are greatly determined by the key light, as the setting often shares the same motivated primary light source, so this must remain consistent.

Specials and Practicals

Specials are low-wattage, unobtrusive lights whose function is to kick up the illumination on a specific object or a small area of the frame for special emphasis. Careful control of specials can help create compositional emphasis to guide the viewer's eye by increasing the relative exposure level (by 1 or 1½ stops) on an important area or object in the image (Figure 13-30, E).

Lights that are included as part of the mise-en-scène, including wall sconces, household lamps, and overhead fixtures, are called **practicals**. In some cases they can provide some illumination but usually they are not powerful or controllable enough for a good exposure. More often than not, they are set dressing and they also provide the motivation for the movie lighting setup by being the ostensible source, as is the case with the chandeliers in the third *Ed Wood* still in Figure 13-32 and the lamp in Figure 13-30.

Three-Point Lighting

Three-point lighting refers to a specific and commonly used lighting strategy that employs a key light (usually a ¾ frontal light, positioned at 45° from the camera and at a 45° vertical angle), a fill light (usually opposite the key), and a backlight (usually a ¾ back) (Figure 13-33). You can see three-point lighting used extensively in television dramas and interviews. Three-point lighting is quick and efficient and occasionally a good starting point for a lighting approach. However, it's important not to think of three-point lighting as a rule that must be observed in every shot, and it's especially problematic to think that one should *always* light people with the three-point lighting scheme. Automatically following conventional approaches by rote can only lead to bland images.

Lighting Ratios

The amount of shadows contained in our scene and their depth relative to the illuminated areas provide our image with a sense of tone, mood, compositional emphasis, and even narrative meaning. Through lighting control, we can easily create an image with relatively few shadows or one in which shadows dominate the composition. We can use artificial lights and manipulate the depth of the shadows to create a naturalistic look or an

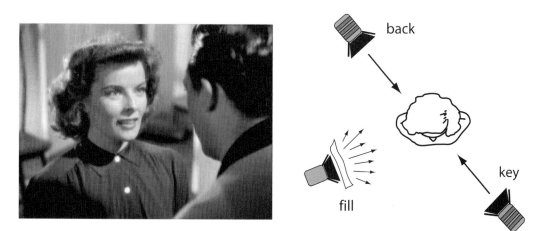

■ **Figure 13-33** A typical three-point lighting setup consists of a key light, a fill light, and a backlight. This setup was considered the standard for decades during the studio system era in Hollywood, as seen in this scene from Hawks's *Bringing up Baby* (1938).

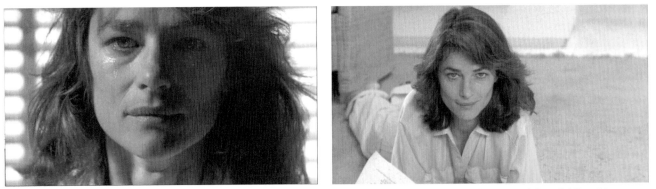

■ **Figure 13-34** Controlling the ratio between the key and the fill produces low-key *(left)* and high-key *(right)* images, and these lighting styles can have profound storytelling impact. These frames from Allen's *Stardust Memories* (1980) (shot by Gordon Willis) show Dorrie (Charlotte Rampling) at different stages of her life. Low-key lighting is employed when she is having a nervous breakdown *(left)* and the high-key image is used during a moment when Dorrie is happily in love *(right)*.

expressionistic tone. The dramatic needs of your story should suggest to you the look you need, but understanding how shadows are measured and controlled is important to getting that look (**Figure 13-34**).

Lighting ratios (also called **key-to-fill ratios**) are an indication of the relative intensities of the major light sources illuminating your subject: the key light and the fill light. The key light, as we know, is the primary source of illumination, but the fill light, being a soft source, not only fills the shadows created by the key light but also spills onto the key side and augments the amount of light falling in the areas lit by the key. For his reason, the ratio between the primary illumination and the fill light is expressed as **key + fill:fill**. This means that to find this ratio, you need to first meter your subject with the key and fill lights falling on the scene. Then you meter only the fill light (by blocking the key from the lumisphere or turning it off, if possible) and then divide these two readings. For example, if the key + fill gives a light intensity reading of 640 footcandles and the fill light alone reads 160 footcandles, then the lighting ratio is 640:160, which can be simplified as 4:1. The *total* illumination (key light plus the fill light) is four times brighter than the fill alone. This ratio can also be arrived at through a comparison of f-stop meter readings. If the key + fill gives you a meter reading of f/8 and the fill only comes in at f/4, then we have a two-stop difference, for a 4:1 ratio again (each stop doubling the light, 2×2).

Lighting ratios help us specifically determine the relationship between light and shadows, especially when shooting on film where you cannot see your image. A lighting setup with a low ratio, like 2:1 or 3:1, means that the fill light is filling in shadows until they are quite light. A lighting ratio of 1:1 would mean that both key and fill are the same intensity and there are no shadows at all. A lighting setup with a *low* key-to-fill ratio is called (somewhat confusingly) **high-key lighting**. High-key lighting ensures visibility in all parts of your scene with overall bright and even illumination. High-key lighting minimizes shadows, texture, and dimensionality.

Conversely, a high lighting ratio, say 16:1 or 36:1, will yield very dark and prominent shadow areas. This occurs when the intensity of the fill light is considerably lower than the key, allowing areas to be submerged in the shadows created by the key. A lighting setup with a *high* key-to-fill ratio is called, you guessed it, **low-key lighting**.

In addition to the key-to-fill ratio, which concerns how the subject itself is lit, there is another important ratio to consider, the **background-to-subject ratio**. This ratio is crucial because it compares the relative brightness of your subject to the background, which in turn determines if and how your subject will stand out from the background. Routinely, filmmakers try to make their subjects anywhere from ⅔ to 1½ stops brighter than the background (approximately 2:1 ratio). In this case, the subjects do not appear glaringly brighter than what's behind them (in fact, most viewers won't even notice the difference in brightness),

It is difficult, and rather pointless, to ascribe absolute and fixed moods to high-key and low-key lighting approaches (as many film books do) (**Figure 13-35**). It is true that many comedies, like John Hughes' *Ferris Bueller's Day Off* (1986) (*top left*), employ high-key lighting to create a lighthearted and cheerful mood. One could even say that high-key lighting is closely associated with this sort of comedy. But many films use high-key lighting to create other moods, like sterility, austerity, or alienation. High-key lighting can also be used in situations where flattening out the image might provide a sense of dramatic irony or could even infuse a scene with a soft, affectionate tone. George Lucas' film *THX-1138* (1971) (*top right*), for example, is a dystopian tale of a future where a subterranean society controls its human citizens through the mandatory use of narcotics that suppress emotions (especially sexual desire). In this film the stark, flat white pallet and shadowless high-key approach creates a sterile and dehumanized world of oppressive uniformity. There are no emotions, no individuality, love, despair, ambiguity, laughter, or humanity in this existence lived under florescent tubes.

There are similar assumptions made with low-key lighting, which is commonly used in the darkly lit film noir and horror genres and psychological dramas. Paul Haggis' 2004 film *Crash* (*bottom left*), for example, employs an overall visual look that is decidedly dark and shadowy for its unflinching exploration of racism and violence in America. But many lighthearted action pictures or horror film parodies have successfully used low-key lighting for laughs. Steven Spielberg's *Raiders of the Lost Ark* (1981) is a good example in which humorous scenes are often lit with heavy shadows and a dark tone to invoke an ominous mood, only to have the actions of the characters humorously undercut the expectations generated by this mood (*bottom right*). In this case, rather than producing an implement of torture as we expect, the device Gestapo Agent Thot (Ronald Lacey) assembles turns out to be a clothes hanger for his jacket.

The specific tone that emerges from your image depends on the unique alchemy between your lighting design and your story, characters, settings, actions, and other creative elements. Remember, there are no absolutes in the creative process of making a film, from writing the script to conceiving your lighting strategy. Indeed, there are conventions associated with high-key and low-key lighting, but conventions are not rules, and you, as a filmmaker, need to marshal all of your creative instincts and technical prowess to make your movie look and feel the way it should to effectively convey your story and ideas.

■ **Figure 13-35** High-key lighting has been used in such dramatically different films as Hughes's *Ferris Bueller's Day Off* (1986, *top left*) and Lucas's *THX-1138* (1978, *top right*). Low-key lighting can be seen in films with completely different emotional tones like Haggis's *Crash* (2004, *bottom left*) and Spielberg's *Raiders of the Lost Ark* (1981, *bottom right*).

in practice

Phil and Olly's 2009 short film *The Black Hole*, which is one of the example shorts in the companion website for this book contains an excellent example of how a shift in lighting ratios and in lighting angles at just the right moment can imply a shift in tone and character. When we are first introduced to the office clerk, he is bathed in the bland, soft fluorescent light of a large office. This high key approach is not only realistic for the environment, but it emphasizes the flat, colorless and mundane nature of the clerk's work life (**Figure 13-36**, *left*). However, after the clerk discovers the power and potential uses for the black hole, his demeanor changes, greed overtakes him, and he decides to break into a locked office to steal money. When he opens the office door and turns on the light, the fluorescent key light now comes from directly overhead and in the absence of any fill light, it creates a low key effect that emphasizes his avaricious urges and the hatching of a sinister plot (**Figure 13-36**, *right*).

■ **Figure 13-36** Reflecting internal character motivation through high-key and low-key lighting in Phil and Olly's short film *The Black Hole*.

but the subjects do pop out from the background and become more vivid (**Figure 13-37**, *top*). However, there are many aesthetic approaches you can take when considering the comparative brightness of the subject versus the background. Shooting your subject as a silhouette, for example, requires that the background be significantly hotter than your subject (**Figure 13-37**, *bottom*).

■ **Figure 13-37** It is common practice to expose principal subjects one stop brighter than the background to make them stand out, as in this frame from *A Serious Man* (Coen Brothers, 2009). Background ratios can be manipulated to create graphically expressive frames, such as this one from Sodergergh's *Solaris* (2002), which reflects Chris Kelvin's (George Clooney) emotional despondency by presenting him as a featureless silhouette.

■ EXTERIOR LIGHTING

Shooting outdoors does not mean simply accepting the light nature has to offer. In fact, the minute you ask your talent to face a specific direction in order to have the sun illuminating them from a particular angle, you are "lighting" the scene. All of the preceding principles about lighting apply to exterior shooting; the only difference is that student and low-budget independent filmmakers usually do not have extensive time, money, or crew to indulge in the sizable lighting equipment (like generators, HMIs, and 20-by-20-foot silks) needed to artificially enhance the available light of exterior scenes. When lighting exterior scenes, we must be crafty concerning the way we control our light sources: the sun during daylight hours and available artificial light during nighttime hours. The following sections offer a few tips.

Location Scouting

When lighting is crucial, take the time to scout your location to figure out the period during which the light is just right, and schedule your production around that moment. Remember, the sun is constantly shifting, so when timing is critical make sure to schedule your call early, allowing for setup time and run-throughs so you'll be ready to shoot when the light is just right. If your schedule doesn't allow this much flexibility and you are required to shoot whenever you can get the location, you should scout the location at the time you anticipate shooting to get a good sense for the angle of the sun during your shooting hours.

My colleague Gustavo Mercado recently shot a scene for his feature film *Becoming* (2007) that involved a simple LS two-shot conversation between two people in front of a river. Mercado wanted to obscure these figures by showing them as silhouettes against the bright sun glistening off the water behind them (an extreme background to subject ratio). The talent would be on the east side of the river, with the camera facing west. Obviously, he needed to shoot somewhat later in the day so that the sun, in the western sky, would be glancing off the water toward the camera. Mercado and his producer took an afternoon to simply sit where the camera would be placed and watch the shifting angle of the sun—occasionally snapping some digital photos. They determined that 5:45 p.m. was perfect. Two days later they arrived on location

■ **Figure 13-38** In this scene from Mercado's *Becoming* (2007), careful research into the position of the sun at a specific time of the day was necessary to capture this arresting shot.

at 4 p.m., set up the gear, ran a few rehearsals, and waited until the moment was perfect. In less than 20 minutes they nailed two good takes and this important scene was in the can (**Figure 13-38**).

Check the Weather

To be fully prepared, part of your production task should involve regularly checking an online weather service to determine if it will be sunny, partly cloudy, or overcast, as well as to determine exact sunrise and sunset times. The degree of cloud cover drastically changes the tone and mood of an exterior image. Overcast days diffuse the sun, creating, in effect, a soft, high-key look. Depending on the thickness of the cloud cover and the angle of the sun, there can be more or less directionality to this soft source. Sunny days produce a hard and bright light, which creates a high-contrast situation between the brightly lit areas of the frame and the areas of deep shadow. Exposures have to be carefully considered on these days. Partly cloudy conditions, especially on windy days when the sun plays hide-and-seek, are particularly challenging because exposures can shift dramatically from one shot to the next or even within a single take. On these days it's not possible to simply set your exposure and forget it (**Figure 13-39**).

Subject and Camera Positions

Just as with shooting indoors using artificial lights, your first lighting consideration when shooting exterior shots is where to place the key light. In this case, you cannot

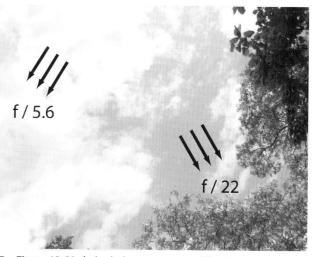

■ **Figure 13-39** A cloudy day can present a difficult exposure challenge, because available light can change seconds. The difference between sunny and cloudy areas can be as much as four or five f-stops!

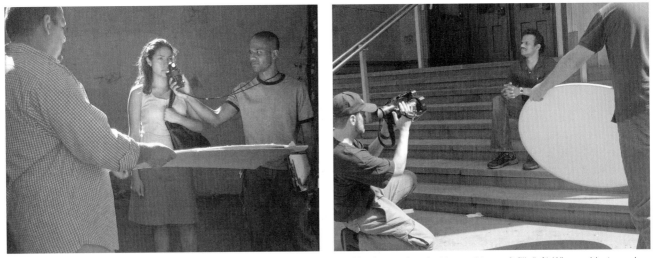

■ **Figure 13-40** Direct sun is used as a hard backlight and also bounced back onto the talent to provide a soft fill *(left)*. When subjects are in the shade *(right)*, a reflector can bounce sunlight back onto the subject to get a better exposure and contrast range.

move your key (the sun) to change its directionality, but you *can* move the orientation of your subject and camera to get the angle you desire. Simply by turning your subject you can get a sidelight, ¾ frontal light, ¾ backlight, and so on.

Sun plus Bounced Light

Perhaps the most useful lighting instrument for exterior shooting is the **reflector board** (also called **bounce board**). A reflector board is a flat, broad, and lightweight board used to bounce light from a source (artificial or sunlight) onto your scene. Whether you make it yourself or buy it, a reflector should have two sides with different reflective qualities. One side has a white, **diffused surface** that simultaneously bounces and diffuses a hard light source, like the sun. The other side is a **specular** (or **hard**) side that reflects and maintains the hard quality of the source, much like a mirror.

If you consider the direct sun as your key light, then you can think of placing a bounce board (diffuse side) opposite the sun, to soften and bounce its light right back to fill in the harsh shadows. One light source (the sun) becomes both a key and fill light (**Figure 13-40**, *left*).

Shade plus Bounced Light

When the direct sun is too intense, you can always simply move your subject into the shade of a tree or a building (if your locations and script allow it). Heavy shade, however, can flatten out the image, and in cases where this is not appropriate, you can always use the specular side of the reflector board to bounce some of that hard sunlight onto your subject in the shade, creating a sharp backlight or sidelight, to provide a little dimensionality to the image in a more controlled way (**Figure 13-40**, *right*).

Diffusing Sunlight

Another option for dealing with the extreme contrast created by harsh sunlight is to diffuse the sunlight itself with a **butterfly scrim**, a large sheet of diffusion material attached to a metal frame (**Figure 13-41**). Because they cannot cover much area, butterflies are usually used for reverse shots and close ups. Their diffusion effect makes it look as if your character has found a shady spot, giving a nice soft light on the subject while the background remains lit by the hard sun.

■ **Figure 13-41** A butterfly scrim being set up to diffuse sunlight for a tight shot. From Sluser's *Path Lights* (2009).

Butterflies scrims are cumbersome and setting them up can take up a lot of time, not to mention that they're difficult if there is any wind at all. So unless you have the crew to deal with them, it's often easier to just find a real shady spot.

Dusk-for-Night

One very convincing and inexpensive method for shooting scenes that ostensibly take place at night is to shoot dusk-for-night. Just after the sun has set, at the moment when there is still ambient light in the sky but streetlights, car headlights, and building lights start to turn on, is the perfect moment to create a full nighttime effect. The dusk-for-night effect is achieved by shooting at dusk and underexposing your film 2 to 2½ stops. Your subject and the surrounding environment will appear dark, but visible, and those street-lamps, headlights, and building lights will glow the way they would at night. What's especially successful with dusk-for-night shooting is that there is still enough ambient light to illuminate building walls that would, at nighttime, be totally dark and indistinguishable. Even at 2 stops under, you will still see some detail, but if you were shooting at night with no lights, the side of an unlit building would appear as black space. Dusk never lasts long; you usually have a window of about only 25 minutes to get your shots and sometimes less depending on the season (Figure 13-42).

Shooting at Night

Given the startling developments in CCD sensitivity and film stocks (Els reaching 500 and even 800!), it is more possible than ever to actually shoot nighttime scenes at night with available light and small portable lighting units to create highlights and emphasis. Obviously, you cannot shoot a scene in a farm field under moonlight and expect to get an exposure, but if you keep your frame tight, shop window lights and bright street lamps can give you more than acceptable exposures. You can also augment these available sources with small, battery-powered lights. Nighttime shooting is tricky, and tests are especially recommended (Figure 13-43, *right*).

Magic Hour

The "*magic hour*" is that time just before sunrise and just after sunset when the Earth's atmosphere bounces the hidden sun's light, creating a diffused and luminous ambient light. People, objects, and landscapes look spectacular during magic hour. Although there is certainly enough light to get fine exposures, the problem with shooting during this time is that the window of opportunity, before night falls (evening magic hour) or daylight breaks through (morning magic hour), is very short. For most of the continental United States, magic hour lasts around 25 minutes, which makes for very limited shooting time, so it's not terribly convenient in terms of production schedules. The actual duration of magic hour depends on a location's latitude and time of year. One reason you see so many luminous shots of polar bears and penguins is that magic hour can last many hours in the Arctic region (Figure 13-43, *left*).

■ **Figure 13-42** Dusk for night shooting. Both images were shot at dusk, when some daylight remained but headlights and streetlights had turned on. The *left* frame was shot with the correct exposure, and the *right* image was taken two stops underexposed, giving the impression of night.

in practice

- *Magic hour.* In the 1978 film *Days of Heaven,* directed by Terrence Malick and photographed by Néstor Almendros, many of the scenes were famously shot during magic hour with no artificial lighting. The film is widely considered to be one of the most visually stunning films in the history of cinema. However, shooting extensively during magic hour severely limited the amount of time available per shooting day (according to Almendros, magic "hour" lasted around 25 minutes each day), so the production schedule was drastically extended, so much so that Almendros, contractually obligated to begin another film, had to leave the project before it was finished and the film was completed by another cinematographer, Haskell Wexler.

- *Shooting at night.* Gustavo Mercado's innovative short film *Yield* (2006) revolves around a brief but violent and ambiguous moment that is witnessed by a woman, the lead character. Trying to figure out exactly what happened, she recalls the moment three times and each time new clues begin to emerge—but we can't be sure if her memories, and the events of the film, are fact or selective perception. In one tense scene, the lead character meets up with a girl she perhaps saw brutalized earlier in the day; the scene takes place at a bus station late at night. Mercado was working fast, small, and with minimal equipment resources, so he carefully scouted for a location that, all on its own, had plenty of light to expose the film well, even in the late nighttime hours. He chose a sidewalk next to a rental car dealership that lit its expansive parking lot with very bright sodium streetlights. To this he added fill from two cheap, portable, battery-powered flood lights he bought at a hardware store. By using what was available in a resourceful way, Mercado was able, even without a generator, HMI movie lights, and a big crew, to create a stunning nighttime image to match this equally stunning moment in the film (**Figure 13-43**).

■ **Figure 13-43** Magic hour cinematography as seen in Malick's *Days of Heaven* (1978, *left*). A night scene shot at night from Mercado's *Yield* (2006, *right*).

■ BASIC LIGHTING AND GRIP EQUIPMENT

As I mentioned previously, film stocks and CCD chips are increasingly capable of shooting in low-light situations. Because of this, the need for huge, bulky, and high-powered lighting units has greatly diminished. For most lighting situations, a student shooting on EI 500, EI 320, or even EI 250 film, or shooting with an industrial grade DV camera, needn't employ any lights that consume more than 2,000 watts of power. Even at that, there is a dizzying array of lights available for low-budget film and DV production, with new ones being developed all of the time. It would be impossible to present them all in this book, but the following sections present some lighting units that are commonly used by students and low-budget independent filmmakers.

Lighting Units

Open-Faced Lights

Open-faced lights are units that consist of an open lamp (no lens) and a specular reflector system. Open-faced lights are a hard light source and act primarily as set lights (and occasionally as key lights) and are either used as a direct source or bounced to soften the beam. The **open-faced spot** is a common open-faced unit that has a movable lamp, allowing it to focus its throw somewhat from a broad to a more narrowly defined area.

Broads, which are open-faced lights with no spotting capability, simply deliver a hard, efficiently bright light. Both lights come in a variety of intensities from 250 watts to 2K (**Figure 13-44**).

Fresnels

Fresnels are one of the most common and versatile lighting units on a film set. What distinguishes a Fresnel is its unique lens and its movable lamp, which allows it to spot its beam with fair precision. Fresnels are named after Augustin Jean Fresnel, the French physicist who designed the shape of the lens. It was already known that plano-convex lenses had the ability to focus light rays and maintain intensity, but they are quite heavy, delicate, and retain a great deal of heat. Monsieur Fresnel simply cut this lens almost in half, but maintained the plano-convex contour by cutting the duplicate curvature into a series of concentric circles. This made the lens lighter and cooler but maintained its ability to focus the beam (**Figure 13-45**). Fresnels are rather hard lights, so the beam is controllable with flags or barndoors, though the textured lens does soften the light somewhat. Fresnels can be either tungsten lights (3,200°K) or HMIs (5,600°K). They also come in various sizes and wattages. The lower wattages (100 w to 650 w) and smaller lens sizes are used as specials and kickers. The medium wattages (650 w to 2 K) are commonly used to light people and can be a key light source. Large Fresnels (2 K to 10 K and large lenses) are used as large area key lights and set lights. Fresnels have specific nicknames depending on the intensity of their lamp and size of their lens. Some Fresnel units commonly used by students and independent filmmakers are **inkie** (100 w to 200 w, small lens), **midget** (500 w, small lens), **tweenie** (650 w, small lens), **baby** (1 K, medium lens, also called **ace**) and **junior** (2 K, medium or large lens, also called **deuce**). These terms are widely used, so you need to know them. On a professional set you'll rarely hear someone say, "Go to the truck and get me 650-watt light with a small lens." They just ask for a tweenie (**Figure 13-46**).

Soft Lights

Soft lights are units that do not throw the light beam directly from the lamp; rather, they emit reflected light. In a soft light, the lamp is nestled in a lamp housing and the beam reflects off the white interior of a **reflector shell,** creating an even and soft source. The larger the reflector shell, the more diffuse the light will be. Very diffuse soft lights are not practical for location shooting because of their girth. The output of a soft light is not particularly efficient, and they are used primarily as fill lights and occasionally as soft keys. Soft lights come in a variety of intensities (**Figure 13-47**); common wattages for small-scale shoots are 650 w, 1 K, and 2 K. Because of the large size of the reflector shell, soft lights can be cumbersome for small crews or tight spaces. When trying to stay light and agile, some filmmakers prefer to create their own soft light source by bouncing light from a hard light unit off a reflector umbrella, a bounce board, or a white wall.

The **Chinese lantern** is a specialized soft light rig that is used exclusively as a fill light. The design of Chinese lanterns is based on the popular collapsible paper lanterns, but the lighting rig that mimics that design is made from flame-resistant material. If you try using a real paper lantern, it will burn! By suspending a low-wattage tungsten lamp, usually 250 w, within a globe made of translucent, light-diffusing material, you have a lightweight soft

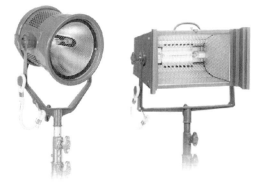

■ **Figure 13-44** The open-faced spot *(left)* has a movable lamp. Broads *(right)* are open-faced lights with no spotting capability. Both deliver a hard, efficient light.

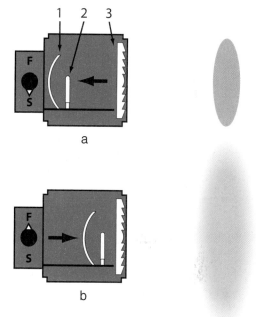

■ **Figure 13-45** Fresnels have a lens (3) that focuses the beam more effectively than open-faced lights. In the spot position (a), the bulb (2) and the reflector (1) are farther from the lens, creating a sharp beam. When flooded (b) the bulb and reflector are brought closer to the lens, creating a wider throw.

■ **Figure 13-46** Fresnel lights come in a variety of sizes and intensities. Shown here are a 220-watt inkie *(left)* and a 1-K baby *(right)*.

■ **Figure 13-47** Soft lights illuminate by bouncing light off some form of diffusing reflector. This Lowell ViP light uses a soft reflector umbrella *(left)* and the 2-K Baby Zip from Mole-Richardson *(right)* has a matte white reflector shell.

■ **Figure 13-48** Chinese lanterns provide a source of soft light, especially for close-ups on faces.

light that can be positioned nearly anywhere, notably much closer to the camera than a stand-alone soft light unit. Chinese lanterns provide a very soft fill that is especially useful for close-ups on faces (Figure 13-48).

Fluorescent Lights

Fluorescent lights are relative newcomers to the shooter's lighting arsenal. Instead of heating a filament to a white-hot point source, florescent lights generate their illumination by passing an electric charge through mercury gas trapped within a hollow tube, causing it to glow. Because of this construction, fluorescent lamps give off a very soft, flattering light. In addition, they are lightweight and draw very little power. Fluorescent units come is a wide variety of sizes, from large banks holding ten 48-inch fluorescent tubes, to tiny nook fixtures holding a single nine-inch fluorescent lamp capable of being tucked under a sun visor for night shots in cars (Figure 13-49). Fluorescent lights have many great advantages: they give off a lovely soft light, they burn cool, they draw very little power, and the units are lightweight and collapsible. Fluorescent lighting units can also be re-bulbed with lamps of various color temperatures, including 3,200°K and 5,600°K. The downside is that they are very delicate.

Reflectors

Reflectors (also called bounce boards) are not artificial lighting units per se, but I'm discussing them here because, as an illumination tool, they are as essential to a cinematographer as is any instrument that contains a lamp. As mentioned

■ **Figure 13-49** Fluorescent light banks *(left)* offer an extremely soft light source, which can be used as a fill light or a soft key. Small, battery-powered fluorescent tubes, like these miniflo lights *(right)* are often tucked into a car to replicate dashboard lights and provide illumination for a good exposure at night.

previously (page 292), reflectors are lightweight, portable surfaces that bounce light. Reflectors usually have two sides with different reflective qualities: a diffused surface (white) that simultaneously bounces and diffuses a hard light source and a specular side (silver or gold to warm the bounced light) that reflects and maintains the hard quality of the source (**Figure 13-50**).

Basic Grip Gear

Throughout the history of film, grips have been the people who make it all happen. The grips are the muscle behind the movie, and after spending enough time on professional sets you come to realize that phrases like "Sorry, but that can't be done" simply do not exist for a professional grip. If something must be lifted, held, propped up, moved, adjusted, or rigged, grips do it. Whatever it takes to accomplish the shot the way the director sees it, the grip will pull it off. Over time an entire arsenal of grip equipment has developed, often by inventive grips themselves, in order to make their jobs more efficient and the set safer. There is so much specialized grip equipment that it would be impossible to cover all of it here, but knowing some of the basic gear is important for knowing what your rigging possibilities are on a set.

■ **Figure 13-50** Reflectors are as essential as lighting units. Foam core reflects diffused light (attached to a C-stand on the left). A foldable reflector can bounce both diffused and hard light.

Stands

Light stands are what we usually position lighting units on, especially in field production. They are collapsible tripod units that have a telescoping center pole to raise and lower the angle of the light as necessary. **C-stands** are your all-purpose holder, used for hanging, holding, or positioning just about anything (**Figure 13-51**). They are heavy and stable and their three legs are at different heights, allowing you to place several C-stands, overlapping, side by side. Combined with a **gobo head** and **gobo arm** (or multiple gobo arms), C-stands become infinitely adjustable and versatile and can firmly hold virtually anything that is fairly lightweight, at any angle and at a wide range of heights.

Gear for Light Control

It should be apparent by now that, when lighting, we want to be able to carefully control where the light falls and where it does not. Blocking light to keep it from falling where you don't want it is called **trimming** the light, and it's easy to do with hard light units. Soft light, on the other hand, is difficult to trim. With the light rays scattering in all directions, soft light will not create the sharply defined shadow edge necessary for precise trimming. Light that falls where it should not is called **light spill**, and soft light tends to spill.

Barndoors are a standard addition to almost every lighting unit and are designed to help control the

■ **Figure 13-51** C-stands are all-purpose holders used on virtually all film shoots. Pictured: a cookie, a net, and a flag attached to three C-stands with the use of gobo arms and gobo heads.

in practice

Whether you're a director, a cinematographer or a gaffer, contemporary filmmaking requires that you be conversant with a wide range of lighting equipment and techniques that can achieve a range of aesthetic results. This doesn't always mean *more* stuff, often it means working successfully with less. Cinematographer Maryse Alberti is an example of a D.P. with consummate technical and aesthetic versatility. Her shooting credits include run-n-gun documentaries like Terry Zwigoff's *Crumb* (1994) and heavily stylized (heavily lit) narratives like Todd Haynes's *Velvet Goldmine* (1998). It was exactly this visual adaptability that made Darren Aronofsky seek her out to shoot *The Wrestler*; his 2008 film about an aging professional wrestler at the rock bottom of his career. The overall style of the film is starkly realistic and to achieve that effect Alberti shot with fast 16mm film for what she calls an "edgier" look than HD. She also went with 16mm because the lightweight cameras allowed her to shoot the film entirely handheld, giving the actors great freedom of movement. Even though much of the film is shot documentary style with available light, augmented by only a few or no additional lighting, some of the scenes, in fact, involved a great deal of theatrical style lighting (**Figure 13-52**).

■ **Figure 13-52** Cinematographer Maryse Alberti shot *The Wrestler* (Aronofsky, 2008) under a variety of lighting situations, including available fluorescents *(top)*, heavy artificial lighting *(center)*, and just one flashlight *(bottom)*.

Darren was interested that I could do a movie like Velvet Goldmine, *which was all about style, and I could really light, but also do a documentary, which I could light with very few tools. So applying that, I could really light a sequence if I had to, like the strip club. But the exteriors, I was not afraid to go with minimal lighting. In the supermarket, or the autograph signing, I just changed a few bulbs. That comes from the world of documentary. Sometimes you're in a place and you say, it looks good, you just have to change a bulb there, or turn something off there, and that's it, we're ready. There's a lightness, you're less encumbered by machines, so it's easier to go with an idea.*
From "Making *The Wrestler* Real" by David Schwartz (The Moving Image Source, February 13, 2009)

Early in the film, the central character, Randy "The Ram," is locked out of his trailer home after a match and must spend the night in his van. The scene was lit and shot entirely with a flashlight. That's the sort of bold choice which infuses *The Wrestler* not only with a sense of realism but also with great visual energy and immediacy. It is this sort of versatility and creative daring that makes Alberti such a sought after collaborator.

You have to master your tools and stay in the creative zone. It begins with knowing what you want your images to look like and why. We lit with everything from an 18K to just a flashlight that The Ram turns on after entering his van. That was the only light in that shot.
From "Cinematographers in action. Shooting 2008 Oscar Nominated Films" by Paulette Brandis, February 24, 2009, www.1000words.Kodak.com.

coverage of the beam. Barndoors fit onto the front of the lighting unit and consist of two or, usually, four foldable black metal leaves (**Figure 13-53**). Two leaves control the vertical and horizontal limits of the beam throw. Right behind barndoors, one can often use **scrims** to reduce the intensity of light. Scrims are wire mesh screens that fit directly in front of the lighting unit. The denser the wire mesh, the more light it cuts. A single scrim cuts the output of the unit by half a stop and a double scrim cuts it by one full stop. You can use multiple scrims to achieve the intensity you need.

When precise trimming is called for, we often used **flags**, which are free-standing frames covered with black felt, to sharply define where the light falls and where it doesn't. **Nets** are netting material stretched across a frame and, like scrims, are used purely to cut the intensity of light. Nets are designed to cut light by one, two, or three stops.

■ **Figure 13-53** Foldable barndoors like these are mounted on the front of most movie lights and help control where the unit's light falls.

Obviously you can reduce the intensity of light simply by moving it, but by placing the net over *part* of the beam, you can cut intensity on only a part of the scene. **Silks** are like nets, but the material is partly opaque, which not only cuts the light intensity, but diffuses it as well. **Gobo** is the general name given to anything that comes between a light source and the scene—that is, anything that throws a shadow pattern. One specific kind of gobo is a **cookie** (short for **cucoloris**), which is metal or foam core that has had shapes cut into it to create patterns on a wall, floor, or other surface (see **Figure 13-52**). Once I found myself shooting a scene with a single character against a white wall. The bare white wall appeared severe, overly bright, and flat, so I needed to throw some sort of vague, diffused shadow pattern against it to beak up the glare and give the image some dimension. With time running short I simply grabbed a C-stand, clamped a plastic milk crate (used to carry power cables) to it, and placed this in front of a slightly diffused light. The mesh of the milk-crate bottom cast a very soft crisscross pattern onto the wall. That's a gobo too, and one that worked well to improve the shot.

Like all specialized professions, film production has specific and often colorful terminology for its tools. The jargon isn't just to be cute: using the proper language, names, and common terms is essential to getting things done quickly and precisely. We certainly wouldn't want our heart surgeon to ask the nurse, "Uh, could you hand me that ... thing ... you know it's yea-long and has a hooklike end on it and it holds stuff." So, too, on the film set you shouldn't be vague by saying things like, "Could you point a light over there?" With a little reading and experience you'll soon be telling your grips, "Grab a stinger and set up that tweenie on a polecat. And let's lose the cookie and go with some spun, so make sure you have enough C-47s" (**Figure 13-54**).

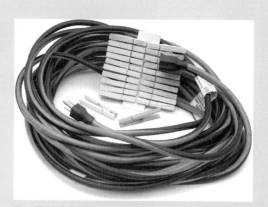

■ **Figure 13-54** Although these may look like wooden clothespins and an extension cord, filmmakers know them as "C-47s" and a "stinger."

■ **Figure 13-55** Polecats let you position lights in places where a light stand cannot be used.

■ **Figure 13-56** Securing cables with gaffer's tape prevents people from tripping on them.

Clamps

There are all sorts of clamps used to hold stuff on a film set, but there are two that can be of special use when it comes to placing lights. **Gator clamps** are heavy-duty spring clamps with rubber teeth to ensure a very tight grip on things like doors and tables, and **mafer clamps** are designed to lock onto pipes. Both clamps are built with posts to which you can attach a small light, like an inkie or a tweenie. These clamps allow you to position or hide small lights in uncommon places. **Polecats** are spring-tension, expandable poles, like a shower curtain rod, that are often used with mafer clamps for hanging lights in window frames, doorways, or narrow hallways (**Figure 13-55**).

Miscellaneous Grip Gear

A few of the other important items in a grip package would include the **stinger**, which is the on-set name for extension cord, **sandbags**, which are placed over the legs of C-stands and light stands to keep them from toppling over, and, of course, the indispensable gaffer's tape. **Gaffer's tape** is the all-purpose utility tape on a film set. Gaffer's tape rips easily into any width and length strip you need, it holds well, and it leaves no adhesive residue behind. It is especially useful for taping down cables (called **dressing cables**) to prevent people from tripping (**Figure 13-56**). Do not substitute common duct tape for gaffer's tape—even though it is much less expensive. Duct tape is designed to be permanent and will leave gum all over your equipment, and anything else it touches.

Given that lighting and grip personnel routinely deal with heavy equipment and thousands of watts of electricity, safety matters are a particular and constant concern. One should never set up a light, rig a jib arm, lay a cable, add a gel, or plug in a stinger without considering all the safety issues involved. Please see Chapter 18 for a discussion of safety on the set, including lighting and grip safety.

■ THE DITTY BAG

A *ditty bag* is a filmmaker's general utility tool kit and is filled with this, that, and the other thing that you might find useful on the set (**Figure 13-57**). Ditty bags are built over time, but here are a few standard items to get you started:

- Lens cleaning fluid/tissues
- Camera tape
- Paper tape
- Sharpies
- Canned air
- White-bristled brush
- Orange sticks
- Tape measure
- Cable ties
- Tweezers
- Magnifying glass
- Small scissors
- Mini-Maglite (penlight)
- AC circuit tester
- Leatherman tool or Swiss Army knife

- Jeweler's screwdriver set
- Screwdrivers: various sizes, regular and Phillips
- Pliers: regular and needle nose
- Allen wrench set
- AC plug adaptors (three-prong-to-two-prong with ground loop)
- Extra take-up cores/spools
- Extra batteries (AA, 9-volt, and whatever your microphones use)
- *American Cinematographer Manual* (or *Kodak Cinematographer's Field Guide*)
- Pencils and small note pad
- Leather grip gloves
- Emergency DV tape stock
- Second edition of *Voice & Vision*!

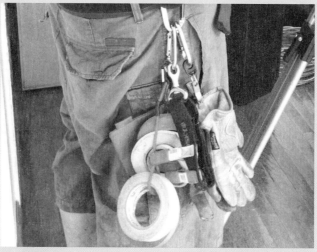

■ **Figure 13-57** A camera grip carrying almost everything he needs for a shoot—including tape, markers, gloves and clamps—right on his hip.

Lighting and Exposure: Beyond the Basics

Now that you are familiar with the fundamental concepts and techniques of exposure and lighting, which are applied everyday on every movie set, we can turn our attention to slightly more intricate issues related to image control. We need to look a little closer at how the film stock or the CCD chip itself actually responds to the various light values in a scene, beyond just its general sensitivity (i.e., exposure index [EI]). Two additional concepts are essential to a more advanced understanding of lighting and exposure for both film and DV: contrast range and exposure range.

■ CONTRAST RANGE AND EXPOSURE RANGE

Contrast range (also called **luminance range**) is the difference between the brightest and the darkest significant areas of your scene. Remember, "bright" and "dark" consist of a combination of incident light intensity and reflectance values. Contrast range can be expressed either in terms of a ratio or in terms of the f-stops difference between the two luminance extremes. For example, it is not unusual to discover, through multiple light meter readings, that a scene's lightest area is 16 times brighter than its darkest area. We can express this as a contrast ratio of 16:1 or as a contrast range of four f-stops. Why? Remember that each stop is a halving or doubling of brightness, so four stops from darkest to brightest is $2 \times 2 \times 2 \times 2 = 16$. It should be noted that four stops is a relatively narrow contrast range. In a complexly lit scene, it's not usual to have a contrast range of 256:1, or eight stops or even more (**Figure 14-1**). One central question concerns how much of this contrast range our film stock or DV sensor can faithfully reproduce.

Broadly defined, **exposure range** (sometimes called **dynamic range for DV**) is the range of luminance values your specific imaging device (film stock or video sensor) can render with detail before falling off into complete overexposure (**blown out** or **clipped whites**) or complete underexposure (**crushed blacks**), where no image detail is visible. Exposure

■ **Figure 14-1** In this scene from Godard's *Masculin Feminin* (1966), we have an example of a wide contrast range *(left)*, where the street outside the café is extremely bright compared to the darker areas inside. In the kitchen *(right)*, there is very little variation between the tonalities, producing a narrow contrast range for this scene.

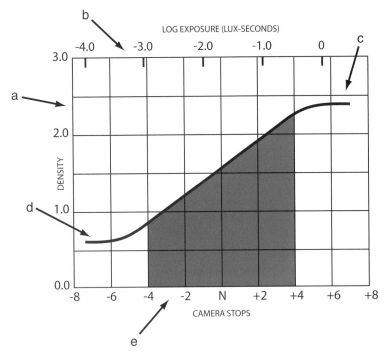

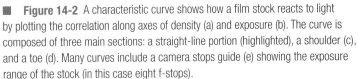

■ **Figure 14-2** A characteristic curve shows how a film stock reacts to light by plotting the correlation along axes of density (a) and exposure (b). The curve is composed of three main sections: a straight-line portion (highlighted), a shoulder (c), and a toe (d). Many curves include a camera stops guide (e) showing the exposure range of the stock (in this case eight f-stops).

range is expressed in terms of stops (i.e., the range of stops within which the imaging device will see detail). It is often the case that the contrast range of a scene exceeds the exposure range of your imaging device, which means that visual detail will be lost in the brightest or darkest parts of your scene, or both. Different film stocks and different DV formats have different abilities to render detail in bright or dark areas of the image; some fall off into total overexposure (blown out white) and total underexposure (crushed black) sooner than others. So if we want to truly control our image, it's important to know both the contrast range of the scene we are shooting and the ability of our imaging device to render those exposure values. Once we know this, we can use lighting to selectively bring areas of our scene into or out of the exposure range of the imaging device to create visual emphasis and interest.

Although the broader concepts of contrast range and exposures are the same for DV and film, the practical application of these concepts plays out very differently, again, because in video, we are able to actually see the true response of our imager (CCD or CMOS) while we are lighting and shooting, especially when we are using a good-quality field monitor. In film, however, careful metering and understanding the exposure range of your specific film stock is essential in order to anticipate and control the final image, which you cannot see until after processing.

Film Stocks: Latitude and Characteristic Curves

There are many different film stocks on the market, each designed for a different shooting situation; there are slow films (EI 50), fast films (EI 500), negative films, reversal films, and color and black-and-white films. Each specific film stock responds to light in a unique way, and that response is plotted on a graph called the characteristic curve. The **characteristic curve** (also called **sensitometric curve**) is a graphical representation of the way a particular film stock responds to light. In a sense it represents that film stock's personality. As we discussed in the section on film stocks and processing (page 181), exposing film is a matter of creating a thicker or thinner silver halide density, depending on the brightness of an object and length of exposure. This is precisely what the characteristic curve measures (**Figure 14-2**).

The vertical axis of the scale measures the thickness of the silver halide **density**, called "**D**," and the horizontal scale measures the exposure increments in lux-seconds, called **log-e**. The log-e scale is commonly translated into a more useful **camera stop** scale on the graph, and that's what we'll use for our discussion. Keep in mind that the graph shown in **Figure 14-2** is for a negative film stock, meaning the light values are reversed from the actual values in the scene. So the range of the "D" scale, as we trace the curve from left to right, goes from **D-min** (complete underexposure) to **D-max** (complete overexposure). D-min means no silver halide crystals were exposed (not enough light and/or exposure time) and the negative image is pure white with no detail. D-max tells us that this area received a great deal of exposure (too much light), which means that the silver halide density is so thick that it registers on the negative as pure black. The straight line between these two luminance extremes (total underexposure and total overexposure) is called, no surprise, the **straight-line portion**, and it shows us the proportional response of the film (density) to exposure. The steady and pre-dictable increase of density/luminance values is in response to an increase in exposure. Exposures that fall along the straight-line portion will show full image detail. The straight-line portion is of primary importance because it tells us the range of f-stops within which a particular film stock can render image detail before fall-ing off into pure white, total overexposure (D-max), and pure black, total underexposure (D-min). The straight-line portion represents a film stock's **latitude**, which is the range of exposure values (brightness values) a film stock can render with substantial accuracy. The longer the straight-line portion of the curve, the more latitude (and therefore the greater exposure range) the film stock has, which means the greater its capacity to "see" detail in the bright and dark areas. On a char-acteristic curve that lists camera stops along the hori-zontal axis, we can easily see how many stops range a film stock has. "N" stands for middle gray normally exposed. Simply find the exact ends of the straight por-tion of the curve, *before* it starts to flatten out, and you can determine how many stops you have where detail will be visible as you move through the various degrees of under-and overexposure. The straight-line portion in Figure 14-2 (blue highlight) shows that with this film stock we will see substantially accurate detail from four stops underexposure to four stops overexposure—a latitude of eight stops.

Negative film stocks typically have a latitude of 8 to 9 stops, meaning around 4 to 4½ stops on either side of "N." However, in film, complete under or overexposure don't occur abruptly, like falling off a cliff. The straight-line portion ends where the exposure detail gradu-ally tapers off, but there is still some visual detail here. Because of this, cinematographers also include the usable range within those curved areas *before* D-min and D-max, which are called the **toe** and **shoulder**, respectively, in order to determine the *total* exposure range of the stock (Figure 14-3). However, the toe and

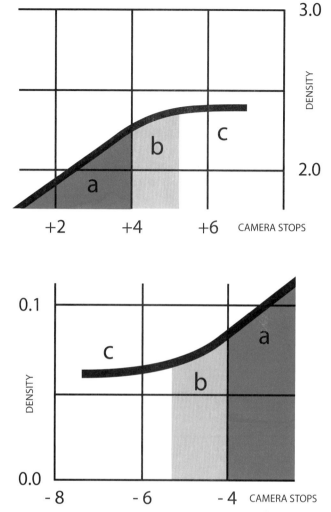

■ **Figure 14-3** The curve of the shoulder *(top)* and the toe *(bottom)* reflect the unequal relationship between density and exposure. When density remains unchanged in the shoulder (c), we have complete overexposure, or D-max. When density remains unchanged in the toe (c), we have complete underexposure, or D-min. Before each of those extremes is extra usable exposure (b), which is not as predictable as the straight-line exposure range (a).

shoulder areas can be tricky. Their curvature tells us that there will still be *some* image detail just before total underexposure (in dark shadows) and total overexposures (bright highlights), but because the film does not respond to light proportionally here (unlike the straight-line portion), it takes some experience to really know what those areas will yield. By including the toe and shoulder we can add another 2 or 3 stops to our latitude — or more, depending on the specific stock — to determine our total exposure range. So the **exposure range** of a film stock is a combination of the film's straight-line portion (latitude) *plus* the usable range within the toe and shoulder areas. An average color negative film stock's usable exposure range (latitude plus toe and shoulder) is around 10 to 13 stops. Reversal film stock and fast film stocks generally have less range than slower stocks and negative film.

Gamma

Closely related to latitude and exposure range is gamma. **Gamma** (also called **contrast**) represents the capacity of a film stock to differentiate between the various luminance tonalities (shades of gray) in a scene and is represented by the angle of the straight-line portion—in other words, the steepness of the slope. The ideal angle for a straight line would be a perfect 45°, meaning a perfectly proportional increase in density to exposure. This would faithfully duplicate all of the subtle shifts in the gray scale (**Figure 14-4**). Although many color negative film stocks come close, no film has yet reached this ideal. The steeper the angle of the straight-line portion, the more contrasty the film is and the fewer shades of luminance it can differentiate. All films go from absolute black to absolute white, so the steeper the slope is, the fewer stops and tonal ranges will exist between these two extreme poles. Reversal film stock and fast film stocks generally have a steeper gamma slope and have more contrast. Slower stocks and negative film usually reproduce a broader range of subtle luminance values. More or less contrast is not the basis for a value judgment about a film stock. Some movies can benefit aesthetically from a high-contrast look (**Figure 14-5**). In fact, given the substantial gamma capabilities of today's negative film stocks, it's quite common for a filmmaker to push film one or two stops (see page 308) to intentionally shift the inherent gamma angle to create more contrast in the negative (**Figure 14-6**).

An additional detail of the characteristic curve that is greatly affected by the angle of the curve slope is the toe and shoulder. When the straight-line portion of the curve is steep, the angles of the toe and shoulder become more acute, which means that the drop into pure white and pure black (D-max and D-min) is more precipitous than with the gently curving toe and shoulder of a lower contrast stock. With high-contrast film, one will see much less into the shadows and highlights of the image, because they plunge more easily into total

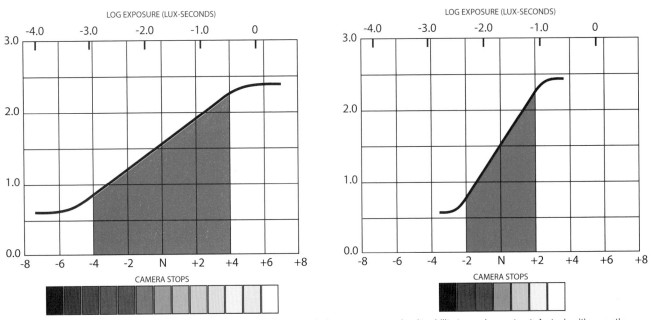

Figure 14-4 The steepness of the curve represents the stock's particular gamma, meaning its ability to render contrast. A stock with a gentle slope has lower contrast *(left)*; it can render more shades of gray. A steep curve *(right)* indicates a stock with a high contrast; it can only render a few shades of gray.

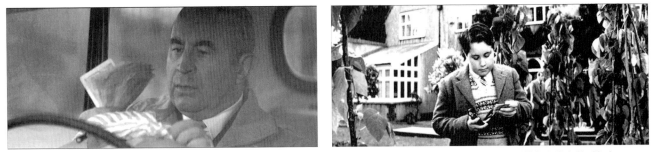

Figure 14-5 Egoyan's *Felicia's Journey* (1999) abruptly changes from a low-contrast to a high-contrast stock when Hilditch (Bob Hoskins) reminisces about his childhood and his domineering mother.

under- and overexposure. This clearly has ramifications for determining the total exposure range of a film stock, which includes toe and shoulder areas.

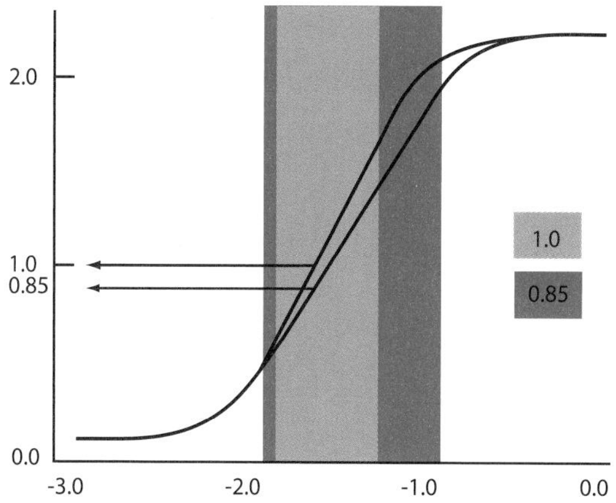

So far, for the sake of simplicity, the characteristic curves we've been looking at have been for black-and-white negative film. Characteristic curves for reversal films, in which the film densities and tonalities are the same as the actual scene, are completely reversed—with D-max representing black areas and D-min representing pure white areas in the image (Figure 14-7, *right*). The characteristic curve graph for a color film stock includes three curves, each one representing a different emulsion layer in the color tripack (see page 183). Each emulsion layer, red, green, and blue, responds to light slightly differently, so each gets its own curve for analysis (Figure 14-7, *left*). Notice how the blue layer is the most sensitive to light.

Quite often, filmmakers select their film stock based on something as simple as exposure index, especially when the lighting situation is somewhat inflexible. For example, when access to artificial lighting is limited and shooting is planned for interiors, one might need to simply go with the fastest film stock available. Other times a filmmaker will approach film selection based on the unique color attributes or the grain structure of the stock. Also, it's not unusual to hear cinematographers speak about exposure range and gamma as one of the deciding factors for their film stock selection. Then, of course, there are the times when filmmakers shoot with film that was given to them or could be purchased inexpensively. When I was a student, my first two movies were made on film stock donated by a production company that had some extra rolls lying around. No matter what criterion (or method) you use in acquiring your film, make sure to study its characteristic curve, which can usually be found on a manufacturer's website.

■ **Figure 14-6** A shift in a stock's gamma (in this case by "pushing" the stock during development from 0.85 to 1.0) can radically alter its contrast. A higher gamma practically shortens the straight-line portion of the curve and increases contrast.

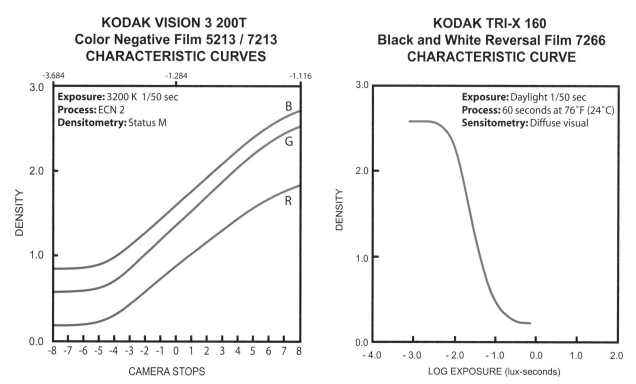

■ **Figure 14-7** A color negative stock has a characteristic curve with three lines, one for each layer of its emulsion *(left)*. Curves for reversal stocks show an inverse relationship between density and exposure, because the image they render is positive, not negative *(right)*.

This basic discussion of the characteristic curve will certainly get you off to a running start, but there is much more to say about how we read a characteristic curve and what it tells us about the way a particular film stock responds to light. I have suggested some additional texts in the Recommended Readings list for a deeper study into the technology and techniques of motion picture photography that would be essential for anyone interested in developing their skills as a cinematographer. And, of course, there is no book as instructive as plain ol' experience, so get out there and shoot, shoot, shoot.

■ WHAT IS PUSHING FILM?

Pushing film (or **push processing**) is a common exposure tactic when we need a little extra film speed to shoot in low-light situations or when we want to intentionally add contrast to our image. Say we're using a film stock with a rating of EI 100 but discover there isn't enough light for a good exposure. Pushing the film one stop means pretending that the film in your camera (EI 100) is twice as sensitive (EI 200) and we set our light meter for that doubled sensitivity and proceed with shooting. Obviously, that film is then one stop underexposed. However, when we send this film to the lab for processing we indicate on the film can label to "push one stop." The lab will process that film longer than normal to compensate for the underexposure. This compensation has the additional effect of increasing grain and contrast in the resulting image. We can push film one, two, three, or even four stops. With each increase the processing time gets longer and the image gets more contrasty. Keep in mind that you cannot push only selected shots. You must push entire rolls of film because the entire roll remains in the chemical processing soup longer.

Putting Latitude, Exposures, and Lighting to Work

Great; so now that we know what latitude is and how we determine the exposure range of our specific film stock, how do we use it? Let's say that we are shooting a simply lit scene with a black-and-white negative stock that has a latitude of 8 stops, 4 stops over and 4 stops under (straight-line portion only) with an extra 1 stop of useful range in both the toe and shoulder for a full exposure range of 10 stops (as in **Figures 14-2 and 14-3**). In reality, you will usually get a fraction more in overexposures than in underexposures, but for the sake of simplifying the example, I'll keep everything to full stops.

Knowing the film's exposure range, I can set out to light my scene. There are five steps to lighting a scene after you've established your basic framing: (1) rough-in the essential lights, (2) measure the exposures, (3) visualize and evaluate the options, (4) peg the exposure, and (5) complete the lighting.

The scene I'm lighting in **Figure 14-8** is an intense chess matchup between Sandor Latzko *(middle),* the great-grandson of chess Grandmaster and legend György Latzko, and Chip *(right),* the sweet, dopey boyfriend of Sandor's daughter Nicole *(left).* Chip stopped by to pick Nicole up for a date when Sandor challenged him to a game, forcing Nicole to wait. In this master shot, Chip is playing some cunning moves, while Sandor feels the pressure of an impending loss to a boy he thinks isn't good enough for his daughter. Sandor is the central character here, as it's his authority as a chess player and parent at stake, but the boy's guileless expression and Nicole's impatience are also important because they add extra pressure to Sandor's situation. So with these three focal points in mind (Sandor, Nicole, and Chip), let's go through the steps:

1. *Rough in the essential lights.* A roughed-in lighting setup is usually little more than the key light and maybe some quick fill. All lights are set up later in relation to the key light and its exposure value. In this case my key is natural light that is already there, the sun streaming into the room through a window (though it could easily be a 2-K Fresnel set up just outside the window). The walls of the room are off white, so they provide some natural fill on their own, but the vestibule where Nicole stands gets none of the direct light and very little of the bounced illumination. I'll start my evaluation just with this available light.

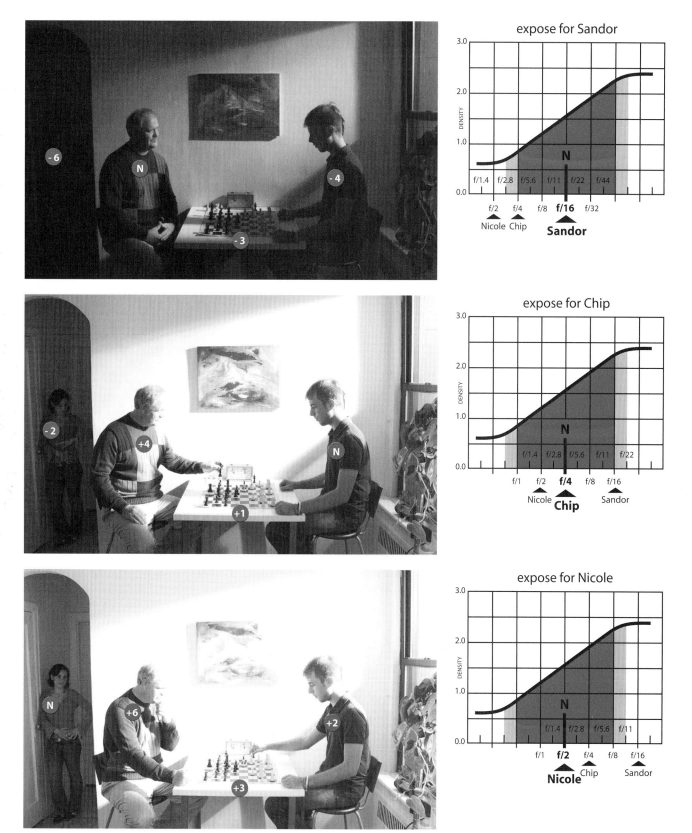

✋ ■ **Figure 14-8** A typical scene will comprise a number of f-stops. In this scene, the darkest area, f/2, and brightest area, f/16, give us a contrast range of six stops. How this scene will be recorded depends on the range of f-stops our stock can handle. Setting the aperture to expose correctly for Sandor *(top)*, Chip *(center)*, or Nicole *(bottom)* causes other areas in the image to fall outside the film's latitude. (Go to www. voiceandvisionbook.com to see this figure in high resolution.)

2. *Measure the exposures.* The next step is to measure the scene thoroughly with a light meter to determine the **contrast range**, which is the range of incident light intensities within the scene. I will pay particular attention to areas that are compositional focal points. Through multiple light meter readings I have determined that the brightest parts of the scene are Sandor's face (focal point), the wall, and the back of Chip's neck, which are all illuminated by the same key source. These areas will be "properly exposed" at f/16. The darkest area of the scene is the vestibule where Nicole waits (focal point), which yields an exposure reading of f/2. There is a difference of 6 stops between these two meter readings, so we say that the contrast range in this scene is 6 stops. All of the other exposure values fall between these poles, like Chip's face (focal point), which is on the shadow side of the key light and reads f/4. The chessboard, which is mostly in Chip's shadow, but getting bounced light from the wall, reads f/5.6. In summary: Sandor = f/16; Chip = f/4; Nicole = f/2; chessboard = f/5.6

3. *Visualize and evaluate the options.* Knowing the latitude of my film and the "normal" exposure for each area in the scene, I can now visualize the scene with some accuracy. This means imagining different f-stop choices and how they will affect the various areas of my scene. You certainly don't need to imagine every possible f-stop, but you do need to know the dramatic context of the scene you are exposing. So ask yourself: Who and what are important in the scene? Where do I want to place visual emphasis? What might I want to expose "normally?" "What's the tone and stylistic approach to the film?" When you hypothetically choose an f-stop setting, you will then be able to imagine how all of the other areas in the scene will be exposed relative to that choice.

As I mentioned earlier, the main character in the scene in Sandor, so I'd like him to be brightest in the scene. No problem there, but I need to see some of Chip's goofy expression and Nicole waiting impatiently in order to realize the pressure that Sandor is under. Also, I'd like there to be a naturalistic feel to this scene—meaning I'd like it to seem like there are no other lights illuminating this space other than the sunlight, direct and bounced. So let's take a look at what happens if I choose to expose for each one of my three focal points, keeping in mind that I have only 4 stops latitude on either side of normal exposure.

■ Shooting at f/16: Sandor's exposure (**Figure 14-8**, *top*).
  ■ Sandor: Sandor is receiving lots of natural light from the window. Shooting at f/16 will expose Sandor's face correctly. This is good, but I lose some of the sense of a brilliantly bright sunny day at this exposure. Only okay.
  ■ Chessboard: The chessboard is 3 stops underexposed. This is within my latitude so there is some visible detail, but in the shadow side it's kind of dark which might not be so good because they're playing chess and the actions could get lost. Passable, but not best.
  ■ Chip: Chip's face is in shadows created by the sun behind his back and f/16 puts Chip 4 stops underexposed, right at the limit of my film's latitude. I still have a little extra exposure range within the toe of the curve, but his face is nonetheless quite dark and facial detail will be murky or lost. Keeping him this dark adds a degree of dark mystery about him, which is definitely not part of my scenario. Not good.
  ■ Nicole: Standing in the darkest area of the scene Nicole is 6 stops underexposed, that's 2 stops beyond my 4-stop latitude, 1 stop past the usable exposure range and therefore well into the D-min part of the curve, so I won't be able to see her at all—the vestibule turns into a dark and ominous void. Not good.
■ Shooting at f/4: Chip's exposure (**Figure 14-8**, *center*).
  ■ Sandor: Sandor is now 4 stops overexposed, right at the edge of the shoulder. That's way too bright. I'll lose some detail in his face and the hot spots on his forehead may start to blend in with the wall. The wall as well (at f/16 and dead center in my composition) will scream. Not good.
  ■ Chessboard: The board is 1 stop overexposed and starting to glow quite bright. Okay.

- ■ Chip: Chip's face is exposed correctly. But he's secondary to Sandor in terms of dramatic emphasis. It also might seem strange for the shadow side of his face to be perfectly exposed while the back of his neck blows out into extreme overexposure. Passable, but not so good.
- ■ Nicole: I can see Nicole! At 2 stops under (well within the film's latitude) she's a little dark, but that's what we'd expect in a vestibule sheltered from the sun. I like this. Good.

■ Shooting at f/2: Nicole's exposure (**Figure 14-8**, *bottom*). This is bad all around. Shooting at f/2 makes Sandor 6 stops overexposed, out of the exposure range of my film and into D-max. I'll lose a lot of his facial features as they blend in with the blanched out wall (both blown out). Chip's face is only 2 stops overexposed, but the back of his neck will also merge with the blown-out wall. I even start to bleach out the tabletop and painting. Not good at all.

4. *Peg the exposure.* **Pegging your f-stop** simply means deciding on the specific f-stop you're going to use for the shot. That decision, in effect, pegs a "normal exposure" (N) f-stop to the center of the characteristic curve (where middle gray will be exposed correctly) and all other values and f-stops fall relative to that. So what f-stop will I go with for this scene? I choose to shoot at f/11. It's the f-stop that brings my overall scene closest to what I'm after and best utilizes my lovely natural key light making it appear bright and strong, but not blinding. This f/stop puts Sandor 1 stop overexposed. With sunlight pouring right on him, I think it would feel right for him (and the wall) to be slightly hot in the scene; it will also accentuate the notion that he's "sweatin' it" in this surprisingly tough game against the kid. Now that I've chosen my f/stop I can go about fixing with lights those areas that have exposure problems. Because I've thoroughly evaluated all of these areas, I know where their exposures fall given f/11 as "normal" and have a good sense for what light I'll need to add or subtract to fix them. Let's take a look.

5. *Complete the lighting.* My approach to lighting this scene will be to maintain a naturalistic look, using the motivation of my strong natural key light and the soft light that would naturally be bouncing around the room. So I'll be using artificial lights to augment the natural light to achieve a naturalistic look. It's the kind of thing we do all the time in film.

The problem areas, according to our evaluation, are Chip (now 3 stops underexpose) and Nicole in the vestibule (now 5 stops underexposed and just out of my exposure range). The chessboard is only 2 stops underexposed, which I think is appropriate for being in Chip's shadow.

To "fix" the scene, I would first add a very soft fill on Chip's face to bring his exposure up 1½ stops to an f/5.6–8 split (1½ stops under normal exposure, but 2½ stops under Sandor's brightness). This will give me more facial detail but keep him on the dark side as we would expect given the direction of the light. Adding more light than that would seem artificial, because his back is to the window and we expect his face to be somewhat in shadow. This soft fill is motivated by the off-white walls of the room. I could use a small soft light unit, but with such nice sunlight streaming in I discover that I can simply use a diffused bounce board off-screen to kick some sunlight back at Chip. In either case, I must be careful not to cast shadows behind Chip or spill more light onto Sandor, because I don't want to boost his exposure level.

I do the same with Nicole, a soft fill to boost the vestibule as if she's getting some of the bounced sunlight as well. I definitely want to bring her well into my exposure range so I can see her, but I definitely do not want to make her too bright because (1) she's in a shadowy corner and (2) if I equalize the exposures I flatten the image and lose the nice depth that the dark vestibule gives the composition. So I'm going to add enough soft fill to bring Nicole up 2 stops, to f/4. At the pegged f-stop of f/11, this makes her 3 stops underexposed but well within the latitude of my film, so her figure and details will be visible, but she'll appear to be in shadows, as we expect. I'll accomplish this with a small Fresnel off-screen left using heavy diffusion (**Figure 14-9**).

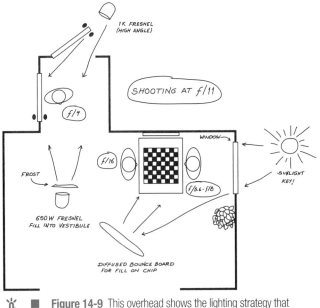

1K FRESNEL
(HIGH ANGLE)

SHOOTING AT f/11

f/4

WINDOW

f/16

FROST

SUNLIGHT
KEY!

f/5.6 - f/8

650W FRESNEL
FILL INTO VESTIBULE

DIFFUSED BOUNCE BOARD
FOR FILL ON CHIP

 ■ **Figure 14-9** This overhead shows the lighting strategy that addresses the exposure problems we had. We now can shoot our scene with the knowledge that all critical areas will fall within the film's latitude.

Okay, exposures are all good, but I still have a problem, Nicole and the vestibule are lit only with fill and it's flat and uninteresting. I imagine cutting to a close-up of Nicole checking her watch and I see bland lighting creating bland skin. So I look at my space and I notice a door behind Nicole leading to another room. If I open that door, the same sunlight that is illuminating the main room will spill into the vestibule. This will give Nicole's shoulders a nice rim light and the light falling on the wall behind her will providing some dimension and snap to her side of the composition. So I open the door and discover that there are no windows in the room behind her. No problem, I set up a 1 K, keep the light hard, and create the sunlight spill *as if* a window were in there. This light must be up fairly high so that it appears to be coming from the same angle as the key light. But wait! Now when I take a reading off Nicole it reads f/5.6 (too bright). What happened? The additional light I set up behind her has also created additional fill in the vestibule, so I need to use a single scrim to lower the intensity of the off-camera fill by half to bring her exposure back down to f/4. *Keep in mind that adding or subtracting light can have repercussions for the other lights already set up.*

Okay, now with all lighting problems solved, I'm ready to shoot (**Figure 14-10**). I laid this little example out in a very methodical way, but in reality, when you're lighting a scene, it's usually not quite this neat; there is a lot of back and forth, constant remeasuring, and comparisons and reevaluation of exposure values. You might add lights that don't work aesthetically, or in fixing one area you might spill light into another area, or you might get new ideas as you go along. Also, keep in mind that sometimes we peg an f-stop for reasons other than accommodating an exposure range. For example, if the dominant visual approach to the scene is to have a deep depth of field, then we might start with f/16 as our f-stop and light specifically for that.

The latitude and exposure range of a particular film stock (how it reacts to various exposure values) are so critical that most film manufacturers provide original negative

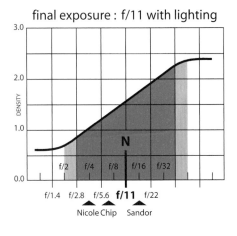

final exposure : f/11 with lighting

 ■ **Figure 14-10** The final scene shot at f/11 and incorporating some lighting, which keeps Sandor, Chip, and Nicole within the film's latitude, yet with a range of appropriate exposures for a naturalistic look. (Go to www.voiceandvisionbook.com to see this figure in high resolution.)

exposure samples for each film stock they sell. This allows you to see for yourself the look and response of a particular film stock. The image used in the exposure samples usually includes a wide range of incident light intensities and objects with various reflectance values (**Figure 14-11**).

Reflectance Values and Exposure Range

In the preceding example, I used an incident meter exclusively. This is the primary metering instrument on film sets, but we know that contrast range and true luminance values also include the reflectance of objects, not just the incident light intensity. Most of the time, incident readings, will give you enough information to imagine how bright or dark that part of the scene will appear on film once you've pegged your normal exposure f/stop. The more film you shoot, the more predictable and intuitive exposures will be. But in some cases, where luminance values are critical, you may want a more accurate assessment. This is where a spot meter and the zone system chart are useful (see pages 258-259).

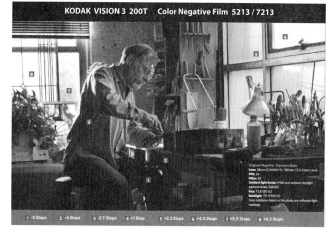

■ **Figure 14-11** Kodak provides "original exposure data" examples for their stocks, letting consumers see how they react to an array of exposure values, including normal (N) over (+) and under (–) exposures. See the color insert.

Let's look at Nicole in the vestibule again. She appropriately remains the darkest area of our frame and we're intentionally underexposing her three stops. This is close to the edge of my latitude so I need to know better how this underexposure will appear, especially given her wardrobe. The choice of a white shirt, a gray sweater, or black jacket will end up looking quite different even given the same incident meter reading, and this will have a huge impact on how Nicole will appear. Clearly, a spot meter reading off her wardrobe will help give us a better idea of the exposure options in this case.

In the final fixed scene (figure 14-10), Nicole is wearing a sweater that is close to middle gray in color (zone V). So a spot meter reading off Nicole's sweater will yield the same result as the incident meter (f/4). When we expose for Nicole at f/4, the sweater looks middle gray. If she were to switch to a black jacket (zone I), it would fall four stops/zones from middle gray and detail in the jacket would be visible. If she were to switch to a white shirt (zone IX), it would fall four stops/zones brighter and the detail would be visible. Finally, Nicole's Caucasian skin (around zone VII) falls between middle gray and white (**Figure 14-12**, *top*). However, when we underexpose Nicole three stops at our pegged aperture of f/11, all these reflectance values shift, so that the white shirt now falls to zone VI, her skin is around zone IV, the middle gray sweater falls to zone II and that black jacket falls right off the zone chart. Notice that her face retains some visual detail (consistent in each shot) and the "white" shirt has lots of detail, but there is no detail in the jacket whatsoever; we can't even detect where her arm crosses her body. It is not the incident light intensity that has pushed her out of the film's exposure range, but the reflectance value of her jacket. It's just a D-min blob (**Figure 14-12**, *bottom*).

An understanding of reflectance values plays an important role in questions of art direction and exposure, it's possible to have an incident reading that remains within your exposure range, but the reflectance value of an object can nonetheless fall outside that range or at least show up in a different way than you had expected. Also, a black jacket, gray sweater, and white shirt are easy enough to figure out, even without a spot meter, but what if Nicole were wearing an orange sweater? Spot meters are very valuable in determining the reflectance values of colored objects, like a green apple, a red suitcase, and a blue jean jacket, and placing them onto the zone scale. These are the reasons that make selective spot metering a regular procedure on film sets when knowing precise luminance values is crucial.

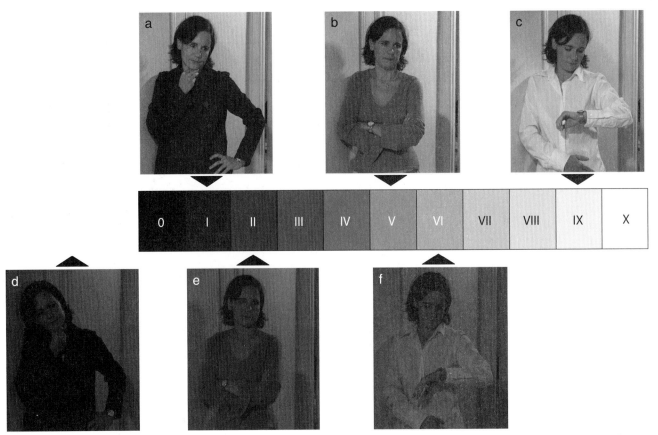

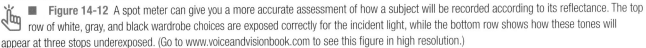

■ **Figure 14-12** A spot meter can give you a more accurate assessment of how a subject will be recorded according to its reflectance. The top row of white, gray, and black wardrobe choices are exposed correctly for the incident light, while the bottom row shows how these tones will appear at three stops underexposed. (Go to www.voiceandvisionbook.com to see this figure in high resolution.)

Film Latitude and Exposure Latitude

As we mentioned previously, **film latitude** can be simply defined as the range of brightness values a film stock can accurately render as represented by the straight-line portion of the characteristic curve. Here is the definition from the Kodak Glossary of Film Terms, which expresses the same thing: "The range of exposure over which substantially correct reproduction is obtained. When the process is represented by an H & D curve [characteristic curve], the latitude is the projection on the exposure axis of that part of the curve that approximates a straight line."

However, this term should not be confused with another, very closely related term: exposure latitude. Again, according to the Kodak Glossary **exposure latitude** is "the degree to which film can be underexposed or overexposed and still yield satisfactory results." By "yield satisfactory results" they mean that an acceptable image (no blown-out whites or crushed blacks) can be attained from this over or underexposed film when transferring or printing to another medium (like making a film print or video transfer). Exposure latitude is determined somewhat by the inherent latitude of the film stock, but it also is determined significantly by the contrast range of the brightness values in the scene. For example, if your film's latitude is 10 stops and you are shooting a scene with a narrow contrast range of 1 stop (say a middle gray card taped to a middle gray wall), you can underexpose that shot 5 stops or overexpose that image 5 stops (each side of normal) and you will be able to "fix" the exposure error in the transfer. In this case you have an exposure latitude of 10 stops. But if you are shooting a scene with a wide contrast range of 8 stops (say a room with a dark vestibule and a window overlooking sunny hills), then you will only have 2 stops of exposure latitude (1 stop under and one stop over) before you exceed the ability of the film stock to render any detail at all in portions of the image. Some people refer to exposure latitude as an emulsion's "room for error" or "range of forgiveness." But my advice is to just control your lighting and exposures and you won't need to rely on the ability of a film stock to forgive your errors.

in practice

Many of the terms in this chapter sound very much alike, and this can cause some confusion, so here's a cheat sheet for four terms that frequently get mixed up:

Contrast range. The difference between the brightest and the darkest significant areas of your scene, expressed as a ratio or as a range of f-stops.

Exposure range. The full range of luminance values an imaging device can render before falling off into complete overexposure or complete underexposure where no image detail is visible. For film, the exposure range is equal to the film latitude *plus* the

usable range in the toe and shoulder of the characteristic curve. In video, exposure range is often called **dynamic range**.

Film latitude. The range of exposure values a film stock can render with substantial and predictable detail as represented by the straight-line portion of the characteristic curve.

Exposure latitude. The degree to which film can be underexposed or overexposed and still yield acceptable results in postproduction transfer or printing through exposure adjustment.

Dynamic Range and Digital Video

Dynamic range (the same as exposure range for film) is one of the central issues that comes up when people compare film and DV images. By now, the reader should know that I'm not a big fan of making value judgments based on film and DV comparisons, because I believe each has its own aesthetic characteristics and a unique and valuable place in filmmaking. Nonetheless, we will build from our understanding of film latitude and exposure range (read the previous sections if you have not yet done so) to discuss dynamic range and the video image, so some objective comparison is helpful. It is true that while DV (especially high-definition video) frequently improves its dynamic range specifications substantially; film manufacturers have answered the challenge with film stocks of unprecedented sensitivity and exposure range. In all likelihood, we will continue to see this game of one-upmanship continue for some time, while we filmmakers reap the benefits of better and better images in both systems.

At this point it's fair to say that the dynamic range of standard definition (SD) video is somewhere around 5 to 6 stops of luminance values before it falls into **clipped whites** and **crushed blacks**. With the SD format quickly phasing out in favor of high-definition video (HD), even on the consumer level, there will likely be no more improvements for SD. The ultra-high-end D-Cinema video cameras (those recording RAW 4:4:4, 2-K to 4-K images with 35mm sensors) can stand toe-to-toe with any film stock on the market in terms of dynamic range and ability to see into shadows and detail. Midlevel and professional HD cameras (those shooting 1080i/p on ½-inch or ⅔-inch CCD sensors with 4-2-2 color sampling) have an average dynamic range of around 9 to 10 stops before the whites clip and the blacks get crushed. Compared with an average negative films' 11 to 13 stops exposure range, that's significantly narrower. However, depending on your camera model, most reasonably high-end HD cameras have a few tricks up their sleeves that can electronically extend the latitude.

The three shortcomings most commonly cited with the digital video image are slightly high-contrast "crispy" images, the inability to see detail in shadows or low exposures without video noise, and the abrupt blowing out of whites when the image exceeds the factory preset dynamic range for that model. All of these image details, taken together, have been labeled by some people as "the DV curse." But others who work with DV

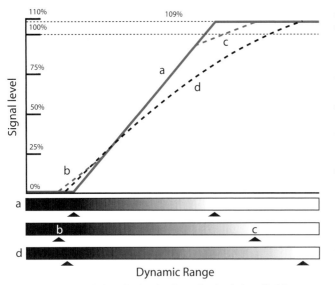

■ **Figure 14-13** Video clips hard as it reaches its dark and bright exposure limits (solid blue line a). Black stretch (b) and knee adjustments (c) can create a toe and shoulder allowing for more visible detail in the dark and bright areas. CineGamma (dotted line d) shifts the signal's contrast for more filmlike exposure details in bright areas and a less acute plunge into crushed blacks.

■ **Figure 14-14** The "black stretch" option found on higher-end video cameras can selectively boost darker areas of a scene, practically creating an artificial toe; note how, after the black stretch option is engaged, some detail can be seen inside the arch. (Go to www.voiceandvisionbook.com to see this figure in high resolution.)

■ **Figure 14-15** Both SD and HD video are susceptible to blown out whites in bright areas like windows and skin highlights. Frame from Mercado's *Becoming* (2009).

extensively use slightly gentler language and refer to these particulars as "artifacts of the digital emulsion" because they understand that much about the performance of the camera's response to light is a function of factory signal presets and that most good cameras are now allowing the user the opportunity to tweak these settings.

Black Stretch, Knee, and CineGamma

One of the central causes of "the DV curse" is that the factory presets of the video compression circuitry create a signal with no toe and no shoulder, which is responsible for the hard clipping of whites and the abrupt plunge into inky blacks when DV approaches the extremes of under- and overexposure (**Figure 14-13**, a). Without the curved toe and shoulder at the ends of the exposure limits of the imaging device, the DV image not only loses out on that gradual tapering off of detail toward total black or total white, but it also loses out on a few stops of "usable exposure range."

Black stretch is a setting that can extend the CCD's sensitivity range in the darkest parts of the image so that you are able to see somewhat more detail in the shadow areas of the shot. Engaging black stretch is the equivalent of creating a "toe" in the response of the CCD (**Figure 14-13**, b). You will see both a little taper to the extreme underexposures and gain about one stop at the bottom end (**Figure 14-14**). Black stretch is like a video gain function that selectively boosts only the darkest portion of the image, like deep shadows. As with video gain, you need to be careful that you don't overdo black stretch because you can introduce video noise into an area that was otherwise clean or you can create blacks that are not rich (called **milky blacks**) in all portions of your image that are black. Some of the work of black stretch can be more accurately and safely accomplished in two ways: careful lighting of the dark areas of the image (when you have lights) so that you bring those areas into your dynamic range or through postproduction color correction (see page 515).

DV is especially vulnerable to clipping in overexposures that commonly shows up in two circumstances; highlights on prominent areas of a subject that reflect the key light, like cheekbones or foreheads, and in situations of extreme contrast ratio, like bright windows visible in a dark interior location (**Figure 14-15**). Extreme clipping can be somewhat avoided by careful use of zebras, but even so, bright

■ **Figure 14-16** The "knee" option found in higher-end video cameras can control the overexposed areas of a frame using compression technology, effectively creating an artificial shoulder. Note how more detail is visible outside the window after the knee option is engaged.

highlights can cause an extreme and uneven loss of color saturation and detail in the image. Clipping occurs at very high signal levels, as you approach pure white. In regular DV this is 100% and with HD it falls around 109% signal level. **Video knee** (or **preknee**) is a signal compression adjustment that is the equivalent of creating a "shoulder" in the signal's response to intense exposures (**Figures 14-13**, c, and **14-16**). Many HD cameras allow for the manual setting of the upper signal levels (near the ultimate white clip level), allowing more detail to be visible as you approach total overexposure. Attenuation of extreme white levels can be set at 80% (low), 90% (mid), and 100% (high). The earlier you set knee to kick in, the more detail you'll see in your highlights. However, the drawback is that setting knee around 80% can make your whites look gray. In my opinion, this is the sort of deep signal adjustment better left to experienced engineers. However, many high-end cameras now have an easily accessible automatic preknee setting, called **auto-knee** (also called **auto highlight control**), which is designed to give you maximum detail depending on the highlight values of the particular image in the frame. Auto-knee is one of the few auto settings that you might consider leaving on while you shoot, but it works best with still frames. A shot that pans across bright areas will reveal the processor adjusting as it detects highlights and corrects on the fly.

CineGamma has become one of the most common signal tweaking settings on DV cameras, especially HD cameras. CineGamma (a.k.a. Cine-like, Cinematone, Film Rec) essentially electronically flattens the straight-line portion of the DV signal's characteristic curve (**Figures 14-13**, d, and **14-17**) and introduces a shoulder to the highlight areas. This accomplishes two things simultaneously: it slightly extends the dynamic range of the camera as well as reducing the contrast of the image, thus ameliorating that "crispy" electronic look that some people don't care for. Some manufacturers claim that CineGamma increases HD's exposure by a full 2 stops (to 11 stops or so) and some claim even more. In effect CineGamma serves the function of black stretch and preknee at the same time because it creates less acute angles at the toe and shoulder of the curve. With CineGamma, you'll see detail somewhat deeper into the shadows and significantly more in the highlights. The drawback of this setting is that the overall reduced contrast of the image can, in some cases, create washed out midtones and colors. Many

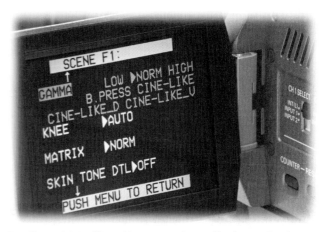

■ **Figure 14-17** Many video cameras have a CineGamma function that electronically creates a toe and shoulder to more closely resemble the way a film stock responds to light.

cameras come with several levels of CineGamma presets to best suit your needs and there is no doubt that this function will become more sophisticated and convincing with each new camera generation.

Always use caution and moderation when you apply any of these settings. Altering the electronic signal of your camera can have unintended ancillary consequences. If you're interested in using black stretch, video-knee, or CineGamma, make sure you shoot tests under similar lighting conditions long before you're on the set and shooting your film. Also remember that adjusting the signal is not a substitute for careful, sensitive, and creative lighting.

■ LIGHTING APPROACHES AND STYLES

As director of photography I am in charge of whatever goes into the making of the image so I am head of the camera, grip, and electric departments. I'm number two to the director so one of the most exciting parts of my job is conceptualizing the visual language that goes into the image. During prep, I sit down with the director and talk about what their visual and narrative influences are. I try to get onto the director's mind's eye in order to be able to enhance and execute that vision. It becomes, for me, a collaborative vision.

**Ellen Kuras, D.P. (From "Cinematography as Poetry,"
interview by Erin Torneo, *indieWIRE*)**

The domain of cinematography is the interpretation of story and character through images and involves composition, color, lighting, and exposure as the primary tools of expression. By now it should be clear that film lighting isn't just a matter of throwing light onto a scene so that we can simply make out the physical subject. Lighting is communicating visual ideas and inflecting the story with a mood, a tone, a visual context, and a narrative meaning. Lighting can help establish a historical era, a season, or even a time of day. It can provide insight into the psychological state of a character or add an ironic edge to the events in the film. Lighting can evoke any mood from ominous to cheerful. But the name of the game with lighting and exposure is "control." Once you have learned to control your image through lighting and exposure, countless expressive possibilities become available to you, and the more you work, the greater your technical and aesthetic repertoire becomes—so much so that the textbooks become irrelevant. At that point it becomes essential to watch movies, study what cinematographers are actually doing in the field, read the trade magazine interviews, and attend screenings where the director and crew make an appearance. Whenever you watch a movie, try to figure out where the lights are placed and what sources are being used, where the D.P. has pegged the exposure, how they handle the camera, and what lenses they have chosen. Consider the quality of the various sources of light and their relationship to the other lights and to the fictive world. And always think about the story and ask yourself why this particular lighting and camera approach was used in this particular film.

Broadly speaking, cinematic lighting approaches break down into naturalistic and stylized designs. But you must always keep in mind that these are not strictly delineated approaches or distinct choices—in fact, naturalistic and stylized lighting designs exist along a highly flexible continuum of aesthetic possibilities for your film. These approaches are often also mixed within the same film. That said, for our introduction we'll discuss the unique principles of each lighting philosophy in discrete terms.

Naturalism and Lighting

A **naturalistic** approach strives to appear as plausible and harmonious with the environment as possible. Lighting direction and sources are always motivated, lighting continuity is observed, and the relationship between the various light sources duplicates what we would expect in a real life situation. Cinematographer Maryse Alberti said in a radio blog interview with *Movie Geeks United* (January 30, 2009) that a naturalistic approach "keeps the world as real as possible. It must work for the drama of the film [but should remain] as real a possible, so you feel that you are in a real place." For this reason, the impact of naturalistic lighting is subtle, unobtrusive, and realistic. In fact, the terms naturalistic and **realistic** are often used interchangeably. Obviously, one way to obtain a raw, naturalistic look is to use no artificial lighting but, rather, to use only available light. Many films have been shot this way, primarily those that try to evoke a documentary look to draw the audience into the realism of the story. The Dardenne Brothers shoot their socially conscious films in a gritty, direct, documentary manner that places very few technical or stylistic layers between

■ **Figure 14-18** In keeping with the documentary style of their cinematography, the Dardenne Brothers shot *The Son* (2002) using mostly available light in real locations (cinematography by Alain Marcoen).

the audience and the subjects of their films (**Figure 14-18**). The Dardennes shoot almost exclusively with natural light in real locations to remain as free from artifice as possible and they consciously use all of the codes of documentary filmmaking. Their visual approach creates the impression that they are not making this stuff up, they are merely reporting on actual human experience from the field.

Naturalistic lighting, however, does not necessarily mean that a filmmaker uses only available light, although many films have been made this way. In fact, naturalistic lighting often requires a lot of artifice, careful light placement, and exposure control in order to look natural. The use of strictly available light does not always translate into what the human eye "naturally" sees because no film stock or CCD chip sees light, as is, quite the way the human eye does. So in an effort to duplicate what an audience expects to see naturally, films employ considerable and careful technique in lighting.

A good example of this can be seen in Erick Zonca's feature film debut, *The Dreamlife of Angels* (1999), which was photographed by Agnès Godard (**Figure 14-19**). The film takes place in the northern French industrial town of Lille during the wintertime, when the skies are overcast and the light is diffused through a blanket of thick, low clouds. The quality of

light during this season is especially thin, gray, and somber, and Godard produced the same quality with the artificial lights to maintain a highly naturalistic feel. For example, the apartment that the two protagonists share in the film had windows that allowed the cold, diffused light to spill in, but Godard nonetheless needed to augment the available light: "Outside it was wintertime, and sometimes we were shooting quite early in the morning—the quantity of light was not high." So she used several HMI lights reflected off bounce boards to bring up the exposures indoors in a way that "duplicated" the natural light of the season. "They were used as a reflecting light, not direct. With the size of the room they were too rude to be used directly."[1] She also used Chinese lanterns for a very soft and subtle source that was more mobile.

■ **Figure 14-19** Zonca's *The Dreamlife of Angels* (1998), shot by Agnès Godard, used bounced HMI lights to maintain the illusion of a typical overcast winter day.

■ **Figure 14-20** The lighting in *Life Lessons,* Scorsese's episode in *New York Stories* (1989), is motivated by where sources would be in the real world, a practice favored by the film's cinematographer, Néstor Almendros.

The legendary D.P. Néstor Almendros summed up the naturalistic approach (**Figure 14-20**) with this statement of his lighting philosophy:

I start from realism. My way of lighting and seeing is realistic; I don't use imagination. I use research. I go to a location and see where the light falls normally and I just try to catch it as it is or reinforce it if it is insufficient; that's on a natural set. On an artificial set, I suppose that there would be a sun outside the house and then I see how the light would come through the windows and I reconstruct it. The source of light should always be justified.

(From *Masters of Light*, by Dennis Schaefer and Larry Salvato)

Stylized Lighting

Stylized (or **non-naturalistic**) lighting approaches, on the other hand, are designed to draw attention to the aesthetic by being overt or exaggerated in ways that make a specific narrative or thematic point. Lighting placement and exposures can be unmotivated or motivated by a logic other than the plausible illumination of the particular physical environment. For example, a stylized lighting scheme might be motivated by the dramatic logic of a scene, by character psychology and point of view, or by the need to create an additional thematic or ironic story layer. Stylized lighting is often associated with nonrealistic film genres, like fantasy films, fables, or films that intentionally invoke an overtly theatrical tone. Film noir is an example of a genre that is associated with an exaggerated lighting scheme whose deep shadows emphasize the dangers lurking in both the dark criminal underbelly of society and the perils of sexual entanglements (**Figure 14-21**).

■ **Figure 14-21** Stylized lighting, commonly found in film noirs like Curtiz' *Mildred Pierce* (1945), can underline the danger lurking around every corner (cinematography by Ernest Haller).

An good example of a theatrical approach to lighting and colors can be seen in Michael Powell and Emeric Pressburger's *Black Narcissus* (1947), which was photographed in Technicolor by Jack Cardiff (**Figure 14-22**). *Black Narcissus* creates a dream world on an operatic scale. The story revolves around the tale of five Anglican nuns who are trying to establish an order in colonial India's Himalayan Mountains. But the surrealistically exotic atmosphere of the remote location causes the nuns to succumb to emotional disorder, sexual desire, and even madness.

■ **Figure 14-22** The hyperstylized look created by the masterful interplay of light, shadow, and color in Powell and Pressburger's *Black Narcissus* (1947) serves to visualize the intense emotions felt by a group of Anglican nuns stationed in the Himalayan mountains (cinematography by Jack Cardiff). See the color insert.

Cardiff would freely mix colors in his lighting approach—for example, using green gels over the fill lights and pink gels in his key light (ostensibly the sun) and blue gels over his set lights—in an effort to represent through color the wild mix of emotions that are overwhelming the Sisters of the order. His virtuosic use of various light qualities—soft, hard, and shadows—adds to a world where narrative dramatic mood above all motivates the quality of light. There is no chance that a viewer could take the intense colors and theatrical lighting for anything resembling realism—that encourages us to look beneath the narrative surface for what all this vibrant imagery could mean. The visual style seems to emerge from, and in turn points the audience toward, the surreal internal landscape of human desire, dreams, and fantasy.

It is essential to understand, however, that naturalistic lighting and stylized lighting do not stand as exclusive options for a filmmaker. There is a sliding scale between these two poles, and most filmmakers find themselves working somewhere between strict naturalism and overt stylization. Working with Tim Burton, a master of stylized film technique, the cinematographer Emmanuel Lubezki was free to use a nonrealistic lighting approach for the mythic horror/fantasy film *Sleepy Hollow,* but in the end his approach was somewhere in between, but leaning toward the stylized end of the spectrum (**Figure 14-23**, *bottom*):

> *[The screenplay] was a wonderful fantasy with a mixture of horror, romance, drama, and humor.... What is great is to take something unreal and make it "real"—or, at least, believable—to create a certain reality with material so completely theatrical. [The lighting style] was between naturalism and pictorialism. The aim of pictorialism is to create photographs that are similar to paintings and to establish photography as a valid art form. In this case, [the purpose was] to make images that felt like illustrations from an old book.... We were going to enhance the reality and make it more beautiful, but still believable.*
>
> **Emmanuel Lubezki (From *Headless Horror*, by Pauline Rogers, The International Cinematographers Guild)**

More subtle is the stylized use of color and lighting in Spike Lee's *Do the Right Thing* (1989), which was shot by D.P. Ernest Dickerson. The setting for the film is the Bedford-Stuyvesant section of Brooklyn and the events take place over the course of one summer day—the hottest day of the year. Dickerson used extremely warm colors and hard lighting to evoke the brutal, oppressive heat of an inner-city heat wave in hyperbolic style. The look is both motivated and slightly exaggerated. This visual style makes the audience really feel the intense sun, the heat, the inescapability of it, and it also transforms the literal heat of the weather into a metaphor for the smoldering, inescapable, and explosive racial tensions between the people in the neighborhood (**Figure 14-23**, *top*).

It is also extremely common for films that are more or less naturalistic in their lighting approach to incorporate scenes and moments with more stylized visual approaches, in order to elevate a particular dramatic moment or bring us into the perspective or psychology of a character. A perfect example can be seen in Roman Polanski's *Repulsion* (1965), the story of Carol, a mentally vulnerable young woman who lives in London with her sister (**Figure 14-24**). When her sister leaves for a vacation, Carol is left alone and her fears become nightmares, then hallucinations, as she falls tragically into madness. Although the film is presented in a more or less naturalistic mode (albeit quite dark), the lighting approach for the scenes in which we are left alone in the apartment with Carol become highly stylized and low key. The starkness of the lighting is exaggerated and the high contrast plunges the audience into the dark shadows of

■ **Figure 14-23** Lee's *Do the Right Thing* (1989) has highly stylized lighting that emphasizes the heat of one particularly hot day in Brooklyn (cinematography by Ernest Dickerson, *top*). D.P. Emmanuel Lubezki tempered the theatrical tone of this ghost story with some naturalistic approaches to create a look for Burton's *Sleepy Hollow* (1999), which was both believable and fantastic *(bottom)*. See the color insert.

■ **Figure 14-24** Stylized lighting can be mixed with naturalistic lighting to effectively emphasize key moments in a film, as Polanski did in *Repulsion* (1965) (cinematography by Gilbert Taylor).

Carol's madness. One cannot say the lighting style here is unmotivated, because Polanski and his D.P., Gilbert Taylor, wish to put us deeply into Carol's point of view, to see the hallucinations as she sees them, so in this case the lighting strategy is motivated by the visions and delusions of a mind in the state of total confusion.

Another film that brilliantly mixes naturalistic and stylized approaches in both lighting and camera work is *Slumdog Millionaire* (2008), which was directed by Danny Boyle and Loveleen Tandan and shot by the digital video pioneer Anthony Dod Mantle. *Slumdog Millionaire* traces the hard scrabble life of Jamal Malik, an orphan who was raised in the slums of Mumbai and who becomes a contestant on a TV game show with the potential to win millions. The film was shot on location with a mix of film, HD, and a digital SLR on burst mode shooting 12 frames per second. As nearly two-thirds of the film was shot on DV, *Slumdog Millionaire* is the first film shot primarily on HD to receive the Academy Award for best cinematography (**Figure 14-25**). Digital video was used especially in the Mumbai slums, where mobility was critical and available light was the only option. However, even though Mantle used natural light exclusively for extended sections, one would not say that *Slumdog Millionaire* necessarily has a naturalistic approach. The richness of the colors, range of exposure choices, creative use of focus, bold compositions, and high-energy camera movement all add up to a style that is too hyperbolic and too dazzling to be labeled "realism," yet the visual style does indeed get at something truthful: the heightened experience of Mumbai and the way one *feels* when one is in the frenzied streets of the world's most crowded city. To capture such visceral imagery in a location so fast paced and demanding, Mantle had to be completely expert in the expressive possibilities of both DV and film technologies and the images he could achieve with both:

> *I wanted to feel really involved in the city. [...] I wanted to be thrown right into the chaos as much as possible. I had to find a [DV] camera set up that would be ergonomic enough for me to throw myself around the slums chasing the children whilst, at the same time, with as much detail in the shadows and highlights. [I] needed a digital camera with enough latitude to hold highlights and something very small so we could enter the children's world at their level.*
>
> **(From Silicon Imaging Press Release, January 2009)**

> *I worked mainly on Fujicolor colour negative ETERNA 500T and Reala 500D.... [I] pushed a great deal of both of the 500 stocks one stop. The artistic reason for pushing the film was to try and attain as much of the local ambience of Mumbai as possible. I also like the effect on colours when the contrast curve of the neg is pushed a little. It somehow fitted my vision of the visceral buzz of the street and the people there.*
>
> **(From Fujifilm Press Release, March 2008)**

■ **Figure 14-25** These two frames from *Slumdog Millionaire* (Boyle and Tanda, 2009) reveal a highly stylized visual approach, despite the use of available light, nonactors and real locations. The D.P. Anthony Dod Mantle was awarded an Oscar for Best Cinematography—the first given to a film shot primarily on DV. See the color insert.

Even though the stylistic approaches of these cinematographers: Almendros and Cardiff, Godard and Dickerson, Alberti and Lubitzky, seem very different, all of them have the very same starting point for adopting a certain technology or applying a particular visual style to a film – they begin with story and character. Here is what Anthony Dod Mantle has to say about the shot in **Figure 14-25**, *right*:

> *I like to experiment, but I only ever experiment because of the story. We thought bringing him really close in the foreground would be good to create that distance between the two boys and create that dramatic comment. One of them is thinking about something else and the other is simply thinking about surviving and moving on. It's a sad image too because you can't help the connotation that these boys have lost their mom, you know. Generally speaking when you're working with Danny, every shot feels as important as every other one. And that shot is an example of the way we work. He'd have an idea for a picture and I'm there to help him as a visually trained composer of images—that's my job.*
> (From *In Contention.com* by Kristopher Tapley, January 14, 2009)

■ FINDING THE APPROPRIATE LIGHTING STRATEGY

So where does one begin to consider the specific approach one should take to lighting a film? In preproduction, of course. The process of devising a lighting strategy is of paramount importance in a movie—even if you're not using any artificial lights at all—and it emerges from the preproduction consultations between the director and cinematographer.

The Overall Look

During the previsualization process, the director and cinematographer examine the script to determine how to visualize the story in terms of lighting (and, of course, camera work as well). Their first task is to determine the overall look of the film. The lighting strategy derives primarily from the story itself. During preproduction meetings, the director and cinematographer ask themselves questions like these:

- What is the film about?
- What is the director's interpretive angle on the script—the central idea?
- What mood or tone is suggested by the events and locations in the movie?
- Does that mood evolve or change over the course of the film?
- What is the primary element driving this film? Dialogue? Character actions? Juxtaposition of images?
- From whose point of view are we shooting this film, and what is their state of mind?
- What is the historic era of the film?
- Does the film reference any existing film genres (screwball comedy, film noir, etc.) that themselves have certain lighting conventions?
- What elements in the script might suggest a lighting approach (i.e., location, season, time of day, set descriptions, character)?
- What might be the balance between natural light and artificial light sources?
- Generally, how can lighting support the tone and ideas of the script?

In answering these questions, the director and D.P. will come closer to figuring out not just a lighting strategy but also the appropriate visual approaches for that specific film expressed through lighting, film stocks, exposures, and camera work that support the story and the director's interpretive idea:

> *Each script is different. Each tells its own story with characters and emotions. It is that which determines the look of the film. This is why each film should look different.*
> (Ernest Dickerson, From "Variations on the Mo' Better Blues," by Al Herrell, *American Cinematographer*, September 1990)

For *Mo' Better Blues* (1990), their fourth feature film as a team, Lee and Dickerson derived the look of the film from the two competing elements in the life of the main character, jazz trumpeter Bleek Gilliam: "cool" jazz and "hot" personal relationships, especially with

■ **Figure 14-26** Cinematographer Ernest Dickerson lights Bleek (Denzel Washington) using colors that stand for his two main interests, jazz (blue) and women (red), in Lee's *Mo' Better Blues* (1990). See the color insert.

women. These are the central narrative elements driving the story. Throughout the film, Dickerson delineates these competing strands of Bleek's life by using cool or warm light sources in various scenes (**Figure 14-26**). In several scenes he even mixes cool light sources with warm light sources in the same frame to create a stylized, thematic point. As Dickerson expresses it:

Hot against cool I felt was the best way to exemplify the music—jazz. It also symbolizes the life of the main character, Bleek, and relationships with ladies and his fellow musicians... . Whenever you play warm against cool light, these opposite wavelengths seem to vibrate against each other creating a visual tension. They pull against each other, just as Bleek was being emotionally pulled between two ladies.

Given the way Dickerson speaks about light and mixing colors to represent emotions, it comes as no surprise that he has often cited Jack Cardiff (and films like *Black Narcissus*) as a major influence on his work.

Visual Research

Often the process of discovering the appropriate lighting style involves some visual research on the part of both the director and the cinematographer. Obviously, as I mentioned in the previous chapter, the history of motion pictures provides cinematographers and directors a wealth of resources and examples to consider when designing a visual approach to a film. However, beyond looking at movies for inspiration, the other art forms, like painting and photography, are also invaluable for visual research. For *Black Narcissus,* Jack Cardiff studied and used many of the lighting techniques from painters like Vermeer (soft directional lighting), Rembrandt (interplay of bright, golden light and deep shadow), and Van Gogh (expressive mix of colors, in shadows and in light sources).

Cinematographer Darius Khondji often acknowledges the extensive visual research he engages in before each film. When preparing to shoot *Delicatessen* (1991)—directed by Jean-Pierre Jeunet and Marc Caro, who themselves employ a unique visual style—Khondji's research incorporated classic silent films and photography (**Figure 14-27**):

■ **Figure 14-27** Cinematographer Darius Khondji saw nothing but silent film masterpieces like Murnau's *The Last Laugh* (1924, *left*), in his preparation for shooting Caro and Jeunet's *Delicatessen* (1991, *right*).

Quai des Brumes (Marcel Carné, 1938) and other French Poetic Realist films inspired Jean Pierre and Marc Caro and they showed me those films or selected clips in preparation for Delicatessen. I remember being much more inspired by the pure cinematic style of silent films. I would watch The Wind (1928) by Sjöström, L'Ange Bleu (1930) by Von Sternberg, Vampyr (1932) by Dreyer, Nosferatu (1922) and Sunrise (1927) by Murnau and Von Stroheim's early films. I was also inspired by the paintings of George Bellows and their texture of black, brown, warm red, yellow, and golden colours. I looked at Pictorialists such as Heinrich Kuhn, early Edouard Steichen, Stieglitz, Cameron, and the illustrator, Martin Lewis.

What I love in Pictorialist photographs is that they were like the "charnier" or "hinge" between painting and photography, neither painting nor photography, and I found that very inspiring for my early movies. Before photographing Delicatessen, I didn't go to the cinema any more. I would only watch black-and-white silent films and avoid being influenced directly by recent movies.

Darius Khondji (From *New Cinematographers*, by Alexander Ballinger, Laurence King, London, 2004)

Small films made on limited budgets can equally benefit from visual research to find their lighting style. I was recently the cinematographer on the short DV film *Flesh & Blade,* which is a dark, 19th-century gothic tale of love and science tragically entangled (**Figure 14-28**). I turned to the wonderful, frightening paintings of Joseph Wright, which depict both the process of scientific inquiry and the romanticized mysticism that characterized science in the 18th century, to help determine the overall look of a film that would take place primarily in a scientist's laboratory.

Other Considerations

As I discussed in the first chapter of this book, the aesthetic of a film, including the photographic look of the movie, is inextricably linked to the practical realities of film production, especially the resources available to the filmmaker. It doesn't do a project any good to imagine a style during preproduction if that style cannot be accomplished in the allotted time or with the resources available. This is a concern, of course, which should be anticipated and addressed during the very conception and scripting of the film. Again, when the director and cinematographer explore the screenplay in preproduction, they need to ask themselves practical questions:

- What is the budget of the film?
- What is the shooting format, and what is it capable of?
- How much time do we have for lighting (days and hours each day)?
- How large is the crew?

■ **Figure 14-28** As part of my visual research for lighting *Flesh & Blade* (2007) (*left* and *right* frames), I looked at paintings like *An Experiment on a Bird in an Airpump* (1768), by Joseph Wright of Derby *(center)*. See the color insert.

- How many and what sort of lighting units (and grip equipment) are available for the shoot?
- How controllable and accessible are the locations?
- How much power is at each location for artificial lights?
- What are the sources of natural light on the set, and how much artificial lighting do we actually need?

However, limited resources never means a lack of style; it means only that the filmmakers need to devise an intelligent, innovative, and resourceful visual approach, which, when perfectly matched with the script, can be as powerful as anything produced with larger budgets. Take the example of the feature film *Personal Velocity* (2002), directed by Rebecca Miller and shot by Ellen Kuras. Kuras recounts the day Miller approached her with the idea of shooting the film:

She wrote a book of short stories and she called me up and said, "Listen, I finally have some money and I can make a short film based on three of my short stories. Would you like to do it?" and I said, "Sure. I'll work with you any time." She said the only thing is "we only have $150,000 and we have to shoot it in mini-DV." I said, "Okay. Well, why don't we shoot it in Super 16?" She said, "We can't, because part of the money is contingent on us shooting mini-DV." Kuras then told Miller, "I'll give you five weeks of my time for free and let's do it—let's make the movie."

(From "Where the Girls Are," by Jennifer M. Wood,
***MovieMaker*, Vol. 2, No. 9)**

Even though the shooting format of the film, the most fundamental technical and expressive tool for a cinematographer, was determined by practical considerations, this didn't mean that Kuras was not able to devise an aesthetic and original interpretation of the project. In fact, she turned a limitation into an opportunity.

Kuras first considered the broader concept of working with DV and with literary material and the freedom that allowed her:

I just said, you know what, I'm shooting with this mini-DV medium, I'm going to think of these as short stories and I'm going to make it look and feel like a poem.... That means I'm not going to do what everybody says you're supposed to do. I'm just going to do what feels right for the movie.

(From "Taking the Digital Medium into Their Hands," by
Philippa Bourke, www.moviesbywomen.com)

Then, in consultation with Miller, Kuras devised a specific lighting and color approach for each woman's story (**Figure 14-29**):

■ **Figure 14-29** Shooting on SD video does not preclude having complex, beautiful cinematography. Ellen Kuras devised three completely different visual styles for the three characters in Miller's *Personal Velocity* (2002). See the color insert.

We had three distinct looks for each of the different narratives. The color palette for Delia's story was warm toned with more yellows and greens and browns. We tried to keep the skin tones neutral.... Greta's story was cool and austere. The camera moves were on a tripod and were much more mannered. Paula's story was much more frenetic so for the color palette, I wanted to put this kind of blue purple to the shadow areas, and to have some cream colored highlights and then have the flashback sequences be a different color which would be in contrast to what the main color palette was.... The contrast is very hard to control using DV unless you have an overcast lighting situation or you're inside. John [Kuras's gaffer John Nadeau] and I basically used the natural light and augmented it, giving it a style unto itself.

(From "Cinematography as Poetry," interview by Erin Torneo, *indieWIRE*)

Kuras has worked extensively on 35mm, Super 16, and DV (both SD and HD); she has worked with large budgets and minimal resources and has been supported by fully staffed professional and skeleton crews alike. Her work on *Personal Velocity* is testament to her versatility and artistic virtuosity.

Sound for Production

The digital revolution has not exclusively revolved around the shooting, editing, and presentation of images alone. Since the beginning of the 21st century, there has been a veritable sea change in the tools and techniques of recording, mixing, and replaying audio as well. There was a time when distribution on video or through broadcast TV meant that people would be listening to your film on little three-inch built-in speakers. Today everyone is fast equipping their home theater units with super-high-fidelity, digital surround sound audio. What this means for the filmmaker is that the audience can hear everything! So we are compelled to create the best sound tracks possible to accompany our carefully composed and exposed images. The first, and most important, step to this end is to gather the best possible sound in the field during production. Unfortunately, sound is often a blind spot for many filmmakers, especially those just starting out. All too often with inexperienced filmmakers, a lot of time, money, and preparation go into the production of the images, but they begin to think seriously about sound only after they hear and try to work with the terrible audio they got during production. The production sound team—those people who record sound in the field—are the unsung heroes of the film world—when they do their job perfectly, no one notices them; when the sound is bad, they are cursed. Good sound people are invaluable, and smart filmmakers understand that getting good sound in production means a stronger sound design in postproduction, more creative options in editing, and saving time and money. This is why good sound people work a lot and why I've devoted two chapters to the craft of sound recording in the field.

◼ WHAT IS PRODUCTION AUDIO?

The final form of a movie's completed sound track consists of layering multiple tracks of sound, anywhere from two to dozens. Although many of the sound elements we hear in a final film are gathered during postproduction (i.e., music, sound effects, voice-overs), there are several crucial elements that are recorded in production while we shoot our images: synchronous sound, wild sound, and ambient sound. For many films, short or feature length, the sound elements recorded in the field, like dialogue, constitute the most crucial audio elements on the sound track. These are the elements we will be exploring in this chapter.

◼ UNDERSTANDING SOUND

In space, no one can hear you scream.

Tag line for Ridley Scott's *Alien* (1979)

In Stanley Kubrick's *2001: A Space Odyssey*, when HAL 9000 severs Poole's life support cable, sending Poole hurtling through space (**Figure 15-2**), the sound that accompanies his sure demise is—total silence. Why did Kubrick choose utter silence for this highly dramatic moment, even though Poole is struggling and likely screaming his head off? Because sound is produced by some vibrating source creating pressure and displacing air molecules. Much like the ripples in a pool of water when a pebble is thrown in, the displacement of the air molecules create acoustic sound waves, which move through the air. If, as in space, there is no air, then there is no sound.

Sounds that appear to be emanating from a single location at a single time are actually constructed from many different elements; some are recorded during production and others are collected later; then the different elements are mixed to create a precise aural impression. Here is a simple scene of two waitresses trying to have a conversation in a noisy coffee shop, just off a busy road, when an off-screen car accident interrupts them (**Figure 15-1**). This scene incorporates several distinct sound elements:

Track 1. The waitresses' dialogue

Track 2. The ambiance of the coffee shop (i.e., coffee machines, cups clattering, patrons' chatter)

Track 3. The sounds of traffic just outside the coffee shop

Track 4. The sound of the car crash that interrupts them

Although it is theoretically possible to record all of these sounds in a single take with a single microphone, it would require a prohibitive amount of time and choreography. Instead, we record (or find) each of these elements separately and later, in postproduction, construct a sound design by layering and mixing independent tracks. Each track can be synced to the picture with frame accuracy and also have the ability for independent volume and equalization adjustments. We will explore postproduction sound in detail in Chapters 22 and 23

Go to www.voiceandvisionbook.com for an interactive example of a scene with multiple tracks.

■ **Figure 15-1** This seemingly simple conversation in a restaurant has a sound track that combines sync sound, sound effects recorded on location, and prerecorded elements from sound effects collections.

■ **Figure 15-2** Poole's silent death from Kubrick's *2001: A Space Odyssey* (1968).

A **sound wave** is in fact a pressure wave, consisting of an alternating pattern of high pressure (compression) and low pressure (rarefaction), traveling through the air. The vibrating source of this pressure can be a guitar string, a tuning fork, the contact between a baseball and a bat, or human vocal chords. These sound waves are eventually received by some sensitive membrane, like an eardrum or microphone diaphragm, which duplicates the vibration patterns of the original source. And what if there isn't a vibration-sensitive membrane to receive those sound waves? Well, you've probably already pondered the proverbial question of whether or not a tree falling in the woods makes a sound if there is no one there to hear it, right?

There are four basic properties of sound that are essential to understanding audio and the techniques of microphone placement and recording for film production:

- Pitch (frequency)
- Loudness (amplitude)
- Quality (timbre)
- Velocity (speed)

We plot these sound wave characteristics on the graph shown in Figure 15-3. This common sine wave graph measures the compression of the air molecules that are caused by a particular sound. With this graph we are able to see certain properties of a particular sound.

Frequency (Pitch)

Sound waves travel in fairly consistent **wave cycles**. One **wavelength** is the length of one cycle, from peak to peak, which then repeats itself. A wavelength is plotted from one highest pressure point to the very next highest pressure point. The number of these waves that pass a fixed point over the course of one second is the measure of the frequency of the sound wave. This measure of **cycles per second** is referred to as **Hertz (Hz)** and is measured along the graph's x-axis.

A sound that generates 10,000 wave cycles every second has a frequency of 10,000 Hz, also written 10 kHz. This frequency of cycles per second is actually measuring the **pitch** of that particular sound. The fewer cycles per second, the lower the pitch of a sound; the more cycles per second, the higher the pitch (Figure 15-4).

Neither the human ear nor a microphone can perceive all sound frequencies. The range of detectable pitches for a given apparatus is called the **frequency range**. An average, healthy human ear can distinguish pitches from 25 Hz to 20 kHz. Dogs can hear frequencies beyond 20 kHz; this is why they can hear high-pitched dog whistles that humans cannot. The frequency range that a microphone or a sound recorder can pick up and duplicate is a common measure of equipment quality. The "hearing" range for a particular piece of gear is called its **frequency response**. Those old cassette decks (good ones!) had a frequency response around 30 Hz to 12 kHz, which is less than the range of human hearing. A typical professional digital audio recorder has a frequency response of 20 Hz to 40 kHz, which is greater than the range of human hearing—just one reason why the cassette tape disappeared.

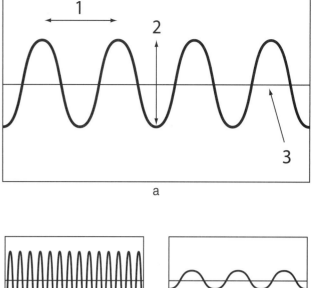
a

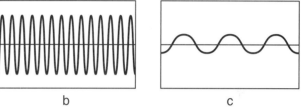
b | c

■ **Figure 15-3** A simple sound (a) can be understood in terms of its wavelength (1), and its amplitude (2), or the degree to which it deviates from normal air pressure (3). The higher the number of cycles per second (b), also called Hertz, the higher the frequency or the sound. Sounds with very low frequencies have fewer cycles per second (c).

5200 Hz   150 Hz - 2000 Hz   45 Hz

■ **Figure 15-4** A piccolo (the highest pitched instrument in an orchestra, *left*) can reach a frequency of 5,200 Hz. A tuba (the lowest pitched instrument, *right*), can create sounds as low as 45 Hz. The human voice is located in the frequency midrange, from 150 Hz to 2,000 Hz.

Amplitude (Loudness)

Each peak high and low pressure point along the graph's y-axis has a specific height or **amplitude,** which is a measure of the **loudness** of a sound (see Figure 15-3). The higher the amplitude peak, the greater is the displacement pressure of the sound wave and the louder the sound. Loudness is measured in **decibels (dB)**. Decibels increase or decrease according to a logarithmic progression. I won't go into the complexities of logarithms; it's sufficient to simply understand that it takes an increase of three decibels (3 dB) to double the loudness and a decrease of three decibels to halve loudness.

The loudness range that the human ear can distinguish falls between the **threshold of hearing** (0 dB) on the lower end and the **threshold of pain** (120 dB) on the upper end. A normal conversation tone is approximately 55 dB. A whisper is around 25 dB and a scream comes in at around 75 dB. At 150 dB, eardrums will rupture—you'll know when *that* happens.

In most recording situations the loudness of your source fluctuates. Sometimes the range of loudness levels is minor and other times it can be extreme. For example, listen to the opening of Richard Strauss' symphonic tone poem *Also Sprach Zarathustra*, Op. 30 (which was used in Kubrick's *2001: A Space Odyssey*). The piece begins with the softest, barely audible drone of the double basses and builds to an all-out, full orchestra fortissimo—led by crashing cymbals, blaring horns, and pounding tympani—in only a minute and a half! The range of different loudness levels is referred to as the **dynamic range**. "Also Sprach Zarathustra" has an extremely wide dynamic range. Comparatively, a song like the White Stripes' "Fell in Love with a Girl" has a narrow dynamic range because it remains at the same loudness level throughout—fairly loud. A conversation that goes from a whisper to screaming has a wide dynamic range, whereas a politician's speech delivered in a monotone has a narrow dynamic range. Wide dynamic ranges can be challenging for both the sound recordist and the equipment (see Chapter 16).

Inverse Square Law

The amplitude of a sound wave diminishes according to the **inverse square law** as it travels through space, which means that the intensity of a given sound decreases by the square of its distance from the sound source. This is the same law that governs the drop-off of light intensity as one moves away from the source of illumination (see page 273), so you can remember it by the same rule of thumb: doubling the distance from the source results in the loudness diminishing four times, and halving the distance from your source will increase the loudness four times. Knowing that sound intensity drops off drastically the farther one moves a microphone away from the audio source is essential in determining microphone placement.

Quality (Timbre)

The sound waves shown in Figure 15-3 represent pure, electronically generated tones with no character or aberrations. When we encounter the waves of sounds from the real world, the curve does not look quite so uniform, with a smooth curve and perfectly symmetrical peaks and dips. Most naturally occurring sound waves include characteristic irregularities in the overall shape and are also accompanied by a series of other waves of lower amplitude and various frequencies, all of which reflect the particular quality of that sound.

The central and dominant shape of the wave is called the **fundamental tone,** but every fundamental tone also resonates with a series of imperfections and coinciding waves that represent **overtones** and **harmonics** (Figure 15-5). These elements constitute **timbre,** which

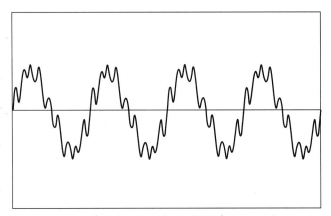

■ **Figure 15-5** Sounds are usually made up of more complex combinations of tiny variations called harmonics and overtones, which mark the difference between, for instance, a piano and a clarinet playing the same note.

a   b   c

■ **Figure 15-6** Waveforms for a piano playing middle C (a), a violin playing middle C (b), and a human voice singing middle C (c).

is the unique tonal composition and characteristics of that sound (i.e., richness, harshness, resonance). Timbre allows us to easily distinguish different instruments playing the very same note. For example, middle C on a piano sounds quite different from the same note played on a trumpet, or on a guitar, or when sung by a human voice (**Figure 15-6**).

Velocity

Sound is a wave that travels through space, so it has both directionality and speed. The **speed of sound** is 1,086 feet per second. This is very slow compared to the speed of light (which is 983,571,056 feet per second). This is why, when you're watching the fireworks display on the Fourth of July, you see the big flash of light first and hear the boom of the explosion seconds later (**Figure 15-7**).

■ PRODUCTION SOUND

There are several names for it—**production sound, field recording, field mixing,** and **audio gathering**—but the name of the game is all the same; get the best quality sound possible. Great quality field recordings allow for maximum creative manipulation in post-production. In some ways it's easier to get away with less-than-perfect images in a film than less-than-perfect sound. Poor quality audio immediately marks your film as that of an amateur. If you're a stop or two underexposed, well, the audience can at least still see what's going on; but if your recording is too low, they can't hear what people are saying and all meaning is lost. A poor original sound recording can be the utter bane of an entire film. It's often impossible to add what is missing or take away what shouldn't be there, and those times when audio *can* be "corrected in post," it's always difficult and often expensive to do. So the primary responsibility of the sound team during the production phase is to get as clean and strong a sound recording as possible. Getting great production sound means understanding sound, knowing your equipment, and practicing good recording technique.

Location Audio

Location sound is any sound that is recorded in the same environment as the images. Location sound breaks down into roughly two categories: **synchronous sound (sync sound)** and **wild sound** (also called **nonsync sound**).

Sync sound is recorded simultaneously with taking the image, so sound and picture correspond to each other with frame accuracy and are said to be "**in sync**" with one another (**Figure 15-8**). This could be a character's dialogue, cars zooming past, or the sound of a door closing—anything in which the sound emanating from the scene is recorded in sync with the picture.

■ **Figure 15-7** In real life, fireworks are usually out of sync with the sound of their blasts, because light travels at a much faster speed than sound. Most films, however, sync them in postproduction, as in Lee's *Brokeback Mountain* (2005).

In DV production this is not difficult because DV can be used as a **single-system** format, meaning that both audio and video are gathered at the same time, with the same apparatus (the camcorder), and are recorded in sync on the same media (videotape or memory card). However, **double-system** film production requires additional and specialized equipment for sync sound shooting to ensure that the audio recorder and camera run precise speeds without fluctuation (see the "Double- and Single-System Recording" section).

Wild sound is audio that is recorded on location, but not simultaneously with the picture, and so has no corresponding picture to be in sync with. Wild sound functions as a sound design element that either doesn't require synchronization or that can be manually synced to an image later in the editing phase. Two common types of wild sound recorded in the field are **ambient sound** (also called **room tone**) and **location sound effects** (also called **spot sound effects**). From time to time we might be prohibited from getting a specific sound because of microphone placement or the size of a frame while we are shooting a scene. In these cases a sound recordist will often rerecord specific sounds from the scene as wild sound (without the camera rolling) to get a better quality representation that can be inserted in postproduction as a special effect. For example, in one of my early films I had a very wide shot of a man getting into his car and trying to start it up. The engine doesn't turn over, so he gets out and walks. After I took

■ **Figure 15-8** The sound crew, usually made up of a sound mixer *(foreground)* and a boom op *(standing),* is in charge of recording sync sound during the shooting of a film.

the shot, the sound team came in and rerecorded the car engine sounds again from much close to get clean audio for use later in editing. Ambient sound refers to the entire group of sounds and tonal qualities of a given recording environment. Ambient sound includes both **room acoustics** (also called **presence**) and **background noise** (also called **atmospheric sounds**).

Room acoustics are the general aural qualities of a given space. For example, the acoustics of a small carpeted room filled with old stuffed furniture is quite different from the acoustics of a bathroom with nothing but tiled floors and walls. In the case of the bathroom, any source of audio is surrounded by hard surfaces that will reflect the sound. Sound bouncing off surfaces is called **reverberation (reverb)**. In this situation a microphone will pick up the audio from the source (**direct sound**) and also pick up the audio reverberating off the walls and floor. The result is a boomy or echoey sound as the signal duplicates itself over and over again. A recording space like this is called acoustically **live**. The carpets and furniture in the small room, however, are poor reflective surfaces and serve to absorb sounds after they leave the source. This allows only the direct sound source to be recorded. This is known as an acoustically **dead** recording space.

The other factor that affects acoustics is room size. A small tiled bathroom is a very reflective space, but the reverberation intervals will be shorter than in a gothic cathedral, where the sound travels a greater distance to a reflective surface and back to the microphone, increasing the time between the recording of the direct sound and its reflection. The audible difference in the acoustic quality between these two live spaces is the difference in **reverb delay**. Very live acoustics are often difficult to work with. Too much reverberation can create muddy audio.

Background noise or atmospheric sounds are all of the sounds that occur naturally in any specific recording location. If we are shooting a scene near a playground, for example, the sound of children playing is part of the environment and therefore is expected to be in the scene. However, we certainly don't want background noises to overwhelm the audio that we are trying to pick up (i.e., the dialogue), so we might want to minimize the sound of children playing while we record our sync sound dialogue as cleanly as possible (through microphone choice and placement) and then record some high-quality "wild sound" of children playing after the camera stops rolling. This way we can place the wild sound under the clean conversation later and adjust the levels to achieve exactly the volume balance we want under the dialogue. We will discuss specific techniques for recording ambient sound later in this chapter.

a   b

■ **Figure 15-9** Single-system sound uses a single device, like a video camera (b), to record both picture and sound. The addition of a boom person (a) can provide greater flexibility to the way the sound is recorded (see also **Figure 15-24**).

Double- and Single-System Recording

Double- and single-system sound simply refers to the number of machines needed to record your image and sound during a shoot. DV can be used as a single-system sound medium that has the capability to record both audio and video in one camcorder and on the same recording medium—sound and picture are automatically and always in sync. Film, on the other hand, is a double-system sound medium, meaning the film camera records the image, and a separate apparatus, a sound recorder, gathers the audio (**Figures 15-9** and **15-10**).

To ensure that sound and image synchronize later in postproduction, it is critical that both pieces of equipment record their portion at a perfectly constant speed. Any variation in speed will throw sync off. For this reason, sync sound cameras are outfitted with a **crystal sync oscillator** to ensure a constant and compatible speed (see **Figure 8-15**). The crystal oscillator emits a steady 60-cycle-per-second pulse that precisely governs the

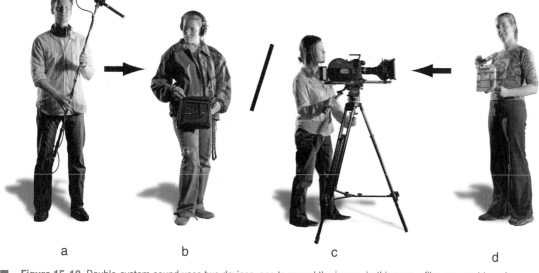

a   b   c   d

■ **Figure 15-10** Double-system sound uses two devices: one to record the image, in this case a film camera (c), and another to record the sound, here a digital sound recorder (b) that captures the signal from the boom op and his microphone (a). Because these two devices work independently, a slate (d) must be used to provide an audiovisual point of reference to sync picture and sound in postproduction.

transport speed of the camera. A crystal sync camera running at sound speed (24 fps) remains accurate to plus or minus half a frame over 400 feet of film (16,000 frames), a standard magazine load. The recording "speed" of digital recorders, on the other hand, is precisely regulated by their constant sampling rate, which is also based on 60-cycle oscillations (see the "Sampling" section). So one second of steady 24-fps film transport will perfectly match one second of steadily sampled digital audio. It's important to know that not all film cameras are capable of shooting sync sound. Nonsync film cameras, like the Arri-S, running at 24 fps, in fact fluctuate between 22 fps and 25 fps. This discrepancy in frame rate isn't noticeable in the image, but it can throw the picture out of sync with its corresponding audio. The other issue concerning shooting sync sound involves camera noise. Cameras designed for sync sound shooting either have a quiet motor or are blimped (encased in metal soundproofing) to keep camera noise from registering on the sound recording. Nonsync film cameras (like a Bolex or Arri-S) tend to have noisy motors, which a microphone will clearly pick up as inappropriate background noise.

It is common for narrative projects shot on DV (SD and HD) to be approached as double-system sound. There are two good reasons filmmakers choose to shoot double-system DV. The first is that the audio components built into DV cameras, especially consumer and "prosumer" grade cameras, do not have the same quality as dedicated digital recorders. While some camcorders have excellent audio specifications, many deliver substandard audio quality (i.e., 32 kHz, 12-bit audio only) and the cheap circuitry can introduce unwanted noise into the signal—especially if they use those dreadful, unshielded ⅛-inch miniplug audio inputs. The second reason is just as valid. Recording your audio with the camera means that you need to be careful of the input levels on the camera itself. Camera operators do not want to (nor should you want them to) be responsible for monitoring audio levels. The trouble is that camera folks don't want sound people hanging around the camera either. For narrative production, it's just a pain for the audio equipment to be on the camera and the sound team to be hovering around checking levels while the D.P. is trying to line up shots.

Figure 15-11 Double-system sound always requires a way to sync the picture and sound in postproduction, with the use of a slate being by far the most common method. Still from Scorsese's *The Last Temptation of Christ* (1988). (Photo courtesy of Pam Katz.)

Whether you're shooting on film or on DV, double-system sound always requires the additional step of syncing audio to the picture in postproduction. This is where the slate comes in (**Figure 15-11**). The **slate** (also called **sticks**) is used for two reasons: one is to place a positive visual identification at the head of every take (including, scene, shot, take, and sound number) and the other is to create a one-frame, easily identifiable reference "moment" with which to line up the picture and sound later in postproduction. That moment is the sharp closing of the slate sticks, which is recorded by the camera and the audio record deck at the beginning of every take. Later, when syncing up the image with the sound, it is easy to find the exact frame in which the slate sticks make contact. Next, you find the "clap" of the two sticks meeting on the audio track, which can be heard and *seen* using the waveform function on your editing software. Then you simply line up the clap image with clap audio and everything after that point, for that take, should be in sync (**Figure 15-12**). (See page 431 for procedure.)

Another method of syncing double-system audio is by using a **timecode slate**. If your recording deck generates timecode (like the Nagra VI or Sound Devices 702T), then you can use a timecode (TC) slate, which receives the same timecode numbers (via wireless or cable link) that are being laid down on the sound track (**Figure 15-13**). When the clapper sticks snap together during slating, the timecode number freezes at that moment and then returns to 00:00:00:00. With a timecode slate, syncing is done by reading the last timecode number off the slate picture and then simply typing in the same timecode number to locate the exact sync point on the sound track. We will discuss syncing footage in more detail later in the postproduction chapter.

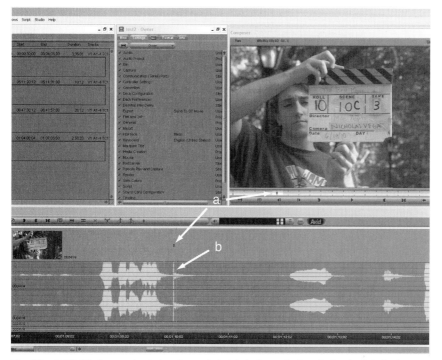

■ **Figure 15-12** A properly shot and recorded slate is the perfect audiovisual point of reference in postproduction. The frame where the slate is clapped is marked in the video file (a), and then the sound file is positioned so that the sound of the slate clapping (b) is aligned with the marker. Video and audio are now in sync.

■ DIGITAL SOUND RECORDING

The Basic Signal Path

Let's look at the basic signal path of a digital recording situation to see how sound starts out as an acoustic source, which is transformed into an electronic signal, then is turned into data, only to be transformed back into acoustic sound again in the end (Figure 15-14):

1. Sound recording begins with the **source** of sound, which emits acoustic energy (sound waves).
2. These sound waves enter the microphone, where a diaphragm, magnets, and coil (see page 345) convert the acoustic energy into fluctuations of electrical voltage that is analogous to the original sound waves. This fluctuating voltage created by a microphone is called a **microphone** (or **mic**) **signal,** which is sent to the digital audio recorder (or a DV camcorder) via a microphone cable.
3. The relatively low-voltage mic signal first passes through a **preamp,** where the signal is boosted, and then goes to an **analog-to-digital converter** (**ADC**), which samples the analog audio information and translates it into binary code (a series of 1s and 0s). The sequencing of binary data ultimately represents the aural characteristics of the source sound. The digital information is stored on some form of recording media; this could be a hard drive, flash drive, or digital audiotape (DAT), depending

■ **Figure 15-13** A timecode slate (a) makes synchronizing even easier, because it displays the timecode being recorded with the audio. The Sound Devices 702T (b) is one of many recorders with timecode capability.

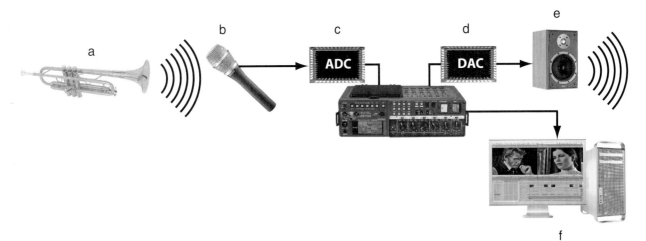

■ **Figure 15-14** An acoustic signal (a) is translated into an electrical charge by a microphone (b) and is then converted into digital information via an analog-to-digital converter (c). These data are stored in the record format (flash memory, hard drive, DAT) and can also be sent via FireWire to a computer for editing (f). A DAC (d) reverses the process when we play the recorded sound (e).

on the recorder you use. In the case of DV camcorders, the audio is recorded onto tape or memory cards.

4. When playing the audio back, the data are sent to a digital-to-analog converter (DAC), which changes them back into electronic energy and outputs a **line signal,** which is the audio signal between audio components. Be careful not to mix up line and mic signals—a line signal is much stronger.

5. The audio line signal can then travel to speakers or headphones, where magnets, sound coils, and cones convert the electronic energy back into acoustic sound waves that travel through the air and are received by our ears.

6. The audio data can also be sent digitally via FireWire or USB connection to the hard drive of a digital editing system.

Digital Audio: Quality Matters

The number one factor in determining the quality of any digital recording has nothing to do with the cost of your equipment, quantizing, sample bit rates, or signal-to-noise (S/N) ratios—any professional sound mixer will tell you that microphone choice/placement and recording technique can make lower-end recording gear sound great, or a state-of-the-art recording system sound terrible. We will discuss recording and microphone technique in depth in the following section.

The other, more objective parameters that determine recording quality are found primarily in the analog-to-digital conversion process, especially as it relates to how thoroughly and accurately the analog information is measured before it is assigned its representative data.

Sampling

Similar to digital video, **audio sample rates** determine how many times a sound (the sine wave of that sound) is measured per second. One **sample** is a single measurement of amplitude, sort of like a snapshot of a piece of that sound, and primarily determines the frequency response of the recording. The more samples (the higher the sample rate), the more accurate the reproduction will be because more frequencies will be measured (**Figure 15-15**). Higher sample rates produce better quality sound, but they take up more storage space on your tape or drive. The most common sample rate for recording audio on either a DV camcorder or a digital audio field recorder is 48 kHz (that is, 48,000 sample measurements per second). As a point of comparison, the standard sample rate for audio CDs is 44.1 kHz, (you'll find this sample rate on a few recorders and camcorders). Occasionally you'll see sample rates on DV camcorders as low as 32 kHz. This substandard rate is used to save space on DV tape and allows for four channels of audio instead

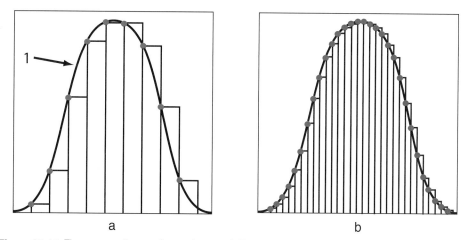

a   b

■ **Figure 15-15** The process of converting analog sound (1) to a digital format involves sampling the signal at regular intervals. The lower the sampling rate (a), the less accurate the digital version will be; a higher sampling rate (b) creates a more faithful reproduction of the original sound.

of the standard two channels. It's a devil's bargain, however, because what you gain in tracks, you lose in quality—having four channels of poor audio does no one any good. On high-end audio recorders you'll find sample rates as high as 96.096 kHz, but most sound mixers agree that this is quality overkill. In general it's best to stick with recording at 48 kHz.

The second, and perhaps more easily perceptible measure of audio quality is bit depth. **Bit depth** (also called **word length**) is a measure of the accuracy and detail of each audio sample, determined by the number of binary digits (bits) assigned to each sample. The greater the bit depth, the better your audio quality will be because the sine wave, in all of its complexity, is more accurately defined. Imagine having a ruler that is divided into ¼-inch units. If any measurement falls between the ¼-inch marks, it will be rounded up or down. This ruler doesn't give you particularly accurate measurements. Now imagine a rule that is divided into ¹⁄₄₈-inch units and another that is divided into ¹⁄₉₆-inch units. These rulers will measure far more accurately because measurements that fall between markings need to be rounded only slightly. Bit depth works the same way, with a sound being measured, more or less accurately, through the number of sampling "levels." A 4-bit sample will measure 16 levels, an 8-bit sample will measure 256 levels, and a 16-bit sample will measure 65,536 levels. With each bit you add, you double the number of values defining that sound, so with 24-bit audio, there are 16,777,216 levels! With greater depth a more accurate picture of the original sine wave can be rendered and consequently the more space the data need for storage. The process of rounding up or down areas of the sine wave that are not measured is called **quantizing**. With more bits, you reduce the quantizing error of the recording. In the field you will often encounter 12-bit audio (substandard), 16-bit audio (great quality, the standard bit depth for CDs and SD DV), 20-bit audio (even better but usually only on HD camcorders), and 24-bit audio (superior quality on professional sound recorders). It's generally recommended that you use the best bit depth you've got.

The mechanism described here, for digitally converting an analog signal by taking a sequence of discrete individual samplings and then storing that data in a sequential binary format, is called **LPCM audio (linear pulse code modulation)**. LPCM audio is an uncompressed encoding method, and it is by far the most pervasive digital recording process for professional audio field recorders and DV camcorders. The most popular audio file formats for audio field recording **.WAV** (PC standard format) and **AIFF** (Mac standard format) use LPCM encoding. So, to summarize, the **standard sample rate** and **bit depth settings** for high-quality film production audio are 48 kHz and 16 bit, but if you have the capability and storage space to go 48 kHz and 24 bit, then by all means use those settings.

■ PRODUCTION SOUND TOOLS

The Digital Sound Recorder

All portable digital sound recorders used for film production record LPCM audio and are essentially the same in their basic features and operation (Figure 15-16). These features include microphone inputs, record level controls and meters, recording controls, and audio outputs. However, the difference between digital recorders centers on how the audio data are stored. We will look at that feature later in this chapter.

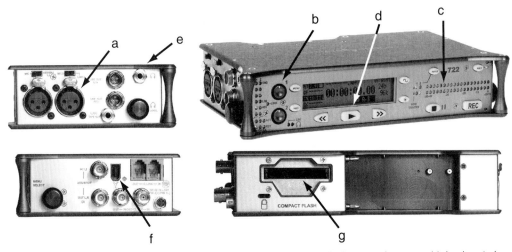

■ **Figure 15-16** Professional sound recorders have the same features: mike inputs and preamps (a), level control potentiometers (b), a peak meter (c), controls for record, play and searching (d), headphone jack (e), audio/data outputs (f), and record media bay (in this case compact flash memory) (g).

Microphone Inputs and Preamps

True XLR microphone (mic.) inputs are essential for film production. XLR connectors are the professional standard connector for microphones and mike cables. If it's possible, stay away from any recorder with miniplug inputs, which you often find on consumer audio equipment. Portable field recording decks typically have between two and four separate microphone **inputs**, also called **channels**, and this allows multiple microphone setups. Each channel can be monitored, controlled, recorded, and transferred as a distinct audio track. Decks with more than four inputs are indeed available, but start to become cumbersome for small-scale film production.

Preamps in the recorder boost the mike signal input. However, the quality of your audio not only depends on the sampling rate and bit depth, but on the quality of the components inside the recorder. Cheap preamps can be a major source of unwanted system noise and will "dirty up" your 48-kHz, 16-bit audio so much that it sounds terrible. **System noise** is electronic junk that contaminates the audio signal we want to record. The specifications for the system noise of any particular recorder are measured by its **signal-to-noise** (S/N) ratio, which is the ratio between the audio that we want to record (signal) and unwanted interference (noise) that contaminates that signal. Signal-to-noise ratio is measured in decibels, and the higher this ratio is, the "cleaner" your audio signal will be when it's recorded. For example, an audio deck that has a signal-to-noise ratio of 55 dB (55:1) means that 1 dB of noise will be detectable when a signal of 55 dB is played back after recording. A signal-to-noise ratio of 95 dB (95:1), however, means that the playback signal can be as high as 95 dB before we detect any noise at all. Professional digital field recording decks should come in at 80 dB or higher—which is extremely clean audio. Again, the first indicators of cheap audio circuitry are miniplug audio inputs (Figure 15-17).

Level Controls and Meters

Adjusting and monitoring the strength of your audio signal is at the heart of the sound recordist's craft. The term **levels** refers to the strength of your audio as it enters the recorder and the degree to which we boost or lower that audio with manual **level controls**, sometimes called **gain controls** or **pots** (short for **potentiometers**). This adjustment determines the strength of the audio signal recorded and is called **setting levels**. On professional recorders you will have one level control for every microphone channel, allowing you to adjust the levels of each microphone independently. Setting levels is aided by a **peak reading meter** (Figure 15-18). The peak meter is a highly sensitive instrument that has a one-to-one level correspondence with all sounds entering the recorder. In other words, it reacts to and measures every sound. This allows the recordist an accurate indication of absolute peak levels in any recording situation. Each mike input will have its own corresponding peak meter. Meter displays can be quite different from machine to machine, including pivoting needles, colored LED lights, or backlit LCD displays, but they are all

■ **Figure 15-17** Low-end audio recording equipment commonly uses a miniplug for connecting microphones. This connection is flimsy and prone to interference and should be avoided if possible.

calibrated in decibels that run from −∞ dB on the extreme low end, through −40, −30, and −20 dB, and so on, to 0 dB on the high end. At −∞ dB there is no signal at all and you will record no sound. If your signal strength exceeds 0 dB your audio is too strong and will become distorted. We will discuss recording techniques and using gain controls and meters in detail in Chapter 16.

Controls and Outputs

Play/Record/Stop control buttons obviously control the starting and stopping of audio recording and playback (to check sound quality and details after recording). A **headphone jack** is standard, because fully isolated headphones are essential for monitoring audio during recording. Headphone outputs often have their own volume control. Beware, however, that you do not mistake the headphone volume level for the record volume level. Headphones are used primarily to monitor the content of your audio, *not* the audio levels as they are being recorded—the peak meter is the device by which we determine record levels (see Chapter 16). When I was a student shooting my first sound film, my mixer had the headphone volume turned all the way up, but the record levels, which he never looked at, were way below standard. The result was audio that he could hear okay in the headphones, but that was recorded "in the mud." In the end I couldn't fix the audio and I was forced to reshoot those scenes. **Audio outputs** send the recorded signal out, either to your computer for capturing with editing software or to whichever format you are transferring your image (i.e., DVCPro) for the direct syncing of video dailies.

■ **Figure 15-18** Peak meters are essential for monitoring the strength of the signal being recorded. Peak meters can be LED based (*left,* showing a two-channel meter) and LCD based (*right,* showing a six-channel meter).

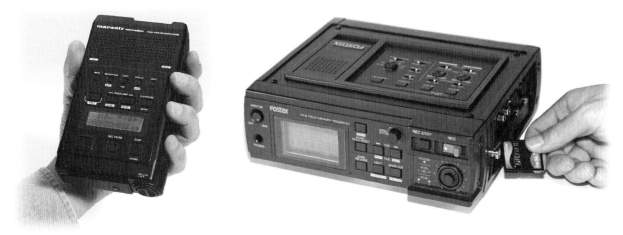

■ **Figure 15-19** With no moving parts and consuming very little power, compact flash memory cards allow for small, yet sturdy digital recorders that are popular with sound mixers.

Digital Recording Media

Beyond the common features of any digital field production recorder, the primary difference between field decks is their **recording media format**—meaning how they store the audio data. Most audio field recorders record in the .WAV file format, but how they store those .WAV files differs. Digital recording formats come and go as the technology evolves, but there are a few standard formats that one is likely to come across.

Flash Memory Recorders

Sound recorders using easily available **compact flash memory** cards as the storage media are a popular and relatively inexpensive choice for students and independent filmmakers. Almost every major sound recording equipment manufacturer has developed portable compact flash recorders. Compact flash (CF) records audio directly to **data cards**, which can be transferred into computer hard drives for storage and then reused again and again. Compact flash also contains no moving parts, which means there is less to break down, they are reliable in extreme conditions, and they use very little battery power. Although the storage capacity of compact flash cards was limited at first, we are currently seeing exponential leaps in storage space even as the price per gigabyte becomes cheaper. If there is one drawback it is that not all compact flash cards are compatible with type 1 and type 2 cards, being different thicknesses (**Figure 15-19**).

Hard Drive Recorders

Hard drive recorders write their data directly to a hard drive—what could be simpler? Most portable units intended for film production use a 2.5-inch shock-resistant internal hard drive. Depending on the size of the hard drive, these recorders can store many hours of audio without changing media. Hard drive recorders also interface with computer editing software seamlessly and have a reputation for being quite robust; temperature, humidity, and motion have little effect on the functions and recording. The convenience and robustness of hard drive recorders come at a price, however, as they are among the most expensive machines available. Ultra-high-end, professional hard drive recorders (like the Nagra VI, Sound Devices 744T, or the Aaton Cantar X-2) include simultaneous secondary media recording to flash memory and even a FireWire connector to record to a tertiary storage device, like an external hard drive (**Figure 15-20**). Now *that*'s safety!

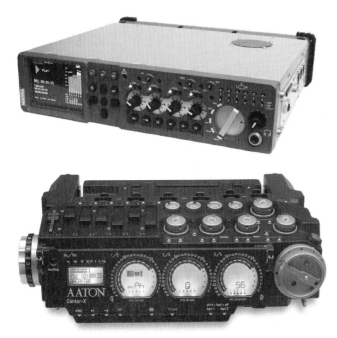

■ **Figure 15-20** Some high-end digital sound recorders like the Nagra VI *(top)* and the Aaton Cantar-X2 *(bottom)* store data directly to an internal 2.5-inch hard disk as well as flash memory cards for safety backup.

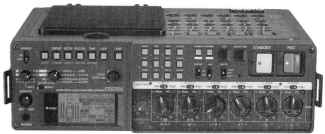

■ **Figure 15-21** Digital audio tape recorders (DATs) record to a proprietary audio cassette *(left)*, and DVD-RAM media like the Fostex PD6 *(right)* make random access possible.

Digital Audiotape and DVD-RAM

Digital audiotape (DAT for short, or **R-DAT** for rotary head digital audiotape) is an audio-only cassette format that uses a magnetic tape 3.81 mm wide and that writes its data in a helical scan pattern with a flying record head—much like a DV video camera. Professional DAT recorders have a frequency response around 20 Hz to 22 kHz and the signal-to-noise ratio is outstanding at around 90 + dB. The drawback to DAT machines is their fragility in the field. They seem especially vulnerable to dust and humidity and can jam up in extreme conditions. The other drawback is their linearity—meaning that one needs to fast-forward or rewind to find sound takes, rather than access them through the instantaneous random access of hard drives and other recording formats. The DAT format is quickly phasing out in favor of digital recorders with no moving parts. Industry reports indicate that there are no new DAT recorder models in the pipeline, but since many production companies and film schools have invested in these machines, they will remain in circulation for a while longer. **DVD-RAM** recorders function similarly to hard disk recorders. DVD-RAMs write the audio data in concentric tracks (like hard drives) instead of one long spiral track (like DVD+R and –R, which are entirely different formats). DVD-RAM does not need DVD burning software and, using a DVD-RAM reader, they can be loaded and read instantly on any PC or Mac computer system. (Figure 15-21).

Sound Recording on DV Camcorders

As I mentioned earlier, for narrative filmmaking it's usually a good idea to go with double system sound recording, even when shooting DV, which has the capacity to record audio (see page 336). But if you have no choice but to shoot single system sound with your camcorder, you can still get great audio. DV camcorders that use tape as their record medium write PCM digital audio along a helical scan with a flying head and file-based media (P2 and SxS) create sound files (see page 208), and this audio is already in sync when you sit down to edit your footage. Most camcorders of any quality have high recording specifications: 48 kHz and 16 bit. In theory, these are great audio specifications; however, as we've discussed before, there are other factors that contribute to audio quality.

Miniplug audio inputs are especially a problem with low-end DV camcorders. The connections are fragile and prone to poor contacts, and miniplugs are unshielded and unbalanced. Many people use an **XLR-to-mini adaptor** (called a **pigtail**) so that they can use professional external microphones. This, of course, is better than nothing, but the problem with this solution is that it converts your lovely balanced, shielded audio into an unbalanced signal, vulnerable to interference and noise. A few years ago I was shooting a short film on DV and using a professional microphone connected to the camera with an XLR-to-mini adaptor. After a few takes into our shooting, the sound recordist noticed that we were picking up a Top-40 radio station. When we played back the tape we could hear it. It was very faint, but sure enough, there was Britney Spears leaking onto my audio track!

■ **Figure 15-22** Although it is possible to get an XLR-to-mini cable *(top)* to use professional microphones with ⅛-inch mike inputs, a mountable adaptor like the Beachtek *(bottom)* provides a sturdier solution.

Camera-mountable adaptors with preamps and XLR connections are available for DV camcorders that have only miniplug audio inputs (**Figure 15-22**). These adaptors allow you to use XLR cables, and some even provide a shielded mini cable to the camera—two big advantages. However, where you find miniplugs you may also find cheap preamps and audio circuitry adding system noise to your signal. Many consumer DV camcorders have terrible signal-to-noise ratios (between 40 dB and 50 dB).

Most industrial and professional camcorders that provide true XLR connectors usually have two microphone inputs with independent level controls. The preset for many cameras is **automatic gain control**, meaning the camera will set your levels for you. Just as with auto focus and auto exposure, you should turn off this blunt tool and set your levels manually. The problem with auto gain is that it doesn't just allow soft noises be soft and loud noises be loud, it tries to bring every sound to a middle volume, so it is constantly responding to peaks and pauses in audio, adjusting levels up when there is quiet and down when a loud noise occurs, however briefly. The background sounds, too, rise and fall very noticeably with each auto adjustment. In Chapter 16 we explore in detail the proper method for setting levels manually.

Portable Field Mixers

Portable field mixers (also **microphone mixers**) are small audio consoles that allow for independent level control of multiple microphone inputs (usually from one to four) and then output this audio as either a microphone or line signal to your camcorder (**Figure 15-23**). Many sound mixers working with DV single-system setups find portable mixers an indispensable tool, because camcorder level controls are located right on the camera itself and it can be very awkward to have the sound recordist hovering around the camera setting levels. Using a field mixer enables the sound recordist to precisely monitor and control levels (and use multiple microphones) at a distance. The output of a field mixer can connect with the camera via a standard XLR cable or via a wireless connection for true independence of movement (**Figure 15-24**). It is vital, however, to calibrate the gain levels of each device (mixer and camcorder or mixer and sound recorder) in order to maintain audio level consistency from mixer to recorder. Again, this process is discussed in detail in the section on setting levels in Chapter 16.

Located in the signal chain between the microphones and the camcorder audio input, field mixers are small enough to be worn in a carrying case over the shoulder, if there is only one sound person who is also holding the boom. Field mixers are also handy when shooting double-system sound because of their capacity for multiple microphone inputs.

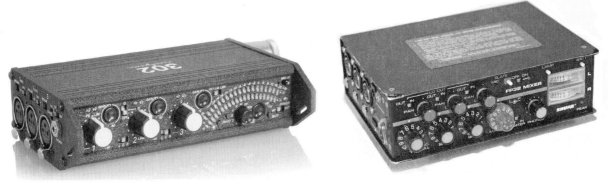

■ **Figure 15-23** Field mixers allow precise control over the recording levels of several inputs. Pictured are two popular three-channel mixers, the Sound Devices 302 *(left)* and the Shure FP33 *(right)*.

■ MICROPHONES

Simply put, a microphone is a device that converts acoustic energy (sound waves) into electrical energy (electrical signal). All microphones are constructed with a diaphragm, a thin membrane that is extremely sensitive to the vibration of air particles. The vibrations of the **diaphragm**, which correspond to the sound waves buffeting it, are translated into fluctuating voltage. One of the ways we identify different microphones is by the method they employ to make this conversion.

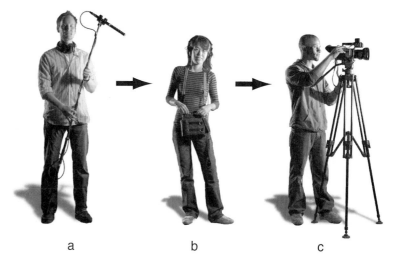

a   b   c

■ **Figure 15-24** A typical single system sound configuration. Boom operator (a), sound recordist adjusting levels with field mixer (b), and audio recorded on camcorder (c).

Dynamic, Condenser, and Electret Condenser

A common type of microphone for film and video field production is the **dynamic microphone**, which generates a signal through electromagnetic principles. This microphone is sometimes called a **moving coil microphone**, after the element that converts the acoustic energy into an electrical signal. Basically, a dynamic microphone element consists of a highly acoustically sensitive diaphragm to which a wire coil, with a permanent magnetic charge, is attached. This coil is called the **voice coil** and is suspended around a permanently fixed magnet. As the diaphragm responds to a particular sound source, the coil moves up and down with the vibrations of the diaphragm. The movement of the magnetized coil through the electromagnetic current of the permanent magnet produces an electrical output that is analogous to the original acoustic vibrations (**Figure 15-25**, *left*).

Dynamic microphones are renowned for their rugged construction, which makes this kind of microphone a favorite on location shooting. They are also less expensive than other types of microphones. Naturally, many of the technical factors, such as sensitivity and frequency range, depend on the manufacturer of the mike, but as a general rule dynamic mikes are fairly sensitive and also have a fairly good frequency response. In close mike situations they are more than adequate, which is why news reporters who report from the field usually use these mikes. When greater sensitivity and frequency response are necessary, then we usually turn to the condenser microphone.

Condenser and **electret condenser** microphones work on a similar principle; however, instead of using an electromagnetic current (like the dynamic mike), condenser and electret condenser mikes work on voltage fluctuations within an electric **capacitor** (another name for condenser). The capacitor is made of two round plates oriented parallel to each other, with a very narrow space between them called the **dielectric**. One plate is the microphone's diaphragm, a movable acoustically sensitive membrane; the other is a fixed plate called the **back plate**. Both of these plates are charged with polarized voltage. When sound waves buffet the diaphragm, the voltage relationship between these plates changes correspondingly, which results in the audio signal. The output signal of this capacitor is very low, so condenser microphones have a **preamplifier** built into the microphone (**Figure 15-25**, *right*).

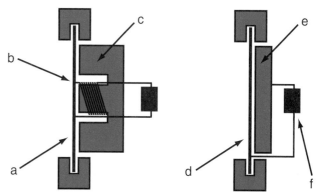

■ **Figure 15-25** A moving coil microphone *(left)* works by converting the movement of a diaphragm (a) into an electrical charge when the coil (b) attached to it moves up and down while suspended around magnets (c). A condenser microphone *(right)* uses a positively charged diaphragm (d) and the negatively charged back plate (e) to form a capacitor; the movement between these two electrically charged plates creates voltage fluctuations that are sent to a preamp (f).

In order for the capacitor to work, both plates require some source of power to provide the necessary polarizing voltage; the preamp also requires some power. Condenser mikes can be powered through the use of **phantom power**, which is power provided by the record deck or a mixer, delivered to the microphone via one of the three XLR cable prongs, or through the use of a **battery power source**, which is usually located in an intermediary capsule connected to the microphone (Figure 15-26).

The **electret condenser** microphone works on exactly the same capacitor principle as does the condenser microphone, but one of the two plates in an electret condenser is manufactured with a permanent charge, so there is no external power source necessary. The preamp, however, still requires power, but much less than is required by a standard condenser. This is usually accomplished by a small battery located in the microphone itself (sometimes AA, or the smaller N battery, or the even smaller LR44 1.5 volt). The low power requirements allow for a more compact design, which is always welcome in field production. Condenser microphones are generally more sensitive than dynamic mikes, both in terms of pickup distance and frequency response. They are especially good with high-frequency audio. However, they cost more than dynamic mikes and are considerably more fragile.

Most professional-quality microphones send a **balanced output** utilizing the standard **XLR** professional microphone connector (Figure 15-27). A balanced output means that the signal is running in opposite directions along two wires within the microphone cable. This effectively cancels out any noise. A balanced line also incorporates a shield, a wire mesh that covers the two hot wires and is connected to ground. This shield greatly protects the signal from interference caused by AC or fluorescent hum and radio frequencies. This is precisely the shortcoming of the ⅛-inch mini microphone inputs on some consumer-level recorders and DV camcorders. In general, miniplugs are neither balanced nor shielded. The other advantage to the XLR connectors and cables is that the actual connectors are rugged and the male end of the connector fits with the female end through a tongue-and-groove fit and a spring lock, providing for a strong and stable connection that cannot be inadvertently pulled loose. This is especially useful when linking a number of cables together to lengthen the reach of the microphone.

Microphone Frequency Response

Frequency response refers to the sensitivity of a given microphone to frequencies in the sound spectrum. This measurement is represented on a frequency response graph (Figure 15-28). The x-axis on this graph measures the microphone's response in dB, and

■ **Figure 15-26**
Condenser microphones, like the Sennheiser shotgun pictured, need a battery to provide the power necessary to charge the capacitor.

■ **Figure 15-27** The standard professional audio cable is the XLR, a tough and inexpensive solution for sending balanced, distortion-free audio between microphones and recorders.

the y-axis measures the frequency. A perfect microphone would have an equal response throughout all frequencies of the sound spectrum. If we were to plot this perfect response on a graph, the line would appear perfectly flat. This would be the theoretical, perfect **flat response**. Flat response in the real microphone world means that, given a large frequency range, a microphone can respond fairly equally throughout. For most microphones, when the extremes of their capabilities are reached, the response dips. All professional microphones come with a spec sheet that will indicate the instrument's frequency range.

Some microphones come with a **low-end roll-off** switch so that one can choose to make the microphone less sensitive to low frequencies, which are often caused by wind or machine noise in the field. A roll-off switch usually has two symbols. It is generally agreed that it's always best, if given a choice, to leave the microphone on flat response, gather as much of the frequency range as possible, and then tweak your audio in postproduction, where graphic equalizers can be much more precise in removing unwanted frequencies (**Figure 15-29**).

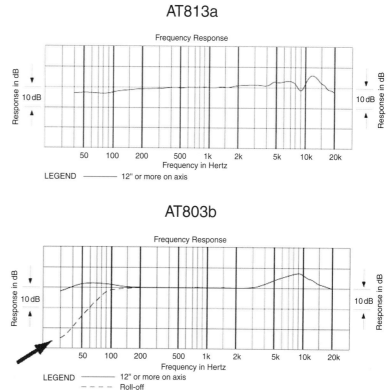

■ **Figure 15-28** A frequency response graph plots how sensitive (measured in dB, on the x-axis) a microphone is to a range of frequencies (measured in Hz on the y-axis). Note that the AT803b, an omnidirectional lavaliere condenser microphone, has a "roll-off" option that affects its sensitivity to low frequencies *(arrow)*.

Microphone Directionality

In addition to the method of generating the electronic signal (dynamic versus condenser), we also identify mikes by their **directionality** (also called **pickup pattern**), which distinguishes the area and range within which the microphone will respond optimally. This is a critical factor in choosing the right microphone for any given recording situation, as different microphones are constructed to have specialized directionality characteristics. In simple terms, directionality is sometimes described by a microphone's basic **angle of acceptance**, which is the area from which a microphone will gather sound. Mikes are often broadly categorized as **nondirectional** (wide angle of acceptance), **directional** (limited to a medium angle of acceptance), and **ultradirectional** (very narrow angle of acceptance). However, the **polarity pattern**, represented in **polarity graphs**, is a more accurate three-dimensional conceptualization of a microphone's pickup pattern.

Omnidirectional

A omnidirectional microphone (**Figure 15-30**) picks up audio from all directions equally (called a broad or wide pickup pattern). This microphone is a good choice for recording general ambient sounds (like crowd noises) or for miking a scene where sound emanates from a number of different directions or for groups of people (e.g., four friends gathered around a table for dinner). This is a good choice for interviews in which you want both the interviewer and the interviewee to be miked and recorded equally. A **lavaliere** microphone (**lav** for short) usually has an omnidirectional pattern but also has a highly specialized function. Lavalieres are tiny, clip-on mikes that can be attached to a lapel or tie or easily hidden under a collar, and

■ **Figure 15-29** Some microphones have a "low-end roll-off" setting (b) that makes them less sensitive to low frequencies, usually caused by wind or machine noise. The flat response setting (a) is preferable for most situations.

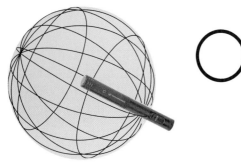

Figure 15-30 The pickup pattern of an omnidirectional microphone allows it to capture sound equally from all directions.

they are used for close miking talent (**Figure 15-31**). However, as tiny omnidirectional mikes, they are handy for hiding in the middle of a scene, say behind a candle during a dinner table sequence. One must be aware, though, that these mikes are intended to be placed near the chest of a speaker, where a great deal of bass is generated, so many lavs employ some degree of low-frequency roll-off (see **Figure 15-28**). Using them as an omnidirectional mike in a crowd situation can result in somewhat thin sound.

Cardioids

The pickup pattern of a **cardioid** microphone (**Figure 15-32**) is just as its name suggests (cardioid/cardiac): heart shaped. The pickup pattern is somewhat directional, so the mike can be aimed specifically at the source of the audio, which minimizes extraneous noise yet still provides a natural ambient feel. Its sensitivity is primarily in front, with some sensitivity to the sides, but the mike picks up very little from behind, which is usually where the equipment and crew are. This is the most common microphone used in film production because it offers both control and extremely high quality. When miking a single person speaking, this is the microphone of choice.

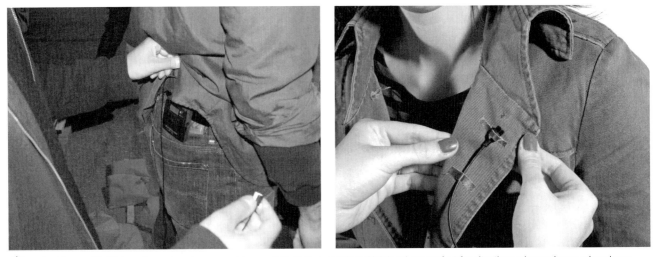

Figure 15-31 Lavaliere microphones must be carefully hidden on talent *(right)* and are perfect for situations where a boom microphone cannot be used or when close miking is needed. If the lavaliere is wireless, the transmitter *(left)* must be concealed as well.

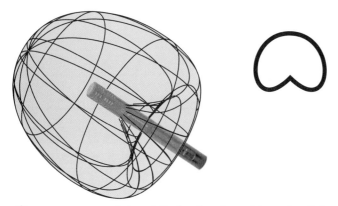

Figure 15-32 A cardioid microphone has a pickup pattern that favors sound coming from the front and sides, but not from behind.

Hypercardioids and Shotguns

Hypercardioids and **shotgun mikes** (also called **supercardioid** or **line mikes**) (**Figure 15-33**) both generally duplicate the heart-shaped pickup pattern, but these mikes are considerably more sensitive than the cardioid and are used when close miking isn't possible (e.g., because of wider camera framings). Their pickup patterns are highly directional, meaning that they are considerably narrower than a cardioid and can be held at a greater distance. The shotgun mike is the more sensitive and directional of the two. There are drawbacks, however, to using both of these microphones. Because these mikes are so sensitive, one must be careful when using them indoors. Not only will they

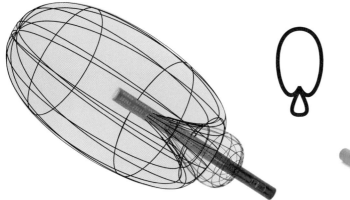

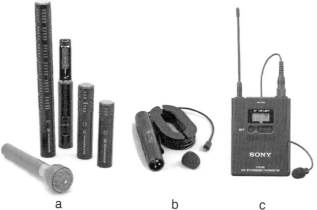

a   b   c

■ **Figure 15-33** A hypercardioid microphone pickup pattern has a narrow range of acceptance and increased sensitivity. It greatly favors sound coming from the front and not from the sides or back.

■ **Figure 15-34** A sound person's basic microphone arsenal: a sturdy dynamic cardioid microphone and a modular condenser system offering three interchangeable heads: omni, cardioid, and supercardioid (a); a lavaliere mike (b); and a wireless microphone system (c).

pick up the sound directly from the source, but also they will easily pick up the reflections of that sound, resulting in a boomy quality to the audio. These mikes are quite successful outdoors, but here, too, one must be careful about sounds reflecting off surfaces within the mike's direct pickup pattern. For example, a couple is seated at a small table in a garden restaurant. There is a wall behind them and a small fountain in the garden. A shotgun microphone can pick up and exaggerate the sound of the fountain reflecting off the wall behind the subjects, even if the fountain is behind the microphone.

in practice

To hear recorded samples of these microphone types so that you can compare their unique pickup qualities, go to Interactive **Figures 15-30 through 15-33** (interior and exterior) at www.voiceandvisionbook.com.

Wireless and On-Board Microphones

Wireless Microphones

Wireless microphones (also called **radio mikes**) consist of a small pocketsize transmitter to which a microphone (very often a lavaliere) is attached, which transmits the electrical audio signal via VHF high-band or FM frequencies to a receiver; the receiver itself is connected to the input of the record deck. Using wireless lavalieres allows close miking while maintaining the talent's freedom of movement, because they carry both the concealed microphone and the transmitter on their person (see Figure 15-31). In addition to wireless lavalieres, there are many radio mike systems on the market that allow you to adapt virtually any professional microphone into a wireless mike with a plug-on transmitter, which means that even the boom operator need not be tethered to the sound recorder by an XLR cable. In both cases, wireless mikes allow a sound mixer to get great audio no matter how wide the framing! If there is a downside to wireless microphones, it is that they are vulnerable to interference, especially the farther the transmitter is from the receiver. Some systems use a "diversity" system that is constantly searching for the clearest transmission channel. Nonetheless, you should always have XLR cables handy (see in practice box next page).

On-Board Microphones

Another microphone that should be mentioned is the **on-board microphone** (or **camera microphone**) found on a DV camcorder. These are factory-provided microphones that are fixed to a mount above the lens. Professional cameras allow you to mount your own microphone. Generally these microphones are for news gathering or down-and-dirty

A filmmaker friend of mine, Didier Rouget, shot his short film *Urban/Suburban* (2006) in the Sahara Desert. He conceived of very wide landscape shots as we followed two yuppies who, even though they are hopelessly lost in the desert, cannot stop talking about real estate investments. Clearly, wireless lavaliere mikes were the best choice, so this is what the sound recordist brought to the desert location. As the crew was setting up for a champion shot that included the actors in the foreground with a dazzling setting sun behind them, they discovered that they could not find a clean VHF channel to transmit the audio. Even though they were in a remote corner of the Sahara Desert, they discovered that this area was North Africa's Grand Central Station for innumerable radio signals, and using their wireless system was impossible. As Didier himself wrote to me, "We actually postponed the shoot until we finally found other wireless mikes with different VHF channels that work in this area. But I never found time enough to take this shot with the sun. Eventually, I was able to take only one shot, under a very cloudy sky. We all called this shot 'the damned shot.'" In the end, only Didier and his crew know that they missed a perfect shot, because the film works

beautifully nonetheless, but what's most important is how Didier concluded his letter to me: "It would have been better to shoot the first day as scheduled without sound, and postsynchronize it. Once more, I learned a lot with this experience." Indeed, in film we learn every single time we're on a set, as much from hardships as from successes (**Figure 15-35**).

■ **Figure 15-35** "Waiting on sound!" Rouget's, film set in the Sahara, sits and waits until a wireless microphone problem is corrected. Production still from *Urban/Suburban* (2006).

■ **Figure 15-36** Camera-mounted microphones are commonly found on even the cheapest video cameras, but the inability to control their position in relation to talent makes them of limited use for narrative filmmaking purposes.

documentary shooting where the camera operator is alone. The controllability of on-board mikes is too limited for most narrative filmmaking needs (**Figure 15-36**). The pickup patterns of these microphones vary from camera to camera. Lower-end camcorders often use an omnidirectional microphone, and broadcast cameras use the more directional supercardioids. Some on-board mikes are switchable from omnidirectional to directional. Obviously, the more directional the on-board microphone is, the more the audio pickup is restricted to the direction the camera is facing. Conversely, omnidirectional camera microphones often pick up noises from the camera operator and from the camera mechanisms like the servo zoom. In any case, the on-board microphone's positioning is obviously restricted by the camera angle and camera-to-subject distance. For this reason, in narrative film production, these microphones are either not used or they are used to pick up general ambient sound when specific audio, like dialogue, is not necessary to the scene.

■ THE SOUND TEAM

The basic production sound team on a small-scale film project usually consists of two people, the **sound mixer** (a.k.a. the **sound recordist**) and the **boom operator**. Occasionally, on shoots with very simple location audio requirements, you'll see one person performing both roles, but when gathering sync sound, like dialogue, is part of the production, two people are highly recommended. On bigger shoots with complex sync audio needs, there is a third person called the **cable wrangler**, who sets up equipment, holds a second boom when necessary, and wrangles the cable when the boom operator follows a moving shot. The sound personnel are a tight team, and they should be chosen with the same diligence as choosing the D.P., A.C., and gaffer. The sound mixer is the head of the sound department and is responsible for getting the best quality audio onto the recording format. This not only means setting the record levels on the sound recorder but also includes understanding the acoustics and ambient qualities of a given location, listening for unwanted noise intrusions on the set, and choosing the most appropriate microphones for the situation. The sound mixer works very closely with the boom operator in strategizing optimal microphone placement. The boom operator is responsible for placing the microphone where it needs to be, whether that means holding it aloft over a scene, hiding it under an actor's collar, planting in somewhere on the set, or any combination of these. The boom operator must know the pickup patterns and capabilities of a variety of microphones and how they function in different acoustic environments (**Figure 16-1**).

As I have mentioned before, getting good location sound is as important to a film as getting great images, but all too often novices think about audio only at the last minute and choose the sound team either from people on the set who don't look busy or from people with utterly no experience but who are "willing to do anything" to be on a film set. But getting good quality audio in the field can make the difference between a smooth postproduction process and a nasty, expensive one. To ensure the success of your shoot and your editing, it is important to choose a competent and knowledgeable sound crew who will dedicate themselves exclusively to the task of getting great sound.

Good recording technique and postproduction mixing are more important now than ever before. The digital revolution has made great quality sound recording and reproduction technology within everyone's reach— even to the point where many homes are equipped with super-high-fidelity surround sound home movie systems. So filmmakers no longer can expect that their final products will be heard through a built-in, three-inch, mono speaker on the family TV set. Nor can low-budget filmmakers expect to show their work only as a 16mm film print with its accompanying poor-quality optical track. These days you really need great sound, because in almost every screening venue, it shows! Three factors play a major role in getting the best audio in the field: recording technique, microphone technique, and simply using your ears.

■ **Figure 16-1** The sound crew for Chu's *The Treasure Hunter* (2009): sound mixer *(right)*, boom op *(center)*, and cable wrangler *(left)*. The importance of getting the best possible sound quality rests on their shoulders, even in hostile environments, like the windswept sands of Inner Mongolia. (Photo courtesy of 3H sound studio.)

While taking a break from writing this book, I was strolling through Washington Square Park and found myself watching a group of students from a nearby university shooting a sync sound film exercise. They, of course, had no idea I was a film professor taking notes for a textbook. The director very seriously selected his shot and blocked the actors' movement through the scene, all the while communicating brilliantly with the cinematographer. Off to the side, lying on the ground unattended, was the sound recording gear. After the actors and camera operator rehearsed the scene two or three times, the director turned to the others in his small production group and asked, "Who's gonna hold the boom this time?" The group shuffled their feet and cast glances at one another, but no one volunteered. "C'mon, we need someone on the boom," pleaded the director. Finally, another actor, who was not in this particular shot, stepped forward and said "Alright, I'll do it." He grabbed the boom, planted its base in his stomach, near his belly button, and dangled the mike in the general vicinity of the camera. The director ran around to the sound recorder, slipped on the headphones and called, "Roll camera!" He then rolled sound and yelled "Action!" As the take played out, he closely watched the movements of the actors, never once looking at the sound levels. "Cut!" he yelled. And then, tossing the headphones aside, said, "That *looked* great! Next shot." He probably had a take that did look good, but he also had one that would undoubtedly give him massive audio headaches in postproduction. And me? I got a nice cautionary tale for my book.

Sound Preproduction

Successful sound recording begins in preproduction. At this stage directors, art directors, and D.P.s tend to overlook sound issues, so if a film relies heavily on location sync sound recording, here are three tips for ensuring that you get the audio you want:

1. The sound mixer should go on location tech surveys to thoroughly scout the environment ahead of time. On the tech survey the sound mixer should check room acoustics and ambience and should look for any "noisemakers" at the location, like refrigerators, fans, fluorescent lights, and radiators. Then the sound mixer should check the larger environment surrounding the specific location for noisemakers such as nearby highways, playgrounds, airports, and construction sites. This can take some time as a location can sound great for a few minutes, but if you remain long enough you may discover that there is a bus stop right outside the front window where a noisy bus passes by every 12 minutes. If you're shooting in someone's apartment, it's perfectly reasonable to ask them how noisy the neighbors are and how loud they play their music or TV?

2. The director (or D.P.) should communicate with the sound team. Give the sound mixer some sense for what the visual strategy of the film will be. Long static shots with carefully composed lighting will require one sort of miking strategy, while handheld shooting on a set which is lit for 360° movement, will need something totally different. Go over the script, scene by scene, and work out what the possible audio challenges might be. All of this helps the sound team anticipate what audio equipment they'll need on the set. In general, this sort of communication fosters a sense of collaboration and quite simply helps them do their job better—which in turn makes the quality of your audio better.

3. The sound team should communicate, before getting on the set, with whomever will be editing and creating the sound design for the film to ensure that they are on the same page as far as technical specs, record media, and delivery details are concerned. Different edit systems, editors and sound designers prefer their sound elements in various formats or recorded at specific settings. It's best to know what editorial requires before the shooting starts.

■ RECORDING TECHNIQUE

The **sound mixer's** job is to get the best possible recording of all field production audio, including dialogue, wild sound effects, wild dialogue, and location ambient sound. This means several things: cleanly picking up and isolating the sounds you want from the unwanted background noise, recording a strong signal, and ensuring the greatest frequency range. It also means being fast, reliable, and consistent; fitting yourself around the lighting, camera, and art department setups; and constantly and creatively adjusting to shifting audio conditions. Solving audio issues on the set is a constant challenge, and it takes resourcefulness, ingenuity, and knowledge. Good sound recordists are not easy to come by, but, by the same token, good sound people are in high demand and work—a lot.

Setting Levels

The term **levels** refers to the **loudness** of a signal as it enters the audio recorder, which in turn determines the strength of the recorded audio signal. As mentioned earlier, all professional recorders offer manual level controls, allowing the sound recordist to control the strength of the signal; this is called **setting levels**. Getting strong audio levels depends on a combination of microphone

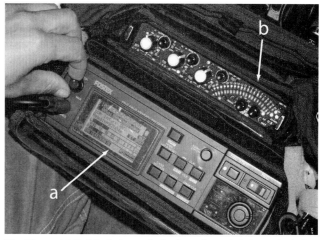

■ **Figure 16-2** A typical sound mixer's equipment chain can include a sound recorder (with a peak meter) (a) and a mike mixer (with a VU meter) (b).

placement and manual audio level adjustment. The craft of the sound mixer centers on the ability to find proper levels, which generally means setting the loudest possible record level without overmodulating. This provides for the best sound signal for playback and postproduction. For the sound mixer, the most important tools for monitoring and setting audio levels on a digital recorder or DV camcorder are the **peak meter** (found primarily on sound recorders) and the **VU meter** (found primarily on field mixers) (Figure 16-2).

Setting Levels on a Peak Meter

Peak meters are found on DV camcorders and stand-alone digital audio recorders and measure the strength of the incoming signal. Peak meters are calibrated in decibels, from –50 dB on the low side to 0 dB on the high side. If your audio level exceeds the maximum, 0 dB, your audio will become **overmodulated** or **overloaded**, which means the signal is too strong to be sampled accurately and the result is distorted sound. Sudden and loud transient sounds, like a car door slamming shut, which **spike** above 0 dB are especially a problem, because even these brief noises can cause crackling on the sound track. You cannot fix overmodulated sound in postproduction. On the other hand, if we record a level that is too low, then we will be required to turn up the volume in postproduction to transfer or even hear this weak signal. By turning up the volume of the recorded signal, we also turn up the volume of the unwanted audio noise and the result is greater background and system noise. Recording too low is called recording **"in the mud,"** the mud being system noise. Be careful, however; recording too low is different than recording soft sounds, which sometimes, appropriately, barely register on the peak meter.

To make sure you obtain a good, strong signal, but protect yourself from overmodulation, you should set your levels so that the loudest audio in the scene peaks around –12 dB on the peak meter. For example, if you have a scene in which a man is arguing with a store clerk and his last line "... and I'm never coming back to this dump!" is the loudest the actor projects in the scene, then, during rehearsals, you will set your levels so this line of dialogue registers around –12 dB on the peak meter. The rest of the actor's dialogue will register lower on the meter, as it should. The range between –12 dB and 0 db is called **headroom** and it gives us a buffer for any unforeseen and sudden audio spikes—like the man slamming the door on his way out. The record level for normal dialogue should generally fall between –20 dB and –18 dB (Figure 16-3).

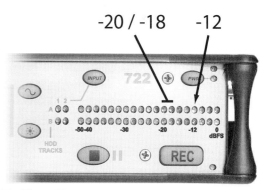

■ **Figure 16-3** Normal dialogue should be recorded around –20 to –18 dB on the peak meter. Loud sounds should peak at –12 dB or else they risk overmodulating.

When we initially set levels for dialogue (usually during on-set rehearsals) this "normal" dialogue level is only our first reference. It is the job of the sound mixer and boom operator to find acceptable mike placement and levels as quickly as possible and then make adjustments to improve the audio with each rehearsal and with each take. This initial **sound check** is usually done with the actors as the crew makes final adjustments to the lights and camera. You should try to find a moment with the actors, before the director runs through the take, to have them speak into the microphone. Sometimes they'll run through a few lines, or you can ask them a question that they need to answer at length. Remember, this is only a starting point. Actors often speak louder or softer than their normal speaking voice once the camera rolls and they're performing. The first run-through or first take will usually help you to tweak your levels (and microphone placement) to get a better signal on subsequent takes.

When setting record levels, it is best to avoid extremes on the level control knobs. We never want to have our gain control set all the way to its loudest point or too close to its lowest setting. These extremes usually mean there is either something wrong with your microphone placement or you have some technical problem along the signal path. Not all sounds need to be recorded between –20 dB and –10 dB, especially when recording soft sounds. Very low sounds, like papers rustling as someone studies in the library, are fine to record at a low level like –40 dB or –30 dB. Trying to get this soft sound to peak at –20 dB will force you to turn the levels up to their maximum, which will increase the extraneous room noise (ambient sound) to an unnaturally high level. This will also exaggerate unwanted system noise. If a fairly strong source, say a person speaking, is registering very low on the meter, then it's preferable to move the microphone in closer instead of boosting the recording levels all the way. And vice versa, if a very loud, consistent noise, like an unmuffled motorcycle engine, is spiking the levels, it's advisable to move the microphone away rather than turning the record levels nearly all the way down. In short, through careful microphone placement (of course, respecting the pickup range of the mike), you should keep your pots within the middle three-fourths of its range.

As already mentioned, the difference between the loudest and softest sounds in any single recording situation is called the dynamic range, and setting levels for a sound situation with a wide dynamic range is a mixer's greatest challenge. It's a temptation to raise and lower the recording levels during recording as the sounds increase and decrease; this practice is called **riding levels** (also called **riding gain**). But riding levels causes unnatural fluctuations in the background noise and it can also be a problem with sudden loud or soft passages that were not anticipated and therefore spike above 0 dB or fall into the mud. The main problem with riding levels is that a range of loud and soft sounds is simply natural. If you constantly raise and lower the levels so that every sound records at the same level, the effect is terribly unnatural. Occasionally riding levels may be necessary, especially in uncontrolled situations. But for most controlled environments, we anticipate (or rehearse through) the loudest possible sound for a given situation, set that level at –12 dB, and leave the sound levels alone.

Setting Levels on a VU Meter

If you use a field mixer for setting levels you will likely have a **VU meter** (short for **volume unit meter**) for reference. As we mentioned previously, peak meters respond to all sounds directly entering the recorder. The VU meter, on the other hand, indicates an average sound level. It is, therefore, not highly sensitive to short, sharp, percussive sounds (transient sounds). For example, a slamming door the middle of a moderately quiet scene will cause the needle to jump a bit, but not to the true decibel level of that slam, because the noise is too brief for the needle to respond directly. In addition, although the VU level range is calibrated in decibels, it has a different scale and runs from –20 on the low end to +3 on the high end, with 0 dB as the audio peak level. The point on the scale from 0 dB to +3 is highlighted by a thicker, red bar on a needle scale or red lights on an LED scale (Figure 16-4).

As a general rule, the loudest sounds in a given recording situation should peak at 0 dB. Occasionally, the reading can peak into the red zone but should not spend too much time there, and in no situation should the VU meter needle "pin" against the +3 side of the scale. A +3 on the VU scale means overmodulation and distorted sound. Normally spoken dialogue voice is usually set to average around –3 dB so that any sudden, loudly expressive moments might peak between –1 dB and 0 dB. Very low sounds, like our previous paper rustling in the library, can be set to register around –10 dB.

Reference Tone and Calibration

Reference tone (also called **lineup tone**) is a 1-kHz pure tone that is used as a reference for calibrating a chain of audio devices in the field. For example, let's say we are plugging our microphone into a field mixer (with VU meters) that we will use to set levels during the shoot. The mike signal then goes from the mixer into either the DV camcorder (with peak meters) or to a sound recorder (with peak meters) where it is recorded (see **Figures 15-24** and **16-2**). This is a very common audio chain, but how do we know where to set our gain control on the camcorder (or sound recorder) so that we get the same audio levels we are setting on the mixer?

-5 / -2   0 / +1

■ **Figure 16-4** The scale of a VU meter is different from that of a peak meter. The loudest signal should peak between 0 dB to +1 dB, with normal dialogue registering between –5 dB to –2 dB.

All field mixers have a button that, when depressed, will generate the 1-kHz reference tone, which allows us to set the recorder levels so that it will record exactly the audio signal levels the mixer is sending. The 1-kHz tone registers exactly as 0 dB on all VU meters; the equivalent level on digital peak meters (according to NTSC) is –20 dB.[1] So when you send the reference tone from the field mixer to the recorder, simply set your peak levels to –20 dB and then forget them; the camcorder (or sound recorder) input level is now calibrated to record the same audio levels you are setting on your mixer (**Figure 16-5**).

One final note about reference tone. It is standard practice to record 30 seconds of reference tone at the head of your record media (Flash card, DVD-RAM, DAT tape, etc.) so that audio transfers and level reference in postproduction can also be calibrated with the original audio recording. This is called **headtone** and it assures the postproduction folks that what they are hearing is exactly what was recorded!

Manual versus Automatic Functions
Camcorder Audio: Manual versus Automatic Level Control

Most camcorders have a setting for **automatic level control**, sometimes called **auto gain**. Auto gain gives away the control for setting audio levels to the recorder, which assumes that there is a single proper level for all sounds. In low-volume situations the record level automatically increases, and in loud environments the signal is depressed — like a robot relentlessly riding the gain. Auto gain is easily fooled by sudden, sharp sounds (called **transient sounds**) or drastic dips in volume. If we are shooting a scene where two people are talking in a normal tone of voice around a dining room table

0   -20

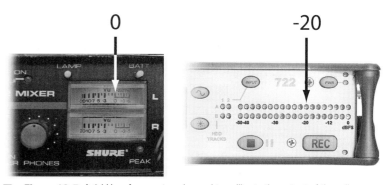

■ **Figure 16-5** A 1 kHz reference tone is used to calibrate the output of the mike mixer with the input of the recorder (or camcorder). The mixer's VU meter reads the tone at 0 dB *(left)*, whereas the recorder's peak meter should be set to register the tone at –20 dB *(right)*.

[1]Many professional sound mixers I've spoken with believe that the –20 dB reference standard is slightly too low and prefer to set their camcorder or digital recorder peak meter at –18 dB against the reference tone.

Figure 16-6 The auto gain control found on many video cameras should be turned off to have precise control over the recording level of the audio signal.

and suddenly a fork is dropped against a plate, the auto gain will compensate for this sudden, sharp noise by immediately lowering the levels. If a character then speaks directly after this, that initial dialogue will be recorded way too low until the gain readjusts itself back to the dialogue level—which always takes some time. Conversely, if two people are speaking in expressive tone of voice and suddenly stop talking, the auto gain will respond to this quiet moment by adjusting the volume up, resulting in a conspicuous boost in room noise. If your camera has the option for **manual override**, use it. If your camera *doesn't* have a manual override option and field audio is important for the project, then reconsider using that camera for audio recording—think double system! A sound recordist is always better off maintaining full control of the audio signal being recorded (**Figure 16-6**).

Limiters and Frequency Filter

Other automatic audio controls that you will encounter on record decks and field mixers are limiters and frequency filters. **Limiters** are volume controls that only come into effect when an audio signal reaches overload. At this point the limiter suppresses the loudness by **clipping** off the sounds before they can peak. The danger with employing a limiter is that it can be difficult for an operator to tell if the levels are properly set, as volume extremes never peak. In controlled audio situations, try not to use the limiter at all, though limiters can be useful when a single person is both booming and setting levels and you anticipate some erratic loud noises in the scene. In these cases, set the levels for the most common audio first, then employ the limiter.

Frequency filters automatically remove unwanted portions of the frequency range (a feature often built into microphones). The most common filters are designed to cut off low frequencies and are variously called **bass**, **bass roll-off**, **low-pass**, or **low-frequency attenuation filters**. Bass roll-off is common because we often encounter wind noise (wind hitting the microphone diaphragm) and low machinery hum (like rumbling HVAC systems) in the field. For example, perhaps we are filming in a factory where there is a constant, low-frequency machinery hum that is making the dialogue between two actors difficult to record. A low-frequency filter will automatically suppress frequencies, say, below 50 Hz (the specific frequencies rolled off are variable depending on the system). In general, it is not a good idea to use any sort of frequency filters in the field. The equalizing capabilities in postproduction are far more sophisticated and precise than those on field recording equipment and should be used instead. The sound recordist should gather the widest possible frequency range and then be more selective (and creative) about equalizing frequencies out of the audio later in the sound mixing stage.

Headphone Monitoring

In the field, sound monitoring is always done through headphones during actual sound recording. Headphones with isolation pads are essential so that the sound people (both mixer and boom op) can be certain that what they are hearing is only the audio being picked up by the microphone. It is important to remember that we use the meters when setting and monitoring audio levels and *not* judge levels by what we hear through the headphones. Most professional audio recorders and camcorders offer a separate headphone level adjustment, so it is quite possible to have the headphone level set so high that audio sounds fine to your ear but is being recorded at an unacceptably low level. First set your audio to the proper levels with your meters, and then set the headphone to a comfortable volume. You shouldn't need to change the headphone volume again (**Figure 16-7**).

Headphones are used to monitor the types of sounds being recorded and to listen for sound problems (loose connections, signal interference, unwanted background noise, etc.). Headphones are also used to evaluate other aural qualities of the recording situation, like the acoustics of the recording location. Once the gain levels are set, the sound mixer and the boom operator (who should be wearing headphones as well) can also monitor the accuracy of the microphone placement; being sure to keep it on-axis and the subject-to-mike distance consistent (discussed later).

Just as a cinematographer is trained to see every light source on the scene, a sound mixer is trained to hear every sound on the location that might wind up on the recording. However, humans have developed highly selective hearing. It is easy for us to ignore or "filter out" inessential sounds and focus only on the sounds we need to hear in a particular situation. It's easy to go through an entire day and never really "hear" the air conditioning droning in the background, or the constant buzz of crickets out your window, or the hum of the cooling fan in your computer. Background noises just like these can be anything from distracting to disastrous on an audio recording, so a sound mixer

■ **Figure 16-7** Large headphones that completely cover the ears should be used to monitor audio, because they block out noise.

needs to develop an "objective ear" and must communicate to the director when unwanted sounds are infiltrating the scene, especially when they are intermittent sounds, like a plane flying overhead, or a news radio coming through the wall from next door, or the refrigerator in the kitchen kicking on. Chances are, no one else on the set has heard any of these noises.

■ MICROPHONE TECHNIQUE

Balance, Consistency, and Being On-Axis

A typical field recording situation includes dialogue (involving one, two, or three characters) and background sounds. The keys to getting good audio in the field are **balance** and **consistency**; balance is finding the right relationship between the audio we want (dialogue) and the background sounds, and consistency is maintaining this balance, as well as audio levels, from setup to setup. Recording in the field always means picking up some background sounds, but too much background noise can obscure the audio. Background sound in recording is like salt in cooking: you can always add a little more later, but you cannot take it out if you've put in too much.

Balance is controlled by two important factors: microphone choice (directionality) and distance. The distance between the microphone and the audio source, say an actor speaking dialogue, is as crucial as proper record levels. Getting the microphone in as close as possible is essential because the stronger the signal from our desired sound source, the lower we can set our record levels and therefore the lower the extraneous noise will be. The farther the microphone is from the source of audio, the more background sounds will infiltrate the recording. This is why we always try to get the microphone as close as possible to our actors. It is also important to understand the pickup pattern of your microphone and to place the projection of the audio source (i.e., the mouth of an actor speaking lines) **on-axis**, which means directly within the microphone's optimal sensitivity range (**Figure 16-8**). As a rule, the boom op first gets the microphone in its optimal position—as close as possible to the sound source and on-axis. "As close as possible" means checking with the camera operator to determine the edges of the visible frame and hovering as close to that limit as you can. Then the sound mixer can adjust gain levels on the recorder to get a strong signal. Remember, boosting the input gain to compensate for a badly positioned microphone (i.e., too far away and/or off-axis) will yield poor results.

■ **Figure 16-8** Microphones should be positioned "on-axis" according to their specific pickup pattern. Note how the microphone is pointing directly at the actor's mouth from above and slightly in front.

The microphone of choice most often for recording voices is the cardioid. It usually offers the flattest frequency response and a certain degree of directionality, so we have control over the source/background balance. Some cardioid microphones are manufactured with a **speech bump**, which means the microphone is especially sensitive to frequencies where the average human voice falls (midrange) and is less sensitive to high and low frequencies. If your framing allows you to position your microphone within 4 feet of the talent, then a regular cardioid will do; if the framing of your shot is wider than this, causing you to position a microphone from 4 to 10 feet, then a hypercardioid is a good choice. Beyond 10 feet, you could use a shotgun microphone, but remember that although this is a fine solution for exterior shots, in interior locations a shotgun will sound "boomy."

in practice

Good sound mixers hear everything. Not only are their ears attuned to the ambient noise, acoustic qualities, and problematic transient sounds of a given location, but they remain aware of aural opportunities as well, including wild sounds that might be useful later in postproduction. This is creative listening! On a recent film of mine, we had to postpone an exterior scene because a flock of crows flew in and squawked obnoxiously over all that nice dialogue I had written. So I decided to break for an early lunch, and later, when the crows had flown off to bother some other neighborhood, we continued the scene in peace. I discovered later that while we were at lunch, Michael (my sound mixer) had remained behind and recorded a few minutes of crows squawking. "Just in case you need it later," he said to me, adding that "it sounded really cool." My short film *FearFall* is about Ray, a middle-class man from the suburbs who descends into paranoia over his new next-door neighbors, whom he never sees. Sure enough, Michael was absolutely right. That little piece of wild sound, recorded impromptu, was pure gold in postproduction. I inserted those squawking, nagging crows as ambient sound in certain scenes later in the film, as Ray's paranoia gets the better of him. Those birds, which seemed to me a nuisance at the time, provided me with the perfect sound to subtly represent Ray's growing anxiety and fearful state of mind.

One indispensable tool for microphone placement, and a common sight on any film production, is the **boom pole** (also called **fishpole boom**), which allows us to position a mike as close as possible to the source but still remain outside the boundaries of the shot (**Figure 16-9**). A boom pole is a long, lightweight pole that telescopes out to various lengths. At one end is a **shock mount** that holds the microphone in place. Shock mounts come in many different styles but the principle for all is the same. The microphone is suspended securely in place by a series of rubber bands that absorb any vibrations or handling noise from the boom pole (**Figure 16-10**).

■ **Figure 16-9** A boom pole is essential to keep microphones as close to the actors as possible while keeping the mike and boom person off frame. Pictured is Antoin Cox booming. (Photo by Sil Stranders.)

■ **Figure 16-10** A shock mount keeps the microphone secured and prevents it from picking up vibrations caused by moving the boom pole.

The boom allows the operator to suspend the microphone on-axis precisely over and in front of the speaker (pointing directly at the source of audio), just out of the edge of the frame. Occasionally, it is advantageous to hold a boom below the talent and angle the microphone upward, but this can be tricky, as you may pick up background noises from above, like airplanes flying overhead if you are outdoors or fluorescent lights buzzing if you're inside.

Boom Technique

Using a boom requires careful technique. Below are a few tips:

1. Consistency is essential. A boom operator must maintain both a consistent distance between the speaker and microphone and the proper on-axis mike angle during a take. Pulling the boom away from a speaker, even a few inches, or slightly positioning the microphone off-axis will drastically shift the balance between the audio you want (i.e., dialogue) and the background noise.

2. Booms should be handled gently to reduce vibration on the pole, which can be transmitted up to the microphone. Take off all rings that can tap against the boom pole. Use your body and fingertips to change the angle of the microphone to keep actors on-axis.

3. Boom operators should monitor the audio with their own headphones to hear exactly what they are picking up.

4. The boom operator must communicate with the camera operator to determine the limits of the frame. During rehearsals and just before each take the boom op tests the framing by slowly lowering the mike into the scene. When the camera operator sees the mike at the edge of the frame, the boom op should back off a few inches to obtain some buffer space.

5. Care must taken not to cast a boom shadow over the set or on the talent. Usually, the boom operator sets up after everything is ready to go and fits in around the existing camera and lighting situation. If the only possible mike position casts a shadow, then the boom op should discuss options with the D.P. or gaffer for flagging or adjusting the light.

■ **Figure 16-11** Talent in motion can be especially difficult to keep "on-axis" while recording sound; rehearsals and knowledge of the script are necessary for good results.

6. Often boom operators are called upon to follow moving talent. Sometimes this means pivoting the body; other times, as with dolly shots, it may mean walking alongside the talent. Care must be taken to move quietly and maintain consistent subject-to-mike distance and pickup axis. Boom operators should practice these moves, know where they are going, and be especially aware of casting boom shadows when moving through a set (Figure 16-11).

7. A boom operator should be familiar with the script in order to anticipate movements and dialogue levels.

8. Remember, rehearsals are not just for the actors—they are for the crew as well. The sound team should perform their duties on every run through as if it were a real take and adjust tweak strategy along the way.

9. Some boom poles are made so that the mike cable runs inside, but in cases where the mike cable swings free, the cable should be loosely wrapped a few times around the pole to avoid having it slapping against the sides and transmitting noise to the mike.

10. In situations that are too tight for a boom pole, it is also possible to mount a microphone on a small handheld device called a **pistol grip** (with a shock mount) (Figure 16-12).

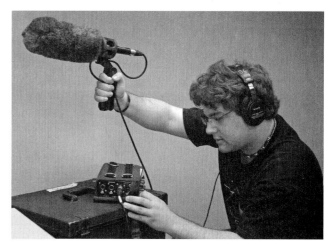

■ **Figure 16-12** Recording sound in close quarters can make handling a boom cumbersome; for these situations, a pistol grip is more convenient.

Using Lavaliere Mikes

There are certain situations for which booming is not a viable option. For example, long shots might not allow you to position a mike close enough to get decent audio, or perhaps character movement is so elaborate that a boom operator could not possibly follow the action. In these cases you may consider using a lavaliere microphone planted on your talent. Hiding lavaliere mikes requires a little bit of ingenuity, tact, and gaffer's tape (see **Figure 15-31**).

Lavalieres are also a good choice in very noisy environments or when you are working within wide shots. The extremely close miking of a lavaliere allows the sound mixer to greatly lower the input level, thereby reducing the background noise; additionally, you can position the actor so that their body acts as an absorbing sound buffer and blocks unwanted sounds.

Although lavalieres can indeed give you great sound, there are a number of other factors to be considered:

1. *Perspective problems.* The close, intimate audio presence of a lavaliere can seem odd in long shot situations. The sound is close but the image is distant. Perspective problems can be fixed in postproduction if you have access to the proper equipment, so before you use this strategy, know what is available to you in postproduction.

2. *Pickup axis.* Lavs need to be placed carefully with regard to vocal projection and possible direction shifts. For example, let's say we've hidden a lavaliere microphone under the left side of a performer's collar, but during the course of the take the performer turns and speaks over the opposite shoulder. The drop-off in the performer's audio level can be extreme (**Figure 16-13**).

3. *Noise.* Hiding a lavaliere microphone on the talent can pose an unwanted noise problem, as this type of mike is particularly vulnerable to "rustle" noises from clothes or fabric. Take care to tape down lavaliere microphones to clothes or to the body, such that there is no possibility of other fabric rubbing against the mike as the actor performs—for example, at the sternum in the little depression between the pectoral muscles. Every working sound person has a home remedy for rustle-free lavaliere mounting. One common method is to wrap a Band-Aid around the body of the lav to keep clothes from direct contact. One guy showed me an elaborate, bent-paperclip cage he made, a sort of teeny-tiny shock mount. It worked well, but unfortunately, I never could duplicate his sculptural creation on my own.

4. *Mobility.* Using a standard lavaliere microphone still means that the talent is tethered to a microphone cable that extends from their body (usually out of their pant leg) all the way to the recording deck. This can restrict movement. In instances where long shots are required and an actor's mobility is essential, a wireless microphone (RF mike) should be used (see page 349).

5. *Feelings.* Hiding a microphone on talent usually means working under a person's clothing, so you need to be tactful when approaching actors to wire them. Less experienced actors will tell you, "Give me the mike and I'll put it on myself." But this isn't a great idea for obvious reasons. It's best to wire your performers in a discreet place (don't, for example, ask them to take their shirt off in the middle of a busy set). Also, let them know

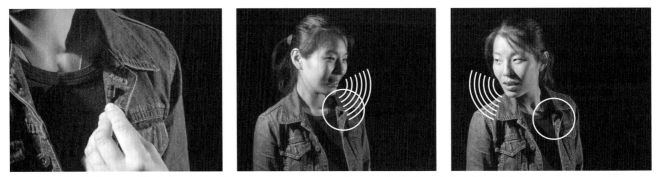

■ **Figure 16-13** Because of their tiny size, lavaliere microphones can be easily concealed in the actor's clothing *(left)*, but special care must be taken to stay "on-axis" *(center)*. A turn of the head can make the signal difficult to record *(right)*.

why all this is necessary; if you tell them that you're trying to record their lovely voice and their brilliant lines as cleanly as possible, then they're more likely to allow you to gaffer tape a microphone to their bra or to run an XLR cable down their pants. Also, if you need to plant a mike on a minor, always make sure their legal guardian in present.

Miking and Perspective

Obviously, the closer we can put the microphone to the speaker, the stronger our signal will be. But when we record for film we also need to consider the **perspective** of a person's voice and how the audio recording will relate to our expectations, given the frame size and the proximity of the camera to the subject. It will feel odd to have an extreme close-up on your characters and to hear their dialogue as if it's coming from a great distance, and vice versa. Fortunately, in narrative production much of this problem is more-or-less solved on its own, because even though we try to get the microphone in as tight as possible, the dimensions of the visual frame determine how close we can actually go before the mike shows up in the frame. A tight close-up allows us to place a microphone close to the subject, which will give us a better frequency response, warmer, more intimate sound, and less ambient noise intrusion. A wide shot will require us to keep the microphone a distance away, and this change in **perspective** is usually appropriate for the camera-to-subject proximity.

Using Multiple Microphones

Occasionally you may have a situation in which one microphone simply doesn't cover all the bases. This is especially the case with shots that involve a dialogue between two people who are far apart, or with long shots that involve substantial character movement. The former situation often requires a combination of booming and planting microphones on the set where characters will stand to deliver lines, whereas the latter case can simply mean hiding wireless lavalieres on your talent (**Figures 16-14** and **16-15**). Each location and each miking situation is unique and poses a variety of challenges. To a large extent, that's the fun of this job! As a sound mixer and boom operator you need to understand the capabilities and limitations of your equipment and be resourceful and creative in devising strategies to obtain the best possible audio under any circumstances.

Audio Continuity: Ambient Sound

Concerning ambient sounds, we also need to consider **audio continuity**. Continuity is usually discussed in visual terms, relating to making sure the actors are wearing the same clothes from shot to shot, or holding their glass with the same hand, but continuity is essential for audio also, and continuity problems usually come from radical shifts in ambiance from shot to shot. This is obviously true if there is some sort of intermittent intrusive noise recorded in, say, a reverse shot which wasn't there when recording the master shot— like a lawnmower or airplane. However, there are more subtle shifts in ambience that the sound team should be aware of. For example, in a simple dialogue scene we would never mike character A with a lavaliere for their close-up reverse shots and then mike character B with a hypercardioid for their close-up reverse shots. We would obviously get a drastic shift in presence and environmental noises. However, this sort of ambient shift also happens when we shoot a wide master shot with a hypercardioid and then switch to a regular cardioid for close-ups, something that would not be uncommon. Ambient shift can also occur if we use the same microphone but change the distance from sound

Figure 16-14 In this scene from Lund's *Snapshot* (2006), the framing made it necessary to use multiple mikes. A boom mike slightly off frame left was used for Nathan (David Andrews, *foreground*), while Marcello (Henry Darrow, *background*) was miked with a wireless lavaliere.

Figure 16-15 In this scene from Altman's *Nashville* (1975), six-way overlapping dialogue is recorded live thanks to the use of wireless lavaliere mikes on all of the talent.

source to microphone from shot to shot; because the recordist is required to change levels in this situation, we'll get a shift in ambient sound and therefore a discrepancy in audio continuity. If the background noises shift from shot to shot, it creates a tough situation for an editor who is trying to invisibly cut two shots together to create the illusion of continuous time and space. For this reason we always record one minute of **ambient sound** (or **room tone**) at each and every location. After the director calls the last "Cut," before anyone starts striking the set, the mixer needs to ask everyone to be quiet for one minute of room tone. The mike is then opened at the normal, speech level and the boom operator announces the sound take by stating (1) the production title, (2) the location, (3) the date, and (4) announcing "one minute of room tone." Then everyone stands stock still while they record one minute of general ambient sound. After one minute, the mixer calls "End ambience" and the set can be struck. It is important to do this while the crew and equipment are still on the set. Remember, they, too, were part of the ambient atmosphere during each take (the bodies absorb echoes, etc.). You must also do this even *before* turning off any movie lights, because they will make little pinging noises as the metal cools.

This is a practice that people usually have very little patience for on a hectic film set, but it pays off big dividends in the editing room, because the editor can use this baseline ambience as a separate track to smoothly suture together shots with differing ambience (see Chapter 23).

■ **Figure 16-16** Sound blankets off screen absorb sound before it bounces off hard surfaces. These blankets will not be visible in this medium close-up shot in a stairwell.

■ **Figure 16-17** Windscreens cut wind noise when shooting outdoors. There are models available for most mikes, even for lavs. Here a Rycote Softie is used on a super-cardioid mike.

Miscellaneous Recording Challenges

When directors scout a location, they are usually evaluating the visual qualities of the set, rather than its aural qualities. Frequently a sound team will find itself on a set that looks terrific to the camera, but that has serious problems for sound recording. **Reverberant spaces** are one such problem. Earlier in the book we spoke about "live" recording spaces with hard surfaces that bounce sound back and forth, creating sound reverberations. Too much reverberation, however, can create indistinct audio with muddy highs and boomy low frequencies. **Sound blankets** (often just mover's blankets) are used often when reverberation threatens to compromise sound quality. By hanging blankets just off screen and laying them on tiled floors, between the sound source and the reflective surfaces, you in effect absorb the sound before it can be reflected. The more blankets, the more sound is absorbed (**Figure 16-16**).

Another common sound challenge—this one for exterior location recording—is **wind noise**. Microphones are particularly vulnerable to wind noise because the wind acts like sound waves and buffet the highly sensitive microphone diaphragm. High winds can sound like a freight train, but soft winds, too, can contaminate sound by generating a low-frequency rumble. To this end, many microphones are manufactured with built-in **windscreens** that are foam wind buffers surrounding the head of the microphone. Windscreens dampen the effects of the wind on the diaphragm without altering the incoming sound waves. Built-in windscreens, however, are rarely enough protection from even the slightest breeze. Thankfully, there are many windscreens on the market that fit the head of almost any microphone—even for lavalieres—and you should always bring one to your exterior locations (**Figure 16-17**). In fact, most sound teams would never shoot outside without a windscreen on the mike.

On-Set Procedures

There are many ways to shoot a narrative film. The complexity of the project, the size of the crew, the nature of the location, and the style of the director all have an impact on what actually occurs on the film set. Director Kelly Reichardt shot her third feature film, *Old Joy,* with a crew of six, a principal cast of two, predominantly exterior locations and available light, and with everyone bunking together on location for the duration of the shoot (see page 18). Filmmaker Didier Rouget shot his second short film, *Vive le 14 Juillet,* in one day, on the streets of Paris, with three other crewmembers, two actors, no lights, and no sound (see this film at www.voiceandvisionbook.com). The shooting processes for these productions are bound to be different than those for your standard industry blockbuster film, with crewmembers numbering into the dozens and a veritable convoy of equipment trucks and trailers. There are many books on the market that explain in complex detail all of the tasks and procedures on a standard commercial feature film, but be careful: a production must adjust its personnel size and on-set procedures to the scale of the project, especially on short films, in order to keep the creative process from being weighed down by excessively elaborate logistics. On the other hand, you must make sure that you have adequate personnel, time, and equipment to pull off the movie you have in mind. This chapter looks at the basic on-set process for an average short narrative film with sync sound. While certain tasks and procedures can be scaled to fit larger or smaller projects and crews, there's nothing in the following discussion that you can cut entirely.

■ WALKING ONTO THE SET

So you've thoroughly completed your preproduction. You've talked to everyone, rehearsed and discussed the script with the cast, and figured out the aesthetic and technical approach to each scene with the crew. Everything and everyone necessary to accomplish the day's shooting is here, the location is secured, and you are armed with your marked shooting script, overheads, and shot list. Now what? Now you get down to the work of building your film one setup at a time, take after take, with the knowledge that being well prepared allows you to respond creatively to what is happening on the set. When you walk onto a film set for the first time, whether you're a director, D.P., actor, art director, or sound mixer, you will feel something remarkable—the energy of a group of people who have come together to make a movie. You will also, probably for the first time, be in the actual shooting space and watching those actors in their costumes moving in that location. As you collaborate with the cast and crew, new ideas will start to emerge. If you know clearly the shots you need to make the film, then you are freer to improvise, cut, alter, or adjust, to accommodate new ideas or unexpected obstacles. Use the chemistry of all of those creative people gathered in one place and the inevitable surprises that occur on the set to improve the project at every turn. So get down to work, but remember that production is rarely just the mechanical realization of the film that had been developed in preproduction; rather, it is another creative stage in the evolution of your idea (**Figure 17-1**).

■ **Figure 17-1** On the set. The creative intensity and collaboration that are generated by a focused and involved cast and crew are among the great experiences of the filmmaking process.

■ WHO DOES WHAT, WHEN

Whatever the scale of your production, the basic stages for a shooting day are the same:

1. Art department arrives at the location to dress the set (also called prepping the set).
2. Camera and sound teams arrive and offload equipment to the staging area.
3. Director and on-camera talent run a tech rehearsal in the actual space.
4. Set up camera, lights, and sound based on that rehearsal while talent get into wardrobe.
5. Run the scene a few more times, tweaking lights, camera, sound, and performance.
6. When all cast and crew feel ready, take the shot!

Repeat these steps until your film is done. After a while, this routine becomes completely automatic for everyone on the project and, at last, you're making a movie. But let's look a little closer at each step for an average short film project, using lights and sound, and fill in some essential details.

Dressing the Set

The first team to arrive on a set, in addition to the director and producing staff, is the art department. The art department **preps the location, dresses the set,** and prepares wardrobe and props in advance of the rest of the crew. Often, the art department will be prepping the next day's location while everyone else is shooting the current day's scenes. On small films, however, it's not always possible to have access to a location a day ahead of time, nor is it necessary if the set needs are minimal, which is often the case for exterior shoots, for example (**Figure 17-2**).

Loading In

When the rest of the crew arrives on the set, they begin the process of **loading in,** which simply means getting all of the necessary equipment onto the location. A very simple shoot might only involve enough equipment to fit in the trunk of one car, while larger projects, especially those with extensive lighting needs, might require trucks full of gear. No matter how much equipment you're using, it is critical that you establish a designated area, near the actual set, where all of it will be held. This is called the **staging area** (**Figure 17-3**). When you need something, you'll know where to find it; when you're done using something, you'll know where to return it. Orderliness is essential! When equipment gets lost, nine out of ten times it's because there is no established staging area and equipment gets sprayed all over the location in the course of a shooting day. In this scenario,

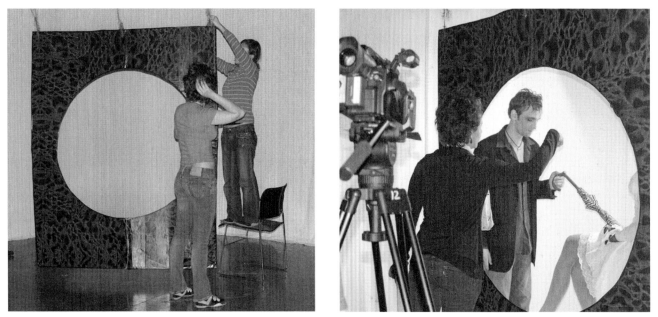

■ **Figure 17-2** Before lights, camera, action! (or sound), the art department arrives and preps the set. Production stills from Vendriger's short *Balloon Girl* (2007).

almost without exception, something gets lost. It may be something small, like a zoom handle or a filter, but it could be something expensive or essential, like a battery cable, a microphone, or a roll of exposed film from the day's shoot!

Tech Rehearsal

With all the equipment now loaded in at the location, the question everyone is asking is, how and where do we set up? Each department should have their own copies of the marked shooting script, overheads, and shot lists, so they should already have an idea of the basic setups, but the director and actors will also stage a **tech rehearsal** in the dressed set (Figure 17-4). This is a basic run-through of the scene to be shot, including dialogue and blocking, so that the various departments get a more accurate sense for where to set up the camera, lights, and sound. The tech rehearsal is also the director's first time running the scene in the actual location and viewing the framings from the camera. Changes to the visual conception of the scene at this point are common. Slight (or major) adjustments to the framing, merging shots, and rethinking the blocking of the actors are all are part of the tech rehearsal. Also, during the tech rehearsal the camera crew might lay **focus marks** on the floor. These are small pieces of tape that follow the path of a character's movement in the space. They are measured to the camera so that focus can be accurately pulled as the character hits their marks, meaning as they move from mark to mark during the scene (see page 229). Once the scene has been staged, the departments get to work.

■ **Figure 17-3** Designating a staging area for equipment is necessary to keep tabs on where everything is and where everything should be once shooting is finished.

Setup

After the tech rehearsal the actors leave the set to get into costume and makeup and, if there is time and it is necessary, the director will run lines or quick rehearsals with them off the set. This is an important time between an actor and director. The director's task at this point is to get the actors **into character,** meaning get them into the emotional and psychological space necessary to pull off the scene, and to remind the actors of the performance decisions that were made during preproduction rehearsals and read-throughs (see the section "The Director and Actors on the Set").

Meanwhile, the camera department preps and sets up the camera, meaning cleaning the camera, selecting the right lens, setting camera speed, mounting the camera on the camera support, and loading the film magazines. If you are shooting on DV, this is where you will white balance the camera, and set all other necessary video adjustments. As the lighting crews set up the lights, the D.P. and A.C. take countless light meter readings and consults the depth-of-field charts to makes sure that lighting setup, exposures, and focus are in line with the visual strategy established in preproduction. If there is movement in the scene, the camera department will rough-in marks for pulling focus. The D.P. may ask an actor to stand here or there, or walk through their blocking again so that lights, camera, and focus can be more accurately established. If an actor is not available (e.g., they're rehearsing or getting into wardrobe), then a **stand-in** is used (Figure 17-5). Ideally a stand-in and the actor have approximately the same height and coloring, and on major film productions there are specific people who are hired as stand-ins for particular stars. But on small shoots a stand-in can be any

■ **Figure 17-4** A tech rehearsal, where actors do a basic run-through of a scene, is essential to establish the lighting, blocking, and camera and sound placement.

Figure 17-5 Using stand-ins instead of actors to focus lighting units can save time during production, especially when actors are in rehearsal or makeup.

Figure 17-6 While the lighting crew sets up, the sound department devises a recording strategy and tests equipment.

available crewmember. During the lighting setup the art department is also on set, laying out the various props for the scene and available to adjust set pieces or furniture in order to create a better composition or accommodate lighting issues.

While all of this is happening, the sound department sets up their equipment (**Figure 17-6**). Their first task is to strategize how to mike the scene given the environment, the blocking, and the framing. Should the recordist decide to boom the scene, they will wait until the lighting crew has finished their work before establishing the position for the boom operator, in order to fit themselves around the lights so boom shadows do not fall onto the set. If lavaliere microphones are used, then the recordist must find the talent and wire them for sound. This should be done while they get into costume and not while the director is working with them. Also, the sound crew will set up and test their recording gear to be certain they are getting a clean audio signal. In a single-system sound situation that means making sure the audio chain (mike → field mixer → camera) is hooked up, calibrated to the 1-kHz reference tone, and transmitting clean audio (see page 355). The same goes for double-system sound (mike → field mixer → recorder), except that the sound recordist will additionally record a **verbal slate** at the head of the record media (i.e., flash card, DAT, etc.), which includes (1) the name of the project and director, (2) the roll number, (3) the date, (4) the recording sample rate/bit depth, and, if your recorder has a tone generator, (5) the headtone level (i.e., −18 dB digital). Then the recordist will record 30 seconds of reference tone, which is used to calibrate the postproduction sound transfers. After this, the sound team is ready for the first take.

From time to time the director will check on the progress of the lighting, camera placement, look of the set and the general readiness of the set-up. On larger shoots an A.D. will serve as the director's proxy and oversee the set-up, communicating anything urgent between director and crew. This leaves the director free to work with the actors.

Final Run-Throughs

When all of the technical setup has been completed and everyone is ready to go—camera in place, lighting set up, sound in position—the director will call for a **run-through** (also called **dress rehearsal**). During the run-through, everyone proceeds as if you're actually filming, without actually rolling camera or sound. This allows everyone to make final adjustments: actors modify movements and performance; the camera operator refines focus, camera moves, and composition; the lighting team tweaks the lights to get them just right; the art department addresses whatever set piece, prop, costume, or makeup issue needs addressing; and the sound team establishes boom position and final record levels. And all of this activity is happening under the watchful eye and instructions of the director, whose job it is to make sure that everyone's creative and technical energies are working toward a single, unified cinematic goal (**Figure 17-7**).

Sometimes a crew will go through several run-throughs before everyone feels they're ready to roll; however, you need to be careful. You can tweak, adjust, fix, and rehearse endlessly. If too much time is being wasted splitting hairs or fixing things that no one would ever notice, the producer, A.D., or P.M. must step in and push things along by reminding everyone how little time there is and how many set-ups they must accomplish before the day is over, and that they generally need to "move it." This efficiency nudge hopefully prompts the director to say, "Okay everyone, let's try a take."

■ **Figure 17-7** Run-throughs are essential to getting your actual takes just right, especially on tricky shots like this moving escalator setup from Mercado's film *Yield* (2006).

in practice

■ THE SLATE AND PRODUCTION LOGS

First Level of Information

The **slate**, the **camera report**, and the **sound log** are all used to keep a running record of every **camera take**. A **take** is defined as the moment the camera is turned on at the beginning of a shot to the moment it is turned off after the director has called "Cut!" Slate and production logs contain two levels of information; the first is general information:

- Title of the project
- Name of the director
- Name of the camera operator (or sound mixer on sound logs)
- Date

This information doesn't change much, but the second level of information, which identifies which scene is being shot and how many times it has been attempted, changes with each and every take on both the logs and the slate (**Figures 17-8** and **17-9**).

■ **Figure 17-8** Roll, scene, and take numbers. The information on a slate is vital in postproduction, so care should be taken to keep the slate updated, accurate, and readable.

Second Level of Information

- *Roll number.* The roll number refers to the DV tape cassette or roll of film or memory card. When you change your DV tape, say after an hour of footage, or put a new roll of film in the camera, or fill up a P2 card, you will change the

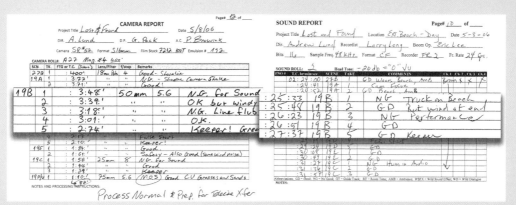

■ **Figure 17-9** The information on the camera report *(left)* and sound logs *(right)* should remain perfectly coordinated with the slate throughout the shoot. Spot checks are recommended. Camera reports and sound logs are available at the Voice & Vision companion website.

roll number. Roll numbers run sequentially, the first being roll #1, then roll #2, roll #3, and so on.

- *Scene/shot number.* The scene and shot you are currently shooting (e.g., scene 19B) is taken from the shot list (which itself corresponds to the marked shooting script, see Chapter 5). The scene/shot number changes to the next on the list after the director believes that a good take, called a **keeper take,** has been achieved.

- *Take number.* This is the number of times you've attempted a scene/shot. This number changes each time you make another attempt at the same shot (e.g., 19B/take 1, 19B/take 2, 19B/take 3, etc.), until you achieve a keeper take.

- *Footage* or *timecode count.* The easiest way to log picture and sound footage is to enter in the *start* timecode or footage count (film) for each take. This not only helps you keep track of how much film or tape you've used and how much you have left before you need to change rolls, but it makes it easy to find and cue specific takes later (especially when using timecode media). It also gives you an accurate time count of how long each individual take is since the *start* number of one take is also the *end* number of the previous take. For example, in **Figure 17-9**, shot 19B/take 4 started at 301 feet and ended at 274 feet (27 feet of film = 45 seconds). When using timecode media, it is even easier. The same take on the sound roll starts at TC 02:26:51 and ends on 02:27:37 (the start TC of the next take) = 46 seconds.

In narrative production, slates and logs are used to label every take, whether you're shooting on DV or film. On small-scale films, like student shorts, the A.C. generally keeps the camera reports and updates the slate, while the sound mixer keeps the sound logs. But if the A.C. is busy with other tasks, like pulling focus or elaborate dolly moves, the A.D. can also load the slate. In either case, establish a routine and stick to it; and compare logs from time to time; it is essential for a smooth and efficient postproduction process that the production logs and the slate are kept in perfect coordination. Also, file-based media, like P2 cards, allow you to enter shot information right into the metadata. This takes time, but if can work it into your routine it can be helpful later.

■ SHOOTING A TAKE

This is the moment of truth. All of the preproduction preparation, all of the setup and rehearsals, boil down to what happens while sound and camera are rolling. A take begins with the director or A.D. asking for "quiet on the set" and for everyone to get into their positions. Actors, camera crew, and sound crew all position themselves where they need to be. Then the A.C. (or whoever was assigned to load the slate) steps into the scene holding the updated slate (clapper arm already opened) for the camera to see. The camera operator must be able to clearly read the slate in the viewfinder. A slate that is halfway out of the frame, out of focus, or too dark to read is useless (**Figure 17-10**).

After everyone is in position and it's quiet on the set, the A.D. (or the director on very small shoots) then calls the shot. **Calling the shot** is a standardized routine for every sync sound take on a double-system film production. The order and commands are designed to make syncing dailies in postproduction routine. Here's how the director calls a shot:

1. A.D. (or Director): "Is anyone not ready?" If no one says anything, then …
2. A.D. (or Director): "Roll sound."
3. SOUND REC.: Starts recorder and after a five-second preroll calls out, "Speed."
4. A.D. (or Director): "Roll camera."
5. CAMERA OP.: Starts camera and calls, "Rolling."
6. A.C. (or other slate person): When the slate person hears "Rolling," they call out the scene and take numbers, "Scene 19B, take 1," clap the slate closed, and move quickly out of the scene and settles down quietly!

■ **Figure 17-10** The slate must always be in the frame, in focus, and readable. Here the A.C. uses a flashlight in a dark location to ensure that the slate is visible.

7. DIRECTOR (after a pause): "Action!"

8. The take plays out and the director will wait a beat after the scene has ended before calling out …

9. DIRECTOR: "Cut!" No one can call cut except the director and no one stops their jobs until the director calls "cut." There may be a great reaction or visual tableau at the end of a scene that the director wants to linger on, and if the camera operator simply turns off the camera because they thought the scene was over, they've lost a great moment. Also, a director should not call "cut" exactly at the end of the shot; it's wise to wait a beat or two to give yourself handles for editing. However, the director can certainly call "cut" before the scene is done if something egregious has occurred, like a piece of the set falling over, the actor speaking the wrong lines, or a police car driving past with the siren wailing.

10. When "cut" is called, the take is over and the camera and sound recorder are turned off.

11. Immediately after a take, the camera report and sound logs are updated as the slate is reloaded for the next take (and if you're shooting with file-based media and you have time, you can enter shot information into the metadata).

Evaluating the Take

Technical: Performance and Continuity

After the take, the director first checks with camera and sound for confirmation. If there was a technical problem, it must be communicated to the director at this point so that he or she can determine if a **retake** is needed:

- *Camera.* If the camera lost focus, or bobbled in the middle of the shot, or if a pan didn't follow the actor or got a light stand in the frame, then a retake might be necessary.

- *Sound.* If the microphone drifted off-axis too much, or the actors delivered their lines so loudly that the levels clipped, or if the mike picked up extraneous noise (like a lawnmower starting up next door), or any other problem like this, you'll probably require another take.

- *Performance or new ideas.* The director also evaluates the performances. Did the actor drop some lines? Was the performance not as good as it could be? Were the actions awkward or incorrect? Maybe everything was fine, but the director got some new ideas while watching the scene unfold. All of these things could also lead to a retake.

- *Continuity.* Continuity issues also must be considered. Did the actor have a cigarette in the long shot but not in this close-up take? Was the actor wearing a coat in the long shot but is now wearing only a shirt for the close-up? Is there a problem with matching screen direction or performance intensity from shot to shot? These issues also can require a retake. On projects that require a lot of continuity shooting, it is a good idea to have a dedicated **script supervisor,** whose job it is to pay attention to continuity details and to mark off shots that have been completed (see "The Lined Script," section). Script supervisors also can do spot checks with the logs and slates to make sure that they're corresponding properly.

If the director decides that another take is needed, then the problem with that take is noted in the camera and sound logs "comments" area and, after making the necessary corrections (technical or performance), the whole process is repeated for "take 2." Keep in mind, the "comments" notes are important because not all "bad takes" are a complete loss. Sometimes a technical or performance problem isn't a problem throughout the take, and there are some good moments that can be used in the editing. These should be noted as well (**Figure 17-11**).

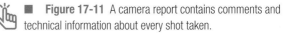

■ **Figure 17-11** A camera report contains comments and technical information about every shot taken.

If the director is happy with the take, then it is marked as a "**keeper**" in the logs and everyone moves on to the next scene/shot on the shot list. After all of the shots from a particular camera setup are completed, the camera and lighting move to the next angle and setup begins again. This system is repeated, take after take, setup after setup, scene after scene, day after day, until you've got your movie "**in the can.**"

Other Retake Factors

There will be times when everything on a take went relatively well, but the actor or D.P. feel that they could have done better or want to try something new, or feel that with one more take they can really do something extraordinary. In these cases they should ask the director for another take. If you can afford the time and the footage, it's a good idea to listen to these requests.

Sometimes, when cast and crew nail the scene on the very first take, a bizarre superstition takes hold of everyone and they think, "It can't have been *that* easy." Or "What if something happens to that take? It's the only one we've got." In these cases, the director may call for another take, "just for safety's sake." This is called a **safety take.** The funny thing is, there is often some problem with the safety take (technical or performance) and then people will inevitably want to do retakes of the safety take, and so on. Still, safety takes are a good idea, if only to give you some options in the editing room.

There will also surely be times when you are running out of time or film or both and simply not getting the entire shot you're after in a single take. This situation calls for the director to be crafty. Perhaps you have everything you need, but it is distributed in good moments among several "imperfect" takes. Maybe all you need to do is shoot a cutaway, or a simple reaction shot of someone else, which will then allow you to piece together the best parts of various takes seamlessly. It's important that a director keep in mind during the shooting process the flexibility that editing affords.

Checking Video

If you are shooting on DV and you are undecided about the quality of a take, you can always rewind the tape, or cue the P2 card, and watch the shot (**Figure 17-12**). People shooting on film can also do this if they have video assist. **Video assist** (or a **video tap**) is a small video pickup device, attached to the camera viewing system, which records low-quality video of each take. Video assist is standard issue on big-to moderate-budget films, but it requires three things that put it out of reach of many introductory film students. First, it requires additional funds for the rental of the videotape; second, it requires an additional crewperson to operate the video assist gear; finally, it requires a camera that can accommodate video assist. Video assist is usually overkill for small film projects, which can do just as well relying on the observations of the director, D.P., sound mixer, A.D., and script supervisor.

■ **Figure 17-12** Checking a take on Zachary Sluser's *(left)* film *Path Lights* (2009). Shooting on video allows reviewing shots. In film, this is only possible with a video assist system.

In either case, evaluating shots by checking the video can be helpful, but it can also be extremely time consuming if you have to rewind videotape to check each and every potential keeper take. Memory cards like the P2 card have the advantage of instantaneous random access, but still you need to watch the take in real time. Watching video also can drive you a little crazy in the quest for absolute perfection. You may find yourself doing retakes for things that no one would ever notice but that you see as a flaw. Some people derisively call the playback monitor the "video village" because of all the people who gather around it to watch takes, which can waste valuable production time. Directors who get into the habit of rewatching everything they've shot on the set can expect, and should schedule, a longer shooting period.

■ TAKES, RETAKES, AND MISTAKES

1. The camera and sound crew must be alert, aware, and honest about evaluating the technical qualities of a take. Everyone makes mistakes; this is what retakes are for. One time, while my class and I were shooting a brief scene on 16mm for an in-class production exercise, we shot a take of two guys playing "rock-paper-scissors" as if their lives depended on winning. The close-up shot involved a slow pan from one player's face, to their hands, then to the other player's face. The actors really nailed the performance and after calling "cut," I turned to the camera operator and asked, "Was that good for camera?" The response was a less than confident "Uh, yeah, s'pose so." "Was it good, or not?" I pressed. "Yeah, yeah, it was good." When we got the dailies back from the lab, we all saw that the pan wasn't great; it mostly missed the hands playing the game and the end of the move didn't really find its final composition on the second player's face, landing instead somewhere around his shoulder. The student knew the pan wasn't good, but he didn't want to admit to his teacher that he messed up the shot so he was less than honest with his evaluation. Unfortunately, and predictably, the photographic evidence was right there and undeniable. Obviously, it's so much better to simply say, "the pan was off" and do another take, than to discover in postproduction that there's only one poor take to edit with. Shooting on DV, I could have checked it in the field myself, but shooting on 16mm film (without video assist), the crew needs to be especially exacting and forthcoming.

2. In one of my own films, I had a scene in which a business executive delivers distressing news about imminent layoffs to his management team. The problem was, I couldn't get the executive to deliver his speech in one clean take. Not only did he flub his lines, but the multiple takes were making him feel increasingly on the spot, and we discovered that when he got nervous, he'd start stuttering. After about five takes I became concerned about the amount of film I was burning on this relatively small moment. Because I planned to intercut the executive's speech with the reactions of one particular worried manager, I came up with a workaround. I figured I had the first three sentences of the speech covered in one of the five takes. Then I imagined exactly where I could cut into the scene and we simply had him deliver two other, tiny chunks of the speech (no more than two sentences each) for the camera. After these two short shots, which he achieved in one take each, I sat with him on location and recorded the entire speech as a sound take only. This way, he could read the speech, sitting down, without the lights and camera on him. He was terrific, and I had both my images for intercutting and the rest of the speech to insert as audio under the anxious face of the manager.

3. A colleague of mine recounted a time when, on her film set, she had an actress who was great during run-throughs but who got "big" when the camera was actually recording. "It was totally unconscious, but she couldn't help it. She would turn up the intensity a few notches whenever she knew we were doing a real take." In addition, retakes only made her performance even bigger. So the director told camera and sound that they'd secretly roll tape during the run-though and then they'd also take some scenes after the run-through, so that the actress wouldn't catch on. Since they were shooting on DV, they put a little strip of black tape over the red light, which indicates when the camera is rolling. The plan worked and the actress' performance in the film was convincing, "but we had no slates for her good takes otherwise; if we had slated, she'd know we were rolling."

Additional Shooting Procedures and Tips
MOS and Single-System Sound

If you are shooting without sound, called shooting **MOS** or shooting single-system sound, all takes are still slated but the commands for the sound recorder are obviously omitted and there is no need to clap the slate because there is no microphone or, in the case of single system, no postproduction syncing to be done. With both single-system and MOS shooting, slating is purely for visual reference, so the slate (with the proper scene information) is simply held in front of the camera for a few seconds after "roll camera." Then the slate person steps away and settles so that action can be called. It is very common to have a mix of sync takes and MOS takes in a single shooting day.

Tail Slates

Sometimes you need to get a shot off right away, or you'll lose a special moment (like a boat cruising unexpectedly in the background or a perfect wind blowing through the trees), or you may simply want to roll camera without breaking the emotional focus of an actor with the whole slating procedure. In these cases we use a **tail slate** to mark the take. A tail slate simply means that the verbal marker and slate clap are done at the end of the shot, but before the camera is turned off. To avoid confusion with the next shot, tail slates are held upside down and called out as "tail marker" by the A.C.

Checking the Gate

When shooting film, the D.P. (or A.C.) should check the gate after each "keeper" take. **Checking the gate** means taking a close look at the aperture plate in the camera's gate to make sure there are no hairs, dust, or debris that would show up permanently on the image. Finding debris in the gate can also be a reason to do a retake. Checking the gate involves using the inching knob to swing the shutter away from the gate, removing the lens, and, with a small flashlight and magnifying glass, looking at all four edges of the aperture plate opening (especially the bottom edge) to make sure it is free of hair and dust. If it is clean, then shooting can continue. If the gate is dirty, then the offending hair should be removed with a soft wooden **orangewood stick.** Outside the film world, "orange sticks" are used for pushing back fingernail cuticles and can be bought at any drugstore. On a film shoot, orange sticks are a standard item in a shooter's ditty bag because they are soft and will not damage the gate and do not leave debris behind (**Figure 17-13**). With zoom lenses, you can check the gate without removing the lens. Simply swing the shutter away from the gate, set the lens aperture to wide open, and bring the zoom lens all the way in. The lens acts like a magnifying glass, so the D.P. need only shine the flashlight through the front of the lens and scan the edges of the gate. If the D.P. finds a hair, then the lens, of course, will need to be removed to clean the gate.

The Lined Script

After each keeper take, that particular scene/shot is then "lined off" with a red squiggly line on a lined script. A **lined script** is a copy of the screenplay that contains a record of what parts of the script have been successfully shot and from what angle. The lined script looks like a marked shooting script (see page 101), but the difference is that it reflects the actual shots taken rather than the shots as they were anticipated in preproduction. Most of the time you will be drawing squiggly lines across the shots you've drawn in during preproduction, but during the production process the coverage might change in some scenes; perhaps some camera angles were added or omitted or merged. Maybe the director decided that the master shot was all that was necessary and that close-ups were not needed. Or maybe the director realized on the set that adding a new close-up angle would

■ **Figure 17-13** An A.C. checks the gate using the zoom lens as a magnifier *(left)*. Soft orangewood sticks are the standard tool for safely cleaning a gate of debris *(right)*.

be a powerful shot to cut to. All of these types of decisions are reflected in the lined script. The lined script also allows everyone to see at a glance if every moment in the film has been covered and how it was covered. Any part of the lined script without a red squiggly line still needs to be shot (**Figure 17-14**). There must be only one lined script on the set, and updating it is the job of a **script supervisor,** but on smaller shoots it can be done by the A.D. or even the director. Any notes about each take or reminders about how a particular scene was covered (especially for scenes that changed during production) should also be noted in the margins or on the back of the corresponding page, making this particular document an important record of the director's ideas during production, which can be highly useful in the editing process.

Roll-Out

When a camera roll reaches its end (the end of a DV tape or the end of a camera load), the D.P. will tell the director, "roll-out," and the production will halt while the film spool or magazine, DV tape, or P2 card is changed. If you've kept careful camera logs, roll-out should be anticipated so that it doesn't happen right in the middle of a long and elaborate shot. If you know you have a minute or so left on a roll, you should inform the director. After removing your DV tape, memory card, or film (in a changing bag if you're using a 400-foot magazine load), you should immediately put it back in its case or can and *label it*. Film cans should also be securely re-taped closed. This point cannot be stressed enough: your footage is the most valuable thing on the set and you don't want an unmarked, unidentified film can, videotape, or memory card kicking around the film set.

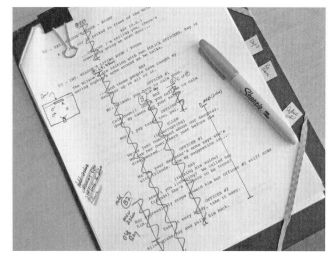

■ **Figure 17-14** A lined script is regularly updated during the shoot to reflect what shots have already been taken; it is also a record of last-minute changes done by the director.

■ AFTER ROLL OUT

Labeling Film Cans and Tape Cases

It's important to take a little time out to properly and neatly label your film cans or tape cases right after roll-out and put them in a secure location (**Figure 17-15**).

■ **Figure 17-15** A properly labeled film can using preprinted labels that are available online from Kodak or the Voice & Vision companion website.

Film cans, DV tapes, and sound rolls must be neatly labeled with the following information:

- Project title
- Roll number
- Director's name and contact information
- Shooting date
- Film cans should additionally contain *processing instructions* (e.g., process normal or pushed one stop), *type of film* (e.g., 7297), and *footage* (e.g., 400 feet).
- Sound rolls should additionally contain *record sample rate* (e.g., 48 kHz, 16 bit) and *headtone level* (e.g., −18 dB).
- If you are splitting a film core (see page 179), then the can containing the unexposed film should be labeled with the *type of film* (e.g., 7297), *footage* (e.g., 220 feet), and *date*.

File-Based Media Workflow on the Set

Once you've filled a video memory card with footage (P2 or SxS), you have two options. You can simply replace it with a new card and keep shooting, gathering all full cards at the end of the day to transfer them after the shoot, or you can download your foot-

in practice

age right on the set and reuse the card. Usually the deciding factor is how many cards you have and how much footage you acquire. Say you're shooting HD and you have only one 16-GB P2 card (16 GB = 16 minutes of HD footage), but you plan to shoot 30 minutes of footage in one day. At some point you'll have to transfer the data off the full card so you can reuse the card.

Transferring on the set requires that you have either a **memory card storage device** or a laptop computer (a PC with a PCMCIA slot or a Mac with a P2 card reader) and two portable hard drives (**Figure 17-16**). It is essential that you transfer your footage to *two* hard drives (one for editing and one for safety backup) before you reuse the P2 card. As you transfer your footage you should label the files with the title and date of the production. In the end, you will have all your foot-

■ **Figure 17-16** Transferring footage from file-based media allows you to reuse memory cards. Two options are dedicated storage devices, such as the Nexto Video Storage Pro, which transfers both P2 and SxS cards to an internal drive and to a second backup drive *(left)*, or using a laptop with a card reader to transfer to two portable drives *(right)*. Always transfer to two drives before reusing your memory card.

age as MXF data files on two hard drives, ready to be "ingested" directly into your editing system. If it's possible, it's a good idea to have at least two memory cards on the set, even if the other is as small as 8 GB, so that while one is being downloaded you can continue shooting with the other.

After the Shoot

Striking the Set

After the last "cut" has been called and the day's final keeper take has been logged, the work is not over. The last task of a film crew's day is to **strike the set.** Because this happens at the very end of a long day, you can be sure that *everyone* on the set is exhausted and wants to get home—and for this reason *everyone* must contribute to striking the set. It is a serious breach of film production ethics to participate in a shoot, but then skip out when it comes time to strike. No one leaves until everything is packed up and squared away. When crewmembers commit to a film, they must commit to the bitter end, which means that they need to clear their schedules and be there when it's time to put all the toys away (**Figure 17-17**). Striking the set must be done neatly, carefully, and thoroughly. If you simply toss the equipment aside to get it out of the way, you will only make the load-in and setup for the next day's shoot all the more difficult and time consuming. Even worse, carelessly striking a set can damage equipment. Each department is responsible for striking its own gear, but everyone pitches in until it's all packed neatly away and the set is put to rights, meaning it's clean and orderly. If you're striking a set to which you will not return, make sure you return that location to its original condition or better (see page 381).

When the director announces to "strike the set," all lights are immediately powered down first, but they are one of the last things to get packed away. This allows them to cool before you fit them back into their cases. Also, the sound mixer, D.P., and A.C. should take some time to organize and label all of the day's camera and sound rolls. If you're shooting film, the D.P. (or A.C.) needs to go someplace quiet to unload the last film magazine,

■ **Figure 17-17** Everyone helps strike the set. Putting gear away should be done carefully and methodically.

which often means splitting the core (see page 179). Remember, exposed film needs to get to the lab for processing and transfer ASAP after a shoot.

That's a Wrap!

After the last "cut" has been called on the very last day of the shoot and all of the coverage for the movie has been accomplished, the director will gleefully exclaim, "That's a wrap!" This means that the production phase is officially over. The last set strike is called the **wrap out** and includes returning the last location to its former state, and all equipment to the rental house, school checkout facility, or wherever it came from, and getting the last of the exposed film to the lab. After the last set strike has been completed, there is nothing left for the film crew to do but attend the wrap party.

The Wrap Party!

The **wrap party** is exactly what it sounds like. It's a party thrown soon after the final shooting day that brings together the entire production team, cast, and crew one last time (**Figure 17-18**). But this time it's not to work on the film, it's to have a good time, eat some good food, dance, share stories, and generally get to know each other outside of the intense and harried environment of a film set. The feeling of camaraderie at a wrap party bonds the team as they communalize the production experience that they have all recently been through. It's also a way the producer and director can express their gratitude for the team's efforts and for a job well done. Take note: I don't mention the wrap party to be cute, I mention it because it's an important part of this process. If your experience with the cast and crew was positive, you very well might call on them again in the future. In fact, they may call each other for their own projects in the future. One director friend of mine always hands out cast and crew contact sheets to everyone involved in the film. A good wrap party leaves everyone with a better final experience than a set strike, and it's quite simply an essential part of creating and maintaining your film community. It should also be a line item in your budget!

■ **Figure 17-18** A group of filmmakers celebrate the conclusion of an intense but successful production period with a well-earned party.

■ THE DIRECTOR AND ACTORS ON THE SET

> *[...] 99 percent of my experience has been that actors, if you treat them with respect and ask for their expertise, they will share that expertise with you.*
> **Mike Figgis (From *Digital Filmmaking*, Faber and Faber)**

> *A director contributes not by instructing the actor but by inspiring him. A performance is wholly the creation of the actor's imagination, of the control he has over his expressive instrument (voice, body), and even more significantly of his emotions, sensory feelings, intuitions and mental attitudes.[...] In reality you are leading the actor on a very short reign, gently coaxing him into a performance that he must believe is entirely his.*
> **Alexander Mackendrick (From *On Filmmaking*, Faber and Faber)**

> *People often ask me what is the secret of directing actors, and they always think I'm being facetious when I answer that all you have to do is hire talented people and let them do their work.*
> **Woody Allen (From *Moviemakers' Master Class*, Faber and Faber)**

In Chapter 7 I discuss the working relationship between directors and actors during preproduction rehearsals and the bond of trust that must be formed. So a productive, collaborative relationship should already be in place when you arrive on the set. However, more should be mentioned about the directing process that occurs on the film set.

In a significant way, an audience can overlook many small problems in a film if the performances are compelling and convincing. By the same token, a film that is technically flawless, or even spectacular, can fall flat if the performances are not persuasive. This is not just an issue on highly dramatic films with complex emotional situations and dialogue. A very simple film, with simple actions, can also be dragged down if the performances go awry. Here is a good example: In an introductory film class, one production group made a very simple silent film about someone doing their laundry. This was, in fact, their first film. The laundromat was beautifully picturesque and the shots were perfectly focused, exposed, and wonderfully composed. The lighting was simple but effective and the scene coverage and editing were sharp. In every way it was a visually successful film, except that the actor, who was not an actor but a friend of the filmmaker, had this slight goofy grin on his face. The grin said, "Hey, I'm on camera!" and it shattered the fictional illusion that the director had so carefully created. The film ended up not being about a guy doing his laundry, but about a guy who was aware of being filmed while trying to perform doing the laundry. It was the director's job to not only organize the sequence of events and compose the shots, but to notice that revealing grin. The director needed to find a way to get the talent to drop it and to do this routine cleaning chore as if he were alone and had done it a hundred times before. Fundamental to the art of film directing is getting performances that are truthful and that emerge from the dramatic moment.

To this end, it's important that a director not allow technical considerations to pull them away from the actors. This is why the producers, the A.D., and/or the P.M. are so important on the set; they transmit the director's wishes to the crew to keep them going, allowing the director to work with the actors right up to the point where the camera rolls. This is also why a reliable and resourceful crew is important; they can take their direction and run with it.

The exact process of working with actors is dependent on many factors, including acting styles, training and experience, directing styles, the tone of the film; the unique circumstances of the production, and the particular actor/director personalities and relationship. This is a topic that is clearly beyond the scope of this book, but I have listed some texts in the Recommended Readings to introduce you to the essential aspects of working with actors in dramatic filmmaking. However, what follows is a basic (if somewhat idealized) description of the way actors and directors work on the set, during the production process.

Tech rehearsals: Tech rehearsals are not just for the crew; the tech rehearsals allow the actor, without the pressure of a rolling camera, to inhabit and move within the real space of the scene, usually for the first time. This has emotional/performance implications for sure, but it also has practical implications as well. If your scene involves any physical business at all—for example, making a cup of tea—this is where the actor will figure out where the tea spoons are located, how to open the tea bag, how well the kettle pours, in what order to perform the task, and so on. Figuring out these little bits of action at this point will not only improve the authenticity of the performance, but it will save you countless retakes because your talent won't be rummaging cluelessly through drawers looking for a tea spoon in a kitchen that's supposed to be their own.

Setup: One of the most important moments between an actor and director happens while the crew is lighting and setting up the shot. There is usually some significant time for work here, and this is when the director reminds the actor where this particular scene falls in the larger story. Remember, we do not shoot a film in sequential order; rather, scenes are rearranged in the shot list to create the most efficient order from a production perspective. It's not unusual, for example, to shoot the end of a film in the first few days of a shoot. It's not easy for a performer to jump around to the various scenes of what is supposed to be an organically unfolding linear story. This means that on the set the director must serve as the guide for the actors, reminding them, with each camera setup, where they are in the story, what their character has been through up to that point, and where they need to be emotionally in the current moment when the camera rolls. Thoughts and approaches developed during the script readings and preproduction rehearsals should be reviewed and any new ideas discussed. It is one of the principle jobs of the director to help the actors understand the story and their characters, speaking in very specific terms about what you want to do with that story and how you intend to present and inflect the characters, actions, and dialogue in the script. This, of course is predicated on the fact that you, as the director, know what you're after first, and then find way to communicate that to the actors so that they can achieve the performance energy, mood, and nuance the movie needs.

Run-throughs: Once everything is set up and the actors are finally in front of the camera, you will do a few run-throughs before you roll camera. With each run-through, first ask the actors how the scene felt to them and what they thought about the way the scene is or isn't working. Use whatever is useful in their comments, and explain why you can't use other aspects of their feedback. Keep all comments and discussion constructive and focused on the story and scene at hand. In other words, simply talk with your collaborator and work it out. The next run-through should be a bit closer and the following one closer still. Just at the point when you think the cast and crew are comfortable, in the zone, and ready to "nail it," that's when the director announces, "Let's try a take."

Takes: It's not uncommon that the actors (and crew) are thrown off a bit on the first take of a new scene (especially early on in the shooting schedule). The added element of being recorded for all posterity can itself impose on a performance. If the take is not what you were after, simply talk with your collaborator again. Start with what was working well in order to zero in on what you think isn't working and why it's not working. Often, it's a simple fix, like more or less physical action, shifting the character's gaze or blocking somewhat, offering a few suggestions for performance adjustments, or simply giving the actors a few more tries to find their focus. Other times it's more complex, like when it becomes clear that the dialogue or scene coverage needs reworking or an actor is emotionally dissipated and simply cannot connect to what you have in mind. In any case, a director needs to be sensitive to all possibilities and do whatever is necessary to get the right performance on film. If that means rewriting a few lines, do it; if it means a few extra takes, do it; if it means letting the actor stir their tea with their left hand instead of their right, do it; if it means taking a few minutes to remind the actor of the scene work you did earlier, do it; if it means finding a new camera angle, do it; if it means clearing the set of unnecessary personnel, do it; if it means rearranging the schedule so that you can take another day to work the scene in rehearsal, do it. Don't go with an unconvincing or inappropriate performance and hope no one will notice. The job of the director is to guide both cast and crew so that their collective creative efforts successfully fulfill a single creative goal, a unified vision of a story told on film. If a director has done the casting right, then the success of the performances depends on the director being able to communicate that vision in specific and workable terms, terms that the actor (trained and nonactor alike) can understand, absorb, and run with. With each take and with each adjustment the director and actors make between takes, you should get closer and closer to a keeper take. Then you move on to the next, and so on.

A final thought: It's easy for a director to get completely invested in their preplanned vision for the film and insist that everything fit within that plan, and usually this isn't necessarily a bad impulse. But a director should remain open and alert to surprises, inspiration, and unplanned gifts. Not infrequently, in the energy of the full production environment, a performer will find something new, fresh, and special. If you're excessively wedded to an old idea for a scene or character, you might just overlook a performance gem and mistake it for a bad take simply because it isn't what you had in mind.

The director Kelly Anderson told me this story of using a simple and ingenious device for getting actors in the right emotional space while she was directing *Shift*, her first narrative film. *Shift* (1999) tells the story of Melanie, an unhappily married waitress who develops an intimate phone relationship with a telemarketer who, it turns out, is also a prison inmate. The scene Anderson was shooting was a wide two-shot of Melanie and Diane, another waitress, behind the counter of the diner, speculating about what Melanie's telephone/inmate boyfriend might look like, since she's never even seen a photograph. They kid around as they refer to various male customers off screen ("I'll bet he looks like him over there"), some cute and some less than attractive. Because they're looking and pointing to guys off screen, Anderson had her first A.D. stand off camera to give the waitresses a point of focus for sightlines. The tone of the scene was supposed to be lighthearted and full of fun, saucy girl talk about guys. But during the run-throughs,

Anderson says, "It was flat. Flat, dull, staged and not fun." She gave her actors some direction but nothing seemed to infuse the performances with the lively spirit she was after (**Figure 17-19**). She did a few takes and it didn't improve. Then she remembered that, while the actresses were in makeup prepping for the scene, she overheard them talking about how "hot" the intern production assistant was. On the next take she switched the A.D. for the intern just as the camera rolled, so that the waitresses would be looking at someone they truly had a little crush on. "Immediately the tone switched. When they saw this really cute intern standing there they were both surprised and started to giggle and blush. Now they had something to work with and I got that fun, girlish spontaneity I was looking for" (**Figure 17-20**).

What made this little directorial ploy possible was that Anderson could spend time with her actors while the crew set up, listening and responding to them even while they were in makeup.

■ **Figure 17-19** One of the primary duties of the director is to help the actors find the right emotional tone for each scene. Here, director Kelly Anderson confers with actors before another take during the shooting of her film *Shift* (1999).

■ **Figure 17-20** Anderson got the performance she was after as Diane (Marla Sucharetza) cannot help but giggle as she talks about guys with Melanie (Alethea Allen).

Set Etiquette and Production Safety

A film set is an exciting, intense, and often pressure-packed environment filled with energetic people who are focused, driven, and usually working with limited time and resources. In this environment there is often a temptation to cut corners to get the job done. But cutting certain corners often proves to be counterproductive—or worse, downright foolish and dangerous. The following sections cover essential set etiquette and safety issues that should always be observed so that your project is safe, productive, and rewarding (**Figure 18-1**).

■ SET ETIQUETTE: RESPECT, COURTESY, AND GOOD WORK

Everyone on a film set should be treated with respect. This is not just a top-down issue (i.e., producers respecting the grips) but goes for all crewmembers toward each other. As they say in the business, when you come onto a film set, leave your ego at the door. Respect has three dimensions on a film set: we must respect the project, we must respect the people on the project, and we must respect ourselves by doing good work. This brief code of conduct outlines the standards of behavior on a film set for showing and earning respect as a member of a film production team:

1. *Do your job, whatever that job is, to the best of your ability.* Films are created by a coordinated group of individuals; one person slacking off can throw the whole thing off and places unfair burden on someone else who has their own job to do. Doing your job well also means knowing your job well. If you sign on to be the sound mixer on someone's film, then you had better know how to be an excellent sound mixer. Educate yourself, train, learn what you need to know to be exceptional at your job, whatever that job is. Doing your job well also means staying alert and being ready when you are needed. Sometimes, there are chunks of downtime on a film set, but you must keep your ears and eyes open for anything that needs doing in your department. Lulls in activity are not invitations to go wandering off to get snacks or make personal phone calls. You never know when the set will suddenly come alive, and the last thing you want is for a producer or director to shout, "Anybody know where the hell [so-and-so] is? We need to shoot a take!" If you are a knowledgeable, conscientious, reliable, and effective worker, whether you're a production assistant photocopying screenplay sides or the D.P., people will want to work with you again and again. Every project is part of the reputation you establish for yourself.

2. *Always be on time, which means be early!* The film industry places a very high premium on promptness. Being late shows a phenomenal lack of respect toward the other people who arrive on time ready to work; in other words, when you are late, you waste other people's valuable time. This goes for everyone on a film during all stages, from directors showing up, to crew meetings starting on time,

■ **Figure 18-1** Film sets involve an intense, focused, and highly coordinated effort by a group of individuals engaging in diverse tasks yet sharing a common goal—to make a great movie. For this "controlled chaos" to work, proper set etiquette must be observed at all times. (Photo by Gary Knight (CC).)

to the makeup person showing up on set on or before call time. Being late can hold up an entire crew and waste valuable production time. I remember being on a set where the crew waited 25 minutes for the guy who operated the teleprompter. No one else could do it, we couldn't shoot without it, so we all just had to wait. When he arrived he was full of excuses (the weather, the traffic, etc.) and he worked that day — but he never worked for that producer again and was fired by the teleprompt company. If you have a reputation for being late (even on the level of film school), you simply will not work much.

3. *Maintain a positive "can-do" attitude.* Film productions involve lots of problem solving: rigging a light where there is no space, getting just the right camera angle, recording useable audio in hostile environments, and so on. A production thrives with people who love a challenge and are innovative when it comes to solving or working around less than ideal circumstances.

4. *Respect the team structure.* It is often said that a film set is "controlled chaos." The thing that keeps this process from devolving into "total chaos" is the way crews are organized and tasks are delegated. No matter what the size of the production team — from 4 students to 34 paid professionals — a film crew is highly organized and specialized. Everyone has a specific job to do and people they report to. You must respect the chain of command, the division of labor, and the areas of the other people on the team. Let's say you're a boom operator and the ideal place to position the microphone catches one of the lights and casts a shadow on the set. It's a serious breech of etiquette to adjust that light yourself. Instead, speak with the gaffer, explain the situation, and between the two of you you'll work it out.

5. *Treat everyone with courtesy.* If you treat people well, they will treat you well. Listen to people. Crew should, of course, listen closely to the department heads, but D.P.s, art directors, directors, and producers should also listen to their crews. Give praise where praise is due and do not take credit if it is not yours to claim. Learn people's names. Don't criticize negatively or humiliate people if mistakes are made. Don't create work or call meetings that are unnecessary. Don't get in the way of the work other people have to do. Crude comments or jokes about race, sex, religion, or specific people on the set are simply not appropriate. Raucous behavior in general can throw everyone's concentration off — stay cool, calm, and focused.

Now, all this does not necessarily mean every film set is a total love-fest. In fact, you will surely find yourself on sets where you don't necessarily like some of the people you're working with. But personal feelings ultimately should not enter into the equation. Everyone has a job to do, and everyone should behave as a professional and do that job regardless of personalities. When you sign onto a film (paid or not), you have a personal obligation to do your job as well as you can and see the project through successfully. Once it's all over, then you can vow never to work with certain people ever again, but for the duration of that film shoot you must do your job.

Food and Breaks

Twelve-hour workdays are not unusual on a film production. When a crew finds its groove and they're knocking down setups and keeper takes with the smooth efficiency of a well-oiled machine, everyone on the set enters an altered state, and time becomes relative. Four hours can pass but will seem like moments. However, the body knows that it's been working hard for hours. To maintain the morale and physical stamina of the crew, well-timed breaks for food are essential. You cannot expect people to work long hours for you if you do not feed them. And a **food break** means all work stops to allow the cast and crew to sit, relax, and eat; it does not mean sandwiches on the run. Giving people meal breaks will only make them a happier, healthier and more productive crew. You also need to make sure that the food is somewhat interesting. When I was a student I once worked as a grip (for free) on a low-budget, seven-day (12 hours/day) film shoot. To save money, the producer decided to serve the crew pizza twice a day. He also decided not to spring for coffee in the morning. The thought of seven days of pizza was more than any of us could bear. After four days he had a disgruntled crew who organized a meeting with the producer to demand some variety for our meals. The next day we had sandwiches, but from that point on the crew referred to him as the "pizza producer." We did our jobs and we did them well, but when it was over we all vowed never to work for him again.

Because film shoots are long and hard, and food is essential, you should take any dietary issues of your crew seriously. A producer or production manager should know before ordering food who is a vegetarian or if people have any food allergies. It's a big problem if you've been shooting for six hours and order pizza only to discover that the sound mixer is allergic to dairy products and therefore cannot eat anything.

Another critical detail is to always have water available throughout the shooting day. Film work is physically strenuous and sets can get hot, so you must have plenty of water on hand to keep your crew hydrated. This is especially critical for exterior locations on hot days. And it only stands to reason that if you want your crew to drink water to stay hydrated, then you'd better make sure that there are bathrooms conveniently available on the set. If you're at an exterior location, do not imagine that people can just go behind trees or bushes. Also, don't assume that the local fast-food joint will allow your cast and crew access to its toilets. Part of preproduction is securing (or renting) the necessary facilities.

Courtesy on Location

Beyond courtesy among cast and crew is the issue of the broader public. Many times you will be shooting in public places like parks, sidewalks, beaches, neighborhoods, and coffee shops. These places are not your private film set, so you must treat the public with respect and try not to disrupt their lives too much. In other words, keep as low a profile as possible. This includes not making excessive noise, not parking in such a way that it obstructs other people's access, being conscientious about litter, and not taking up more space than is necessary. I remember going to a café in my neighborhood where the owner allowed a student film crew to shoot before working hours. But this crew was running late and the café had to open while they continued shooting. Making matters worse, they had totally commandeered the place by strewing pieces of equipment on every table and chair, preventing patrons from sitting down to enjoy a cup of coffee. I took my coffee to go and the owner admitted that he regretted his decision to let them shoot there. The next time a film crew asks, that owner will surely reject the request. Being rude, taking up more space than you need, and bossing the public around so you can get your shot is a sure way to engender hostile feelings for your project and any other film project that tries to work in the same public space. Think of yourself as an ambassador for filmmaking in general—if you leave people with a bad impression, then you'll spoil it for others.

Respect and Protect the Location

Making movies often involves renting or borrowing locations that are ordinarily not film sets. The unwritten rule in these cases is that, when the shoot is over you should leave a location in exactly the same condition you found it, *or better*. It's important to observe this rule if we are to maintain the good faith of those kind people who open their homes, shops, restaurants, and property for the sake of our movies. This requires that you instruct everyone on the team to be careful to protect the location. Additionally, a few extra precautions are standard:

1. Lay clean tarps over carpets before you load in your equipment.
2. Carefully assess the electricity distribution so you don't overload internal wiring.
3. Designate a single place for the production team to dispose of garbage.
4. Place delicate objects well out of harm's way, and ask the location owners to secure their valuable items in another place.
5. Be aware of the placement of hot movie lights: they can blister paint and burn drapes. Also, don't use tape directly on walls as it will peel paint off.
6. Assign someone the job of monitoring the condition of the location. If necessary, this person can suggest that the crew take some time out to clean the space.
7. Take photographs before you move furniture around so that you know exactly where everything belongs when it comes time to return the space back to normal.

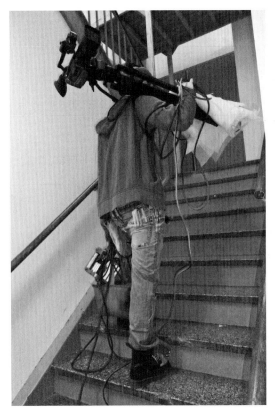

■ **Figure 18-2** Careless handling of equipment will result in damage, production delays and even injury. This guy is doing everything wrong. By carrying too much gear and dragging improperly coiled cables, not to mention the camera slung recklessly over his shoulder, he's tempting a production calamity.

From time to time an accident may occur and the location might sustain some damage (e.g., you accidentally gouge the wall while moving a C-stand). Don't try to hide the damage and get away with it; tell the owner of the property and offer to fix it. Also make sure you have some contingency money in the budget to professionally clean or repair the location if necessary.

Respect Your Equipment

Filmmaking is a highly technical art form, and you cannot make a film without equipment. Neglecting, manhandling, or misusing your equipment will undoubtedly hurt you because your gear will either not function properly or cease to function at all. In the case of electrical equipment, misuse can be especially dangerous and even deadly. Respecting equipment includes educating and training yourself in the proper use of the gear long before you get on the set, using the specific item for its intended use only, handling all gear with care, not physically modifying or customizing equipment that is not yours, maintaining an orderly set and staging area, packing equipment away properly, and using common sense at all times (**Figure 18-2**). Obviously, when you are renting equipment, you will be charged for damages and your reputation will be scarred. In a school situation, where all students desperately rely on the quick turnaround of common and properly functioning equipment, your manhandling of gear can not only result in a fine or loss of privileges (as in the school where I teach) but it could also jeopardize other students' ability to complete their work, and therefore their film and their grade is put at risk.

■ PRODUCTION SAFETY AND SECURITY

The information in this chapter is designed to alert you to some of the major issues concerning production safety and security and to prompt you to take them very seriously. These guidelines are here to help you avoid risk of death, injury, arrest, equipment loss and damage, lawsuits, project collapse, and a bad reputation. Absolutely nothing else in this book means anything if your project is not a safe one and catastrophe occurs. This discussion, however, is in no way comprehensive, nor can it address the safety concerns of every production and circumstance. For this reason I urge you to do further research into the specific safety contingencies of your particular project and to check with all the applicable labor union, state government, local government, location, and school safety regulations and procedures before you start rolling the camera.

Every semester, I discuss safety practices in my production classes, first in a general lecture and again when I meet with production crews to discuss their specific projects. I'm happy to say that I have a very good record when it comes to my students pulling off their films without incident; nonetheless there are those occasions, as any production teacher can attest, where students insist on doing things that are strongly ill advised. I collect these experiences (and those from other schools and professional film shoots) to share with future classes, hoping that they will learn from the mistakes of others. I recount some of the most boneheaded and unsafe things I've heard of people attempting in the pressure and stress of a film production. I tell the story of the crew who put their camera operator on rollerblades and had him hold onto the rear bumper of a moving car with one hand while shooting with a $10,000 film camera in the other—it was cool until they drove over a pothole. I recount the story of the students who improvised a climactic scene of a woman burning a photo of her boyfriend, but they did not give the actress a place to drop the burning photo when the flame got close to her hand—so she dropped the fireball into a waste paper basket filled with, well, waste paper. I tell them about the team who wanted to shoot in an abandoned public pool so they ignored the "No Trespassing" sign, cut through the chain-link fence, and started shooting—they were surprised when the police officers wouldn't accept "But we're only shooting a movie!" as a legitimate excuse. You'll hear more stories later in the chapter. Every time I tell these stories my students rolls their eyes and snicker at the ridiculousness of the actions. The laughter seems to say, "What an idiot. Who would *do* something like that!?" And yet, from time to time one of those snickering students who was shaking their head ends up doing something like that. Thinking that you're immune to doing stupid stuff can quickly evolve into thinking that you can *get away with* doing something stupid. And the minute you think that you can get away with it is when something bad happens, to equipment or people. So the first step to avoid stupid accidents is to acknowledge that we are all capable of poor judgment and therefore must remain vigilant, stay smart, follow rules, heed warnings, and listen to others who have the experience and expertise to tell us how things should be done and when we're being unwise and reckless (**Figure 18-3**).

■ **Figure 18-3** This is an exuberant idea for an improvised traveling shot in a time when cars were rare and car mounts nonexistent; however, these days you'd get in serious trouble for trying a move like this. This is one of the rare times I'll tell my readers, "*Do not* do what this master filmmaker is doing!" From Vertov's *Man with a Movie Camera* (1929).

■ THE TREE COMMANDMENTS OF FILM PRODUCTION SAFETY

1. Every filmmaker has a moral and legal obligation to keep the cast and crew, and the public, safe. Lack of funds is never an excuse for poor safety practices.
2. Safety is everyone's responsibility. You are first responsible for safety in your specific department, but if you see something dangerous or excessively risky anywhere on the set you *must* mention it. *If you see something, say something.*
3. Learn and follow all safety regulations and guidelines that apply to your specific project (union, government, school, location).

Prepare for Safety

A great deal of the effort and attention for ensuring a safe production process happens in preproduction. Don't think that your project is so small or so blessed by the filmmaking gods that you can get away with avoiding these steps:

1. Research, study, and follow all safety regulations and guidelines that apply to your specific project. This may include guidelines from the state or local governments and law enforcement; regulations of the specific location where you are shooting; safety requirements of unions that represent your cast and crew, if any; and the safety guidelines established by your school or department as well as the production parameters expressed by your instructor (in the syllabus or verbally) for the class. I have a colleague who was reviewing a student script and saw that the last scene took place on a building rooftop. He was assured that they had permission to shoot on the roof, that the rooftop had high walls around all edges, and that they would not be shooting near these walls. When he saw the dailies, however, there was a shot of the lead actress sitting on the *other* side of the wall, perched on the edge of the rooftop—very stupid and reckless and in clear violation of the safety regulations of the building and the school. Teachers do not create arbitrary limitations or seek to restrict your creative freedom. We impose limitations because we want you and your team to have a safe and successful production so that you may live to make many more films in the future.

2. Someone on the production team should be assigned the role of **safety coordinator**. On small shoots this can be the producer, production manager, or A.D. On larger shoots with many locations and safety challenges, this should be a dedicated position.

3. Location surveys should include looking for and noting any safety concerns on the set. It's important to bring along one person (safety coordinator) who is responsible exclusively to note all safety issues. This includes a careful assessment of electricity capabilities (discussed later), structural condition, hazardous materials, potential fire hazards, weather exposure, proximity of high voltage lines and traffic, dangerous natural terrain, neighborhood crime trends, hospital proximity, a secure staging area, and so on. This person should also note all emergency exits, fire extinguishers, and access points.

4. Hold safety meetings with the department heads and producing team. These meetings are especially important after a location survey so that each department can anticipate and address its specific safety concerns before the shoot occurs.

5. For every location, everyone on the film team should have the emergency contact information for the police, fire department, and ambulance as well as know where the nearest hospital is. It's a good idea to put this information right on the call sheet, which everyone gets (see **Figure 5-11**).

6. Consult (or hire) the appropriate safety specialists if you plan to do anything with fire, automobiles, stunts, prop weapons, water, etc. (discussed later). They are good at their jobs and a little money in the budget for this will pay off in a safe, trouble- free, and dramatically convincing production.

7. Schedule reasonable hours. Allow enough time for the crew to rest between shooting days, and schedule enough time to allow your crew to do their jobs thoroughly and thoughtfully (see page 118). Don't cram so many setups in each day that everyone is rushing and cutting corners just to stay on schedule. Give people time to do their jobs properly.

8. Everyone must know how to operate their gear before getting on the set, especially large and potentially dangerous items like dollies and generators. Speaking of large and dangerous equipment, *do not* rent or attempt to use equipment for which you are not qualified, and do not attempt to use equipment (or do procedures) that requires a trained and certified technician. And *no,* watching a how-to video on YouTube does *not* constitute training. Specifically, do not try to use large trucks, cranes, generators, or high-wattage lights if you're not trained, qualified, and licensed.

Production Insurance

The boom operator is holding the microphone aloft over the scene, the actor walks two steps farther than in the previous take, so the boom operator steps back but trips over a sandbag, falls, and breaks an arm. It can happen to anyone. When the boom operator gets back from the emergency room, he's got a cast and a hospital bill for $5,000. If you've arranged for production insurance, you're covered; if not, well then your low-budget movie isn't so low budget anymore. Production insurance is necessary for all film shoots, regardless of the size, scale, and budget. Insurance protects the project from catastrophe should there be any injury to the cast or crew or damage to the equipment. In fact, if you want to use SAG actors, you must show proof of insurance before they can enter into a contract with you. Additionally, many rental houses and locations require proof of insurance (some rental houses will provide insurance on equipment for an extra rental fee). Be aware! Finding and securing insurance does not happen instantly—it takes a long time to find an insurance company, determine what kind of insurance you need, and complete the application process, so give yourself plenty of time to go through the process. If you're a student, your department should have information about where and how to acquire production insurance. If you're an independent filmmaker, then there are several insurance companies catering to low-budget films. The Independent Feature Project (IFP) website is a good place to start your search (www.ifp.org). There are more links to insurance resources in the Web Resources appendix.

Common Sense

By far, the preponderance of accidents that happen on the set occur because people forget to use common sense. I've already mentioned this earlier in the book, but it bears repeating; no one on a film set should do or request anything of anyone that would even remotely jeopardize their safety. Asking a camera operator to climb up onto a steep rooftop to get a panoramic shot constitutes a willful and dangerous lack of common sense, as is jerry-rigging a structurally unsound and untested camera mount to a moving car (or any other support). Both cases constitute **negligence**, which is defined as conduct that falls below the standards of behavior established for the protection of others against unreasonable risk of harm (Figure 18-4).

■ **Figure 18-4** Do not attempt under any circumstances. No amount of liability insurance or skating prowess will ever make this kind of thing a good idea.

Here is a true story of a staggering lack of common sense that turned dangerous. A group of students in one of my classes (I'm sorry to say) were making a film outside an all-night bodega. The scene they were shooting involved a big American car pulling up to the bodega and the lead character strutting out. They thought it would be cool to set the camera up in the parking spot on the street so that when the car came to a halt, the front grill would be framed in a tight wide angle (ECU!). Already we can see that common sense was not in play here. A wide-angle ECU meant that the car would need to stop about twenty-four inches in front of the camera. But they, and I mean a crew of five with no objections from anyone, decided to go with it and put the tripod and D.P. off the curb, right where the car would pull in. The driver of the car, another member of the crew, all on his own decided that it would be even cooler to come to a *hard stop*, with the tires skidding a bit and the front grill bouncing in front of the lens. Well, you can guess what happened. The car hit the camera, smashing the lens, and breaking the D.P.'s finger. The entire crew was banned from using school equipment after that and, needless to say, the movie never got made. It's a sad story, but hopefully it'll encourage everyone reading this book to weigh creative impulses against potential risks and to use common sense.

In addition to willful negligence, ordinary, unintentional carelessness can also create serious problems. I was recently on a set where, in a rush to get a setup done before losing the daylight, I saw a grip struggling to single-handedly carry a 1-K baby, a light stand, a sandbag, a bounce board, and a tangle of extension cables up a steep flight of stairs. Even though I was on set to take photos for this book (i.e., not my department), I stopped the guy and helped him schlep equipment so he wouldn't break his careless neck. You should also avoid (or ban) all possible set distractions, like pets, visitors, iPods, and the reigning king of all distractions, the smartphone. I once visited a student film set and saw someone trying to set up a big 2-K softlight while talking to a friend on a cell phone squeezed between her ear and shoulder. If you see something, say something, right? I told the student to hang up and pay attention to what she was doing. I was amazed that she didn't seem to think what she was doing was all that risky. On a film set, all cell phones should be *off* during work hours unless making a project-related call.

Although this next point should be obvious, which is why it's here in the "common sense" section, it must be stated in no uncertain terms. No drugs or alcohol on a film set. By drugs I am not only talking about illegal substances, but you must also be careful with many prescription medications and over-the-counter drugs that cause drowsiness or fuzzy thinking. Many allergy and flu medications are also very effective sleep aids, so before you get on a set, read about the side effects of any medication you're taking.

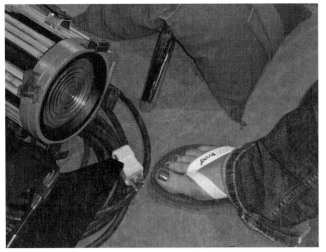

■ **Figure 18-5** Film crews should always show up to a set dressed appropriately to their task. Baggy jeans sagging below the butt, short skirts, high heels, and flip-flops are not only fashion "don'ts" on a film set, they can cause injury.

Also, it's up to each crew member to dress appropriately for their particular role on the set. This is especially important for crew who work with or around heavy equipment and electrical gear. Leather palmed gloves to protect your hands from scorching hot movie lights are obvious, but it should be equally obvious that high heels or open toed shoes are not appropriate footwear if you're required to move equipment, build sets, or work in the middle of a C-stand jungle. Always wear shoes or boots that protect your feet. You should also wear pants which cover your legs, but *not* baggy jeans that slouch half way down your butt. You surely do not need the added encumbrance of your waistband wrapping around your knees while you're carrying a 2-K Fresnel (**Figure 18-5**).

Finally, it's important for safety's sake to keep your set neat and orderly with room for movement. Use your staging area, put things away that are not being used. Don't leave gear where people can trip on it and never, ever block emergency exits with equipment.

Rest and Health

Filmmaking on any level is strenuous work. Keep yourself healthy and mentally sharp by getting enough sleep and eating well during your production period. Also, allow your crew the same. Without rest, your thinking and coordination will be blunt and you'll lack the energy to deal with the general intensity level of filmmaking—no one is an exception. Also, be sensitive to driving times. If you're shooting 250 miles out and expect to wrap at midnight, arrange for hotel accommodations; do not ask anyone to drive 4 hours to get home after a 12-hour workday.

Weather

The entire production team must watch the weather and dress appropriately. In cold conditions wear extra clothes, beyond what you would normally wear on a cold day. When you are working in cold weather for hours, the cold eventually seeps in. In extreme cold conditions, an exterior location should always have a sheltered, heated area nearby where cast and crew can warm up. If you're in a remote area, this could be a tent or shed with a portable heating unit.

In extremely hot weather, lots of drinking water is especially crucial and if you're outside, protect your crew from sun exposure. This means providing sunblock and shade in the form of tarps and umbrellas (which also protects equipment from direct sun). Finally, don't shoot in hostile weather just to stay on schedule. Ice storms, rainstorms, heavy snow, and gale force winds not only make for a miserable experience and compromised footage, but are simply dangerous. Don't risk injury to personnel and damage to equipment, just reschedule.

Risky Locations

You should know, long before you arrive to shoot, if your location is safe through your location scouting (see Chapter 6). If during the location scouting or tech survey you discover that a location is not structurally secure, that there are hazardous materials on the site (asbestos, flammable or toxic compounds), or that the electrical wiring is not up to code, then simply look for another location. It's also best to avoid dangerous locations like steep cliffs, soft riverbanks, and busy highways. Dangerous neighborhoods or buildings known for high crime or gang activity can put your crew and equipment at risk. If you must shoot in dangerous neighborhoods, contact the local police and find out what provisions are available for security. I tell my classes the true story of a small crew who were making a fiction/documentary hybrid film and wanted the capture some gritty reality so they followed the subject of the film, a true heroin addict, as he went to a dealer to score drugs. The next thing they knew, the crew had guns pointed at them and all of their money and equipment was taken. Did it not occur to them that these are dangerous people? Did they think their status as filmmakers would protect them?

Picture Vehicles

We use automobiles in films quite a bit, and extreme caution must be exercised around them at all times. Whenever a person drives a vehicle in a distracted state, like while talking on a cell phone, they are prone to accidents; this also includes acting. When performers are acting (i.e., recalling lines, staying in character, finding emotions), they are very aware of being on film and much less attentive to the road.

Car camera mounts must be rigged and tested by people who know what they're doing and should never be driven on public roads without a permit. I often tell a story, which comes from another film school, of the director and camera operator who wanted to get some pickup shots from out of a window of a moving car. While the camera operator hung out the window, the director drove the car and gave direction. They weren't going fast, but distracted as they were, they crashed the car, damaged the camera, and had to deal with police, school administration, insurance companies, and so on and so on. They were lucky no one was hurt. For inexperienced filmmakers, car chases, screeching tires, and car stunts of any kind are very bad news and absolutely not recommended. The majority of stunt-related deaths and injuries involve vehicular accidents. Automobile stunts, including driving fast, must always be accomplished by trained "precision drivers" driving prepared picture vehicles, and these professionals are often out of budget reach for students. In addition, there is an enormous amount of coordination, permit work, and insurance coverage involved in car action sequences. Even the "simplest" car stunt is dangerous. The story related earlier about parking the car inches in front of the camera attests to that.

Weapons and Violence

Never use a real weapon in a movie. No real guns ever and no real knives. You must always use prop weapons. Prop knives are blunt and often made of plastic. Prop guns come in three flavors: **rubber guns**, which are made of heavy rubber material; **nonfiring "function" guns,** which are made of metal and have working hammers, slides, triggers, and cartridges but have no chamber and cannot fire anything; and **blank-firing guns,** which make a bang and produce a flash out of the barrel (**Figure 18-6**). Blank firing guns can still injure or kill you when not used properly and they require additional permits and insurance to use on a set. It is best not to use a blank-firing gun at all, and many schools prohibit their use for student films. You must also be careful with nonfiring guns, as they are designed to look authentic and can easily be mistaken for a real gun if taken anywhere off your set. If you have a prop gun in your film (nonfiring or blank firing), here are a few essential rules: (1) Review all state and federal laws concerning theatrical weapons use. (2) Always rent from a certified and reputable prop weapons rental house. (3) The people handling the gun (actor and prop master) must be trained in how to use the prop. (4) Treat every gun, even a nonfiring prop, as if it's a loaded weapon. (5) No one else may touch the prop weapon or blanks. (6) You must have a secure place to store prop guns when not in use. (7) You must always notify the local police about your intention to use a prop weapon, whether indoors or outdoors, and arrange for police supervision. It does not matter if you are shooting on a sidewalk or an interior scene on private property. Passers-by and neighbors can see inside homes, stores, or any other location. If they see someone pointing a gun at someone else, they will call the police. Recently, an independent filmmaker making a mafia movie on Long Island was shooting a scene of a convenience store robbery. The action included actors holding guns on a store clerk *inside* a rented convenience store. The crew was very small and they were shooting with a small-format camera using mostly available lights, so there were no overt signs that filming was in progress. Someone driving by saw what was happening through the windows and called the police. The next thing they knew, real cops stormed the shop with real guns drawn

■ **Figure 18-6** The nonfiring prop guns used in the film excerpt *Kiarra's Escape* (see Chapter 5) were handled exclusively by the prop master and actors who were trained in their use. The prop guns were also securely locked away when not in use.

■ **Figure 18-7** News stories of vehicle accidents, accidental fires, misuse of prop guns, and real arrests on film shoots. This is not the way you want your movie to make it into the news.

and disarmed the actor "with force." Luckily, very luckily, no shots were fired before the police realized that this was a film shoot and the guns were props. The producer and director placed their entire cast and crew, and the police officers, in grave danger by not making a simple phone call to notify the police ahead of time of the project (Figure 18-7). More on prop weapons safety can be found at www.moviegunservices.com/mgs_safety.htm.

You should notify the police of any scene of aggression or violence that takes place at an exterior location, even if it does not include weapons. I tell the story of a group of students who ended their film with a scene of a man beating up a former friend who stole everything from him. At the last minute, they decided to change the location from inside an apartment to the courtyard between apartment buildings. Neither actor was trained in fight choreography, so they decided to shoot it in an extreme long shot from the apartment window for believability's sake. As the scene unfolded in the courtyard, people from the surrounding apartments looked out their window to see what the commotion was all about. They saw two men fighting, cursing, and screaming with each blow—but they did not see a film crew or a camera, as they were shooting from inside a third-floor apartment. Because these were very convincing actors, it did not appear to be kids fooling around. So the police precinct received emergency calls about a terrible assault in progress, and cops surrounded the courtyard.

Fire and Open Flames

Fire is unpredictable and flames of any size can quickly get out of hand, so fire should always be avoided. Many schools and locations absolutely forbid open flames of any sort on film shoots, so make sure you check all regulations that apply to your project. If your film absolutely must have a fire of any size at all (like a campfire) and you are legally allowed to have one, then you should have a trained, bonded, and insured pyrotechnics expert on the set. The same goes for any type of legal fireworks (illegal fireworks are, of course, forbidden).

Even if your film has something as small and ordinary as birthday candles or a match lighting a gas stovetop burner, always designate a person to watch that open flame, and make sure they are armed with a fire extinguisher (**Figure 18-8**). Here is a story I heard from another film school. The scene was a birthday party of an elderly man. The art department thought that 65(!) birthday candles would look better than two candles (a 6-shaped candle and a 5-shaped candle). Sixty-five small candles add up to a lot of fire! As the students were lighting the candles, they forgot to start with the inside candles and work their way out—so someone burned their hand, jumped, and knocked the cake over; the lit candles fell on the paper napkins, and a fire quickly started. Luckily, the crew doused it with the punch from the punch bowl, but they narrowly escaped a serious disaster. Fire is no joke. Always make sure that matches, lighters, or anything else used to ignite a flame are put securely away after the scene and not just left around. Always have a fire extinguisher on the set (either bring your own or, in public buildings, locate the nearest available one) whether you're using open flames or not.

■ **Figure 18-8** Even though this romantic scene from Shelton's *Bull Durham* (1988) uses common household candles, the many open flames pose a huge fire risk, which must be taken seriously. For shots like these, a dedicated safety supervisor should oversee the art department setup to ensure that the flames are not near flammable materials and this person must also be on set, with a fire extinguisher, during production.

Water

I discuss electricity and water (showers, pools, etc.) later (see page 394), but if you are shooting on a boat or near any large body of water, do not use electricity at all; rather, since you'll be outdoors, use bounce boards. Additionally, life vests and safety lines are mandatory. Don't use "tippy" boats, and don't overload boats. Many scenes that ostensibly take place in open water are actually shot with the crew and equipment on a pier and the talent in the water only a few feet away. No one knows what's off-screen, so be creative, cheat the shot, and you won't find yourself tipping over in a rowboat and dumping that $25,000 RED One camera to the bottom of the lake (**Figure 18-9**).

Physical Stunts

Here's a comedy scene: a woman races down a grocery store aisle, turns the corner, and knocks the store manager over with her cart. This can be funny, but it's also a stunt and can cause injury. For very simple stunts like this you, should first cast a performer who is in good physical shape and knows how to fall without breaking bones. Then you must protect the actor with body pads and floor mats off-screen. Also, rehearse the stunt until the actor is comfortable with the fall. However, in many cases (e.g., your store manager is played by a frail elderly actor) even a simple fall like this could pose a danger. Some actors will just never fall well or convincingly. Don't take risks. Most physical stunts require a **professional stunt performer**. If your script calls for someone to, say, crash a bicycle on the sidewalk, fall down a short flight of stairs, climb over a chain-link fence, or engage in a fight sequence, you cannot do these things with regular actors. First, you stand a good chance of hurting the talent, no matter how well padded they are, and second, most actors will never give you a convincing fall because they just

■ **Figure 18-9** Scenes that take place in open water can often be cheated closer to the shore so that crew and equipment remain on solid ground. In this production still from *De Daltons, VPRO* (2007), the film crew remains on the pier while shooting a scene in the water. Notice the extra personnel standing by the camera *(right)* and wrangling cables *(left)* to make sure everything and everyone remains dry. (Photo by Sil Stranders.)

don't know how. Professional stunt people are worth the extra expense and insurance precisely because they know how to do stunts so that no one gets hurt and yet are dramatically (or comically) convincing (**Figure 18-10**). Veteran stunt performer and stunt coordinator Matt Anderson, whose many credits include feature films and TV, describes his job like this:

> *If I'm just working as a stunt man, my job is to simply make something look as dangerous as possible, while actually taking as little risk as possible. That's the profession. [...] You don't really want to hire an actor to go down a flight of steps, so you hire a stunt man that can do the job. As a stunt coordinator, it is your job to know the people that can do these things. Usually, they've worked in the business for a longer period of time, they know how to do the stunts and know how everything is set up. But first and foremost as a stunt coordinator, your job is safety. You have to make sure you can make something look spectacular without crashing a lot of people and putting them in the hospital.*

Matt Anderson (From www.pollystaffle.com)

The two critical aspects here are the emphasis on safety (which should be your emphasis as well) and the ability to make even simple stunts completely convincing. There are many agencies, like Stuntworks.com, where you can consult with stunt coordinators before you undertake any sort of physical stunt and cast stunt performers. When casting for a stunt performer, you'll notice that each person specializes in different things—some are good at falls, and others (usually martial arts trained) are expert at fight choreography—and they will be very specific about their physical type so that you can make a good physical match with your talent in cases where you're looking for a stunt double.

■ **Figure 18-10** A trained stunt performer can make physical stunts look very dramatic while keeping everyone safe. Pictured is stuntman Matt Anderson in Davis' *Forget About It* (2006).

Security

In addition to safety, you must think about the security of people, equipment, and personal belongings when you are shooting, especially on location. Theft of equipment and the personal belongings of cast and crew is a common problem on film sets. A producer must ensure that the staging area for equipment is secure and that the actors have a safe place to store their personal belongings while they are on set and in costume. This is especially challenging when you are shooting in a public exterior location. In some cases you may need to assign a person the job of locking away and watching over people's belongings. Never just leave valuables and equipment in a car. Cars get broken into all the time. I have many stories of lazy students who left equipment in a locked car overnight (rather than unload and lock it away indoors) only to find everything gone the next morning. My colleague told me a story of driving home from a long shoot with her D.P. and stopping to have a bite to eat. They tried to find a bonded (insured) parking lot because they had some equipment in the van, but they couldn't find one so they parked on a fairly busy street. When they returned to the van, all the locks had been popped off and the equipment was gone. In this instance she was lucky on three counts: (1) she had paid extra for theft insurance when she rented the van, (2) the D.P. did what any professional would do—he took the camera into the restaurant with him (never leave a camera in an unattended vehicle), and (3) the thieves were not interested in all those DigitBeta tapes in the van and left them behind—these contained all the footage they had shot up to that point!

Gear also gets stolen when there are not enough people loading or returning equipment. One person must be assigned the job of watching the vehicle while others take equipment inside. Loss also often happens on messy, disorganized sets. When set strikes are rushed and haphazard, things get left behind. Leaving equipment in a public hallway while the entire crew is in the apartment shooting is asking for it to get stolen. People will steal your equipment, boxes, extension cords, gels, C-stands, tape, purses, computers, whatever, if you give them the opportunity,

Security also means providing a safe place for cast and crew to work and not asking them to go into unsafe territory just getting to or from a location. For example, if people must travel through dangerous areas late at night, provide escorts or shuttle transportation.

in practice

■ ADDITIONAL SAFETY INFORMATION RESOURCES

There is much more to learn about safety and there may be areas of specific concern for your particular project that were not covered. To find more information, the best place to start is with the Contract Services Administration Trust Fund (CSATF). Within the CSATF is an Industry Safety Committee, which is composed of guild, union, and management representatives active in industry safety and health programs. This committee researches and publishes bulletins and guidelines that provide detailed guidance for film and television industry safe practices.

The CSATF publication *General Code of Safe Practice for Film Production* is a basic summary of safety standards and is a *must read* for everyone involved in film production. You can download this document from the *Voice & Vision* companion website or the CSATF website:

www.voiceandvisionbook.com, (Cht. 18), or www.csatf. org/pdf/GenCodeoSafePractices.pdf

The CSATF *Safety Bulletins* are much more detailed recommendations for safety standards as they pertain to specific issues and circumstances, like the use of prop weapons, stunts, animals, cold weather, etc. You can find the bulletins at www.csatf.org/bulletintro. shtml.

Another highly informative publication is the *Safety Guidelines for the Film and Television Industry in Ontario*, which is published by the Ontario Ministry of Labour. Whether or not you are shooting in Canada, this is a well-researched, cogently organized, and highly informative publication concerning film production safety. You can find a pdf of these guidelines on the *Voice & Vision* companion website or on the Ontario Ministry of Labour website: www.labour. gov.on.ca/english/hs/pubs/filmguide

■ ELECTRICITY AND SAFETY

Film and video production often requires the use of many lights, adding up to thousands of watts of power; using lots of lights means that a filmmaker is harnessing a great deal of electricity. Electricity is dangerous stuff and must be treated properly. A few safety principles and common sense are all it takes to ensure a safe and successful production experience (**Figure 18-11**).

How Much Electricity?

Before you start plugging lights in, you need to determine how much electricity you have at your location and how it's distributed. This will help you figure out how many lights you can work with and where they can be set up and plugged in. This simple procedure for determining how much power you have and where it is should be done during your location survey. It can save you a lot of time and labor by keeping you from lugging more lights than you could possibly use or by keeping you from having to completely overhaul your lighting scheme when you discover the layout you envisioned at your desk isn't possible, given the facts of electricity distribution on the location:

1. Locate the **breaker box** (or fuse box) for your particular location. A breaker box brings the raw power from the utility company into a building and breaks it out into various circuits distributed throughout the rooms. Each circuit is rated in **amps** (short for amperes) and has a dedicated breaker switch (or fuse) with the amp rating written

■ **Figure 18-11** Electricity can kill you. Care, common sense and knowledge are required even when using minimal movie lighting.

right on it. The amp rating tells us how much electricity can safely flow through that circuit. Common circuit ratings found in homes and apartments are 15 amps (most rooms) and 20 amps (rooms that use heavy-draw appliances, like kitchens and bathrooms), but you'll need to check your breaker box to be sure. If you exceed the circuit's rating by plugging in too many lights, the breaker will trip and cut the electricity (with a fuse; a metal filament embedded in the fuse melts and breaks the connection). If the breaker trips, you can simply reset it with the flick of a switch, but you also need to reduce the amount of electricity you are drawing on that circuit or it will trip again (fuses must be replaced). The purpose of breakers is to keep the building from burning down. Excess electricity can heat the internal wiring so much that the insulation melts, leaving super hot and exposed wires to start a fire. If you're using extensive lighting and you do not have access to the breaker box, then it may be too risky to shoot at that location; if you blow a fuse, it's lights out for the rest of the shoot (**Figure 18-12**).

2. The next step is to determine which wall outlets are on which circuits. Usually there are several outlets per circuit, but it's impossible to know exactly how many and how they are clustered without testing them. To determine the distribution, simply turn on one breaker at a time and plug a small lamp or a circuit tester into each outlet. Take note of which breaker controls which outlet throughout your location. Occasionally breakers will be labeled "kitchen," "living room," "master bedroom," etc., but these labels are often flat-out wrong, so it's best to simply figure out for yourself which outlets are connected to which breaker switch.

3. Calculate the amount of electricity you can draw on each circuit. To determine how many watts you can plug into any single circuit, use the following formula:

$$\textbf{watts} = \textbf{volts} \times \textbf{amps}$$

We already know what amps are and their rating can be read straight off the breaker of each circuit. **Volts** (voltage) are the measure of the electromotive force of the electrical current in a system. Volts are standardized by country. In the United States household voltage fluctuates slightly, ranging from 110 to 120 volts. This voltage fluctuation is why our electricity is called AC (for alternating current). Out of respect for electricity, we always use the conservative figure for our calculations:

$$110\,\textbf{(volts)} \times 15\,\textbf{(amps)} = 1{,}650\,\textbf{(watts)}$$

$$110\,\textbf{(volts)} \times 20\,\textbf{(amps)} = 2{,}200\,\textbf{(watts)}$$

So we can plug in up to 1,650 watts of light on each 15-amp circuit and 2,200 watts of electricity on a 20-amp circuit (**Figure 18-13**). Many gaffers feel that it's not safe to go right up to the limit; if there is a dip in power, you could blow a fuse. Also, be careful to take into account or unplug any appliances at the location that can also draw power. It's easy to forget that the refrigerator is plugged into the kitchen's 20-amp circuit. If lights adding up to 2,100 watts are plugged in while the refrigerator compressor is off, invariably the fridge will kick back on just as an actor is delivering the most moving performance of their career, and BLAM!—the breaker trips and the lights go out. Cut!

Lighting and Grip Safety Tips

1. The first rule of safety is to use common sense at all times. Things can become quite hectic on a film shoot—but you should always take your time and do things correctly. Never cut corners on safety to save time and don't try to get away with untested, unsafe jerry-rigging.

2. Never attempt to do things that require the expertise of a trained and certified electrician. This includes doing repairs on high wattage units, opening up breaker boxes to tie into the mains, rewiring outlets, and so on. And again, watching a "how-to" video on YouTube does not constitute adequate training. I once had a student who was planning an exterior night shoot and he asked about the possibility of tapping into the power of a public streetlamp. "It can't be that hard," he said; "I've seen people pop off the covers and rig their own plug-in right on the street." When he saw the incredulous look on my face he added, "Yeah, maybe it's not such a good idea." Indeed!

3. Maintain a professional attitude toward your equipment. Abused and manhandled gear will break and, in the case of lighting equipment drawing thousands of watts of electricity, can bite back!

4. Movie lights get very hot and can burn everything from hands to walls. Keep flammable items away from lights. When bouncing lights off walls, keep them back far enough that they will not blister the paint. Be aware of all flammable materials on the set (costumes, set dressing, etc.) and keep lights clear. Always wear leather-palmed grip gloves when handling hot lights. For lighting units of 500 watts and more, never put gaffer's tape or gels in direct contact with the unit's housing or even the barndoors; they will melt. When attaching gels to barndoors, clip several C-47s to the barndoor first and then clip the diffusion to the C-47s (Figure 18-14).

5. Gels designated with the "tough" (tough spun, tough blue, etc.) are flame resistant and can be used near lights but will melt if not mounted properly. Also, carefully handle the scrims that are used in lights to cut the intensity—they also get super hot. Back when I was a student I was on the set of a classmate who removed a scrim from a 1-K baby and dropped it on his mother's carpet. When the shoot was over he went to pick it up and discovered that it had melted the nap and was fused to the carpet. When his mom came home, he lost the one location he thought he could always count on.

6. Always turn off lights when not in use; and after a shoot, turn them off right away and let them cool down completely, on their stands, before you pack them away.

7. Never touch the lamp of a movie light, even if it is cool. Lamps get extremely hot and will obviously burn you. But touching a cool lamp with your bare fingers is also dangerous because your fingers leave oil on the bulb; the oil cooks when the lamp is turned on and eventually causes the bulb to explode. Always use the plastic or paper sheath provided with a new lamp to handle the bulb when you are replacing it.

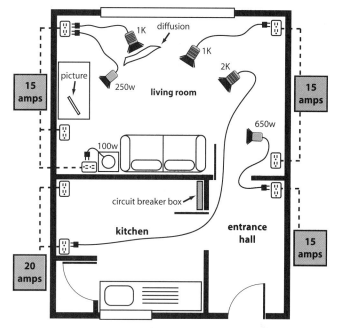

■ **Figure 18-13** Overhead diagrams that detail both the distribution of electricity at a location and where each lighting unit will be plugged in are essential to keep from tripping breakers during your shoot. Notice that the cumulative wattage plugged in to any given circuit does not exceed its amp rating.

■ **Figure 18-14** Diffusion and gels should be attached to barndoors using a couple of C-47s to avoid melting and fires. Always wear leather-palmed gloves when handling lights.

■ **Figure 18-15** All lights should always be set up so that the cable is flush against the stand (a), the light is stabilized with one or more sandbags (b), and cables are taped to the floor to prevent accidents (c).

8. Electricity and water do not mix. Duh! When shooting scenes involving water, like bathtubs and swimming pools, it's best to go with available light. If you must use lighting for interior bathroom scenes, do not set up lights where they could fall into the water. In fact, my students are not allowed to have movie lights in the same room with a full bathtub or running shower. They must bounce light from a unit set up outside the door. In addition, they are required to station a grip at each unit for added safety.

9. When setting up a lighting unit or a C-stand, try to keep the weight as evenly distributed as possible. An unbalanced C-stand can easily topple over; so can a fully extended light stand with a heavy instrument on top. Use a sandbag to stabilize every stand (**Figure 18-15**, *left*). Try not to create unbalanced gobo extensions. In addition, rotate the gobo arm such that the weight of the object pulls the gobo arm in the direction of tightening the gobo head. Do not allow gravity to pull the arm in a direction that would loosen the head.

10. Keep your cables neat. Use stingers to allow cables to fall straight down from the unit to the ground rather than stretching out diagonally to reach an outlet (**Figure 18-15**, *right*). In areas where there is a lot of foot traffic, tape down your cables with gaffer's tape (called **dressing cables**). And always coil unused cables and put them out of the way, safely in the staging area.

11. All hanging lights, barndoors, and any other item rigged overhead should be secured with a safety chains.

PART IV TOOLS AND TECHNIQUES: POSTPRODUCTION

Postproduction Overview and Workflow

After the director has gleefully announced, "that's a wrap," after all of the equipment has been packed up and returned, after you shake the last hand at the wrap party, and after the last video daily comes back from the lab, there's still quite a way to go before you've finished making your movie. The next step is postproduction. **Postproduction** encompasses all of those creative and technical processes that go on after the shooting stops:

1. Review and evaluating footage (page 434).
2. Transfer footage (and other media elements) into your edit system and organize (page 429).
3. Edit the picture and sound (rough cuts to fine cut) (pages 435 - 439).
4. Add visual transitions and effects (page 439).
5. Create and mix the sound design (Chapter 23).
6. Correct color and exposures and add credits (Chapter 24).
7. Master the project and distribute (Chapter 24).

Most of these stages offer tremendous creative potential for the continuing evolution of your motion picture. The possibilities range from large structural changes, like cutting out entire characters or rearranging the events of the plot, to subtle alterations in dramatic tone by tweaking the image color palette. You can also develop new thematic layers by adding a music track that creates a new subtext or associations with the image or subtly alter the mood of a scene by manipulating the ambient sound. In other words, the possibilities are endless.

Naturally, the director follows the project into postproduction. Often, you will find directors actually editing their own film; this is especially true on short projects, but less so on feature-length films. Just as there are creative specialists in the other areas of filmmaking (cinematographers, art directors, sound mixers, writers, etc.), there are also specialists in postproduction who can bring fresh conceptual perspectives, imaginative energy, and technical expertise to the movie. Editors, sound designers, composers, rerecord mixers, and colorists are the postproduction contingent to the filmmaking team. Again, if you are shooting a five-minute film for an introductory film class you will probably do most, or all, of the postproduction tasks yourself. In fact, when you are starting out, it's a good idea to do as much of the postproduction as possible yourself. The more postproduction you encounter first hand, the more you will understand the expressive possibilities of this phase. This is especially true of editing. It is equally useful to edit footage shot by someone else. In both cases, you will be a better filmmaker. If you end up on the production side of filmmaking (director, D.P. etc.), you'll have a better sense for what an editor needs to cut a movie together, or you may just end up loving the creative impact of postproduction so much that it could become your chosen métier. Remember, film is an integrated art form, and editing is a storytelling tool of equal power and importance to cinematography, directing, screenwriting, and art direction.

■ WORKFLOW AND FORMAT INTERFACE

One essential factor that a filmmaker must consider from the very beginning of a project is workflow. **Workflow** is the process and format path your project will take from acquisition (sound and image) to exhibition, including the shooting format, editorial format, finishing process, mastering format, and distribution formats. At this point in the evolution of the medium, there are a wide variety of pathways one can take, and each course has a significant impact on the budget of the film, the technical process, and the range of exhibition possibilities. More than any other technical area, filmmakers can lose their way in the workflow stream, with unexpected and often expensive results. A little bit of research, from the very beginning, into the technical stages of your project and the way various production phases and formats interface with each other, will go a long way toward minimizing nasty surprises. In preproduction you must ask yourself these primary questions right up front:

1. What is my shooting format: film, broadcast DV (HD or SD), uncompressed video (2K or 4K), resolution, frame rate?
2. How am I editing: format, frame rate, resolution?
3. How do I want to finish and master the movie: HD, film, uncompressed media files?
4. How do I want to distribute (screen) the project: broadcast format, film, Digital Cinema, DVD, Blu-ray, web, or a combination?

With the advent of inexpensive and user-friendly editing software, **digital nonlinear editing (NLE)** system has totally eclipsed film editing, so generally speaking, we're all cutting digitally (see Chapter 20). However, the *format details* between the NLE system and the shooting and finishing variables determines an enormous amount concerning the technical postproduction pathway and, consequently, your budget. On a broad level, workflows can be similar, but in the details, things can get tricky and can change from year to year. This is why you need to research your complete workflow before you start shooting. This includes speaking with people who have taken a similar path and anyone who you'll be working with including sound mixers, editors, and especially film labs if your workflow requires their involvement. A little bit or research up front will save headaches, money, and wasted time down the road.

Two Common Workflow Paths: DV to DV and Film to DV

Most low-budget projects, whether shorts or features, finish on one of the HD digital videotape formats and are ultimately screened on a television monitor or with video projection. This is the case for most films that are made in a film class, films that are festival bound, and films that are made for broadcast. Here are the two most common workflows.

1. **Shoot:** DV (HD or SD)/**Edit and Finish**: Digital NLE/**Master**: HD tape/**Release**: Broadcast, Blu-ray, DVD, web (**Figure 19-1**).

2. **Shoot**: Film/**Transfer**: HD tape/**Edit and Finish**: Digital NLE/**Master**: HD tape/**Release**: HD tape, Blu-ray, DVD, web (**Figure 19-2**).

You'll notice that the major difference here is the acquisition format and the additional transfer step shooting on film requires before you can edit. After that, these workflows are essentially the same. You'll also notice that neither one of these workflows finishes

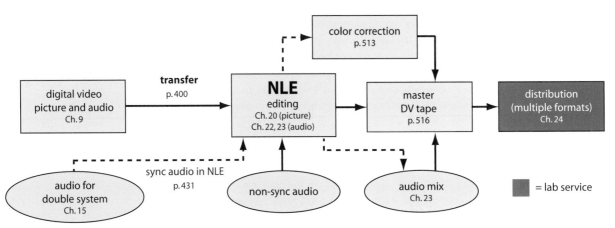

■ **Figure 19-1** Picture and audio paths for workflow #1: Shoot: DV/Edit: Digital/Master: DV tape/Release: multiple formats.

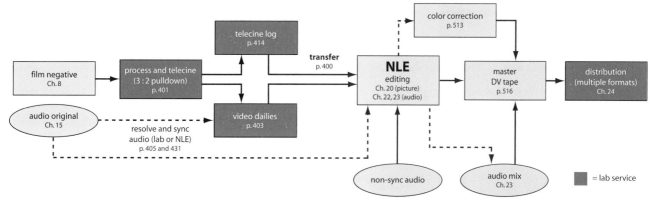

■ **Figure 19-2** Picture and audio paths for workflow #2: Shoot: Film/Transfer to DV/Edit: Digital/Master: DV tape/Release: multiple formats.

on film. The world of film festivals has realized that projecting
submissions on digital video is
essential if they are to represent
the full spectrum of films out
there—documentary or narrative—regardless of their acquisition format. In 2008 the Tribeca
Film Festival in New York City,
one of the world's elite festivals, screened well over half
their programs on HDCAM, and
the Avignon International Film
Festival (that showcases emerging filmmakers) is 100% digital
projection. Add to this that the

■ **Figure 19-3** Daschbach's award-winning short film *Waking Dreams* (2004, *left*) followed workflow
#1: it was shot on video (DVCPRO50) at 24p, edited at 29.97, and color corrected with the NLE system's
native color tool. The film was then mastered to DVCPRO as well as BetaSP for festival distribution. Lu's
film *When I Was Young* (2003, *right*) followed workflow #2: it originated on 16mm film, was transferred
to video, edited, and color corrected on a NLE. The film was mastered right out of the NLE to BetaSP and
distributed in multiple formats. (See both of these films at www.voiceandvisionbook.com.)

only affordable film release format (16mm) is all but dying out; 16mm projectors (with
their horrible optical audio) are getting harder to find, while good-quality digital projection is ubiquitous. So although Super 16mm remains a viable shooting format, "film
release" essentially means 35mm, and that is always an expensive proposition (see page
410) **(Figure 19-3)**.

■ TECHNICAL PROCESS OF POSTPRODUCTION WORKFLOW

Each of these workflow options has its own advantages and challenges. It's important
to keep in mind that the picture and audio often follow different technical paths, especially in double-system sound production. We've covered the production formats (image
and audio) in earlier chapters: Chapter 8: *The Film System*, Chapter 9: *The Digital Video
System*, and Chapter 15: *Sound for Production*. Now let's look closer at the specific postproduction technical process for each workflow scenario.

Setting Up Your NLE Project

Before you bring footage into your editing system and start cutting away, you need to take
the time to properly set up your NLE project. Setting up your project means establishing
the postproduction format workflow so that every stage is consistent and compatible.
Obviously, we can't cover every specific variation for setting up a project in this book, but
in general you must access the audio/video settings **(Figure 19-4)** and enter the following
information for your particular project:

1. *Source format.* The format of the media you're bringing into the NLE (including resolution, frame rate, scanning mode, timecode, and codec). For SD and HD projects, this
   is your shooting format, but for projects that shoot on film and D-Cinema (see page
   407), your source format is what you've transferred to for editing.

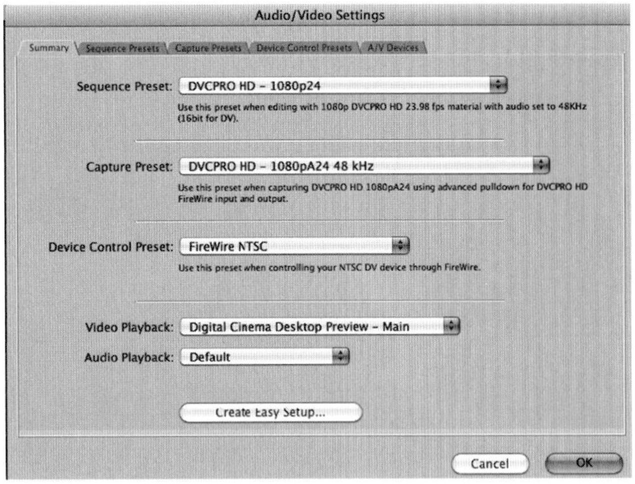

■ **Figure 19-4** The audio/video settings window in FCP used to set up the editing format workflow.

2. *Capture preset settings.* How you want the system to capture your footage—with these two workflows, the capture settings should simply match your source format. However, if you've shot on a high-resolution (storage hungry) format (like 2 K or 4 K) and have limited storage space, you might capture footage with high compression to save space and then **relink** (or **conform**) the original footage to the final edit, using only the high-res footage that matches the exact shots in the final cut. Using compressed footage for cutting is called **offline editing**, and editing with footage at its native resolution is called **online editing** (see page 408). For projects shot on film and destined for one of the 24fps release formats (film or DCP), you should capture with "reverse telecine" to remove the extra frames, allowing you to edit with the original frames at 24 p (see *telecine* later).

3. *Sequence settings.* The format you'd like to work with in the sequence—again, this usually matches the other two formats. There are exceptions, however. Again, if you've shot film (24 fps) and wish to finish on film (24 fps), you should edit at 24 fps even though the video dailies are 29.97 (see page 413).

4. *Output.* Determines what format you'd like to output for mastering. For mastering your project, this usually also just matches the input format. However, depending on the anticipated distribution, you could output a number of different formats (see Chapter 24).

In most cases, especially with these two workflows, a project maintains the same format from beginning to end. For example, if you shoot with a Panasonic HVX200 (DVCPRO HD format) at 1080/60i (source format), you simply use the same format details for your capture, sequence, and output settings. This is why there is always some form of "easy setup" option in your NLE. Projects that require more complex settings include those that involve media from various sources (mixed formats, HD and SD, mixed frame rates, etc.), those for which the anticipated output format is very different from the source format, and shooting formats that are not natively supported by the NLE system. In all these cases, you'll need to consult the NLE system manual to determine the proper project format setups.

One additional and critical setup step: before you start transferring footage into your NLE system, it's important to set a *single destination folder for all your media files* on your external hard drive (called a **capture scratch file** in Final Cut Pro) or you run the risk of spraying footage throughout your system and ultimately losing some.

Transferring DV and Film Footage

Staying entirely in the digital domain—shooting on DV (SD or HD) capturing the footage directly from your memory cards (P2 or SxS) or camera original tapes into the nonlinear editing system, and outputting back onto digital videotape—is by far the most straightforward and cost-effective workflow process because nowhere does it rely on the services of a laboratory. Working with footage originating on film requires a few extra steps and the involvement of a lab, but we'll get to that later.

The process of transferring your original DV footage into your NLE system is called a number of things: **capturing** (tape media)**, ingesting** (file based media), or **transferring** (Figure 19-5). If your footage is on tape (either originating on tape or film transferred to tape), capturing is usually done with a DV deck via a FireWire cable and the deck functions are controlled by the computer interface with **external device control**. If your footage is on memory cards or has been transferred in the field to a hard drive, then the interface can be FireWire or USB 2.0. In both cases you *can* use your camera to do the transferring, but it's best not to add extra wear and tear on a valuable piece of production equipment with this task.

Transferring video turns your raw elements into media files that the NLE software can work with. This is done through **container formats**. Final Cut Pro is a **QuickTime (.mov)** based editing system and natively supports all QuickTime compatible formats (which include most of the shooting formats out there). The Avid system, on the other hand, saves all media in one of two open media container formats: **Open Media Framework (.omf)** (the old format) or **Material Exchange Format (.mxf)** (the new format).

■ **Figure 19-5** The log and capture window in FCP (for capturing tape-based media) allows you to see the clip you are capturing (a) and log each one with scene and take numbers and comments, (b) as you go (see also log and transfer window, Figure 20-20).

in practice

■ WHAT'S A CONTAINER FORMAT?

Okay, we already discussed ATSC display formats, SD and HD shooting formats, and codecs in Chapter 9. At the risk of giving you serious brain fatigue, let me introduce *one more* type of video format that you'll see in editing systems: the **container format** (a.k.a. **wrapper format**). All video data downloaded for use into an editing system is "wrapped" within a system container format. Basically, the container format used by an editing system (Avid or Final Cut Pro) wraps around all the shooting format data (codec compressed video) and metadata (timecode, etc.) in order for the system to efficiently store, move, and "work with" this material. In a way, you can think of a container format as standardizing all the video and audio data you import into the editing system so that it can be read by the system and therefore seamlessly stored and manipulated *without changing the original shooting format encoding*.

QuickTime File Format (.mov) is the container format for all video imported into Final Cut Pro and AVID currently uses the **Material Exchange Format** (.mxf). If, for some reason, the editing system *does not* support the video-shooting format (meaning that it does not recognize the format codec), then you will be required to transcode your footage. **Transcoding** means converting the original encoding to another, compatible encoding format that the edit system's container format will support. For example, as of the writing of this book, Final Cut Pro does not natively support footage shot with H.264 coding (i.e., DSLR footage and AVCHD format), but this does not mean you cannot edit this footage in FCP. You simply need to transcode your footage to the native Apple ProRes codec first. Transcoding can sometimes result in a loss of quality and always involves more technical hoops to jump through. This is why you should check the compatibility of your shooting format with your editing system *before* you start shooting.

The Film-to-Tape Transfer

Whenever we choose to shoot on film (usually for aesthetic reasons), the workflow is not as self-contained. Clearly, we have to have some way of converting our original camera negative into a digital format so that it can be captured in the same way as footage originating on DV. For this we must use a laboratory, not only for processing but also to transfer that footage to a digital video format. This service, of course, costs money, and like all format conversions there are some technical considerations that must be carefully observed to make the process run smoothly. Of primary concern is the transfer between a format with one frame rate (film's 24 fps) to a format with a different frame rate (DV's 29.97 fps). Tangled up in this format conversion is synchronous audio, which, if it is to remain in sync, must undergo its own conversion. Even though this transfer process is very common, it is easy to be confused by all of the associated details, minutiae, and extenuating factors.

It's not difficult to find very cheap, down-and-dirty, film-to-tape transfers, called **film chain** transfers. Basically, a film chain is a projector that pushes light through your negative onto a CCD chip mounted where the projector lens usually sits. Although film chain transfers are cheap, they give you thoroughly wretched results. Contrast is extreme, color is dull, and a stroboscopic throb is evident, caused by the crude method for (not) reconciling the different frame rates. In the end, this method is cheap but totally counterproductive because it eliminates all of the reasons we shoot film in the first place (namely, rich image quality, and detailed response to light).

Figure 19-6 A Rank/Cintel flying spot scanner telecine machine.

To maintain all of the hard work you put into your lighting and exposures (not to mention your story, performances, sound, etc.), you should go the final yard and get a professional **telecine** transfer. The telecine is the standard machine used for film-to-tape transfers, which are sometime also called "rank" transfers, after the commonly used Rank/Cintel flying spot scanner, telecine machine (Figure 19-6). The **flying spot scanner** is a **cathode ray tube (CRT)** telecine system. A photon light beam scans the negative film frame, passing right through and registering the color and brightness information, pixel-by-pixel, onto red, green, and blue photodiodes. However, many labs also use the Philips **CCD telecine** system, which uses light from a xenon bulb; the light passes through the negative and into a prism block, which in turn separates the image into red, green, and blue components to be registered by respective R, G, and B CCD chips, similar to the CCD camcorder (Figure 19-7).

The film-to-tape transfer process accomplishes four things: (1) it converts the film image into digital data to be recorded on a DV tape format, (2) it reconciles the difference between film and DV frame rates, (3) it inverts the colors from negative film into a positive image on your tape, and (4) it allows for color and exposure correction. Let's look at each procedure:

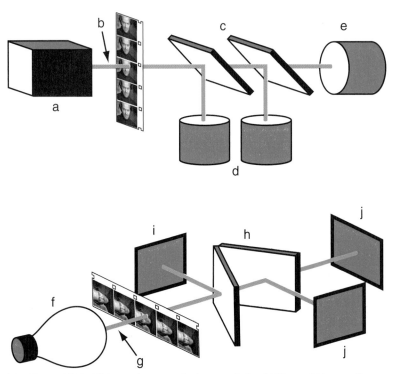

1. *Converting the film image into digital data.* As your camera original negative film runs through the telecine machine, it scans your negative, separating the color components (RGB and luminance information) and converts these values into binary code (or digital data), ready to be recorded on whichever DV format you need for your NLE system: MiniDV, DVCPRO, DVCAM (for SD projects), or DVCPRO HD, DVCAM HD (for HD projects). It is essential that you tell the lab to which DV format you wish to transfer.

2. *Reconciling the difference between film and DV frame rates.* The telecine scanning process allows us to reconcile the difference in frame rates between film and video through a process called **3:2 pulldown**. There are two components to this process, the "3:2" part and the "pulldown" part. We know that the frame rate of film is 24 frames per second and the frame rate for standard video is essentially 30 frames per second. We also know that each video frame is made up of 2 fields (30 frames per second = 60 fields per second). The 3:2 process involves duplicating every other film frame as 3 fields, instead of 2 fields. If we look at how the

Figure 19-7 A flying spot scanner *(top)* uses a photon light beam (a) to scan the negative (b); the resulting beam is separated by dichroic mirrors (c) into primary colors, and their output is received by photodiodes (d, e). A CCD scanner *(bottom)* uses a xenon bulb (f) to scan the negative film frame (g). Dichroic mirrors (h) separate the resulting beam into primary colors that are registered by CCD chips (i, j).

3:2 process affects four frames of film, we see that frames A and C are each scanned onto 2 fields (1 video frame each), and frames B and D are each scanned onto 3 fields (1.5 frames each). So after 4 frames of film we will have 10 fields, or 5 frames of video (**Figure 19-8**). Following this pattern, after 24 frames of film, we will have created an extra 6 video frames, to arrive at 30 frames of video (60 fields).

But wait a minute! By now we all know that video really runs at the slightly slower rate of 29.97 frames per second (see page 197), so what are we going to do about that? This is where the "pulldown" part of the process comes in. The 29.97 video frame rate is precisely 0.1% slower than 30 fps, so, to compensate, the telecine machine actually slows down the running speed

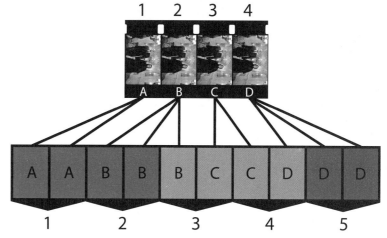

■ **Figure 19-8** To reconcile the different frame rates between film and video, the 3:2 pulldown transfer process creates five video frames from four film frames by duplicating every other film frame across three video fields.

of your film to 23.976 fps, which is exactly 0.1% slower than 24 fps. Both of the adjustments in the 3:2 pulldown, film-to-tape transfer process (adding extra fields and slowing the film transport speed) are amazingly imperceptible to the human eye.

Incidentally, this elaborate process of converting frame rates with 3:2 pulldown is not a global problem. For example, if you're a filmmaker in a country that uses DVB-T or PAL (like all of Europe, for example) the standard frame rate for video and film are the same, 25 fps, so the transfer from film-to-tape is a simple frame-for-frame conversion.

3. *Inverting the colors from negative film into a positive image.* Once the frame rate issue is resolved and the image information of each frame has been scanned and turned into binary code, the telecine outputs that data to a highly sophisticated console called a color corrector. The primary job of the color corrector at this point is to invert the color values of the negative film so that you get a positive image on the DV tape. However, the color corrector console can do much more than simply invert a negative image to a positive image.

4. *Correcting color and exposure.* Two of the most common film-to-tape color correction consoles are the DaVinci and the Pandora systems. In the hands of an experienced **colorist** (the person who operates the color corrector), you can have significant control over the tonalities and exposures of each scene. During the telecine transfer process, the colorist is able to adjust the red, green, blue, and luminance values of each scene independently and with a remarkable degree of flexibility (**Figure 19-9**). Adjusting the original image is called **color correction** or **color timing.** Subtle and common adjustments include fixing inconsistencies and minor problems with color temperatures and exposure. Extreme color timing can include shifting an entire color palette of a scene or altering the contrast for an entire film. Yes, all of this can be yours! For a price!

Film labs offer several different levels of color correction that you can use, depending on the stage of your project. At this early stage, when transferring all raw footage to video in preparation for editing, what comes back from the lab are called **video dailies** (**Figure 19-10**). For making video dailies we generally use one of two **unsupervised color correction** processes. The quickest and cheapest is called the

■ **Figure 19-9** A colorist using a DaVinci color correction station to fine-tune color and exposures during a film-to-tape transfer.

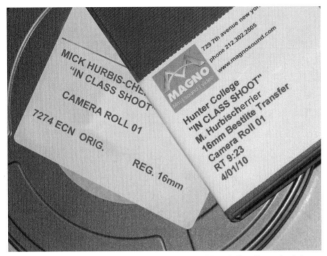

Figure 19-10 My original negative and video dailies from the lab. Notice on the DV tape label that I had requested a best light transfer for this in the class shooting exercise.

one-light transfer: the colorist establishes the transfer settings based on the skin tones and the color chart at the head of each film roll—if you remembered to shoot it. Once set, the entire roll is run through the telecine and transferred. So what you shot is what you get. If you've underexposed a few scenes, it'll show. The other option is called a **best-light transfer.** This costs more, but the colorist resets the chrominance and luminance settings for each change in location or lighting situation on the roll (for which there should be a new color chart). With this transfer, minor color temperature and exposure problems will be fixed and often your video dailies will be of high enough quality to take you pretty close to your finished movie—with a little additional color correction toward the end of the process, either with your own software (e.g., color correction in Final Cut Pro) or in a supervised session at the lab. A **supervised color correction** session involves the filmmaker sitting with the colorist at the color correction console as adjustments are made to each and every scene. This service is charged by the hour, which is why we tend not to use this service for making video dailies from all our raw footage. Usually, supervised transfers are reserved for after the editing process, when you can color correct only those shots that actually made it into the final cut.

In any case, once the lab has processed and transferred your film to DV tape and delivered your dailies, you are ready to capture the footage into your NLE system, as we mentioned previously.

SHOOTING A COLOR CHART AT THE HEAD OF EVERY FILM ROLL

A **color chart** (also called **chip chart**) is a piece of cardboard with a series of standardized colored squares. The chip chart is shot at the head of every roll of film to help the colorist achieve accurate and consistent colors when transferring your film to DV tape. It is standard procedure to shoot a color chart at the head of every roll of film, but some film crews will also shoot a chip chart on the first shot whenever the lighting situation changes dramatically (e.g., moving from outside to inside in the middle of a roll). Here are a few tips:

1. Shoot just a few feet of film. Don't waste film on the chip chart; the colorist will freeze one frame to set up the telecine transfer colors.
2. Always shoot the chip chart under the representative light for the scene (e.g., tungsten or daylight) but without using any special color effects (gels or filters) you wish to add into the scene. If, for example, you are shooting indoors with tungsten lights and you want to create a red edge to the image by adding red gels to some of the lights, this effect could easily be "corrected" right out of your image if you've shot the chip chart under the red glow. In this case, shoot the chip chart under tungsten lights first, *then* add the red gels. This will signal to the colorist that the red glow in the image is intentional.
3. Include skin for fine-tuning. Many colorists ultimately will rely on skin tones to fine-tune the color balance. For this reason, many labs prefer that you include the face of the crewmember holding up the color chart (**Figure 19-11**).

Figure 19-11 It's important to shoot a few feet of a color chart (with skin tone) at the head of each camera roll to help the colorist make color adjustments during the film-to-tape transfer

The Audio Transfer

If you have shot single-system sound on DV, then the audio is captured in sync along with the picture. However, if you shoot DV in a double-system sound setup, then your audio is captured separately and stored as .wav files. Then, each scene must be synced in the NLE timeline, either by lining up the image and audio reference timecode or by lining up the image and audio of the slate closing (see page 431). All nonsync audio sources, music, sound effects, etc., must also be captured from their original format, into the NLE for editing and mixing.

As we mentioned earlier, film shooting is always a double-system sound process, so all synchronized audio must be captured separately and synced with the picture before editing. A film shooter has two options for this. You can send your field audio to the lab with your film (and your sound logs) and request that they sync your audio for you, take for take. This service, as with all lab services, costs money and is charged by the hour. If your slating and logging procedures on the set were inconsistent and sloppy, then you can expect it to take them many more hours to figure out exactly where sync is on each take. The final cost can be significantly reduced if your slates are readable, your audible markers are clearly articulated on each take (e.g., "scene 2b, take 3"), and your logs are accurate and readable. Using a timecode slate that is receiving timecode from the audio recorder also makes the job go much faster, because syncing is simply a matter of reading timecode off the image and typing the corresponding number into the audio transfer deck to find the sync point (see page 336). When you ask the lab for this service, what you get back are video dailies with the audio synced on the same tape, ready to be captured. Or to save on your budget you can sync your transferred footage with the audio yourself in your NLE system. This process is discussed in detail on page 431.

Sync Drift and Audio Resolving

There is one additional step that must be accomplished before film, transferred to DV, and field audio can be manually synced up: **resolving the audio.** As we just discussed, when film is transferred to tape, the 3:2 pulldown process effectively slows the film down by one-tenth of one percent (0.1%). With the image running slightly slow, our synchronous audio is now slightly faster than the picture; image and sound are out of sync. Although a 0.1% difference doesn't seem like much, over long takes the difference becomes more and more pronounced; this is called **sync drift.** The pulldown speed's discrepancy amounts to an offset of 1.8 frames every minute; that's 18 frames every 10 minutes. Loss of sync becomes noticeable after only 20 or 30 seconds. To compensate and resolve our audio, we need to perform the pulldown process on the audio as well (i.e., slow *it* down 0.1% too). Film labs, of course, resolve audio as a matter of course when you ask them to sync your audio. But if you're syncing dailies yourself, NLE systems have some type of "modify speed" command that will quickly and easily resolve your audio, essentially by playing it a 99.9% speed (**Figure 19-12**). You will then be able to easily sync up picture and audio by lining up the slate (see page 431).

Editing and Sound Design in the NLE System

Once you've successfully set up the audio/video format settings for your project and transferred all your media to an external hard drive through the NLE capture/ingest function, you're ready to edit. The editing phase is complex, involving technical knowledge of the NLE system, good organization and a number of creative stages. As this chapter is dedicated to general issue of workflow and formats, I have dedicated four other chapters to

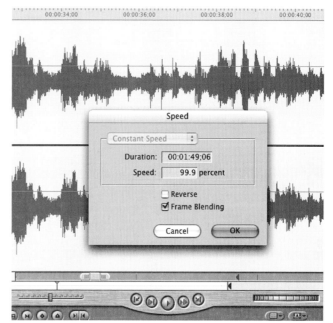

■ **Figure 19-12** The modify speed command in Final Cut Pro allows you to easily resolve your audio to your pulled-down footage when syncing dailies yourself.

3:2 PULLDOWN: IT'S NOT JUST A FILM ISSUE!

3:2 pulldown, as you know, is the process that allows us to convert from 24 fps to 29.97 fps so that we can display our footage in a standard definition NTSC digital system. However, this process is not only for film, but for 24p video (both SD and HD) as well. In fact, 24p video doesn't exactly capture at 24 fps; it captures at 23.976 fps for the same reason we slow film's 24 fps frame rate down by 0.1%—for a compatible transfer to 29.97. The important thing to remember is that although 24p cameras *capture* at 23.976, they in fact *record* at 29.97. The 3:2 pulldown is accomplished in your camcorder's digital signal processor (DSP),

■ **Figure 19-13** The Panasonic DVX100b is just one of many cameras that has the option to shoot 24p video.

which then sends the 29.97 DV (with extra fields, interlacing, and all) to be written onto your record media. In fact, all video outputs in 24p mode are actually 29.97 video. So when you view your 24p DV footage on a monitor or even on the camera LCD screen, you're seeing the standard 29.97 frame rate (**Figure 19-13**).

With software like Cinema Tools, most NLE systems are able to easily remove the extra frames when you capture, so that you may edit in 24p mode with the **original frames.** Whether you plan to go back to film for distribution, finish for Digital Cinema projection or on Blu-ray, distribute on DVD, staying in the 24p mode throughout your workflow is advantageous. In the first case, the 1-to-1 frame transfer to film is much simpler. In the second case, Digital Cinema and Blu-ray are native 24p formats, and in the third case, while DVDs are capable of storing media at many frame rates, 24p reduces the amount of data you need to pack onto your disc, as compared with 60i, so there will be less need for compression.

---

the picture and audio editing phase. Chapter 20 discusses the NLE interface, logging and organizing your elements, syncing dailies, and the creative steps used to get your film from a rough cut to a fine cut (picture and essential sound tracks). Chapter 21 discusses the art and expressive concepts behind common editing techniques. Chapter 22 explores the conceptual and creative dimension of the sound design, while Chapter 23 zeroes in on the technicalities of working with multiple sound tracks and doing a final mix. So please refer to those detailed chapters for this stage of the workflow. Additionally, the final finishing and distribution phases for the two common workflows discussed previously, which are essentially the same because they finish in the same formats, have also been given a complete and detailed chapter, Chapter 24. As I mentioned earlier, the majority of projects on the introductory, intermediate level, and even lowbudget independent projects use these common workflows. So if this is your case, proceed to these other chapters.

■ HIGH-END FINISHING WORKFLOWS

Let's jump off from what we know about workflows so far to look those high-end workflows that finish on 35mm film or 2K/4K Digital Cinema formats. Finishing, mastering, and distributing on **film** (called **film out**) or as a (2K and 4K) **Digital Cinema Package** (**DCP**) for theatrical release is always expensive, primarily because they involve extensive lab services. This fact means that these processes are undertaken when a filmmaker *knows* that they have the budget to go this route or after a filmmaker secures theatrical release or is accepted into a prestigious festival that requires a film print or DCP. In the case of a film gaining theatrical release, the distribution company will usually foot the bill; in the case of satisfying the requirements of a festival, the filmmaker finds the money in the hope that a distribution deal will result from the exposure. In all cases, if you anticipate that you'll be finishing on film or DCP, you'll need to plan for this workflow long before the camera rolls because all labs have their own requirements in terms of formats, processes, and elements (edit decision list format, timecode format, etc.). Also, many of the services you'll be needing are billed by the hour, so mistakes, indecision, or lack of knowledge can be costly. For these reasons, it's important that very early on in the preproduction stage you introduce yourself to your lab and find a consultant who can guide you through the lab's workflow process.

Generally, workflows that include high-end (and high expense) finishing and mastering are appropriate when you've shot on a high-resolution format as well, namely Super16 or 35mm film, or uncompressed (4:4:4) video formats (i.e., Redcode RAW, ArriRaw, CineAlta uncompressed, etc.). However, premium shooting formats have never automatically determined the artistic quality of a movie. Many projects shot on professional HD formats, like DVCPRO HD and XDCAM, can also transfer very well to film or DCP. Indeed, many projects shot on low-end formats like standard definition NTSC video and consumer HDV have nonetheless been of such strong artistic merit, that they've garnered theatrical release and therefore needed to be finished on film (see page 413). What's important to remember, whether you're shooting film, HD, or 4K video, is to shoot at 24p for a smooth workflow as both 35mm film and Digital Cinema are 24 fps formats.

Digital Cinema Finishing

In 2007 the seven major film studios (20th Century Fox, Universal, MGM, Paramount, Warner Bros., Sony, and Disney) came together in a joint venture called the **Digital Cinema Initiative (DCI)** to establish common technical specifications and quality standards for Digital Cinema (the digital theatrical presentation of 2D and 3D films).[1] These standards do not conform to the ATSC broadcast standards; rather, they exceed them (see Chapter 9). In the few years between the first edition of *Voice & Vision* and the publication of this second edition, the number of commercial theaters equipped for Digital Cinema projection went from a few hundred to nearly 20,000. This rapid expansion is not entirely in response to issues of quality; rather it is largely driven by economics. It's in the best economic interest of studios, distribution companies, and theaters to handle hard drives and data rather than reels and reels of celluloid. Why ship a 35mm film print weighing more than 75 pounds to 1,000 theaters across the country when you can send a hard drive weighing only a few pounds or, even better, simply upload your movie to 1,000 theaters at the scheduled projection time. Also, film prints are susceptible to damage (scratches, torn sprockets, etc.) in a way that data are not. However, the ubiquity of 35mm projection will ensure that both release formats will remain side by side for a while.

The **DCI standards** of primary concern for the filmmaker are projection resolution and delivery standards. Currently, the two most prevalent projection resolutions are 2K (2048 × 1080 pixels) and 4K (4096 × 2160 pixels), although, as always, there are rumblings of greater pixel counts in the future. The frame rate for digital cinema projection is 24p for both 2K and 4K (and also 48p for 2K projection). The video encoding standard is JPEG 2000 and the audio file format is PCM WAVE (.wav). Picture, sound and subtitles are delivered in the MXF file container format (see page 401). These elements in these particular formats and files constitute the **Digital Cinema Package (DCP),** which is stored on a hard drive and sent to theaters where it is then ingested right into the 2K or 4K projector server for exhibition (Figure 19-14). The DCI standards are very complex and sufficiently rigorous to require a filmmaker to use a lab to create the DCP. Virtually any acquisition format can be transcoded to meet the DCI standards, although the new breed of high-end cameras, shooting 24p, 2K, and 4K, aim for a smooth workflow from production to screening (see page 217).

■ **Figure 19-14** The Sony SXRD 4K Digital Cinema Projector can achieve a maximum resolution of 4096 × 2160 pixels and can be used on screen sizes as large as 60 feet.

[1]Go to www.dcimovies.com for more information.

From Finished DV Movie to DCP

Let's say you've shot and finished your short movie on DVCPRO HD at 1080, 60i following workflow #1 on page 398. You send it to festivals and it's a surprise hit! In fact, you've won a best-in-category prize at an Academy of Motion Picture Arts and Sciences qualifying festival, which makes you eligible for an Academy Award nomination in the live-action short category. Great! However, you read the application and it says, "Short films must be submitted to the Academy on 35mm or 70mm film or as a DCP formatted according to the digital qualification standards described in Paragraph III.A.1." Those qualification standards are the DCI specifications I've listed here. In other words, you need a DCP! The only thing to do, since you've already finished the film, is to go to a lab and have them create your DCP. There are a number of ways to do this, but they're all some variant of (1) send the lab an uncompressed QuickTime file of your movie and your mixed audio track, (2) the lab will convert the video frames to 24p, (3) the lab encodes the video to JPEG 2000 2K (2048 × 1080), (4) the mixed audio is resolved to the new video frame rate and converted to the .wav format (if it isn't already), (5) everything is wrapped up nicely in the MXF container format to create the DCP and delivered to you on a hard drive. This process is currently rather expensive but is getting less so every year. Many labs also offer student and prorated independent filmmaker rates.

Shooting 2K and 4K Video for DCP

If you've shot at 24p on one of the 2K or 4K video formats like ArriRaw, RedCode Raw, etc.) (see page 217) and from the very beginning anticipated finishing to a DCP (or even to a film print), then your workflow will involve a few more steps (**Figure 19-15**). Primarily, uncompressed video files are way too large to store and work with in a standard NLE system. So low-resolution copies, called **low-res clones,** must be made of all your footage for offline editing (at 24p). In Final Cut Pro, this usually just involves transcoding the footage to a compressed Apple ProRes format. Understanding the need for offline editing, some HD cameras simultaneously record uncompressed video (to a high-capacity hard drive) and compressed video like QuickTime/Apple ProRes (to memory cards) so that you can start offline editing immediately without the need to transcode (**Figure 19-16**). In either case, once all the creative editorial decisions are done and you've reached picture lock in this low-res format, you go back to the original, full resolution source video and bring only those shots that you've used in your final film, called **the selects**, into a color grading session. The **color grading process** is where you correct problems with exposures and color temperature, match the look of shots across scenes, and enhance the image to create the precise look you want for your film. We only color grade the selects because this is a supervised session billed by the hour, so it makes no sense to color correct footage you do not use in the film. After color grading, the lab then **relinks** these original source video files to the offline sequence, which is fairly simple because the low-res and full-res footage share all the same meta-

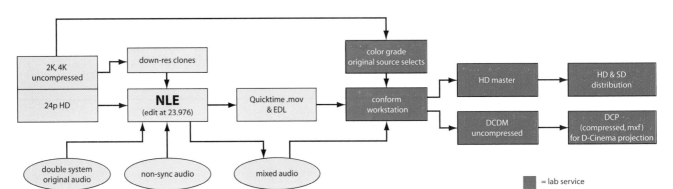

■ **Figure 19-15** Picture and audio paths for workflow #3: Shoot: uncompressed video/Transfer: Lo-res for offline edit/Conform: source selects/ Master: DCDM/Distribute: DCP and various formats.

data like filenames and timecode. This full-resolution reassembly of the project is called **conforming** because you are conforming your original uncompressed footage to your offline edits cut for cut and frame for frame. This list of all your offline edits (timecode in-points and out-points) is called the **edit decision list** (**EDL**). During the conforming process, the mixed sound track is also brought in and matched to the full-resolution picture to create your **Digital Cinema Distribution Master (DCDM)**. The DCDM is your master, which contains your completed movie in an uncompressed state. From here the lab compresses it with JPEG 2000 to create the DCP. The DCDM and DCP are usually stored and delivered on hard drives; however, during this process you can also master your film to HDCAM SR tape, which is capable of recording up to 4K uncompressed resolution. This tape master can be used to create distribution copies in a variety of HD and SD formats.

■ **Figure 19-16** The Arri Alexa digital camera saves uncompressed 2K or 3.5K video to high-capacity hard drives and simultaneously records NLE-ready Apple Pro Res files to onboard SxS cards *(arrows)* for instant offline editing.

in practice

■ SHOOTING SUPER 16MM FILM FOR DCP: A WORKFLOW CASE STUDY

We can, of course, shoot on film for DCP delivery. Let's follow the step-by-step workflow of a project shot on Super16 that went to DCP (as well as HD distribution formats). Shanti Thakur's short film *Sky People* (2008) is a surreal satire that imagines a future following the scientific discovery that the farther you are from Earth, the slower time passes and therefore, the longer you'll live. This discovery leads to a new form of class division, those who live above the 13th floor (the elites) and those who are ground dwellers. From the beginning of the project, Thakur planned and followed a crafty workflow to save money and ensure maximum distribution flexibility (**Figure 19-17**):

1. *Sky People* was shot on Super 16 and the raw footage was transferred to standard definition

■ **Figure 19-17** Shanti Thakur's award-winning short film *Sky People* (2008) followed a complex workflow, which was carefully planned out in consultation with her lab during preproduction

DVCAM via a relatively inexpensive one-light telecine transfer. Thakur knew that all necessary color correction would be accomplished later on.

2. The transferred footage was captured and edited at 24p because Thakur anticipated going back to a 24 fps final product (either DCP or film print). This means employing a **reverse telecine** process, which removes the extra fields created during the 3:2 pulldown transfer, so that editing is done to original frames only. Keep in mind, there is no reason to edit at 24p if one masters on any HD format based on 29.97 frame rates.

3. When she finished editing, the lab went back to her original Super 16 negative and scanned the selects at 4K resolution.

4. These files were brought to a workstation and conformed to her EDL. The color grading was done here as well; however, Thakur knew that this process could be hard on the budget, so she paid careful attention during production to shoot her film as closely as possible to the look she desired. As Thakur explained "Some filmmakers find their 'look' here. I didn't have the money or interest to find the look in post. I selected the color palettes in advance and used color filters while shooting the film. I also pushed the film different stops to create distinct looks for the different worlds. This saved time and money in color correction—all the colorist needed to do was minor color tweaking and scene matching."

5. After conforming and color grading *Sky People* was mastered at 4K (4:4:4) resolution

on HDCAM SR. So, Thukur was *ready* to go to a DCP, but didn't have any reason to incur this expense at this stage because the festivals she wanted to enter didn't require one.

6. Thakur down-converted from this HDCAM SR master to create film festival copies in whatever format was required (HDCAM, DigiBeta, and Beta SP). Thakur was also able to use the master to include the film on a DVD compilation. Happily, the film was a hit and won a number of awards including Best Experimental Film at the Los Angeles International Short Film Festival, which is an Oscar-qualifying festival.

7. Riding the success of her film, Thakur then created a DCP from the HDCAM SR 4K master in order to comply with the Academy's technical requirements. The DCP was more economical than going film-out to a 35mm print.

Given all the various permutations and possibilities for workflow, the most important thing to remember is to figure out your path and the costs involved *before* you start shooting. Thakur's workflow involved extensive lab services, so she established a working relationship with a lab consultant early on in preproduction.

Finishing on Film and the Digital Intermediate Process
Broadcast HD or Uncompressed Video to Film

In olden days (only a few years ago), video was a TV format only; it was unheard of to shoot a project on video and release it on film. But then, at the turn of the century, successful films like *The Celebration* (1998), *Dancer in the Dark* (2000), *Bamboozled* (2000), and *Ten* (2002) showed the world that filmmakers could capitalize on the unique storytelling qualities of DV (these films were all shot on consumer format SD camcorders) and on the advantages of extremely small and mobile production gear to energize their camera work and their ideas to such an extent that SD video was transferred to 35mm film for release and people flocked to the theaters (see page 413). The inherent image compromises this process entailed were cleverly incorporated into the very concept and aesthetic of the film, and the quality of performances, story, and ideas trumped conventional notions of a proper "look" for theatrically released films. This opened the floodgates and video became a viable acquisition format for filmmakers who had hopes of a broad theatrical release. The video shooting formats of today, from HD 1080 and 720 to uncompressed 2K and 4K formats, are improving video footage resolutions so much so that very few viewers even notice the difference between film or video acquisition.

These days, the process for completing a project (shot on film or video) as a film print is called **film out** and it requires the creation of a **digital intermediate** (**DI**) to transform your original shooting format into a format that can be printed out to 35mm film at high resolutions. This is exactly why we must not be overly optimistic about the shoot video/finish film workflow when it comes to budget savings. The substantial costs involved in striking a film print from video source material are somewhat contradictory to video's capacity for ultra low-budget production. Because staying within the DV workflow (see **Figure 19-1**) is so simple and because of the hefty additional cost of the of the tape-to-film transfer, people tend not to go this route unless there is a real demand to put the film into theatrical distribution where a commercial distributor will pay the tab. The D.P. Ellen Kuras (**Figure 19-18**) commented on this issue concerning Spike Lee's *Bamboozled*, the first film she shot on MiniDV:

> *Digital definitely does have its advantages and is appropriate in certain applications. With my strong desire to give the film a look and the need for a full color correction, we ended up spending quite a bit on the back end in post. Unless aesthetics or theory dictate choosing video—whether Hi-def or mini-DV—I caution everyone to consider all costs involved, not just the dollars you'd save during a production shoot.*
>
> **(From *The Digital Cinematographer*, by Kevin H. Martin, The International Cinematographers Guild)**

Again, if you have a sense that you will, or might, strike a film print, then you to must consult with the film lab in preproduction to get all of the details. Each lab has its own process and proprietary system and therefore prefers specific camera settings, capture settings, editorial sequence settings and edit decision list (EDL) formats for compatibility with their system.

Whether you have followed the compressed HD workflow (see **Figure 19-1**) and are working from a HD master or followed the uncompressed (2K, 4K) workflow from (see **Figure 19-15**), the film-out stage of this workflow is essentially the same—and the work mostly happens in the lab. In both cases, the process works from your EDL, pulls the selects from your original footage masters (HD or uncompressed video), and converts this footage into a 2K or 4K format, which can be used for striking a 35mm print. Although there are several viable formats, the most popular one used to create a digital intermediate is the **digital picture exchange (DPX)** file. The **digital intermediate (DI)** process is the conversion of your original source format into a high-resolution intermediate digital form (2K or 4K) that is capable of output to film via a film recorder. The term "digital intermediate" is often misconstrued as a process for working only with material originating on film; however, anytime your workflow culminates in a film-out process, even if your source material is HD video, you need a DI. During this process, any foot-

■ **Figure 19-18** Cinematographer Ellen Kuras is one of the most versatile and sought-after D.P.s working today. She has produced brilliant images on 35mm and Super 16 film as well as HD and SD DV.

age shot at frame rates other than 24p are de-interlaced and converted to 24 fps. How a lab extracts 24 discrete frames from interlaced video shot at 29.97 is a complex process that involves proprietary software, reverse pulldown algorithms, and lab-specific procedures. In other words, every lab has its own method. Shooting and editing at 24p eliminates this procedure.

In any case, the conversion of source video to DPX files essentially creates a sequence of discrete pictures of every frame at 2K or 4K (4:4:4) and up to a 16-bit data rate. This not only creates files requiring enormous storage space, but it in turn allows for phenomenal flexibility in **color correction** and **color grading**. Once your original footage has been converted to the DI format, you have the opportunity to make substantial corrections and adjustments to exposure and color to enhance the look of your project. Color grading at this point is a supervised process in which the filmmaker sits with the colorist and goes over each and every scene (**Figure 19-19**). You should always know exactly what you're after *before* you go into this session, or you can seriously hemorrhage money as you spend time adjusting this and tweaking that hunting for the right look.

After color grading, the lab uses a **conforming workstation** to conform the DPX files to your EDL (adding all transitions and special effects) to create a 4K, 4:4:4 digital master. A conforming workstation is similar to your NLE except that it has the capacity to work with DPX files of enormous size. These new DPX image frame sequences are then recorded onto film with a film recorder. A **film recorder** is a machine that scans the digital image onto a strip of unexposed 35mm negative film one frame at a time to create an **internegative** from which positive release prints can be struck. Some film recorders use a **cathode ray tube (CRT)** scanning method (less expensive), whereas others, like the Arrilaser film recorder (**Figure 19-20**), utilize a **laser scanner** (more expensive).

■ **Figure 19-19** The DI color grading suite at Final Frame Post. (Photo by Dag Bennstrom.)

■ **Figure 19-20** The Arrilaser film recorder scans 2K and 4K DPX video files, frame by frame, onto raw 35mm film stock to create a film print.

■ **Figure 19-21** Optically printed sound tracks on a married 35mm film print. (a) Dolby Digital audio and (b) stereo optical tracks. (Image courtesy of Adakin Productions.)

But wait! Where's our mixed audio track in all this? The mixed audio from your master tape follows a slightly different path. First it's transferred and delivered in the format your lab specifies. Sometimes the lab prefers a digital audio file, sometimes they'll take it off your master tapes. After resolving the audio to the 24 fps film rate (if necessary), the lab transfers the audio track to a **negative optical sound master** on 35mm film. Motion picture film projection predominantly uses optical sound tracks. Standard **optical tracks** are an analog audio system in which the film's sound track is represented by a clear stripe of varying widths photographically printed right into the black edge of the film (**Figure 19-21**, b). An exciter lamp pushes light through this clear stripe and onto a photodiode. Changes in the width of the stripe create varying pulses of light hitting the photodiode, which in turn transforms the fluctuating voltages into analog audio. The concept is not unlike the jagged grooves of an LP record, only created and read with light instead of with a needle, and this would be a pretty good metaphor if LP records still existed! Another common option is to create Dolby Digital audio tracks (5.1 audio) (**Figure 19-21**, a). In this case, your mixed audio track files must first be shipped off to Dolby labs; there your digital files are converted to an optical impression, which they then send to the lab for printing onto the negative optical sound master. Nothing else is on this strip of 35mm film except the sound track printed along the edge of the sprockets. Once the lab has created both a picture internegative and optical sound negative master, they are each photographically printed (and permanently joined) to another strip of negative print film (neg + neg = positive image) to create a positive image, **married film print** ready for projection in a theater.

For projects originating on HDCAM or DVCPRO HD video formats, it's overkill to go for a 4K, 4:4:4 conversion. Generally, in the DI process these formats are handled at slightly lower resolutions like 2K, 4:2:2. Alternately, you could hand the lab your HDCAM master, which has already been color corrected (i.e. the result of workflow #1; see **Figure 19-1**), and the lab can do a basic tape-to-film transfer without the color correction stage. The primary problem with this solution is that the color correcting you've accomplish on your NLE may look great on an HD monitor, but that does not tell you how your project will look once it's scanned to celluloid. Since you're already spending the dough to go to a 35mm print, you might as well indulge in the added creative benefits of true DI color grading and know for certain what your film print will look like.

The video-origination to film-distribution barrier was first broken down by documentary films that were so compelling they found an audience in the commercial theatrical market despite the obvious image compromises inherent in transferring a project shot on standard-definition NTSC video to 35mm film. *Hoop Dreams* (directed by Steve James) was one of the early examples of this groundbreaking phenomenon. The storyline of this film, which closely followed the lives of two talented young boys as they strove to become professional basketball players, was so captivating that no one really cared about the unusual technical specifications. Once it was clear that audiences didn't resist the look of films shot on SD video, pioneering fictional narrative filmmakers quickly developed stories that incorporated the "video aesthetic" and benefited from the enormously reduced production budget (**Figure 19-22**).

Eduardo Sánchez and Daniel Myrick's *The Blair Witch Project* (1999) was an early example of a film that was shot on 16mm and the now obsolete Hi8 consumer video format and was transferred to film for national release. This movie proved to be one of the great independent film success stories of all time,

partly because of its fearless use of a consumer video format. Lars von Trier and the Danish Dogme filmmakers made the consumer DV format the liberating centerpiece of their look and their minimal intervention, minimal contrivance, production philosophy. Thomas Vinterberg's landmark Dogme film *The Celebration* (1998) even won the Jury Award at 1998 Cannes Film Festival. You can go to www.dogme95.dk to read the "Dogme 95" manifesto and their "vow of chastity." Even today, there is much to be gained from understanding the creatively liberating impulses of these innovative filmmakers (**Figure 19-23**).

Following the success of the Dogma films, there was a virtual wave of films by upstarts and major filmmakers alike produced on standard definition DV, including *Bamboozled* (2000), *Timecode* (2000), *Chuck & Buck* (2000), *Personal Velocity* (2002), *24 Hour Party People* (2002), *Pieces of April* (2003), and *Open Water* (2003), to mention just a few. Today, because of its ubiquity and low cost, HD has largely replaced SD as a shooting format, but this revolution was precipitated, in no small measure, by the fearless pioneers who produced brilliant films with a video format that most industry folks dismissed as insufficient.

Figure 19-22 *Hoop Dreams* (1994), a documentary directed by Steve James, was one of the first movies shot on video to achieve a wide theatrical release on film.

Figure 19-23 Sánchez and Myrick's *The Blair Witch Project* (1999, *left*) was shot on both 16mm film and Hi8 video and Vinterberg's *The Celebration* (1998, *right*) was shot on consumer format SD DV. Both films enjoyed wide theatrical release on 35mm and inspired many filmmakers to turn to video as a production format.

Shooting on Film and Finishing on Film

The use of digital intermediates has been around for several decades in limited applications, but its use as an essential workflow step for shooting and finishing motion pictures on film is relatively recent. The first use of DIs for conforming, color grading, and printing an entire commercial film was on the Coen Brothers' film *O Brother, Where Art Thou?* in 2000 (**Figure 19-24**). Since then, the transformation from finishing films via a cutting and photo-chemical process to a digital film-out process is nearly total.

Figure 19-24 The film *O Brother, Where Art Thou?* (Coen Brothers, 2000) was the first commercial movie to use exclusively a DI for conforming, color grading, and film-out printing. (See the color insert).

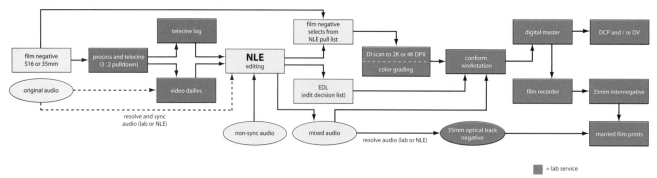

■ **Figure 19-25** Picture and audio paths for workflow #4: Shoot: Film/Edit: Digital/Finish: DI/Master: Film-out to 35mm.

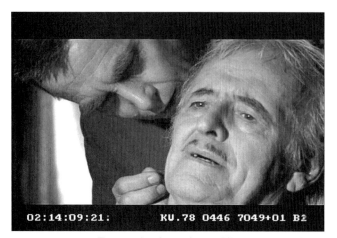

■ **Figure 19-26** The metadata from a frame of film-to-tape transferred footage reveals both the transfer video timecode *(lower left)* and original film edgecode numbers *(right)*, providing an easy reference for conforming back to film. (Frame from Lund's *Snapshot.*)

The early stages of the shoot film/finish film workflow (Figure 19-25) is very similar to the first half of workflow #2 (see Figure 19-2). One shoots negative film, sends it to the lab for processing and telecine transfer with 3:2 pulldown, and cuts the movie on a NLE system. In cases where we *know* we'll be finishing on film, we usually set up our NLE to edit at 24p (capturing dailies with reverse telecine to remove the extra frames). A **telecine log report** provided by the lab is the basis for a database that keeps track of the film edgecode (Keycode) numbers on the original negative and their relationship to the timecode numbers in the transfer (Figure 19-26). Once editing is completed, the NLE is capable of exporting not only the program edit decision list but also a **matchback cut list,** which interpolates every edit from timecode number to precise film edgecode frame numbers for every in-point and out-point of every edit (Figure 19-27).

The next step is to go back to the original negative and reconstruct the film according to the EDL using the full resolution of the negative film in a process called **conforming**—and it is here where the DI revolution changed everything.

Back in the day—not that many years ago—conforming was a brutal "cutting/photochemical" process that required finding all of the shots on the original negative (in- and out-points from the matchback cut list) and physically slicing them out of the camera original negative roll then gluing them together in the order following the edited project. The person who did this was called *the negative cutter*! Negative cutters had to do all their work wearing gloves, and in a specially ventilated dust-free room to avoid scratching or getting dust or hand oils on the original negative (Figure 19-28). The glued together negative was then run through a contact printer to photographically create a print. Color correction and transitions (dissolves, fades, etc.) were accomplished with a color timing console called a Hazentine color analyzer, which controlled the balance of red, green, and blue printer lights during the print process. Several different prints (answer prints and intermediates) had to be color timed, printed, developed, projected, and scrutinized before the final release prints (married with the mixed audio, optical sound track) were struck.[2] This photochemical process is now only rarely used and will soon disappear altogether in favor of a digital process that leaves the original camera negative uncut and pristine.

Let's get back to the here-and-now and pick up the workflow at the stage where we have finished editing (picture lock) and are ready to go back to our negative film to conform it

---

[2]If you would like a much more detailed and less flippant description of the film finish workflow involving negative matching, please go to www.voiceandvisionbook.com.

to the EDL. Instead of cutting and gluing, we now bring the intact rolls of camera original negative into a high-resolution **film scanner** (also called a **datacine**) and we scan only those shots that made it into the film without cutting them out. These shots are identified by their keycode number from a pull list (or assembly list) exported by your NLE. A **pull list** identifies all the shots used in your edited program (in- and out-points, with extra frames for transitions) in the order in which they can be found on the original negative rolls. These shots are called your **selects**.

A film scanner is similar to a telecine in that it pushes light through the film negative and registers the color and light values onto CCD chips for recording as digital information (in fact, many film scanners serve both purposes). The difference is that film scanners used for the DI process have the capacity for ultra-high-resolution scanning at 2K and 4K resolutions, 4:4:4 color space and up to 16-bit data rate. These scanning specs fully realize the color and luminance range resolution of the original Super 16 or 35mm film frame. In other words, you lose nothing in terms of quality. This sort of high-detail scanning also takes time (8 fps for 4K) and it's expensive; that's why we generally transfer only those shots that made it into the film—the selects. In the end, the selects are scanned at a high resolution and saved as, you guessed it, 24p DPX files.

The process from here to film-out is similar to the one we discussed beginning on page 411 for the video to film-out workflow. These full resolution DPX files are extremely malleable and now the project goes through a color grading session in which the filmmaker has remarkable latitude to create the final look for the movie. One can, for example, manipulate individual colors and objects in a scene and emulate lighting effects, camera filters, and lab processing techniques. In fact, the DI color grading process is so powerful that the director and D.P. need to carefully discuss what effects they wish to create during the shooting and processing of the film versus what they can accomplish during the DI color grading process. For example, in the DI color grading stage you can easily mimic the look of the bleach by-pass chemical process, the high-contrast look of pushed film stock, or the look of a graduated camera filter.

Once the color grading has been completed, the DPX files are brought into the conforming workstation and conformed, cut for cut, to the picture lock EDL. It's here too that transitions and special effects are incorporated. At the end of this process you have a 4K, 4:4:4 digital master, which can be screened and approved before moving on to the film-out step. If something about the color grading isn't working, you can go back to the DPX files and tweak the look. Once everything has been approved, the conformed DPX sequences are then scanned back onto a strip of unexposed 35mm negative film with a laser (or CRT) film recorder creating an internegative film print.

```
Avid Cut Lists
Project: AX Matchback
List Title: 35mm Matchback

35mm Matchback                10 events       handles = -1
Picture 1                     0 dupes         total footage:   74+04
Assemble List                 0 opticals      total time: 00:00:49:13
-----------------------------------------------------------------------------
      Footage  Duration   First/Last Key    Address TC  Cam Roll   Sc/Tk   Clip Name

 1.     0+00    10+04   KW 42 9137-4866+15   06:22:47:24   A85    A10G/2  A10G/2
       10+03            KW 42 9137-4877+02   06:22:54:18

 2.    10+04     8+04   KW 35 3532-5791+11   06:18:07:29   A83    A10B/1  A10B/1
       18+07            KW 35 3532-5799+14   06:18:13:13

 3.    18+08    11+08   KW 42 9137-4884+05   06:22:59:11   A85    A10G/2  A10G/2
       29+15            KW 42 9137-4895+12   06:23:06:29
     Matchback lengthened the tail of the clip by 1 frame.

 4.    30+00    12+04   KW 35 3532-5812+01   06:18:21:16   A83    A10B/1  A10B/1
       42+03            KW 35 3532-5824+04   06:18:29:20

 5.    42+04     5+06   KW 42 9137-4904+14   06:23:13:03   A85    A10G/2  A10G/2
       47+09            KW 42 9137-4910+03   06:23:16:20
     Matchback shortened the tail of the clip by 1 frame.

 6.    47+10     4+00   KW 46 7331-2663+04   06:25:54:15   A87    A10K/1  A10K/1
       51+09            KW 46 7331-2667+03   06:25:57:04

 7.    51+10     2+09   KW 42 9137-4914+01   06:23:19:06   A85    A10G/2  A10G/2
       54+02            KW 42 9137-4916+09   06:23:20:26

 8.    54+03    10+11   KW 35 3532-5907+07   06:19:25:04   A83    A10C/1  A10C/1
       64+13            KW 35 3532-5918+01   06:19:32:07

 9.    64+14     4+12   KW 42 9137-4926+01   06:23:27:06   A85    A10G/2  A10G/2
       69+09            KW 42 9137-4930+12   06:23:30:10

10.    69+10     4+10   KW 35 3532-5923+00   06:19:35:15   A83    A10C/1  A10C/1
       74+03            KW 35 3532-5927+09   06:19:38:16

(end of Assemble List)
```

■ **Figure 19-27** The matchback cut list generated by an NLE system automates the conforming process by matching the original negative film edgecode numbers to the exact EDL edits.

■ **Figure 19-28** An old-school negative matcher literally cut film and then used cement glue and a hot splicer to connect the shots. Delicate handling and a clean environment were required around the camera original negative.

The audio mix track follows the same path discussed on page 412. The mixed digital track is first resolved to the 24 fps film rate if necessary and then transferred to a negative optical sound master (via Dolby if necessary) on 35mm film. Finally, the picture internegative and optical sound negative master are each printed to another strip of 35mm negative film, which creates a married film print—a positive film image with a sound track strip along the sprocket holes. If all went well, you are the proud owner of a **release print**—ready for distribution and exhibition in theaters.

One happy by-product of the film-out workflow is that you have also created a high-quality digital master that can easily be used for finishing as a DCP or for making distribution copies in any number of HD or SD release formats.

Twenty-first-century filmmakers have had an extraordinary array of powerful tools and aesthetic capabilities available to them, but the digital revolution has also opened up so many more workflow avenues that, quite frankly, it boggles the mind. The workflow overviews in this chapter are designed to help you understand the basics of the technical stages and the format interfaces involved in the most common production routes. Just as a road map cannot show you every sight, building, or pathway, it would be impossible for me to explain every detail in every workflow scenario—especially given the fact that these days workflows change regularly. These are details you need to discover for yourself by talking to the lab, talking to filmmakers who have been through the same process, and hitting the web for the most up-to-date information. By now you know that this book concentrates on ideas, aesthetics, and creativity as the most important tools for a filmmaker. But film is a technical art form, and just as all technical knowledge is worthless without imagination and a story to tell, so, too, all of the creativity in the world remains unnoticed if you can't get your movie to an audience. Thankfully, technology is not like talent; there really is no mystery to it—it can be taught and you can learn it. And you can harness it for your creative goals to get your story onto a screen. A little bit of forethought, research and legwork is all it takes. It will always pay off.

The Process of Digital Editing

■ DIGITAL EDITING FUNDAMENTALS

Virtually all film projects, whether they're destined for broadcast, DVD, or theatrical release, regardless of being shot on film, standard DV, or HD, are edited on a **digital, nonlinear editing system** (or **NLE** for short). Editing in the digital domain means that all visual and aural components of the project, no matter what their original form, must be transferred as digital data called **media files** and brought in to a computer running specialized editing software. In data form, any piece of visual footage or any piece of sound can be instantly accessed through a computer's **random access** capability and easily labeled, organized, duplicated, cut, arranged, rearranged, trimmed, mixed, and manipulated with a mere drag and click of a mouse. This simple fact is why, even in the technologically conservative arena of narrative filmmaking, digital editing completely revolutionized the postproduction process in only a few years (**Figure 20-1**).

What Is Nonlinear Editing?

So why *do* they call it **nonlinear editing**? The label "nonlinear" basically means that we are not limited by the linear characteristic of videotape. For example, if you want to preview a shot in a digital editing system, just a click will open it up on the screen in a flash, and another click will instantly position you on any frame within that shot. A nonlinear system allows us to move around in the footage in any direction, instantaneously. On videotape, if the shot we wanted to preview happened to be at the end of the tape, we would have to wait while the tape fast forwarded to the cue point; and if the next shot we wanted to preview happened to be at the head of the tape, we'd have to rewind all the way to the beginning again. Even more significantly, however, is the fact that, with digital editing, we can delete (or insert) a shot anywhere along our edited sequence and all succeeding shots will move up to close the gap or push down to accommodate the new shot. In short, inserting or deleting shots has no effect on the other shots in the sequence. At this point, I can imagine a young film student, weaned exclusively on hard drives and data, blinking hard and saying, "Yeah? So?" The fact is, there are those of us who, in the dark ages, struggled with tape-to-tape video editing, which is essentially a process of rerecording material from a source tape directly onto a record tape. We remember a time when you would string together, say, 25 edits, only to realize that you wanted to insert a new shot after edit #4. Videotape's "linearity problem" meant that if you inserted (literally recorded) a new shot #5, you covered over the old shot #5 and so had to rerecord it as shot #6, which covered over the next shot, which you had to then re-lay, and so on. Every time you inserted or deleted a shot in an existing sequence you had to re-lay every shot that came after that point. I'd rather not contemplate the hours of my life I lost doing exactly this in videotape editing rooms. Digital editing, on the other hand, never actually lays any media down onto tape until you are completely done editing. Instead, it uses the computer's **random access memory (RAM)** to perpetually "preview" all of the edits in your program. You can insert shots, delete shots, rearrange sequences, and build several versions and still make it home in time to get eight hours of sleep. So the term "nonlinear editing" was introduced to announce that, although digital editing was done electronically, it didn't have video's "linearity problem," and hearing this, we all traded in our play decks, record deck, and RM440 edit controllers for a mouse and a hard drive, in record time!

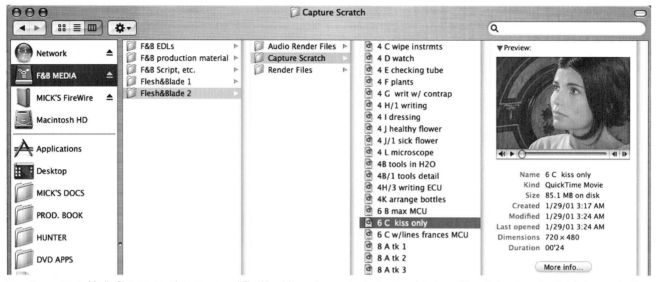

■ **Figure 20-1** Media files are saved on an external FireWire drive and are not actually altered during editing. Pictured are the QuickTime media files for a project on Final Cut Pro located in the capture scratch folder.

Nondestructive Editing

To be fair, editing on film was also a form of nonlinear editing. Yes, you still had to rewind and fast-forward through rolls of film to find specific shots, but if you had a 25-edit sequence cut together and decided to insert (or delete) a shot early in the sequence, you would simply unsplice two shots and insert the new shot (or remove a shot) and redo the splice. The rest of the shots in the sequence would slide up or down. This is why videotape editing, despite all predictions, did not win over many film editors, especially in the feature film world. However, "cutting" on film literally meant cutting a strip of cellulose acetate to define the shot you wanted to edit into the film. If you changed your mind often and recut many times, you had little pieces of film scattered across the flatbed like spilled cornflakes, and every one of these frames had to be saved and labeled just in case you changed your mind again. Additionally, film editing was done on a workprint (a low-resolution print struck from the original negative), and because a workprint costs money to make, there was usually only one copy—especially for students. After cutting together a sequence, it was painstaking to pull it apart and try another version of the sequence. If the new version didn't work, you'd have to redo the old sequence. So although film editing was nonlinear, it was unfortunately also "destructive editing," which means that the physical material you were editing with was permanently changed (damaged) with each cut. Digital nonlinerar editing (NLE) is **nondestructive editing,** which means that any cutting, arranging, trimming, corrections, or effects you might perform occur only virtually, in a preview mode. The original media files that you captured are not altered in any way.

All editing is done via **media file indicators,** which only "point" to the original data without ever altering the media file. For example, let's say you have a camera take that is 10 seconds long and you want to use 2 seconds from the middle of that media file for an edit. In film you would have to literally cut that portion out of the longer take. But digitally, you simply indicate the timecode numbers where you want the shot to begin (the **in-point**) and end (the **out-point**). Then you edit that portion of the shot into program sequence. However, you are in fact not cutting any actual media into the sequence, rather, only the numbers (or pointers) that tell the computer what piece of that QuickTime media file to load into RAM and play back at that point. This is why it's easy to make changes to that shot, to trim it a few frames longer or shorter, to try numerous versions of the same sequence using the same shots: because you're simply altering the data indicators, the numbers, not the media file itself. Nothing is actually recorded until the last stage, when all of the editing has been completed and you send your final project out to be recorded onto DV tape for mastering.

All of the editing decisions you make—length of shots, order of shots, layering of audio, and so on—that are simply pointer numbers referencing the media files constitute your **edit decision list** (**EDL**). Without any actual media, an EDL is a very small file. For this reason, it is not uncommon to have two sets of hard drives with the same raw media files on them—say, one with the movie's director in New York and another with the editor in Chicago, who then can email the EDL file back and forth. This way the director is able to see and respond to the work of the editor, several times a day, if necessary, without ever leaving New York.

Nonlinear and nondestructive editing solved two of the most pernicious drawbacks of previous editing methods, film and video, which is why NLE systems pushed both film and video editing into obsolescence in very short order. Add to this the fact that the cost for all of this power is considerably cheaper than for the old processes, because so many procedures and capabilities have been taken out of the hands of labs, rental facilities, and technical specialists (and their assistants) and placed in our hands, making the process of filmmaking easier, faster, more accessible, and cheaper, and that's great. But the digital revolution is not without its own drawbacks.

Too Much of a Good Thing?

These days I can edit a short film, with titles, effects, sound mix, and color correction by myself, in no time flat and in the comfort of my own home or on my laptop. So what's to complain about? In the past, I've done a lot of editing on both film and video. My first three student films were edited on a cantankerous machine called an upright Moviola (**Figure 20-2**). Our professor kept telling us not to complain when the "green monster," as we called it, ate our film. He'd remind us, "Think of all the great movies that were made on machines just like this one, including *Citizen Kane*!" At the mention of *Citizen Kane,* we were all obliged to stop our whining. We'd looked at the green monster and conclude that Orson Welles should be considered a genius, if only for his ability to actually finish a movie with this beast! I, for one, will tell you that if I never have to get on my hands and knees to hunt for three missing film frames that dropped behind the flatbed or spend an hour re-laying 20 edits just so I could add one new shot in a videotape sequence, it will be too soon (**Figure 20-3**).

However, as I started writing this second edition, I bought the latest version of one of those popular, relatively inexpensive NLE programs that are on the market. The software for all that power and technical capacity came on just a few slim little disks—but the box it came in was *huge!* Why was the box so big? Because the user's manual came in five(!) volumes of around 300 pages each. The manual for this "easy-to-use" editing software takes up more than twice the space on my bookshelf as the complete works of William Shakespeare. Think about that. I looked at these NLE tomes, after nearly dislocating my shoulder putting them on the shelf, and wondered, is this *really* going to simplify my life? Or even more to the point, will all this technology really make me a better filmmaker? Is *all* of it really necessary? Does one need to read all 1,500+ pages before one can call oneself an editor? Sometimes, when I sit in front of my hyper-turbo-charged editing software, I acutely feel the burden of an excess of riches. I think about the sort of editing resources truly great filmmakers like Robert Bresson, Yasujiro Ozu, Roberto Rossellini, and Satyajit Ray had when they were making the films that profoundly resonated around the world and established cinema as an artistic force. Take a look at any one film from each director (*A Man Escaped, Tokyo Story,*

■ **Figure 20-2** The upright Moviola. Even though countless wonderful movies have been edited on this machine, it is thankfully a relic of a bygone era.

■ **Figure 20-3** The convenience of today's editing software. Two students do some last-minute cutting in the hallway before their film production class begins.

■ **Figure 20-4** Ozu's masterpiece *Tokyo Story* (1953) is told using only straight cuts, two fades, and no "spinning 3D cubes."

Rome: Open City, and *The World of Apu)* and you'll see mostly simple cuts and occasionally you'll see a fade-out or fade-in, maybe a few dissolves, and only very, very rarely a slow motion shot. But you'll *never* see a "shattering-glass" transition effect, or a "chroma key composite" layering two images, one with a "radial blur filter" and the other with a "ripple effect" and both spinning through space inside a "cube-spin 3D motion effect." I can do that! I can do what these legendary filmmakers never imagined, in a matter of minutes. But how important is this ability, truly (**Figure 20-4**)?

What you *will* see in these films is eloquent and thoughtful visual storytelling using simple, precise, and fundamental editing techniques that have become the essential vocabulary for anyone wishing to make movies. With all this technology, *how* we make a dissolve is super easy, but *why* we use a dissolve is still the most important question, the complexity of which cannot be changed by technology. If we are not careful with all of this technological power we are gaining, we run the risk of losing much (**Figure 20-5**).

How to Approach Surplus Technology

The boon and the burden of the digital revolution is the remarkable ease with which we can manipulate sound and image. We are offered so many bells and whistles in our editing software, not because we *asked* for six different kinds of image blur filters, but simply because engineers could easily include them. The best way to approach your software is to learn the basic functions first, the essential tools. Learn how to choose the shots you want, how to perform cuts and make a sequence. Learn how to arrange those shots and how to trim them longer or shorter as you need. Learn how to layer a few tracks of audio and adjust sound levels and keep your footage in sync. Maybe try a dissolve or two. That's all you really need at first. Now go make a movie. If your shots don't work together with a cut, then a "page-peel" transition isn't going to help. If your images aren't carefully composed, spinning them across the screen won't make them more eloquent. If your actors aren't convincing, not one of the numerous image-effect filters will make their performance ring more true. Strengthen your fundamental storytelling techniques and use only what you need to tell your story. Don't worry: those 1,500-page user manuals are waiting for you. As soon as you discover that you truly need to use a wipe transition, then look it up and learn

■ **Figure 20-5** The NLE surplus. Does anyone truly need the "checkerboard wipe" *(left)* or the "jaws wipe" *(right)* to tell a good story?

how to do it. When you find that your film will be improved by adding an image filter to reduce contrast; it's there, it's not hard, go learn it. There may come a day when you want to try a green screen key effect; no problem, it'll be there when you need it. As you make your movies, you will be adding one useful technique at a time—but on your schedule and as your movies require. The tail should not wag the dog. Make the technology work for your ideas and resist the temptation to let snazzy technology lead the way.

in practice

The film director Michel Gondry developed his filmmaking skills in the world of music videos before he tackled feature-length narrative films. He created memorable videos for such pop musicians as Björk, the Chemical Brothers, Cibo Matto, and others. Although he has a reputation for fairly low-tech special effects, his music video works are nonetheless highly stylized and technically flamboyant. However, when it came to feature film storytelling, the music video director surprisingly used no extreme digital technology or even fancy transitions in his 2004 film *Eternal Sunshine of the Spotless Mind*. In telling a complex story—which traces the labyrinth of a man's mind as he slowly loses his memories of a woman through a scientific process designed to erase her from his brain—Gondry opted for a highly stripped down style including a handheld camera and natural lighting. His editing approach is equally simple. In the entire film, Gondry uses exclusively straight cuts with only four exceptions: one fade-in, two fades to black, and one fade to white. It is the structure of the film itself that conveys the layered storyline, and not the flashy effects (**Figure 20-6**).

The Dardenne Brothers' highly influential film *La Promesse* (1997) (**Figure 20-7**) presents a fictional drama in a cinema vérité documentary style. The film derives its realism and credibility from the immediacy of the raw, unembellished documentary approach. In this case, the use of digital effects, dissolves, or other fancy transitions in video or audio would be completely inappropriate for the realist content and corresponding style and would weaken the film's impact.

However, I certainly wouldn't want to close off any of a filmmaker's potential creative avenues. If your story will benefit from all of the bells and whistles, if the fancy transitions, key effects, and digital processing are appropriate and can actually enhance your story, then by all means use them. In *The Matrix* trilogy (1999-2004) (**Figure 20-8**), the Wachowski Brothers certainly exploited technology for all it was worth in creating the matrix, an entire world and consciousness, a complete construction of technology. In

this case the filmmakers are practically obligated by the subject matter and themes of the film to push high technology to its limits.

■ **Figure 20-6** Michel Gondry needed little more than straight cuts to intricately explore the mind and memories of Joel (Jim Carrey) in *Eternal Sunshine of the Spotless Mind*.

■ **Figure 20-7** In *La Promesse*, the Dardenne Brothers tell the story of Igor's (Jérémie Renier) moral awakening in a documentary style, devoid of any flashy techniques that would detract from the gritty realism of the film.

■ **Figure 20-8** The Wachowski Brothers had to push the limits of filmmaking technology to render the dystopian future world of *The Matrix*.

■ THE BASIC NLE SYSTEM

Nonlinear editing systems are a lot like camcorders. There are the bare-bones consumer programs, like iMovie, which are usually free and ultra easy but are not flexible enough (especially in their limited sound-editing abilities) for anyone who seriously wishes to make narrative films. Then there are the midrange programs, like Final Cut Pro HD, Avid Xpress Pro, and Adobe Premiere Pro, which are extremely reasonable in price for their capabilities and quality—especially with the educational discount. Finally there are the ultra-high-end systems, like Avid's Symphony Nitris DX system, which can claim the mantle of highest image finishing quality and most visual effects. The truth is, however, that the midrange systems add new features and higher quality by the bucket full every year. The watershed moment for affordable editing software came in 2003 when Walter Murch cut Anthony Minghella's feature film *Cold Mountain* with "off-the-shelf" Final Cut Pro software and won an Academy Award for Best Editing (**Figure 20-9**). These days many filmmakers—students, independents, and commercial filmmakers alike—find no practical advantage to moving beyond these highly accessible editing systems.

Although there are a number of nonlinear editing systems around, they all work on the same basic principles and interface. True, there are enough differences in terminology, layout, and small details to keep most people from switching around once they're comfortable with one particular system, but learning one system certainly prepares you for working with any other system. It's like learning to drive in a Ford and then getting behind the wheel of a Honda. Sure, you need to figure out where the headlight switch is, where the windshield wipers are, and if the gas cap is on the driver's or passenger's side, but other than that, you can drive.

The Hardware Setup

The hardware for a typical, low-end, nonlinear editing station consists of a computer and monitor(s) (Mac or PC) running NLE software, external FireWire hard drives, a media transfer device (DV deck or card reader), speakers, and a comfortable chair (**Figure 20-10**). Editing sound and picture, especially if you plan to incorporate any effects at all, requires a fairly powerful personal **computer**, and maxing out the RAM is always recommended. It is important that your computer **monitor** be of high resolution so that you can have some sense for the picture quality of your footage and any image effects you may employ. Many editing setups will use two monitors, with one (often a high definition LCD monitor) dedicated to a full-screen display of the program.

■ **Figure 20-9** Walter Murch edited Minghella's *Cold Mountain* (2003) and Mendes's *Jarhead* (2005) using off-the-shelf Final Cut Pro software. Still from Apple's *The Cutting Edge* (2004).

External FireWire hard drives store your media files. Most NLE software instructions recommend not putting media files onto the internal drive of your computer where your software resides. This is a speed issue and also a convenience issue. Media saved on a portable, FireWire hard drive can be used on any editing station running the same software. Keep in mind that media files take up a lot of space so you must calculate storage needs before you transfer your footage. Storage space depends entirely on your shooting format. Five minutes of standard definition video (DV25) with sync sound will take up a little more than 1 GB of drive space. Five minutes of DVCPro HD footage shot at 1080i60 will require 5 GB of drive space. Any number of free format/storage calculators can help you figure out the storage needs for your format's data rate (see Page 219). However, in addition to holding your original media files, your NLE system will also create new media each time you add and render a transition, special effect, or text and graphics, which all require additional space. It's a good idea to have at least an extra one-third of free space for these render files. It's also recommended that your hard drive have a spindle speed of 7200 rpm.

The **media transfer device** is used to download your footage into the NLE system. Again, this depends on your shooting format. If you're shooting MiniDV, then you'll require a MiniDV deck interfacing with the computer via a FireWire cable, but if your shooting on memory cards (P2 or SxS hard drive), then you'll need a card reader hooked in via a FireWire or USB 2.0 cable. If you've already transferred your footage to a portable hard drive in the field, then you can simply hook in the hard drive and edit. Transferring footage can be accomplished with your camcorder in a pinch, but this not only ties up a piece of production equipment for a mundane task, it also causes unnecessary wear and tear to the camcorder. Remember, with tape media you have the original to fall back on should your hard drive crash after the transfer, but memory cards are usually erased to be reused, so *always* transfer your footage to a second drive for a safety backup.

A good set of powered **speakers** is important to get a true sense for your audio. Often, in editing facilities where there are multiple systems in a single room, you'll be forced to edit with headphones so that no one disturbs

■ **Figure 20-10** A typical NLE system setup: (a) computer, (b) external FireWire hard drive, (c) DV deck, (d) speakers and monitor, (e) comfortable chair.

the other editors in the room. Headphones are fine while you're constructing the first few rough cuts of your movie, but the final sound track mix should always be done with high-quality speakers to get an accurate sense for how the balance and presence of the audio will sound to an audience who will themselves be listening to speakers.

A **comfy chair** is a must. The familiar film industry saying, "Never trust an editor with a tan," reminds us that editing requires that you remain inside an editing room, sitting on your behind, in front of an NLE system for hours and days on end. For this reason, a comfy, adjustable, ergonomically correct chair is important. A comfortable editor is a happy, creative, and productive editor; an uncomfortable editor takes frequent breaks to go to the beach.

The Software Interface

In standard editing mode, all NLE systems divide the **edit environment** (or **desktop**) into four main windows (**Figure 20-11**): (a) the browser (Final Cut Pro [FCP]) or project window (Avid), (b) the viewer (FCP) or source monitor (Avid), (c) the timeline window (FCP and Avid), and (d) the canvas (FCP) or composer monitor (Avid). FCP and Avid may refer to these windows by different names, but their functions are the same.

The Browser (FCP) or Project Window (Avid)

The **browser window/project window** is the main window for storing, organizing, and accessing all of the visual and audio elements for your project. These elements, which you use to edit your film, are organized in folders called bins. A **bin** is where you store and organize all of your separate editing elements, including **video clips** (the individual camera takes), **audio clips** (music, sound effects, voice-over, etc.) and **graphics files** (photos, text, animations, etc.). The clips in the bins are saved on the internal hard drive and are not actual media; they are simply the pointers that reference the original media files that are stored on the external hard drive (**Figure 20-12**).

You can create as many bins as you need within the larger browser window. Organizing your bins so that you can easily find the material you need is essential for efficiency—but *how* you organize the bins is a personal matter. Usually, editors will create one bin for each scene, and this bin will include all of the elements (camera takes and audio) needed to edit the scene. Most NLE systems provide great flexibility for customizing, organizing,

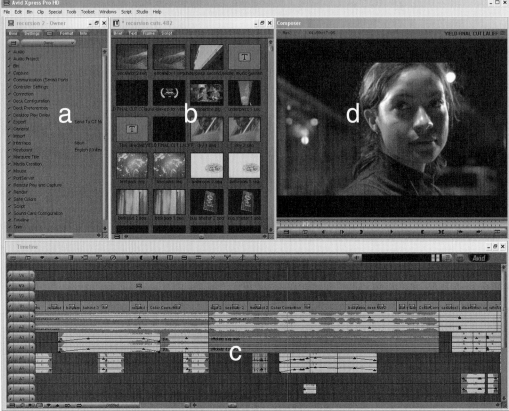

■ **Figure 20-11** The four main editing windows are essentially the same in Final Cut Pro HD *(top)* and Avid Xpress Pro HD *(bottom)*: (a) the browser (FCP) or project window (Avid), (b) the viewer (FCP) or source monitor (Avid), (c) the timeline window (FCP and Avid), and (d) the canvas (FCP) or composer monitor (Avid).

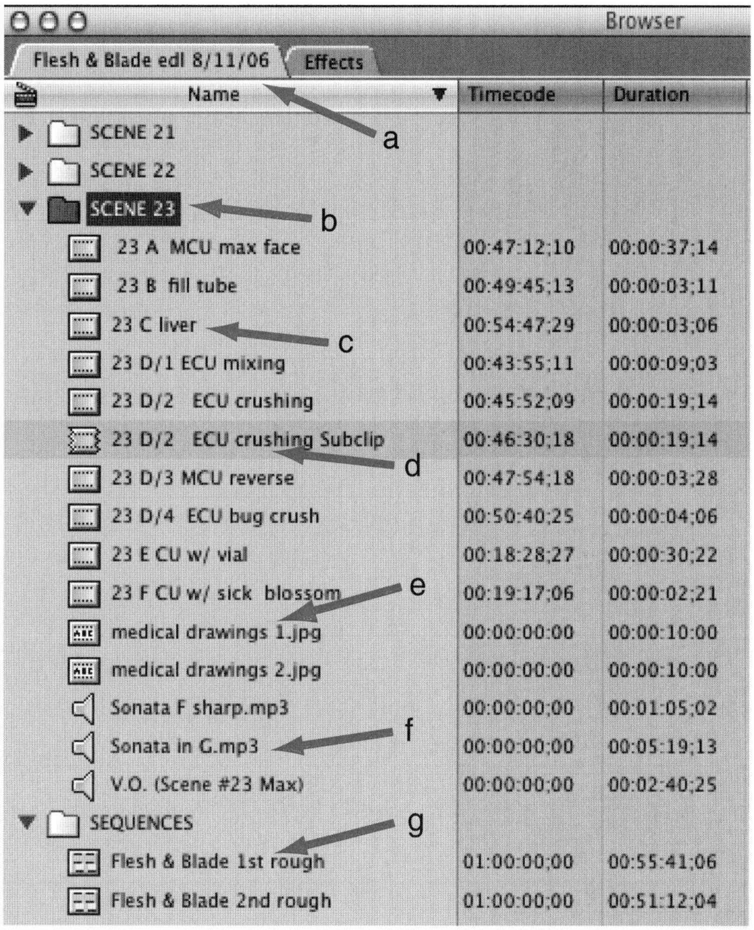

Figure 20-12 The organization of project files in Final Cut Pro: The project folder (a) contains all project files including the bin folders (b) that themselves hold all necessary files for each scene including master clips (c), subclips (d), graphic files (e), and sound files (f). Sequences (g) are also found in the project folder.

and identifying clips. Clip information can include the scene, take, and camera roll numbers that correspond to the slate and marked shooting script. You can also see the *in* and *out* timecode numbers, shot duration, audio channels, frame rates, compression, formats, pixel ratio, and so on and so on (sometimes it's more than you need to know). However, one feature that is very useful for an editor is the ability to include your screening notes on the clips. For example, you might write the note "sound is NG, but good reactions toward end" on a clip (**Figure 20-13**).

The Viewer (FCP) or Source Monitor (Avid)
If you want to view, evaluate, and work with any particular video clip, you simply click on it and the shot will open up in the FCP **viewer** (or **source window** on the AVID). In the viewer you can view the entire shot and then set **in-points** and **out-points** to delineate the exact piece of footage from the longer shot that you want to edit into your film. If you're working with a sound clip in the viewer, like a piece of music, you will see the magnified audio waveform in the viewer, which can be enormously helpful in finding beats or sound peaks and determining where you want to cut into and out of the sound track (**Figure 20-14**).

The Timeline Window (FCP and Avid)
Once you've decided on the specific parameters of the shot you'd like to insert into your film, you place it into the **timeline.** The timeline is where all the action is—this is where you truly edit your movie by inserting, deleting, arranging, rearranging, and fine-tuning your clips as you build your movie, both sound and image, one cut at a time.

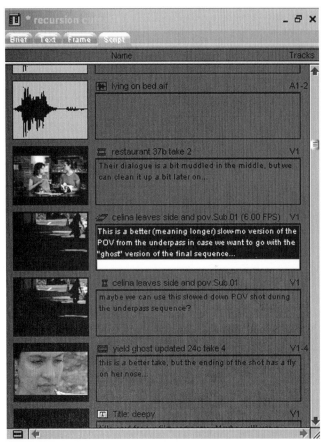

The timeline is divided into discrete **video** and **audio tracks** for maximum creative flexibility. You have the option to cut, rearrange, or apply effects to only the picture, or only the sound, or any combination of picture and sound tracks, or all tracks simultaneously. A typical timeline will automatically provide one video track and four audio tracks when you start a project, but you can add as many audio tracks as you need. Additional video tracks can also be added when you want to create superimpositions, text over image, and other image layering effects (Figure 20-15).

As you lay down a string of shots and audio tracks in the timeline, you are creating a **sequence,** which is a graphical representation of your edited movie. Sequences should be clearly named and saved frequently. Sequences are also saved in the browser, along with the clips. One of the great flexible advantages of digital editing is that you can create multiple sequences, copy sequences, create versions of sequences, and treat a sequence like a clip and insert it into other sequences.

In both Avid and Final Cut Pro, the number of tools and the possibilities for working in the timeline are staggering. Some capabilities, like the ability to trim shots shorter or longer with frame precision, are essential tools for editing, other timeline functions you will use only occasionally, and others you may never need at all.

■ **Figure 20-13** Most NLE systems, like AVID Xpress Pro HD *(pictured),* allow you to keep fairly extensive notes on each take with the clip itself.

It is not possible to cover timeline functions in detail in this book, so I refer you to the software instruction manuals. Both Avid and Final Cut Pro have a "Getting Started" manual, which is the best place to begin. Also, there are many third-party books on the market that are written in a much more intuitive and useful way than the full software manuals. I have mentioned a few of the more popular publications in the Recommended Reading list in the back of the book.

■ **Figure 20-14** The viewer in Final Cut Pro can toggle between soundtrack view *(left)* and picture view *(right).* The in-point and out-point on the clip timeline *(arrows)* show exactly what portion of the entire clip you have chosen to use.

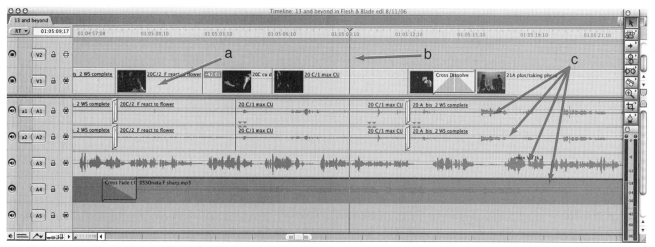

■ **Figure 20-15** The timeline consists of the picture track(s) (a); sound tracks (c), and playhead (b).

Inside the timeline is a **playhead,** which is a horizontally scrolling vertical line running through all edited tracks. The playhead tells you where you are in the timeline and is used to move around your sequence quickly. We also use the playhead to determine where edit points are placed and where shots are inserted. With the mouse, you can drag the play-head across the sequence to locate a specific shot quickly, or, if you hit play, the playhead moves across the sequence in real time.

The Canvas (FCP) or Composer Monitor (Avid)

Wherever the timeline playhead rests, that frame of video is viewable in the FCP **canvas** (or composer monitor on an AVID). The canvas is where you watch your sequence to see how your shots are holding together. You can move through the sequence in real time by using the **transport control buttons** at the bottom of the window, or scroll through in slow motion (forward and backward) with the **shuttle control,** or frame-by-frame with the **jog control wheel.** Or you can drag the playhead with the mouse to move around the sequence extremely quickly. The playhead in the canvas window is a duplicate of the playhead in the timeline window (**Figure 20-16**). Notice that the viewer window (see **Figure 20-14**) has all of the same playback controls for viewing clips.

In addition to the four main windows, there are other auxiliary windows that you should include on your desktop for the sake of convenience. The two most common are the **sound levels window,** to monitor your sound as you lay down audio, and the timeline **toolbar window,** which allows you to access timeline tools and various edit modes with the click of your mouse (**Figure 20-17**).

in practice

■ SUMMARY: THE FOUR BASIC NLE WINDOWS

1. *Browser/bin.* This is where you store and organize your editing elements: video clips, audio clips, and graphics files and sequences.
2. *Viewer window.* This is where you preview clips and determine edit parameters for your shots.
3. *Timeline.* This is where you edit and arrange your shots and sound tracks to create a sequence.
4. *Canvas.* This is where you view and move through the sequence

Menu, Icon, or Keyboard: Take Your Pick

One thing you'll discover on all NLE systems is that there are usually *three* ways of doing exactly the same thing. You can find any given command inside pulldown menus or you can trigger the same command by clicking an icon on the desktop, or you can use a

Figure 20-16 The Final Cut Pro canvas includes transport control buttons (a), a shuttle control slider (b), and a jog control wheel (c), allowing you to view your footage at practically any speed you desire. You can also grab the timeline playhead in this window (d) and slide it through the entire program.

Figure 20-17 Optional auxiliary windows include the sound levels window and the timeline toolbar window *(arrow)*.

keyboard shortcut for the same action. For example, setting in- and out-points in the viewer can be accomplished three ways: by hitting the "i" or "o" button on the keyboard, by clicking on the *mark in/mark out* icons on the viewer window, or by scrolling down the "mark" menu to the "mark in" or "mark out" command (**Figure 20-18**). You don't need to memorize all three ways of doing every task. If you don't like to take your fingers off the keyboard, then learn the keyboard shortcuts; if you're a mouse person who loves to click on icons, learn what the icon symbols stand for; if your brain organizes the world through lists and menus, then use the pulldown menus; or, if you're like me, and like to mix it up, then go that way. I use the keyboard for some functions (setting in- and out-points) and icons for others (taking an edit). In short, customize your process, find the easiest and fastest route (for you) for each function and ignore the alternatives!

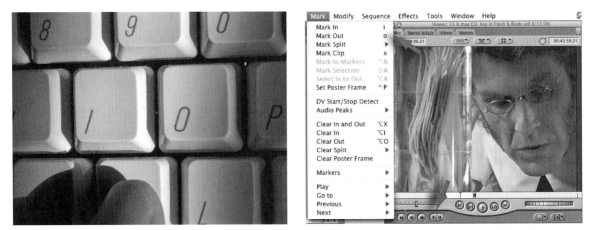

Figure 20-18 Many functions can be accomplished in multiple ways. For example, you can set in- and out-points on the keyboard *(left)*, through a menu *(middle)*, or by clicking icons.

That said, there are two special keyboard functions that are extremely handy to know:

1. The J, K, and L buttons are universal, transport control buttons. J is play/reverse, K is pause, and L is play/forward. Pressing J and L multiple times increases or decreases the play speed from normal speed (one press) to 2× to 4× to 8× (four presses) (**Figure 20-19**).

2. The **command + Z** keystroke combination instantly undoes your last action. Inevitably, as you edit, you will click a wrong icon or drag and drop something where it doesn't belong, or accidentally delete an entire sequence. Well, if you've made a mistake, simply hit command-Z, and voilà!—all is forgiven and put back where it was before your little blunder. I've often wished for a command-Z function in the less technological areas of life, but alas most things are not so easily undone.

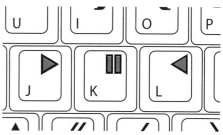

■ **Figure 20-19** Some keyboard shortcuts, like the J, K, and L buttons for playing footage, can be extremely helpful.

Transferring, Logging, and Organizing Media

Before you can start editing, you must set up your NLE audio and video format settings for your project. This establishes the format workflow during the editing stage (see page 399 for details). Then you need to get your raw materials into the computer environment to edit. In fact, all other film elements you plan to use in the film—music, sound effects, graphics, and so on—need to be put into the computer for editing. This process is called **capturing** (tape media), **ingesting** (file-based media) or **transferring**. If your footage is on tape capturing is usually done with a DV deck via a FireWire cable and the deck functions are controlled by the computer interface with **external device control**. If your footage is on memory cards or has been transferred in the field to a hard drive, then the interface can be FireWire or USB 2.0. As I mentioned earlier, if you've shot on film you obviously must convert those celluloid images into digital bits through a film-to-tape transfer process (explained on page 401).

Transferring video turns your raw elements into media files that the NLE software can work with. This is done through container formats: QuickTime (.mov) in Final Cut Pro and Material Exchange Format (.mxf) in Avid systems (see page 401). But putting technical format issues aside, what is crucial during the editing stage is the organization of your elements. And organization begins as soon as you start transferring your media into the NLE. The first important step in staying organized is to establish a *single destination folder for all your media files* on your external hard drive (called a **capture scratch file** in Final Cut Pro). This is especially critical when using shared NLE systems where others might have set the media capture destination to who-knows-where.

As you capture, you will be **logging** your footage, which involves labeling your clips, adding descriptive information, and creating bins to organize the clips (**Figure 20-20**). Even though you might be anxious to start cutting right away, it's important that to take your time at this stage to label and log your media carefully and to organize your sound and video clips into a logical bin structure. A little extra time up front will save a lot of time later as you hunt for clips during the editing stage. Generally, bins are organized such that you have *one bin per scene* that

■ **Figure 20-20** The FCP log and transfer window for ingesting file-based media (also see Figure 19-5 for tape media log and capture window).

contains all the video and audio clips necessary for editing that particular scene. The bins themselves are then organized in the scene order as they appear in the movie (see **Figure 20-12**)

There are a number of ways you can capture footage (called **ingesting** for file based formats), but the two most common are **clip capture** and **batch capture**:

1. *Clip capture.* As you view your footage one camera take at a time, you decide if this take gets transferred at all, and if it does, determine where you'd like the capture to begin and end. You then fill in the log information (roll number, scene number, take number, and notes) and execute the clip capture. This will give you one **media file** in your hard drive and one **master clip** (that references the media file) to place in your bin. Then you move on to the next camera take, and repeat. With this method you watch, log, and capture one take at a time. If you're capturing from tape, you could capture the multiple takes of each scene and split them up later into subclips (see **Figure 20-12**). **Subclips** are smaller clips that reference master clips, which in turn reference media files. Be careful, however: if you lose your master clip, then you lose your associated subclips. File-based media doesn't work this way, as it provides a separate file for each take.

2. *Batch capture.* With this method, you identify and log all of your select clips first, naming shots and entering the in and out timecode numbers for each clip from the DV tape. Then with the "batch capture" command, the editing software takes over and automates the entire capture process. It shuttles to the cue points, captures, and moves on to the next shot on the tape. If there are multiple tapes, the computer will prompt you to insert the next tape when the previous one is finished. This method saves time on the editing system but requires that you compile the timecode numbers for your selects as you view dailies. This method of capturing is primarily used with tape-based media because unlike file-based formats, the capture takes real time and you cannot review and log the next clip until the capture process is over. Batch capture is especially useful for *both* tape- and file-based formats when, for some reason, you lose or need to delete your original media files from the hard drive *after* you've already captured your shots. In this case, your clip information in the bins (pointers to media, remember?) still contains the roll number and timecode metadata for every shot. So you simply choose the clips and batch capture the media back onto the hard drive (**Figure 20-21**).

One additional note about capturing: With narrative film we generally capture complete takes, even if we think we'll use only a small portion of the shot. This will give you room for trimming and transitions like dissolves. The extra frames and seconds you need for transition effects are called **handles**. If you capture entire camera takes—from slate to "Cut!"—then you'll have all the handles you need.

Syncing Audio

If the footage you're capturing is single-system DV footage or if you shot film and had the lab sync your dailies for you, then both sound and picture are captured in sync at this stage. However, if you shot film or double-system DV and planned to sync the footage yourself in the NLE system, then you must capture the image (from tapes or files) and sound (from original recording media) individually, creating separate clips and media files. You will then need to perform one extra step before you can start editing: syncing dailies manually (see the accompanying box).

	Name		Timecode	Duration	In
▼	📁 roll 1				
	🎞 7 A CU "blight"		00:08:06;16	00:00:04;02	00:09:12;29
	🎞 10 (?) pick up CU		00:26:13;20	00:00:00;01	Not Set
	🎞 10 A WS w/ plant etc.		00:24:52;01	00:00:03;25	00:25:12;09
	🎞 10 B CU hands		00:25:40;23	00:00:16;25	Not Set
	🎞 10 B CU hands1		00:26:00;25	00:00:13;05	Not Set
	🎞 7 J coat off–leave		00:16:06;19	00:00:18;15	00:16:18;11
	🎞 7 B "blight"		00:04:20;15	00:00:39;00	Not Set
	🎞 7 B bis "blight"		00:06:49;01	00:00:06;11	00:07:12;06
	🎞 7 C bis m w/ apparat WS		00:00:07;06	00:00:11;12	00:00:14;10
	🎞 7 C m w/ apparatus WS		00:17:14;03	00:00:07;11	00:17:51;01
	🎞 7 C/ 1 dropper CU		00:01:20;17	00:00:12;20	00:02:24;17

Browser — Flesh & Blade edl 8/11/06

■ **Figure 20-21** In FCP, clips that have had the original media files deleted appear in your bin with a red slash. It's an easy procedure to choose all clips that have lost their media and batch capture new media without relogging.

■ SYNCING DAILIES IN A DIGITAL EDIT SYSTEM

The procedure for *syncing dailies* is very simple and uses the basic edit interface windows we explained earlier. Syncing dailies takes a little time at first, but once you get the hang of it, it's quick and easy. For each sync take you will be working with the two related clips, the sound clip and the image clip, and the all-important slate, so you must be sure to capture the slating in all of your sync clips (**Figure 20-22**):

1. Open the image clip in the viewer and, using the jog control wheel, find the exact frame where the clapper arm on the slate closes. Place a marker on that frame with the **marker**

■ **Figure 20-22** The marker button (a) is extremely helpful for lining up the slate closing frame with the slate closing sound *(bottom arrows)* when syncing dailies.

button. A marker is not an in-/out-point: it just tags a specific frame, the way a bookmark marks a page. Finally, drag the video clip into an empty timeline sequence.

2. Open the corresponding sound clip. You will see a sound wave representing the audio on that clip. (If you have shot on film, at 24 fps, then you'll need to compensate for the speed slowdown of the 3:2 pulldown process (see page 405). With the "modify speed" command, simply enter 99.9% and the clip will be slowed down the required 0.01% to match the image [see **Figure 19-12**]). Now, find the exact point on the timeline with the "clap" sound of the clapper arm meeting the slate. You will also be able to see a drastic peak in the sound wave at this point. **Audio scrub,** which allows you to hear frame-by-frame audio as you drag the viewer playhead, is a helpful tool here. Again, place a marker at the "clap" point and drag the clip into the timeline audio track just below the image.

3. Slide the video clip until the two markers are lined up. Make sure the **snap** function is on, which will line the markers up with a snap when they are brought close to each other. When the markers are perfectly aligned, the clips are in sync, but can still easily be moved out of sync.

4. The next step is to choose the video and audio tracks and, using the **link** command, merge them together. Link simply associates the two tracks as one **merged clip.** You can now drag the new synced and linked clip back into the browser window. You should create a separate bin for your synced clips to distinguish them from the unsynced sound and video clips as you proceed.

5. Once you have created new, synced clips (that point to the original media files), you can delete the unsynced clips to avoid confusion.

6. Now you're ready to edit!

Making a Simple Edit

The more you edit, the more tools, edit modes, and shortcuts you will incorporate into your routine. As I mentioned earlier, the best way to learn software is one function at a time, as the need arises. It only takes cutting a few short films before you have a thorough knowledge of a program's capabilities. However, the place to start, where you'll do the majority of your editing, is using the four basic windows to do simple cuts. Let's go through the process of using the basic windows to make two simple, but extremely common, edits.

As an example we will use one of the sample scenes we explored in Chapter 5 from *Kiarra's Escape.* The moment we'll edit is the sequence in which Kiarra is sitting at her table when she hears a car pull up outside her apartment. She rushes to the window, looks out and sees Smith and Vogler approaching her building. She closes the blinds (see **Figure 5-1**, shots 13-B, 13-C, and 13-D; see also **Figure 4-15**). The moment is made up of three shots: (1) MS Kiarra at the table hearing the car and getting up, (2) CU Kiarra at the window looking out and reacting to what she sees, (3) ELS Kiarra's POV of Smith and Vogler on the street. The first edit—from table to window—moves us elliptically from one area of the apartment to another. The second edit involves dropping the POV shot into the CU window shot, splitting it in half to create a POV sequence (looking/POV/reaction). To begin, we have already laid down shot 13-B (MS of Kiarra at the table); now we want to add the next shot to get her to the window.

1. *View and evaluate the shot.* In your bin (within the browser window), locate the shot you wish to cut into the film (shot 13-C: CU of Kiarra going to the window, looking out and reacting) and click on it. The entire clip will be loaded into the viewer. If the clip includes sync sound, then both sound and image will be loaded. Play through the clip a few times to determine what portion of the camera take you want to edit into the film at this moment. When you have a sense for where you want the shot to start and end, set an in-point by using the mark in-point button (or by hitting the "i" key on the keyboard) and an out-point by using the mark out-point button (or by hitting the "o" key on the keyboard).

2. *Make the edit.* Once the parameters of the shot have been established, you can simply drag the shot from the viewer window into the timeline and place it where you'd like it (**Figure 20-23**). Again, if the shot includes sync sound, you will simultaneously be dragging and adding the picture track and the sync audio tracks. This drag-and-drop editing approach is used primarily for simply putting one shot after another. In this case, we simply drop the shot after the previous shot of Kiarra at the table and getting up to go to the window. But, again, you can "take" this edit in other ways (keyboard or menu), as you'll see in the next cut.

3. *Evaluate the edit.* Play through your timeline and watch your edit in the canvas window. How does the shot work with the other shots in the sequence? Is it right? Does it belong there? How is the rhythm? Perhaps the shot order is great, but the precise edit point, where the two shots meet, is a little off and needs adjusting. Adjusting the out- and in-points of adjacent shots from within the timeline is called **trimming,** and that's the next step.

4. *Fine-tune the edit.* When you enter **trim mode,** you are shown two screens, the left shows the very last frame of the first shot and the right screen shows the very first frame of the next shot—in other words the splice where the shots meet. Here you can trim the edit points of either or both shots. In trim mode you can add or subtract 1, 5, or 10 frames at a time. At first, trim mode can be tricky, but with a little practice, this tool becomes the editor's primary implement for fine-tuning edit points. Trim mode is one of the most powerful features introduced by digital nonlinear editing (**Figure 20-24**).

The Three-Point Edit

Now, the next shot we want to cut in is Kiarra's POV shot for the sequence: Kiarra looking shot (shot 13C) → POV of Smith

■ **Figure 20-23** Simple edits can be accomplished by choosing your clip from the bin (a), setting your in- and out-points in the canvas (b), and drag-and-dropping the clip image into your timeline (c).

and Vogler (shot 13D) → Kiarra's reaction (shot 13C). Although the edited sequence consists of three shots, Kiarra's looking and reaction shots are originally only one shot, with the POV inserted and splitting it in two (see marked script page 101). For this sort of edit, dragging and dropping isn't accurate enough. We need to perform a common cut called the **three-point edit,** in which three in- and out-points (two on the source material and one in the timeline, or vice versa) determine the cut.

As usual, we find the POV shot in the bin and click on it to bring it up in the viewer. After deciding on the in- and out-points for the shot, we turn to the timeline and position (or **park**) the playhead on the precise point where we want to insert the POV shot, which will be somewhere in the middle of the looking shot, and we mark an in-point on the timeline (**Figure 20-25**). When we

■ **Figure 20-24** When you place your playhead on an edit point and enter trim mode (a), you will get two windows that show the very last frame of the outgoing shot (b, *left*) and the very first frame of the incoming shot (b, *right*), allowing you to adjust the precise frames of the cut.

click on the "insert edit" icon, the shot will be inserted at that exact frame in the timeline, splitting the looking shot and pushing everything after the in-point down the timeline. We now have Kiarra's looking shot, next to the POV shot, followed by her reaction. Again, you can go into trim mode to finesse where each of the three shots begins and ends in relation to the shots immediately adjacent.

These two sample edits pretty much describe the predominant cutting routine for editing any movie. As I mentioned before, there are many other tools, functions, and capabilities in your software with which you will no doubt become familiar as you need and use them. (To watch this edited sample scene, go to www.voiceandvisionbook.com.)

■ **Figure 20-25** Inserting a shot with a typical three-point edit. Mark the in- and out-points of the shot you wish to cut in (a); mark the in-point on the timeline where you wish to place that shot (b), and click on "insert edit" to make the edit (c). Notice how the looking and reaction shot (along with its sync audio) has been split by the newly inserted POV shot *(right)*.

■ **THE EDITING STAGES**

You know you've achieved perfection in design,
Not when you have nothing more to add,
But when you have nothing more to take away.

Antoine de Saint-Exupéry

The editing process is one that has become somewhat standardized over time, yet it remains extremely flexible to fit the scale of the specific project and the working preferences of the editor. The filmmaker for a large-budget Hollywood film has no trouble shooting 500,000 feet of 35mm film, and features shot on HD, where scene coverage is often extreme because of the low cost, can easily generate well over 100 hours of footage to wade through, consider, evaluate, and edit. Because of the volume of material and the cost of production, most commercial feature film editors begin cutting during the shooting of the film. As the dailies come back from the lab (or as memory card footage is downloaded to a portable drive), the editor immediately starts reviewing footage and cutting scenes. This way, if there are serious holes in the coverage of scenes, the director can reshoot while the cast, crew, and equipment are still assembled. I've seen many students also who will shoot by day and quickly cut together the day's scenes that night. In this sense, to call editing a "postproduction" process is a bit of a misnomer. Yes, it deals with material that emerges from the production process, but it also often commences along with production.

On the other hand, when budgets are low and shooting days are few and compressed, there is often simply no time to edit along the way, especially if the director is also the editor. In these cases, editing tends to truly be a postproduction process, starting once the shooting is over.

In either case, whether you're dealing with 100 hours of raw footage and a team of editors cutting scenes while the film is in production or just 20 minutes of footage being cut by the director, after the shooting stops, the process is similar.

Viewing Dailies

The total footage that is the result of your production process, whether you're shooting on DV or film, is your **raw footage.** Raw footage is also known as **dailies,** especially when lab processing is involved. The term "dailies" comes from the early vernacular of Hollywood studio productions, where film was shot on one day, processed overnight, and viewed the next day, so that any reshoots could be undertaken before the set was taken down. It still works that way in commercial filmmaking, only now, with digital editing, not only is the raw footage being viewed, but rough cuts of scenes as well. If you're shooting on film, what comes back from the film lab after processing are **video dailies,** which are the processed footage transferred to DV (see page 403).

Viewing dailies means watching your footage for the first time and evaluating each and every camera take for exposures, composition, scene coverage, and performance. This should be done on the highest-quality monitor (or projection) you can find so that your image is as clear and true as possible. As you view your dailies, take detailed notes on which shots are great, called **selects,** which shots simply don't work, called **outtakes,** and which shots have some portion that can be used. Selects, which have an abundance of great material for editing, are naturally marked for downloading by noting the camera roll and timecode information for the shot. Outtakes, usually early takes of a shot, do not need to be downloaded into the computer. This saves hard drive space and helps with organization and efficiency because you only have what you can use. Still, you should always know where to find your outtakes, just in case you need a piece of one later. It is not unusual to be cutting a scene and remember just a look or a gesture from an outtake that would fit perfectly into the edit. Some shots are neither

When shooting *Bamboozled* (2000), director Spike Lee and his D.P. Ellen Kuras usually had three MiniDV cameras, shooting from different angles, running at the same time. The MiniDV format was used for the "real-world" sections of the film, which constitute nearly 90% of the movie, while the television broadcast segments were photographed on Super 16mm film. In one scene, in which the Mantan TV show is filmed along with the live studio audience reactions, Lee and Kuras had 15 cameras running simultaneously: 3 Super 16mm film cameras and 12 DV camcorders. The scene coverage on *Bamboozled* was staggering; there was more than 100 hours of footage to consider. This is where editor Sam Pollard's experience editing documentary films, which routinely generate much more footage than narrative films, came in handy. Also, Pollard started editing the day after the first day of shooting, meaning he sifted through and logged the raw footage, selected and narrowed down the potential shots he would use, and edited quick rough cuts of scenes, in an effort to remain on top of the avalanche of footage (**Figure 20-26**).

■ **Figure 20-26** For *Bamboozled* Lee used multiple cameras, generating an enormous amount of footage for editor Sam Pollard to work with.

selects nor outtakes. They are great in one part, but lacking in another. These shots are marked for downloading, too, but notes should be made about what you liked about them and what wasn't working. As an aside, if you're shooting short exercises or a short film and have very little footage (and no storage issues), you could simply transfer *all* your footage into your NLE right away and view your dailies after transferring and not before.

Viewing dailies can be an emotional experience. All of the effort, struggles, victories, and tears from the production process are in that footage, yet filmmakers need to detach themselves from what went on during the shoot and watch the footage as objectively as possible. You need to keep reminding yourself that no one in the audience will know what went into making these shots; no one knows what's just out of the frame or how you struggled or how much money you spent or how ingenious you were to get that shot. Only the image on the screen counts, and that is exactly what you need to evaluate when you watch dailies. Often, when I mention to a student that a particular shot simply isn't working, I get the response, "But it took me all day to get that damned shot so it's got to be in the film!"

In addition, it's easy to succumb to the "daily blues," which is a sort of letdown feeling you can have viewing your raw footage. You've put so much time, effort, and money into production that you'd like to sit down and just watch your movie! But it's not a movie yet. It's still in pieces and there's a lot of work yet to be done. The daily blues happens to me every time. The footage never looks quite as good as I thought it would, and everything seems lifeless and flat. But then once I start editing, and the individual shots start connecting and talking to other images, and the sound track adds its alchemical dimension, the story and emotions start to emerge from the edited sequences, and my original excitement returns as the film starts to become what I thought it might be at the beginning.

First Assembly Edit

The **assemble edit** means placing end-to-end all the shots of a scene, or a sequence of scenes, or even an entire short film, without selecting too precisely the parameters of each shot. The shots are slapped in "very fat" without any finessing. The assemble edit is your first opportunity to see the broad strokes of the general order of the shots, to get a sense of the relationships between scenes and to get a feel for the overall flow of the story. Because it's like a preliminary sketch, rearranging shots and scenes is quick and simple and allows you to see various versions without too much effort. During the assemble edit stage you will ask yourself the larger questions of sequencing: How is the story unfolding scene by scene and shot by shot? Do these scenes belong next to each other? How many shots and which shots should I include to cover this scene? It is more efficient to make structural adjustments in this very broad form, than to waste time carefully finding precise edit points and frame-accurate transitions for five consecutive shots, only to discover that they really don't belong in that order at all.

> *The first assembly is a first draft. When you first put an assembly together, you put in everything the director shot. You don't try to give it too much shape yet. Then, you attack it in the second cut. So, it's like a first draft of someone's writing.*
> **Thelma Schoonmaker (editor, *Raging Bull, Goodfellas, The Aviator*)**
> **(From *MovieMaker*, Vol. 5, No. 2)**

Rough Cuts

Once you've laid down the general structure off the film, it's time to dive into the individual scenes to rearrange, add, eliminate, split, or trim footage to make each scene work on its own. A **rough cut** is a version of the film in which all scenes have been edited fairly tightly, but usually with the blunter tools available in the edit system, like straight cuts instead of other transitions effects. Rough cuts are edited with picture track and the essential audio tracks only. For example, if your scenes involve extensive sync sound dialogue, then you should be editing picture and dialogue; if your film has no dialogue, but instead a music sound track throughout, then you'll cut picture to the music; if voice-over is a major component of a sequence, then you'll need to lay that down on the audio track and cut to it. Usually, you will cut several rough edits of your movie, tightening and improving the film with each version. Remember, the idea here is not to spend too much time on the ultrafine points until you know absolutely that all of the cuts are just right.

Cutting Dialogue

If your film involves extensive dialogue, then you will probably start to cut audio during this stage as well. Remember, all of our film elements, audio and video, are on separate tracks and can be edited and manipulated independently. Therefore, sync audio does not necessarily need to remain with the corresponding images. When editing picture and dialogue there are three basic cutting techniques: the straight cut, the split edit, and the insert cut (**Figure 20-27**).

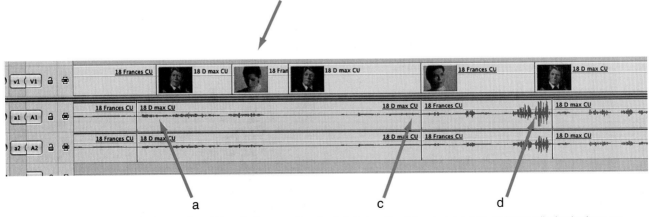

■ **Figure 20-27** A variety of dialogue edits within a single scene. Sound cuts in before the picture in a J-cut (a), an insert edit simply places an image over the ongoing sound of a shot (b), sound and picture cut at the same time in a straight cut (c), and picture cuts in before sound in an L-cut (d).

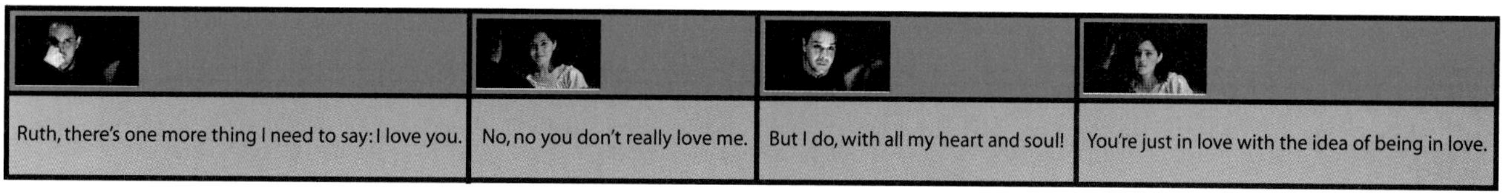

Ruth, there's one more thing I need to say: I love you.	No, no you don't really love me.	But I do, with all my heart and soul!	You're just in love with the idea of being in love.

■ Figure 20-28 A scene with all straight cuts on dialogue has a predictable pattern and rhythm.

As the name suggests, the **straight cut** cuts the picture and sound on the same frame. When the picture cuts to another image, the sound cuts as well. When using straight cuts for dialogue, we go from one person speaking to the other speaking, then back to the first person speaking and so on, as in the example in Figure 20-28. This sort of back-and-forth dialogue cutting has a certain rhythm that can be effective at times, but in most instances the predictable edits, always coming between lines of dialogue, are too monotonous to use for an entire scene. **Split edits** (also called L-cuts and J-cuts) are edits in which the transition from one image to the other happens at a different time than the transition in the audio track. In an **L-cut,** the picture cuts to the next shot first, and the audio cuts occur later. The **J-cut** is the opposite: the audio cuts out first, while the picture plays a bit longer before cutting to the next shot. The timing of these edits—how many frames or seconds to displace the cut in image versus the cut in audio—depends on a number of factors, some creative and some practical. Split edits are used frequently in dialogue scenes to produce smooth edits that are practically invisible.

Beyond invisibility, however, split edits are an essential technique for dialogue editing and play an important role in establishing the internal rhythm of an encounter, in the dramatic timing of reactions, and in the construction of character point of view, which are all key story-telling considerations. Holding the camera on a character's face, a few seconds longer as someone else speaks, can communicate a strong sense of point of view in the scene; like-wise, cutting to someone on just the right word is a juxtaposition that can make powerful, subtextual, and emotional associations.

An **insert cut** involves completely disconnecting either the sync audio or video from its original linked clip and inserting it over a shot that is continuous. This is commonly done with reaction shots where you wish to continue one person's dialogue during the reaction of the other person and then return to the image of the first person talking. All that's needed in this case is the image of person 2 laid over the dialogue. Conversely, you can insert someone else's dialogue only, without ever cutting to their image.

Most films liberally combine J-cuts, L-cuts, and insert cuts even within the same scene. Figure 20-29 is an example of three additional versions of the melodramatic scene, with exactly the same dialogue, but cut using various dialogue editing options in order to alter the tone and POV of the dramatic moment. Bob and Ruth are coworkers out for lunch, and Bob takes the opportunity to announce that he's in love with Ruth. As you can see with these simple illustrations, dialogue editing can have a substantial impact on the shaping of performances and the interpretation of a scene. The first version (see Figure 20-28), using only straight cuts when each person speaks, presents the moment in a rather neutral way. The second version (Figure 20-29, A) allows two moments where Ruth reacts while Bob delivers his most ardent lines. The L-cut in particular brings Ruth in at a crucial moment ("I love you"), giving her a great moment for a reaction. This dialogue edit announces that Ruth's reaction is more important than Bob's proclamation and therefore draws the audience into a closer identification with Ruth, who clearly does not share Bob's feelings. The third version (Figure 20-29, B) draws us closer to Bob's POV, who now gets to respond to what Ruth is saying. The last insert, in particular, leaves us with Bob's forlorn reaction at the end of the scene. The final version (Figure 20-29, C) is all Ruth's POV: not only does she get that strong L-cut reaction on "I love you," but Ruth also gets the rest of the scene, in a close-up, and we get to watch her struggle with Bob's declaration of love. (A more elaborate example of dialogue editing is available online. Go to www.voiceandvisionbook.com.)

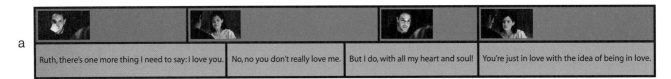

a — Ruth, there's one more thing I need to say: I love you. | No, no you don't really love me. | But I do, with all my heart and soul! | You're just in love with the idea of being in love.

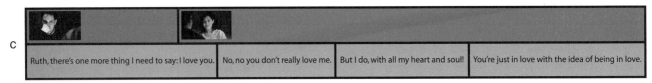

b — Ruth, there's one more thing I need to say: I love you. | No, no you don't really love me. | But I do, with all my heart and soul! | You're just in love with the idea of being in love.

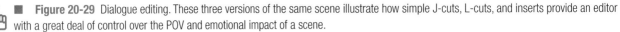

c — Ruth, there's one more thing I need to say: I love you. | No, no you don't really love me. | But I do, with all my heart and soul! | You're just in love with the idea of being in love.

■ **Figure 20-29** Dialogue editing. These three versions of the same scene illustrate how simple J-cuts, L-cuts, and inserts provide an editor with a great deal of control over the POV and emotional impact of a scene.

On a more practical note, split edits are frequently used to fine-tune continuity edits, especially when cutting to match action or to hide continuity errors altogether. Although the dialogue may cut perfectly on a particular point, the gesture in the video might not exactly match, so simply trimming only the video a few frames earlier or later than the audio cut might just give you either the perfect action match or the ability to avoid the problematic movement all together.

Rough cuts are where you spend the majority of your time and creative thinking. There is a lot of cutting and re-cutting during this stage as you discover the final style, shape, order, and rhythm of your movie. And as you edit, you become intimately familiar with every frame of your footage. Because of this, new ideas will emerge as you notice more details, connections, and possibilities between shots. Experimenting with different juxtapositions will reveal the full potential of your footage over the course of the editing process.

However, be careful: familiarity can also be a liability when you start seeing things in the footage or assuming information in a sequence that a first-time viewer would never be aware of. It happens with some frequency that a student will screen a film that, let's say, includes a conversation between two people, with the scene consisting entirely of close-ups. The audience will become disoriented, wondering where this scene is taking place. The response of the director/editor is usually something like "They were in her father's house. Didn't you see the yellow walls behind her head? That was the same house as in the first scene!" The fact is no, we didn't notice the yellow walls. While the director/editor, who knows the script and has seen the footage a million times, can immediately match the wall color between two disparate scenes, *we*, drawn in by the close-ups, looked at faces, not walls. The editing did not establish the location because it all seemed clear enough to the editor. By the same token I have seen students struggle for hours to fix a teeny-tiny continuity problems, which no one watching the film would ever notice.

One remarkable skill that all great editors share is the ability to step back and look at the footage and sequences with fresh eyes, like they were watching it for the first time—the way an audience will experience it in a theater. It's also important to show rough cuts to selected people for a fresh perspective and to get some constructive criticism while you are editing and can do something about it. It's better to have a few people raise red flags during the rough-cut stage than to have a theater full of confusion at your premiere.

The Fine Cut and Picture Lock

Once you're happy with the basic editing of your film, and all of the sequences are working the way you need them to work, and you've determined that there will be no more big changes to the film, you can start to fine-tune the rough cut. **The fine cut** involves finessing all of the edits one by one; it's the time to make those small edit adjustments to, for instance, get that cut on action just right, add the dissolve between two scenes, or trim a few frames off a POV shot to get the timing of the reaction just perfect. The fine cut is also where we make final decisions concerning visual effects and transitions. Although you can preview many effects while you edit, like fades and dissolves, most need to be rendered before you can output them to your master. **Rendering** is the process of combining the video and audio with the applied effect to create a new media file. For example, a dissolve involves a slow fade-in of the incoming shot simultaneously with the slow fadeout of the outgoing shot. We can see two images superimposed for the duration of the dissolve. But there is no actual media like this, so, by rendering, the edit system creates this media. It's most efficient to render during the fine-cutting stage after you've decided on the type and duration of your effects and when you can simply render all of the effects on any single track at the same time.

This stage is also where you add additional sound tracks (like sound effects, ambience, music, etc.) and get the film into its final form. Once the film is perfect, all of the creative editing decisions are done, and you've decided you will not trim a single frame more, you have arrived at **picture lock.**

in practice

CHROMA KEY EFFECTS

The principle behind the **chroma key** effect is simple: shoot a subject in front of a solid color background and in post-production place this shot on a video track in the timeline and digitally remove the color of the background. Then, place footage of a background of your choosing on a 2nd video track, and this image will replace (or show through) the areas where the color was removed giving you a new background. Theoretically, you can key out just about any color, but the most popular and technically successful background colors used for this effect are **blue screen** and **green screen** primarily because these colors are far from human skin tones. Most of us are familiar with chroma key effects: the simplest ones we see are used during weather forecasts to insert a weather map background behind the meteorologist. Ultra complex green screen effects are used in big budget Hollywood fantasy extravaganzas for which many sequences are shot on a sound stage that is *completely* chroma green and then the entire environment is created through computer generated imaging (CGI). Quite literally, the final visual result represents a post-production digital construction rather than images captured with a camera. This is an elaborate and expensive manifestation of the green screen process. However, much simpler applications are commonly used for low budget films needing special effects or simply to put your subject in a location which would be impossible for you and your crew to travel to. Duncan Jones' 2011 film *Source Code* made extensive use of a very simple green screen effect in order to make production faster and more flexible (**Figure 20-30**). The train interior was constructed on a sound stage with a green screen outside the train window. The green in the window was later keyed-out and replaced with a landscape rushing past the train. This allowed the filmmakers to create a train set with with no ceiling and with removable walls so that they could position lights and camera with greater freedom than if they shot on a real train.

Technical tips

The chroma key process is done in post production with the **chroma keyer** (found under video filters). After you initially key-out the color (blue or green) you should see your background emerge behind the subject – but you'll still see color artifacts lining the edges subject of your subject. It often takes a considerable amount of tweaking with the chroma, luminance and saturation sliders (and adjustments with the edging and softening tools) to get a very clean key. However, the real secret to a clean, convincing key is in the lighting of the subject and chroma background.

1) Use a soft source to light the chroma background independently and make sure there are no shadows, wrinkles or hot spots.

■ **Figure 20-30** *Source Code* (Jones) used a simple green screen effect to create a moving background for a stationary train set built on a sound stage. (See the color insert).

2) Light your subject in a way that matches the background image.

3) Be careful that there are no reflective surfaces on the set or subject (like eyeglasses) that will catch the chroma color – these patches will also key-out.

4) Keep your subject five feet or more from the green screen to keep the green tint from spilling on their skin.

5) Avoid set and wardrobe colors that are close to the key color.

The *Voice & Vision* example short film *The Black Hole* by Phil and Olly uses a green key to create the "black hole special effect." Can you figure out how it was done? See the film and then check out the *Black Hole* storyboards for clues. Both can be found at www.voiceandvisionbook.com.

Finishing

Picture lock does not mean all of the creative the work is over, however. The film still needs finishing, which means that you turn your attention to three areas: the sound design, the visual effects, and color correction. Once all of the images are locked in place and the film has been edited to the essential sound track(s), you can then start to do the serious work of building the broader sound design, which includes adding music, sound effects, and ambience tracks, which will ultimately lead to the mixing down of all of the audio tracks into one mixed track. The sound design for a film is a major creative endeavor, and I have devoted an entire chapter to the art and craft of postproduction sound (see Chapter 22).

Visual effects finishing, like green screen keys or inserted graphics, are fine tuned during this stage as well as color correction. **Color correction** is the process of tweaking the tonalities and exposures in each scene for balance and consistency and to polish the final visual impression of the film. Digital editing systems like Final Cut Pro and Avid are becoming increasingly sophisticated in their color correction capabilities. For most short and low-budget films finishing on tape, there is more than enough power to make your final adjustments within your editing system. If you are finishing on film or a high-resolution Digital Cinema format (2K, 4K), however, the film lab will do the color correction. Color correction for film prints and video masters is covered in Chapter 19.

Mastering

The final step in the editing process is to master the film. This means outputting the final film to a sturdy, archivally sound digital form from which distribution copies can be made. Although most NLE systems offer a wide range of output options, you will, no doubt, want to master to a format that does not involve any further video data compression. The robust DV tape formats, like DVCPRO HD and HDCAM, are recommended over standard MiniDV, but MiniDV is certainly sufficient for most introductory film projects if the output is SD video. Because of their flimsiness and limited data space (4 GB), DVDs are not recommended as a mastering format. If your project exceeds that space, you will be forced to compress the image and this means making image compromises, which is never a good option for a project master. You can certainly distribute on DVD, but you do not want to master onto it (see Chapter 24 for more on mastering).

Think!

Everything we've discussed so far has revolved around the process and even the technology of editing, but I have saved discussing the most essential part of the editing process for last—creative thinking, imagining how the film will hold together, and thinking about how one shot will work next to another shot. This is not something you do with your fingers on a keyboard or something that is saved for one specific moment in the process. Imagining the way the story will reveal itself and the way the film will play out on the screen is something that is done, as one of my students said, with the "technology of the mind."

In his book *In the Blink of an Eye,* editor Walter Murch devotes a chapter to figuring out how much time he (and his editing associates) actually spent *physically* cutting Coppola's *Apocalypse Now.* His calculations included the number of days the editors worked divided by the number of cuts in the finished film. The rate of cuts, per editor for each 12-hour day, came out to 1.47. He then goes on to figure that for each cut in the film, there were probably five "shadow splices," which were cuts that were undone. His conclusion?

> Since it takes under ten seconds to make one-and-a-half splices, the admittedly special case of Apocalypse Now *serves to throw into exaggerated relief that fact that editing—even on a "normal" film—is not so much a putting together as it is a discovery of a path, and that the overwhelming majority of an editor's time is not spent actually splicing film.*
>
> [T]he remaining eleven hours and fifty-eight minutes of each working day were spent in activities that, in their various ways, served to clear and illuminate the path ahead of us: screenings, discussions, rewinding, re-screenings, meetings, scheduling, filing trims, note-taking, bookkeeping and lot of plain deliberative thought.
>
> **Walter Murch (From *In the Blink of an Eye*)**

What Murch is telling us is that, like all other aspects of filmmaking, the creative work of the editor is not about the technology, it's about the ideas and the imagination, which are then expressed through the technology. Interestingly, he reminds us that all of those seemingly mundane organizational tasks, like logging and bookkeeping, have their role in allowing us to think, consider, and reflect.

Murch also makes the point that making an actual cut on film takes no time at all, and this is doubly true in the digital age. It's so easy to perform many editing procedures these days that we run the risk of confusing the creative task of the editor, which takes time, with the practical task of making a cut, which takes no time at all. Sam Pollard expressed it this way in an interview with Jennifer M. Wood (*MovieMaker,* Vol. 3, No. 4):

> What's happened now with the digital medium, because everything can be done so fast, is that people don't have the tendency to understand that editing is really about what you think—not about what you do physically. It's really how you think in terms of conceptualizing the way a sequence should unfold [...] How the sequence should build structurally—it's a real thinking process. To me that's the one downside to digital technology. People are so impatient now and things are on TV so quickly, there's no opportunity to think.

An editor should never lose sight of the fact that "why" we make an edit is much more important than "how" we make an edit. This is as important and powerful a question as "Why put the camera here, instead of there?" or "Why use this lens, instead of that lens?" or "Why cast this person in the role instead of that person?" In the next chapter we'll look at the "why" of it, the creative and storytelling dimension of the art of editing.

in practice

Editing Stages Summary

1. *Viewing dailies.* All of the footage must be reviewed, evaluated, and logged. This is done on a high-quality playback system.
2. *Capturing and logging.* All usable footage and double system sound audio (and other project elements) are transferred into the computer for editing, labeled with all logging information, and organized in bins.
3. *Sync dailies.* Done for projects using double system sound and, in the case of film-to-tape material, if the lab has not previously synced dailies.
4. *First assembly.* Scenes and sequences are loosely arranged to determine broad scene sequencing and story structure.
5. *Rough cuts.* Scenes are cut and recut with essential audio through several versions, progressively tightening the film.
6. *Fine cut.* Transitions, small edit adjustments, visual effects, and additional sound tracks are added to finesse the movie into its final form.
7. *Picture lock.* The film is ready for finishing, after all creative editing decisions are done and not another frame will be added or subtracted.
8. *Finishing.* The picture is corrected for color and exposure consistency and all visual effects are fine tuned. The various tracks in the sound design are polished, sweetened and mixed down into one track and the picture is corrected for color and exposure consistency (see Chapter 23 for mixing and Chapter 24 for color correction).
9. *Mastering.* The final film is outputted to tape for mastering (see Chapter 24 for mastering).

The NLE Project Structure (Figure 20-31)
Media Elements

- *Source media* (a.k.a. *original media*). Your media elements *before* they are brought into the NLE environment for editing. This includes your original footage (e.g., DV tape, telecine transfer, or file-based video and audio), music or sound-effects CDs, and graphic files from third-party software (e.g., Photoshop or Illustrator files).
- *Media files.* The media that are created when you capture video or audio from the original source, including video and audio. In FCP the video container format is QuickTime (.mov), and in the Avid system it is MXF. The standard audio format for both is AIFF (.aif). Media files can also be text, photos, or graphics imported from other software applications. Media files are saved on an external HD.
- *Render files.* Media files that are created by the NLE system from rendering special effects (like dissolves, superimpositions, motion effects, etc.).

Editing Elements (in project window/browser)

- *Master clips.* A master clip references the media file. Clips are trimmed, altered, and manipulated during the edit session, but because they are only "pointers" to the media file, all edit decisions occur only virtually, leaving the media unaltered.
- *Subclips.* Smaller clips made from, and referencing, the master clip. Subclips do not reference

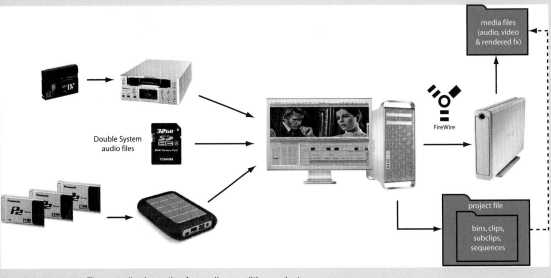

■ **Figure 20-31** The overall schematic of a nonlinear editing project.

in practice

the media file; if you delete the master clip you will lose the subclip information and it will not play.

- *Sequences*. The edited sequence of video, audio, and graphic clips arranged in the order you need to tell your story. Clips used in the sequence are essentially "edited copies" of the information from the master clip, known as "associated clips," and therefore they directly reference the media files. If you delete a master clip, the associated clip within the sequence will play nonetheless. Your movie can comprise only one long sequence or you can create multiple sequences and bring them together later. Multiple sequences can also be used to edit various versions.

Organizational Elements

- *Project*. A top-level folder (located in the project/browser window) that includes all of the elements of the movie, including sequences, bins, clips, and graphics.
- *Bins*. Second-level folders that are used to organize all audio and video clips and graphic files. You can create as many bins as you need to organize your footage.

The Art and Technique of Editing

THE GOLDEN RULE OF POSTPRODUCTION

The one piece of advice that I would impart to anybody who is looking to be an editor or any other aspect of this business is always remember that making movies is about investigating all possibilities. You should always be open to different options. If you get focused into making something one way, you may not make the best film.

The thing that you learn when you're writing a film is that it's the template; it's the foundation. [...] Then when you go into the editing room, that process is the next level of the template. First you have it on paper, now you have it visually and then you have to make it a film.

**Sam Pollard (From "Things I've Learned
as a Filmmaker," *MovieMaker*, Vol. 3, No. 4)**

Professionals who work in postproduction—primarily directors, editors, and sound designers—understand this one fundamental principle: *make the film from what you have, not solely from what is written in the script.* Some time ago I was discussing the process of editing with Sam Pollard (**Figure 21-1**), an accomplished editor (*Mo' Better Blues, Juice, Bamboozled*), producer (*When the Levees Broke, The Blues:"Feel Like Going Home"*), and educator, who told me that he tries not to read the script more than once or twice before he starts to edit—and after that he rarely refers to the script again. Why would this be? There are two reasons.

First, if the director, cinematographer, and art director have done their jobs correctly, they will have improvised here and there and altered details to improve the film from its incarnation as a screenplay. So the actual results—the scenes, performances, footage— coming from production may be quite different from the script. Hopefully the footage reflects a beneficial transformation of the material and one that has taken the editing process into account. Second, as anyone who has been on film sets will tell you, "stuff happens." Just as you may find shots and scenes that weren't in the script that improve the project, you might equally have run out of time and left a few things out or even forgotten a detail or two; the sound from one day can be junk, or an actor had an off day, or the camera was running at 30 frames per second and no one noticed—it happens to everyone. This certainly doesn't mean you don't have a film; it just means you have a slightly different film, one that you will find in the editing process. Whether the footage contains everything called for in the shot list and then some or is missing pieces here and there, the bottom line is that when you bring your footage into postproduction, stay loose and work from what you have. Don't stubbornly hang on to preproduction ideas that are not in the footage, or even if they are—let the movie evolve. Look for new possibilities that will emerge during the cutting and sound design process—they will present themselves to you.

One of the primary reasons that filmmakers break a film-in-process down into little pieces—every shot separate from the others and every type of audio distinct from the others and from the picture—is to allow for maximum creative flexibility in

postproduction. We can put any shot next to any other shot as we see fit, we can lay down any audio track under any sequence, or we can layer tracks and tracks of audio in any configuration that our heart desires—whatever works best for the film. So remember: postproduction isn't just the mechanical construction of the original idea, but postproduction also constitutes the further creative development of your story. It is often said that "editing is your second chance at directing." Something happens when you start connecting one shot with another—a whole new chemistry occurs and new storytelling options emerge. And when you put a piece of music behind your sequences or a slightly different ambient background, the film takes on new life and new energy again. That's the power of postproduction.

■ **Figure 21-1** Producer and editor Sam Pollard works extensively in both narrative and documentary forms.

■ "FIXING IT IN POST"

We've all heard the old adage that we can learn as much, or more, from our mistakes as from our successes; but just like Alexander Fleming's accidental discovery of penicillin, mistakes can be more than hard-knock lessons: they can also be blessings in disguise—if you stay open to the creative possibilities available in postproduction.

Bad Color, Good Concept

Wong Kar-Wai's 1995 movie *Fallen Angels* is widely considered to be the most visually bold, original, and groundbreaking of his early films. The deliriously hedonistic, over-the-top visual style of *Fallen Angels*, which was shot by cinematographer Christopher Doyle, was celebrated by critics and audiences alike (**Figure 21-2**). "We f***** up with the film stock. It was old," said Doyle in an interview with Vicente Rodriguez-Ortega ("Zen Palette," *reverse shot online*, summer

2004). "We couldn't reshoot … so of course it was foggy in color. We said: 'maybe this can represent something so let's pick some other pieces,' and that's what we did. Because of a mistake, a certain structure came out of the film. … What happened was that we gave it a system, so we made the most important parts of each scene in black-and-white. But that was a solution to the problem, not an original concept. We just appropriated the mistake and made it work." It not only worked but it also firmly established the Kar-Wai/Doyle team as a force of stylistic innovation in international cinema. Turning your mistakes into cinematic achievement in the edit … *that* really is innovative.

Sound Design Saves the Picture

In the bold documentary/narrative hybrid film *Close Up* (1990), Abbas Kiarostami follows the real trial of Hossain Sabzian, a man who posed as the famous Iranian film director Mohsen Makhmalbaf, and ingeniously intercuts this documentary footage with a recreation of the events of the crime—showing how the man gradually insinuated himself into the good graces and home of the unsuspecting Ahankhah family. Sabzian and the family portray themselves in these reenactments. Kiarostami planned all along to have the film culminate with a surprise meeting between Sabzian (the imposter) and the real Makhmalbaf on the day he is released from jail. Like the rest of the film, this scene was shot in a documentary style, but with a telephoto lens, from a long distance so that the men wouldn't feel as if they were under a microscope. Each man was wired with a wireless lavaliere to pick up his dialogue from a distance as Kiarostami's film and sound crew

■ **Figure 21-2** Cinematographer Christopher Doyle and director Wong turned a mistake into stylistic innovation by artfully integrating footage shot on bad film stock at key points in *Fallen Angels* (1995).

follow them, in a trailing van, as they drive from the jailhouse to the home of the Ahankhah family on a small motorcycle (**Figure 21-3**).

The first moment is shattering. When Sabzian encounters Makhmalbaf outside the jail, he breaks down in tears and embraces his idol, whom he impersonated. But then, as Kiarostami tells it, Makhmalbaf dominated the conversation and it veered into territory that dissipated the intensity and honesty of Sabzian's moment. Kiarostami felt that his climactic scene was ruined and with it his entire film. This was not a scene that could possibly be reshot, and he felt that he had lost the only possible ending for his movie. Kiarostami says that he went four sleepless nights wondering how he could salvage his film. Then the solution came to him: creative postproduction sound mixing. Kiarostami created a staticky sound effect as if there was a bad microphone connection, which allowed him to simply cut the sound intermittently whenever he chose. He then inserted the off-screen voices of the ostensible "director" and the "sound man," from the trailing van, complaining about the bad connection and about the sound coming in an out. The contrived sound equipment malfunction allowed Kiarostami to preserve what

■ **Figure 21-3** A faux microphone malfunction, created in postproduction, allowed Kiarostami to salvage the emotional climax at the end of his film *Close Up* (1990).

was best about the scene and eliminate what might have destroyed it. It was also a device completely in keeping with the vérité style of the movie. In the end the climax remains Sabzian's moment—utterly moving. *Close Up* went on to establish Kiarostami as one of the foremost directors in the world. The filmmaker himself has said that this is one of his favorite moments in all of his films.

■ WHY WE EDIT I: NARRATIVE ORDER AND EMPHASIS

For my style, for my vision of cinema, editing is not simply one aspect; it is the aspect.
Orson Welles (From *Cahiers du Cinéma*, n°84, 1958)

As an editor, you decide the meaning the spectator is going to get from the combination of pictures and sounds you give. Film [is not] a film until it is edited and that's so important you almost don't see it.
Mathilde Bonnefoy (editor, *Run, Lola, Run*) (From *Edgecodes.com: The Art of Motion Picture Editing* [2004; directed by A. Shuper])

I love editing. I think I like it more than any other phase of filmmaking. If I wanted to be frivolous, I might say that everything that precedes editing is merely a way of producing film to edit. Editing is the only unique aspect of filmmaking which does not resemble any other art form—a point so important it cannot be overstressed. (I know I've already stressed it!) It can make or break a film.
Stanley Kubrick (From *Stanley Kubrick Directs*, by Alexander Walker)

When I was a student, I remember taking an introductory editing class in which the teacher gave seven students exactly the same batch of found footage (which, in fact, consisted of outtakes from several films). Using the outtakes, each student created a film. It was a surprise to the students that the same footage yielded seven very different films; one was even a comedy, while another was edited as a mystery. Now, as a professor, having seen this phenomenon repeated many times, the range of films that can emerge from the very same footage comes as no surprise at all. The differences between all of those student films, made from the same raw materials, were the result of the conceptual plasticity and creative flexibility of the editing process.

The art of telling of a story, even a verbal or written story, involves carefully ordering the events of that tale, controlling the unfolding information, and elevating certain dramatic details over other, more utilitarian, details. We, as filmmakers, don't just objectively show actions; we narrate, which means interpreting the story through the voice of a storyteller. And much of the filmmaker's voice is located in the domain of the editing process. The primary reason we edit is to tell a particular story in our unique way: to guide the audience to see what we want them to see, to understand what we want them to understand, and at the moment when we want them to see and understand it. And, of course, all of this story manipulation is to get them to feel what we want them to feel.

Although one could write volumes trying to define the art of editing in narrative filmmaking, for the sake of concise definitions we could say that **editing** is the process of selecting, arranging, and assembling the essential visual and sound elements to tell a unique version of the story of the film.

Editing for Story Order

Here is a simple three-shot sequence:
a. Sandra drives up to her house and gets out of her car.
b. Sandra walks to the front door, opens it, and discovers …
c. A burglar is in her house stealing her TV!

a   b   c

■ Figure 21-4

These three shots (Figure 21-4), put in this order, tell us the story of Sandra, who comes home one day and discovers a burglar in her house. The film is told strictly from Sandra's point of view, and because of that, we discover the burglary at the same moment she discovers it. It's a shock to all of us, character and audience, when that front door opens.

One of the broader and essential creative considerations in the editing process is **story order**: the shot-by-shot and scene-by-scene unfolding of the events of the story. The same material can yield very different approaches to the same story when placed in a different order. Let's reedit the preceding sequence by simply rearranging the order of shots (Figure 21-5):

a   b   c

■ Figure 21-5

a. A burglar is in Sandra's house stealing her TV!
b. Sandra drives up to her house and gets out of her car.
c. Sandra walks to the front door, opens it, and discovers the burglar.

This sequence no longer develops strictly from Sandra's point of view. Showing the burglary in progress to the audience, before Sandra herself discovers it, gives the audience more information than Sandra has. And what will the audience do with this information? Well, they will certainly anticipate Sandra stumbling upon the burglary in progress, and we hope that they start to fear for her, to worry about what will happen when she opens that door. This is the essence of suspense: give the audience a little bit more information than the character has so that they anticipate the conflict. Not only has the audience's perspective on the events been completely altered simply by rearranging the same shots, but the emotional effect changes also. In the first sequence the emotional effect is surprise, and in the second it is suspense. Both are powerful, so now the director and editor need to choose which one works best for the story.

Editing for Dramatic Emphasis

Imagine the inside of an office in someone's home (**Figure 21-6**):

> *LONG SHOT; A man enters the office and crosses to the desk. Looking for something, he moves stuff around the desktop, knocks a picture frame over, and then opens a drawer and pulls out a letter. He stuffs it into his pocket and leaves.*

Surely we can present this scene in real time—long shot, from one angle, in one single take, with no edits—much the way we would see it in live theater. Some might say that this would be the most democratic way to present the scene, allowing the audience to pick and choose what they wanted to look at and when. But now, let's add emphasis by "cutting into" the scene and highlighting certain details. Here's one interpretation of the preceding scene (**Figure 21-7**):

■ Figure 21-6

a. LONG SHOT; A man enters the office and crosses to a desk. Looking for something, he moves stuff around the desktop and knocks a picture frame over.
b. CUT TO a MEDIUM CLOSE-UP on the drawer as he opens it, revealing a letter.

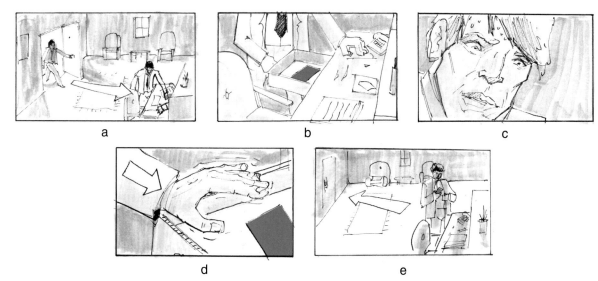

■ Figure 21-7

c. CUT TO a CLOSE-UP of his face looking at the letter; we can see sweat forming on his anxious brow.
d. We CUT back to the drawer (CU) as his trembling hand enters the frame and takes the letter out.
e. CUT back to our LONG SHOT; the man stuffs the letter into his pocket and leaves.

Cutting into the scene with close-ups at just the right moments creates **dramatic emphasis**, a moment of discovery, and turns that letter into a LETTER! In addition, the back-to-back close-ups of the man's anxious face and the letter imply a complicated relationship; it may not be explicit, but clearly that letter is of great importance to him, and we've already started a mystery. The audience is led to wonder, "What is it with that letter?"

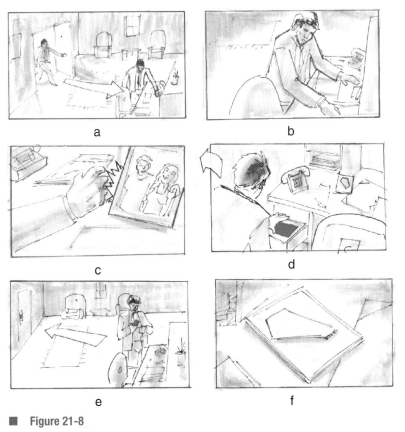

a   b

c   d

e   f

■ **Figure 21-8**

Now, let's try another interpretation through cutting (**Figure 21-8**):
a. LONG SHOT; A man enters the office and crosses to a desk.
b. CUT to a MEDIUM shot as he moves stuff around the desktop, looking for something.
c. CUT TO a CLOSE-UP of a framed photograph of him and a beautiful woman; he carelessly knocks over the photo.
d. CUT back to the MEDIUM shot; as he opens the drawer, pulls out a letter, and stuffs it in his pocket.
e. As he leaves the room we CUT back to the CLOSE-UP (**f**) of the picture frame, tipped over on its face.

Now the scene is no longer about the letter, it's about that photo. We're no longer asking why the man is so anxious about getting that letter; we're asking what it means that he knocked over the photo. We suspect that it will become a clue—someone will know he was here when they notice the photograph knocked out of place. We might even be wondering who that woman is in the photograph.

Beyond the editing, these interpretations obviously also involve slightly different scene coverage, and this is where shooting and editing are absolutely linked. When shooting a scene we must anticipate what the editor will need to create the particular emphasis we are after. This is why the director and D.P. need to "think like editors" on the set—and editing your own films in the beginning will help you understand, in a practical way, what editors need.

> *In telling a story, the task of a director is to emphasize what is significant by underemphasizing what is less so. The actor's performances, the camera's coverage of the performances and the film editor's re-construction of these during post-production: all are designed to make certain things more significant than others to an audience.*
>
> **Alexander Mackendrick (From *On Filmmaking*, 2004)**

Although Mackendrick is talking about the larger task of the director as storyteller, there is a significant lesson in this quote for the editing stage. Films rely extensively on editing to create those dramatically elevated moments and details. However, you can't have dramatic peaks without a few valleys. Most films have moments that must be elevated through expressive or stylized editing to reveal their true dramatic importance, with, say, a well-timed cut to a close-up, or a series of graphically stunning juxtapositions, or energetically disjunctive jump cuts, or whatever visual acrobatics the scene needs. But all narrative films also have many fairly utilitarian passages that just get us from narrative point A to narrative point B, and these should be cut simply and efficiently. And then there are those scenes of enormous dramatic importance that acquire their power *without* the intervention of editing. In these cases, the primary dramatic weight is not necessarily carried by the editing but perhaps instead by the dialogue or the mise-en-scène. These scenes, too, are either cut very simply or, in some cases, not edited at all. Keep in mind that *not* cutting is an editorial decision, too, and it can be a powerful one.

in practice

Martin Scorsese's *Raging Bull* (1980) brilliantly illustrates the use of stylized editing, functional editing, and expressive nonediting approaches, all within the same film. Editor Thelma Schoonmaker, a long-time collaborator with Scorsese, won an Academy Award in 1980 for her work on *Raging Bull*, which itself constitutes a complete textbook on editing and sound design.

Stylized editing: "Sugar Ray Robinson, Round 13"
Among the great achievements in cinema for editing (and sound design) is the "Sugar Ray Robinson, Round 13" fight scene (**Figure 21-9**). It stands as a tour de force of rhythm, energy, and raw impact accomplished through editing and sound. This scene is central in the movie because it is more than a boxing match: it is the moment when Jake LaMotta allows Robinson to savagely beat him as an act of contrition and sacrifice for the violence he has visited on the people he loves, namely his wife Vickie and his brother Joey. In planning the scene, Scorsese looked to the famous "shower" murder sequence in Hitchcock's *Psycho* for inspiration. What he admired about that scene was that "every shot had its own energy." Scorsese meticulously storyboarded each and every shot in the fight sequence himself—shot

■ **Figure 21-9** The speed, power, ferocity, and pain as Jake LaMotta (Robert De Niro) is pummeled by Sugar Ray Robinson (Johnny Barnes) is vividly conveyed through the stylized editing of Thelma Schoonmaker.

size, movement, and angle. Continuity was not a huge concern for this sequence, as Scorsese said during a filmmaking master class: "I wanted every shot to have enough raw energy that we could edit them in any configuration and it would work."

Thelma Schoonmaker worked with that visual energy and employed everything from perfectly matched action edits to intentional jump cuts to convey to the audience what it must feel like to be in a ring with a prizefighter who is trying to knock you out. In her hands, time becomes completely elastic; moments are extended by packing in multiple shots between a raised fist and its crushing blow, yet later a flurry of ferocious punches are cut so quickly that they all seem to land on LaMotta's face within a fraction of a second. Relatively long shots are juxtaposed with images just a few frames long; Schoonmaker duplicates actions and creates jarring edits between radically different angles and different frame rates. Scorsese and Schoonmaker vividly create an altered state in which time itself alternately slows down and abruptly lurches forward. There's pain, numbness, power, brutality, and beauty. The walls spin, punches come out of nowhere; what you thought was up is down. This is precisely the feeling they wanted to convey. Strict adherence to rules of continuity and the 180° line would be antithetical to the chaotic, visceral experience of being in the boxing ring getting your head beaten in.

Simple editing, shot/reverse shot: "Pelham Parkway, 1950"

Earlier in the film, after Jake wins the boxing title from Cerdan, his personal life completely falls apart and he succumbs to jealous paranoia about his wife being unfaithful. One scene (**Figure 21-10**), which begins innocuously with Jake and his brother trying to get a TV to work, carefully traces the workings of his deluded mind as he falls so deeply into suspicion

that he asks his own brother if he's had sex with his wife. This scene is the beginning of a slow burn sequence that culminates, several scenes later, in a violent rage against those who love Jake the most. Here we recognize the point of the scene through the dialogue, which reveals the tangled logic of a dangerously warped mind. The scene is shot and edited in a simple shot/reverse shot structure—starting wide and moving in tighter as the conversation becomes more intense. It adheres to the principles of continuity, maintaining proper looking direction and angles and never once crossing the line of action. Understanding that the dialogue is doing the heavy lifting in the scene, Thelma Schoonmaker knows that the editing doesn't need to be acrobatic, despite the tension and simmering violence, and should simply support the rhythms of this disturbing interrogation.

Unbroken shots: "Dade County Stockade"

Toward the very end of the film, Jake LaMotta's fall from glory is nearly total. He's an overweight has-been running a tacky nightclub in Florida. He has no friends and has long alienated anyone who once loved him, most importantly Vickie and Joey. He is picked up by the police for allowing a 14-year-old girl into his nightclub and is thrown into the Dade County stockade. Totally alone, stuck in a cage, Jake hits rock bottom. The realization of what he is and what he's done overwhelms him and he releases his anger onto himself. Screaming "Why, why, why?" and calling himself "stupid," he ferociously beats his head and fists against the concrete walls of the jail cell (**Figure 21-11**), inflicting the same physical punishment on himself that he's inflicted on everyone else throughout the film, whether a boxing opponent or family member. When his anger is spent, he collapses onto the jail cell bed and cries, "I'm not an animal." In this devastating scene, a man is realizing that he is an animal, like a raging bull, and Robert De Niro's performance is

■ **Figure 21-10** The unobtrusive editing in the "Pelham Parkway, 1950" scene supports the tension that is simmering in the dialogue.

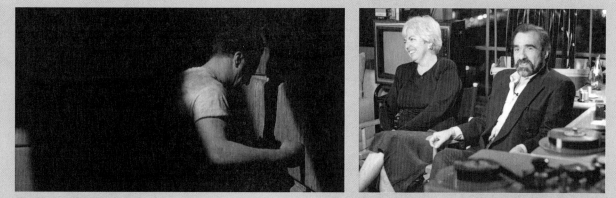

■ **Figure 21-11** A good editor also understands when it is more powerful *not* to cut into a scene, as in the "Dade County Stockade" scene *(left)*. Editor Thelma Schoonmaker with Martin Scorsese in the editing room *(right)*.

shattering. The scene lasts for over two minutes and there is only one discrete cut. Knowing that editing would diffuse the power of the scene, Scorsese and Schoonmaker allow the moment to play out, in real time—essentially unbroken. Because the scene is unbroken, the audience becomes not so much viewers but witnesses to this man's most private and pathetic pain. It's so uncomfortable for the audience that we want to look away; we're begging for a cut to show us something else, and we secretly want a little bit of "editing style" as an emotional buffer, reminding us that it's only a movie. We need anything that could take us away from Jake's naked misery. But Scorsese and Schoonmaker don't cut away and they don't flinch; they keep us right in there, in that cell with Jake as he reaches the nadir of his life. We thought it was tough being in the boxing ring with Jake, with all of those punches coming out of nowhere, but the Dade County stockade proves to be much rougher.

We have already discussed many of the fundamental shooting and editing patterns in Chapters 3 and 4. It might be helpful to review them again in the context of this editing chapter:

- Shots, sequences, and scenes (page 43)
- Juxtaposition and cumulative meaning (page 44)
- Continuity shooting and editing (Chapter 4)
- 180° principle and the 20mm/30° rule (pages 68–70)
- Match action cuts (page 70)
- Shot/reverse shot technique (pages 73–77)
- POV sequences (page 79)
- Moving people through space and elliptical editing (pages 82–84)
- Meeting and chase/follow sequences (page 85)
- Parallel action sequences (including temporal, graphic, and action matches) (page 86)
- Jump cuts and long takes (pages 94–95)

Fundamental Image-to-Image Transitions

To be sure, there are many ways to get from one shot to another, but in the world of narrative filmmaking, there are really only three bread-and-butter transitions that constitute the vast majority of visual transitions in films throughout history: the cut, the dissolve, and the fade. Sure, there are others transitions, but they're specialty effects that are concocted when the need arises from a special circumstance. But these three—cuts, dissolves, and fades—are the core.

The Cut

For the most part in this chapter and in the previous chapters, we're exploring the function, power, and versatility of the cut, which is the joining of two shots such that the last frame of the first shot is directly spliced to the first frame of the next shot. The visual shift in a cut from one shot to the next is sequential, instantaneous, and complete. First we're looking at a man running out of an apartment ... CUT; now we're looking at a picture frame on a desk. A direct cut is by far the most commonly used shot-to-shot transition in film, and we have already explored some of the vast spatial, temporal, and narrative associations created by adjoining two images and some of the numerous techniques for making a cut work. This chapter sheds some light on a few additional creative considerations, beyond the formally conventional, for making cuts work expressively in your films.

in practice

One of the most famous cuts in motion picture history is the elliptical edit from Kubrick's *2001: A Space Odyssey* (1968), in which the image leaps hundreds of thousands of years, from man's first major evolutionary step, the discovery of "tools" (a bone notably used as a weapon) to our next evolutionary step, a moment in the space-age in which the dominance of man and technology over nature is superseded by an alien intelligence, perhaps a deity, which is unfathomable. This single instantaneous edit seems to imply, by skipping over our entire history, that everything in between these two evolutionary points was comparatively insignificant, amounting simply to the development of more tools with which to conquer nature on Earth, in space, and even man's own nature (**Figure 21-12**).

This is an **intellectual edit**; yes, it moves the story forward, fast forward as it were, but it also invites us to think thematically about why these two particular moments are juxtaposed. Encouraging this deeper connection is the fact that this is a **formal edit**; it is both a **match on action cut** (see page 70) and a **graphic match** (see page 464). The physical similarities between the shape of the bone and the orbiting nuclear-powered satellite make the point that the primitive tool and the sophisticated satellite are fundamentally more similar than they are different. Kubrick does not want us to be awash in emotions in this film; he wants us to put the pieces together, and, in encouraging us to think about the relationship between shots and events of the story, we are also inevitably led to ponder our own place in the universe.

■ **Figure 21-12** Elliptical edit, from Kubrick's *2001: A Space Odyssey* (1968) (editor, Ray Lovejoy). This single cut takes us from the "dawn of man" to the end of mankind as we've known it.

The Dissolve

The dissolve is a transition in which the first shot gradually disappears (fades out) as the second shot gradually appears (fades in). With a dissolve we see, for a moment, the merging of both images on the screen simultaneously. A dissolve can have any duration the filmmaker needs, from a few frames that overlap to dissolves that occur over many seconds, becoming a prolonged superimposition (two images layered over one another) before giving way to the second shot entirely. Because the dissolve holds both images and is a shot-to-shot transition that occurs over time, the audience is invited to think about the deeper relationship between the two shots. Dissolves are often used to imply a temporal shift, or a change in location on a more thematic level. They're also used as a transitional device that implies a character-based psychological motivation for the transition, like moving into a memory, dream, or fantasy. A dissolve

■ THE DISSOLVE

Anthony Minghella's *The English Patient* (1996) (edited by Walter Murch) is set during the final days of World War II and revolves around the memories of Hungarian Count Almásy, a cartographer, who has been severely burned in a plane crash. Almásy recounts to his attending nurse the story of his complex and tragic involvement with Katherine Clifton. Dissolves are often used to bring us into and out of the flashback sequences, which take place much earlier in North Africa (**Figure 21-13**).

In one flashback scene Almásy and Katherine are stranded in a truck during a fierce sandstorm. As Almásy talks to her, Katherine reaches up and touches the window of the truck, behind which the sandstorm is raging. This image dissolves slowly into the horribly burned face of the "present day"

Almásy, bringing us out of the memory. The merging of her hand and his face looks for a moment as if she, a woman who in the present tense is dead, is caressing his face. The dissolve not only brings us back in time, but it intimately and viscerally connects Almásy to his now dead lover. It is as if he, by conjuring her memory, can still feel Katherine's caress, her hand on his face.

Michael Ondaatje, the author of the novel on which the film was based, said this of that specific dissolve: "It's a remarkable scene and it suggests so many things, of compassion and forgiveness; all of these things that are there, again, is that emotional result of that technical device that makes it work" [from *Edgecodes.com: The Art of Motion Picture Editing* (2004; directed by A. Shuper)]. Once again we hear expressed the interconnection between technology and artistic expression.

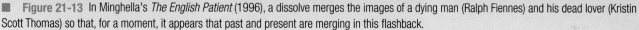

Figure 21-13 In Minghella's *The English Patient* (1996), a dissolve merges the images of a dying man (Ralph Fiennes) and his dead lover (Kristin Scott Thomas) so that, for a moment, it appears that past and present are merging in this flashback.

is a transition that promises something to the audience. It says, "look at these two images merging, think about it"; the complex associative relationship between these images is developing.

The dissolve can be a powerful transition, but it is frequently abused, especially in the era of digital editing where a simple movement of a mouse can create a dissolve. Any film professor can tell you stories of students whose footage isn't cutting together well and who simply plop a dissolve between every shot, hoping to "smooth out" the rough edges. The effect of using dissolves willy-nilly is to strip them of their expressive potential, which they can retain only through careful and restrained use.

The Fade

The **fade-out** is a slow disappearing of an image into a color, and a **fade-in** is the slow appearing of the image from a color. Most commonly, one sees a fade to (or from) black, and a little less frequently, a fade to (or from) white. Very often a fade-out and fade-in are used back to back as a transition from one image to another. In other words, from the first image we fade to black and then we fade up from black to bring in the second image. Again, the duration of the fades and the black between the images can be short or long, depending on the effect you want. The **fade-out/fade-in** technique is frequently used as a time ellipse or to punctuate a major shift in the dramatic direction of the movie. There is a strong sense of closure after a fade-out, and if followed by a fade-in, the audience feels a sense of a new beginning.

■ THE FADE

Orson Welles' seminal film *Citizen Kane* (1941) tells the fictional life story of the powerful and imposing Charles Foster Kane through the device of a reporter, Mr. Thompson, who is trying to solve the mystery of the last word Kane uttered on his death-bed, "Rosebud." Thompson follows up on numerous leads, hoping to discover the essence of Kane's life, primarily by interviewing anyone who knew Kane personally. In the end, the film compiles an intricate and multifaceted portrait of a man through multiple perspectives. Each source of information is handled as a separate chapter, and Welles often uses fades to delineate these various accounts. For example,

early in the film Thompson tries to interview Susan Alexander Kane, "the second Mrs. Kane." But Miss Alexander is drunk and in no mood to talk. When it's clear that the "Alexander chapter" has yielded everything it can concerning "Rosebud," which is essentially nothing, Welles fades out to black and then fades up on a statue of Walter Parks Thatcher at the Thatcher memorial library, where Thompson is given access to Mr. Thatcher's journals. We then begin a new account of Charles Foster Kane from the perspective of Thatcher's diary, pages 83 to142 to be precise. The use of this fade-out/fade-in is Welles' way of turning the page, closing off one chapter and opening on the next (**Figure 21-14**).

■ **Figure 21-14** This fade-out/fade-in from *Citizen Kane* (1941) effectively closes off one investigative lead and introduces another "chapter" (Editor, Robert Wise).

■ WHY WE EDIT II: EXTRA-NARRATIVE CONSIDERATIONS

Although we've looked at some of the more systematic approaches to cutting shots and sequences in previous chapters, let's now fill in some of the gaps and add a few more creative considerations that inform editing decisions. Editing for dramatic structure or continuity is only part of the editor's expressive vocabulary. When you listen to professional editors talk, they often use words like "rhythm," "feeling," "pace," and "energy." Great editors and great musicians are a lot alike: great musicians, while thoroughly understanding the formal aspects of their craft (i.e., how to play their instrument, musical scales, harmonic modulation), also play from their gut to "get it right." As jazz great Duke Ellington reminds us, "It don't mean a thing if it ain't got that swing." Well, it's the same with film-making, and the editing process is where a movie finds its "swing."

Given that editing is a craft that involves sequencing, action, and movement played out over time, there are limits to what can be illustrated with words and still frames. I have used a lot of examples from films in this section and encourage the reader (the serious student of film) to rent the films and watch these examples play out in time and in the context of the larger story, to really fill out these lessons.

Temporal Editing: Condensing and Expanding Time

Time is an endlessly elastic entity in the hands of a screenwriter, director, and editor. Some films tell a story whose events take place over two hours, in two hours; these are **real-time** films. Other films will take two hours to tell stories that occur over two days, or two years, or two hundred years. Look at the example from *2001: A Space Odyssey* (see **Figure 21-12**). One edit covers 200,000 years! Some people call this **reel time** (alluding to a film reel).

There are a few notable examples in the history of cinema of entire feature films that play out in real time—Hitchcock's *Rope* (1948), Chantal Akerman's *Jeanne Dielman, 23 Quai du Commerce, 1080 Bruxelles* (1976), Aleksandr Sokurov's *Russian Ark* (2002), and

Agnès Varda's *Cleo from 5 to 7* (1961) (**Figure 21-15**), to name a few. But for the most part, these films are exceptions, even within the broader oeuvres of these particular filmmakers. When speaking about examples of real time, it is far more common to see films that follow a one-shot-per-scene pattern. For many filmmakers, like Jim Jarmusch, Abbas Kiarostami, Agnès Varda, Andrei Tarkovsky, Tsai Ming-Liang, and Hou Hsiao-Hsien (to name only a few), most scenes (short or long) unfold in real time with unedited shots—then it is only the cut from one scene to the next that provides any sort of time ellipsis from one moment to the next. The one-shot-per-scene strategy often requires careful choreography between camera and subjects (especially if both are moving) and can provide a direct connection between the viewer and the actions on the screen because it feels as if there is no third-party inter-

Figure 21-15 Varda's *Cleo from 5 to 7* (1961) is one of a handful of films that play out in real time.

mediary manipulating space, time, or our attention through editing. Cristian Mingui's 2008 film *4 Months, 3 Weeks, 2 Days* is a brilliant example of the intense intimacy that can be created by this method (**Figure 21-16**).

We decided from the beginning to have, as much as possible, one shot per scene. There are a lot of ways to shoot one shot per scene. Finally, we decided what would serve the story was not to make ourselves visible as authors. We wanted to tell the story so the audience would feel that they witness the emotions of the girls in front of them. [...] We couldn't make any sketches or storyboard because we had to stage everything like in theater. There is no editing, basically. It's important to find the right rhythm of the film and figure out the right place to put the camera for which to capture the scene; this generated the position of the characters.

Cristian Mungiu (From *Q&A: Cristian Mungiu* by Patrick Z. McGavin, StopSmiling Online, February 26, 2008)

One primary task of film editing, from larger structural choices to cutting within scenes, is to **compress time** for efficiency's sake, and we've already explored the temporal and spatial economy of elliptical editing (see page 83). However, beyond simple storytelling efficiency (i.e., taking out the unnecessary bits), the elliptical edit can also be used as a strategy to create highly expressive moments. A great example is the abduction scene from Stephen Gaghan's *Syriana* (2005) (edited by Tim Squyres). The scene (**Figure 21-17**) begins with CIA operative Bob Barnes returning to his hotel room, having just been told by another CIA agent that the Prince Nasir Al-Subaai will be kidnapped and killed. While standing at his window, watching for evidence of the pending kidnapping, Barnes is suddenly grabbed from behind by four men who throw him to the ground, tie him up, drag him out of his room, and toss him into the back of a waiting SUV. Barnes was set up. It was he who was the kidnapping target after all. But by whom? Why?

The kidnapping sequence, which in real time would likely take several minutes at least, takes 35 seconds and is accomplished in 18 quick shots. The quickness of the actions and rapid edits reinforces the fact that this was totally unexpected and takes Barnes (and us) completely by surprise. The action is over "in a flash," certainly before he (or we) can figure out what's going on. Just like Barnes, we're left in a state of breathless confusion about what just happened. The highly elliptical, noncontinuity, rapid cutting also infuses the scene with the "feeling" of the brutal efficiency and the instantaneous change of fortunes on this level of espionage.

Figure 21-16 The verbal banter is totally banal in this long static shot from Mingui's *4 Months, 3 Weeks, 2 Days* (2008), yet the dramatic tension is excruciating as we must sit at the table with Otilia (Anamaria Marinca) for a full 11 minutes knowing she is desperately needed elsewhere but cannot leave.

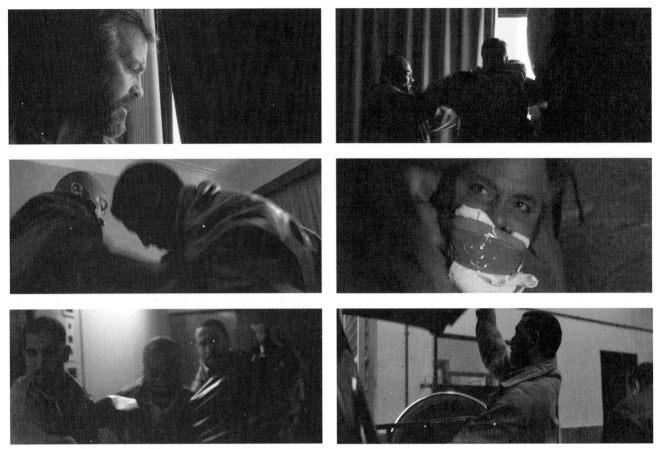

■ **Figure 21-17** In *Syriana* (2005), the six shots of Bob Barnes' (George Clooney) kidnapping are edited with rapid jump cuts to connect the audience to the confusion that Barnes must be experiencing, as well as to the professional efficiency of this brutal act.

■ **Figure 21-18** Dissolves *(top)* and jump cuts *(bottom)* are used in this party scene from Soderbergh's *Traffic* (2000) to both condense time and convey a sense of drug-induced disorientation.

In a central scene in Soderbergh's *Traffic* (2000) (edited by Stephen Mirrione), the drug czar's daughter, Caroline (Erika Christensen), and her friends are having a drug party in her living room. This scene uses two different edit transitions to imply the passing of time (**Figure 21-18**). Frequent jump cuts lurch us forward in little, discontinuous bits of time, while slow dissolves give us the feeling that hours and hours are passing while these kids do nothing but drink, snort coke, and engage in mindless banter. The cumulative effect of these two elliptical devices is remarkable because, while the editing does in fact greatly condense time (the scene lasts only 3 minutes and 10 seconds), it "feels" like they, and we, have been in that living room all night long. In addition, the jump cuts reinforce the partiers' disorientation as a result of their drug-induced state.

Although the majority of temporal editing is done to condense time, editing also has the ability to **expand** or even **suspend time** as well. There are more or less obvious ways to use this technique, depending on how apparent you want the device to be. Rob Reiner's *Misery* (1990) (edited by Robert Leighton) employs a subtle but effective time expansion device that is commonly used to heighten suspense. The famous novelist Paul Sheldon is wheelchair bound and literally imprisoned by the violently unpredictable Annie, his most ardent fan, after she rescues him from a terrible car accident. In one scene, while Annie is away, Paul picks the lock on the door of his room and ventures into the rest of the house to find a way out. He is some distance from his room when he hears Annie's car coming up the driveway.

■ **Figure 21-19** The edits in this sequence from Reiner's *Misery* (1990) add tension and drama by making it seem that it takes forever for Paul (James Caan) to travel a few feet in his effort to avoid Annie (Kathy Bates).

Paul must not be discovered out of his room or he'll face Annie's wrath, so he races down the hallway to his room, and that action is intercut with Annie walking to the house and up the front stairs (**Figure 21-19**). But each time we cut back to Paul, furiously rolling his wheelchair down the hall, he seems to be getting nowhere; it's taking him forever to get down that short little hallway! Editorially speaking, each time we cut to Paul he is a bit farther back than we left him in the previous shot, so he is in fact traveling over some of the same territory. So not only time but also distance seems to be elongating for Paul, while Annie makes quick progress to the front door of the house. The longer it takes Paul to get down the hallway, the more anxiety the audience feels for him. The editor expands Paul's trip down the hallway, not so much that it's visibly obvious, but just enough that we feel the suspense more intensely, causing us to scream to ourselves, "Go faster, Paul. Go!" Horror, action, and mystery genres thrive on this sort of emotional manipulation, this delicious, suspenseful anxiety.

Overlap editing is one of the more stylistically overt devices for suspending time, and it is often used to punctuate a heightened moment. **Overlap editing** is the obvious repetition of the same moment, action, or gesture several times—sometimes from different camera angles. In Mike Nichols' *The Graduate* (1967) (edited by Sam O'Steen), the recently graduated Benjamin finds himself alone with Mrs. Robinson, an old friend of his parents, in her house. She proceeds to seduce the highly confused Benjamin. When he refuses her advances, she slyly manages to get him into her daughter's bedroom, where she pounces. The moment Mrs. Robinson enters the bedroom, totally naked, and locks the door behind her, Benjamin's head turns in total surprise—not once, not twice, but three complete times (**Figure 21-20**). Benjamin's stupefaction at that moment—his shock, confusion, and panic—is brilliantly punctuated by duplicating the gesture and extending the moment of discovery with an overtly stylistic flourish (not to mention that it's funny, too). The continuation of the scene is also wonderfully edited. Benjamin doesn't want to, but he can't help looking at Mrs. Robinson's body, and his attracted-but-reluctant POV is reflected in little rapid close-up insert shots of various parts of her naked body, intercut with his furtive glances (**Figure 21-21**)—which brings us to our next editing consideration: timing, rhythm, and pace.

Timing, Rhythm, and Pace

Timing

Timing refers to the specific placement of a shot within the sequence, meaning the precise moment one cuts to a new shot for maximum impact. Good editors have a sixth sense for timing: it seems to be in their bones; the rest of us experiment—we try an edit

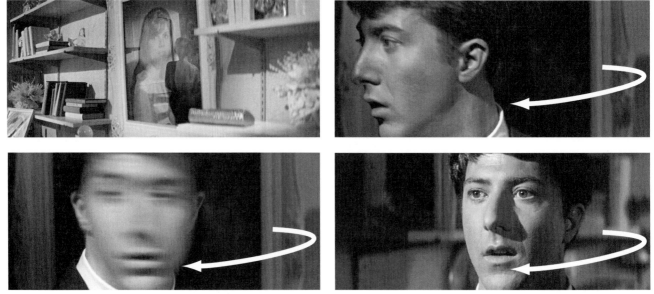

■ **Figure 21-20** In Nichols' *The Graduate* (1967), the moment when Benjamin (Dustin Hoffman) sees Mrs. Robinson (Anne Bancroft) naked is punctuated by three quick shots of him turning his head, edited together.

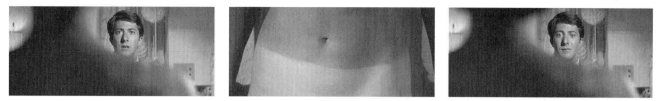

■ **Figure 21-21** The rapid intercutting between Mrs. Robinson's naked body parts and Benjamin's stare in *The Graduate* mimic his inability to keep his eyes off her even though he doesn't want to look.

here or there and then trim it until it's right. One good example of a sharp, perfectly timed edit is the first moment of death for Charlie Company in Terrence Malick's World War II film *The Thin Red Line* (1998) (edited by Saar Klein), which is edited with absolutely precise timing.

At 45 minutes into *The Thin Red Line,* Charlie Company has already landed on Guadalcanal and the men have made their way to the front lines, where the Japanese are firmly dug in. Up to this point the company has seen only the aftermath of war during encounters with American soldiers returning from battle but they have suffered no casualties themselves. At the edge of the Japanese fortifications, a Second Lieutenant, on orders from the First Lieutenant, sends the first two soldiers out to press forward and scout. Slowly, carefully, they move toward the heavily armed Japanese bunkers while everyone watches (**Figure 21-22**). Although the audience can feel the apprehension, visually the journey doesn't seem so dangerous—the soldiers travel across a stunningly beautiful hill covered with long, brilliantly green grasses, gently swaying in a soft breeze. Suddenly, seemingly out of the blue—Bap! Bap!—two quick gunshots from the top of the hill, and both men drop. Before they even hit the ground, Malick cuts to the stunned Second Lieutenant and then quickly to the stunned First Lieutenant. They blink hard, staring in disbelief, trying to comprehend what just happened, in a flash—Bap! Bap!—just like that, two men dead. Is that possible? That swiftly, that easily, life is gone? We, too, like the First and Second Lieutenants, are stunned and disbelieving. Malick's strategy, not to linger on the deaths but to rapidly show the witnesses who are just as shocked as we are, compels us to ask the same questions they must be asking. The environment seemed so beautiful and quiet—how can death be so close? The precision of the editing, just a few quick cuts, constructs a huge existential moment from very little and dramatically understated material.

■ **Figure 21-22** The rapid cutting, from the falling soldiers to their stunned commanding officers, reflects the fragility of life in a war situation in Malick's *The Thin Red Line* (1998).

Verbal and visual timing are, of course, essential for comedy, too. A genuinely funny joke will elicit only a polite chuckle if the punch line isn't delivered with just the right timing—trust me on this one: I know! On the other hand, something decidedly silly can have people rolling on the floor in hysterical laughter, if the delivery is sharp. It's the same with editing a film that hopes to provoke laughter, and in comedy everything is secondary to making people laugh. The comic timing in Bobby and Peter Farrelly's 1998 comedy *There's Something about Mary* (edited by Christopher Greenbury) is flawless. One editing tactic the Farrelly Brothers frequently use is to allude to something off screen but not reveal it until the moment is just right.

Early in the film, when teenage Ted is getting ready to take his dream girl to the prom, he goes to the bathroom to relieve himself. As he does so, he glances out the window at a pair of cooing doves—the perfect image for how he feels, but when the doves fly away they reveal a half-naked Mary, with her mother, at her bedroom window getting dressed. They naturally assume Ted is a peeping tom, and in his haste to get out and explain himself, he zips up too quickly and, well, gets his "frank and beans" mangled in his zipper. A few scenes later, the bathroom is filled with Mary's parents, a police officer, and a fireman, all staring at his zipper predicament.

■ **Figure 21-23** The careful timing of the edits in this scene from the Farrelly Brothers' *There's Something about Mary* (1998) creates a terrific punch line to a painfully funny situation.

The cop decides to resolve the situation and approaches to unzip his fly to free him from the zipper's teeth. He tells Ted it'll be "just like taking off a Band-Aid" (Figure 21-23). Below the frame line, the cop takes hold of the zipper and counts "A-one, and a-two, and a-...." Just then, the they cut to a close-up of a person we've never seen before—now outside. Huh? And the person screams, "We've got a bleeder!" The next quick cut is a wide shot. Poor Ted is on a stretcher, a towel covering his wound, and the entire neighborhood is watching as he's rushed into a waiting ambulance by the EMTs. All of the audience's anxiety, built up while anticipating the pain of the cop's brutal action, is funneled through those two quick edits into the punch line of the joke. We feel the pain, understand the bloody aftermath, and laugh, all at the same time. At the conclusion of Ted's tragic and traumatic prom night, as the ambulance takes him to the hospital, he starts to cry and the Farrellys cut to ... years later, a scene in which adult Ted is on a therapist's couch. Again, a sharp edit efficiently and comically tells us that he's still suffering the psychic wounds of that fateful night at Mary's house.

Rhythm

Rhythm within a sequence refers to the duration of the shots relative to each other, and the patterns of emphasis, or pulses, these durations create. If you consider an edited shot as a pulse or a beat, like a musical beat, then you will be able to manipulate the duration of these image "beats" to create regular, irregular, or syncopated visual rhythms. For example, if you were to edit a sequence such that every shot was exactly 24 frames, then the sequence would have a constant rhythmic beat, as if it were cut to a metronome, and each image would have equal weight in the sequence. Cutting a sequence of shots that are all 48 frames long would obviously be slower and longer, but it would also have a very even rhythm. If, however, you were to cut your film in a pattern in which three shots had 12 frames and the fourth shot had 48 frames, and repeated this twice, you would get a visual rhythm in which there was a strong accent on the fourth and eighth shots, not unlike the opening of Beethoven's Fifth Symphony (da, da, da, duummmm/da, da, da, duummmm).

Obviously, finding a cutting rhythm is much more organic than arbitrarily imposing frame counts to edited shots. The visual cutting strategy of a sequence can find the drive for its rhythm in a number of places, especially action within the frame, camera movement, dialogue rhythms, or beats in the music sound track. The opening sequence in Fernando Meirelles and Kátia Lund's film *City of God* (2002) (edited by Daniel Rezende) intercuts between

■ **Figure 21-24** A clever POV sequence serves as a metaphor for the violence found in the favelas of Meirelles and Lund's *City of God* (2002).

■ **Figure 21-25** The jarring editing style and lapses in continuity augment the energetic introduction of the street gangs in *City of God*.

two scenes with contrasting visual rhythms. The very first scene plunges the audience into the sounds, colors, people, food, music, and dangers of the favelas of Rio de Janeiro. A street party is in progress with food being prepared and music playing. The sequence is put together with familiar editing patterns. For example, there is a POV sequence involving a tied up chicken; the chicken looks (looking shot) and sees a knife cutting the throat of another chicken (POV shot), and when we cut back to the chicken (reaction shot) we see panic in his eyes (thank you, Mr. Kuleshov) (**Figure 21-24**). The chicken then tries to pull free of his bindings (cause and effect). Once the chicken is free, a chase sequence ensues, with gun-wielding kids trying to kill the frantic chicken in the alleys of the favela (**Figure 21-25**).

However, while the basic patterns are familiar, the editing (and camera work) does not strictly adhere to the rules of continuity. Through rapid cutting, combined with dynamic visual discontinuity and percussive jump cuts, the editor creates a visual equivalent for the driving and syncopated Brazilian Batucada rhythms that play on the sound track. By varying the length of shots, which creates surprising accents throughout the scene, the cutting assiduously avoids a constant rhythm. Instead, the cuts create a complex syncopated visual rhythm that instantly holds the audience through its momentum and visual audacity. The propulsive energy of the scene would be destroyed by smooth, continuity style cuts, perfect matches on action, strict adherence to the 180° rule, and editing that was too metrically regular. When you watch this sequence, you can turn off the sound track and still dance to it!

During the dynamically rhythmic chicken chase scene, the film cuts to Buscapé, the level-headed protagonist of the film, who is casually walking and talking with a friend (**Figure 21-26**). Buscapé has a calm, thoughtful,

■ **Figure 21-26** Buscapé's (Alexandre Rodrigues) introduction in *City of God* is marked by a shift in editing and cinematographic styles, immediately establishing him as a level-headed, decent character.

and sensible demeanor (and no gun). The editing abruptly stops and yields to a long, steady shot that reveals this shift in character energy. Within the first minutes of the movie, we "feel," through the shift in editing rhythm, the contrast between Buscapé and the activity of the streets around him—which is one essential dimension of the conflict driving the film.

Pace

Pace (also called **tempo**) is, of course, related to rhythm, in that it is determined by the duration of shots next to other shots, but pace refers specifically to the rate of speed that a scene, or sequence of scenes, plays out. A **fast-paced** editing approach can suggest intensity, excitement, energy, or even confusion or chaos, depending on the narrative context. **Slowly paced** editing can lend a feeling of casualness, fluidity, calm, contemplation, or even torpor or stasis to a movie, again depending on the story.

The storyline of a film often suggests an overall pace, or tempo, and is an important consideration that can be incorporated right up in the scripting stage by carefully controlling the length of scenes on the page. Overall tempo is then carried through in the production phase by controlling the length of shots, number of shots, and camera movements, and then is finally realized in the editing room. However, very few films strictly maintain a single pace from beginning to end. Contrasting the pace of scenes is an important tool for creating narrative emphasis and a general sense for overall story shape.

Thomas McCarthy's film *The Station Agent* (2003) (edited by Tom McArdle) is about Finbar McBride, a dwarf who inherits a pathetic little plot of land in New Jersey and simply wants to live his life in calm solitude doing what he loves the most, train watching (**Figure 21-27**). The pace of this film is broad, calm, and contemplative; Finbar is in no hurry, so neither is the editing pace. However, as Finbar becomes reluctantly involved in the dramatic personal lives of his neighbors, he is eventually forced to confront that which he sought to escape—his own loneliness. In one extraordinary scene (**Figure 21-28**), Finbar becomes drunk in a bar, and the suppressed anger and frustration he's been holding suddenly erupts and this normally quiet and reserved man becomes publicly confrontational. To emphasize this profoundly disquieting moment, the editing pace accelerates and the length of each cut decreases.

Associative Editing

Associative edits are cuts that are designed to build additional meaning by juxtaposing two shots together with a stylized technique that encourages the audience to *think* about the connection. Broadly speaking, associative editing works by comparing or contrasting the content of the shots to create an association that is not contained in the individual shots. The connective content can be either the **formal/graphic** compositional elements of the frame (e.g., color, shape, and movement) or the **thematic/metaphoric** elements (based on actions and other visual detail), and these properties provide a link between

■ **Figure 21-27** The leisurely pace of McCarthy's *The Station Agent* (2003) is exemplified by this 30-second shot of the main characters watching a train roll along.

■ **Figure 21-28** A change in the pace of the cutting effectively foreshadows Finbar's (Peter Dinklage) outburst in this scene from McCarthy's *The Station Agent* (2003).

shots that don't otherwise have an immediate, direct, or obvious narrative connection. We have already explored this phenomenon of creating an association between two juxtaposed images in its most basic form, with the examples from Kuleshov and Lucas (see page 45). But there can be more overt and complex connections created through associative editing; these encourage the audience to think instead of merely responding emotionally, which is why this technique is also referred to as **intellectual editing.** Again, we saw a classic example of this technique in our discussion of *2001: A Space Odyssey.* In the cut shown in **Figure 21-12**, Kubrick used a strong **formal/graphic edit** (on shape and movement) to forge a metaphoric connection between a bone and an orbiting satellite.

In *Natural Born Killers* (1994), Oliver Stone and editors Brian Berdan and Hank Corwin use extremely fast, disjunctive, highly associative editing and wildly stylized camera work to depict the vicious anarchy of Mickey and Mallory's killing sprees. In several episodes, Stone cuts in (or projects right onto the scene) images of horses, snakes, spiders, and rabbits that do not come from the world of the film but are inserted to create metaphoric visual links that force us to consider the murderous brutality of Mickey and Mallory in the context of predator and prey and the cruel laws of nature (**Figure 21-29**). Where does the ability to kill come from? Is it natural or is it a by-product of our particularly violent culture? These questions are posed relentlessly through associative editing. Are Mickey and Mallory natural born killers, as the title suggests? Or have they been shaped by a violent upbringing and a sick society? Stylized devices like this never allow the audience to become entirely taken in by the fictive world; we are consistently reminded that we are watching a movie, a construction, an artifice from which we are deriving a perverse, prurient pleasure through a narrative of mass murder and mayhem. Hey, that's entertainment, no? This self-reflectivity is nowhere more apparent than at the end of the film, when Stone creates a didactic juxtaposition by cutting from the movie's final fictional events to true news events, such as the O.J. Simpson trial (**Figure 21-30**).

Intellectual editing is a product of early Soviet filmmakers and their rigorous writings on, and uses of, an editing theory that has been labeled "Soviet montage." Soviet montage eschewed the smooth, invisible Hollywood style of continuity editing, which historically had been primarily about facilitating the dramatic goals of the story, for a more intellectually engaging, overtly visible and political style. Associative editing, like many Soviet montage techniques, is meant to call attention to itself as a device. Consequently, the audience is encouraged to thoughtfully participate in the

■ **Figure 21-29** The violent journey of Mickey (Woody Harrelson) and Mallory (Juliette Lewis) in Stone's *Natural Born Killers* (1994) is punctuated with documentary images from the natural world.

■ **Figure 21-30** Oliver Stone juxtaposes the fictional world of Mickey and Mallory with real news events to illustrate his central theme concerning the American public's insatiable appetite for violence as entertainment.

construction of the film's meaning. The early Soviet filmmakers, like Vertov, Eisenstein, and Pudovkin, who each developed their own theories of montage, had a profound influence on the art of editing in general and on specific filmmakers, including Welles, Hitchcock, Godard, Kubrick, Scorsese, and Coppola, to name only a few. At this point in cinema history, the editing theories and practices of Soviet montage, Hollywood editing, French New Wave styles, Hong Kong cinema, and the rest of the cumulative history of national and individual editing approaches have merged into one big, global aesthetic, cinema toolbox, available and accessible to any filmmaker, for any project, anywhere on the planet.

in practice

■ EDITING AND DEVELOPING CHARACTER

In his book *Making Movies,* director Sidney Lumet says about editing, "To me there are two main elements to editing: juxtapositioning images and creating tempo." He then goes on to talk about how his careful control over editing tempo was used for narrative emphasis and characterization in his classic film *Long Day's Journey into Night* (1962) (**Figure-21-31**):

On Long Day's Journey into Night, *I found that I could use editing tempos to reinforce character. I always shot Katherine Hepbu rn in long,*

sustained takes, so that in editing, the legato feel of her scenes would help us drift into her narcotized world. We would move with her, into her past and into her own journey into night. Jason Robard's character was edited in exactly the opposite way. As the picture went on, I tried to cut his scenes in a staccato rhythm. I wanted him to feel erratic, disjointed, uncoordinated.

(From *Making Movies,* by Sidney Lumet, Vintage Books, 1995)

Another good example of how editing rhythm aids in the development of character is in Jason Reitman's

■ **Figure 21-31** In Lumet's *Long Day's Journey into Night* (1962), the characterization of Mary (Katherine Hepburn) and Jamie (Jason Robards) is reinforced through editing tempo.

2008 film *Up in the Air*. The central character, Ryan Bingham, spends much of his time flying from city to city. He's an experienced frequent flier; suitcases, airports, security gates, and bonus miles constitute a large part of his life. As Ryan himself puts it, "To know me is to fly with me; this is where I live." In an early sequence, in the introduction to Ryan's character, Reitman and editor Dana Glauberman unfurl a brief 1 minute and 15 second montage of Ryan packing his suitcase, arriving at an airport, and going through security check. This sequence is cut together with quick, dynamic, elliptical edits showcasing Ryan's consummate skills in luggage packing and negotiating airport security protocol. His movements have the sophisticated timing, balance, precision, and master technique of a samurai. And just as there is nothing extraneous in Ryan's movements or method, the cutting is accurate, efficient, and economical, in both the shot selection and duration. At the end of the montage, in no small part because of the editing style as well as shot content, we are in awe of his skill; when it comes to navigating a business trip, he's the best—the Michael Jordan of airport check-in (**Figure 21-32**) (see also the "Montage" box).

■ **Figure 21-32** In *Up in the Air* (Reitman, 2008) Ryan's (George Clooney) expertise at packing and airport check in is highlighted through sharp, highly dynamic editing.

Emotion

We started this chapter by talking about cutting to tell a story, but a story without emotion is lifeless. Notice how in many of the examples we have discussed the word "feel" is used. Many editors believe that the first consideration of an editing strategy, and indeed the motivation for individual edits, is emotion—how you want the audience to feel at any given moment. Do you want them to laugh? Worry? Jump in their seat? Do you want them to feel an impending doom, or a sense of relief? Do you want them to feel what your protagonist is feeling? Emotion is aroused in the audience when they become participants in the drama. The editing principle for the Robinson fight sequence from *Raging Bull* (see **Figure 21-9**) was not to be stylistic for its own sake, but to make the audience feel what it's like to be in a boxing ring, to feel the surreal malleability of time as your adrenaline surges, to feel the powerful blows from a prizefighter.

The Farrelly Brothers also want us to feel pain, in *There's Something about Mary* (see **Figure 21-23**)—the pain of catching your "frank and beans" in a zipper; but they also want to make us howl with laughter as we simultaneously grimace in pain; Rob Reiner, in *Misery* (see **Figure 21-19**), wants us to feel anxiety that our hero will not make it to the room in time—and so on.

■ MONTAGE

"Montage" is one of the more slippery terms in filmmaking. When speaking of (1) **Soviet montage**, the term refers to the various theories of the early Soviet filmmakers concerning a style of editing that was, by and large, a noncontinuity method that juxtaposed images to suggest ideas that are not obviously present in each individual shot. In French, (2) **montage** means "editing." To edit a film is *faire le montage*. Often in English, you will also come across the term used simply as a synonym for editing in general. In the parlance of traditional American film, a (3) **montage sequence** refers to a sequence that greatly condenses time, space, or narrative activity through broad elliptical editing as a way of quickly getting from one point in the story to another. We're all familiar with *Rocky*-type montages that collapse time and highlight only key moments in the long development of, say, a mediocre boxer training to become a prizefighter. We saw a similar elliptical montage in the example from *Up in the Air* (see **Figure 21-32**). Trey Parker and Matt Stone playfully spoof this sort of montage sequence in the "Montage Song" sequence from their film *Team America: World Police* (2004) (**Figure-21-33**).

A great example of the temporal flexibility of editing can be seen in the brief "falling off the train" montage from *Slumdog Millionaire* (2008) which was edited by Chris Dickens. This sequence begins with the brothers Jamal and Salim (each around 6 - 8 yrs old), who are traveling through India atop trains, trying to steal food. While Salim holds Jamal by the ankles,

dangling him over the side of the train, Jamal grabs food through the train window. Unfortunately, they are caught and are both pulled off the moving train. A series of quick edits trace their plunge down the dusty embankment. When they finally hit the bottom and, dazed from the fall, sit upright, the brothers are now teenagers. This little montage, edited to feel like one continuous fall and tumble from the train, in fact is an elliptical device moving us years forward. This sequence also informs us that these boys have spent all this time riding and hustling on the trains of India, until now, in their teen years, when they begin a new hustle at the Taj Mahal (**Figure-21-34**).

■ **Figure 21-34** This montage from *Slumdog Millionaire* (Boyle and Loveleen, 2008) transforms young Salim (Azharuddin Mohammed Ismail) and young Jamal (Ayush Mahesh Khedekar) into teenage Salim (Ashutosh Lobo Gajiwala) and teenage Jamal (Tanay Chheda) during what appears to be one continuous fall down a train track embankment.

■ **Figure 21-33** Parker and Stone parody a common cinematic device, the montage sequence, in *Team America: World Police* (2004).

Never forget that we are telling a story to move people emotionally in very particular ways. So the next time you're watching a movie and have an emotional reaction, pull yourself out of the filmmaker's spell and try to figure out how they did that. Try to recall, cut for cut, how the filmmaker drew that emotion out of you. If you can do that, then you'll *really* be learning how to make movies.

So of course there are basic rules. But even today, people are struggling with new ways of telling stories through film, and they're still using the same old tools— establishing shots, medium shots, close-ups—but not necessarily with the same intent. And it's the juxtaposition of these shots in the editing process that is creating new emotions or, more precisely, a new way to communicate certain feelings to the audience.

**Martin Scorsese (From *Moviemakers' Master Class*,
by Laurent Tirard)**

The Sound Design in Film

We gestate in Sound, and are born into Sight
Cinema gestated in Sight, and was born into Sound
Walter Murch (From the foreword to *Audio-Vision,* by Michel Chion)[1]

Roughly, the first 33 years of film's early history—between the introduction of Edison's kinetoscope in 1894 and the commercial success of Warner Brothers' *The Jazz Singer* in 1927—established the "motion picture" as a fundamentally visual art form, with images telling the entire narrative. In those early decades, before the introduction of "talking pictures," the movies themselves were silent and sound was incorporated almost exclusively in the form of live musical accompaniment played during the screenings, long after the production of the motion picture. Even though it's been roughly 80 years since *The Jazz Singer* transformed film production into an art form with multiple layers of synchronized audio, filmmaking is all too often still considered (and taught) as a primarily visual art form—with sound as a sort of addendum. However, as Walter Murch, Michel Chion, Randy Thom, and others have so eloquently expressed, the filmmaker's art has evolved to the point where the aural dimension of a movie is at least as important as, and sometimes even more dominant than, the picture for creating tone, mood, and meaning. For too many filmmakers, the audio component remains at one of two poles; for some it plays a purely supporting role as an auxiliary to the image, an accompaniment (often redundant) to the story being told through the visual action, and others shackle it to the hard labor of expository dialogue that explains the film story in the absence of truly expressive imagery. Because of its powerful dramatic potential, you should consider sound as a costar of your movie, capable of much more than expository drudgery—capable, in fact, of profound and nuanced narrative eloquence. The filmmaker who learns to harness the power of a film's aural realm and fully develops sound as an essential storytelling component that enhances, but does not duplicate, the visual dimension of a movie will have vastly more opportunity and territory for creative expression. This requires imagining and incorporating aural story elements from the earliest scriptwriting stages straight through to postproduction. It's unfortunate that all too often, filmmakers think about sound only after the shooting is done.

■ SOUND DESIGN OVERVIEW

The final form of a movie's total aural impression is called the film's **sound design**. A film's sound design consists of layering multiple tracks of sound, anywhere from two to a dozen. The creative manipulation, placement, layering, enhancing, composing, juxtaposing, and mixing of these audio tracks is done in the postproduction stage. It is important to understand that in film production visual and aural components remain separate for as long as possible to allow for maximum creative manipulation, right up to the very end of the filmmaking process, when the movie (picture) and all sound tracks are locked together and prepared for distribution. For this reason, we gather and lay down the elements of the sound design, each separate and distinct from the others. For example, as we construct our movie in postproduction we may have three separate audio tracks for our sync sound dialogue, a fourth track for the music, a fifth track for sound effects, and maybe a sixth track for ambient sound. Taken as a whole, all of these audio tracks and the way they are mixed together comprise the sound design. (See **Figure 15-1**)

---

[1]*Audio-Vision,* by Michel Chion, Columbia University Press, New York, 1994.

Whether you are cutting to only a single music track or layering 15 tracks of audio, there is virtually no end to the contributions a well-crafted sound design can bring to a film. Sound can establish a tone or mood with unmatchable nuance, and it can vividly establish the legitimacy and emotional impression of a location. Sound is able to bring dramatic emphasis to actions or details inside or outside of the frame; in fact, sound can create an entire world off screen (how many times have we seen characters reacting to the sound of a terrible car crash just outside the frame's edge?). Sound can contribute to establishing a character's point of view even to the point of reflecting their particular psychology. In short, sound is an essential cinematic storytelling component that deserves considerable attention throughout all phases of the film production process.

■ SOUND DESIGN I: SOUND, SYNC, AND SOURCE

In closely exploring or devising the sound design of a motion picture, we need to consider three closely related aspects of the movie's sonic world: (1) What kinds of sounds make up the sound design? (2) Is the sound synchronous (in sync) with the picture or not? (3) Where are those sounds emanating from, or where is the source?

Sounds: Speech, Sound Effects, and Music

The sound components of a film, the aural elements of the sound design, can pretty much be organized into three broad categories: **speech, sound effects,** and **music**. These sounds constitute the way a film can aurally communicate to an audience, but not every scene within a film will have all three types of sound. For example, many scenes are edited to music without any dialogue or sound effects at all, while other scenes may

■ **Figure 22-1** A scene from Polanski's renowned short film *Two Men and a Wardrobe* (1958), which includes no dialogue.

■ **Figure 22-2** The powerful realism of Mingui's *4 Months, 3 Weeks, 2 Days* (2008) would be subverted by the inclusion of a musical score.

have dialogue and no music. Short films often tell their stories without the use of the human voice at all, either as dialogue or voice-over. One of the most famous examples is Roman Polanski's celebrated short, *Two Men and a Wardrobe* (1958), which is a complex social satire about two men who are ostracized from "civilized" society because they carry a huge wardrobe around with them. This 14-minute short film, which garnered prizes all over the world, has no dialogue or voice-over whatsoever. The sound design consists only of a music track and a few sound effects (**Figure 22-1**). Not using dialogue isn't something that only occurs in short films; there are many feature films with extended periods in which there is no dialogue: the famous 30-minute heist scene in *Rififi* (1955), Luc Besson's postapocalyptic *Le Dernier Combat* (1983), which has no dialogue whatsoever, and the opening 20 minutes of *There Will Be Blood* (2007) are three that come to mind.

It is also not uncommon to find narrative films, even feature films, that do not have any music at all. A good example is the Romanian film *4 Months, 3 Weeks, 2 Days* (2007) by Cristian Mungiu. The power of this film comes from its strict adherence to realism, without emotional broadcasting or editorializing. The addition of music, even just once, would undercut the brutal honesty and integrity of its tone and therefore the audience's direct connection to the situation (**Figure 22-2**). Many filmmakers, especially those working in a more realist mode, like Abbas Kiarostami (*Taste of Cherry*) and the Dardenne Brothers (*Rosetta*), assiduously avoid the overt infusion of emotion that music supplies.

The general categories of speech, sound effects, and music can obviously be broken down into more detailed categories, which we will do, but first let's look at the question of sync and source that also informs the more specific elements of a sound design.

Synchronous, Nonsynchronous, and Postsynchronous Audio

The second consideration for sound is whether the audio as it is realized in the sound design is **in sync** with the picture or not, in which case it is called **nonsync audio** (or **asynchronous sound**). Sync audio has a frame-accurate, direct correspondence with the image and appears to be generated from what we are watching, like a character speaking lines of dialogue or the sound that accompanies the image of a car starting up and driving off. Sync sound that is recorded on location and in sync with the image (for example, the car image and the sound of the car) is called **direct sound**. As we explored in Chapter 15, if we're not happy with the quality of the sync sound (perhaps the camera framing didn't allow us to position our mikes for optimum sound), we can always get another, better recording in the field, of a car starting and pulling away without the camera rolling, as **wild sound**. In the postproduction world, sound effects recorded on location are called **pfx**, for **production sound effects**. This sound is recorded nonsync, but it will be aligned to appear in sync later in postproduction. But perhaps in building our sound design we don't like *either* car sound from the field recordings. Well, we can easily replace it with a "car starting and drive away" sound from a **prerecorded sound effects** library; such libraries are found on CDs or through online sound effect resources. In this case, the sound will also be aligned with the image in postproduction (i.e., just as the key is turned in the ignition). Both the pfx and prerecorded effects are called **postsynchronous** sound effects because their synchronous relationship to the picture is accomplished in postproduction rather than in the shooting.

Nonsync audio (either speech, sound effects, or music) is sound that has no corresponding image and so has no visible source. For example, just as the car drives off screen, we hear the sound of a car crash. Nonsync audio always carries with it the question: Where is this sound coming from? Because there is no visible source, nonsync sound is often used to create a sense for the area outside of the camera's field of view (as in the car crash example) or to layer an additional emotional tone over the image. In the climactic scene in the 2008 vampire film *Let the Right One In*, director Tomas Alfredson plunges the camera (and therefore the viewer) underwater with the central character Oskar as he is being drowned by a bully (**Figure 22-3**). A moment later, we hear wild screeching, thuds, and screaming, indicating that terrible violence is being wrought just above the water, off screen. It is not until later, when we come out of the water, that we fully understand that Oskar was saved by his friend who unleashed horrific carnage while he and we were underwater.

Source

The question of the location of the source of a sound has a profound interrelationship with all categories of sound. The film theorist Michel Chion makes the astute observation, in his book *Audio-Vision,* that in film, all images are contained within the frame. But sound, the aural universe of the film, has no such "container," no such strictly delineated limits. Not only are we free to layer as many sounds as we want on top of other sounds, but we can also have various rationales for where those sounds are ostensibly coming from. As we just mentioned, sounds can emanate from **on screen** (a source within the frame) or from **off screen** (a source outside the frame). In addition, sounds can have different relationships to the fictive world that the film has created. In film theory terms, the world of the film—consisting of the characters, actions, objects, locations, time, and story—is called the film's **diegesis**. A sound track can have sounds that seem to come from

■ **Figure 22-3** *Let the Right One In* (Alfredson, 2008) uses off-screen sound to provoke us to imagine the horrific carnage we're missing while the camera keeps us submerged underwater.

the world of the movie, called **diegetic sound**, and it can have **nondiegetic sounds**, which don't come from anything in the world of the film. These are supplementary sounds, like music, included by the filmmaker to add further emotional or narrative dimensions.

Examples of diegetic sound would be the dialogue spoken by a character, music playing on a radio that is visible in the scene, or the sound of a car crash that our characters respond to, whether it is on screen or not. All of these sounds come from the world of the movie and can be heard by the characters in the film. Nondiegetic sound, on the other hand would include the voice of a narrator commenting on the scene we are watching, music that has no source in the world of the film (like the romantic orchestral music that surges when two characters kiss), or the sound of a car crash just as an infatuated boy says something stupid to the girl he's trying to win. There is no literal car crash in the world of the film, neither the boy nor the girl hears this sound, but the filmmaker is making a sound metaphor for the boy's crash-and-burn attempt to get the girl.

MEL BROOKS, JOKIN' AROUND WITH DIEGESIS

Off screen, on screen, diegetic, nondiegetic—these terms may sound theoretical, but their application is simple and evident in practically every film you see. Mel Brooks even found a way to play to the audience's expectations concerning diegetic and nondiegetic sounds for laughs. In his 1977 comedy *High Anxiety*, which is a hilarious spoof of Alfred Hitchcock thrillers, Dr. Richard H. Thorndyke is the new chief administrator for the prestigious "Psychoneurotic Institute for the Very, Very Nervous." But Dr. Thorndyke quickly discovers that there are some *very* sinister goings-on at the hospital. On his first day, as he is being driven from the airport to the institute,

his chauffer Brophy announces that the sudden demise of the previous chief administrator was "highly suspicious!" True to the genre conventions, ominous orchestral music (nondiegetic music) punctuates this portentous revelation.

As soon as the music kicks in, Dr. Thorndyke and Brophy start looking around. The audience wonders: What are they looking for? And at that moment a bus carrying the entire Los Angeles Philharmonic passes their car, playing the very ominous orchestral music that we (and they) are hearing. In one moment, the music that we assumed was simply the musical score becomes diegetic music coming from just outside their car (**Figure 22-4**).

■ **Figure 22-4** Mel Brooks pokes fun at cinematic conventions by exposing the "true source" of the ominous music that underscores this scene from *High Anxiety* (1977).

SOUND DESIGN II: THE SOUND ELEMENTS IN DETAIL

Now let's look in more detail at those basic audio categories (speech, sound effects, and music), with the added aspects of sync and source. When we consider these other factors, we are able to break down the general categories even further and define all of the kinds of sounds we can employ in a sound design. Remember, not every film uses every kind of sound.

Speech

Sync Dialogue and Off-Screen Dialogue

Sync dialogue is dialogue that is recorded in sync with the picture during the production phase. The picture and sound from the shot are both used and sync is maintained during editing. **Off-screen dialogue** is dialogue that comes from a person who is assumed to be in the time and space of the film (diegetic sound) but simply is not in the view of the camera. For example, in Orson Welles' *Touch of Evil* (1958), Susie Vargas (Janet Leigh) talks through the wall with a mysterious young woman who is in the adjacent motel room. The voice from next door warns her that boys are looking for a key to get into her room to drug her. Susie's dialogue is sync dialogue,

■ **Figure 22-5** "Do you know what a mainliner is?" Welles' *A Touch of Evil* (1958) incorporates both on-screen sync sound and off-screen non-sync sound in this one shot.

while the woman talking through the wall is off-screen dialogue (because there is no visual reference in the frame, this is a nonsync sound element) (**Figure 22-5**). Keep in mind that these categories are not fixed in production. We often use sound that was recorded as sync sound, but in the edit we decide not to use the corresponding image. For example, say we shoot a scene of a girl getting dressed in the morning and include a shot of her mother at the foot of the stairs calling up to her, "Honey, hurry up. You're going to be late!" When we edit, we could easily toss out the mother's picture and simply place that dialogue under the image of the girl getting dressed, as if it's coming from off screen.

Voice-over Narration

Voice-over narration (V.O.) is also nonsync sound and has no direct visual sync reference in the frame; however, it differs from off-screen sound in that it is understood by the audience that the voice cannot be heard by the people in the scene. This means that the voice-over is either not in the time and space of the film world (nondiegetic sound), as in the case of narrator who is commenting on the events or narrating the story of the film, or it can be the unspoken thoughts of a character in the scene.

ADR

ADR is the acronym for **automatic dialogue replacement**, which is the rerecording, of sync dialogue, in a studio, in cases where the production sound is not usable. ADR is also referred to as **looping** because the method of rerecording and syncing up the dialogue involves the actor standing in a studio in front of a microphone watching a loop of the scene whose dialogue needs replacing over and over again (**Figure 22-6**). The actor watching the scene also listens to the field recordings of their performance (called **guide tracks**) on headphones while trying to duplicate the words, timing, and emotional intensity. ADR can be used to replace poorly recorded audio, improve articulation or performance, or even "revoice" a character (meaning to replace one actor's voice with another's).

ADR can be an expensive and elaborate process, especially if you have to pay Tom Cruise to come back into a rented ADR studio to redo the dialogue for entire scenes. But on shorts and independent films, where field recordings are mostly used, ADR can simply mean replacing an unintelligible line or two here and there, while the talent watches the scene on a laptop computer in a soundproof room.

■ **Figure 22-6** In this scene from Haneke's *Code Unknown* (2000), he replicates a typical ADR session, where actors are brought back to rerecord their lines as they watch themselves on screen.

■ SPEECH IN FILMS

Dialogue

With very few exceptions, narrative films after the silent era have used some degree of sync dialogue. In some film genres, dialogue is *the* dominant storytelling element. The screwball comedy genre is known for its reliance on wall-to-wall, fast-paced, witty verbal repartee, as in the following conversation between two recently divorced newspaper reporters, from *His Girl Friday* (1940), by Howard Hawks (**Figure 22-7**):

■ **Figure 22-8** Much of the sparse dialogue in Kubrick's *2001: A Space Odyssey* (1968) is given to HAL 9000 (voiced by Douglas Rain), allowing the audience to identify with it more than with the human protagonists.

Hildy: Walter!

Walter: What?

Hildy: The mayor's first wife, what was her name?

Walter: You mean the one with the wart on her ...?

Hildy: Right.

Walter: Fanny!

■ **Figure 22-7** Fast and witty repartee is central to the screwball comedy genre as epitomized in Hawks' *His Girl Friday* (1940), with Cary Grant and Rosalind Russell.

Stanley Kubrick, on the other hand, used quite a different approach in *2001: A Space Odyssey*, where his use of dialogue was extremely spare. In his article "*2001: A Space Odyssey* Re-viewed" (from the book, "The Making of *2001: A Space Odyssey*"), Alexander Walker claims that, "there are barely forty minutes of dialogue in a 141 minute film." By far, the most

verbal character in this film is the computer HAL 9000, whose dialogue expresses much more emotion than do any of the human beings in the movie (**Figure 22-8**). In fact, while crewmember Poole dies a quick and silent death in space, Kubrick gives HAL 9000 a very talky and stirringly melodramatic death scene. As crewmember Bowman is shutting HAL 9000 down by removing one artificial intelligence bank at a time, HAL at first protests, but then, weakened, it (he?) comes to terms with its (his?) impending death:

HAL: I'm afraid. I'm afraid, Dave. Dave, my mind is going. I can feel it. I can feel it. My mind is going. There is no question about it. I can feel it. I can feel it. I can feel it. I'm afraid. Good afternoon, gentlemen. I am a HAL 9000 computer. I became operational at the H.A.L. plant in Urbana, Illinois, on the 12th of January 1992. My instructor was Mr. Langley, and he taught me to sing a song. If you'd like to hear it I can sing it for you.

Bowman: Yes, I'd like to hear it, HAL. Sing it for me.

HAL: It's called "Daisy."

[HAL progressively slows down as he sings]

Daisy, Daisy, give me your answer do. I'm half crazy all for the love of you. It won't be a stylish marriage, I can't afford a carriage ...

[slows down further]

But you'll look sweet ... upon the seat of a bicycle ... built ... for two....

---

in practice

Off-Screen Voice

Alfred Hitchcock uses the physical absence of a character as an essential element of mystery and suspense in his film *Psycho* (1960) (**Figure 22-9**). After the brutal stabbing of Marion, we hear the off-screen voice of Norman Bates shouting, "Mother! Oh God, mother! Blood! Blood!" By keeping Norman off screen we assume he's addressing his mother and that she may have been the one who killed Marion, but we can't be entirely sure. Randy Thom, in his article "Designing a Movie for Sound" (1999, www.filmsound.org), says "starving the eye will inevitably bring the ear, and therefore the imagination, into play." This is exactly Hitchcock's strategy: by suggesting the presence of Norman's mother strictly through off-screen dialogue, he piques the audience's curiosity (Where is she? What does she look like?) and a mystery forms in their minds.

Voice-over

François Truffaut's classic short film *Les Mistons* (1957) (**Figure 22-10**) uses a sound track with two primary elements: voice-over and music. There are also a few sound effects and postsynchronously dubbed dialogue, but it is the voice-over that dominates and recounts the story of a group of preadolescent boys who spy on, tease, and torment Bernadette and Gérard, a young couple in love. When Gérard leaves to go on a mountain-climbing expedition,

■ **Figure 22-10** Truffaut's use of voice-over in *Les Mistons* (1957) adds emotional complexity and poignancy to this story of five mischievous boys.

the boys play a trick on Bernadette, sending her a postcard that suggests that Gérard is not being faithful while he is away, but after they mail it to her they learn from the newspapers that Gérard was killed in a mountaineering accident.

Voice-over as a storytelling element is frequently poorly used. It's so easy to tell a story simply by slapping on a voice-over, but one must be sure that this technique contributes additional layers of meaning to the image rather than simply duplicating what we are seeing, or, worse, doing all of the storytelling while the images accomplish nothing. *Les Mistons* is a great example of well-used voice-over. The story is told from the point of view of one of the boys (we never know which), who is now a man. The young boys could not possibly understand at the time that they are experiencing a profound, tragic, and indelible life lesson as they struggle with their newly emerging and confusing desires—their first romantic crush on a woman. But it is the now grown man, reflecting on his childhood experiences in the voice-over, who reveals the emotional complexity of what would otherwise be seen simply as the irritating antics of a group of childish brats.

■ **Figure 22-9** Hitchcock's use of off-screen dialogue expertly manipulates audience expectations in this scene from *Psycho* (1960).

Sound Effects and Ambient Sound

Hard Effects

Hard effects are sound effects that are essentially gathered as a nonsync sound and then inserted into the sound design either as postsynchronous sound (synced up to a corresponding image in the editing) or as an asynchronous sound effect. Hard effects are sounds like shattering glass, dog barks, gunshots, explosions, creaking stairs, doorbells, telephones, exotic birdcalls, and a Huey helicopter fly-by. A hard sound effect can come from the production wild sound track (pfx) (e.g., a clean, nonsync recording of

25. Small group gasp - astonished.:01	48. High performance car - engine turning over - won't start.................:19
26. Party - social gathering - medium..................................1:04	49. High performance car - fast departure (burn out).................:05
27. Shopping in supermarket 1:00	50. High performance car - driving - interior perspective ....:30
28. Pool hall - general atmosphere 1:00	51. Motorcycle passing..................:10
29. Patchinco - continuous play .....:30	52. Light traffic............................1:00
30. Karate workout atmosphere ..1:00	53. Medium traffic.......................1:00
31. Boxing match - small arena...1:00	54. Outboard boat - approach ....:16
32. Hot air balloon rising...........:18	55. Tractor - start idle & stop 1:00
33. Hot air - 1 long blast ....:09	56. Tractor - driving by ....:30
34. Sailing with surf 1:00	57. Harp - diminished glisses down and up ....:10
35. Golf Swing - driving club whoosh ....:01	58. Harp - C chord - cracked ....:05
36. Factory with automated machines 1:00	59. Harp - C chord - cracked slower:07
37. Sleigh Bells - jingling 1:00	60. Slide whistle - gliss up slow ....:04
38. Door Bell - Avon type - 1 ring ...:04	61. Slide whistle - gliss down slow :03
39. Clock - church - strikes 1/2 hour ....:13	62. Vibra - slap - accent ....:03
	63. Boat whistle - orchestral - 2 blasts ....:06

■ **Figure 22-11** An enormous repository of prerecorded hard effects and ambient sounds can be found through commercial sound effect libraries on CDs or on the Internet.

the actual car starting), or can be found as a prerecorded sound effect from commercial sound effects libraries (on CDs or the Internet), or can be constructed from a collection of sounds, like mixing a car starting sound with a lion's roar to reflect a character's anger as he starts the car and pulls away (**Figure 22-11**).

It's extremely important to record, create, or find the sound effect that will have the particular impact you need, and this is a task that requires great attention to detail. One doesn't just say, "Hey, I need a dog barking." That's way too general. To get just the right one, each sound effect needs to be considered from a number of different angles. You need to have a specific sense for the size and kind of dog (the "yap" of a Yorkie or the lazy "woof-woof" of a hound dog), the kind of bark (playful, serious, or rabid barking), and the dramatic context for the bark (Is the film a drama or comedy? Is the barking realistic or expressionistic?), and so on.

Foley Effects

Foley effects, named after Universal Picture sound department head Jack Foley, differ from hard effects in that they are created and recorded in synchronization with the edited film. A foley session involves watching a scene in a soundproof room, with whatever objects or surfaces you need to create the right noise, and creating and recording the sounds as you watch the film. The recording is done onto a digital sound recorder and input into the NLE system to be aligned with the scene. The intention of a foley effect is always to create a sound in sync with the picture. Just like ADR, a foley session can be an extremely elaborate and expensive event, requiring professional **foley artists** and a special **foley room** equipped with, among other things, different floor surfaces (gravel, concrete, wood, carpet, etc.), in order to create the right "walking sounds" (**Figure 22-12**). But for shorts and independent films, a foley session can simply mean watching your footage on a laptop computer in a soundproof room and re-creating a sound effect or two onto a digital recorder, then putting it back into the NLE and making the necessary frame adjustments to slide it into sync.

■ **Figure 22-12** Professional foley rooms are sound studios designed to record post-synchronous sound effects while the foley artist watches the scene projected. As you can see here, they are outfitted with a wide array of objects that can make a variety of noises.

■ USING SOUND EFFECTS IN FILM

When Real Is Not Real Enough

Anyone who has seen a fight in real life knows that a real punch doesn't sound like much—it sounds quite a bit like a slap, only a little more solid. It certainly doesn't sound as bad as it *feels*. A real punch sound is decidedly undramatic, which is why many "punch" sound effects are constructed out of layers of other sounds (not to mention that you can't go around hitting people just to get the pfx of a punch). But when constructing a sound effect, like a punch, you need to consider the visual and dramatic context for the effect. The sound of a bare-fisted punch would be different than one with a boxing glove; a punch to the jaw should sound different than a punch in the gut. Also, the sound of a punch seen in a long shot would have less vivid presence than would a punch in a close-up shot. Additionally, a punch in a comedy film will sound very different than the same punch in a hard-hitting drama. A student of mine, in an editing class exercise, created a punch sound effect for his "found footage" that included one quick shot of a knockout punch from a boxing match. He blended the sound of a baseball bat hitting the soft cushion of a sofa, for the low "thud," and the sound of crushing a small head of lettuce, for the high "crunch" of damaged nose cartilage, and his own fist hitting his wet palm, for the "slap" of leather on flesh. The effect was pretty darn good, if a little bit too visceral for his exercise. The "knockout punch" effect stole the show.

In the world of sound design, it's universally recognized that supervising sound effects editor Frank Warner created some of the greatest "punch" sounds in the history of movies for Scorsese's *Raging Bull*. Warner created punches that acutely reflected the subjective *feel* of receiving blows from a prizefighter. Not only do the boxers get punched, but everyone in the audience *feels* each uppercut right on their own jaw. How did Warner construct these sound effects? So far, he hasn't shared with anyone this particular sound effect recipe, and he has since destroyed the original multitrack tapes. Although there are rumors that melons and tomatoes were involved, no one really knows exactly how he created those punches. It has remained a secret even from Martin Scorsese himself, who admits that he indeed asked, but wasn't told (**Figure 22-13**).

When Real Is Too Real

Sometimes with sound effects, less is more. A former student of mine in an intermediate production class made a simple, high-energy comedy chase scene, in which a high school kid on a skateboard is being chased by his mother, who turns out to be

■ **Figure 22-13** Among the most famous and mythologized sound effects in film history are Frank Warner's "punch" sounds in Scorsese's *Raging Bull* (1980).

the superior athlete. She ultimately catches the kid and forces him to finish his breakfast. The end. At one point, as the mother chases her son, the boy bumps into an old lady carrying groceries, knocking her onto her fanny (the mother later hurdles right over the woman as she picks up her oranges). The old lady was played by a sophomore dance major (wearing loads of makeup) and she was miked with a super-cardioid to get good sync sound. The stuntwoman did a great job of getting knocked backward, sprawling, onto the sidewalk. But when the student showed his synced dailies in class, rather than laugh, the students groaned with sympathetic pain. The sounds were too good, too real, too close. We could hear flesh and bone hitting the hard concrete and we felt this poor old woman's pain; it was anything but funny. Clearly, the student filmmaker needed a different "fall" sound effect. He removed the sync sound and found a funny "yelp and fall" sound effect on a sound effects CD that had a huge selection of "cartoon" sound effects. The new "fall" sound included a soft "splat" and comical "boioing," clearly not realism. When he showed the edited film, the old lady's fall was now a truly comic pratfall (**Figure 22-14**).

■ **Figure 22-14** To keep us laughing, the slapping, poking, punching, and falling sounds in the *Three Stooges* are given a comedic rather than a visceral tone. Mo is no Jake LaMotta. From White's *Nutty but Nice*, (1940).

Simple Foley

I once edited a scene that had no dialogue and involved a man standing in a bathtub, up to his ankles in water, bathing (**Figure 22-15**). After his bath he steps out of the tub and leaves the bathroom. The scene was shot MOS (without sound) so I needed to create all of the sounds in foley. After the scene was cut, I simply brought the footage on my laptop into a music practice room (a soundproof space) along with a plastic tub of water and a microphone hooked up to a digital recorder. I positioned the mike above the water and plunged my hands in. When the man moved in the tub, I swirled my hands around, making the sound his legs might make. When he stepped out of the tub, I quickly removed both arms from the water, to make the right "splash" sound, and when his feet hit the tiled floor, I patted my wet hands on the linoleum floor to make the "pit-pat" sound of wet flesh on tile. After downloading the sound into my NLE, it took only a little tweaking and the entire scene had perfectly convincing sound to accompany the image. All that was left was to slide each sound into sync with the picture on the sound track, add ambience to the location, and tweak the levels.

■ **Figure 22-15** Simple foley effects were used to create all the bath water sounds in K. Hurbis-Cherrier's short film *Ode to a Bar of Soap* (1998).

Ambient Sound and Walla-walla

Ambient sound is the overall aural environment in which a scene takes place—the background noises and other acoustic properties of a location. Ambient sound can come from the field recordings at the actual locations or can be pulled off commercial sound effects libraries, which can offer hundreds of different ambient environments ("rainforest with birds," "city streets/rush hour," "small restaurant," "children's playground," and so on). Ambient sound in a final sound design can be a combination of the ambience which is already part of the sync field recordings augmented by added sounds to create the precise aural space for the scene. It is not uncommon to use multiple ambient tracks in a single scene to get the atmosphere just right.

It's important to note that "silence" in film, as well as in real life, does not mean "utterly no sound." During "silent" passages, we should be able to hear the ambient sound of the environment, the naturally occurring background noises. What this means is that there is never a time when a sound track has no audio track. At the very least, it will contain very quiet ambient sound that only feels like silence.

Walla-walla is the term used for ambient sound that involves the general, unintelligible chatter of a group of people. You can have, for example, the walla-walla of a theater audience before the curtain goes up, or of a cocktail party, or an art gallery opening. Walla-walla is a great resource for a low-budget filmmaker, because it is often used under a scene to give the impression that there are many more people in the location (off screen) than there actually were in production. For example, a medium close-up of two people sitting in a restaurant may have been shot in an empty restaurant during off hours, but by putting "crowded restaurant ambience and walla-walla" under the scene, it will feel like the place is full. Like ambient sound, you can record this yourself as wild sound or you can get it from a sound effects library.

As with everything else in film, ambient sound has a practical use and a creative application. Practically speaking, the ambient track is used to smooth out any ambient shifts that would be apparent when cutting from one shot to another in the same scene. For example, in a scene in which we cut between two people sitting at a sidewalk cafe, one facing the traffic and another facing away, there might be a noticeable discrepancy between the traffic noise we hear in their respective sound recordings. Often, this ambience shift (the amount of traffic picked up by the mike) can be too abrupt for continuity's sake when cutting from one shot to the other. Although we can't get rid of the traffic noise from one character's audio, we could add a little traffic ambience on another track, under the character who has less, in order to even them out.

The creative dimension of ambient sound is not to be underestimated. Finding just the right ambient sound for a scene can, with any degree of subtlety, establish an environment that adds additional narrative information or an emotional tone. Ambience is also often used to create a subjective sound space, meaning that the sound environment the audience hears is a reflection of what a specific character is feeling.

in practice

■ PRACTICAL AMBIENCE AND WALLA-WALLA

Andrew Lund's *Snapshot* (2006) is a low-budget short film that revolves around the kidnapping of the wildly popular photographer Marcello (Henry Darrow), who has enjoyed a lucrative career taking candid photos of people on the street (**Figure 22-16**). His kidnapper is Nathan, the disgruntled subject of one of his photos who believes that Marcello ruined his life when he published the fateful photograph showing Nathan at a highly compromised moment. In order to establish the popularity of the photographer, the film opens with an elaborate and well-attended museum retrospective of the photographer's work. But Lund did not have the time or money to wrangle a large, well-heeled crowd of extras to populate the museum opening. So he and his editor/sound designer, Dave Monahan, created the crowd through sound. In the museum scene Lund kept his framing fairly tight and

carefully selected several ambience and walla-walla tracks to sonically create the excited buzz and murmurs of a large crowd—but just off screen! Once in a while Lund would have an extra pass in front of the lens, implying that people are milling about, but we never see more than a few people. The effect is totally convincing; the audience gets a clear sense of a huge turnout for Marcello's big museum retrospective.

Dramatic Tone and Ambient Sound

Ramin Bahrani's *Chop Shop*, revolves around the struggles of Alejandro, a 10-year-old boy who works at an auto repair shop in a very rough neighborhood to support himself and his teenaged sister. Late in the film, after Ale discovers that his sister is selling sexual favors for money, he decides to catch her in the act and confront her. Twice, Ale walks through the barren, decrepit neighborhood, to a remote parking area where she meets the men (**Figure 22-17**).

Figure 22-16 Clever use of ambience and walla-walla, along with tight framing, in his short film *Snapshot* allowed Lund to convincingly conjure a crowded museum without having a real crowd.

Figure 22-17 Bahrani and special effects designer Abigail Savage carefully controlled the ambient sounds in the 2007 film *Chop Shop* to create dramatic emphasis within a naturalistic design.

The first time she is not there, the second time she is. For many reasons, this is a highly perilous act for Ale and this is subtly underscored and amplified by the ambient track during his journey through the neighborhood. Without undercutting the realist tone of the movie, Bahrani and sound effects designer and editor Abigail Savage worked with sounds that would be perfectly plausible for the location to evoke a sense of threat and anxiety. The first time Ale goes to the parking lot, the normal ambience of the nearby highway is layered over with the unsettling sounds of sirens, crashing metal, and a barking dog in the distance, increasing Ale's (and our) anxiety level. The second time Ale goes to confront his sister (this time he finds her), Bahrani and Savage utilized an even subtler, yet more unnerving ambient effect. They manipulated the ubiquitous buzzing of the sodium vapor security lamps that are characteristic of the environment. At the beginning of Ale's journey, the buzzing sound track was slowed down 50% so that its pitch was lower than normal. Then, down each new street, getting closer and closer to his sister, the buzzing sound track was sped up, raising its pitch, with each edit. The effect creates an edgy, intensification of emotional tension which is practically imperceptible on a conscious level. Consequently the film's realist tone is never broken.

Music

Source Music

Source music is the name for any music that has a visible source in the scene—for example, a song playing from a jukebox in the corner of a bar, the guitar that a character is playing, or the orchestral music of the Los Angeles Philharmonic in a bus driving down the highway (see **Figure 22-4**). Source music is always diegetic music, but it is not always direct sound (recorded in sync). Many times source music is postsynchronous sound, either gathered from prerecorded music (the jukebox playing in the bar) or recorded in postproduction (the orchestral music on the bus) and synced up in the editing. The guitar music, however, could easily be recorded on location as sync sound or handled as postsynchronous sound (**Figure 22-18**).

■ **Figure 22-18** The music emanating from Radio Raheem's (Bill Nunn) boom box in Lee's *Do the Right Thing* (1989) is a prime example of source music, even though it was dubbed in later.

■ **Figure 22-19** On major motion pictures an entire orchestra plays and records score music while the conductor watches the scene on a monitor for timing. Pictured is a scoring session for the *Lord of the Rings* trilogy.

The Score

The **musical score** (or **background music**) is nonsync and nondiegetic music that generally accompanies action or dialogue to underscore the events of a scene with a tone, a mood, or musical commentary. Most people understand how scary music can underscore frightening scenes, how lush and sweeping violins can infuse passion in a romantic moment, and how a jaunty score can encourage laughs for a funny scene. This use is so common that audiences barely notice score music, but they feel it deeply. Score music is often composed specifically for the film. In this case, the edited film is given to a composer who, in close consultation with the director, composes music timed to the actions, rhythms, and durations of specific scenes. Sometimes, the performance and recording of scored music are done while the performers watch the scenes projected to ensure perfect timing, not unlike ADR or foley sound effects (**Figure 22-19**). Other times, the composer will record a number of **musical motifs**, smaller musical phrases, which can be easily combined, elongated, and rearranged in the editing process to fit the temporal dimensions of the sequences.

Motifs can have a close association with an emotion, a psychological state, or an event such that the repetition of that musical phrase will evoke that feeling or event. For *Gone With the Wind*, Max Steiner created one of the most famous motifs in film history, called "Tara's Theme," a grand, sweeping melody that conjured the glory of the plantation and Scarlett's love for the land. Motifs can also be associated with a character and repeated whenever that character appears in the film or when you wish to evoke them. A character motif always contains something of the spirit of the character—for example, accompanying the shark in *Jaws* (1975) is the frighteningly efficient "duum-dum, duum-dum, duum-dum," which gathers momentum and malevolence the closer the shark gets. Once the association is made, all Spielberg needs to do is play the motif and everyone in the theater thinks, "Aaaak, shark!" even if we're only looking at blue water. In either case, the music is aligned with the scenes in editing. You can also use prerecorded music from CDs for your background music, like a jazz tune or a baroque suite from a CD. Using prerecorded music, however, means that you'll be cutting your picture to a musical track that is fixed. This is a major difference between these two types of background music. With one, the editing rhythm and tempi of the picture determine the music, and with the other, the music determines the rhythms and pace of the editing. Also, the length of prerecorded music is fixed, and getting into or out of a piece can be tricky—especially if you want the score to be somewhat understated.

Film music has been around for the entire history of cinema and is in itself a complex art form. It's beyond the scope of this book to elaborate in complete detail the uses of music in films, but a few concepts might be helpful. Obviously, the **tempo** and **rhythm** of music can infuse a scene with fast and explosive energy, as in the opening of *City of God* (see page 462), or with slow sensual fluidity, as in the case of Wong Kar-Wai's *In the Mood for Love* (**Figure 22-20**).

We are also all familiar with music that provides an **emotional tone** or **mood** in a scene. No one can resist feeling the exhilaration of victory in *Star Wars: Episode VI—Return of the Jedi* (1987) when the Rebel Alliance destroys the Death Star (**Figure 22-21**) and restores justice and order to the galaxy— especially when the heroism is underscored with John Williams' exuberant and energetic orchestral score. Incidentally, throughout the *Star Wars* series, Williams also created individual musical motifs for Darth Vader, Princess Leia, Luke Skywalker, and other major characters.

■ **Figure 22-20** Shigeru Umebayashi's bittersweet theme for Wong's *In the Mood for Love* (2000) perfectly encapsulates the film's slower pace and sad story, and is frequently repeated, particularly during slow motion sequences.

Prerecorded Music and Copyright Clearance

Using a prerecorded music track from a commercial CD, whether it's a pop song from last year, a folk song recorded in the 1950s, or a classical symphony from the 18th century, will usually require **copyright clearance**. Copyright clearance means that you have been given, or you have purchased, the rights to use specific music in your film. Getting copyright clearance requires a number of steps. Sometimes the

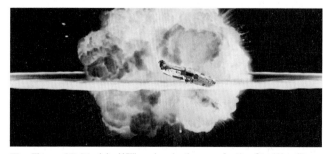

■ **Figure 22-21** John Williams' majestic score for the *Star Wars* films is designed to augment the emotional tone of the action, as seen in the triumphant final destruction of the second Death Star in Lucas' *Star Wars: Episode VI—Return of the Jedi* (1983).

■ FOREGROUNDING MUSIC TO ADD EXTRA LAYERS

Audiences are so familiar with the traditional role of music supporting the emotions of a scene that this music can fade in and fade out again without them being consciously aware of it. But music, like sound effects, can do much more than simply reinforce the existing mood, tone, or rhythm of a scene. Music can supply an extra, and sometimes surprising, layer of emotions or even commentary, and in these cases, the music is noticeable. In the famous "ear scene" in Quentin Tarantino's 1992 film *Reservoir Dogs,* an upbeat pop song ("Stuck in the Middle with You" by Stealers Wheel) plays on the radio as the cold-blooded killer, Mr. Blonde, tortures a captured police officer by slicing off his ear (**Figure 22-22**). The audience absolutely notices this music because the peppiness of the song completely plays against the horror we're witnessing on the screen, and this ironic juxtaposition only accentuates the cruelty of the moment. Another example of the overt use of music comes from Sean Penn's 2009 film *Into the Wild.* In addition to a traditional score, the director frequently interjects complete ballads sung by Eddie Vedder into the film. In these sequences, the narrative progress slows down, while the songs infuse a sense of the fatal innocence and social valor of a true folk hero into the actions of the central character Chris McCandless, a young man who wants to live free of material possessions and closer to nature. These sequences, which are cut to the rhythms of the songs, invoke the romanticism of a rambling man, a traveling seeker, a "supertramp" (**Figure 22-23**).

■ **Figure 22-22** The pop music that plays on the radio as Mr. Blonde (Michael Madsen) cruelly taunts a captured police officer creates a highly disturbing tonal dissonance in this scene from Tarantino's *Reservoir Dogs.*

■ **Figure 22-23** Penn's *Into the Wild* incorporates ballads sung by Eddie Vedder to provide a heroic subtext to the actions of the main character Chris McCandless (Emile Hirsch).

process is painless, especially for students who do not expect to make any money from the exhibition of their project, but other times it can be prohibitively difficult and expensive:

1. First you must ascertain and contact the person (or entity) who holds the rights to the song. This can be anywhere from simple to impossible. As a student, I once tried to get the rights to use a Rolling Stones song in a film of mine. After tracking down and contacting four of the numerous entities who held a piece of that song, I simply gave up. Each person passed the buck and I eventually realized that no one wanted to say yes to a proposition that held absolutely no financial gain for them. I was also discouraged because I knew that for me to legally use the song in my film I would need not just one rights holder to grant permission, but *all* of them. Obviously, the more popular the performer and composer, the more difficult it becomes because you enter into the corporate world of big money. In general, the music publisher owns the musical composition (music and lyrics) and the record company owns the recordings.

2. Once you have contacted the rights holder, you need to state specifically (a) what you want, (b) how much of it you want, (c) in what context it will be used, and (d) how the music will be credited. As you can understand, people who create or control artistic works are very careful about how the works are used. A composer who wrote a lovely ballad may not want his song used in and associated with a slasher film bloodbath. Complicating matters is that there is often not just one "right" you need to acquire, but a bundle of rights, including clearance for lyrics, clearance

for music composition, clearance for performance, and so on. Also, obtaining the right to cover a song is a totally different proposition than trying to get rights to prerecorded material from a CD. In other words, you really need to know what you're asking for. But let's move on.

3. If the rights holders are okay with your use of the music, then you negotiate the price of getting the rights. What's important to the rights holder here is how much money the filmmaker stands to make from the film for which the music is helping to sell tickets. So you need to be honest about what sort of distribution your film is expected to get. If your movie is a short movie made for a class and you hope to show the movie only at a few film festivals, then what you're asking for is called "festival rights." The cost of festival rights is often manageable. Occasionally, my students are given permission to use commercial music in their films for nothing.

If you have any intention of getting your film into festivals (which is a public screening), then you should take the time to acquire the necessary clearance. You never know. It's not uncommon for low-budget, independent films to become surprise festival hits, ones that attract commercial distributors. One of the first questions an interested distributor will ask is, "Do you have the rights to all of the music?" If you don't, then they'll probably back away. Why? A music rights holder is more likely to give a filmmaker a cheap price for rights *before* it has a distribution company attached, because they think the film is small, but if you attempt to buy music rights after your festival success (i.e., it has commercial value), then the earning potential of the movie skyrockets, as does the price for the music. The price for clearance can easily become more than a distributor wants to pay and so they pass, even though they love the movie. This is such a sad story and so common, but so crushing for the filmmaker that I dare not name examples, though I could.

I certainly cannot cover this topic in nearly enough detail, but it is necessary for you to be alerted to the fact that you cannot simply grab music from your CD collection to use in a film you plan to distribute to festivals or broadcast on TV. In the Recommended Readings and the Web Resources at the back of the book you will find some resources that can help you negotiate this complex terrain. Obtaining clearance, in any case, is usually a time-consuming process that requires patience, research, and persistence. Filmmakers on tight schedules, like students, are usually better off finding musicians to write original music for their films. There are many benefits to this: namely, you can acquire perfectly matched, custom-made music *and* collaborate with more creative people along the way.

---

in practice

■ COMMON MUSIC PITFALLS

Music, when used correctly, can be a profoundly expressive option in the filmmaker's toolbox of storytelling elements. The use of music to enhance a motion picture's impact can seem so easy, and yet there are a number of pitfalls to be wary of. A poorly employed musical score can bury what would otherwise be a fine film. Most problems with poorly used music come from "too much." Music is like a strong cooking spice—just because a little bit is good does not mean that more is better.

1. Use music only where it is necessary. **Wall-to-wall music** is the phenomenon of the excessive and indiscriminate use of music from the beginning to the end of a film. Music that relentlessly "cues emotions" from the audience can be exhausting and counterproductive because it ultimately impedes authentic audience involvement.

2. Don't try to evoke an emotion that is not in the film. It doesn't help to throw music under a scene simply because the scene isn't working. If a suspenseful scene does not create suspense in the actions, adding suspenseful music will not necessarily help. It will simply become an unsuspenseful scene with mismatched music.

3. Too loud! Often in student films the music is mixed in so loudly that it dominates anything else in the scene. In especially bad cases, loud music makes dialogue unintelligible. This is a sound mixing issue.

4. Watch out for mismatched tempo. Rhythm and tempo come from many places: the cutting pace, the actions in the frame, the camerawork, and the dialogue. Be careful that your music fits well with the tempo you've established in the picture editing. This doesn't necessarily mean to duplicate the rhythms beat-for-beat, because music can often serve as a rhythmic counterpoint.

5. Lyrics can be difficult to manage, especially in dialogue scenes. Lyrics tend to fight with dialogue for attention, even if you're using low-level source music, like a radio softly playing in the background. The more compelling the lyrics, the more they'll scream "listen to me!"

6. A related problem is inappropriate lyrics. I've seen many films where students will use a piece of music because they love the beats or the melody, but they're so familiar with the song that they've stopped really listening to the words. Remember: the words are expressing

something. They will invariably add a layer of meaning to your film. Make sure it's something you want to include.

7. Emotional associations are not fixed. While music is especially useful for conjuring emotions, the relationship between the particular music and the individual listener can be highly subjective. This is especially a problem when using popular music. You may decide to use a song in a love scene because it was on the radio two summers ago when you fell madly in love, so that piece of music resonates, for you, with all of those feelings. But this may not be a universal feeling about that song; in fact, there are no universal feelings about any song. When you use a very popular song, people bring their feelings about that song (and that band or that musical genre) with them into your movie instead of gleaning the emotional context from within the world of your movie.

■ SIMPLE SCORE MUSIC

Keep in mind that you certainly do not need the Los Angeles Philharmonic and a professional recording studio to score a film. One of my own short films, *Ode to Things* (1997) (7 minutes), was scored by Byron Estep, a very talented musician playing only a guitar, and the music was recorded in a small soundproof recording room Byron built in his apartment. *Ode to Things* is an adaptation of a poem by Pablo Neruda; it follows a day in the life of a married couple, detailing the myriad "things" they use over the course of that day: keys, pencils, napkins, shoelaces, spoons, sunglasses, and so on. Byron and I sat in his apartment and watched the film a few times, discussing the overall feeling I wanted to evoke in the

film, which was affection. The film, I told him, was an affectionate and appreciative look at those simple objects that help us live our daily lives but that we scarcely even notice. It was a paean to common objects. I also pointed out to him the place where the film/poem shifts from a literal discussion of "things" into a more metaphysical mode. I indicated to him that there needed to be a marked shift in the tone of the music right at that point, telling him where the music needed to dig a little deeper. As we watched and talked he played me a few riffs on the guitar and together we found the musical mood and themes we were looking for. Then Byron moved to his soundproof room, opened a mike, and, as he watched the film one more time, expertly improvised on those themes, modulating into a minor key and slowing the tempo just a hair when the film shifted into its metaphysical mode; then he resolved back to the bright major key just as the final images faded to black. He nailed it in one go! I took that track, which was recorded on DAT, and downloaded it into the Avid, laid it into my sound track, and adjusted a few frames, and voilà, my scored sound track was done. All in all it took one great musician and about four hours (**Figure 2-24**).

Figure 22-24 The lovely original score music for Hurbis-Cherrier's short *Ode to Things* was conceived, written, performed, and recorded by Byron Estep—in his apartment!

■ SOUND DESIGN STRATEGIES

> *Sound may be the most powerful tool in the filmmaker's arsenal in terms of its ability to seduce. That's because "sound," as the great sound editor Alan Splet once said, "is a heart thing." We, the audience, interpret sound with our emotions, not our intellect.*
> **Randy Thom (sound designer, *Wild at Heart, Forrest Gump, The Incredibles*)**
> **(From "Designing a Movie for Sound," 1999, www.filmsound.org)**

In film production we have a great degree of control over the actual sounds used in the sound design and we are able to create a sound environment that can be anything from highly objective, using a direct sound, documentary approach, to highly subjective, reflecting the emotional or psychological state of a character. A sound design can provide a tone of irony or hyperbole, or even create fantastic or intellectual associations between sound and image. Moreover, one can combine any number of approaches in a single film. The possibilities are endless. The question to ask yourself is: What are you trying to say with this film and how can sound help you accomplish that?

From Realism to Stylized Approaches

The continuum from **realism** in sound to a **stylized** sound design, as with cinematography, cannot be broken down into strict categories. The differences between approaches can be subtle and practices can overlap. Films that overall employ a realistic sound design often use stylization to elevate certain dramatic moments.

Realism obviously can be achieved through **direct sound**, which is the use of sounds recorded at the actual location (usually in sync). This "realism" is a documentary type of realism, but depending on microphone placement it can be more or less convincing. Realism is also achievable through the careful and judicious addition of other nondirect sounds, which are motivated by the scale of a shot (close-ups requiring "closer" sounds and long shots requiring remote sounds), by the dramatic magnitude of the actions, or by character psychology. For example, the sound of a gun firing in an extreme long shot is expected to sound lower and farther away than a gun going off in a close-up. However, the direct sound of a man firing a gun in a long shot might be "realistic," but will also, in all likelihood, be thinner than what most movie audiences expect from a gunshot in a fictional narrative film. If the narrative context calls for a big and violent sound, then adding a closer, darker gunshot sound effect will be necessary and not necessarily unrealistic. Using a sound that enriches the image and adds an expressive or emotional feel to the action from which it emanates is referred to (originally by the sound theorist Michel Chion) as **added value sound**. This "hyper-real" sound effect doesn't in and of itself create a stylized sound approach. Although it is an artifice, it in fact gives a stronger impression of realism by reinforcing the emotional energy of the dramatic moment. Remember, "sound is a heart thing." However, if we should add a sound effect of a lion's roar inside the gunshot to augment the menace and power of the gun, we would then be pulling away from realism into stylization.

A simple example of this can be seen in Akira Kurosawa's *Dreams* (1990) (Figure 22-25). In "The Tunnel" segment, an officer walks along a small mountain road, returning home from a battle in which his entire platoon has been annihilated. As he enters a tunnel, he is confronted by rabid dog, which bares its teeth and growls at him. Through a layered sound design, each bark and growl of the dog includes real vicious dog barks with what sounds like gunshots and cannon fire. The sound effect not only increases the ferociousness of the dog, but through it we understand that this is not a "real" dog, it's a hound from hell, a dog from the hell of war. In keeping with the otherworldliness of this particular "dream" (or nightmare, in this case), Kurosawa employs an otherworldly, stylized sound approach.

■ **Figure 22-25** The barking of this dog in Kurosawa's *Dreams* is manipulated to sound much more aggressive than in real life. Michel Chion calls this type of sound manipulation "added value sound."

in practice

The Sound of Strict Realism

The Dardenne Brothers' 1996 film *La Promesse* is an excellent example of a realist film that uses a direct sound approach almost exclusively to express its tragic story in an utterly honest and immediate way. The Dardenne Brothers' aesthetic approach to this film, as with all of their other films, is a fairly strict vérité documentary style: handheld camera, real locations, natural light, and almost exclusively direct audio recorded by the microphone in the field. An example of the effectiveness of the Dardennes' uncompromis-

■ **Figure 22-26** Realistic and stylized sound design. In *La Promesse* the Dardenne Brothers maintain audio that matches the documentary style of the cinematography *(top)*. *The Wrestler* maintains a realist tone for most of the film, but includes two moments of subjective sound design *(center)*. In Demme's *The Silence of the Lambs*, sound designer Skip Lievsay often interjects stylized, subjective sounds when the dramatic tension is elevated *(bottom)*.

ing approach occurs early in the film, when the main character, Igor, a 15-year-old boy, is running through a building under construction, warning all of the illegal immigrant workers to flee because inspectors are on their way. As he climbs a staircase, Igor hears Amidou, an illegal immigrant from Africa, fall several floors from the scaffolding. Igor races down the stairs; when he reaches Amidou, Igor sees that he is badly hurt. Just before the man dies, he asks the boy to take care of his wife and the boy promises that he will. It's a central and highly dramatic moment in the film—but the audio remains absolutely realistic and without any embellishment. What the boy hears in the stairwell is the very faint and simple clank of a scaffolding pipe breaking loose. It's easy to miss, and we certainly don't know what has happened until the boy reaches Amidou outside. During the dialogue between them, not one additional sound is used to pull pathos from the moment. There is no sad music, no added value sound effects, no special ambience to enrobe these characters at this moment in which everything is suddenly and dramatically changed. The track consists of whatever was picked up on the boom mike in the field. The strict use of nothing but direct sound leads the audience to feel that this is not a constructed fictional film, that this did indeed truly happen. In this unembellished moment we feel as if we are kneeling right next to Amidou and Igor (**Figure 22-26**, *top*).

Realism with Elevated Moments

Darren Aronofsky's film *The Wrestler* (2008) follows the bitter end of an aging professional wrestler's career as he struggles to find a new life after a devastating heart attack. *The Wrestler* can be described as having a realistic style, both visually and aurally. Indeed many people have noted its "documentary-like" look and feel. True to form, the ambient sound throughout the film faithfully reflects the locations of each scene. But there are two notable deviations, which add nondiagetic sounds in an attempt to get us inside the main character's perspective. The first exception takes place when Randy "The Ram" has his heart attack following a particularly brutal wrestling match. As Randy doubles over in pain, the ambience of the locker room is replaced by a high-pitched whine and echoes of voices, which draw us into what Randy is experiencing during this brush with death. The second instance, later in the film, is an even greater stylistic departure from realism. Randy has secured a new job working the deli counter at a supermarket. As he walks through the hallways, stockrooms, and loading areas in the back of the supermarket on his way the deli counter, the ambience of the supermarket slowly fades out and is replaced by the sound of a cheering crowd. These are the cheers Randy would have heard in his wrestling prime, when he was star, making his way through the sports arena tunnels from the locker room to the ring. Placed here, the cheers are a commentary by the filmmaker, reminding us of who Randy once was and showing us what he's become. It's a brief moment in the film, but it's heartbreaking because it reinforces the fact that wresting is still this man's life, his entire identity; but now, as he pushes through the plastic curtains, he is not entering the ring to fight in the main event, he is entering a deli counter to sling potato salad (**Figure 22-26**, *center*).

Story and a Stylized Design

Jonathan Demme's *The Silence of the Lambs* (1991) is a classic example of a film, shot in a highly dramatic style, which uses added value sounds (ambience and sound effects) in a more or less "realistic" way throughout most of the film, but then selectively elevates other, exceptionally dramatic moments by incorporating overtly stylistic flourishes to the sound design. For example, early in the film, just as the lead character, Clarice Starling, is about to meet the serial killer, Hannibal Lecter, for the first time, the chief administrator of the institution, Dr. Chilton, shows Clarice a photograph of one of Hannibal's victims. We do not see the photograph she is looking at, only her reaction, but the sound track leaves no doubt as to the gruesomeness of the image and the savagery of Lecter's actions.

On the dialogue track Chilton talks about the attack on a nurse, "When she leaned over him he did *this* to her ... they managed to save an eye, reset her jaw more or less" and his voice is recorded oppressively close, too close for comfort, like he's right at our ear. The ambience track suddenly becomes thick with a portentous low bass rumble and a sound effects track additionally layers the diabolical groans and malevolent breathing of a madman. Although Clarice is trying to remain professional and confident, the sound track infuses the scene with fear. This is not objective fear, it is *her* fear, escalating like a spiking pulse rate, and we share her dread that when she sees Hannibal, she will be seeing the face of evil. A few moment later, as Clarice enters the secure cell block where Hannibal is imprisoned, the automatic prison bars close behind her with a decisive, resounding, and exaggerated *clang*, giving her and us the feeling that she is well and good locked in with a madman who eats people's faces. Then, the moment she begins her tentative progress toward Hannibal's cell, the music track slips in. A slow, low-pitched dirge, a frightening musical scale, descends lower and lower the closer she gets to "Hannibal the Cannibal," who, once he sees her, greets her with a surprisingly courteous "Good Morning." All of these sounds (ambience, sound effects, and music) are not merely hyper-real, they are downright expressionistic. The sound design not only amplifies the terror that the young FBI agent is feeling at meeting her first serial killer face-to-face, but it communicates her emotional point of view so directly that we feel what she is feeling as well (**Figure 22-26**, *bottom*).

■ SOUND DESIGN IN THE V&V ONLINE FILMS

The five *Voice & Vision* online example films provide an excellent study in sound design. One reason these films were chosen was for the variety of approaches they take to sound. It's instructive to consider and compare how their different approach to sound design correlate with their particular stories. Two of these films use no dialogue whatsoever, one is primarily voice-over, another is essentially dialogue driven. One film uses no music, another uses source music, and three others incorporate score music. Be sure to check them all out at www.voiceandvisionbook.com.

The Black Hole

There is no dialogue in this brief, action-driven film, so without the need for sync sound, *The Black Hole* could be shot entirely MOS. There is no music in this

film either. All the narrative and emotional sound work is achieved through a well conceived ambient track and sound effects (all added in postproduction). This is a very efficient way to work. In terms of hard sound effects, listen to the otherworldly hum in the shots from the underside of the hole (as if that POV were from another dimension) and the dark electrical buzz when the character puts a finger or hand into the hole. Listen carefully at the moment when he gets the idea to plunder the safe—he's eating the candy bar and takes a big, greedy bite out of it; the heightened, wet sound of his smacking lips underscores his avarice. It's subtle and sharp. More overt is the climax of the film, which is intensified by the escalation of the black hole buzzing sound and his heavy breathing as he plunders the safe. Also, listen closely to the ambient track. At first it seems like an ordinary office environment, with the rhythmic beeping of a photocopier making multiple copies, but the filmmakers never let up on that beeping sound. Throughout the film, that beeping takes on various overtones depending on the actions of the main character and in the end (it seems to me), the beeping mocks him; life goes on as usual, the task he's supposed to be performing—photocopying papers—continues without him.

Plastic Bag

The ambience and sounds effects in this film are more or less realistic. The sounds of the plastic bag, wind, water, beach, bulldozers, seagulls, bugs, etc. are all what we'd expect. There is notably one stylized moment when the plastic bag is "born" early on in the film, when it take its "first breath," and the ambient sound of the supermarket becomes clear. This little aural moment seems to imply that before the bag is opened and put to use, it was in a state of silent, pre-consciousness. Clearly the dominant sound track in this film is the voice-over track (spoken by Werner Herzog). As I mentioned before, voice-over works best when you do not use it to tell the entire story or duplicate what we see on screen; instead it should add another layer to our understanding of the story. Turn off the sound and you will still get the very basic story: A plastic bag from the supermarket goes home with a woman who uses it for other tasks. After she uses it to clean up a dog's mess, the bag is discarded and winds up in the landfill. It is then blown around by the winds through a landscape that is utterly devoid of human life, and it winds up in the ocean with a lot of other plastic bags. But include the voice-over and you'll see all the new layers it adds to this simple journey. Primarily, the voice infuses the bag with human consciousness and motivation. Not only does the bag refer to its "skin," "hand," and "mind," but it also speaks of desires, fear, hope, beauty, joy, madness, despair, and needing a purpose in the world. The bag is more than a sentient being—it's a sensitive soul. This "humanity" means that it also perceives its condition of loneliness, purposelessness, and immortality as a human would—as a terrible tragedy. Also critical to *Plastic Bag* is the score (by Kjartan Sveinsson of *Sigur Ros*). Though quite subtle, the music underscores the various emotional shades in the film, and it also helps to change narrative direction. Listen carefully to when the music comes up and when it falls out again and when it changes (slightly) in tone. The first time music enters is fully six minutes into the film, when the bag learns to "navigate the winds" and decides to look for its maker. Watch this film and take note of when the music enters and drops out, and you'll see how Bahrani uses the score to skillfully delineate the narrative beats and emotional progression of the journey.

Waking Dreams

Turn off the sound in this film and you won't get it at all. Waking Dreams is a heavily dialogue-driven film and relies on location sync sound. Character, motivation, and the central existential question play out in the verbal interactions between the office temp Becky and the executive Mr. Saroyan. As I mention on page 39, Daschbach handles the dialogue extremely well. His characters do not tell us the story or their feelings in words; rather the dialogue is part of dramatizing their reactions to this rather bizarre encounter. There is clearly some added ambient sound of the office environment (off-screen typing, phones ringing, etc.) to provide authenticity to the location, and for most of the film Daschbach stays with a highly realistic sound design. There is not much in the way of music or sound effects in the film except as transition devices (i.e., the airplane and Caribbean steel pan drums to efficiently indicate that time has passed and Mr. Saroyan took his vacation, and a few notes played backward to suture scenes together). However, in the last scene, piano score music is laid over the street ambience to add a new emotional layer to Mr. Saroyan's indecisiveness at this critical moment, which elevates this final scene into a genuinely existential dilemma.

When I Was Young

Strict realism is the general sound design approach for this film. It would be inappropriate to be too polished or hyperbolic with a film that has a quasi-documentary feel and might contradict the emotional tone of this story of a woman who feels she's fallen into a life of compromise. In addition to the sync sound, music plays an important role in this film. In keeping with the realist tone, the music is not underscore music but in-scene source music from her radio or played by musicians or whistled by another character. Take note of how Lu uses music as a sound bridge to get us from present day Philadelphia to her memories of the American boy she knew in China.

Vive le 14 Juillet

With no sync dialogue, this film was shot entirely MOS with a small crew. The playful music track (composed of source and prerecorded underscore music) not only identifies this as a distinctively French film (set during Bastille Day after all) but it also carries important narrative functions. Songs like Serge Gainsbourg's "Sea, Sex and Sun" put an extra edge on the wayward girlfriend's flirtatiousness, the military band music at the parade serves to contrast this mild guy with the military brawn around him, and the return to the tender accordion music at the end implies that he has re-won her heart and they are in love again. All the ambience and source sounds were recorded as wild sound (the tank) or were prerecorded sound effects (morning birds) and were mixed with a slightly exaggerated presence, more like cartoon noises than strict realism. Again, this is perfectly consistent with the playful tone of the whole film.

Cutting Sound and Working with Multiple Tracks

One of the things that I try to hold on to is some sort of creative constraint. For example, one of those creative constraints might be: "I'm going to only give myself eight channels to edit" ... and if I can't make something interesting in that eight channels, I am going to get rid of something and replace it with something else until I get something that is, in fact, interesting. And the reason why that's an important way to work is that it helps you focus on what the music and the sound is truly about. Because if you can't figure out the essence of "what it's about" within a creative constraint of a minimum amount of channels then you're probably doing something wrong.

Ren Klyce (sound designer, *Panic Room, Fight Club, The Social Network*)
(From DVD extras, *Panic Room,* 2002)

■ WORKING WITH MULTIPLE TRACKS

In the previous chapter we defined a film's sound design as the complete aural impression of a movie created through the layering of multiple tracks of sound, and we concentrated on defining the various sound elements and discussing their creative application. In this chapter we will look closely at the more practical aspects of building the sound design, specifically how to work with multiple tracks within a nonlinear editing timeline. The most basic principle of multiple tracks is that it allows us to layer sounds that occur simultaneously in the film—for example, music playing under dialogue while we also hear waves crashing on the shore, which would involve three layered tracks running simultaneously (**Figure 23-1**).

There are four fundamental tasks in audio postproduction: **finding, positioning, enhancing, and mixing**. The first task we have already covered in detail (choosing the best lines of dialogue, the perfect sound effects, and the most appropriate music). The second task means to locate the precise placement for each sound element in your sound design, meaning the right dramatic moment (horizontally along the timeline) and the best track for individual equalizing and creative sound manipulation (vertically along the layered tracks). The third task involves the enhancement of each sound element to craft a multilayered sound design that works toward the same goal as the writing, directing, cinematography, and editing—telling your story in the style you choose. The last task, mixing, includes fixing the perfect interplay and relative dynamic levels of each sound element to all the others in the final version of the sound track.

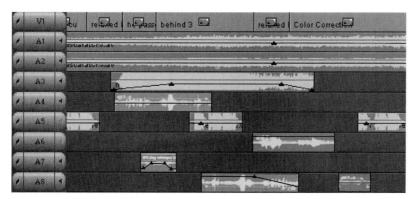

■ **Figure 23-1** The timeline for this project has 8 tracks of audio—1 stereo pair and 6 mono tracks. NLE systems can layer upward of 99 tracks of audio.

Building Your Audio Tracks

Even though popular NLE systems allow us to create 99 audio tracks, clearly most films use only a small fraction of this capacity. The sound design for *Apocalypse Now* included more than 75 audio tracks, but short films and low-budget productions can easily be made with anywhere from 3 to 12 tracks of audio.

The construction of your sound design follows various stages, from the most important sounds (those that are essential to understanding the story) to the supplementary sounds (those that add tone, mood, or other sonic dimensions to the film). We begin to build our tracks from the moment we start to put shots together in the first assembly and first rough cut. If your film is driven primarily by a music track, then start with that. If you're cutting a narrative that is dialogue based, then picture and dialogue editing will happen simultaneously. As you edit your early rough cuts, you will find it necessary to start adding other sound track layers that also play a vital role in the progress of the story and are therefore necessary for picture editing. Again, the basic rule for rough editing applies: don't fine-tune something that may have to be undone later. Start with the cake, and then later add the icing. The typical progression for the gradual buildup of audio tracks for a narrative film with sync sound dialogue goes something like this:

- Audio tracks from rough cut to fine cut:

1. *Dialogue.* The first assembly and first rough cut include rough picture and production dialogue editing involving only a few tracks of audio (see Chapter 20).
2. *Essential sound effects.* Subsequent rough cuts add a sound effect track for important hard sound effects, especially those that are central to the story and to which characters in a scene respond.
3. *Music–I.* If necessary, an additional track is then added for sequences that are intended to be edited to music (for example, chases or montage sequences cut to prerecorded music).

- Audio tracks after picture lock.

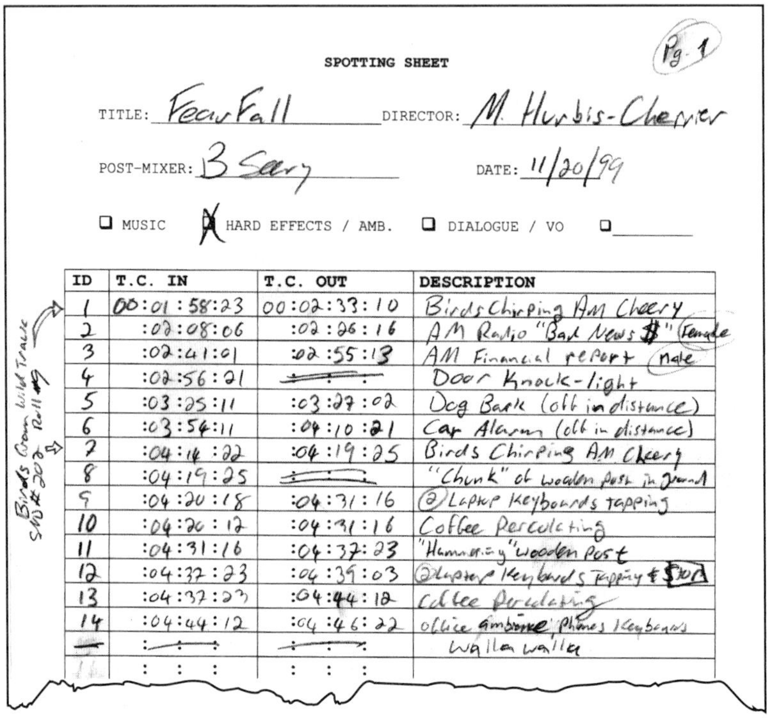

SPOTTING SHEET

Pg. 1

TITLE: FearFall DIRECTOR: M. Hurbis-Cherrier

POST-MIXER: B Sary DATE: 11/20/99

☐ MUSIC ☒ HARD EFFECTS / AMB. ☐ DIALOGUE / VO ☐

ID	T.C. IN	T.C. OUT	DESCRIPTION
1	00:01:58:23	00:02:33:10	Birds Chirping AM Cheery
2	:02:08:06	:02:26:16	AM Radio "Bad News $" (Female)
3	:02:41:01	:02:55:13	AM Financial report (male)
4	:02:56:21		Door Knock-light
5	:03:25:11	:03:27:02	Dog Bark (off in distance)
6	:03:54:11	:04:10:21	Car Alarm (off in distance)
7	:04:14:22	:04:19:25	Birds Chirping AM Cheery
8	:04:19:25		"Chunk" of wooden post in ground
9	:04:20:18	:04:31:16	(2) Laptop Keyboards tapping
10	:04:26:12	:04:31:16	Coffee Percolating
11	:04:31:16	:04:37:23	"Hammering" wooden post
12	:04:37:23	:04:39:03	(2) Laptop Keyboards Tapping & [illegible]
13	:04:37:23	:04:44:12	Coffee Percolating
14	:04:44:12	:04:46:22	Office ambience, Phones, Keyboards
			Walla walla
	: : :	: : :	

■ **Figure 23-2** The first page of the sound effects spotting sheet for *FearFall* (2000). After picture lock, all missing sound effects are listed in the order they occur in the program with their approximate timecode in- and out-points. You can download a blank spotting sheet from the book's website.

- Once you have arrived at picture lock, with the image and essential audio tracks in their fixed places, you then turn your attention to the supplementary sounds—those sounds that provide extra layers of mood, tone, and information. This is where much of the creative sound design work begins. The first step in this process is called **spotting for sound** (or just **spotting**). Spotting is the process of sitting down and closely watching the picture-locked movie to identify, scene by scene, the placement and character of any additional sound effects, ambience tracks, or music that are needed. Notes are taken on a **"spotting sheet"** detailing the location (scene, shot, and time-code reference) of each sound effect and music track (sync and nonsync), along with your thoughts on the tone, mood, or other contribution that each sound is supposed to provide in the film (**Figure 23-2**). Do you want to add an off-screen siren under a tense confrontation? What sort of siren? How far off? On what line exactly does it come in and how long can we hear it before it fades away? If someone else is composing the music or creating the sound design, then this process is done in collaboration between them and the director.

Continuing with the track progression, the next steps involve:

4. *Adding final hard sound effects.* Once the film has been thoroughly spotted, all of the sound effects must be composed (or found) and placed in the appropriate audio track. This usually involves adding a few more tracks if several effects overlap. This step is where you replace all scratch sound effects as well.

5. *Room tone tracks.* An additional track is added for production room tone when it is needed to smooth over dialogue edits and fill in dialogue gaps. Remember: with extremely rare exceptions, there should be no place in your sound design where there is utterly no sound. Silence almost always means adding quiet room tone. A complete absence of sound signals to viewers a technical problem with the audio.

6. *Ambient tracks.* Further tracks can be added if you need additional ambient sounds to add a mood or sense of location for a certain scene (like adding the ambient sound of off-screen waves on the beach to indicate that a scene takes place in a beachfront home).

7. *Score music and background source music.* Finally, after the composer has created the score (specifically to the locked picture edit) and/or you've located any background source music used in the film, you'll need to add still more tracks to accommodate these elements.

By now you should be getting a good idea how a film like *Apocalypse Now* ended up with close to 75 tracks of audio! However, remember that many films need only 5 or fewer tracks.

■ WHAT ARE SCRATCH TRACKS?

Scratch tracks (also called **temp tracks**) are audio cuts (either music, voice-over, or sound effects) that are slugged in temporarily during the editing process when the actual sounds still need to be composed, recorded, or located. Rather than hold up the picture cutting, we insert scratch tracks that have a similar character (rhythm, feel, duration) to the sound we will ultimately use. Scratch tracks are often used in editing the rough cuts to establish basic placement and timing and are replaced when the actual sound is finished and ready to cut in.

■ BASIC SOUND DESIGN: ANALYSIS OF AN AVERAGE SCENE

Figures 23-3 and **23-4** shows an example of the audio track layout for a relatively ordinary scene that has a few stylistic flourishes. This scene, from the final moments of a film I made in 2000 called *FearFall,* takes place in an average, middle class, suburban neighborhood. Ray Wilson has become completely paranoid about the people who recently moved in next door, although he's never met or even seen them. His mania has caused

■ **Figure 23-3**
The scene from *FearFall* (2000) in which detailed attention to sound design was considered early in the scriptwriting stage.

INT. WILSON BEDROOM - NIGHT

Ray is standing at the window, eyes fixed on the Jones house. Ellen sits up in the bed, telephone next to her, re-reading Sophie's note.

Ray sees a light go on and for the first time he sees a figure next door: against the closed curtains a man's silhouette crosses from the front of the house to the back. The light goes off. Then Ray faintly hears the Jones' BACKDOOR open and close. The dog BARKS, then stops. A METALLIC SCRAPE, the lock on his gate? Some RUSTLING outside...

A beat of silence, suddenly Ray cocks his head to listen.

                    RAY
              (whispering)
         Did you lock the back door?

                         ELLEN (O.S.)
              Ray, I'm not...

                    RAY
              (sharp but still a whisper)
         Ssshhh! Did you lock the door?

Ellen is getting scared.

                    ELLEN
              (whispering)
         I think so...I don't know.

Suddenly, a dull THUD downstairs, definitely *IN* their house! They freeze.

                    RAY
              (very softly)
         They're in here.

INT. WILSON KITCHEN

Sophie has just opened the refrigerator which has caused bottles to rattle. She pokes around for munchies and beer.

his 15-year-old daughter to "run away" from home, which means she's just hanging out at a friend's house (which she explains in a note to her parents). Ray, however, is sure that she's been lured next door by the neighbors, who he is convinced are very dangerous.

In this scene, sound was central to the progress of the story and psychology of the character. Ray hears a collection of ambiguous noises that, in his paranoid state, signify that the neighbors have broken into his house. To him, the sounds are clear evidence of someone moving from the Jones' house, to the backyard, and into his house. On screen, Ray's head pivots as his eyes follow exactly this path. In fact, the sounds are a circumstantial combination of noises from the neighbor's house and from his own daughter, who has snuck back home to nab some food for her friends. Although these sounds have real (off-screen) sources, the scenario Ray spins with them emerges from his paranoid imagination (**Figure 23-4**).

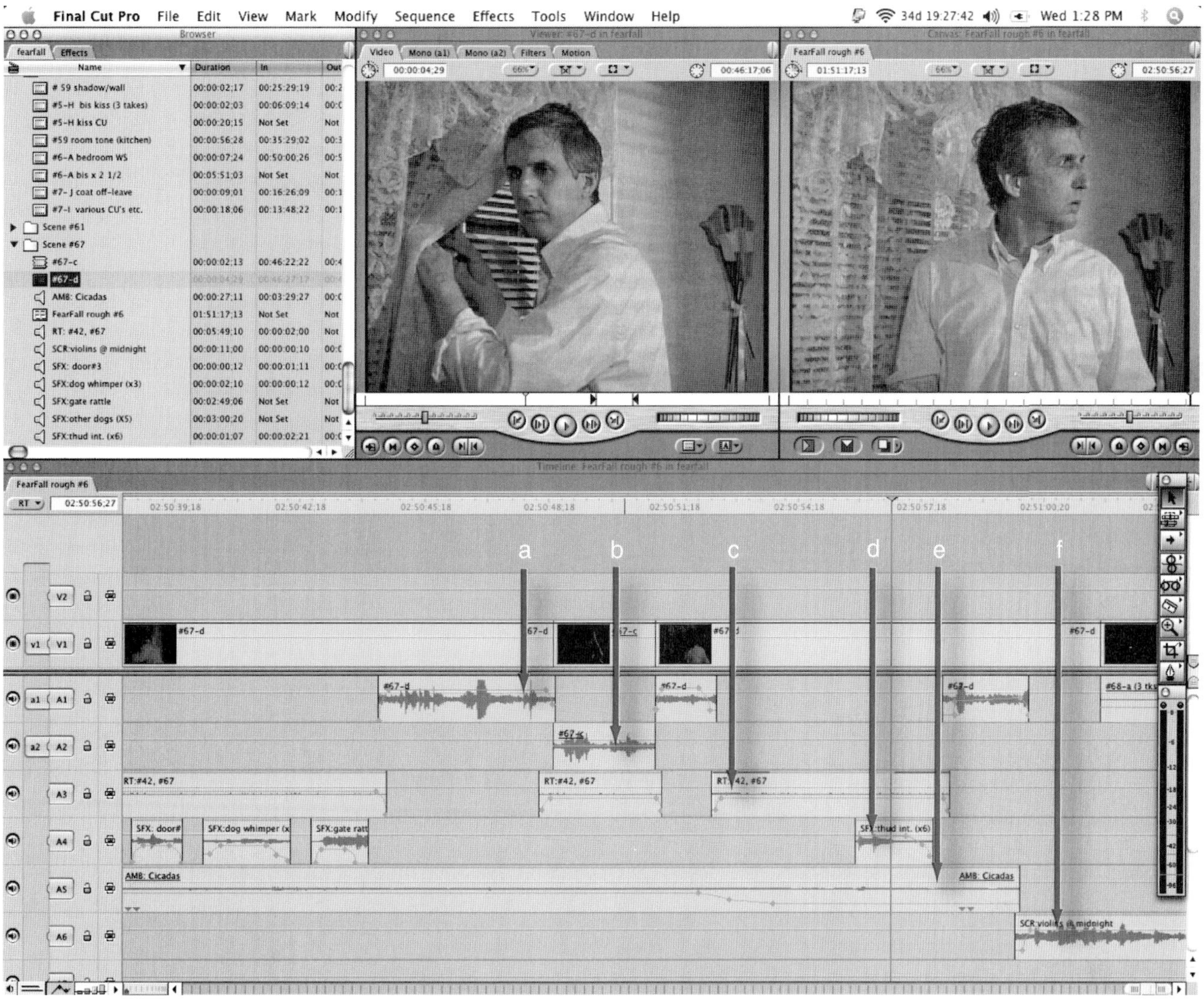

■ **Figure 23-4** A careful selection of sounds serves to deepen Ray's (James Rutledge) paranoia in this scene from *FearFall*. Audio tracks: (a) Track 1, Ray's dialogue; (b) Track 2, Ellen's dialogue; (c) Track 3, production room tone; (d) Track 4, sound effects; (e) Track 5, ambience; (f) Track 6, music.

Dialogue Tracks

We have already discussed the craft of dialogue editing and the role of L-cuts, J-cuts, and insert edits for creating dialogue rhythms, point of view, and emphasis (see Chapter 20). Now let's look at a few technical aspects of handling dialogue on the timeline.

The dialogue for the *FearFall* scene discussed in the preceding section was edited as **split tracks**, meaning each character's dialogue is placed on its own audio track (Ray: Track 1; Helen: Track 2). The idea behind splitting tracks that occur in the same location and same time is that you have greater ability to equalize (or EQ, for short) each track separately. **Equalizing** basically means adjusting the various frequencies and characteristics of a sound to achieve a specific quality (see "The Sound Mix," later in the chapter). In the case of dialogue, a shift in microphone proximity, recoding quality, or ambient sound can make the edits between lines of dialogue too apparent for continuity's sake. Splitting the dialogue allows you to easily EQ one or both tracks so that they match better. In the case of *FearFall,* Ellen's shots were taken later, after it had gotten very hot at the location. There was a fan going in the next room, which no one on the set noticed, but that gave her sync audio a slight low-frequency hum. By splitting her dialogue off, it was easy to select her clips and remove selected low frequencies until the ambient sound of Ellen's dialogue matched Ray's perfectly (**Figure 23-5**). The EQing of tracks is not done in the editing stage but is accomplished during final sound mixing (discussed later). Splitting Ray's and Ellen's dialogue onto

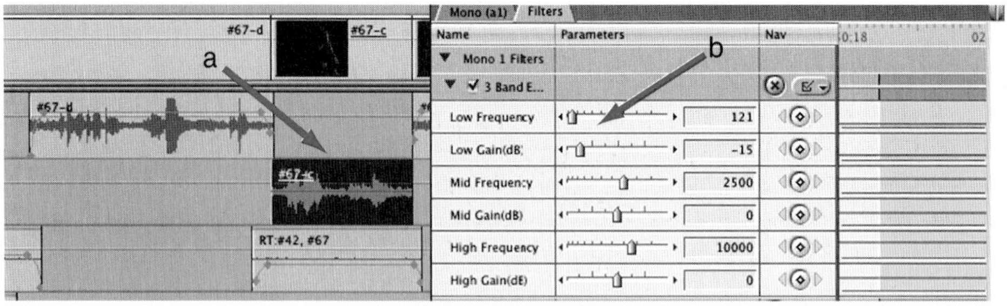

Figure 23-5 By applying the three-band equalizer filter to a specific clip (a), you can select and attenuate specific frequencies in the sound spectrum (b).

separate tracks also allowed me to create a slight overlap when Ray interrupts her. Scenes in which people step on each other's lines can be created by overlapping split dialogue.

If the sound quality of your dialogue matches perfectly and you have no overlaps, then you don't necessarily need to split tracks, and any slight smoothing out of cuts can be accomplished with quick cross-fades (four frames or so) between dialogue edits to smooth out the cut point (**Figure 23-6**).

Room Tone

The room tone you gathered during the production of the film is downloaded into the computer and saved as a sound clip with the other editing elements for the each scene (Room Tone: Track 3). Room tone is used primarily to fill in "silent" gaps between lines of dialogue. Remember that silence in film, as in real life, does not mean the total absence of sound. Background noises in the environment are always present and audible (with the exception of outer space, where there is no sound) (see page 330). So in the moment when Ray remains quiet, listening, the ambient sound of the room must fill in that space (**Figure 23-7**).

You may wonder why I didn't simply use the sync take as Ray looks around and hears noises. A sync take would have had the same room tone, so why did I have to slug in new room tone? New room tone was necessary here because to get the performance I needed—that is, the very sharp reaction to a series of noises—I "verbally cued" each noise

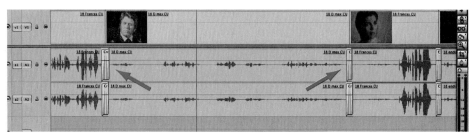

Figure 23-6 The arrows point to the four frame cross-fades that are commonly used to smooth over sound edits when cutting dialogue on a single track.

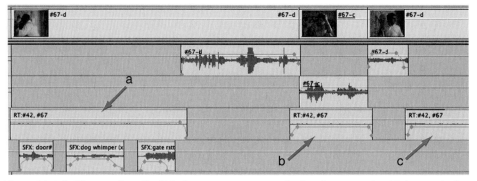

Figure 23-7 In this scene from *FearFall,* clean room tone was cut in along its own track to fill the gaps in the sync audio (a and c) and to even out the ambience in Ellen's shot (b).

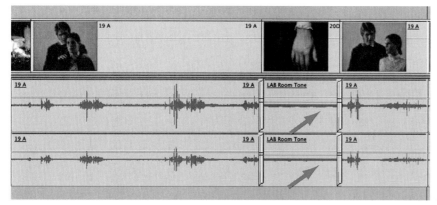

■ **Figure 23-8** When cutting single-strand dialogue, matching room tone can be seamlessly added under MOS shots using quick (four-frame) cross-fades at the edit points *(arrows)*.

at precisely the moment Ray was supposed to hear them. During the take I would say, "the dog barks ... stops ... The gate, they're opening the gate! What's that rustling?" and so on. The sound recordist, of course, picked up all of this, so the original sync take was cut out and replaced with nice, clean room tone. This illustrates another use of room tone: replacing any parts of the existing ambience that contains noises the recordist picked up, but that you'd rather not have in the sound design. For example, if a motorcycle roars past in what is otherwise a perfect take, you just need to replace the motorcycle section with clean ambience you recorded at the location. If your dialogue ambience matches perfectly and you wanted to cut the dialogue on a single track, then ambience would be used between the lines to fill in the "silent" gaps (**Figure 23-8**). This is why it's important to remember to record at least 1 minute of room tone/ambience at every location before you break down the set.

Hard Effects Track

Hard effects are either downloaded from a digital recording or from the Internet, or they are imported from an audio CD as sound clips; they are then logged, named, and, like room tone, saved along with the sync takes and other editing elements for each scene for quick access.

Even though all of the hard effects in the Ray/Ellen scene are nonsync (Effects: Track 4), they nonetheless required careful alignment with Ray's head and eye movements, which precisely indicated where his attention was focused and when he heard a noise. So I created an effects track right in the first rough cut with the dialogue (**Figure 23-9**). Two of these effects were recorded on location. We got a great recording of the "screen door"

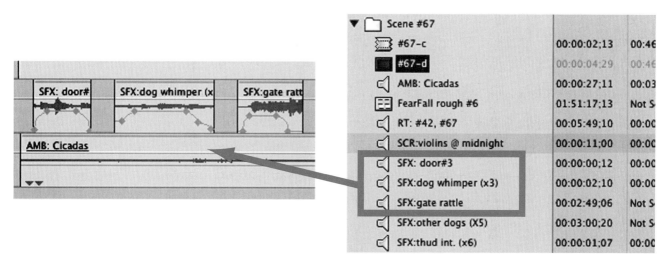

■ **Figure 23-9** Detail of the sound effects and ambient tracks from *FearFall*. All sound files for a particular scene should be saved in the same folder as the scene clips.

opening and closing (with a squeak and a tinny latch sound) right in the house where we were shooting. And the "rustle" effect was stolen from another scene entirely (one in which Ray is in the bushes, hiding from his neighbors), but was tweaked a bit; it worked beautifully in the scene. These effects I cut in right away. Initially, I had to use a scratch "dog bark" and "metal gate" sound because it took me some time (and two CD sound effects libraries) to find just the right dog and I had to create the metal gate sound from scratch a few weeks later.

It's important that your sound effects be as pure as possible, without too much ambience behind the noise you want. Also, cut the effect as tightly as possible, without clipping off any of the sound. When adding additional tracks, you want to avoid piling

in practice

■ SOUND FX LIBRARIES

Sound effects collections come either on CDs or can be found through numerous sites on the Internet, where you pay per sound effect download. A good sound effects library can provide you with sounds you could only dream of recording on your own: dozens of factory noises, hundreds of airplane and helicopter fly-bys, and more dog barks than you can imagine. If you need the sound of a 1965 Mustang starting up and pulling away, you'll find it. If you want the wheels to screech, they've got that too (**Figure 23-10**).

But beware, not all commercial effects libraries are created equal and some are mostly garbage. Wading through the bad stuff to find the sounds you can actually use can take a lot of research time. Also be aware that sound effects libraries come from different countries and can, for many effects, sound

different. The difference in police sirens is an obvious example, but interestingly, even though you cannot make out any words, walla-walla also contains national characteristics. When I was an undergraduate (before there was such a thing as online sound FX libraries), my department had only one sound FX library, which was produced by the BBC. In one of my first sync sound films I had a scene in a restaurant and tried to use the "restaurant walla-walla" from this collection. The effect was not exactly what I was after. While my actors were clearly from the American Midwest, the restaurant patrons in the background were right out of Notting Hill. And forget about using a "car starting up" sound: our choices were a Mini-Cooper, a Jaguar, an Austin-Healey, and a Rolls Royce. Sure, they've got motors, but they also had a British accent.

Apocalypse Now "This Is War" (The American Zoetrope SFX Collection)

Disc Number	Track Number	Duration	Description
AZ-01	01	0:21	Radio spot: 'Psychedelic Music Show'. Mono.
AZ-01	02	0:38	A-6 Intruder: power-up and takeoff. Stereo.
AZ-01	03	0:30	F-4 Phantom: takeoff medium-distant, 2 versions. Stereo
AZ-01	04	1:42	F-4 Phantom: taxi, idle and takeoff. Stereo.
AZ-01	05	0:41	F-4 Phantom: idle, power-up adn takeoff. Stereo.
AZ-01	06	0:43	F-4 Phantom: in, by and afterburner distant. Stereo
AZ-01	07	0:06	Fighter jet: hot fly-by, close-up. Stereo
AZ-01	07	0:08	Fighter jet: fly-by. Medium close-up. Stereo
AZ-01	07	0:12	Fighter jet: fly-by distant overhead. Stereo
AZ-01	07	0:08	Fighter jet: fly-by medium-distant. Stereo
AZ-01	08	1:10	C-130 Hercules: taxi by, medium close-up. Stereo
AZ-01	09	1:11	AH-1 Cobra: hover overhead, medium-distant. Mono
AZ-01	10	0:39	AH-1 Cobra: fly-by while firing 2.75' rockets. Mono
AZ-01	11	0:46	Ch-46 Chinook: idle on ground, medium close-up. Stereo
AZ-01	12	1:01	CH-46 Chinook: takeoff and hover. Stereo

■ **Figure 23-10** This excerpt from the extensive list of sound effects used in Coppola's *Apocalypse Now* (1979) illustrates how precise sound effects must be in order to be convincing, including specific model, action, and distance perspective. The sound designer was Walter Murch.

ambience on ambience each time to cut in a different sound effect. This is why good CD and Internet sound effects libraries are useful: the sounds are generally quite pure. If you record your own hard effects, try to find as quiet a location as possible and close-mike the recording. You can always create sound perspective later in the mix (discussed later).

Ambience

Ambience is related to room tone, which is a kind of ambience also. However, in sound cutting terms, ambience is a background effects track that creates a unique sense of space and location. Many films work quite well with just the production ambience recorded in the field, but ambience can be manipulated, as we saw in the previous chapter, to add another layer of narrative meaning or emotional tone.

For *FearFall,* I added a nighttime ambient track with cicadas (Track 5). Initially I was interested in cricket sounds, but after trying few tracks, I found they didn't add anything to Ray's highly agitated psychological state. The cicadas, with their extra annoying buzzing, were a better emotional fit, because their sound seemed to push Ray's anxiety further. In general, this track level remained quite low and worked on a more subliminal level. But you may notice (**Figure 23-11**) that I dipped the level of the ambient sound just a little bit when Ray is listening hard and imagining what's going on. I wanted at that moment to create a subjective sound space for Ray, who is focusing hard on the sounds next door, mentally filtering out extraneous noises. I was hoping that this would bring the audience slightly further inside his head.

Adding separate ambience allows us to shoot our scenes in as quiet a location as possible, and concentrate on getting the best possible recording of the dialogue, knowing that we can create the specific sonic background context for the location and the scene in the sound editing. We can also control volume levels and equalize all of these tracks totally independently.

Music

The music in *FearFall* was composed by Randy Wolff (Track 6). For some scenes he scored music to the picture lock edit, and for other scenes, like the one shown in **Figure 23-12**, he provided me with short motifs that I could easily adapt to the picture editing. The music here is simply a strident, dissonant violin chord that starts the minute the narrative takes a new turn; Ray, now convinced "they" are inside his house, must do something. The music

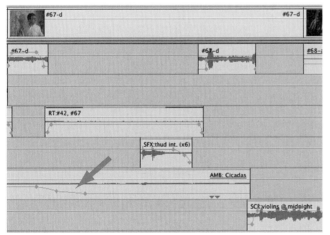

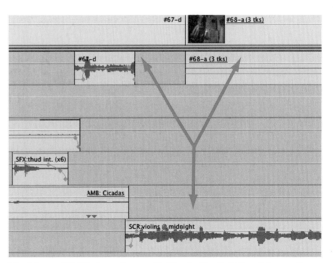

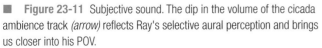

■ **Figure 23-11** Subjective sound. The dip in the volume of the cicada ambience track *(arrow)* reflects Ray's selective aural perception and brings us closer into his POV.

■ **Figure 23-12** A music sound bridge in *FearFall*. The violins on the music track begin slightly before the end of scene 67 and continue into scene 68, creating a strong connection between the two scenes.

was cut in right after his line "They're in here" to punctuate this dangerously flawed realization and to infuse the moment with tension and foreboding, but it continues into the next scene, in which his daughter Sophie is innocently getting food out of the refrigerator. This is called a **sound bridge** and it is designed to carry the emotional tension from one scene to the next.

Sound Levels and Effects during the Edit Stage

During the editing stage you will need to manipulate the audio levels of all your tracks somewhat to give yourself an idea for the perspective and balance of the various tracks in relation to the others. This is especially important if you plan to screen rough cuts to

in practice

■ THE SOUND BRIDGE

Sound bridges are a very common sound editing technique involving any sound that overlaps from one scene into another. Sound bridges can involve a sound from one scene continuing into the following scene (as in the *FearFall* example, **Figure 23-12**) or, vice versa, the sound from the second scene beginning early, at the tail end of the preceding scene. Sound bridges create a strong and smooth connection between scenes by carrying over the emotional content of one scene into the other. Musical sound bridges are the most common, but sound effects and dialogue can also be used as sound bridges. Like any other technique that creates strong associations, sound bridges can be extremely powerful and adaptable in their specific application.

Music Sound Bridge

The story of Bernard Rose's *Immortal Beloved* (1994) (**Figure 23-13**) revolves around the mystery of Ludwig van Beethoven's famous love letter to his unnamed "immortal beloved." The ending sequence of the film includes a sound bridge constructed around Beethoven's most famous and influential composition, the mighty Ninth Symphony. The sequence begins with an investigator talking to one of Beethoven's presumed mistresses, while the last movement of the Ninth Symphony underscores the scene (as nondiegetic music). The music continues as we cut to a concert hall, which shows an orchestra playing the symphony (the music is now diegetic).

When Beethoven comes onto the stage, the sound is drastically muted and muffled to reflect his near total deafness (now it is subjective sound). The full dimension of the music returns as the film cuts to a flashback of Beethoven as a child, tormented by his father. The Ninth Symphony in this sequence serves as a sound bridge for three scenes that take place in three different eras and locations. In addition, the music transforms into three different sounds modes: nondiegetic score music, diegetic source music, and subjective sound.

Dialogue Sound Bridge

Fritz Lang's *M* (1931) contains perhaps one of cinema's earliest sound bridges and it remains one of the most eloquent and moving moment on film. After we see the little girl Elsie lured away by a man who has bought her a balloon, Lang cuts to her mother, who anxiously waits for her child to come home. The mother goes to her window, opens it wide, and calls for her little girl, "Elsie!" "Elsie!" (**Figure 23-14**). The sound of her voice bridges the next few edits, which take us out of the apartment, to the staircase, and to an attic, places where the little girl should be and that are still in earshot of the mother's continuing cries of "Elsie!" Elsie!" But suddenly the calling stops and Lang presents us with three stunning shots in silence. Elsie's empty place at the family table, the little girl's toy ball rolling out of a thicket of brush, and the balloon, tangled in the wires of an electrical pole. The meaning couldn't be clearer: Elsie is another victim of the child killer.

■ **Figure 23-13** Rose's *Immortal Beloved* (1994) uses the music from the premiere of Beethoven's Ninth Symphony to bridge several scenes in one of the last sequences of the film.

■ **Figure 23-14** Although made only a few years after the introduction of sync sound in film, Lang's *M* (1931) experimented with sophisticated techniques, such as using a dialogue sound bridge.

get feedback along the way. All NLE systems offer some sort of easily accessible level control right in the timeline (Figure 23-15). You can adjust tracks globally, by selecting the entire track, or adjust individual clips. Adjusting clip levels in the timeline does not alter the master clip or the original media in any way. You can also add simple transitions like sound fades and cross-fades into your sequence very simply as well (Figure 23-16).

But be careful. It's very easy to waste hours tweaking the volume or dissolve parameters for this shot, that shot, and the other. Don't take too much time fine-tuning details that will only be undone and redone later. The editing stage is not the place to get the sound absolutely perfect. Finessing the track levels, creating transition effects, and enhancing the sound through equalization and audio filters are done in the next and final stage of the sound design process—sound mixing.

■ THE SOUND MIX

For most student and independent films that are edited and finished on an NLE system, it's hard to strictly delineate the editing and sound cutting phase from the sound mixing stage. To be sure, as you work with your rough cuts and build your sound design, you will be doing some rough sound mixing along the way, especially if you screen test your rough cuts for feedback. But at some point, after picture lock and after you've more or less gathered all of the actual sounds you will use for your sound design and placed them more or less where they need to be, you need to turn your attention exclusively to perfecting the way your movie sounds. The **sound mix** is the process of polishing and finalizing the various audio tracks in your sound design and creating a single

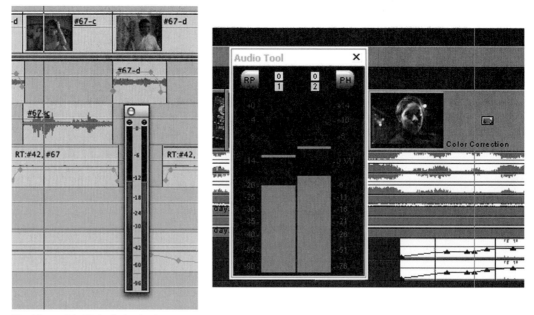

■ **Figure 23-15** Audio level adjustments are done right on the timeline and can be monitored on the sound tool's level meter window. Final Cut Pro *(left)*; AVID *(right)*.

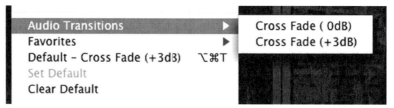

■ **Figure 23-16** The audio transition menu in Final Cut Pro. Simple audio effects, such as preset cross-fades, can be applied as you edit, but save the more detailed sound work for the mixing stage.

mixtrack, which is the mono or stereo sound track that is then married to your images and accompanies your film into distribution and exhibition. The ultimate goal of a sound mix is to create a harmonious sonic environment for your film, harmonious meaning that the completed sound design is both believable and appropriate for the conceptual and aesthetic aims of your motion picture. In this respect, the sound mix should not be viewed as merely a polishing process; rather there are substantial creative decisions to me made here.

The Sound Mixing Steps

The sound mix process involves five steps, generally in this order: (1) final sound selection and placement, (2) audio sweetening, (3) creating audio transitions, (4) audio level balancing, and (5) the mix down.

Step 1: Final Sound Selection and Placement

As we discussed previously, the editing process involves the somewhat expeditious use of sound in order to get the film to a picture locked phase. This means using some sounds that will end up in the final film (like dialogue, production sound effects, or pre-recorded music) and inserting scratch tracks as placeholders until you find or record the perfect sound (like sound effects, voiceover, or score music). But the final sound mix is the moment of truth: you must select (or record) all final sounds that make up your sound design and precisely place these sounds into your timeline, replacing all scratch tracks.

Step 2: Audio Sweetening

Audio sweetening simply means making your audio sound better. This is accomplished by evaluating, and adjusting when necessary, every individual audio clip, across each audio track (i.e., dialogue, sound effects, ambience), one track at a time. Sweetening includes a variety of audio signal processing tools that can be employed to accomplish three goals: to generally enhance the quality of the audio, to repair poor audio, and to create audio effects. Remember, like every other effect in nonlinear editing, changes you make to an audio clip or track are nondestructive, meaning the original media are not affected in any way, so feel free to experiment; you can always undo anything you try.

Audio Filters

At the heart of audio sweetening is the application of **audio filters**. Audio filters are audio signal processors that digitally alter the audio data, and therefore the characteristics of your sound, in some way. Each audio filter manipulates the spectrum in a unique way to produce a specific effect. It is certainly not possible to explore in this chapter the capabilities of every processing tool found in most NLE systems, but a few basics should get you started. The effect and function of a specific audio filter generally falls into one of three categories: (1) equalization, (2) reverb/echo, and (3) compression/expansion.

Filters for Frequency Equalization and Noise Reduction

Equalization, or **EQ**, means the manual manipulation of the various frequencies in your signal. Generally, we divide the frequency spectrum of an audio signal into three **frequency bands:** low frequencies, which are the deep, bass quality (around 25 Hz to 250 Hz); midrange frequencies, which are the most perceptible range for the human ear and includes the human voice (250 Hz to 4 kHz); and high frequencies, which include the bright, treble quality of the sound (4 kHz to 20 kHz). Most NLE systems offer a filter called a **three-band equalizer**, which allows you to manipulate these three broad areas of the sound spectrum more or less independently (Figure 23-17).

So when might we use an EQ filter? Let's say you have a romantic scene (shot in fairly tight close-ups) of a couple talking and clearly falling in love. In this situation, you may want to boost the low end of your audio just a bit, to "warm up" the audio, make it sound close, resonant, and intimate. Or let's say you shot a scene with a microphone that accentuated the high, treble end of the audio and, to your ear, it sounds too "crispy." You can use the EQ filter to bring down the high frequencies. Completely removing high frequencies and low frequencies, leaving only the midrange, will make voices sound like they're coming through the telephone or over a PA system.

Primarily, however, EQ is used to fix audio that includes some sort of unwanted noise. In the *FearFall* sound design analysis (beginning on page 493), I mentioned that Ellen's dialogue was recorded while an unnoticed fan hummed in the next room. The microphone picked up this vibration as a low-frequency hum. So I split Ellen's dialogue onto its own track, selected all of her clips from that scene, and equalized the low frequencies until that low hum was mostly eliminated. High frequencies can also be equalized out. One of my students shot a scene that took place around a computer, and when he listened carefully to the recoding he discovered an extremely high-pitched whine coming from the computer monitor. This sound was fairly easy to eliminate through EQing. In both his film and in mine, the frequency of the offending noise was either higher or lower than any other sounds, especially the voices in the scene, so there was no discernible change to the quality of the voices. However, if you need to EQ out a

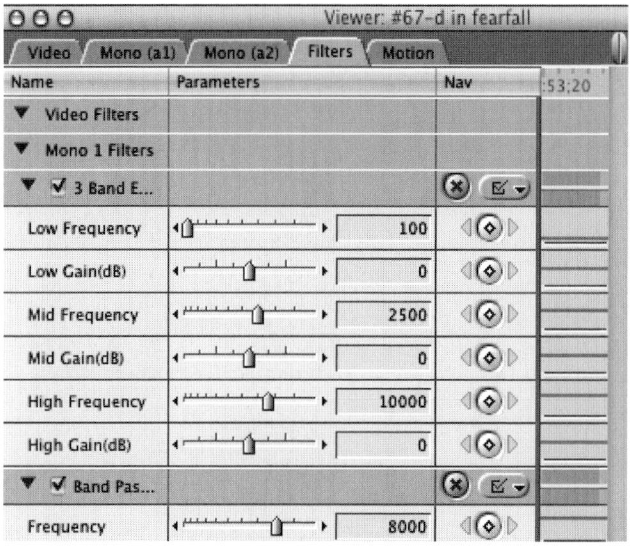

■ Figure 23-17 The three-band equalizer in Final Cut Pro. A common audio filter used in sound mixing.

frequency that is found in other areas of the recorded sound spectrum, then the EQing will remove that frequency throughout the recording and will alter sounds you want to alter, as well as those you don't want changed. Also keep in mind, as a general rule, you can fairly successfully remove (or accentuate) frequencies that are in the recording, but you cannot add frequencies that are not in the audio in the first place. The removal of high- and low-frequency noise is so common in sound mixing that you'll find numerous **filter presets** for high-end and low-end roll-off filters designed exactly for these problems.

Filters for Reverb and Echo
Echo and **reverb** are similar in that they both involve the reflection and return of sound after a slight delay. The return delay for reverb is fast (e.g., small tiled bathrooms and concrete stairwells). The return delay for an echo is much longer (e.g., Gothic cathedrals or the Grand Canyon). Reverb and echo effects change the audio signal to make it sound as if it were recorded in an acoustically live space, where sound reverberates off hard surfaces.

There are several preset filters (small hall, large hall, tunnel, etc.) (Figure 23-18) or you can control the loudness and delay of the return manually. Reverb and echo can sound great, but be careful not to use too much or to use it without narrative and visual justification. Inappropriate reverb can sound cheesy and too much will make otherwise clear sound, especially dialogue, murky and unintelligible. Also remember that *reverb filters do not remove reverberation—they can only add it!* So when do we use these filters? Let's say you have a scene in which a man is being chased up a concrete stairwell by an unseen dog. You want that dog to be barking and growling (off screen) as the man makes a desperate dash up the stairs to the rooftop doors. If you found your barking sound effect from a sound effects library, it's likely that the "mean dog barking" will have been recorded as closely and as flat as possible. All you need to do to make it sound as if that dog is only one landing below him in the stairwell is to add the appropriate amount of reverb to the "barking" clips.

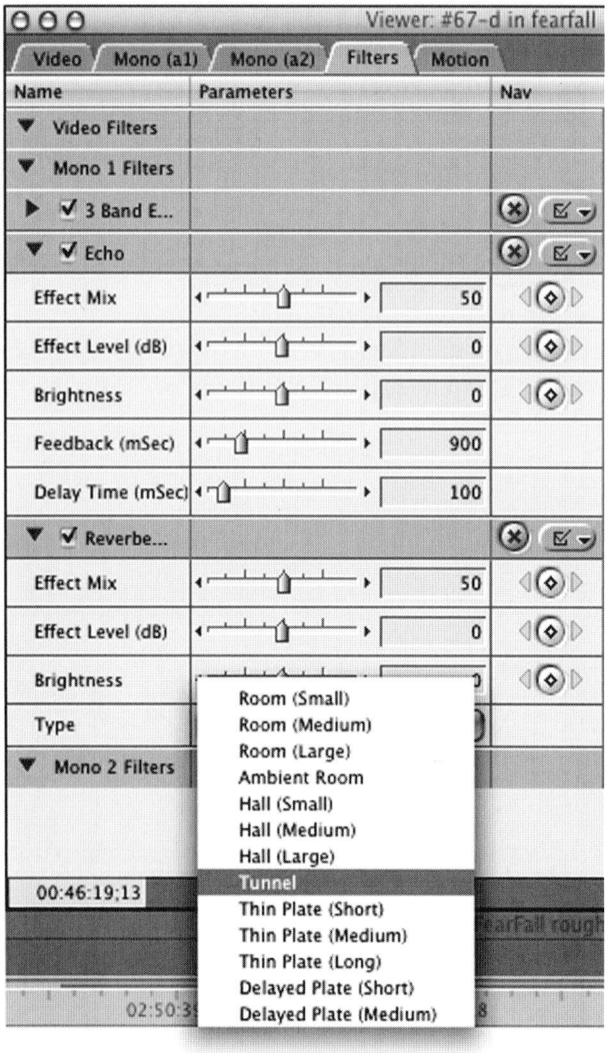

Filters for Amplitude Compression or Expansion
Compression and **expansion filters** work on the amplitude of a sound signal or, more accurately, on the dynamic range (see page 332) of a given recording. As I mentioned previously (page 353), the result of audio that peaks above 0 dB on a peak meter is distortion. In digital audio this means the loss of data and noticeable crackling in the sound. A compression filter detects when a sound will peak above 0 dB and it will suppress the sound to keep it within range without affecting the average audio levels of the track.

This is very different than simply lowering the overall (or average) audio level to keep loud sounds from peaking above 0 dB, which would also lower everything on that track. Here's an example: Let's say you've shot a scene in which a married couple is talking while the husband washes the dishes. The sound recordist did their job well and kept the sound from peaking above 0 dB in the field recordings, but now that you're mixing your sound, you want to be able to hear the dialogue clearly, and so you've set the audio levels for the dialogue track fairly high. But now you discover that every time the husband bumps a plate in the sink or in the dish drainer, the audio spikes above 0 dB and crackles. If you simply lower the average

■ **Figure 23-18** Do you want your audio to sound like it's reverberating in a tunnel? A large hall? In Final Cut Pro you can choose from a range of acoustic effects when you apply the reverb filter.

track level overall so that this doesn't happen, you'll be lowering the dialogue as well. The solution here is a compression filter, which will suppress only the audio that threatens to peak above 0 dB, leaving the rest at the level established in the timeline.

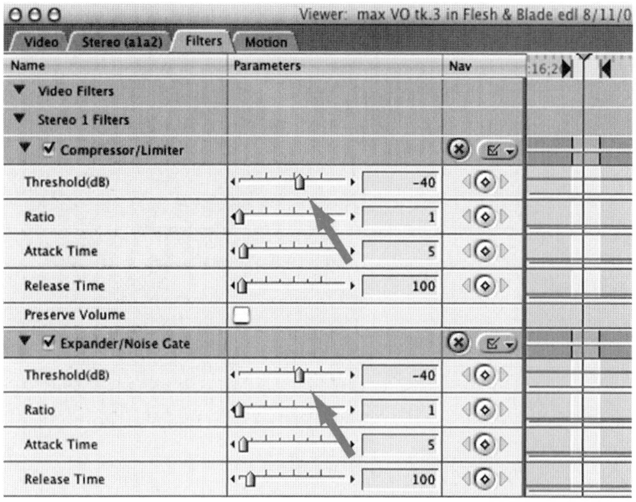

While compression filters lower loud, peaking sounds, **expansion filters** lower the amplitude of extremely low-level sounds in order to drop them below the level of audibility. Let's say you finally go into your sound mix, with super high-quality speakers, and suddenly notice that during the shooting of a tight, close-up monologue, the microphone picked up the ticking of the boom operator's watch. It's very, very faint but, by revealing the presence of a crewperson, the fictive world you're trying to create is shattered. An expansion filter will drop this very quiet noise even lower, hopefully out of the range of hearing, without affecting the rest of the audio on track. Expansion filters can also be used to minimize the room tone in a dialogue

■ **Figure 23-19** The manual threshold level adjustments for the compressor audio filter *(top arrow)* and the expander audio filter *(bottom arrow)* in Final Cut pro.

recording, allowing you to more successfully replace it with another ambient track without worrying about compounding ambience over a noticeably different presence. With both compression and expansion, you can manually set the **threshold level** (Figure 23-19), which is the amplitude level above which (compression) or below which (expansion) the sound must be in order to be affected by the filter.

Step 3: Creating Audio Transitions

Most of the creative audio editing choices, like split edits for dialogue, sound bridges, and ambient track layering, are accomplished during the rough cut and fine cut stage. During the sound mixing phase, what concerns us most is the smooth transition from sound to sound across an entire track. This includes the use of room tone to fill in gaps of "silence" on the sound track and to even out the ambience quality of two pieces of audio that are supposed to sound continuous. However, most audio edits that are straight cuts, especially in dialogue editing, also require a little extra attention. A straight cut between two audio clips not only magnifies small ambient shifts, but the inconsistent waveforms of the two directly abutted audio clips will also result in a audible "pop" or "click" right at the edit point. To correct this, sound editors routinely add a very quick, four- to six-frame **cross-fade** right at the edit point between two connected sound clips, and two- to four-frame **fades** (in and out) at the beginning and end of sound clips that are not directly joined to another audio clip (Figure 23-20).

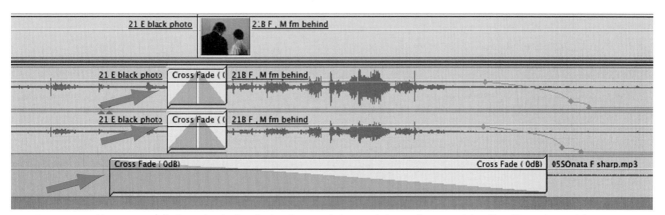

■ **Figure 23-20** You can manually determine the length of audio cross-fades to suit the requirements of the effect. Pictured are a 6-frame cross-fade *(top arrows)* used to create an invisible dialogue edit and a 60-frame fade-in from silence to gradually introduce music on the sound track.

Cross-fades and Handles

A **cross-fade** is the audio equivalent of a dissolve in the image. As the level of the first audio clip fades out, the level of the incoming clip fades up. Obviously, like an image dissolve, you can create long cross-fades of many seconds to, for example, slowly introduce some background music. But quick cross-fades are extremely helpful in smoothing a cut from one audio clip to another. Very often, cross-fades of 12 to 24 frames is enough to smooth an edit between two dialogue clips with more noticeable room tone differences.

When you cross-fade between two clips, the audio of the first clip is extended beyond the cut point by half the duration of the cross-fade in order to accommodate the full fade-out, and the incoming shot is extended at the head by half the cross-fade duration to accommodate the fade-in. This is called a **center on cross-fade.** For example, if you decide that a cut point needs a 30-frame cross-fade to smooth out an ambience discrepancy, then the first shot will end 15 frames after the cut point before it completely fades out, and the second clip will begin 15 frames before the edit point to accommodate the fade-in. These extra frames are called **handles**, and you must be sure that there are no unwanted sounds, like the tail end of some dialogue that you wanted to cut out, within those extra frames (Figure 23-21).

Step 4: Audio Level Balancing

Once all of the tracks sound good on their own, and all of the edit points are clean and smooth, it's time to think about adjusting the overall volume balance between the clips in each track and between the various tracks in relation to the others. This stage is critical not only for the intelligibility of your sound (for example, important dialogue shouldn't be drowned out by music that is too loud), but it also is critical for the general believability of the world of your film. An ambience track that is too loud can make a scene ring false; dialogue levels that are all over the map can make the editing painfully obvious; music that is too low will cause the audience to turn around and scream "louder!" at the poor projectionist. If all tracks have equal volume levels, then all you'll get is a sonic stew. The dynamics of track levels helps you to create emphasis and direct the ear and the eye to what is most important at a particular moment. Keep in mind that when you screen your film for an audience, you cannot ride the levels; the final sound track has to work all on its own from start to finish. Once, when I was judging a student film festival, we had an entry that came with a little note marked "URGENT!" The note said something like, "Please be advised, sound dips at TC 00:08:12:13 (after scene under tree) but it goes back up at TC 00:09:18:23." Even though this is totally unacceptable, we, the three judges, decided to watch it anyway, but we were certainly not disposed to like it.

The Reference Track and Establishing Average Level Range

When establishing audio levels we start with the most important tracks first and then adjust all other tracks relative to this central reference. For example, if a film is primarily music driven, with an occasional special effect tossed in here and there, then you'll set

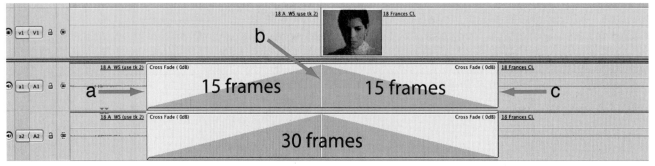

■ **Figure 23-21** Handles. To accommodate a 30-frame cross-fade, the incoming audio clip requires 15 additional clean frames (a) before the cut point (b) and the outgoing audio clip needs an additional 15 frames beyond the cut point (c).

levels for the music track first. For dialogue-driven projects, start with dialogue tracks and then later adjust the effects, music, and ambience tracks relative to the dialogue. In either case, the first, and most important, track we mix is called our **reference track**.

Just as with field recording, we use a peak meter as our primary reference tool as we adjust levels. Yes, we monitor with the headphones as well (discussed later), but the peak meter helps us maintain consistency **across time**, meaning from clip to clip, from start to finish, across your timeline. The first track that we adjust, our reference track, establishes our **average audio level range** (also called **headroom)** (Figure 23-22).

Let's say we're adjusting dialogue first. Just as with field recording (see page 353), the level for normally spoken dialogue is around –20 dB, and the loudest peaks in your sound mix should not exceeded –6 dB (to give you a comfortable margin before the ultimate limit of 0 dB). The area, between –20 and –6 dB, becomes our average audio range. Now you can adjust the levels of each and every clip, across the dialogue tracks, relative to this reference. A whisper should obviously dip below –20 dB, loud voices will register around –16 dB, and a scream will clearly be even louder, but should not peak above –6 dB. If prerecorded music is your most important track (say you're making a music video), then you'd simply find the loudest peak in the track and adjust the levels so that it falls on –6 dB. The rest will fall into place below that top headroom point.

■ Figure 23-22 The Final Cut Pro mixing tool allows you to adjust and meter the levels for each track independently. You should first establish your headroom by adjusting your dominant audio track, and then adjust the others to that reference.

As you adjust your clip levels for the reference track across time, you should use the peak meter to maintain consistency from clip to clip to clip. For example, if character A's average voice in the first scene held around –20 dB, then in the last scene it should also be at the same level. By comparing the levels of the two clips, you can easily see if your mix levels have drifted over time.

Dramatic Sound Perspective
Keep in mind that composition and dramatic content can have an important effect on audio levels. The sound of a man talking in a close-up should obviously be somewhat louder than the same dialogue shot in a long shot or extreme long shot. For this reason it's important not only to *listen* to your sound mix but also to *watch* and consider the images you're trying to match the sound to. Dramatic content also has a profound effect on levels, especially when working with **subjective sound**, in which you are trying to represent the POV and selective aural perception of a character. Just as we can either "tune out" or concentrate on someone who is talking to us from across the table, you can use your audio level mixing to duplicate this effect.

Bob Fosse's *All That Jazz* (1979) (Figure 23-23) tells the story of hard-living and hardworking Joe Gideon, a musical theater director on Broadway who is putting up a show while his life and health fall apart. During the first reading of the play, with the entire cast and principal crew of the production gathered around him, Gideon has a mild heart attack. At this moment, Fosse completely mutes all sounds, except for those that Gideon himself makes, which are amplified. Although we see everything going on around him, we cannot hear the obvious sounds, like lines being read or the uproarious laughter of the people gathered in the room. Instead we hear his fingernails scratching on a metal pipe, the rustle as he removes yet another cigarette from its box, his pencil snapping, and his spent cigarette landing on the floor. The effect is one of extreme character subjectivity in which we are enclosed completely and deeply in Gideon's perspective and consciousness.

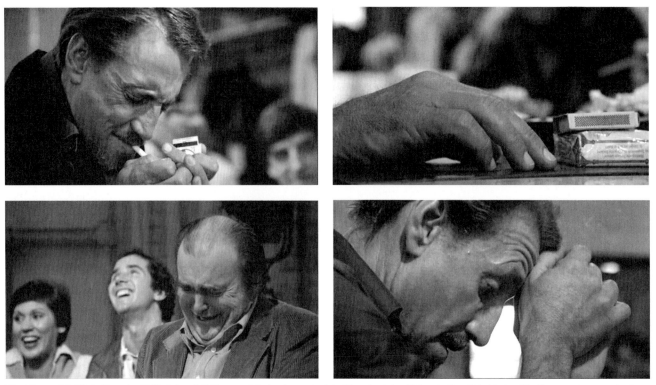

■ **Figure 23-23** In Fosse's *All That Jazz* (1979), sound design is manipulated to reflect Joe Gideon's (Roy Scheider) subjective experience as he has a mild heart attack.

Adjusting the Other Tracks

Once you have established the levels of your reference track, you can then adjust the other tracks (sound effects, ambience, music) relative to this one. Keep in mind that "reference track" does not mean that this is always the loudest track in the movie. There are many times, for example, when music levels will be set well under dialogue levels and then later fade up to become the most prominent track in the sound design. Also, some sound effects, like explosions, should clearly be mixed louder than average dialogue; other sounds can be mixed hotter than dialogue to intentionally drown out the speakers for dramatic value.

A good example of a music track taking over in prominence and volume level can be seen in the famous "Albert Hall" sequence in Alfred Hitchcock's *The Man Who Knew Too Much* (1956) (**Figure 23-24**). In this film an average American couple finds themselves unwittingly

■ **Figure 23-24** The famous Albert Hall sequence from Hitchcock's *The Man Who Knew Too Much* (1956). The diegetic orchestral sound track drowns out all other sounds in the scene and playfully recalls the silent era films of Hitchcock's early career.

tangled in a plot to assassinate a prime minister; to keep them quiet, the plotters kidnap their son. Looking for their son, the couple finally converges on one of the kidnappers as he is about to carry out the assassination during an orchestral concert at the Royal Albert Hall. The killer's plan is to shoot the diplomat when the music reaches its climax, with a crash of cymbals, to cover the sound of the shot. The sequence dramatically intercuts the police and parents searching for the killer, while the killer takes aim at the diplomat and the audience simply enjoys the orchestral music. Although the rest of the film is primarily dialogue driven, in this sequence the music itself becomes the driving force of the narrative as we get closer and closer, measure by measure, to the assassination. Additionally, the music completely drowns out all dialogue exchanges, essentially creating a sequence that harkens back to the silent era.

NLE Systems and Audio Levels

As with most other functions in NLE systems, there are a number of ways to adjust the audio levels of clips and tracks. The most controlled and accurate method for adjusting audio levels is a combination of using the timeline and the viewer. Most NLE systems make it extremely easy to adjust audio levels right in the timeline. To do this, you must select the timeline setting that shows the clip **audio level overlay** within each track (**Figure 23-25**). The line that you see drawn through each clip is the system's default level. Using your mouse, you can simply grab the audio overlay and manually raise or lower it to raise or lower the entire clip level.

If you have a clip that has multiple dynamic level adjustments (for example, music in which the volume dips and then rises again), you can use the **pen tool** to create key frames. Audio levels between key frames can be adjusted independently. You can create as many key frames as you need, allowing for enormous flexibility for dynamic level adjustment (**Figure 23-26**). If you require a much more detailed view of the audio track than you see in the timeline, you can simply bring your clip into the viewer and you will see both a waveform representation of the sound and the audio level overlay. You can also magnify or reduce the audio clip. The viewer also allows you to work with key frames and dynamic adjustments, but with a much more detailed and precise picture of the sound (**Figure 23-27**).

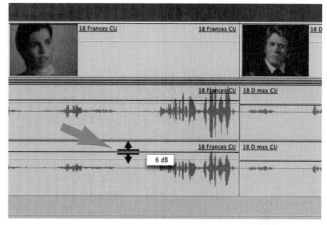

■ **Figure 23-25** In most NLE systems, audio levels can be adjusted right in the timeline by clicking/dragging clip overlays. Notice the box showing the changing dB levels on this Final Cut Pro timeline.

Obviously this discussion only scratches the surface of the capabilities and procedures for adjusting levels in an NLE system. You should look over the manual for your particular system carefully to fully understand how to achieve the audio balance you are after.

Step 5: The Mix Down

Finally, with all of the tracks sounding their best and mixed to the perfect balance relative to the other tracks, you are ready to mix down and output your multiple tracks to create a master **mix track**. Your NLE program's mix tool is used for this purpose

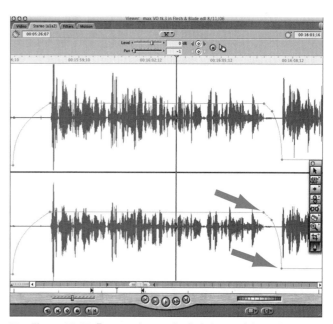

■ **Figure 23-27** For a much more detailed picture of the audio waveform, level adjustments can be made in the viewer where you can clearly see the end of one musical phrase and the beginning of the next. The arrows show where a pen tool was used to drop the audio out during this pause.

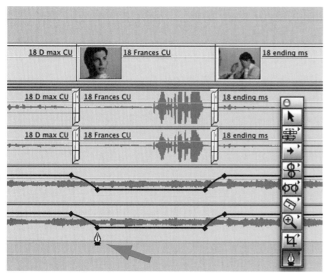

■ **Figure 23-26** The pen tool allows you to create multiple level adjustments within a single clip.

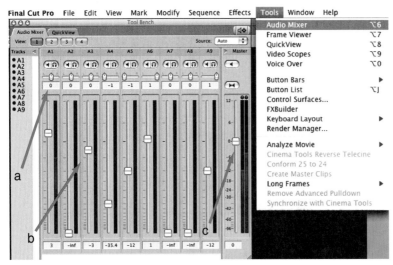

■ **Figure 23-28** The audio mixer in Final Cut Pro mixes all your audio tracks down to two master output stereo channels (c). With the panning slider (a) you can send each track to either one or both stereo channels. Each track also has its own fader (b) for independent level adjustment. Both the panning slider and faders automatically respond to all the choices you made in the timeline.

(Figure 23-28). When you open the mix tool, you will see one audio gain slider for every audio track in the program, and as you play through your sound design, the gain sliders will move, corresponding to the level adjustments you made in each clip. At the top of each level slider is a **pan slider**. Generally, whether you are finishing on film or on DV tape, you will be outputting your audio as a two-channel stereo master. The pan sliders allow you to select which channel each audio track should be recorded to and later play from. If you want both channels of audio to be the same, then all of the pan sliders remain in their central position. This is especially important if you plan to finish on a 16mm film print, because 16mm optical sound is a mono format. In any case, if you are mastering to DV tape, you will output your audio mix down along with your program to the master tape, creating a master that has both video and stereo sound.

If your workflow involves finishing on film, then you will need to output the audio only to a DAT tape (or whatever format the lab requires) and take that master mix track to the laboratory, where they will use it to strike an optical sound track master (see page 412).

(see page 412)

■ MORE SOUND MIXING TIPS

The Mix Environment

Sound mixing should be done in an environment that most accurately represents a high-quality exhibition space. In a professional mixing facility, the **rerecording mixer** handles the hardware and the mixing tasks while the director and editor watch the film projected on a fairly large screen and listen to the sound mix on high-quality reference speakers. The whole mixing suite is also sound baffled to minimize reverberation. Most students in introductory or intermediate production courses, however, mix right on their NLE system—which is certainly fine—but it is recommended to mix in a space that is quiet and to use good speakers. Be aware of what the mixing environment itself sounds like; traffic noise, reverberant surfaces, and the cooling fan of a CPU all blend with what's coming out of your speakers. Mixing with headphones is also a viable alternative, but again, make sure the headphones are of very high quality and are isolation-type headphones, meaning that they have foam that surrounds your ears to keep external noises from leaking in. Poor-quality headphones, especially those that do not press firmly against your ear, can give you a less than accurate impression of your sound track. Also, if you do mix with headphones, be sure to check your sound on a good set of speakers from time to time to get a more accurate impression of how the audience will hear it.

Audio Monitor Reference

When setting audio levels during the sound mix, it is essential that you keep the output level to your speakers, or headphones, absolutely consistent. Audio levels are relative, so if your headphone level is low one day, you might raise the levels of your clips higher than you need, and if the headphone levels are higher another day, then you may be tempted to set clip levels lower than on the previous day. So set the output volume to a comfortable level and leave it alone for the duration of the sound mix. This includes the computer audio output volume settings and the monitor out on an external mixer, if you're using one.

Audio Filter Toggle for Reference

The human ear is a very adaptable and intricate mechanism that subconsciously equalizes, attenuates, filters, and selectively perceives the sounds in the world around us in order to reduce what we perceive to the essentials. For example, sitting around a table talking with our friends, it's automatic that we no longer perceive the hum of the air conditioner or the sound

in practice

of traffic outside the window. For this reason, all filter effects have the ability to toggle instantly on and off. To really hear what effect an audio filter is having on your sound, you need to compare it regularly to the reference of the original track. Without toggling back to your reference, your ear can get lost as you apply effect after effect, straying further from the parameters of acceptable audio manipulation (**Figure 23-29**).

Summary

Clean dialogue edits and consistent levels are essential for the maintenance of continuity in dialogue-driven films. Here is a summary of techniques we use to keep an edited sequence feeling like it's unfolding seamlessly and continuously:

1. Stay in sync.
2. Use split audio edits.
3. Maintain consistent room tone.
4. Use cross-fades for hard cuts.
5. Never let audio peak above 0 dB.
6. Maintain consistent and appropriate audio levels from clip to clip and scene to scene across time.

▼ ✓ 3 Band E...		
Low Frequency		100
Low Gain(dB)		0
Mid Frequency		2498
Mid Gain(dB)		0
High Frequency		10000
High Gain(dB)		0
▼ ☐ Echo		
Effect Mix		50
Effect Level (dB)		0
Brightness		0

Figure 23-29 The audio filter toggle icon *(arrows)* enables you to easily switch a filter effect on and off, allowing you to compare the effect to your original audio for reference.

■ ADVANCED SOUND MIXING PROGRAMS

The audio sweetening and sound mixing capabilities found in most NLE systems are truly remarkable, but to a professional sound mixer they offer only basic functions. As your films get more complex and your sound track needs become more demanding, you may find yourself needing to use more advanced, stand-alone, sound mixing programs. Remember, Avid and Final Cut Pro are picture editing programs, and professional sound mixers would never use these to mix sound; instead, they use a **digital audio workstation** (or **DAW**, for short). There are numerous DAWs on the market, but many are exclusively for mixing music. **Soundtrack Pro** (from Final Cut Pro Studio software bundle) and **Pro Tools** (from AVID/Digidesign) are designed to mix both music and film sound tracks and contain many more features and capabilities compared to NLE picture editing programs (**Figure 23-30**). Both mixing programs offer dozens more (and much more powerful) audio filters for special effects and "audio fixing." They have several more precise equalizers and many more transition effects. Their ability to make subframe edits and stretch audio without changing pitch allows for highly precise sound edits and ADR syncing.

These programs are also designed to import both your edited video (for visual reference) as well as all of the sound tracks and adjustments you've made along the way. Sound track Pro is designed to let you move seamlessly from Final Cut Pro and back again without any format conversions. Pro Tools, on the other hand, requires that all sound files be converted into the **open media framework (OMF)** file format. Realizing that most sound mixing professionals use Pro Tools, Apple has made it relatively easy to migrate and has an option for exporting all audio clips and timeline information in the OMF format (**Figure 23-31**). You can even set the conversion to export each clip with handles, extra frames on either end of the edit points to accommodate cross-fades, or trims to the individual audio clip during the mix.

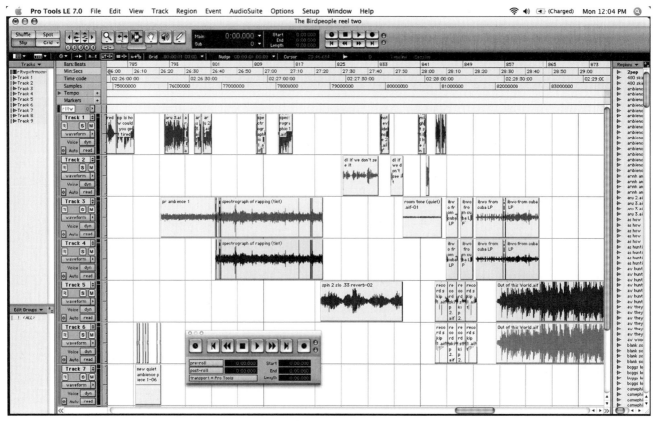

■ **Figure 23-30** DAWs are substantially more precise and powerful for audio work than NLEs. Pictured is the Pro Tools desktop.

Why Go Pro?

Venturing into the territory of highly advanced software applications for sound mixing means acquiring the not insubstantial expertise to use them. This itself begs the question, why not go to a professional sound mixer?

Certainly, as you are starting out, the benefits of mixing your own sound tracks on your first, fairly simple films are enormous. Mixing your own sound gives you an intimate and nuanced understanding of the power of layered audio tracks. Creating an intricate sound design, placing a sound effect with perfect timing, adjusting the audio balance to create dramatic emphasis, changing the mood by inserting a different ambient track, and literally seeing the way a music track can weave its way throughout a film and therefore in and out of a viewer's consciousness are all invaluable lessons that will inevitably have an impact on the way you look at movies and how sound is used in your future projects. To actually lay your hands on the stuff and make it happen, quite simply, will make you a better filmmaker; it may even convince you that you'd like to be a sound designer like Walter Murch, Ben Burtt, Randy Thom, or Ren Klyce.

But at some point you may find that your ideas and sound requirements have become more complex than your abilities. It's then time to turn to those people who absolutely adore

■ **Figure 23-31** The "export audio" menu allows you to convert audio from a Final Cut Pro timeline into OMF files for importing into a Pro Tools sound mix session.

postproduction sound, those who have dedicated their careers to it and have a talent for it, those people who know exactly what every one of those audio filters and third-party plug-ins in a Pro Tools system does—those people called professional **postproduction sound mixers**.

I remember the first film for which I had a professional digital mix on a Pro Tools system (before that, my mixes were done on 16mm magnetic stock, which is a different experience entirely). I dutifully brought in my video and all of my audio and sound track data in OMF format to the postproduction mixer, Bill, having carefully arranged and "fixed" my tracks. I had a very small budget and needed the mix session to proceed as quickly as possible, so, to save time, I had done meticulous level balancing, inserted quick cross-fade dissolves for every cut, and applied a few simple filters. I thought that by doing that, all Bill would have to do is tweak things here or there, replace a few special effects, and I could go home. When Bill loaded my sound design into his Pro Tools system he indeed told me to go home and we would start the next day. When I returned I found that overnight he had undone everything I had done, with the exception of the basic sound cutting and placement. All of the lovely audio smoothing and finessing I had labored over for more than a week was gone. Bill had removed all audio filters and transitions, undone all level settings, and split all dialogue onto individual tracks. I went from 6 tracks to about 20 in less than 10 hours! Then Bill got down to work.

Yes, he had a high-end mixing program with audio processors, scopes, and equalizers I had never even heard of, but more important he had experience and a sensibility for the world of sound that I simply couldn't match. He not only made everything sound much better with his more accurate and powerful mixing tools and his vast selection of sound effects and ambient tracks, but he heard problems in the tracks that I couldn't hear until after he fixed them. Most important, he made creative suggestions, especially for sound bridges between scenes, which quite frankly improved the movie. And that's why we go to a professional, in any area of filmmaking; experience, talent, and technical experience will enhance the expressive impact of your movie.

When you decide to start using professional sound mixers, it is important to consult with them before you start shooting your film. They will tell you the details of the mixing system they use and how it interfaces with your particular editing system. They will tell you what resources they have, what they need, and in what format they prefer the audio data and video delivered. It is especially important to consult with them ahead of time if you have problematic sound that will need significant fixing in the mix. Some things can be fixed; others, like too much reverb in a recording, are nearly impossible to correct.

Keep in mind that the options are not limited to DIY or going with a professional sound mixer charging $200 an hour or more. Just as with acting, cinematography, directing, writing, and any other filmmaking task, there are people who have a talent for sound design and mixing, who are good, but not yet professionals. This person might be your classmate or it might be you! These people need to establish themselves in the field and gain experience, and the only way to do that is to work and practice and show what they've got—so they are looking to mix your movie, and you are looking for a postproduction mixer. Sounds like a perfect match.

Finishing, Mastering, and Distribution

■ FINISHING ON DV (SD OR HD)

Once you have a picture-locked film and a mixed sound track, the big creative choices are over. Yet there is still some finishing work to be done, and this phase has a few additional aesthetic considerations to think about before you transfer your film from your NLE system and onto a format that will allow you to send it out into the world. This chapter looks at the finishing process for the two common workflows discussed on page 398, namely, projects finishing on HD or SD broadcast formats. For details on finishing projects to 35mm film or DCP, workflows which require extensive lab services, please see Chapter 19.

Digital Color Correction

The standard **color correction tool** incorporated into many NLE systems is, in fact, quite a powerful image correction device; it takes some time and patience to learn, but once mastered it can put a truly professional and individualized polish on the look of your motion picture. Color correction is used primarily to accomplish four things:

1. **Match** color and brightness values across all clips in a single scene.
2. **Correct** color temperature or exposure problems.
3. **Enhance** colors to create subtle tonalities for a specific "look" or mood.
4. **Create** color effects, like stripping an image of all but one specific color.

The simplest color filter to use for correcting your image is called the **three-way color corrector** (Figure 24-1). The three-way color corrector allows you to alter the **luminance values**, which are the brightness of gray tones from black to white, and the **chrominance values**, which are **hue** (the color) and **saturation** (the intensity of color) within three separate areas of your image, more or less independently of one another. Altering the chrominance values in an image is called **color balancing**. The three areas within which we make adjustments are the **blacks**, **mids**, and **whites**, and each area has its own **color wheel** and **luminance slider** for executing the modifications. Brightness or color adjustments made with the blacks control will affect the darkest parts of the image, like dark objects, dark clothing, and shadows. Using the whites control will affect the very brightest parts of the image, like practical lights, windows, and white objects. The mids control has the broadest range and generally includes everything in between blacks and whites. Keep in mind that these areas are not strictly distinct; they do overlap somewhat, as will the adjustments you make (Figure 24-2).

To make changes to the brightness of the image, you simply click and drag the luminance slider. Adjustments are made to

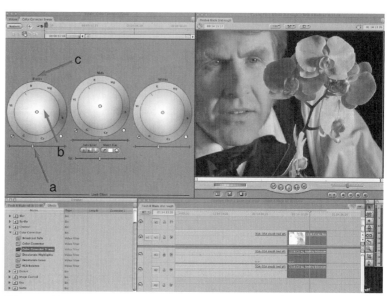

■ **Figure 24-1** The Final Cut Pro three-way color corrector interface. (a) The luminance slider; (b) the color balance controls (with the balance indicator at center); (c) the color correction control range (blacks, mids, or whites). Notice that the shot selected in the timeline is brought up in the viewer for color correction. See the color insert.

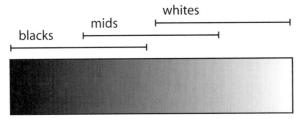

Figure 24-2 The color correction controls for blacks, mids, and whites actually overlap somewhat, which means that changes to a specific area of the image will have some effect on other areas as well.

a

b

c

Figure 24-4 Most color correction adjustments are subtle. The original image (a) appears somewhat flat and pale. By adjusting luminance values we can create sharper contrast and more depth to the image (b). Adjusting the color further refines the image. In this case adding a slight amber hue provides a sense of the heat of the summer sun (c). See the color insert.

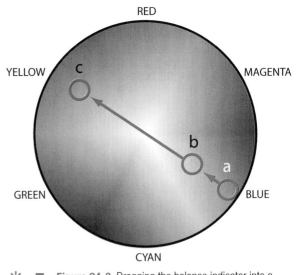

Figure 24-3 Dragging the balance indicator into a specific area of the color wheel balances the image toward that particular color. The closer to the edge you go, the more intense the color becomes. (a) Intense blue; (b) lighter blue; (c) intense yellow. See the color insert.

the color balance by clicking and dragging the **balance indicator**, which starts at the middle of each color wheel by default. Dragging the indicator toward any area of the color spectrum infuses the image with that particular color; the farther you move away from the center, the more intense the color becomes (**Figure 24-3**). **Complementary colors**, like blue and yellow, are opposite each other on the color wheel because, by adding more of one color, you are reducing its complement. Beyond correcting wayward white balancing or removing color to make your film black and white, there are an enormous number of visual possibilities with this tool. You can, for example, use the luminance slider in the blacks to brighten up the shadows a tad so that we can see some detail in the shadows, or if in one scene the light outside a window is a little too bright, you can use the luminance slider in the white areas to bring it down a bit. Perhaps you want to push a little blue into the shadows to create a certain mood. Just click and drag the blacks color balance indicator slightly further into the blue range of the color wheel (**Figure 24-4**).

If you're using the three-way color correction filter for the first time, you'll quickly realize that simply pushing sliders and dragging your mouse around the color wheel can create a visual mess: skin tones suddenly take on a Martian quality, or an image that had fine exposures suddenly looks terribly dull or overly crispy, or while you're adjusting the color of the grass, the sky takes on a sickly tone. The color correction tool is something that should be researched thoroughly before you go grabbing sliders and whanging them around. Also, color correction is not just about the buttons you need to push: there is considerable technique and aesthetic judgment involved that goes beyond the scope of this book, so I have listed some resources in the Recommended Readings to help familiarize you with this step of the finishing process.

One more word of caution: color correction, like any other visual effect, should be used with intelligence and some restraint. Creating red highlights in the shadows might look cool, but you need to consider what its purpose is in your film. Once again, technology is there to serve our ideas, so we need to be clear about what our ideas are in the first place in order to use these tools only when they are really called for. To be sure, if your shooting, lighting and exposures were controlled and accurate, you may not need extensive color correction; perhaps you'll just need to even out a few shots or scenes. If it ain't broke, don't fix it, but if you can improve your movie's look with this tool, then by all means, use it. That's what it's there for.

Titles and Credits

The final step, before we can send our film out of the computer and onto a format we can show to our eager public is to put titles and credits on the film. Again, most NLE systems contain a titling generator with more typographical options than you could ever use in a lifetime (Figure 24-5). You can choose from dozens of fonts, sizes, and colors; you can adjust the opacity of the text, create drop shadows or fuzzy edges, make the text scroll up and down, or crawl sideways, or fly in from the four corners of the screen; you can have your credits fade-in, wipe-in, or all of the above at the same time. You can, of course, create titles against simple color backgrounds, like any color text on black or any color on white. Or by adding an additional video track to your timeline, you can superimpose your opening credits over scenes from your film (Figure 24-6).

Despite the myriad titling options included in all popular NLE systems, some filmmakers who have a very specific graphic ideas for their title designs might go to an even more powerful third-party graphics or typography software, like Adobe Illustrator, to create customized titles and import those files back into the NLE system to cut into the program like any other media clip.

One important word of advice: take your time creating your credits. The people who worked on your movie deserve proper credit. Especially for people initiating their careers in film, credits can be as important as pay. It is not unusual for talented people to work only for the credit, especially if they believe the film will be good. If you slap your credits together at the last minute, you run the risk of forgetting people, giving them improper credit, or misspelling their names. All of these are serious faux pas and can alienate the people you've worked with, who are among your most important resources as a filmmaker.

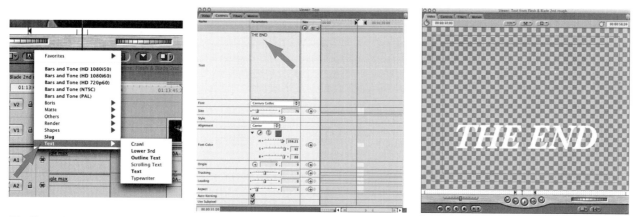

■ **Figure 24-5** The titling generator in Final Cut Pro allows you to select from a wide variety of effects and fonts. Superimposed titles are written over a checkerboard background that is later replaced by the image.

■ **Figure 24-6** Superimposed titles are placed on a second video track, and the final result can be seen in the viewer. Notice the title-safe overlays that help your text remain within the "safe area" of all monitors.

In Chapter 18 I talked about treating everyone on the film with respect. Giving proper credit is at the core of this respect. Also, do not forget to acknowledge those people who helped make your film a reality, though they may not have directly worked on it, by putting them on a "thanks to..." or "special thanks to..." list.

■ MASTERING YOUR PROJECT

Picture locked, sound mixed, color corrected, and titles on, you are ready to take your film out of the computer and into the real world. The first step is to create full-resolution **program masters**. Mastering simply means getting your film onto a high-quality DV tape format, both for archiving and so that you can make distribution copies for exhibition. This chapter discusses mastering projects that finish on SD or HD video; if your project involves a workflow that finishes on 35mm film or with a D-Cinema ready digital master (2K or 4K), please see "High-End Finishing Workflows" in Chapter 19.

Output Formats

NLE systems offer a huge range of output options depending on your intended distribution avenues. Each output option uses a different **codec** (compression/decompression) mathematical algorithm that reduces the amount of video information (compression) to match your exhibition needs (Figure 24-7) (see page 216 for a discussion of compression). Different codecs are compatible with different uses. For example, the MPEG 2 codec is used for making DVDs and MPEG 4 and H.264 are commonly used for distribution over the web.

You can also export a QuickTime movie of your project at different levels of compression depending on your distribution outlet. Outputting SD or HD is done via FireWire to a DV tape, but many of these other output options, like QuickTime movies or MPEG 2, simply create media files on your hard drive; these files can be exported into third-party programs for multimedia playback, for further compression, for uploading to the web, or for authoring DVDs. Indeed, you can output a number of different formats if you like. For example, you can output to DV tape with the "print to video" function *and* later output a QuickTime movie file through the "File > Export..." function. That said, the *very first* output you should undertake is creating your program master.

When we make **program masters** of our film, we want the highest quality possible. Masters are used for archiving our final film and as the source for subsequent duplication in order to create distribution copies. *The recommended method for mastering your film is to simply output your project to a DV tape with the same codec and to the same format in which you shot and captured*. For example, if you shot DV NTSC 29.97, then this should be your output option. If your acquisition and capture format was DVCPRO HD 720p 29.97, then you will likewise output using the same codec to create your master. Mastering to the same format ensures that you will lose no image quality at all from acquisition to output and it also ensures that all of your elements, raw footage and program master, are in the same compatible format.

Whether you are editing on Final Cut Pro or Avid, outputting to tape is simply a matter of hooking up a record deck to the NLE system via a FireWire cable. You should always master

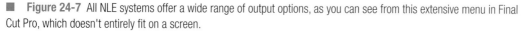

Tools Window Help

Animation
Apple DVCPRO HD 720p60
Apple Intermediate Codec
Apple Pixlet Video
Apple ProRes 422
Apple ProRes 422 (HQ)
Apple ProRes 422 (LT)
Apple ProRes 422 (Proxy)
Apple ProRes 4444
DV – PAL
DV/DVCPRO – NTSC
DVCPRO – PAL
DVCPRO HD 1080i50
DVCPRO HD 1080i60
DVCPRO HD 1080p25
DVCPRO HD 1080p30
DVCPRO HD 720p50
DVCPRO HD 720p50
DVCPRO50 – NTSC
DVCPRO50 – PAL
✓ H.264
HDV 1080i50
HDV 1080i60
HDV 1080p24
HDV 1080p25
HDV 1080p30
HDV 720p24
HDV 720p25
HDV 720p30
HDV 720p50
HDV 720p60
JPEG 2000
MPEG IMX 525/60 (30 Mb/s)
MPEG IMX 525/60 (40 Mb/s)
MPEG IMX 525/60 (50 Mb/s)
MPEG IMX 625/50 (30 Mb/s)
MPEG IMX 625/50 (40 Mb/s)
MPEG IMX 625/50 (50 Mb/s)
MPEG-4 Video
None
Photo – JPEG
PNG
Uncompressed 10-bit 4:2:2
Uncompressed 8-bit 4:2:2
XDCAM EX 1080i50 (35 Mb/s VBR)
XDCAM EX 1080i60 (35 Mb/s VBR)
XDCAM EX 1080p24 (35 Mb/s VBR)
XDCAM EX 1080p25 (35 Mb/s VBR)
XDCAM EX 1080p30 (35 Mb/s VBR)

Compression Type

Motion

Frame Rate: Current

Key Frames: ○ Automatic
● Every   2
○ All

☑ Frame Reorder

Compressor

Quality

Least   Low   Medium

Encoding: ● Best quality (M
○ Faster encode

Format: QuickTime
Use: Default Se

☑ Hide extension

Automatic
Restrict to   kbits/sec
Download

Cancel   OK

cel   Save

■ **Figure 24-7** All NLE systems offer a wide range of output options, as you can see from this extensive menu in Final Cut Pro, which doesn't entirely fit on a screen.

on the most robust tape format you have access to and always use a fresh tape for each master. DVCAM, DVCPRO, and DigiBeta formats are better than MiniDV for standard-definition projects, and HDCAM and DVCPRO HD are used for mastering HD projects. DVDs and Blu-ray are considered distribution formats and not mastering formats.

As usual, NLE software offers various methods for outputting, but for creating a master tape you should use the method that allows you to add a **program leader** to the head of your tape before your film begins; leaders include **color bars** and **tone**, a **slate**, and **countdown** (Figures 24-8 and 24-9). In Final Cut Pro, this output method is called **print to video**.

You should always make several master tapes, called **safety masters**, and then you can export your movie as a QuickTime movie file (or MPEG 4) in preparation for distribution over the web, or as an MPEG 2 file that you can later bring into a DVD authoring program (like iDVD or DVD Studio Pro) in order to create DVDs for distribution. None of these other options need, or should have, the added program leader.

Print to Video

Leader
Element: Sec:
☑ Color Bars — 60 — Tone Level ——————— -12 dB   Preview
☑ Black —— 10
☑ Slate —— 10 — Text   "Mick's Movie"
                              TRT: 15 min.
☑ Black —— 10   Mick Hurbis–Cherrier
☑ Countdown —— Built-in

Media   Trailer
Print: In to Out   ☑ Black —— 10 Seconds
Options: Duration Calculator
☐ Loop —— 1 Times   Media: 00:14:10:23
Between each loop place: Total: 00:15:55:23
☐ Black —— 5 Seconds

☐ Automatically Start Recording

Cancel   OK

■ **Figure 24-8** Bars, tone, slate, and countdown; everything you need for a professional program leader can be found in the "Print to Video" dialogue box in Final Cut Pro.

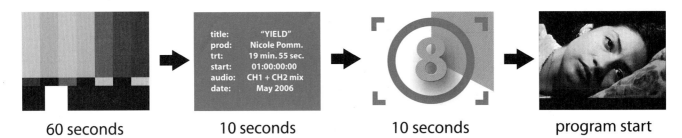

<table>
| 60 seconds | 10 seconds | 10 seconds | program start |
</table>

title: "YIELD"
prod: Nicole Pomm.
trt: 19 min. 55 sec.
start: 01:00:00:00
audio: CH1 + CH2 mix
date: May 2006

■ **Figure 24-9** The standard elements and timing for the program leader.

■ ELEMENTS OF THE PROGRAM LEADER

The program leader is inserted at the beginning of your master tape and has a standardized order and duration for each element.

Bars and Tone (60 seconds)

If you plan to broadcast your movie over television or cable, or submit it to film festivals, it's important to give the recipient of your film some way to accurately calibrate their equipment so that your images (color and brightness) and your audio levels will play back accurately. The standard calibration tools, which we lay down at the head of our tape, are **color bars** and **tone**. We have already mentioned color bars with respect to calibrating field monitors (see page 264). The leader elements discussed here are the same Society of Motion Picture and Television Engineers (SMPTE) standard color bars, which allow the projectionist or broadcast engineer to accurately calibrate the chrominance and luminance of their playback equipment. The 1-kHz reference tone, which is recorded on the sound track under the color bars, allows them to calibrate the audio so that your program is played back neither too soft nor too loud.

The Program Slate (10 seconds)

In addition, standard professional tape leader includes a **program slate**, which is a simple list of all of the information that would be important to a broadcaster or programmer, including (a) the film title, (b) producer, (c) total running time (TRT), (d) starting timecode (standard start timecode is 1:00:00:00), (e) audio configuration (i.e., mixed or stereo unmixed), and (f) production date.

SMPTE Countdown (10 seconds):

SMPTE countdown is a numeric countdown in seconds, from 10 to 2, which cuts to black for the last 2 seconds of the countdown. Your project then begins precisely after the end of the 2 seconds of black. Countdown allows the broadcast engineer or projectionist to easily cue your tape for screening. By simply pausing in the black, after the #2 frame, they can be sure to begin your program with a little buffer of black before the first images appear on screen.

■ DISTRIBUTION COPIES

Once you have created your program and safety masters, you need to think about distribution. In the not so distant future, distribution will mean simply a video-on-demand, full-resolution transfer of data via the web or satellite download. Indeed, there are a number of distribution avenues for a filmmaker to take these days, but in broad terms these pretty much break down into the disc and the web.

DVD and Blu-ray for Distribution

As of the writing of this book, the common coin of exchange for mass distribution is still the disc: DVD for standard definition and Blu-ray disc (BD) for high definition. However, whereas DVDs play on practically all players (DVD, Blu-ray, and computers), BDs will not play on standard DVD players or on Mac computers! Even though Blu-ray was designed to replace the DVD disc, that hasn't quite happened yet. This makes the DVD disc your most reliable way of getting your movie out there. In fact, most film festivals, television programmers, museum curators, online festivals, and online sales and distribution outlets usually require DVD submissions for initial screening and consideration. Also, if you want to send a sample of your work to a production company, ad agency, or producer, you will most likely send a DVD because they are nearly universally compatible. Whether

DVD or BD, these discs are called **screening copies** (or **screeners**). The more polished and professional your disc package, meaning a disc with extras, printed covers, and a plastic case, the better your film will be represented. Offering DVD or BD is also standard for selling your own film (online) and for giving your movie to family, friends, and especially the people who participated in the production.

Both **Blu-ray** discs **(BD)** and **DVD** (for **digital versatile disc**) are optical storage discs that store the binary data for your sound and images as microscopic bumps and indentations, called **pits**, in the surface of the disc. These pits are written as one long, ultrafine spiral called the **data track** and are read with a laser beam as the disc spins in the drive bay. The primary difference between these two formats is the precision of the laser and the size and number of the data pits. The red laser found in the DVD system is capable of reading data tracks that are 0.74 microns wide, while the much sharper blue laser (hence the name) with its shorter wavelength can read data off tracks that are 0.32 microns wide (**Figure 24-10**). This allows for much more data information to be packed on a disc, and the blue laser also provides for greater data rates. Here is the comparison: a single-layer DVD holds 4.7 GB of data, and a dual-layer DVD can hold 8.5 GB. A single-layer BD, however, can hold 25 GB, and a dual-layer BD holds 50 GB. The audio/video data transfer rates are similarly different with DVDs clocking in at 10.08 Mbps, and BDs at a much faster 54.0 Mbps. What this adds up to is resolution potential, and this is why DVDs can only support standard-definition video resolutions (720 × 480/720 × 576) whereas Blu-ray is capable of 1920 × 1080 (1080p) high definition.

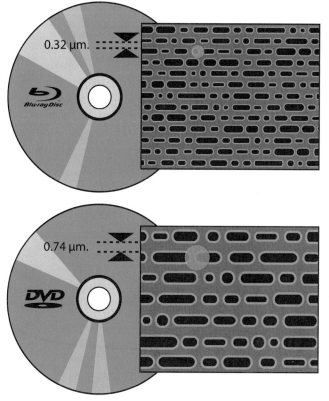

Figure 24-10 The ultra-sharp blue laser used in the Blu-ray HD format reads data tracks that are 0.32 microns wide *(top)*. This allows much more video data to be packed onto a disc, compared to the DVD format, which can only read data tracks that are 0.74 microns wide *(left)*.

DVDs encode the image and sound data using the MPEG 2 compression codec. So your software encodes your film as MPEG 2 when you create the disc, and your DVD player contains the MPEG 2 decoder to uncompress the data as you watch it. Blu-ray can use either MPEG-2 or the much more advanced H.264/MPEG-4 AVC codec. What is also essential to know, for projects shot on film or 24p and edited at 24p or 23.976 fps, is that you can output, encode, and author either type of disc at these frame rates as well. Keeping your frame rate at 24p or 23.976 fps allows you to put more footage, less compressed, onto the disc, because you have fewer frames and less data per minute. Not only that, but it keeps your 24p movie really looking like 24p. This is the encoding method used for most commercial films released on disc.

Pressed or Burned?

Not all DVD and Blu-ray discs are created equal. **Pressed discs** physically mold the pits of the data track into the surface of the polycarbonate plastic, which is then coated in aluminum. This is the kind of disc you find when you buy a commercial movie. **Burned discs** use recordable media and are created using a laser to burn a color dye layer in the media surface, which turns various colors and densities that mimic the depth and shadows of the physical pits in a pressed disc.

Pressed discs offer much better compatibility and physical longevity but must be created by a professional disc mastering service. The cost for having discs professionally mastered is quite low, but they are only available in bulk quantities, which means 300 or more discs! That's a lot of distribution. If you plan to go this route, the disc mastering

■ **Figure 24-11** The interface for Adobe Encore DVD, a powerful DVD authoring program.

service you choose will instruct you as to the specific file format they prefer to work with. Usually, whether you are going to DVD, BD, or both, the service will want uncompressed files and will do any necessary compression in-house, so be sure to check with the facility. But what if you don't need 500 discs? What if you only need 12 or so? Then you're likely to burn your own using **recordable discs.** Recordable DVDs come in four flavors: **DVD+R** and **DVD–R** are record-once-only formats, and **DVD+RW** and **DVD–RW** can have their data erased and rewritten. Recordable Blu-ray discs are **BD–R** (record once only) and **BD-RE** (rewritable). In both cases, rewritable discs are not a good choice for distribution. When we create a DVD+R or BD–R copy, it's called "burning" a disc, instead of "pressing" a disc, because the record laser essentially burns faux "pits" (color dye layers) into the disc surface, which fool the playback laser into thinking that it's scanning and reading into the dimensions of a pressed pit. Encoding, authoring, and burning your own DVDs or BDs requires a computer with a DVD burner or Blu-ray burner and a DVD authoring program like DVD Studio Pro or iDVD (for simple projects) on the Apple platform, or Adobe Encore or Pinnacle Studio for the PC (**Figure 24-11**). It is usually recommended that you import your projects as an uncompressed file into these programs (i.e., uncompressed QuickTime movie) and do the necessary encoding from within the program. Make sure you thoroughly research the capabilities and options these programs offer before you encode, author, and burn your discs.

Screening Dubs for Film Festivals and Broadcast

Cable television and film festivals are two of the most visible and important outlets for your film, so screening your movie at its best quality is essential. Although most festivals and broadcast stations require DVDs for application submissions or as a preview copy, once you are accepted for screening, you must find out what their preferred exhibition format is and use one of your safety masters to make a **screening dub**. *Do not send your master!* You should assume that the handling of this projection tape will be rough and it may not survive the journey to the festival and back. Common formats used for projection at film festivals and broadcasting include DVCAM, HDCAM, DVCPRO HD, and DigiBeta.

■ WEB DISTRIBUTION AND THE FUTURE

The web is a fact of life for the student and independent filmmaker. There are many, many vitally useful websites for any stage of production. For example, during the preproduction phase, **kickstarter.com** or **indiegogo.com** are fundraising platforms that can help you raise money, and **backstage.com** can help you cast your film. While in production, **cinematography.net**, **Kodak.com,** and **dofmaster.com** can provide valuable information for shooting and, of course, you'll find all the necessary production forms and log sheets for your project at **www.voiceandvisionbook.com.** For postproduction, you'll find the complete (searchable) manual for Final Cut Pro online at **apple.com/support** and an indispensable promotion, distribution, and festival resource at **withoutabox.com.** These are just a few examples, and although online resources are multiplying annually, web culture is also notoriously unstable and subject to constant change, so it would be folly to commit to a list of the most popular sites in print here. I have listed some currently available and useful sites in the Web Resources section of the book's companion website. Hopefully they will still be around when you try to visit them.

Getting back to distribution; whether you intend to distribute your film in a traditional way, through the festival circuit or TV broadcast, or if you've designed your project exclusively for Internet distribution, you need to create some sort of presence on the web. Almost all traditionally distributed films, short or long, create a promotional website for their movie and often that film site is contained in a larger site designed around the filmmaker. These sites also incorporate blogging and social network dispatches (i.e., Facebook, Twitter, MySpace) to keep fans abreast of the progress of the movie from preproduction through to distribution. **Figure 24-12** shows the website for John Daschbach's short film *Waking Dreams* (a film you can screen at www.voiceandvisionbook.com). The website contains everything a potential festival programmer, film critic, film writer, film buyer, or other interested person needs to know. It lists the cast and crew and provides filmmaker contact information; it announces all screening and awards; it furnishes a quotable synopsis of the film as well as

■ **Figure 24-12** Director John Daschbach went to Michael Richardson at Hand Eye Design to create the promotional website for his short film *Waking Dreams*.

high-quality stills for reproducing on the web and in print. It also contains a complete online press kit (downloadable). In addition, it gives easy links for streaming the film online or purchasing a DVD copy.

■ WEB-BASED PROMOTION AND DISTRIBUTION: TWO CASE STUDIES

Filmmakers Susan Buice and Arin Crumly created both a website and an ongoing series of video podcasts around their first feature film, *Four Eyed Monsters*, which was shot on DV and screened at numerous film festivals. The strategy of the filmmaking duo was to generate interest in the film by "creating an audience" through regular, five-minute podcasts. These podcasts were not episodes from the film; rather, they were ongoing, behind-the-scenes documentaries about the filmmaking process and the couple's developing romantic and creative relationship during the period of making and distributing the movie—the podcasts were the movie about the movie, delivered in five-minute episodes (**Figure 24-13**).

"In about nine months, we went to 16 film festivals and 3,000 people saw the film. Yet in the first 36

■ **Figure 24-13** Filmmakers Susan Buice and Arin Crumly successfully promote and self-distribute their film *Four Eyed Monsters* (2005) through the use of a website and regular podcasts.

hours [our podcasts] were viewed 3,000 times online" (from *The Independent*, May/June 2006). Buice and Crumly self-distribute their film, which has opened to sold-out audiences around the country. Most of those in attendance are primed and eager to see the film because they've been closely following the story of the film and the couple via the podcasts.

In podcast episode 7.6, in which the couple screen their film in New York City, Susan and Arin interview audience members standing in line to attend their film. Many speak of the connection they felt with the filmmakers, even though they had yet to see the film itself: "I guess since I've been seeing the podcasts for a little while, I feel like I have a connection." "I'm really invested in Susan and Arin as people even though I don't know them; it's creepy." "I like you guys and I want things to work out."

Looking at their website, especially through the "Friends" links, it's clear that the feature film is only one part of what Buice and Crumly have accomplished; the podcasts have a life of their own and have essentially created a broader film community through innovative online outreach.

Not feature film, not a short film, watch it on your cellular telephone, on your television, at the movie theater, on your toaster oven—Stingray Sam is the first episodic thriller developed for these modern technologies!
From the Stingray Sam trailer

Director Cory McAbee and his producing partners Becky Glupczynski and Robert Lurie brought back the idea of the serialized drama and updated it for the 21st century. Their 2009 multi-format, micro-budget, genre mash-up film *Stingray Sam* is equal parts musical, cowboy film, sci-fi flick, and social satire. *Stingray Sam* follows the exploits of the titular character (played by McAbee) and his former prison cellmate the Quasar Kid as they begin their postincarceration life by saving a cute little girl in distress.

Although the plot description sounds like a project destined for a small cult following, *Stingray Sam* has in fact found wide acclaim with festivals, audiences, and the critical press. This was largely the result of two groundbreaking ideas that were built into the very conception of the project. The first was to devise a story format that could be screened equally successfully on cell phones, televisions, and in movie theaters.

The plot of the film was carefully constructed in six, 10-minute episodes that can be easily downloaded into a cell phone to watch individually and sequentially. Each episode contains a little bit of plot progression, a little bit of social commentary, a musical number, and a few laughs. The six episodes, however, can also be stitched together to form a feature length film, which can be screened in movie theaters or on DVD at home. It is in this long form that *Stingray Sam* made the initial rounds on the film festival circuit, gaining fans, press, and positive word of mouth along the way. Visually, the film's campy, low-tech, black-and-white aesthetic also plays perfectly well on anything from a 2-by-2-inch cell phone LCD to a 30-foot movie theater screen (**Figure 24-14**).

The second strategy was to retain all rights to the film and self-distribute by developing a web-based "direct to fan" marketing strategy. The fan base came from the film festival buzz, the success of McAbee's previous movie *The American Astronaut*, the success of McAbee and Lurie's rock band the Billy Nayer Show, and carefully moderated releases of free episodes on YouTube, Vimeo, and the Cory McAbee website in order to get people hooked and wanting more. This fan base and its broader network is diligently (but not obnoxiously) cultivated via email, official blogs, fan blogs, Facebook, and Twitter, and all marketing roads lead back to the

■ **Figure 24-14** "Coming soon to screens of all sizes!" The website for McAbee's innovative Stingray Sam (2009).

in practice

website—which one quickly realizes is not just a promotional tool for a single film; rather it is a synergistic collection of related creative media and artist information. You can buy movie episodes, sound tracks, DVDs, posters, music CDs, T-shirts, stickers, as well as find out where the next *Stingray Sam* screening or the next Billy Nayer Show concert will be, or read the latest reviews, and so on. The band ties-in to the movies, which ties-in to the graphic arts, which ties-in to the band and movies—everything is related to everything else and it all revolves around the singular voice of this multi-talented artist Cory McAbee. The remarkable creativity of McAbee's artistic vision and distribution strategy has made *Stingray Sam* something of a prototype for other filmmakers wishing to directly reach a wide public through self-distribution on the web.

Another critically important use of the web for filmmakers is online streaming. More and more films, especially shorts, are being streamed on one of the many film outlets proliferating on the web. Some of these sites are **video hosting sites**, which provide a wide variety of services, from video-on-demand to online marketing, distribution, and DVD sales. Some of these sites hold online film festivals, and others simply lay out a smorgasbord of media and keep a running tally of the most popular works (those that get the most hits) on the site. Divining who the major players are in the web video hosting world can be difficult, again because they come and go quickly, but some of the most stable video streaming sources are the conventional film festival websites. Sundance, the Tribeca Film Festival, and Slamdance, to name just a few, all stream some of their short film winners from their websites. Other web platforms, like individual **filmmaker websites** and **video podcasting**, are also significant new outlets for the promotion and self-distribution of films. Without much trouble, filmmakers can create a series of video podcasts of their work, list the video podcast on Apple's music store, or post them on their own personal website, and subscribers will receive new video episodes downloaded to their video iPods automatically. Another recent trend in media for the small screen is cell phone distribution. Cell phone companies are currently in a mad scramble to find "byte-sized" video content for downloading onto their cell phones. This means there is a whole new outlet for very short, low-resolution films. By and large, cell phones also use MPEG 2 encoding.

Video-sharing websites, like YouTube and Vimeo, have emerged as significant outlets for sharing short films, rough cuts, or trailers with friends, potential employers, or for fundraisers, or for the pubic in general. Most web-based video-sharing sites that stream (or download) video require that you keep files fairly small, meaning a total file size no more than 2 GB to 5 GB, and they often limit the length of downloads to something like 15 minutes. MPEG 4, QuickTime (.mov), and Windows movies (.wmv) are the current standard encoding formats, and all webstreaming is done with progressive scan, so if your project was mastered in an interlaced format (like 1080i) you'll need to de-interlace it before you upload. It's important that you carefully read the format standards and uploading requirements for the particular video-sharing site you're interested in using, as they are not uniform and are frequently changing (Figure 24-15). Since the adoption of the H.263/MPEG-4 AVC codec in 2008, many sites are capable of offering multiple resolutions from 320 ×240 (very poor, but fast stream) to 720p HD (much better but slower) to 1080p HD (best resolution but slowest) (Figure 24-16). It is this relatively recent bump in image quality that has made these services viable for filmmakers. Personal websites, of course, can hold and stream longer films in larger resolution, but all of these factors increase the download time for the viewer.

In any case, however, what the web is able to handle, in general, at this point are short movies, in small containers, at fairly low resolutions. But this assessment can only serve as a snapshot of this rapidly changing arena. The current level of technology and quality isn't causing many filmmakers to abandon the large screen yet, but they are monitoring the web's progress very carefully. Currently the World Wide Web is a space that is more appropriate for advertising your film than actually distributing it with any quality; it is, as yet, an emerging distribution outlet—not a fully developed one. But web and satellite

■ **Figure 24-15** Every video sharing service provides technical guidelines to help you output your film correctly for web streaming.

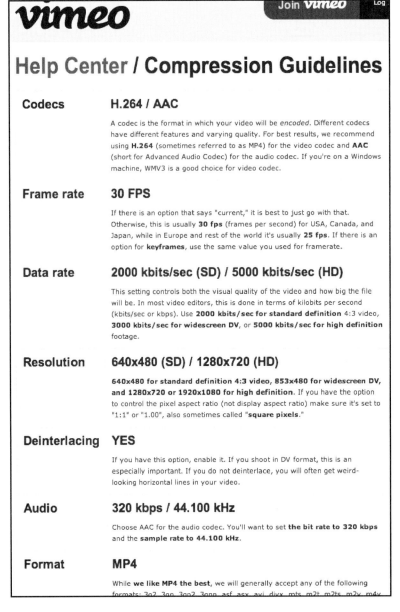

Join **vimeo**   Log

Help Center / Compression Guidelines

Codecs   **H.264 / AAC**

A codec is the format in which your video will be *encoded*. Different codecs have different features and varying quality. For best results, we recommend using **H.264** (sometimes referred to as MP4) for the video codec and **AAC** (short for Advanced Audio Codec) for the audio codec. If you're on a Windows machine, WMV3 is a good choice for video codec.

Frame rate   **30 FPS**

If there is an option that says "current," it is best to just go with that. Otherwise, this is usually **30 fps** (frames per second) for USA, Canada, and Japan, while in Europe and rest of the world it's usually **25 fps**. If there is an option for **keyframes**, use the same value you used for framerate.

Data rate   **2000 kbits/sec (SD) / 5000 kbits/sec (HD)**

This setting controls both the visual quality of the video and how big the file will be. In most video editors, this is done in terms of kilobits per second (kbits/sec or kbps). Use **2000 kbits/sec for standard definition** 4:3 video, **3000 kbits/sec for widescreen DV**, or **5000 kbits/sec for high definition** footage.

Resolution   **640x480 (SD) / 1280x720 (HD)**

640x480 for standard definition 4:3 video, 853x480 for widescreen DV, and 1280x720 or 1920x1080 for high definition. If you have the option to control the pixel aspect ratio (not display aspect ratio) make sure it's set to "1:1" or "1.00", also sometimes called "**square pixels**."

Deinterlacing   **YES**

If you have this option, enable it. If you shoot in DV format, this is an especially important. If you do not deinterlace, you will often get weird-looking horizontal lines in your video.

Audio   **320 kbps / 44.100 kHz**

Choose AAC for the audio codec. You'll want to set **the bit rate to 320 kbps** and the **sample rate to 44.100 kHz**.

Format   **MP4**

While **we like MP4 the best**, we will generally accept any of the following formats: 3g2, 3gp, 3gp2, 3gpp, asf, asx, avi, divx, mts, m2t, m2ts, m2v, m4v

Official Teaser Trailer for "Saturnalia" by Gustavo Mercado

dektarium 1 videos Subscribe

You Tube HD

▶ ◀) 0:41 / 1:23   720p

■ **Figure 24-16** Improvements in resolution have made web-based video-sharing services a useful tool for disseminating short films or portions of features, like this trailer from Mercado's feature film *Saturnalia* (2011), uploaded in 720p HD.

distribution will surely arrive at this point in the near future. As **video on demand** (**VOD**) and web-based video streaming services like Netflix get better, faster, and sharper with each passing year, we will see more filmmakers taking advantage of the web as a distribution outlet for feature-length films. The technology and capacity advance monthly and it is consistently improving, step by step, achieving better and better visual resolution. A published book like this one can never remain current with a developing organism like the web; it is up to you, the emerging filmmakers, to stay current with the technological state of the art. You must also carefully consider all of the creative, aesthetic, and formal implications that the web, cell phones, video podcasts, 3D, and all other screening formats that await, right around the next evolutionary bend, will have on your art form—filmmaking (**Figure 24-17**).

■ **Figure 24-17** An audience enjoys the action on the big screen *(left)*, from Keaton's *Sherlock Jr.* (1924). The convenience and portability of your own pocket-sized movie screen *(right)* with Apple's iPhone.

When I read that the newest generation of Apple's iPod allows for movie as well as music downloads, I was taken aback. An iPod screen is, I believe, an inch and a half by an inch and a half. Now, the iPod is a tremendous product. But can this really be called an innovation? In other words, if you're watching a movie on a screen that small, are you actually watching a movie? What, in fact, are you looking at?

Martin Scorsese (From the Tribeca Film Festival Catalogue, 2006)

Scorsese poses a central and vital question for all of us to consider. What are we looking at? Is this a new mode of media, one that requires its own approaches, its own aesthetic, its own forms? Or is this simply another outlet, a further extension of filmmaking as we've always known it? That's not just for you to decide, it's for you to define!

Recommended Readings

GENERAL FILM STUDY

Looking at Movies: An Introduction to Film
by Richard M. Barsam and Dave Monahan; W.W. Norton and Co.

The Film Experience
by Timothy Corrigan and Patricia White; Palgrave Macmillan.

The Cinema Book
by Pam Cooke and Mieke Bernink; British Film Institute Publishing.

Film Style and Technology: History and Analysis
by Barry Salt; Starword.

SCREENWRITING AND SCREENPLAYS

The Shooting Script (Newmarket Shooting Script Series)
(especially *Pieces of April,* by Peter Hedges; *The Squid and the Whale,* by Noah Baumbach;
and *Sideways,* by Alexander Payne and Jim Taylor); New Market Press.

Rushmore
by Wes Anderson and Owen Wilson; Faber and Faber.

Developing Story Ideas
by Michael Rabiger; Focal Press.

Crafting Short Screenplays that Connect
by Claudia Hunter Johnson; Focal Press.

Alternative Scriptwriting
by Ken Dancyger and Jeff Rush; Focal Press.

The Screenwriter's Manual: A Complete Reference of Format & Style
by Stephen E. Bowles, Ronald Mangravite, Peter A. Zorn; Allyn & Bacon

PREVISUALIZATION

Film Directing Shot by Shot: Visualizing from Concept to Screen
by Steven D. Katz; Michael Wiese Productions.

PRODUCING

A Killer Life by Christine Vachon with Austin Bunn: Limelight Editions.

Producing and Directing the Short Film and Video
by Peter W. Rea and David K. Irving; Focal Press.

Contracts for the Film & Television Industry
by Mark Litwak; Silman-James Press.

IFP/Los Angeles Independent Filmmaker's Manual
by Eden H. Wurmfeld and Nicole Laloggia; Focal Press.

Film Budgeting: Or, How Much It Will Cost to Shoot Your Movie?
by Ralph S. Singleton; VNU Inc.

Clearance and Copyright: Everything the Independent Filmmaker Needs to Know
by Michael C. Donaldson; Silman-James Press.

■ DIRECTING

On Filmmaking: An Introduction to the Craft of the Director
by Alexander Mackendrick; Faber and Faber.

Film Directing Fundamentals: See Your Film Before Shooting
by Nicholas Proferes; Focal Press.

Directing Actors: Creating Memorable Performances for Film & Television
by Judith Weston; Michael Wiese Productions.

The Film Director's Intuition: Script Analysis & Rehearsal Techniques
by Judith Weston; Michael Wiese Productions.

Directing Feature Films: The Creative Collaboration between Director, Writers, and Actors
by Mark W. Travis; Michael Wiese Productions.

Directing: Film Techniques and Aesthetics
by Michael Rabiger: Focal Press.

■ ART DIRECTION

What an Art Director Does: An Intro to Motion Picture Art Design
by Ward Preston; Silman-James Press.

Production Design and Art Direction (Screencraft Series)
by Peter Ettedgui; Focal Press.

The Art Direction Handbook for Film
by Michael Rizzo; Focal Press.

■ CINEMATOGRAPHY

The Filmmaker's Eye
by Gustavo Mercado; Focal Press.

Cinematography for Directors: A Guide for Creative Collaboration
by Jaquiline B. Frost: Michael Wiese Productions

Lighting for Film and Digital Cinematography
by Dave Viera and Maria Viera; Wadsworth Publishing.

Motion Picture and Video Lighting
by Blain Brown; Focal Press.

Contemporary Cinematographers on Their Art
by Pauline B. Rogers; Focal Press.

New Cinematographers
by Alex Ballinger; Collins Design.

Cinematography (Screencraft Series)
by Peter Ettedgui; Focal Press.

Masters of Light: Conversations with Contemporary Cinematographers
by Dennis Salvato and Larry Salvato; University of California Press.

■ SOUND

Audio-Vision
by Michael Chion; Columbia University Press.

Practical Art of Motion Picture Sound
by David Yewdall; Focal Press.

Sound for Film and Television
by Tomlinson Holman; Focal Press.

■ PRODUCTION TECHNICAL REFERENCE

American Cinematographer Manual
by Stephen Burum; American Society of Cinematographers.

Selected Tables, Charts and Formulas for the Student Cinematographer from the American Cinematographer Manual
by ASC, Stephen Burum (Ed.); American Society of Cinematographers.

ASC Video Manual
by Michael Grotticelli (Ed.); ASC Holding Corp.

Camera Assistant's Manual
by David E. Elkins; Focal Press.

The Professional Cameraman's Handbook
by Sylvia E. Carlson and Verne Carlson; Focal Press.

Digital Cinematography
by Paul Wheeler; Focal Press.

■ POSTPRODUCTION

In the Blink of an Eye
by Walter Murch; Silman-James Press.

Technique of Film and Video Editing: History, Theory, and Practice
by Ken Dancyger; Focal Press.

On Film Editing
by Edward Dmytryk; Focal Press.

Avid Editing: A Guide for Beginning and Intermediate Users
by Sam Kauffmann; Focal Press.

Apple Pro Training Series: Final Cut Pro
by Diana Weynand; Peachpit Press.

Visual Quickpro Guide: Avid Express Pro
by James Monohan; Peachpit Press.

■ ON FILMMAKERS AND METHODS

Digital Filmmaking
by Mike Figgis: Faber & Faber.

Notes on the Cinematographer
by Robert Bresson; Green Integer.

Hitchcock
by Helen G. Scott and François Truffaut; Simon & Schuster.

On Directing Film
by David Mamet; Penguin.

Making Movies
by Sidney Lumet; Vintage.

Who the Devil Made It: Conversations with Legendary Film Directors
by Peter Bogdanovich; Ballantine Books.

Moviemakers' Master Class: Private Lessons from the World's Foremost Directors
by Laurent Tirard; Faber and Faber.

Catching the Big Fish
by David Lynch: Jeremy P. Tarcher; Penguin.

Web Resources

The World Wide Web offers an enormously wide range of resources for the filmmaker. The usefulness of individual websites ranges from absolutely indispensable to completely disposable fluff. Here I have listed some of the more useful websites for a working filmmaker. Many of these websites also provide links to additional useful websites, so try them out. Also, as anyone who visits the web regularly knows, it is a rather unstable organism—websites come and websites go. I have tried my best to list the most reliable resources out there, but I cannot guarantee that all of these links will still be up and running when you try to visit. Best of luck. (Go to the Voice & Vision companion website at www.voiceandvisionbook.com for hot links to all these resources.)

■ GENERAL FILM INFORMATION

http://www.aivf.org/	www.ascmag.com	www.studentfilmmakers.com
www.ifp.org	www.filmmakermagazine.com	www.filmmaking.net
www.imdb.com	www.filmthreat.com	http//filmmaking.com
www.moviemaker.com	www.film4.com	www.studiodaily.com/
www.premiere.com	www.filmmaker.com	filmandvideo
www.sensesofcinema.com	www.indiewire.com	

■ FUNDING, PREPRODUCTION, CASTING, CREW

www.kickstarter.com	www.backstage.com	www.breakdownservices.com
www.creative-capital.org	http://home.castingnetworks.com	www.crewconnection.com
www.massify.com	www.nowcasting.com	www.productionhub.com
www.indiegogo.com	www.ReelACT.com	www.stuntworks.org

■ SCRIPTS

www.wga.org	www.scriptcity.net	www.creativescreenwriting.com
www.wgaeast.org	www.screenwriting.info	www.screenwritersutopia.com
www.copyright.gov	http://wordplayer.com	http://celtx.com

■ GUILDS, UNIONS, AND ORGANIZATIONS

www.wga.org	www.aivf.org	www.ifp.org
www.theasc.com	www.sagindie.org	www.smpte.org
www.editorsguild.com	www.wif.org	www.atsc.org
www.dga.org	www.ufva.org	www.dcimovies.com
www.mpaa.org	www.pbs.org/independentlens	

■ SAFETY, INSURANCE AND LEGAL

http://www.filmins.com	www.marklitwak.com
www.independent-magazine.org/	csatf.org (essential)
magazine/07/2009/filmmakerinsurance	www.labour.gov.on.ca/english/hs/pubs/
www.ifp.org	filmguide (Canada)
	http://moviegunservices.com (prop gun laws and safety guidelines)

■ CINEMATOGRAPHY

www.theasc.com   www.cinematographers.nl   www.motion.kodak.com
www.cinematography.com   http://nofilmschool.com/dslr   www.fujifilmusa.com
www.cinematography.net

■ SOUND AND MUSIC

www.filmsound.org   www.soundonsound.com   www.ascap.com
http://cinemasound.ning.com   www.cinemaaudiosociety.org   www.bmi.com

■ PRODUCTION TOOLS AND TECHNICAL REFERENCE

www.fdtimes.com   www.hdforindies.com   www.dofmaster.com
www.highdef.org   www.creativecow.net   www.aja.com
www.adamwilt.com   www.freshdv.com   www.davideubank.com
http://digitalcontentproducer   www.dvcreators.net
.com   www.panavision.com/tools.php

■ FESTIVALS AND DISTRIBUTION

www.withoutabox.com   www.ifc.com/media-lab   http://sxsw.com
www.filmfestivals.com   www.atomfilms.com   www.current.com
www.triggerstreet.com   www.indieflix.com   www.indiepixfilms.com
www.filmfestivalworld.com   www.slamdance.com

Bibliography

■ INTRODUCTION

Broughton, James. *Making Light of It,* City Lights Books, San Francisco, 1992.

Figgis, Mike. *Digital Filmmaking*, Faber & Faber, New York, 2007.

Mackendrick, Alexander. *On Filmmaking*, Faber & Faber, New York, 2004.

Tirard, Laurent. *Moviemakers' Master Class*, Faber & Faber, New York, 2002.

■ CHAPTER 1

Hedges, Peter. *Pieces of April: The Shooting Script*, Newmarket Press, New York, 2003.

Locarno International Film Festival, 1996. Excerpt from an interview with Houshang Golmakani, "48th Locarno International Film Festival." Available July 27, 2006 at www.pardo.ch/1995/95ret1.htm.

Mamet, David. *On Directing Film*, Penguin Books USA, Inc., New York, 1991.

Pfeiffer, Mark. "A Conversation with 'Pieces of April' director Peter Hedges," *The Film Journal*, November 2003. Available at www.thefilmjournal.com/issue7/hedges.html.

Tirard, Laurent. *Moviemakers' Master Class*, Faber & Faber, New York, 2002.

■ CHAPTER 2

Kieslowski, Krzysztof and Piesiewicz, Krzysztof. *Decalogue: The Ten Commandments*, Faber & Faber, London, 1991.

■ CHAPTER 3

Mackendrick, Alexander. *On Filmmaking*, Faber & Faber, New York, 2004.

Tirard, Laurent. *Moviemakers' Master Class*, Faber & Faber, New York, 2002.

■ CHAPTER 4

Tirard, Laurent. *Moviemakers' Master Class*, Faber & Faber, New York, 2002.

■ CHAPTER 5

Bourke, Philippa. "Taking the Digital Medium into Their Own Hands: Storytelling by Women Filmmakers Evolves with DV." Available at www.moviesbywomen.com/articles (posted August 9, 2002).

Mackendrick, Alexander. On *Filmmaking*, Faber & Faber, New York, 2004.

Truffaut, François and Scott, Helen G. *Hitchcock*, Simon & Schuster, France, 1985.

■ CHAPTER 7

"A Conversation with Michael Ballhaus, ASC" *ASC Magazine*, November 20, 2006 (available at www.theasc.com/news/News_Articles/News_77.php).

Cronin, Paul. "Four Golden Rules," *The Guardian*, June 17, 2005 (available at http://film.guardian.co.uk/interview/interviewpages/0,6737,1508057,00.html).

Figgis, Mike. *Digital Filmmaking*, Faber & Faber, New York, 2007.

Hart, Hugh. "Filmmakers Find Fresh Talent on MySpace," www.wired.com, March 14, 2008.

Sells, Mark. "From Law School to Oscar: Courtney Hunt Talks Frozen River," *MovieMaker Magazine*, February 11, 2009 (available at www.moviemaker.com/directing/article/courtney_hunt_frozen_river_oscar_20090210).

Vachon, Christine (w/Austin Bunn). *A Killer Life*, Simon & Schuster, New York, 2006.

Wood, Jennifer M. "Where the Girls Are: DP Ellen Kuras Talks about Shooting Rebecca Miller's 'Personal Velocity,'" *MovieMaker Magazine*, February 3, 2007 (available at www.moviemaker.com/cinematography/article/where_the_girls_are_2739).

■ CHAPTER 8

Anderson, Joseph, and Anderson, Barbara. "The Myth of Persistence of Vision Revisited," *Journal of Film and Video*, Volume 45, Issue 1 (Spring 1993): 3–12.

Doyle, Christopher. *R34G38B25*, Gingko Press, Berkeley, 2004.

Eastman Kodak Corp. "Kodak Cinema Tools." Available at the iTunes Store.

■ CHAPTER 9

Coo, Ryan. "The DSLR Cinematography Guide" (available at http://nofilmschool.com/dslr).

■ CHAPTER 10

Burum, Stephen H. *American Cinematographer Manual*, 9th ed. ASC Press, Hollywood, CA, 2004.

DOFMaster. "Hyperfocal Distance and Depth of Field Calculator" (available at www.dofmaster.com).

Figgis, Mike. *Digital Filmmaking*, Faber & Faber, New York, 2007.

■ CHAPTER 12

Brown, Blain. "Cinematography," Focal Press, Boston, 2002.

McDonough, Tom. "Light Years: Confessions of a Cinematographer," Grove Press, New York, 1987.

■ CHAPTER 13

"A Conversation with Michael Ballhaus, ASC," *ASC Magazine*, November 20, 2006 (available at www.theasc.com/news/News_Articles/News_77.php).

Brandis, Paulette. "Cinematographers in Action: Shooting 2008 Oscar-Nominated Films," Kodak: 1000 Words, February 24, 2009 (available at http://1000words.kodak.com).

Schaefer, Dennis, and Salvato, Larry. "Masters of Light," University of California Press, Berkeley, 1986.

Schwartz, David. "Making *The Wrestler* Real." Museum of the Mocing Image / Moving Image Source, February 13, 2009 (available at www.movingimagesource.us/articles).

■ CHAPTER 14

Ballinger, Alexander. *New Cinematographers*, Laurence King/Harper Design, London, New York, 2004.

Bourke, Philippa. "Taking the Digital Medium into Their Own Hands: Storytelling by Women Filmmakers Evolves with DV" (available at www.moviesbywomen.com/articles; posted August 9, 2002).

Calhoun, John. "Photographing Angels," *Live Design Online*, April 1, 1999 (available September 4, 2006 at http://livedesignonline.com/mag/lighting_photographing_angels/index.html).

Fujifilm Press Release, March 2008.

Herrell, Al. "Variations on the Mo' Better Blues," *American Cinematographer*, September 1990.

Kodak Glossary of Motion Picture Terms (available at www.motion.kodak.com/US/en/motion/Education/Film_Video_Glossary).

Kristopher, Tapley. "The Top 10 Shots of 2008: Pt. 1," InContention.com, January 14, 2009.

Rogers, Pauline. "Emmanuel Lubezki, ASC Puts a Twisted Look on the Macabre Myth of *Sleepy Hollow*," The International Cinematographers Guild (available at www.cameraguild.com/index.html?magazine/stoo1199.htm~top.main_hp).

Schaefer, Dennis, and Salvato, Larry. *Masters of Light*, University of California Press, Berkeley, 1984.

Silicon Imaging Press Release, January 31, 2009 (available at www.siliconimaging.com/DigitalCinema/News).

Torneo, Erin. "Interview: Cinematography as Poetry: Ellen Kuras Talks about the DV Challenges of 'Personal Velocity,'" *indieWIRE*, November 25, 2002 (available at www.indiewire.com/people/int_Kuras_Ellen_021125.html).

Wood, Jennifer M. "Where the Girls Are: DP Ellen Kuras talks about shooting Rebecca Miller's 'Personal Velocity,'" *MovieMaker Magazine*, February 3, 2007.

■ CHAPTER 17

Figgis, Mike. *Digital Filmmaking*, Faber & Faber, New York, 2007.

Mackendrick, Alexander. *On Filmmaking*, Faber & Faber, New York, 2004.

Tirard, Laurent. *Moviemakers' Master Class*, Faber & Faber, New York, 2002.

■ CHAPTER 18

CSATF publication General Code of Safe Practice for Film Production (available at www. csatf.org/pdf/GenCodeoSafePractices.pdf).

Polly Staffle Q&A with Matt Anderson (available at www.pollystaffle.com/questionsandanswers/mattanderson.shtml).

Safety Guidelines for the Film and Television Industry in Ontario (available at www.labour.gov.on.ca/english/hs/pubs/filmguide).

■ CHAPTER 19

Martin, Kevin H. "The Digital Cinematographer: Ellen Kuras, ASC, discusses *Bamboozled* and the travails of digital filmmaking," The International Cinematographers Guild (available at www.cameraguild.com/technology/bamboozled.htm).

■ CHAPTER 20

Doughton, KJ. "A Cut Above: Editor Thelma Schoonmaker Celebrates in Seattle," *MovieMaker Magazine: Hands on Pages*, Issue 35 (available at www.moviemaker.com/hop; go to "editing" and Issue 35).

Murch, Walter. *In the Blink of an Eye,* Silman-James Press, New York, 2001.

Wood, Jennifer M. "Life with Spike: Moviemaker Sam Pollard Discusses His Most Frequent Collaborator," *MovieMaker Magazine: Hands on Pages*, Issue 22 (available at http://moviemaker.com/hop; go to "editing" and Issue 22).

■ CHAPTER 21

Bazin, André, et al. "Entretiens avec Orson Welles," *Cahiers du Cinéma* (June 1958), no. 84: 1–13.

Lumet, Sidney. *Making Movies*, Vintage Books, New York, 1995.

Mackendrick, Alexander. *On Film-Making: An Introduction to the Craft of the Director*, Faber & Faber, New York, 2004.

McGavin, Patrick Z., "Q&A: Cristian Mungiu" *StopSmiling Online*, February 26, 2008.

Pollard, Sam "Things I've Learned as a Moviemaker," *MovieMaker Magazine*, Volume 3, Issue 4 (available at www.moviemaker.com/editing/article/things_ive_learned_as_a_moviemaker_2690;).

Rodriguez-Ortega, Vicente. "Zen Palette: An Interview with Christopher Doyle," *reverse shot online*, summer 2004 (available at www.reverseshot.com/legacy/summer04/doyle.html).

Tirard, Laurent. *Moviemakers' Master Class: Private Lessons from the World's Foremost Directors*, Faber & Faber, New York, 2002.

Walker, Alexander. *Stanley Kubrick Directs,* Harcourt Brace Co., New York, 1972.

■ CHAPTER 22

Chion, Michel. *Audio-Vision*, Columbia University Press, New York, 1994.

Schwam, Stephanie (Ed.). *The Making of 2001: A Space Odyssey,* Modern Library, New York, 2000.

Thom, Randy. "Designing a Movie for Sound," *FilmSound.org*, 1999 (available at www.filmsound.org/articles/designing_for_sound.htm).

■ CHAPTER 24

Kaufman, Anthony. "Caught in the Web: Netting Higher DVD Sales Online." The Independent May/June 2006, Vol. 29 No. 4.

Filmography

 ■ **VOICE & VISION ONLINE SHORT FILMS STREAMING AT
WWW.VOICEANDVISIONBOOK.COM**

The Black Hole. Dirs. The Diamond Dogs Phil & Olly. Prod. Nicola Doring, Claire
Neate-James, and Ben Sullivan. @ HSI London Ltd., 2009 (Chapter 1, Chapter 2,
Chapter 4, Chapter 5, Chapter 13, Chapter 22)

Plastic Bag. Dir. Ramin Bahrani. Noruz Films, Gigantic Pictures, ITVS & Lucky Hat
Entertainment, 2009 (Chapter 1, Chapter 4, Chapter 22)

Waking Dreams. Dir. John Daschbach. Mirror Movies, 2004 (Chapter 1, Chapter 2,
Chapter 4, Chapter 7, Chapter 19, Chapter 22, Chapter 24)

When I Was Young. Dir. Huixia Lu. Produced by Huixia Lu, 2004 (Chapter 1, Chapter 4,
Chapter 19, Chapter 22)

Vive le 14 Juillet. Dir. Didier Rouget. OVNI Films, 1995 (Chapter 1, Chapter 4, Chapter 22)

■ CHAPTER 1

Pieces of April. Dir. Peter Hedges. IFC Productions, 2003. (DVD distribution: MGM Home
Entertainment) (Figure 1-5)

Chop Shop. Dir. Ramin Bahrani. Noruz Films, 2007. (DVD distribution: Koch Lorber Films)
(Figure 1-3 L)

The Social Network. Dir. David Fincher. Columbia Pictures, 2010. (DVD distribution: Sony
Pictures Home Entertainment) (Figure 1-3 R)

Nine Lives. Dir. Rodrigo Garcia. Mickingbird Pictures, 2005. (DVD distribution: Sony
Pictures Home Entertainment) (Figure 1-6)

Raiders of the Lost Ark. Dir. Steven Spielberg. Lucasfilm Ltd., 1981. (DVD distribution:
Paramount Home Video)

La Jetée (short). Dir. Chris Marker. Argos Films, 1962. (DVD distribution: BijouFlix
Releasing) (Figure 1-7 R)

Dwaj ludzie z szafa (*Two Men and a Wardrobe*) (short). Dir. Roman Polanski. Panstwowa
Wyzsza Szkola Filmowa, 1958. (DVD distribution: Available on *Knife in the Water*. The
Criterion Collection, 2003)

Meshes of the Afternoon (short). Dir. Maya Deren, 1943.

Available on *Maya Deren: Experimental Films.* Mystic Fire Video, 2002. (Figure 1-7 L)

Nan va Koutcheh (*Bread and Alley*). Dir. Abbas Kiarostami, 1970 (Figure 1-8)

El Mariachi. Dir. Roberto Rodriguez. Columbia Pictures, 1992. (DVD distribution: Columbia Tristar). (Figure 1-9)

Old Joy. Dir. Kelly Reichardt. Washington Square Films, 2006. (DVD distribution: Kino International Corp.) (Figure 1-10)

■ CHAPTER 2

The Miracle (short). Dir. George Racz, 2006. (Figures 2-1, 2-2, 2-14)

Ocean's Eleven. Dir. Steven Soderbergh. Village Roadshow Pictures, 2001. (DVD distribution: Warner Home Video) (Figures 2-5, 2-7, 2-8, 2-9)

The Thin Red Line. Dir. Terrence Malick. Fox 2000 Pictures, 1998. (DVD distribution: 20th Century Fox Home Entertainment) (Figure 2-6)

The Silence of the Lambs. Dir. Jonathan Demme. Orion Pictures Corporation, 1991. (DVD distribution: The Criterion Collection) (Figure 2-10)

Sideways. Dir. Alexander Payne. Fox Searchlight Pictures, 2004. (DVD distribution: Twentieth Century–Fox Film Corporation) (Figures 2-11, 2-12)

■ CHAPTER 3

Psycho. Dir. Alfred Hitchcock. Shamley Productions, 1960. (DVD distribution: Universal Home Entertainment)

Russian Ark. Dir. Aleksandr Sokurov. Egoli Tossell Film AG, 2002. (Distribution: Wellspring Media)

The Wrestler. Dir. Darren Aronofsky. Protozoa Pictures, 2008. (DVD distribution: 20th Century Fox Home Entertainment) (Figure 3-1)

The Thin Red Line. Dir. Terrence Malick. Fox 2000 Pictures, 1998. (DVD distribution: 20th Century Fox Home Entertainment) (Figure 3-2)

Star Wars: Episode VI—Return of the Jedi. Dir. Richard Marquand. Lucasfilm Ltd., 1983. (DVD distribution: 20th Century Fox Home Entertainment) (Figure 3-3)

Down by Law. Dir. Jim Jarmusch. Island Pictures, 1986. (DVD distribution: The Criterion Collection) (Figure 3-4)

Young and Innocent. Dir. Alfred Hitchcock. Gaumont British Picture Corporation, 1937. (DVD distribution: Delta Expedition, 2000) (Figure 3-5)

Yield (short). Dir. Gustavo Mercado. Gustavo Mercado, 2006. (Figure 3-6)

A Serious Man. Dir. Ethan & Joel Coen. Focus Features, 2009. (DVD distribution: Universal Studios Home Entertainment) (Figure 3-7 T)

The Double Life of Veronique. Dir. Krzysztof Kieslowski. Sidéral Productions, 1991. (DVD distribution: The Criterion Collection) (Figure 3-7 TM)

Russian Ark. Dir. Aleksandr Sokurov. Egoli Tossell Film AG, 2002. (Distribution: Wellspring Media) (Figure 3-7 BM)

Raging Bull. Dir. Martin Scorsese. Chartoff-Winkler Productions, 1980. (DVD distribution: MGM Home Entertainment) (Figures 3-7 B, 3-17 through 3-24)

Stranger than Paradise. Dir. Jim Jarmusch. Cinesthesia Productions, 1984. (DVD distribution: MGM Home Entertainment) (Figure 3-8 T)

Le Samouraï. Dir. Jean-Pierre Melville. TC Productions, 1967. (DVD distribution: The Criterion Collection) (Figure 3-8 B)

Letyat zhuravli (*The Cranes Are Flying*). Dir. Mikheil Kalatozishvili. Ministerstvo Kinematografii, 1957. (DVD distribution: The Criterion Collection) (Figure 3-9 T)

Smala Sussie (*Slim Susie*). Dir. Ulf Malmros. Götafilm, 2003. (DVD distribution: Home Vision Entertainment (HVE)) (Figure 3-9 M)

Masculin/Féminin: 15 faits précis. Dir. Jean-Luc Godard. Argos Films, 1966. (DVD distribution: The Criterion Collection, 2005) (Figure 3-9 B)

The Usual Suspects. Dir. Bryan Singer. Polygram Filmed Entertainment, 1995. (DVD distribution: Polygram Home Video) (Figure 3-10)

Vozvrashcheniye (*The Return*). Dir. Andrei Zvyagintsev. Ren Film, 2003. (DVD distribution: Kino International) (Figure 3-11 T)

Naked. Dir. Mike Leigh. Thin Man Films, 1993. (DVD distribution: The Criterion Collection, 2005) (Figure 3-11 B)

Tetro, Francis Ford Coppola. American Zoetrope, 2009 . (DVD distribution: Lionsgate Home Entertainment) (Figure 3-12)

Avatar. Dir. James Cameron, Twentieth Century Fox, 2009 . (DVD distribution: 20th Century Fox Home Entertainment) (3-13)

A Zed & Two Noughts. Dir. Peter Greenaway. Channel Four Films, 1985. (Distribution: Skoures Pictures) (Figure 3-14 L)

L'eclisse. Dir. Michelangelo Antonioni. Interopa Film, 1962. (DVD distribution: The Criterion Collection, 2005) (Figure 3-14 R)

The King's Speech. Dir. Tom Hooper. See-Saw Films, 2010. (DVD Distribution: Anchor Bay Entertainment) (Figure 3-16)

Der himmel über Berlin (*Wings of Desire*). Dir. Wim Wenders. Argos Films, 1987. (DVD distribution: MGM/UA Home Entertainment) (Figure 3-25)

Amélie (*Le fabuleux destin d'Amélie Poulain*). Dir. Jean-Pierre Jeunet. Victoires Prod., 2001. (DVD distribution: Miramax Home Entertainment) (Figure 3-26)

Le fils (*The Son*). Dirs. Jean-Pierre Dardenne and Luc Dardenne. Archipel 35, 2002. (DVD distribution: New Yorker Video) (Figure 3-28)

The Crying Game. Dir. Neil Jordan. Channel Four Films, 1992. (DVD distribution: Live Home Video) (Figure 3-29)

Lourdes, Dir. Jessica Hausner. ARTE, 2009. (DVD distribution: Palisades Tartan)
(Figure 3-30 R)

Angst essen Seele auf (*Ali: Fear Eats the Soul*). Dir. Rainer Werner Fassbinder. Tango Film, 1974. (DVD distribution: The Criterion Collection) (Figure 3-30 L)

La belle et la bête (*Beauty and the Beast*). Dir. Jean Cocteau. DisCina, 1946. (DVD distribution: The Criterion Collection) (Figure 3-32)

Elephant. Dir. Gus Van Sant. HBO Films, 2003. (DVD distribution: HBO Films)
(Figure 3-33)

The Silence of the Lambs. Dir. Jonathan Demme. Orion Pictures Corporation, 1991. (DVD distribution: The Criterion Collection) (Figure 3-34)

Raising Arizona. Dir. Joel Cohen. Circle Films, 1987. (DVD distribution: 20th Century Fox Home Entertainment) (Figure 3-35)

The Lives of Others (*Das Leben der Anderen*). Dir. Florian Henckel von Donnersmarck. Arte, 2006. (DVD distribution: Sony Pictures Home Entertainment) (Figure 3-38)

Creation. Dir. John Amiel. Recorded Picture Company, 2009. (DVD distribution: Icon Home Entertainment (UK)) (Figure 3-39)

Reservoir Dogs. Dir. Quentin Tarantino. Dog Eat Dog Prods., 1992. (DVD distribution: Artisan Entertainment) (Figure 3-40)

■ CHAPTER 4

Bamboozled. Dir. Spike Lee. 40 Acres & A Mule Filmworks, 2000. (DVD distribution: New Line Home Video)

My Own Private Idaho. Dir. Gus Van Sant. New Line Cinema, 1991. (DVD distribution: The Criterion Collection) (Figure 4-2)

New Jack City. Dir. Mario Van Peebles. Warner Bros. Pictures, 1991. (DVD distribution: Warner Home Video)

River of Things: "Ode to Things" (short). Dir. Mick Hurbis-Cherrier, 1998.
(Figure 4-7)

Sideways. Dir. Alexander Payne. Fox Searchlight Pictures/Michael London Prod., 2004. (DVD distribution: 20th Century Fox) (Figures 4-8, 4-12)

Down by Law. Dir. Jim Jarmusch. Island Pictures, 1986. (DVD distribution: The Criterion Collection)

The Savages. Dir. Tamara Jenkins. Fox Searchlight Pictures, 2007. (DVD distribution: 20th Century Fox Home Entertainment) (Figure 4-9)

Up in the Air. Jason Reitman. Paramount Pictures, 2009. (DVD distribution: Paramount Home Entertainment) (Figures 4-10, 4-33)

Blade Runner. Dir. Ridley Scott. The Ladd Company, 1982. (DVD distribution: Warner Home Video) (Figure 4-11)

The Squid and the Whale. Dir. Noah Baumbach. American Empirical Pictures, 2005. (DVD distribution: Sony Pictures) (Figure 4-13)

The Diving Bell & Butterfly. Dir. Julian Schnabel. Pathé Renn Productions, 2007. (DVD distribution: Miramax Home Entertainment) (Figure 4-14)

Amélie (*Le fabuleux destin d'Amélie Poulain*). Dir. Jean-Pierre Jeunet. Victoires Prod., 2001. (DVD distribution: Miramax Home Entertainment) (Figure 4-16)

L'Avventura. Dir. Michelangelo Antonioni. Cino del Duca, 1960. (DVD distribution: The Criterion Collection) (Figure 4-17)

Raising Arizona. Dir. Joel Cohen. Circle Films, 1987. (DVD distribution: 20th Century Fox Home Entertainment) (Figure 4-19)

Strangers on a Train. Dir. Alfred Hitchcock. Warner Bros. Pictures, 1951. (DVD distribution: Warner Home Video) (Figure 4-23)

Diva. Dir. Jean-Jacques Beineix. Les Films Galaxie, 1981. (DVD distribution: Anchor Bay Entertainment) (Figure 4-24)

Romuald et Juliette (*Mama, There's a Man in Your Bed*). Dir. Coline Serreau. Union Générale Cinématographique, 1989. (Figure 4-25)

The Godfather. Dir. Francis Ford Coppola. Paramount Pictures, 1972. (DVD distribution: Paramount Home Video) (Figure 4-26)

The Constant Gardener. Dir. Fernando Meirelles. Potboiler Productions, 2005. (DVD distribution: Focus Features) (Figure 4-28)

Breathless (*À Bout de Souffle*). Dir. Jean-Luc Godard. Impéria, 1960. (DVD distribution: Fox Lorber)

Dancer in the Dark. Dir. Lars von Trier. Zentropa Entertainment, 2000. (DVD distribution: New Line Home Video) (Figure 4-30)

Happy Together (*Cheun gwong tsa sit*). Dir. Wong Kar-Wai. Jet Tone Prod. Co., 1997. (DVD distribution: Kino Video) (Figure 4-31)

Aiqing wansui (*Vive L'Amour*). Dir. Tsai Ming-Liang. Central Motion Pictures Corporation, 1994. (DVD distribution: Strand Releasing) (Figure 4-32)

■ CHAPTER 5

The Miracle (short). Dir. George Racz, 2006. (Figure 5-4)

Sideways. Dir. Alexander Payne. Fox Searchlight Pictures/Michael London Prod., 2004. (DVD distribution: 20th Century Fox)

Sabotage. Dir. Alfred Hitchcock. Gaumont British Picture Corporation, 1936. (DVD distribution: Laserlight Entertainment) (Figure 5-7)

Finders Keepers (short). Dir. Andrew Lund, 2006. (Figure 5-10 L)

Snapshot (short). Dir. Andrew Lund, 2005. (Figure 5-10 R)

■ CHAPTER 6

Pieces of April. Dir. Peter Hedges. IFC Productions, 2003. (DVD distribution: MGM Home Entertainment) (Figure 6-1)

The Lives of Others (*Das Leben der Anderen*). Dir. Florian Henckel von Donnersmarck. Arte, 2006. (DVD distribution: Sony Pictures Home Entertainment) (Figures 6-2, 6-6, 6-7)

Chop Shop. Dir. Ramin Bahrani. Noruz Films, 2007. (DVD distribution: Koch Lorber Films) (Figure 6-3)

Sleep Dealer. Dir. Alex Rivera. This is That Prod., 2008. (DVD distribution: Maya Entertainment) (Figure 6-4)

Before the Making of Sleep Dealer. Dir. Alex Rivera. 2008. (DVD distribution: Maya Entertainment)

Looking for Richard. Dir. Al Pacino. 20th Century Fox, 1996. (Distribution: Fox Searchlight Pictures) (Figure 6-5)

■ CHAPTER 7

Frozen River. Courtney Hunt. Harwood Hunt Productions, 2008. (DVD distribution: Sony Pictures Home Entertainment) (Figures 7-2, 7-15 T)

Brief Reunion. Dir. John Daschbach. Mirror Movies, 2011 (Figure 7-4)

The Last Temptation of Christ. Dir. Martin Scorsese. Universal Pictures, 1988. (DVD Distribution: The Criterion Collection) (Figure 7-5)

Super Spree (short). Dir. Matt Post, Drewstone Productions, 2011 (Figure 7-6)

The Miracle (short). Dir. George Racz, 2006. (Figures 7-9 L)

Chop Shop. Dir. Ramin Bahrani. Noruz Films, 2007. (DVD distribution: Koch Lorber Films) (Figure 7-9 R)

Paranoid Park. Dir. Gus van Sant. MK2 Productions, 2007. (DVD distribution: IFC Films) (Figure 7-10)

Ballast. Dir. Lance Hammer. Alluvial Film Company, 2008. (DVD distribution: Kino Video) (Figure 7-15 B)

Vive le premier mai (short). Dir. Didier Rouget, 1999. (Figure 7-16)

■ CHAPTER 8

2001: A Space Odyssey. Dir. Stanley Kubrick. Metro-Goldwyn-Mayer, 1968. (DVD distribution: MGM/UA Home Video) (Figure 8-4 T)

A Clockwork Orange. Dir. Stanley Kubrick. Warner Bros. Pictures, 1971. (DVD distribution: Warner Home Video) (Figure 8-4 B)

Creation. Dir. John Amiel. Recorded Picture Company, 2009. (DVD distribution: Icon Home Entertainment (UK)) (Figure 8-5)

Zindeeq. Dir. Michel Khleifi, 2009 (Figure 8-6)

What's up, Tiger Lily? Dirs. Woody Allen & Senkichi Taniguchi. Benedict Pictures, 1966. (DVD distribution: Vestron Video) (Figure 8-11)

Fa yeun nin wa (*In the Mood for Love*). Dir. Wong Kar-Wai. Paradis Films, 2000. (DVD distribution: The Criterion Collection) (Figure 8-16 T)

Women without Men (*Zanan-e bedun-e mardan*). Dirs. Shirin Neshat & Shoja Azari. Essential Filmproduktion GmbH, 2009. (DVD distribution: IndiePix Films) (Figure 8-16 M)

Requiem for a Dream. Dir. Darren Aronofsky. Artisan Entertainment, 2000. (DVD distribution: Lions Gate Films) (Figure 8-16 B)

Manhattan. Dir. Woody Allen. Jack Rollins and Charles H. Joffe Productions, 1979. (DVD distribution: MGM/UA Home Entertainment) (Figure 8-35 B)

Good Night, and Good Luck. Dir. George Clooney. Warner Independent Pictures, 2005. (DVD distribution: Warner Bros. Pictures) (Figure 8-35 T)

Hero (*Ying xiong*). Dir. Zhang Yimou. Beijing New Picture Film Co., 2002. (DVD distribution: Miramax Films) (Figure 8-38)

Pi. Dir. Darren Aronovsky. Harvest Filmworks, 1998. (DVD distribution: Lion's Gate Films) (Figure 8-43)

The Miracle (short). Dir. George Racz, 2006. (Figure 8-44)

The Wrestler. Dir. Darren Aronofsky. Protozoa Pictures, 2008. (DVD distribution: 20th Century Fox Home Entertainment) (Figure 8-48 T)

Cidade de Deus (*City of God*). Dirs. Fernando Meirelles and Kátia Lund. O2 Filmes, 2002. (Distribution: Miramax Films) (Figure 8-48 M)

The Queen. Dir. Stephen Frears. Pathé Pictures Int'l, 2006. (DVD distribution: Miramax Home Entertainment) (Figure 8-48 B)

■ CHAPTER 9

The Informant! Dir. Steven Soderbergh. Warner Bros. Pictures, 2009. (DVD distribution: Warner Home Video) (Figure 9-7 L)

Crank: High Voltage. Dirs. Mark Neveldine & Brian Taylor. Lionsgate, 2009. (DVD distribution: Lionsgate Home Entertainment) (Figure 9-7 R)

Dancer in the Dark. Dir. Lars von Trier. Zentropa Entertainments, 2000. (DVD distribution: New Line Home Video) (Figure 9-8)

Taste of Cherry (*Ta'm e guilass*). Dir. Abbas Kiarostami. Abbas Kiarostami Productions/ CiBy 2000, 1997. (DVD distribution: Criterion Film Corp.) (Figure 9-16 L)

Ten. Dir. Abbas Kiarostami. Abbas Kiarostami/Key Lime/MK2 Productions, 2002. (DVD distribution: Zeitgeist Films) (Figure 9-16 R)

The Rocking Horse Winner (short). Dir. Michael Almereyda, 1997. (Figure 9-33 L)

November. Dir. Greg Harrison. IFC Productions, 2004. (DVD distribution: IFC Films) (Figure 9-33 R)

Star Wars: Episode II—Attack of the Clones. Dir. George Lucas. Lucasfilm Ltd., 2002. (DVD distribution: 20th Century Fox Home Entertainment) (Figure 9-38)

Tiny Furniture. Dir. Lena Dunham. Tiny Ponies, 2010. (Distribution: IFC Films) (Figure 9-40)

■ CHAPTER 10

Goodfellas. Dir. Martin Scorsese. Warner Brothers Pictures 1990. (DVD distribution: Warner Home Video) (Figure 10-4)

The Fisher King. Dir. Terry Gilliam. Columbia Pictures Corp., 1991. (DVD distribution: Columbia Tristar Home Video) (Figure 10-5 T)

Searching for Bobby Fischer. Dir. Steven Zaillian. Mirage Entertainment, 1993. (Distribution: Paramount Pictures) (Figure 10-5 M)

Man Push Cart. Dir. Ramin Bahrani. Noruz Films, 2005. (DVD distribution: Koch/Lorber) (Figure 10-5 B)

No Country for Old Men. Dirs. Ethan & Joel Coen. Paramount Vantage, 2007. (DVD distribution: Miramax Home Entertainment) (Figure 10-10)

Let the Right One In (*Låt den rätte komma in*). Dir. Tomas Alfredson. EFTI, 2008. (DVD distribution: Magnolia Home Entertainment) (Figure 10-11)

Ed Wood. Dir. Tim Burton. Touchstone Pictures, 1994. (DVD distribution: Buena Vista Home Video) (Figure 10-13)

Sideways. Dir. Alexander Payne. Fox Searchlight Pictures/Michael London Prod., 2004. (DVD distribution: 20th Century Fox) (Figure 10-18)

■ CHAPTER 11

Café Lumière (*Kôhî jikô*). Dir. Hou Hsiao-Hsien. Shochiku Co., 2003. (DVD distribution: Fox Lorber) (Figure 11-1 T)

Elephant. Dir. Gus Van Sant. HBO Films, 2003. (DVD distribution: HBO Films) (Figure 11-1 M)

The Hurt Locker. Dir. Kathryn Bigelow. Voltage Pictures, 2008. (DVD distribution: Summit Home Entertainment) (Figure 11-1 B, 11-19)

Eternal Sunshine of the Spotless Mind. Dir. Michel Gondry. Focus Features, 2004. (DVD distribution: Universal Studios Home Video)

La Promesse. Dirs. Jean-Pierre and Luc Dardenne. Eurimages, 1996. (DVD distribution: New Yorker Films)

Dancer in the Dark. Dir. Lars von Trier. Zentropa Entertainments, 2000. (DVD distribution: New Line Home Video)

Chelovek s Kino-Apparatom (*Man with Movie Camera*). Dir. Dziga Vertov. VUFKU, 1929. (DVD distribution: Kino Video) (Figures 11-3)

Tokyo-Ga. Dir. Wim Wenders. Chris Sievernich Filmproduktion, 1985. (DVD distribution: Gray City/Pacific Arts) (Figure 11-8)

Rocky. Dir. John G. Avildsen. Chartoff-Winkler Productions, 1976. (DVD distribution: MGM Home Entertainment)

Marathon Man. Dir. John Schlesinger. Paramount Pictures, 1976. (DVD distribution: Paramount Home Video)

The Shining. Dir. Stanley Kubrick. Warner Bros. Pictures, 1980. (DVD distribution: Warner Home Video) (Figure 11-12)

Breathless (*À Bout de Souffle*). Dir. Jean-Luc Godard. Impéria, 1960. (DVD distribution: Wellspring Media) (Figure 11-14)

The Evil Dead. Dir. Sam Raimi. Renaissance Pictures, 1981. (DVD distribution: Anchor Bay Entertainment) (Figure 11-15)

Miss Julie. Dir. Mike Figgis. Red Mullet Productions, 1999. (DVD distribution: MGM Home Entertainment) (Figure 11-16)

Blood Simple. Dir. Joel Coen. Foxton Entertainment, 1984. (DVD distribution: Columbia TriStar Home Video)

The Celebration (*Festen*). Dir. Thomas Vinterberg. Nimbus Film, 1998. (DVD distribution: Universal Studios)

Barry Lyndon. Dir. Stanley Kubrick. Hawk Films Ltd., 1975. (DVD distribution: Warner Home Video) (Figure 11-17)

Nine Lives. Dir. Rodrigo García. Mockingbird Pictures, 2005. (DVD distribution: Sony Pictures Home Entertainment) (Figure 11-18)

No Country for Old Men. Dirs. Ethan & Joel Coen. Paramount Vantage, 2007. (DVD distribution: Miramax Home Entertainment) (Figure 11-20)

■ CHAPTER 12

The White Ribbon (*Das weiße Band - Eine deutsche Kindergeschichte*). Dir. Michael Haneke. X-Filme Creative Pool, 2009. (DVD distribution: Sony Pictures Home Entertainment) (Figure 12-1)

There Will Be Blood. Dir. Paul Thomas Anderson. Paramount Vantage, 2007. (DVD distribution: Paramount Home Entertainment) (Figure 12-4 T)

No Country for Old Men. Dirs. Ethan & Joel Coen. Paramount Vantage, 2007. (DVD distribution: Miramax Home Entertainment) (Figure 12-4 M)

The Graduate. Dir. Mike Nichols. Embassy Pictures Corporation, 1967. (DVD distribution: MGM DVD) (Figure 12-4 B)

Personal Velocity: Three Portraits. Dir. Rebecca Miller. IFC Productions, 2002. (DVD distribution: MGM Distributing Corp.) (Figure 12-17 T)

Still Life (*Sanxia haoren*). Dir. Zhang Ke Jia. Xstream Pictures, 2006. (DVD distribution: New Yorker Video) (Figure 12-17 M)

The Celebration (*Festen*). Dir. Thomas Vinterberg. Nimbus Film, 1998. (DVD distribution: Universal Studios) (Figure 12-17 B)

■ **CHAPTER 13**

Masculin/Féminin. Dir. Jean-Luc Godard. Argos Films, 1966. (DVD distribution: The Criterion Collection) (Figure 13-1 TL)

Personal Velocity: Three Portraits. Dir. Rebecca Miller. IFC Productions, 2002. (DVD distribution: MGM Distributing Corp.) (Figure 13-1 TM)

Chungking Express (*Chung hing sam lam*). Dir. Wong Kar-Wai. Jet Tone Production Co., 1994. (DVD distribution: Miramax Home Entertainment) (Figure 13-1 TR)

Leaving Las Vegas. Dir. Mike Figgis. Initial Productions, 1995. (DVD distribution: MGM/UA Home Entertainment) (Figure 13-1 BL)

Nénette et Boni. Dir. Claire Denis. Canal+, 1996. (DVD distribution: Strand Releasing) (Figure 13-1 BM)

Ali: Fear Eats the Soul (*Angst essen Seele auf*). Dir. R. W. Fassbinder. Tango Film, 1974. (DVD distribution: The Criterion Collection) (Figure 13-1 BR)

The Blair Witch Project. Dirs. Daniel Myrick and Eduardo Sánchez. Haxan Films, 1999. (DVD distribution: Lions Gate Films) (Figure 13-2 R)

River of Things: "Ode to a Bar of Soap." Dir. Katherine Hurbis-Cherrier, 1998. (Figure 13-3)

Persona. Dir. Ingmar Bergman. Svensk Filmindustri AB, 1966. (DVD distribution: MGM Home Entertainment) (Figure 13-4)

Lost in Translation. Dir. Sophie Coppola. American Zoetrope, 2003. (DVD distribution: Universal Home Entertainment) (Figure 13-9 L)

Reconstruction. Dir. Christoffer Boe. Nordisk Film, 2003. (DVD distribution: Palm Pictures) (Figure 13-9 R)

Path Lights (short). Dir. Zachary Sluser. Prod. Jonathan Lynch, Mathew Goldberg, Brian Morrow, & Zachary Sluser, 2009. (Figure 13-14)

Der himmel über Berlin (*Wings of Desire*). Dir. Wim Wenders. Argos Films, 1987. (DVD distribution: MGM/UA Home Entertainment) (Figure 13-15 and 13-18)

Veronika Voss. Dir. R. W. Fassbinder. Tango Film, 1982. (DVD distribution: The Criterion Collection) (Figure 13-20)

The Godfather. Dir. Francis Ford Coppola. Paramount Pictures, 1972. (DVD distribution: Paramount Home Video) (Figure 13-26 L)

Mr. Arkadin. Dir. Orson Wells. Mercury Productions, 1955. (DVD distribution: The Criterion Collection) (Figure 13-26 R)

Beauty and the Beast (*La belle et la bête*). Dir. Jean Cocteau. DisCina, 1946. (DVD distribution: The Criterion Collection) (Figure 13-29 TL)

Sweet Smell of Success. Dir. Alexander Mackendrick. Hill-Hecht-Lancaster Prods., 1957. (DVD distribution: MGM/UA Home Entertainment) (Figure 13-29 TR)

The Last Laugh (*Der Letzte Mann*). Dir. F.W. Murnau. Universum Film A.G., 1924. (DVD distribution: Kino Video) (Figure 13-29 BL)

Citizen Kane. Dir. Orson Welles. Mercury Productions/RKO Radio Pictures, 1941. (DVD distribution: Warner Home Video) (Figure 13-26 BR)

Night of the Hunter Dir. Charles Laughton. Paul Gregory Prod., 1955. (DVD distribution: MGM/UA Home Entertainment) (Figure 13-31)

Ed Wood. Dir. Tim Burton. Touchstone Pictures, 1994. (DVD distribution: Buena Vista Home Video) (Figure 13-32)

Bringing up Baby. Dir. Howard Hawks. RKO Radio Pictures, 1938. (DVD distribution: Warner Home Video) (Figure 13-33)

Stardust Memories. Dir. Woody Allen. Rollins-Joffee Productions, 1980. (DVD distribution: MGM Home Entertainment) (Figure 13-34)

Ferris Bueller's Day Off. Dir. John Hughes. Paramount Pictures, 1986. (DVD distribution: Paramount Home Video) (Figure 13-36 TL)

THX-1138. Dir. George Lucas. American Zoetrope, 1971. (DVD distribution: Warner Home Video) (Figure 13-36 TR)

Crash. Dir. Paul Haggis. Bull's Eye Entertainment, 2004. (DVD distribution: Lions Gate Films Home Entertainment) (Figure 13-36 BL)

Raiders of the Lost Ark. Dir. Steven Spielberg. Lucasfilm Ltd., 1981. (DVD distribution: Paramount Home Video) (Figure 13-36 BR)

A Serious Man. Dir. Ethan & Joel Coen. Focus Features, 2009. (DVD distribution: Universal Studios Home Entertainment) (Figure 13-37 T)

Solaris. Dir. Steven Soderbergh. Twentieth Century Fox, 2002. (DVD distribution: 20th Century Fox Home Entertainment) (Figure 13-37 B)

Becoming. Dir. Gustavo Mercado (2007) (Figure 13-38)

Days of Heaven. Dir. Terrence Malick. Paramount Pictures, 1978. (DVD distribution: Paramount Home Entertainment) (Figure 13-43 L)

Yield (short). Dir. Gustavo Mercado, 2005. (Figure 13-43 R)

The Wrestler. Dir. Darren Aronofsky. Protozoa Pictures, 2008. (DVD distribution: 20th Century Fox Home Entertainment) (Figure 13-52)

■ CHAPTER 14

Masculin/Féminin. Dir. Jean-Luc Godard. Argos Films, 1966. (DVD distribution: The Criterion Collection) (Figure 14-1)

Felicia's Journey. Dir. Atom Egoyan. Alliance Atlantis Communications, 1999. (DVD distribution: Artisan Entertainment) (Figure 14-5)

The Son (*Le Fils*). Dirs. Jean-Pierre and Luc Dardenne. Les Films du Fleuve, 2002. (DVD distribution: New Yorker Films) (Figure 14-21)

The Dreamlife of Angels. Dir. Eric Zonca. Diaphana Films, 1999. (DVD distribution: MGM Columbia Tristar Home Video) (Figure 14-19)

New York Stories, "Life Lessons." Dir. Martin Scorsese. Touchstone Pictures, 1989. (DVD distribution: Touchstone Home Video) (Figure 14-20)

Mildred Pierce. Dir. Michael Curtiz. Warner Bros. Pictures, 1945. (DVD distribution: Warner Home Video) (Figure 14-21)

Black Narcissus. Dirs. Michael Powell & Emeric Pressburger. Independent Prods, 1947. (DVD distribution: The Criterion Collection) (Figure 14-22)

Do the Right Thing. Dir. Spike Lee. 40 Acres & A Mule Filmworks, 1989. (DVD distribution: The Criterion Collection) (Figure 14-23 T)

Sleepy Hollow. Dir. Tim Burton. Paramount Pictures, 1999. (DVD distribution: Paramount Home Video) (Figure 14-23 B)

Repulsion. Dir. Roman Polanski. Tekli British Productions, 1965. (DVD distribution: The Criterion Collection) (Figure 14-24)

Slumdog Millionaire. Dirs. Danny Boyle & Lovleen Tanda. Film4, 2008. (DVD distribution: 20th Century Fox Home Entertainment) (Figure 14-25)

Mo' Better Blues. Dir. Spike Lee. 40 Acres & A Mule Filmworks, 1990. (DVD distribution: Universal Pictures) (Figure 14-26)

The Last Laugh (Der Letzte Mann). Dir. F.W. Murnau. Universum Film A.G., 1924. (DVD distribution: Kino Video) (Figure 14-27 L)

Delicatessen. Dirs. Jean-Pierre Jeunet and Marc Caro. Miramax Films, 1991. (DVD distribution: Miramax) (Figure 14-27 R)

Flesh & Blade (short). Dir. Katherine Hurbis-Cherrier, 2009. (Figures 14-28 L and R)

Personal Velocity: Three Portraits. Dir. Rebecca Miller. IFC Productions, 2002. (DVD distribution: MGM Distributing Corp.) (Figure 14-29)

■ CHAPTER 15

Alien. Dir. Ridley Scott. 20th Century Fox, 1979. (DVD distribution: 20th Century Fox Home Entertainment)

2001: A Space Odyssey. Dir. Stanley Kubrick. Metro-Goldwyn-Mayer (MGM), 1968. (DVD distribution: Warner Home Video) (Figure 15-2)

All That Jazz. Dir. Bob Fosse. Columbia Pictures Corporation, 1979. (DVD Distribution: 20th Century Fox Films) (Figure 15-4 M)

Brokeback Mountain. Dir. Ang Lee. Focus Features, 2005. (DVD distribution: Universal Home Entertainment) (Figure 15-7)

The Last Temptation of Christ. Dir. Martin Scorsese. Universal Pictures, 1988. (DVD Distribution: The Criterion Collection) (Figure 15-11)

Urban/Suburban (short). Dir. Didier Rouget, 2006. (Figure 15-35)

■ CHAPTER 16

The Treasure Hunter (Ci Ling). Dir. Yen-ping Chu. Yen-ping Films Prod., 2009 (Figure 16-1)

Snapshot (short). Dir. Andrew Lund, 2006. (Figure 16-14)

Nashville. Dir. Robert Altman. American Broadcasting Co. (ABC), Paramount Pictures, 1975. (DVD distribution: Paramount Home Video) (Figure 16-15)

■ CHAPTER 17

Old Joy. Dir. Kelly Reichardt. Washington Square Films, 2006. (Distribution: Kino International Corp.)

Balloon Girl (short). Dir. Sharone Vendriger, 2007. (Figure 17-2)

Path Lights (short). Dir. Zachary Sluser. Prod. Jonathan Lynch, Mathew Goldberg, Brian Morrow, & Zachary Sluser, 2009. (Figure 17-12)

Shift. Dir. Kelly Anderson. Anderson Gold Films, 1999. (Figures 17-19, 17-20)

■ CHAPTER 18

Chelovek s Kino-Apparatom (Man with Movie Camera). Dir. Dziga Vertov. VUFKU, 1929. (DVD distribution: Kino Video) (Figure 18-3)

Bull Durham. Dir. Ron Shelton. The Mount Company, 1998. (DVD distribution: MGM Home Entertainment) (Figure 18-7)

Forget About It. Dir. BJ Davis. Beverly Hills Film Studio, 2006. (DVD distribution: Big Screen Entertainment Group) (Figure 18-9)

■ CHAPTER 19

Sky People (short). Dir. Shanti Thakur. Lucida Films, 2008 (Figure 19-17)

Bamboozled. Dir. Spike Lee. 40 Acres & A Mule Filmworks, 2000. (DVD distribution: New Line Home Video)

Hoop Dreams. Dir. Steve James. Kartemquin Films, 1994. (DVD Distribution: The Criterion Collection) (Figure 19-22)

The Blair Witch Project. Dirs. Eduardo Sánchez and Daniel Myrick. Haxan Films, 1999. (DVD distribution: Artisan Entertainment) (Figure 19-23 L)

The Celebration. Dir. Thomas Vinterberg. Nimbus Film ApS, 1998. (DVD distribution: Universal Studios) (Figure 19-23 R)

O Brother, Where Art Thou. Dir. Joel Coen. Touchstone Pictures, 2000. (DVD distribution: Touchstone Home Video) (Figure 19-24)

■ CHAPTER 20

Un condamné à mort s'est échappé ou Le vent souffle où il veut (A Man Escaped). Dir. Robert Bresson. Nouvelles Éditions de Films, 1956. (DVD distribution: New Yorker Video)

Tokyo monogatari (Tokyo Story). Dir. Yasujiro Ozu. Shochiku Films, Ltd., 1953. (DVD distribution: The Criterion Collection, 2003) (Figure 20-4)

Roma, città aperta (Rome, Open City). Dir. Roberto Rossellini. Excelsa Film, 1945. (DVD distribution: Image Entertainment Inc.)

Apur Sansar (*The World of Apu*). Dir. Satyajit Ray. Satyajit Ray Productions, 1959. (DVD distribution: Columbia TriStar Home Entertainment, 2003)

Eternal Sunshine of the Spotless Mind. Dir. Michel Gondry. Focus Features, 2004. (DVD distribution: Universal Studios Home Video) (Figure 20-6)

La Promesse. Dirs. Jean-Pierre Dardenne and Luc Dardenne. Touza Productions, 1996. (DVD distribution: New Yorker Films) (Figure 20-7)

The Matrix. Dirs. Andy Wachowski and Larry Wachowski. Warner Bros. Pictures, 1999. (DVD Distribution: Warner Bros. Pictures) (Figure 20-8)

The Cutting Edge: The Magic of Movie Editing. Dir. Wendy Apple. A.C.E. Prod., 2004. (DVD Distribution: Warner Home Videos) (Figure 20-9)

The Miracle (short). Dir. George Racz, 2006. (Figures 20-21, 20-22, 20-23, and 20-25)

Bamboozled. Dir. Spike Lee. 40 Acres & a Mule Filmworks, 2000. (DVD distribution: New Line Home Video) (Figure 20-26)

Source Code. Dir. Duncan Jones. Mark Gordon Company, 2011. (Distribution: Summit Entertainment) (Figure 20-30)

Apocalypse Now. Dir. Francis Ford Coppola. Zoetrope Studios, 1979. (DVD Distribution: Paramount Home Video)

■ CHAPTER 21

Bamboozled. Dir. Spike Lee. 40 Acres & A Mule Filmworks, 2000. (DVD distribution: New Line Home Video)

Fallen Angels. Dir. Wong Kar-Wai. Jet Tone Production Co., 1995. (DVD distribution: Kino International Corp.) (Figure 21-2)

Close Up (Nema-ye Nazdik). Dir. Abbas Kiarostami. Kanoon, 1990. (DVD distribution: The Criterion Collection) (Figure 21-3)

Edge Codes.com: The Art of Motion Picture Editing. Dir. Alex Shuper. Travesty Productions Inc., 2004.

Raging Bull. Dir. Martin Scorsese. Chartoff-Winkler Productions, 1980. (DVD distribution: MGM Home Entertainment) (Figures 21-9, 21-10, and 21-11 L)

2001: A Space Odyssey. Dir. Stanley Kubrick. Metro-Goldwyn-Mayer, 1968. (DVD distribution: MGM/UA Home Video) (Figure 21-12)

The English Patient. Dir. Anthony Minghella. Tiger Moth Prod./Miramax Films, 1996. (DVD Distribution: Miramax films) (Figure 21-13)

Citizen Kane. Dir. Orson Welles. Mercury Productions/RKO Radio Pictures, 1941. (DVD distribution: Warner Home Video) (Figure 21-14)

Rope. Dir. Alfred Hitchcock. Warner Bros. Pictures, 1948. (DVD distribution: Universal Home Entertainment)

Jeanne Dielman, 23 Quai du Commerce, 1080 Bruxelles. Dir. Chantal Akerman. Paradise Films, 1976. (DVD distribution: The Criterion Collection)

Cléo de 5 à 7 (*Cleo from 5 to 7*). Dir. Agnès Varda. Rome Paris Films, 1961. (DVD distribution: The Criterion Collection) (Figure 21-15)

4 months, 3 weeks, 2 days (*4 luni, 3 saptamâni si 2 zile*). Dir. Cristian Mungiu. Mobra Films, 2007. (DVD distribution: IFC Films) (Figure 21-16)

Syriana. Dir. Stephen Gaghan. Warner Bros. Pictures, 2005. (DVD distribution: Warner Bros. Entertainment) (Figure 21-17)

Traffic. Dir. Steven Soderbergh. USA Films, 2000. (DVD distribution: Focus Entertainment) (Figure 21-18)

Misery. Dir. Rob Reiner. Castle Rock Entertainment, 1990. (DVD distribution: MGM DVD) (Figure 21-19)

The Graduate. Dir. Mike Nichols. Embassy Pictures Corporation, 1967. (DVD distribution: MGM DVD) (Figures 21-20 and 21-21)

The Thin Red Line. Dir. Terrence Malick. Fox 2000 Pictures, 1998. (DVD distribution: 20th Century Fox Home Entertainment) (Figure 21-22)

There's Something About Mary. Dirs. Bobby & Peter Farrelly. 20th Century Fox, 1998. (DVD distribution: 20th Century Fox Film Corporation) (Figure 21-23)

Cidade de Deus (*City of God*). Dirs. Fernando Meirelles & Kátia Lund. O2 Filmes, 2002. (Distribution: Miramax Films) (Figures 21-24, 21-25, and 21-26)

The Station Agent. Dir. Thomas McCarthy. SenArt Films, 2003. (DVD distribution: Miramax Films) (Figures 21-27, 21-28)

Natural Born Killers. Dir. Oliver Stone. New Regency Pictures, 1994. (DVD Distribution: Warner Home Video) (Figures 21-29 and 21-30)

Long Day's Journey into Night. Dir. Sidney Lumet. Embassy Pictures Corporation, 1962. (DVD distribution: Embassy Pictures Corp.) (Figure 21-31)

Up in the Air. Jason Reitman. Paramount Pictures, 2009. (DVD distribution: Paramount Home Entertainment) (Figure 21-32)

Team America: World Police. Dir. Trey Parker. Paramount Pictures, 2004. (DVD distribution: Paramount Home Entertainment) (Figure 21-33)

Slumdog Millionaire. Dirs. Danny Boyle & Lovleen Tanda. Film4, 2008. (DVD distribution: 20th Century Fox Home Entertainment) (Figure 21-34)

■ CHAPTER 22

The Jazz Singer. Dir. Alan Crosland. Warner Bros. Pictures (as The Vitaphone Corporation), 1927. (DVD Distribution: Warner Home Video)

Dwaj ludzie z szafa (*Two Men and a Wardrobe*) (short). Dir. Roman Polanski. Panstwowa Wyzsza Szkola Filmowa, 1958. (DVD distribution: Available on *Knife in the Water* (*Nóz w wodzie*). Dir. Roman Polanski. The Criterion Collection) (Figure 22-1)

4 months, 3 weeks, 2 days (*4 luni, 3 saptamâni si 2 zile*). Dir. Cristian Mungiu. Mobra Films, 2007. (DVD distribution: IFC Films) (Figure 22-2)

Let the Right One In (Låt den rätte komma in). Dir. Tomas Alfredson. EFTI, 2008. (DVD distribution: Magnolia Home Entertainment) (Figure 22-3)

High Anxiety. Dir. Mel Brooks. Crossbow Productions, 1977. (DVD distribution: 20th Century Fox Film Corporation) (Figure 22-4)

A Touch of Evil. Dir. Orson Welles. Universal International Pictures, 1958. (DVD distribution: Universal Studios Home Video) (Figure 22-5)

Code inconnu: Récit incomplet de divers voyages. Dir. Michael Haneke. Canal+, 2000. (DVD distribution: Kino International Corp.) (Figure 22-6)

His Girl Friday. Dir. Howard Hawks. Columbia Pictures Corporation, 1940. (DVD distribution: Columbia Classics Home Video) (Figure 22-7)

2001: A Space Odyssey. Dir. Stanley Kubrick. Metro-Goldwyn-Mayer, 1968. (DVD distribution: MGM/UA Home Video) (Figure 22-8)

Psycho. Dir. Alfred Hitchcock. Shamley Productions, 1960. (DVD distribution: Universal Home Entertainment) (Figure 22-9)

Les Mistons (short). Dir. François Truffaut. Les Films du Carrosse, 1957. (DVD distribution: The Criterion Collection, 2003) (Figure 22-10)

Raging Bull. Dir. Martin Scorsese. Chartoff-Winkler Productions, 1980. (DVD distribution: MGM Home Entertainment) (Figure 22-13)

Nutty but Nice. Dir. Jules White. Columbia Pictures Corporation, 1940. (Figure 22-14)

River of Things: "Ode to a Bar of Soap" (short). Dir. Katherine Hurbis-Cherrier, 1998. (Figure 22-15)

Snapshot (short). Dir. Andrew Lund, 2006. (Figure 22-16)

Chop Shop. Dir. Ramin Bahrani. Noruz Films, 2007. (DVD distribution: Koch Lorber Films) (Figure 22-17)

Do the Right Thing. Dir. Spike Lee. 40 Acres & A Mule Filmworks, 1989. (DVD distribution: The Criterion Collection) (Figure 22-18)

Gone With the Wind. Dir. Victor Fleming. Selznick International Pictures, 1939. (DVD Distribution: Warner Home Video)

Jaws. Dir. Steven Spielberg. Universal Pictures, 1975. (DVD distribution: Universal Studios Home Video)

Fa yeun nin wa (In the Mood for Love). Dir. Wong Kar-Wai. Paradis Films, 2000. (DVD distribution: The Criterion Collection) (Figure 22-20)

Star Wars: Episode VI—Return of the Jedi. Dir. Richard Marquand. Lucasfilm Ltd., 1983. (DVD distribution: 20th Century Fox Home Entertainment) (Figure 22-21)

Reservoir Dogs. Dir. Quentin Tarantino. Dog Eat Dog Prods., 1992. (DVD distribution: Artisan Entertainment) (Figure 22-22)

Into the Wild. Dir. Sean Penn. Paramount Vantage, 2007. (DVD distribution: Paramount Home Video) (Figure 22-23)

River of Things: "Ode to Things" (short). Dir. Mick Hurbis-Cherrier, 1998. (Figure 22-24)

Yume (Dreams). Dir. Akira Kurosawa. Akira Kurosawa USA, 1990. (DVD Distribution: Warner Home Video) (Figure 22-25)

La Promesse. Dirs. Jean-Pierre Dardenne and Luc Dardenne. Eurimages, 1996. (DVD distribution: New Yorker Films) (Figure 22-26 T)

The Wrestler. Dir. Darren Aronofsky. Protozoa Pictures, 2008. (DVD distribution: 20th Century Fox Home Entertainment) (Figure 22-26 M)

Silence of the Lambs. Dir. Jonathan Demme. Orion Pictures Corporation, 1991. (DVD Distribution: The Criterion Collection) (Figure 22-26 B)

■ CHAPTER 23

Apocalypse Now. Dir. Francis Ford Coppola. Zoetrope Studios, 1979. (DVD Distribution: Paramount Home Video)

FearFall. Dir. Mick Hurbis-Cherrier, 2000.

Immortal Beloved. Dir. Bernard Rose. Majestic Films International, 1994. (DVD Distribution: Columbia Home Video) (Figure 23-13)

M. Dir. Fritz Lang. Nero-Film AG, 1934. (DVD Distribution: The Criterion Collection) (Figure 23-14)

All That Jazz. Dir. Bob Fosse. Columbia Pictures Corporation, 1979. (DVD Distribution: 20th Century Fox Films) (Figure 23-23)

The Man Who Knew Too Much. Dir. Alfred Hitchcock. Paramount Pictures, 1956. (DVD Distribution: Universal Home Video Inc.) (Figure 23-24)

■ CHAPTER 24

Four Eyed Monsters. Dirs. Susan Buice & Arin Crumley. Less Life Lived LLC, 2005. (Figure 24-13)

StingRay Sam. Dir. Cory McAbee. BNS Productions, 2009. (DVD distribution: www .corymcabee.com/stingraysam) (Figure 24-14)

Saturnalia. Dir. Gustavo Mercado, 2011 (Figure 24-16)

Shirlock Jr. Dir. Buster Keaton. Buster Keaton Productions, 1924. (DVD Distribution: Kino Video) (Figure 24-17 L)

Photograph and Illustration Credits

Figure 1-1 Photo by Seifolla Samadian; **Figure 1-2** Courtesy of Photofest; **Figures 1-8** and **1-9** Photos by Simon Max Hill; **Figures 2-7** and **2-8** Excerpt from *Ocean's Eleven* granted Courtesy of Warner Brothers Entertainment Inc.; **Figure 2-12** Excerpt from *Sideways* © 2004, Courtesy of Twentieth Century Fox. Written by Alexander Payne and Jim Taylor. All rights reserved.; **Figures 4-1, 4-4,** and **4-6** Photos by Catherine Riggs-Bergesen; **Figure 5-6** Courtesy of: Diamond Dogs, Phil and Olly; **Figure 5-10** (L) Photo by Chip Hackler; **Figure 6-4** Courtesy of Alex Rivera; **Figure 6-11** Courtesy of Abel CineTech; **Figure 7-1** Photo by Henny Garfunkel; **Figure 7-2** (L) Photo by Jory Sutton, Courtesy of Don Harwood and Heather Rae; **Figure 7-4** Photo by Pierce Varous; **Figure 7-5** Photos by Mario Tursi, Courtesy of Pam Katz; **Figure 7-6** Courtesy of Matt Post; **Figure 7-9** (L) Courtesy of George Racz, (R) Courtesy of Noruz Films; **Figure 7-15** (T) Photo by Jory Sutton, Courtesy of Don Harwood; **Figure 8-6** Courtesy of Michel Khleifi; **Figure 8-32** Courtesy of DuArt Inc.; **Figures 8-34** and **8-42** Courtesy of Kodak Inc.; **Figure 9-15** Courtesy of (L) Sony Corp of America (R) Panasonic; **Figure 9-19** Courtesy of Panasonic; **Figure 9-24** Courtesy of (L) Panasonic (R) Sony Corp of America; **Figure 9-31** Courtesy sphl; **Figure 9-32** Courtesy of Canon USA; **Figure 9-34** Courtesy of Arri Group; **Figure 9-39** Courtesy of AJA Systems; **Figure 9-41** (T) Courtesy of Red Rock (B) Courtesy of Panasonic; **Figure 10-19** Courtesy of Don Fleming at DOFmaster; **Figure 10-24** Courtesy of Letus; **Figure 11-2** (L) Photo by David Pavlosky (R) Courtesy of Rain Li; **Figures 11-4** and **11-6** Courtesy of Sachtler; **Figure 11-11** Courtesy of Didier Rouget; **Figure 11-13** Courtesy of (L) Sachtler, (R) Glidecam; **Figure 11-14** Copyright Raymond Cauchetier-Paris; **Figure 11-13** Courtesy of Mike Figgis; **Figures 12-3, 12-6,** and **12-12** Photo by Catherine Riggs-Bergesen; **Figures 13-10, 13-44, 13-46, 13-47** Courtesy of (R) Mole-Richardson; **Figures 13-14** and **13-41** Courtesy of Zachary Sluser; **Figure 13-48** (L) Courtesy of Matt Post; **Figures 14-7** and **14-11** Courtesy of Kodak Inc.; **Figure 14-28** (C) Photo © The National Gallery, London; **Figure 15-11** Photo by Mario Tursi, Courtesy of Pam Katz; **Figures 15-13(R)** and **15-16** Courtesy of Sound Devices; **Figure 15-18** Courtesy of (L) Sound Devices (R) Fostex; **Figure 15-19** Courtesy of Marantz; **Figure 15-20** Courtesy of (T) Nagra, (B) Aaton S.A.; **Figure 15-21** (L) Courtesy of HHb (R) Fostex; **Figure 15-23** Courtesy of (L) Sound Devices; **Figure 15-28** Courtesy of Audio Technica; **Figure 15-34** (R) Sony Corp of America; **Figure 15-35** Courtesy of Didier Rouget; **Figure 15-35** Courtesy of 3H Sound Studio; **Figure 16-3** Courtesy of Sound Devices; **Figures 16-8** and **16-16** Photo by Catherine Riggs-Bergesen; **Figure 16-9** Photo by Sil Stranders Courtesy of Antoin Cox; **Figure 17-12** Courtesy of Zachary Sluser; **Figure 17-16** Courtesy of (L) NextoDI USA (R) Panasonic; **Figure 17-17** Photo by Catherine Riggs-Bergesen; **Figure 17-18** Photo by Kim Spiegler; **Figure 17-19** Courtesy of Kelly Anderson; **Figure 18-1** photo by Gary Knight (CC); **Figure 18-8** Photo by Sil Stranders Courtesy of Antoin Cox; **Figure 18-8** Courtesy of Matt Anderson; **Figures 19-6** Courtesy of DuArt Inc.; **Figure 19-9** Courtesy of Color Lab; **Figure 19-14** Courtesy of Sony Corp of America; **Figures 19-16** and **19-20** Courtesy of Arri Group; **Figure 19-17** Courtesy of Shanti Thakur; **Figure 19-18** Photo by Kerwin Devonish; **Figure 19-19** Photo by Dag Bennstrom; **Figure 19-21** Courtesy of Adakin Productions; **Figure 19-28** Courtesy of DuArt Inc.; **Figure 21-1** Courtesy Sam Pollard; **Figures 21-4, 21-5, 21-6, 21-7,** and **21-8,** Illustration by Wes Simpkins; **Figure 21-11** (R) Photo by David Leonard ©, Courtesy of Thelma Schoonmaker; **Figure 22-12** (R) Courtesy of Sound One/Ascent Media; **Figure 24-12** Courtesy of John Daschbach; **Figure 24-13** Courtesy of Susan Buice and Arin Crumley; **Figure 24-14** Courtesy of Cory McAbee and Becky Glupczynski; **Figure 24-15** Courtesy of Vimeo.

■ ADDITIONAL PHOTOGRAPHY BY

Gustavo Mercado, Mick Hurbis-Cherrier, Peter A. Jackson, Jessica Webb, Alessandra Kast, and Nicole Pommerehncke

■ ILLUSTRATIONS BY GUSTAVO MERCADO

Index

Note: Page numbers followed by *b* indicate boxes, *f* indicate figures and *t* indicate tables.

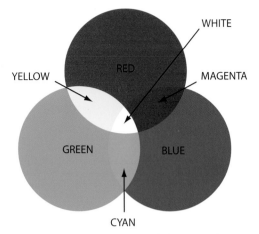

Figure 8-37 The color wheel shows at a glance the three primary colors of light, red, green, and blue, and their respective complementary colors directly opposite, which are cyan, magenta, and yellow.

Figure 8-38 Scenes from Zhang's *Hero* (2002).

Figure 8-44 In George Racz' *The Miracle* (2006), special attention was put into selecting a stock that would render the little girl's environment, toys, and clothing as colorfully as possible.

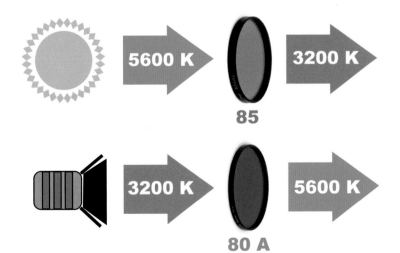

Figure 8-45 Color conversion filters. Two of the most commonly used filters are the 85 (amber), which turns 5,600°K daylight into 3,200°K tungsten light, and the 80A (bluish), which turns 3,200°K tungsten into 5,600°K daylight.

■ **Figure 9-12** Just like camera sensors, color flat-screen displays (LCD or plasma) are made up of millions of pixels. Each individual pixel contains red, green, and blue subpixels (outlined).

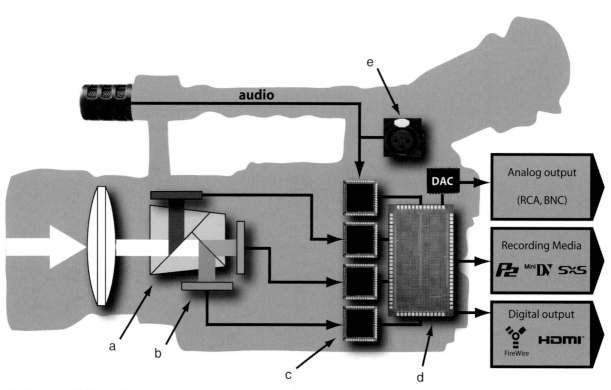

■ **Figure 9-30** A three-chip video camera produces an image by first dividing the light entering the lens into primary colors with a prism block (a), which are read by three CCD chips (b), their signal outputs are converted into digital data by an ADC (c), and they are processed by the DSP (d), ultimately outputting the data to the record media. Audio inputs (e) have their own ADC as well.

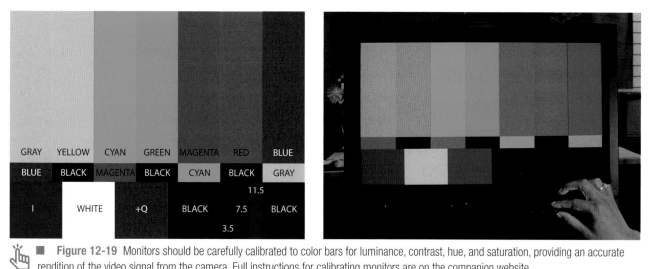

GRAY	YELLOW	CYAN	GREEN	MAGENTA	RED	BLUE
BLUE	BLACK	MAGENTA	BLACK	CYAN	BLACK	GRAY
I	WHITE	+Q		BLACK	7.5	BLACK

11.5

3.5

■ **Figure 12-19** Monitors should be carefully calibrated to color bars for luminance, contrast, hue, and saturation, providing an accurate rendition of the video signal from the camera. Full instructions for calibrating monitors are on the companion website.

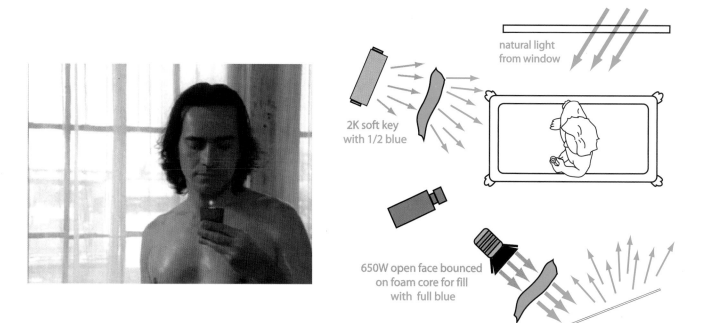

natural light from window

2K soft key with 1/2 blue

650W open face bounced on foam core for fill with full blue

■ **Figure 13-3** In this scene, from Katherine Hurbis-Cherrier's *Ode to a Bar of Soap* (1998), mixed lighting (artificial and sunlight) has been balanced for color temperature and quality.

■ **Figure 13-14** Diffusion filters are used to soften the image while maintaining sharp focus. Notice in this shot, from Sluser's *Path Lights* (2009), the glow on the metal highlights and hair and the softness added to Bobby's (John Hawkes) face.

■ **Figure 13-21** Gels come in hundreds of colors and intensities, including color correcting, neutral density, and diffusion media.

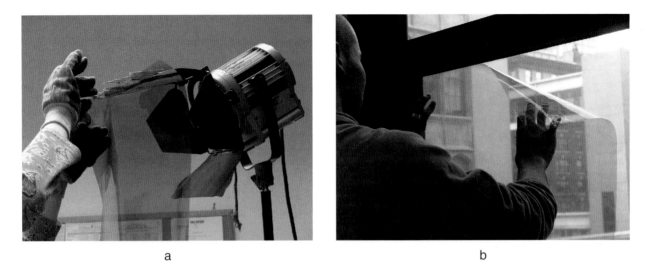

a

b

👆 ■ **Figure 13-22** CTO and CTB gels are used to correct the color temperature of a light source. CTBs are placed on movie lights to make them "daylight," and CTOs are placed on windows to make them "tungsten."

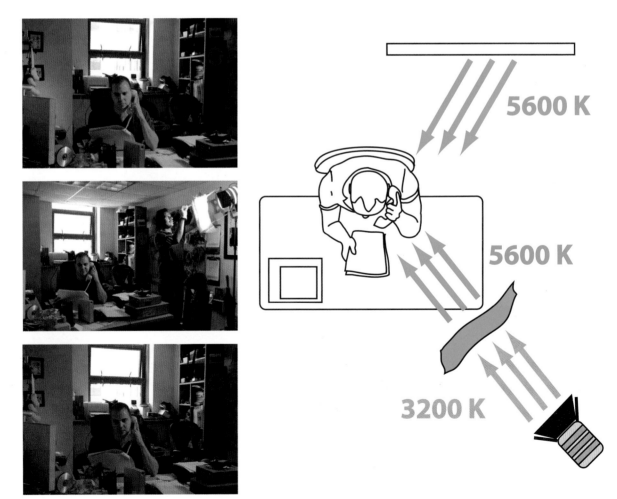

5600 K

5600 K

3200 K

👆 ■ **Figure 13-23** Shooting with daylight film (or DV balanced for daylight) matches the sunlight coming through the window but records tungsten light as excessively orange (A). Placing a CTB gel over the tungsten unit changes it to daylight (B), matching the color temperature of all sources (C).

Original Negative Exposure Data
Lens: 38mm (CANON 11 - 165mm T2.5 Zoom Lens)
FPS: 24
Filter: 85
Incident light levels: (HMI and ambient daylight
approximately 5660K)
Key: T2.8 (80 fc)
Backlight: T11 (1200 fc)
Stop notations listed on the photo are reflected-light
readings.

| 1 -5 Stops | 2 -4 Stops | 3 -2.7 Stops | 4 +1 Stop | 5 +2.3 Stops | 6 +4.4 Stops | 7 +5.3 Stops | 8 +6.3 Stops |

■ **Figure 14-11** Kodak provides "original exposure data" examples for their stocks, letting consumers see how they react to an array of exposure values, including normal (N) over (+) and under (–) exposures.

■ **Figure 14-22** The hyperstylized look created by the masterful interplay of light, shadow, and color in Powell and Pressburger's *Black Narcissus* (1947) serves to visualize the intense emotions felt by a group of Anglican nuns stationed in the Himalayan mountains (cinematography by Jack Cardiff).

■ **Figure 14-23** Lee's *Do the Right Thing* (1989) has highly stylized lighting that emphasizes the heat of one particularly hot day in Brooklyn (cinematography by Ernest Dickerson, *left*). D.P. Emmanuel Lubezki tempered the theatrical tone of this ghost story with some naturalistic approaches to create a look for Burton's *Sleepy Hollow* (1999), which was both believable and fantastic *(right)*.

■ **Figure 14-25** These two frames from *Slumdog Millionaire* (Boyle and Tanda, 2009) reveal a highly stylized visual approach, despite the use of available light, nonactors and real locations. The D.P. Anthony Dod Mantle was awarded an Oscar for Best Cinematography—the first given to a film shot primarily on DV.

■ **Figure 14-26** Cinematographer Ernest Dickerson lights Bleek (Denzel Washington) using colors that stand for his two main interests, jazz (blue) and women (red), in Lee's *Mo' Better Blues* (1990).

■ **Figure 14-28** As part of my visual research for lighting *Flesh & Blade* (2007) (*left* and *right* frames), I looked at paintings like *An Experiment on a Bird in an Airpump* (1768), by Joseph Wright of Derby *(center)*.

■ **Figure 14-29** Shooting on SD video does not preclude having complex, beautiful cinematography. Ellen Kuras devised three completely different visual styles for the three characters in Miller's *Personal Velocity* (2002).

■ **Figure 19-24** The film *O Brother, Where Art Thou?* (Coen Brothers, 2000) was the first commercial movie to use exclusively a DI for conforming, color grading, and film-out printing.

■ **Figure 20-30** *Source Code* (Jones, 2011) used a simple green screen effect to create a moving background for a stationary train set built on a sound stage.

■ **Figure 24-1** The Final Cut Pro three-way color corrector interface. (a) The luminance slider; (b) the color balance controls (with the balance indicator at center); (c) the color correction control range (blacks, mids, or whites). Notice that the shot selected in the timeline is brought up in the viewer for color correction.

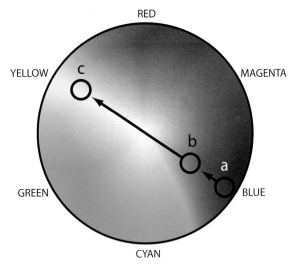

a

b

c

Figure 24-3 Dragging the balance indicator into a specific area of the color wheel balances the image toward that particular color. The closer to the edge you go, the more intense the color becomes. (a) Intense blue; (b) lighter blue; (c) intense yellow.

Figure 24-4 Most color correction adjustments are subtle. The original image (a) appears somewhat flat and pale. By adjusting luminance values we can create sharper contrast and more depth to the image (b). Adjusting the color further refines the image. In this case adding a slight amber hue provides a sense of the heat of the summer sun (c).